THE
ENCYCLOPEDIA OF
SCHIZOPHRENIA
AND THE
PSYCHOTIC DISORDERS

THE
ENCYCLOPEDIA OF
SCHIZOPHRENIA
AND THE
PSYCHOTIC DISORDERS

Richard Noll, M.A.
Foreword by
Leonard George, Ph.D

Facts On File
New York • Oxford

The Encyclopedia of Schizophrenia and the Psychotic Disorders

Copyright © 1992 by Richard Noll

Facts On File, Inc. Facts On File Limited
460 Park Avenue South Collins Street
New York NY 10016 Oxford OX4 1XJ
USA United Kingdom

Library of Congress Cataloging-in-Publication Data
Noll, Richard.
    The encyclopedia of schizophrenia and the psychotic disorders / Richard Noll.
        p. cm.
    Includes bibliographical reference and index.
    ISBN 0-8160-2240-2 (alk. paper)
    1. Schizophrenia—Encyclopedias. 2. Schizophrenia—Information services—Directories. I. Title.
    [DNLM: 1. Psychotic Disorders—encyclopedias. 2. Schizophrenia—encyclopedias. WM 13 N793e]
RC514.N63 1991
616.89′003—dc20
DNLM/DLC
for Library of Congress   91-19999

A British CIP catalogue record for this book is available from the British Library.

Facts On File books are available at special discounts when purchased in bulk quantities for businesses, associations, institutions or sales promotions. Please call our Special Sales Department in New York at 212/683-2244 (dial 800/322-8755 except in NY, AK or HI) or in Oxford at 865/728399.

Composition by the Maple-Vail Book Manufacturing Group
Manufactured by Hamilton Printing Company
Printed in the United States of America

10 9 8 7 6 5 4 3 2 1

This book is printed on acid-free paper.

*I dedicate this book with love to
my parents, Richard Dean Noll (1929–   ) and
Betty Ann Noll (1937–   ),
and to my maternal grandparents,
Stanley Vincent Adamczak (1908–1957) and especially
Belle Marie Adamczak (neé Tipniski) (1910–   ),
who has given me a lifetime of joy.*

Unumquemque move lapidem, omnia experire,
nihil intentatum relinque.

("Move every stone, try everything,
leave nothing unattempted.")

Erasmus
Adagia, I.IV.xxx

TABLE OF CONTENTS

ABOUT THE AUTHOR

Richard Noll, M.A., is a clinical psychologist and a free-lance writer. He is in private practice in Philadelphia. He completed an externship at New York University Medical Center in New York City and was a staff clinical psychologist for four years at Ancora Psychiatric Hospital in Hammonton, New Jersey. Noll is a doctoral candidate in clinical psychology at the New School for Social Research in New York. The author of many scholarly articles and three books on psychiatric and anthropological topics, he has a long-standing interest in unusual psychiatric syndromes and in the history and folklore of psychopathology.

In October 1991 the author completed an invited lecture tour in Eastern Europe during which he spoke on both psychiatric and anthropological topics. He delivered an invited presentation on the latest scientific research on multiple personality and the dissociative disorders to an interdisciplinary organization of Polish scientists and academics at the Royal Castle in Warsaw. Noll also lectured on both multiple personality and shamanism at the universities in Warsaw, Kielce and Krakow, Poland. Following this, he gave an invited presentation on the psychological aspects of shamanism to the Hungarian Academy of Sciences in Budapest, Hungary.

FOREWORD
THE IMPORTANCE OF PSYCHOSIS

Madness, like disease, pain and death, is a topic that affects most people in a paradoxical manner. On the one hand, we are disturbed, perhaps even horrified, that such things occur and tend to avoid contact with these domains if at all possible. As a society, we apply cosmetics to the dead to simulate "the glow of life" before displaying them. We do not discuss the gory details of illness and pain in "polite" conversation—and we do not like to visit, or even to think about, the back wards of psychiatric hospitals, where a significant number of people spend much of their lives.

On the other hand, our aversion to madness (in contemporary technical parlance, "psychosis") is mixed with an irresistible fascination. We sense that, no matter how thick are the walls we erect between ourselves and the phenomenon of psychosis, the world of madness is somehow very relevant to our own lives. In some cases, the walls are blown away by the occurrence of psychosis in a loved one or in ourselves. Then, we no longer have the luxury of pretending that psychosis is important only to someone else.

The world of psychosis is, in some inescapable sense, our own. We can choose to ignore this reality. Or we can decide to be aware, to become knowledgeable and to consider how the human encounter with psychosis can be meaningful.

In order to understand the importance of psychosis in human life, we must first consider what is shared in common by psychosis—the painful loss of contact with the everyday reality in which most people live—and everyday reality. The most significant commonality is that both psychosis and normal-world perceptions are species of *experience*. The definition and understanding of psychosis have changed dramatically through the years. It has variously been thought to arise from, for example, demonic invasion, moral failure, poor upbringing, faulty genes. Despite these vicissitudes, we still identify the presence of psychosis in terms of an unusual experience. Although there is a lot of current speculation regarding biological aspects of schizophrenia, the diagnosis of schizophrenia is still based solely on reports of disturbed experience and the expression of this disturbance in behavior.

As psychosis and normal functioning are both types of human experience, they have in common a fundamental feature of all experience—its *constructed nature*. Our experience of the world and the self does not seem to be constructed; rather, it appears as if we discover features of the world that exist independently of our perceptual or conceptual acts. However, contemporary philosophy and social science, as well as much traditional thought, holds that this seeming neutrality of experience is illusory. In actuality, the expectations, assumptions, dreams and fears we bring into a situation strongly shape our contact with whatever exists in that situation. This shaping of experience by the framework of belief is highlighted by the accounts of travelers, who find their own assumptions and realities contrasted to those of other cultures. For instance, the anthropologist Colin Turnbull recounted how he invited some African pygmies, who had never set foot outside of their dense jungle home, to visit the open plains. As they travelled across the flatland in their jeep, they sighted some cattle in the distance. The pygmies at first thought that the cattle were ants, because of the animals' tiny size from a distance. As they approached the cattle, which seemed to grow larger with the shrinking distance, the pygmies became disturbed, thinking that the increasing size represented a magical transformation of ants into giant creatures. The pygmies, because their home environment gave them no experience with perceiving distant objects, did not possess the assumption that psychologists call "size-distance invariance"—the idea that the variation in the size of an object at varying distances is only apparent.

All experience, then, whether normal or deviant, is an act of personal construction, even though we may be unaware of the processes underlying this construction.

The formation of human experience generally involves many influences. The state of the body is always involved, of course; everyone has noticed that the world is a more pleasant and inviting place when we are physically healthy. Mental states are pervasive also. Moods and thoughts, images and memories, all contribute to the present world as we experience it. In addition to such individual factors, the social and political context of individuals plays an important role in determining the characteristics of experience.

These observations about the constructed nature of experience, and the role of biological, psychological and social factors in its determination, apply not just to our perception of the world, but also to our sense of self and embodiment. "I" may seem to be a changeless pivot of awareness, around which the events of a life orbit, but some reflection reveals that "I," too, is a construct: My self-worth, for instance, is not at all fixed but depends on such continually shifting influences as appraisals of my physical attractiveness, the presence of positive self-images and thoughts, memories of achievements, and the supportive behaviors of others. Even our experience of our bodies, the physical ground of our being, is mediated by processes of psychosocial construction. This fact is most dramatically revealed in the condition known as chronic pain, in which an injured person continues to feel physical discomfort long after the bodily healing processes have completed their work. Research has demonstrated that the experience of pain depends not just on somatic conditions, but also on psychosocial variables such as the meaning of the pain in the person's life and the extent to which attention is focused on the pain by family members.

International studies reveal that our general sense of health and illness is affected by cultural factors. For instance, in Germany, heart disorder is admired as a sign of sensitivity, and heart medicines are proudly displayed and respected, whereas in America, heart problems are highly aversive experiences. Many illnesses that are thought to be unrelated to each other everywhere else in the world are regarded by the French as arising from liver dysfunction, and treated accordingly.

In summary, all human experiences result from a process of synthesis in which biological, psychological and social forces play a role. The external world, the body and the inner domain of the self, insofar as they are experienced, are influenced by the biopsychosocial context. Psychosis, as an experience, is a constructed entity.

Our paradoxical reaction to psychosis—fascination and horror—suggests that it has a special importance that distinguishes it from most other forms of experience. We can understand this importance by examining the ways in which psychosis itself illuminates various features of the processes that create our experience of reality.

Perhaps the most obvious significance of psychosis to society is that the experience of the psychotic is profoundly debilitating and unpleasant. The processes that construct experience generally aim to provide a coherent and meaningful world, within which we can minimize anxiety and achieve satisfying goals. In psychosis, this orienting function of the cognitive framework seems to break down, leaving the sufferer, to varying degrees, disoriented and unable to access sources of pleasure and meaning. We are moved to compassion—and some are moved to compassionate action—by this suffering, yet repelled by the possibility that we too could be trapped within such a hell. As the behaviors and verbal expressions of psychotics are often so ambiguous, and the origins of the disorder mysterious, some tend to romanticize madness as a "wisdom beyond reason" or demonize the sufferer into a "homicidal maniac." Neither image is particularly relevant to the reality of psychosis.

A second significance of psychosis lies in the lessons it imparts concerning nonpsychotic mental functioning. Since the inceptions of psychology and psychiatry, it has often been observed that the mental processes involved in psychotic experience are the same as those underlying less disturbed domains. For instance, many schizophrenics complain that they are unable to control the focus of their attention, and that, consequently, they experience a paralyzing flood of information. This observation highlights the importance of focal attention in organizing the more controlled and useful perceptions of nonpsychotic perception. Psychosis may not be a state of enlightenment, but it does offer a useful mirror of normal psychology, in a distorted and exaggerated fashion.

Psychosis is also important because it is related to creativity. This is not to say that all creative people are mad, nor that all psychotics are creative. There is, however, a link, which has been intuited and enshrined in folklore over the centuries. Historians of the mind have noted that a surprising number of notable creative figures seem to have suffered from bipolar disorder, a form of psychosis involving painfully extreme mood states and strange thought patterns. Psychosis has proven magnetically attractive as a subject for artistic expression. And some researchers have observed that schizoprehnics and unusually creative individuals do have some similarities (and some important differences) on psychological tests. A deeper understanding of psychosis may teach us much about the nature of productive innovation, if we avoid the error of simply identifying the two.

Psychosis is important for a fourth reason: Unlike ordinary experience, the experience of psychotics is obviously the result of the process of construction described above. While those of us sharing the everyday world support each other in the shared (and generally unquestioned) certainties that comprise our reality, few of us are as uncritical when it comes to the experience of a psychotic. We can clearly see that the psychotic perception arises from unusual biological states, strange thoughts and odd emotional conditions. Close examination of the psychotic domain also reveals how social conditions influence psychotic experiences and behaviors. And historical studies reveal how the beliefs concerning psychotics, held by those responsible for their care and management, shift over time and are often embedded in changes regarding more general beliefs about the nature of reality. The thoughtful student of psychosis might be prompted by these observations to ask some important questions: If the psychotic world and self are constructed by biopsychosocial forces, what about MY world and MY self? Are the certainties in my own life anchored in some fixed truth or merely on assumptions that have proven useful in my life so far? Such relativizing meditations can be very unnerving. They can also help us to be more flexible and creative in our definitions of ourselves. If we are willing to examine our own construction of experience in light of the evident artifactuality of psychosis, we might discover that some of the limits to our wisdom, freedom and kindness that we have been so certain about are not immutable features of reality but are only constructs, too.

Richard Noll's book, *The Encyclopedia of Schizophrenia and the Psychotic Disorders,* is a unique tool with which to explore the importance of psychosis. It enables the reader to consider the many facets of psychotic experience, both the subjective and the behavioral.

Noll lucidly discusses the qualities of psychotic consciousness; major conceptual approaches, such as altered states of consciousness and daseinanalyse, are introduced, and the important categories of experience, including body image and perceptual anomalies, are examined. Many contemporary writings concerning psychosis neglect these subjective aspects. But if we do not cultivate our understanding of psychosis from the point of view of the sufferer, we risk losing sight of the fact that psychosis afflicts human beings who are not so different from the rest of us. This insight is the motor that drives our efforts to alleviate the suffering of the psychotic individual. As Manfred Bleuler, the great researcher of schizophrenia wrote, the schizophrenic "hides a warm and human heart behind his sometimes shocking affective behavior. We must know how to approach the schizophrenic. We must enter and feel with him his vision of reality. We must never relinquish this endeavor."

Noll's book is rich in material highlighting the biopsychosocial construction of the psychotic experience. Regarding the biological aspects, he summarizes the major biochemical theories and genetic studies, as well as the dominant antipsychotic drugs currently being used to manage psychotic symptoms. The psychological factors contributing to psychosis are explored under such major headings as cognitive studies and attention disorders. Regarding social influences, Noll has included important material on the cross-cultural studies of psychosis, including descriptions of disorders that occur only in certain cultures (such as boufée délirante aigue in Haiti and kitsune-tsuki psychosis in Japan). These descriptions of how psychotic symptoms are molded by cultural expectations establish that psychosis is determined in part by social factors. He amplifies this point in his presentation concerning the relation between socioeconomic status and schizophrenia.

This volume is a compendium of information concerning the intense suffering experienced by psychotics. Noll's consideration of the subjective features, as noted above, makes it clear that these disorders are profoundly unpleasant in themselves. This suffering is often amplified by the "treatment" offered to the sufferers, much of which is well-described as noninjurious torture. The author's recitation of the medical "aid" offered to psychotics in the past reads like a description of a chamber of horrors: bleeding; various forms of constraint such as confinement in cages and the spread eagle cure; flogging; psychosurgery; ovariotomy; the bath of surprise (being suddenly thrown into cold water); even the induction of hemorrhoids. Has the situation improved today? In some respects it has, but there is no room for complacency—see Noll's descriptions of the abuse of psychiatric patients.

Readers journeying through this encyclopedia will learn much, not just about psychosis, but about normal psychological functioning as well. Noll explores the categories of mental disorder that bridge psychosis and the milder, neurotic disturbances to which we are all prone to some degree; the borderline personality disorder and schizotypal personality disorder are examples of these intermediate forms of psychological dysfunction. A careful consideration of the author's descriptions of psychotic features, such as delusions and hallucinations, may sensitize the reader to the fact that strange thoughts and perceptions frequently occur in the normal stream of consciousness, even if only for a moment and in the margins of awareness.

This book discusses the mysterious relationship between the maladaptive novelties of psychotic experience and the useful novelties of highly creative persons. In his consideration of schizophrenic art, for instance, Noll summarizes over a century of research on this topic. He notes the similarity between the artistic productions of psychotics and modern abstract art, and notes that famous artists like Vincent van Gogh and Jackson Pollock suffered from severe mental disturbances. Research comparing the psychological functioning of creative individuals and psychotics is discussed under the heading of creativity and psychosis.

This volume contains a vast amount of information on the history of the concept of psychosis in Western culture. Noll provides a panoramic view of the many transformations in conventional belief regarding the nature of madness over the years—from belief in demonic possession to the medical model, which describes psychosis as a disease—and the continuous shifts in the defining symptoms, types and subtypes of psychosis as discerned by the experts in the field. One can easily sense the fact that the concept of psychosis is always embedded within the larger framework of assumptions concerning reality, and that as these assumptions change, so also do our basic beliefs regarding psychosis. Through contemplating this historical process, the intelligent reader will discern the relativity of his or her own beliefs and expectations.

An implication of the incessant changes evident in the historical perspective is that the prevailing understanding of psychosis is not the last word on the matter. Indeed, perhaps there cannot be a final and complete understanding of such a complex realm. However, a thorough exploration of Richard Noll's compendium of knowledge about schizophrenia and the other psychotic disorders will give the reader full access to the richest levels of understanding available today. As the ancient alchemists said, "Ora, lege, lege, lege, relege, labora, et invenies."—"Pray, read, read, read, reread, work, and you will find!"

Leonard George, Ph.D., R. Psych.
Columbia Centre for Integrated
Health Services
Vancouver, British Columbia

ACKNOWLEDGMENTS

No book is created *ex nihilo,* and I have stood on the shoulders of three giants who have given me the insights and strength to wrestle with such a powerful demon as the disease we call schizophrenia: Eugen Bleuler, for his empathetic dedication to understanding, studying and then colorfully describing those anonymous institutionalized persons with schizophrenia who live out their lives in a tragic obscurity. The descriptions of the words, hopes, fears and desperate actions of his patients in his 1911 landmark book on the "group of schizophrenias" are so accurate even now that it is as if Bleuler were alive today, making his rounds in the back wards of some state hospital, conversing with his patients, observing them and then sharing his insights with us about what it is like to be a person with schizophrenia in the 1990s. Unfortunately, despite our technological advances in research, some things have not changed since Bleuler's psychiatric apprenticeship in the 1890s.

C.G. Jung, for his insights into the personal symbolic meaning of the signs and symptoms of psychosis, for his phenomenological approach to the psyche, and for the tremendous impact his life and work have had on my life, both personally and professionally.

And E. Fuller Torrey, for his exceptionally creative mind—he has frequently introduced new problems or approaches to the study of schizophrenia—his humane spirit and his heartfelt advocacy for the improvement of the life of the mentally ill in America. Torrey has guts, and he has often risked the ire of his colleagues by drawing attention to certain controversial issues regarding the treatment of the mentally ill. He has often placed himself in the front lines and has personally devoted his time to working in shelters for the homeless mentally ill. Torrey has also written two important books on their plight *(Surviving Schizophrenia: A Family Manual* and *Nowhere to Go: The Tragic Odyssey of the Homeless Mentally Ill),* which I read and reread when I worked as a clinical psychologist in a state psychiatric hospital. They simultaneously aroused my anger about the present injustices of the mental health system in the United States and sparked the hope in me that somehow, someday, my patients with schizophrenia would not have to live the torturous, inhuman existence that is the lot of so many—in the streets, in the shelters and boarding homes and in the back wards of psychiatric hospitals, where there still exist secret hells that only those who have been employed or incarcerated in such a place could believe would exist in our day and age.

Two reference works in particular were of great value: Daniel Hack Tuke's two-volume *A Dictionary of Psychological Medicine* (London: J. & A. Churchill, 1892) is an exemplary source of knowledge about what psychiatry was like a century ago. I spent countless hours in the rare books section of the Medical Library of the College of Physicians and Surgeons in Philadelphia, absorbed in reading Tuke (and Pinel and Rush and Esquirol and Griesinger and Maudsley . . .), feeling quite often as if I were transported in time back to the 19th century, and I sincerely hope that Tuke's volumes are reprinted soon to make this wonderful reference more accessible to scholars. John G. Howells and M. Livia Osborn's two-volume work, *A Reference Companion to the History of Abnormal Psychology* (Westport, Conn.: Greenwood Press, 1984) is a rich source of cultural information relating to psychopathology and was also quite helpful.

The Schizophrenia Research Branch of the National Institute of Mental Health in Bethesda, Maryland, was quite generous in providing me with back issues of *Schizophrenia Bulletin* and other materials that were essential to the writing of this book.

The National Alliance for the Mentally Ill, the national self help/advocacy organization for families and friends of persons suffering from serious mental illnesses, was helpful to me in many ways. I particularly want to thank NAMI's executive director, Laurie Flynn, for her assistance and for her efforts on behalf of those who are in any way personally or professionally involved with the mentally ill.

Four persons who were directly involved in the genesis of this book deserve my thanks: My literary agent, Bert Holtje, of James Peters Associates in Tenafly, New Jersey, was responsible for landing this project for me; and my editors, Kate Kelly, who was there at the conception, and Neal Maillet, who patiently nursed this book (which we've nicknamed "Fred" for the sake of brevity in our communications); and Kathy Ishizuka, who carried it to full term and delivered it in its present form.

Leonard George, Ph.D., of Vancouver, British Columbia, Canada, always the "bearer of light," deserves special thanks for his help and wisdom in areas far too numerous to mention.

L. Erlenmeyer-Kimling, Ph.D., Barbara Cornblatt, Ph.D., and Canadian genetics researcher Anne Basset, M.D., all of the Departments of Psychiatry and of Genetics and Development of the College of Physicians and Surgeons of Columbia University in New York City all were very helpful to me for my understanding of the genetics and high-risk areas of research.

Many of my mentors about schizophrenia are experts whom I have never met but whose published research has been an invaluable source of knowledge for me. Through sharing their thoughts and discoveries in their writings they have influenced my thinking. They include: John A. Talbott, M.D.; Irving Gottesman, Ph.D.; Nancy Andreasen, Ph.D.; Thomas McGlashan, M.D.; Herbert Y. Meltzer, Ph.D.; David Rosenthal, Ph.D.; Seymour S. Kety, M.D.; Timothy J. Crow, Ph.D.; Peter A. Magaro, Ph.D.; William T. Carpenter Jr., M.D.; John S. Strauss, M.D.; Manfred Bleuler, Prof.Dr.Med.; Leopold Bellak, M.D.; Monte S. Buchsbaum, M.D.; Jeffrey A. Lieberman, M.D.; Keith H. Nuechterlein, Ph.D.; John Wing, M.D.; John Cutting, Ph.D.; Michael Shepherd, Ph.D.; Roy Porter, Ph.D.; Andrew Scull, Ph.D.; Jan Goldstein, Ph.D.; John J. Bartko, Ph.D.; Norman Garmezy, Ph.D.; John Gunderson, M.D.; John M. Kane, M.D.; Norman Sartorius, M.D.; Allan S. Bellak, Ph.D.; Douglas S. Levinson, M.D.; Racquel Gur, M.D., Ph.D.; Ruben C. Gur, Ph.D.; Ming T. Tsuang, M.D., Ph.D.; Richard Jed Wyatt, M.D.; Carol Tamminga, M.D.; Stephen Marder, M.D.; Darrell G. Kirch, M.D.; Malcom B. Bowers Jr., M.D.; Malcom Bowers Sr., M.D.; David L. Braff, M.D.; Paul Meehl, Ph.D.; Nina Schooler, Ph.D.; Loren J. Chapman, Ph.D.; Jean P. Chapman, Ph.D.; Emil Kraepelin, M.D.; Pierre Janet, M.D.; Albert Deutsch; and Clifford Beers.

Others who deserve recognition for their treatment of persons with schizophrenia are: T. Stephen Patterson, Ph.D., chief psychologist for the state of New Jersey; Robert Eilers, M.D., clinical director of Ancora Psychiatric Hospital in Hammonton, New Jersey; Stephen Sachson, Ph.D., director of psychology, Ancora Psychiatric Hospital; Gene Nebel, Ph.D., of Marlboro Psychiatric Hospital in Marlboro, New Jersey; Aisha Ahmed, M.D.; Jackie Weintraub, Ph.D.; Donna Hallworth, M.S.W.; Barbara Zwicker, R.N.; Fran Langer, R.N., B.S.N.; Doris Simmerman, B.A.; Esther Reid, R.N.; Gloria Williams, H.S.T.; Bill Helfand, M.A.; Tom Schwartz, Ph.D.; Wade Johnston, Ph.D.; Michael Scott, Ph.D.; Michael Lieberman, Ph.D., and Carl Welte, M.A., clinical psychologist and doctoral candidate at

Temple University in Philadelphia. Special thanks also goes to Larry Seifer, Ph.D., my internship supervisor.

My greatest teachers, by far, were my patients. Two persons who taught me the most about schizophrenia were themselves afflicted with the disease and shared their lives with me over the many hundreds of hours we spent together, whether on the wards, in McDonald's, or at the "flower concert": Robert Ciocca (1960–1987) and Bruno C. (1933–   ), two superior personalities who taught me the differences in a very human way between Type I and Type II schizophrenia. I could not have written this book without them.

A special note for the future goes to Dylan James Patterson of London, Ontario, Canada, who awakens daily, questioning, and who one day will know the truth.

Richard Noll, M.A.   Haddonfield, New Jersey
                                                            August 1990

A BRIEF INTRODUCTION TO THE HISTORY OF SCHIZOPHRENIA

The history of schizophrenia is the history of psychiatry. The earliest clear description of this disease dates to only 1809—at about the time that the very first psychiatric textbooks were being written by dedicated physicians who worked in "madhouses" and "asylums" with the "insane." They collected their observations of the "mentally ill," devised classifications for them, speculated as to the causes of their afflictions and even performed crude autopsies on their bodies to see if they could discover the secret of madness. The profession of psychiatry grew out of the efforts of these physicians to understand and cure diseases of the mind, particularly those tragic, chronic mental illnesses that condemned thousands to debilitated lives in institutions. Therefore, the psychotic disorders, and schizophrenia in particular, have always been at the very heart of the concerns of the psychiatric profession and are in fact responsible for its existence.

As we enter the 1990s, hardly a month goes by in which some new discovery in genetics is not announced, and the mission to explore the genetics of schizophrenia will no doubt occupy a prominent position in the research of the next decade. But our late-20th-century cultural persona of schizophrenia as primarily a "genetically transmitted disease" forces us to reexamine certain historical problems related to schizophrenia: Specifically, what is its ever-changing story over the centuries? What other masks has it worn on the various stages of human history? What guesses have been made as to its possible etiology? What have been the fads and fashions in its research?

The many individual entries in this encyclopedia provide detailed synopses of these topics, but below is a brief summary of the highlights of the history of this disease.

DID SCHIZOPHRENIA
EXIST IN ANTIQUITY?

If schizophrenia is truly a brain disease that has a strong basis in genetics, then there should be evidence that this severe mental disorder has afflicted people for hundreds, if not thousands, of years. "Madness" has been reported in every society on record, no matter how ancient or how primitive, and descriptions of hallucinations, delusions and bizarre behavior are often reported in association with "madness." For example, in an attempt to trace schizophrenia back to ancient Babylonian accounts (3000 B.C.) or to early Sanskrit texts from India, translations of descriptions of mental illness from these cultures have been collected in articles published in 1985 by D.V. Jeste and his colleagues and in 1984 by C.V. Haldipur. But it is still not clear from this historical evidence that schizophrenia—as we know it, as a disease with a particular course that begins in adolescence or early adulthood, with characteristic signs and symptoms and a chronic deteriorating course (at least in the type of schizophrenia that seems to be the most "genetic")—existed in ancient eras. This point (and the larger ramifications of this entire issue) has been eloquently argued and documented by psychiatrist E. Fuller Torrey in his book *Schizophrenia and Civilization* (1980).

There are many reasons for this doubt. First, ancient descriptions of madness that involved delusional, hallucinating or confused individuals could be accounts of any number of physical or mental disorders. The same argument holds true for 19th- and 20th-century anthropological descriptions of "schizophrenia" or "psychosis" in preliterate (formerly called "primitive") societies. For example, these same symptoms could be produced by head trauma, brain infections, injury due to birth complications, strokes or by any number of other known organic mental disorders. Or they could be descriptions of the other psychotic disorders, such as bipolar disorder (manic-depressive psychosis) or any of the acute reactive psychoses. What is missing in these accounts are descriptions of the full course of the disease process over time.

Another issue regarding "schizophrenia" in so-called primitive societies should also be addressed. In the 20th century there has been a long tradition among some anthropologists (usually psychoanalytically oriented) and certain psychiatrists and psychologists who are "armchair anthropologists" that the magico-religious healers and diviners known as "shamans" have perhaps been persons who would otherwise be labeled schizophrenic or certainly psychotic in our culture. The theory goes: Since their bizarre behavior is accepted (visions, ecstatic trances, etc.) and since prominent social roles have been created for them, they seem to adapt just fine without any further deterioration. This absurd ethnocentric notion has unfortunately persisted with some very prominent proponents, often with those who have little or no true expertise in the study of shamanism, schizophrenia or both. The "schizophrenia metaphor" of shamanism is unfounded.

PSYCHOSIS IN EUROPE UP TO 1600

Since antiquity, persons with psychotic disorders and other forms of mental illness have been left to themselves, sent off in "ships of fools," locked in cages, "flogged into reason," chained or simply killed, in some instances. Until the 1500s, the care of the insane in Europe—what little was offered—had been the responsibility of monks and nuns. For example, the oldest institution for the insane in England, the Bethlem Royal Hospital ("Bedlam"), was first established in 1247 as a priory, and by 1329 it functioned as a hospital. The patients were serviced by a 13th-century religious order known as the "Bethlehemites," and on their habits they wore the special insignia of a red star with a dark blue center. The city of London took control of the place in 1346, and in 1547 it was made into a royal institution, headed by physicians, and the name was changed to St. Mary of Bethlehem. This was later changed to its present name, the Bethlehem Royal Hospital.

The reigning theory of madness was based on the antiphlogistic or humoral theory of disease. This theory had been in vogue since the time of Hippocrates (460–377 B.C.) and was elaborated upon by Galen (A.D. 129–199). Both mental and physical disorders were considered by Galen to be caused by an excess *(plethora)* of one of the four humors: black bile, yellow bile, blood and phlegm. The cure was to remove the excess by bleeding the patient or by using purgatives or laxatives. Remnants of the humoral theory formed the basis of asylum treatment for persons with schizophrenia and the other psychotic disorders until well into the 19th century and are graphically described, by the fathers of psychiatry in the earliest psychiatric textbooks.

THE "NEW PHILOSOPHY" AND MADNESS—
THE 1600S

Many social and historical changes converged in the 17th century (especially in England) to change this dark state of affairs for people with mental disorders. First, societies began to incarcerate mentally ill people in central institutions (jails, hospitals) where many of them could be observed together for long periods of time. Second, physicians (crude as their art may have been at the time, an era that medical historian Guy Williams has dubbed "the Age of Agony") began to be put in charge of the care of the mentally ill in these institutions, in England and France. The institution of private madhouses for the care of the insane (at a profit) also began in this era and also involved physicians. And third, with the influence of Francis Bacon's "new philosophy," which sparked science as we know it, the concept of "disease" began to take on new meaning. This was largely due to the influence of the English physician Thomas Sydenham (1624–1689), often referred to as the "English Hippocrates," who emphasized the direct observation of illnesses and suggested their classification according to syndromes, or groups of symptoms. This differed from the centuries-old identification of diseases usually by a single symptom, such as was the case with the ancient mental disorder known as "fury."

THE 1700S: MADNESS IS CLASSIFIED

Throughout the 1700s, physicians who doctored to the mentally ill in madhouses (both public and private) began to be recognized for their medical specialty and were called "mad-doctors" or "lunatic-doctors" in England and its colonies. The more scientifically minded "mad-doctors" began to study the symptoms of mental illness for the first time in terms of syndromes, and many of them contributed treatises and classifications of their insane patients. In this endeavor the British led the way, and such figures as William Battie of St. Luke's Hospital in London, John Haslam of "Bedlam" in London and William Cullen of Edinburgh became world-famous authorities through their written observations on madness. Daringly, Haslam even reported on his autopsies of corpses of Bedlam patients, in an age where such practices were discouraged by British laws and "bodysnatchers" supplied medical students and professors with such commodities. Each author devised his own unique classification system for mental disorders, often borrowing concepts used for centuries, as well as coining new terms and phrases. It is certain that many cases of what we would now call schizophrenia were probably classified under one or more of these early attempts to devise a more scientific method of understanding mental illness.

THE 1800S: PSYCHIATRY (AND
SCHIZOPHRENIA) BEGINS

Following the early lead of the British, after 1801 it was the French who dominated the medical study of the mentally ill until mid-century, when the Germans began their domination of this field. Indeed, the devotion of the early French *alienistes* (Pinel, Esquirol and the members of the "Esquirol Circle") to the study and classification of mental disorders directly led to the development of a distinct medical specialty for mental illness, which is now universally known as "psychiatry." The French were the first to include lectures on mental illness in their medical schools, and the British followed suit by the 1820s.

In 1801 French physician Philippe Pinel published his famous treatise on insanity (*l'aliénation mentale,* or "mental alienation," which led physicians who specialized in the care of the mentally ill to be called "alienists" in England). The first edition of Pinel's *Traité médico-philosophique sur l'aliénation mentale, ou la manie* established him as the world's leading authority on mental illness, and helped to persuade the world that the mentally ill could be treated in a more humane manner through his philosophy of "moral treatment." When Pinel was put in charge of the large institution for insane men in Paris following the French Revolution, he became famous for freeing 53 patients from their chains—without any disastrous consequences. Indeed, one of them, a former French soldier named Chevigné, became his bodyguard. The legend of Pinel unshackling the insane fit well with the revolutionary and democratic spirit of the times, and it helped to free the psychological chains in the minds of caretakers of the mentally ill, that their charges were nothing more than beasts and should be treated as such. Variations of the "moral treatment" were already being developed in England by William Tuke at the York Retreat and by Vincenzo Chiarugi, often referred to as "the Pinel of Italy." This more humane treatment philosophy was not widely adopted in Europe until the mid-1800s, and even in England it took the reformist physician John Conolly's "nonrestraint movement" in the 1840s to finally bring lasting changes in the asylums in that country.

In the young United States, Philadelphia physician Benjamin Rush of the Pennsylvania Hospital began to study the insane patients within his institution and published a book on the subject, his *Medical Inquiries and Observations upon the Diseases of the Mind* of 1812, the only major American textbook of psychiatry to appear until the 1880s. Thus, American physicians played almost no role in the scientific description and classification of mental disorders until the 20th century.

Schizophrenia now enters the picture. In 1809, the very first clinical descriptions of schizophrenia as we know it appeared in print in two separate works. Working independently in their respective countries, John Haslam of the Bethlem Royal Hospital in London and Philippe Pinel of the Salpêtrière asylum in Paris both produced expanded second editions of books on mental illness that had been published previously; they contain the first complete reports of what we now know as schizophrenia in its "chronic" (or "Type II") form. The expanded second edition of 1809 of Pinel's original 1801 treatise has never been translated into English (a translation of the first edition appeared as early as 1806). Pinel's description of *démence* in the first edition strongly resembles the thought disorder of schizophrenia, and this concept was apparently illustrated with case material in the second edition that seemed to confirm this connection. However, the following case history reproduced here from Haslam's 1809 *Observations on Madness and Melancholy* may be the first valid historical evidence in the English language for schizophrenia:

There is a form of insanity which occurs in young persons; and, as far as these cases have been the subject of my observation, they have been more frequently noticed in females. Those whom I have seen, have been distinguished by prompt capacity and lively disposition; and in general have become the favorites of parents and tutors, by their faculty in acquiring knowledge, and by a prematurity of attainment. This disorder commences, about or shortly after, the period of menstruation, and in many instances has been unconnected with hereditary taint; as far as could be ascertained by minute enquiry. The attack is almost imperceptible; some months usually elapse before it becomes the subject of particular notice; and fond relatives are frequently deceived by the hope that it is only an abatement of excessive vivacity, conducing to a prudent reserve, and steadiness of character. A degree of apparent thoughtfulness and inactivity precede, together with the diminution of the ordinary curiosity, concerning that which is passing before them; and they therefore neglect those objects and pursuits which formerly proved sources of delight and instruction. The sensibility appears to be considerably blunted; they do not bear the same affection towards their parents and relations; they become unfeeling to kindness, and careless of reproof. To their companions they show a cold civility, but take no interest whatever in their concerns. If they read a book they are unable to give any account of its contents; sometimes, with steadfast eyes, they will dwell for an hour on one page, and then turn over a number in a few minutes. It is very difficult to persuade them to write, which most readily develops their state of mind; much time is consumed and little is produced. The subject is reportedly begun, but they seldom advance beyond a sentence or two; the orthography becomes puzzling, and by endeavoring to adjust the spelling the subject vanishes. As their apathy increases they are negligent of their dress, and inattentive to personal cleanliness. Frequently they seem to experience transient impulses of passion, but these have no source in sentiment; the tears, which trickle down at one time, are as unmeaning as the loud laugh which succeeds them; and it often happens that a momentary gust of anger, with its attendant invectives, ceases before the threat can be concluded. As the disorder increases, the urine and feces are passed without restraint, and from the indolence which accompanies it, they generally become corpulent. Thus in the interval between puberty and manhood, I have painfully witnessed this hopeless and degrading change, which in a short time has transformed the most promising and vigorous intellect into a slavering and bloated idiot.

(Haslam is describing what 20th-century British psychiatrist Timothy J. Crow has named "Type II schizophrenia" or the "Pinel-Haslam syndrome": insidious onset, negative symptoms [attention deficits, problems in information processing, apathy, poverty of speech, loss of curiosity in people and activities] and gradual cognitive deterioration.)

The cognitive deterioration described by Haslam, or *démence*, as Pinel termed it, was later elaborated upon by French *alieniste* Benedict Augustin Morel in his descriptions of mental "degeneration," for which he coined the term *démence précoce* in 1852. Whereas the concept of degeneration probably referred to cases that we would label schizophrenia today, it also referred to cases of one of the most frequently encountered psychotic disorders of the 19th and early 20th century, the "general paralysis of the insane," which was later found to be caused by tertiary syphilis.

After Morel's contribution of the "mental degeneration" concept in the 1850s, and Jules Baillarger's very first description of the "double-formed insanity" (what we now call bipolar disorder) in 1854, the French alienists subsided in importance, and it was the Germans, led by Wilhelm Griesinger, who began to dominate psychiatry until well into the 20th century (except, perhaps, for Charcot's contributions in Paris in the 1880s to the understanding of hysteria and the use of hypnosis). Griesinger's 1845 textbook, *Die Pathologie und Therapie der Psychische Krankheiten (The Pathology and Therapy of Mental Disorders)*, provided a detailed classification of mental disorders that was based on the notion that they were organically based, indeed, that they were all largely diseases of the brain. Although not a new notion, the work of Griesinger and later German psychiatrists and neurologists helped to establish the biological approach in psychiatry. Because of the contributions of the Germans, the biological approach is the central research strategy in the study of schizophrenia and the psychotic disorders today.

The 1840s was the pivotal decade in the history of the profession of psychiatry. By this time the actual word "psychiatry" was in use in both Germany and England, and the very first professional associations of such physicians were formed in Germany, England, France and in the United States. In 1844, 13 superintendents of state asylums from across America met together in Philadelphia and formed the organization that is now known as the American Psychiatric Association. In the 1870s, following the study of wounded veterans of the American Civil War, the first professional society for the medical specialty of neurology was founded. Thus the study of mental disorders now had two branches of medicine with two very different philosophies, which remained at odds with one another until well into the 20th century.

With the Germans taking the lead, psychiatry began to resemble its present form. Indeed, by the end of the 19th century our present notion of psychosis as a disorder involving a gross impairment in reality testing (a "break with reality") and the creation of a new reality had taken shape. Even today psychosis encompasses phenomena that were labeled "insanity," "alienation" and "dementia" or degeneration in the 19th century. German psychiatrists such as Karl Kahlbaum and Ewald Hecker described specific psychotic disorders that are still included in our present definitions of schizophrenia—catatonia (first named by Kahlbaum in 1869) and hebephrenia (described by Hecker in 1874). By the end of the 19th century, the stage was set for the decisive definition of the psychotic disorders.

DEMENTIA PRAECOX (1896)

At the end of the 19th century psychiatry could not yet agree on a universally recognized classification system for mental disorders. Classification systems would differ from hospital to hospital (by 1900, no longer officially called "asylums"), and often one of the first questions to be asked by visiting colleagues upon arrival at a mental hospital they had never been to before was, "Whose classification system do you use?" Some might use Griesinger's or Kahlbaum's or some other authority's, but by the 20th century a universally recognized authority had emerged—German psychiatrist Emil Kraepelin. It was the successive editions of his constantly revised textbook, *Psychiatrie,* that were eventually adopted as the standard in Europe and the United States.

In 1896 the fifth edition of *Psychiatrie* came out and introduced the world to the chronic, progressively degenerative psychotic disorder that Kraepelin called *dementia praecox.* The name referred to the disorder's rapid mental deterioration. Kraepelin combined a degenerative form of the ancient psychotic disorder known as paranoia with Kahlbaum's catatonia and Hecker's hebephrenia. Kraepelin's concept of dementia praecox was based on its poor prognosis: All cases eventually ended up with severe mental degeneration and without remission. This was in distinction to the "recoverable psychoses," the primary one of which he later named manic-depressive psychosis. Thus, Kraepelin classified the psychotic disorders according to good prognosis psychoses (manic-depressive psychosis) and poor prognosis psychoses (dementia praecox).

In his very first published descriptions of dementia praecox, Kraepelin outlined the characteristics that are still largely true today for schizophrenia: It is a disease that begins in late adolescence or early adulthood; it afflicts more men than women; it is largely hereditary; and it is first and foremost a brain disease due to a "tangible morbid process in the brain." Indeed, Kraepelin believed a toxin in the brain caused it to "autointoxicate" itself, thus producing the progressively degenerative symptoms and course of dementia praecox. Kraepelin considered negative or deficit symptoms to be of greater clinical significance, but the characteristic symptoms of this disorder have increased or decreased with the broadening or narrowing of its definition by others over the last century (Andreasen and Flaum, 1991).

SCHIZOPHRENIA (1908)

Not everyone agreed with Kraepelin's emphasis on classification by prognosis. Indeed one Swiss psychiatrist, Eugen Bleuler, began to question the notion, observing that there were many different courses to the disorder, and that some persons with dementia praecox would plateau at a particular level of deficit and stay at that level for the rest of their lives, without degenerating any further. In 1908 Bleuler published a paper challenging Kraepelin's views, and suggested that the disorder be renamed *schizophrenia* (from two Greek words meaning "to split" and "mind") to remove the emphasis on prognosis suggested by the term dementia praecox. Bleuler had been using the term "schizophrenia" in lectures to his medical staff at the Burghölzli Hospital in Zurich, Switzerland, prior to this time. In 1911 Bleuler published his classic monograph, *Dementia Praecox oder die Gruppe der Schizophrenien*. His description of schizophrenia (to which he added a fourth subtype, Otto Diem's "simple schizophrenia") was hailed as a major contribution, and the ideas in Bleuler's 1911 book are still largely reflected in the classification systems in use today. No one has ever matched Bleuler's insightful description of this disease.

THE 20TH CENTURY: PSYCHIATRY BECOMES PSYCHOANALYZED

Although Kraepelin continued to search for the biological causes of mental disorders (including the establishment of a series of laboratories in Munich to study neuropathology, histology and even [a first] to develop drugs to battle mental illness), much of the rest of psychiatry became enamored of the theory of psychoanalysis of Viennese neurologist Sigmund Freud. As his one-time associate, Swiss psychiatrist C.G. Jung, wrote, Freud "put the psychology into psychiatry." As such, psychiatrists became more and more interested in the psychodynamics that might lead to mental disorders and began to ignore their possible physiological causes—even for such chronic and debilitating disorders as schizophrenia. Although much has been gained in the understanding of neurotic disorders and psychotherapy from psychoanalysis, the "psychoanalyzing" of psychiatry (particularly American, French and British psychiatry) from about 1920 to the 1960s largely diverted the search for biological causes of the psychotic disorders into a blind alley, perhaps prolonging the needless suffering of millions. Psychoanalysis led to blaming "refrigerator mothers" or "schizophrenogenic mothers" for causing schizophrenia in their children, and the "family interaction theories" of the 1950s and 1960s placed the blame on unhealthy communication patterns within the entire family—thus sharing the blame for the cause of schizophrenia. It took advances in medical technology to finally swing the pendulum back to the search for biological causes of psychosis.

THE 1970S: SCHIZOPHRENIA BECOMES A PHYSICAL DISEASE ONCE AGAIN

Advances in the technology to study biochemistry, brain function and structure, genetics and the development of brain imaging techniques (e.g., the CT scan) all converged to stimulate a biological renaissance in the study of schizophrenia and the psychotic disorders in the 1970s. Suddenly it was appropriate to speak of schizophrenia as a "brain disease," and psychoanalytic and family interaction models largely began to be ignored as legitimate causes of this disease (although it was found that psychosocial factors can have an effect on relapse rates in persons with schizophrenia). Genetic transmission was now estimated to be responsible for about 80% of the cause of schizophrenia, with other unknown environmental factors comprising the other 20%. Viral theories of the cause of schizophrenia were also resurrected after first being mentioned by Kraepelin and Bleuler almost a century before. Perinatal factors in the development of schizophrenia again began to be studied in earnest. Cross-cultural studies of the prevalence rates of schizophrenia were initiated by the World Health Organization. Twins studies and adoption studies conducted in the 1960s helped to form new and complex theories of the genetic transmission of schizophrenia in the 1970s and 1980s. After decades of disappointment and neglect, the search for the causes of schizophrenia once again was viewed as a promising endeavor.

THE 1980S AND BEYOND: THE GENETIC QUEST

By 1980, enough evidence had accumulated from a variety of sources (clinical phenomenology, brain imaging studies, biochemical and neurophysiological studies) to allow British psychiatrist Timothy J. Crow to postulate "Type I" and "Type II" schizophrenia, each with different symptoms, different organic causes (one primarily biochemical, the other primarily genetic) and different outcomes. Much of the earlier research has been reanalyzed according to this "two syndrome" hypothesis.

Advances in the technology of molecular genetics led to the first report (in the April 1988 issue of the British medical journal *The Lancet*) of the discovery of a chromosomal abnormality in schizophrenia by Canadian researcher Anne S. Basset and her colleagues at the University of British Columbia. The abnormality was discovered on chromosome 5. Shortly thereafter other research reports were published that also implicated chromosome 5, as well as some that implicated other chromosomes. With the Human Genome Project commencing in the late 1980s to begin the arduous task of mapping the entire human genome, thus theoretically enabling the location of the genes that cause diseases suspected to be genetic in origin (such as schizophrenia and bipolar disorder), the 1990s may be the era when the psychotic disorders are finally understood and—quite possibly—point to the day when they can be prevented.

Andreasen, N.C. & Flaum, M., "Schizophrenia: The characteristic symptoms," *Schizophrenia Bulletin*, 17 (1991), 27–49.

Haldipur, C.V., "Madness in Ancient India: Concepts of Madness in Charaka Samhita (1st century A.D.)," *Comprehensive Psychiatry*, 25 (1984), 335–344.

Haslam, J., *Observations on Madness and Melancholy*. London: J. Callon, 1809.

Jeste, D.V., "Did Schizophrenia Exist before the Eighteenth Century?" *Comprehensive Psychiatry*, 26 (1985), 493–503.

Pinel, P., *Traité médico-philosophique sur l'aliénation mentale*, 2nd ed. Paris: J.A. Brosson, 1809.

Torrey, E.F., *Schizophrenia and Civilization*. New York: Jason Aronson, 1980.

Williams, G., *The Age of Agony: The Art of Healing, ca. 1700–1800*. Chicago: Academy Chicago Publishers, 1986.

A NOTE TO THE READER ON THE USE OF THIS BOOK

This volume points both forward and backward in time.

The information source you have before you about schizophrenia and the psychotic disorders begins at about the year 1750—when the first stirrings of interest in psychiatry began—and includes more than two centuries of historical, biographical and clinical information about how the medical sciences have tried to understand these devastating diseases. Biographical entries have been provided only for those persons who are deceased, since many of the major figures in schizophrenia research living today continue to make contributions.

This book is first and foremost a compendium of detailed information on schizophrenia. More detailed information on bipolar disorder (manic-depressive psychosis)—which is not covered with the same depth as schizophrenia—can be found in the masterpiece *Manic-Depressive Illness* (New York: Oxford University Press, 1990) by F.K. Goodwin and K.R. Jamison and in the other reference works suggested in this book.

The entries in this book have been carefully selected for their usefulness in the years to come. Many technical terms relating to the field of genetics have been included, since much of the scientific research on schizophrenia and the psychotic disorders in the years to come will be in this field. Therefore, whether the reader is a concerned family member, a person with schizophrenia, or a mental health professional who wants to be able to read the new scientific literature on the genetics of schizophrenia, the extensive entries in this book will help that person decipher these highly technical articles and books.

Throughout the entries in this book there will be many references to *ICD-9* (1978) and *DSM-III-R* (1987), the two most often used diagnostic manuals for mental disorders throughout the world. Full descriptions of these books are provided in the entries listed under the acronyms for these volumes.

Rather than including a huge bibliography at the end of the book, in order to prevent all of the flipping of pages back and forth as the reader attempts to locate a particular reference, full citations of references are included after each entry. These reference sources have been chosen carefully according to three criteria: (1) the source is recommended as the best single review of the relevant research in a particular area; (2) the source represents the first mention of an important theory or research finding in print; and (3) the source refers directly to a passage quoted in the entry, or cites a major representative work of the person listed in a biographical entry. The users of this book are encouraged to read further, and it is hoped that the extensive references provided with the entries will encourage further exploration in the spirit of the proverb that was a favorite among the medieval alchemists, *liber librum aperit* (essentially, "one book opens another").

There are many long citations from very rare psychiatric texts and especially from autobiographical accounts. Our best feeling for what life must have been like for both patients and psychiatrists alike over the past two centuries comes from such vivid reports. Many of these quotations are from books that are so rare that they can be found only in the rare book collections of *some* specialized libraries, and care has been taken to select those passages that particularly make psychiatric history "come alive" for the reader.

No other book like this presently exists for understanding schizophrenia and the psychotic disorders. It is hoped that the reader will find it of value when trying to come to grips with a subject that has mystified humankind for centuries.

A

abaissement du niveau mental Literally, a "lowering of the level (or threshold) of consciousness." Today, this idea is usually expressed by the term ALTERED STATE OF CONSCIOUSNESS.

French psychiatrist Pierre JANET (1859–1947) coined this term to refer to the apparent weakening of volitional control of consciousness, and the subsequent dissociation (or 'splitting') of consciousness into autonomous parts that may not even be aware of one another. Although Janet noted that this *abaissement* was common in forms of psychological automatisms such as found in multiple personalities, hysterics, the trance behavior of mediums and in automatic writing, the term was adopted and used extensively by Swiss psychiatrist C.G. Jung (1875–1961) in his famous 1907 monograph, *Über die Psychologie der Dementia praecox: Ein Versuch (The Psychology of Dementia Praecox)* to describe dementia praecox (later "schizophrenia"). This monograph was the first to apply the controversial psychoanalytic concepts of Sigmund Freud (1857–1939) to dementia praecox. Jung felt that the *abaissement* was the "primary condition" and "the root of the schizophrenic disorder." He thought it resulted from both psychological and physiological causes. In dementia praecox, Jung argued that the *abaissement* caused the following effects commonly observed in schizophrenics: (1) the loss of whole regions of normally controlled contents of consciousness; (2) split-off fragments of the personality; (3) the prevention of normal trains of thought from being consistently carried through and completed; (4) a decrease in the responsibility and proper reaction of the ego; (5) constriction and distortion of thoughts and feelings; and (6) a lowering of the threshold of consciousness (as in an altered state), thereby allowing normally inhibited content of the unconscious to enter consciousness in the form of autonomous invasions.

Jung was briefly (in 1902) a student of Janet's in Paris and was greatly influenced by him. *Abaissement du niveau mental* was a term used frequently by C.G. Jung in his later writings.

Janet, P., *L'Automatisme Psychologique*. Paris: Alcon, 1890.

Jung, C.G., *Über die Psychologie der Dementia praecox: Ein Versuch*. Halle a.S.: 1907.

ablation studies In the late-19th and early-20th centuries, the modern neurosciences (then called the "brain sciences") were coming into being, just as the clinical syndromes of dementia praecox and manic-depressive psychosis were simultaneously being identified and described by Emil KRAEPELIN (1856–1926). It was natural that the investigative techniques of gross anatomy and neuropathology of the new "brain sciences" would be applied to the study of the brains of deceased patients that had suffered from these mental disorders. The many ablation studies of the brains of schizophrenics and manic-depressives involved the removal and systematic destruction of the brain tissue in order to look for structural abnormalities. Brain tissue was commonly ablated slice by slice, with careful records kept to document unusual formations. Not surprisingly, most of these studies were inconclusive due to the imprecision of this gross procedure. Modern brain imaging techniques and biochemical and genetic strategies of investigation have been more successful in detecting the subtle physiological abnormalities in the brains of people suffering from schizophrenia or manic-depressive psychosis. (See also BRAIN ABNORMALITIES IN SCHIZOPHRENIA; BRAIN IMAGING TECHNIQUES).

Abraham, Karl (1877–1925) A close friend of Sigmund Freud (whom he first met in 1907), Abraham founded the Psychoanalytic Society in Berlin in 1908. Freud reports that he was the first German psychoanalyst. For many years he worked at the BURG-HÖLZLI HOSPITAL in Zurich, Switzerland, with two pioneers in the study of schizophrenia: Eugen BLEULER and C.G. JUNG. He was somewhat pessimistic about the psychoanalytic treatment of schizophrenics in his early career, but his views became more hopeful in later writings. He is remembered most for his work on depression, and most of the patients he treated fit into the then-accepted diagnostic description of manic-depressive illness formulated by Emil Kraepelin. Two of Abraham's early, influential papers on these psychotic syndromes are "The Psycho-Sexual Differences Between Hysteria and Dementia Praecox" (1908) and "Notes on the Psycho-Analytic Investigation and Treatment of Manic-Depressive Insanity and Allied Conditions" (1912).

Abraham, K., *Selected Papers in Psychoanalysis*. New York: Basic Books, 1953.

abuse of psychiatric patients   The mentally ill have been ridiculed and scorned throughout human history. Although the efforts to humanize the treatment of the mentally ill through the "moral medicine" movement of the early 19th century resulted in many reforms in some asylums for the insane, reports have continued until present times of periodic abuses—both psychological and physiological—in psychiatric facilities throughout the world. It is often thought that the tremendous power that the staff of such institutions wields over the (usually) involuntarily committed, mentally ill patient can sometimes corrupt even the most empathetic and well-intentioned caregiver at stressful times.

Through the centuries a massive and disturbing literature of first-person accounts has been created that documents such abuses. A small book published anonymously in London in 1752, entitled *Low-Life, Or One Half Of The World Knows Not How The Other Half Lives,* describes the torturous condi-

tions of the chained patients at the Bethlem Royal Hospital ("Bedlam"), in which the author reports observing the nurses stealing for themselves the best portions of food that were originally intended for the patients. Sadly, even today such abuses by staff are frequently reported in large mental institutions, and not only food but also property and even money often mysteriously disappear from patients who, when they complain, are told they are either confused, delusional or lying. In *The New York World* newspaper in 1887 a serialized story entitled "Ten Days in a Mad House" described similar abuses. It was written by journalist-celebrity Elizabeth Seaman (*née* Cochrane) who, under the pseudonym Nellie BLY, faked mental illness and gained admission to the New York City Lunatic Asylum on Blackwell's Island (briefly named "Welfare Island" in the 1940s but now changed to "Roosevelt Island"). This account was published in book form in 1888.

Perhaps the most famous—and influential—autobiographical account was Clifford Beers' *A Mind That Found Itself* (1908). Beers, a businessman who underwent a brief psychotic episode, was first put in a private sanitarium and then a state hospital. He described the repeated abuses of patients by attendants and how kindly new staff members were soon transformed into sadists through peer pressure. Beers writes:

I soon observed that the only patients who were not likely to be subjected to abuse were the very ones least in need of care and treatment . . . The patient too weak, physically or mentally, to attend to his own wants was frequently abused because of that very helplessness which made it necessary for attendants to wait upon him.

He also relates the following anecdote, still familiar to those who work in today's mental institutions:

One attendant, on the very day he had been discharged for choking a patient into an insensibility so profound that it had been necessary to call a physician to restore him, said to me, 'They are getting pretty damned strict these days, discharging a man for simply *choking* a patient.' This illustrates the attitude of many attendants.

Beers eventually improved, wrote his autobiography and founded the MENTAL HYGIENE MOVEMENT in the United States. His early efforts are still bearing fruit with the many mental patients' advocacy groups, especially the NATIONAL ALLIANCE FOR THE MENTALLY ILL.

As much as we may prefer not to believe it, abuses are still a part of the world of almost any institution that serves an inpatient population of people who have chronic mental illnesses. A short autobiographical account by Leopold Bellak, a prominent psychiatrist, schizophrenia researcher and professor at the Albert Einstein College of Medicine in New York City, includes a story that almost anyone today who has ever worked in such facilities will find familiar. These are the sort of events that go on *sub rosa* in the culture of the mental hospital but that no one will openly admit to, especially administrators, who often do not want either to hear of such cases or believe them when reported. This leaves the honest witness to suffer the brunt of the negative consequences for his or her accusations, with the actual abuser often remaining unaffected. Bellak describes his first clinical experiences as a psychiatric aide on a chronic psychotic ward in 1938 and 1939:

> The utter sense of hopelessness fostered in institutions run in very poor and dictatorial fashion by an ill-trained staff was often hardly better than that described in *One Flew Over the Cuckoo's Nest*. Acts of sadism were tolerated, if not encouraged. On my first day as a psychiatric aide in a high-class sanitarium, I was put under the tutelage of an experienced psychiatric aide. Among his first words of wisdom to me were that if I should find it necessary to hit a patient, I should hit him in the abdomen in order to leave no telltale marks. Seeing a patient put into wet packs was the closest thing I could imagine to a rape.

In many countries today political prisoners are sometimes incarcerated and abused in mental institutions, a practice that led to the withdrawal of the Soviet Union from the World Psychiatric Association in 1983, when it became clear that the U.S.S.R. was likely to be expelled. As a result of the *glasnost* of the Gorbachev era, an official delegation of 26 Americans (including 14 psychiatrists and 2 lawyers) selected by the National Institute of Mental Health, visited four Soviet mental hospitals in February and March 1989 to investigate such reports. In July 1989 the investigative team released its report, claiming that many of the patients they examined had no discernible mental disorders and that the maximum security prisons in the Soviet Union still had the characteristics of "psychiatric prisons." They found that many patients had been incarcerated for "anti-Soviet thoughts" or undesirable political behavior. Drugs were used for "punitive rather than therapeutic purposes," and patients were denied most rights, especially the right to have a say in their treatment. Based on these grim findings, the delegation recommended that the Soviet Union not be readmitted to the World Psychiatric Association. However, due to the political climate of openness and optimism toward the changes in Soviet society, on October 18, 1989, the World Psychiatric Association voted to readmit the Soviet All-Union Society of Psychiatrists and Narcologists, but with the stipulation that it would be subject to suspension if the Soviets do not end their misuse of psychiatry against political dissidents. Despite the negative report and recommendations of the NIMH, the American Psychiatric Association voted in favor of readmission. (See also BEERS, CLIFFORD; CHEMICAL RESTRAINT; MECHANICAL RESTRAINT.)

Beers, Clifford, *A Mind That Found Itself: An Autobiography*. New York: Longmans, Green, 1908.

Bellak, L., "An Idiosyncratic Overview," in L. Bellak (ed.), *Disorders of the Schizophrenic Syndrome*. New York: Basic Books, 1979.

Peterson, D. (ed.), *A Mad People's History of Madness*. Pittsburgh: University of Pittsburgh Press, 1982.

accessory symptoms   The name given by Eugen Bleuler in his 1911 classic, *Dementia Praecox, Or The Group of Schizophrenias,* to the symptoms of schizophrenia that may also appear in other types of mental illness. This is in contrast to the "fundamental symptoms" that uniquely characterize schizophrenia. Among the most easily recognizable of the accessory symptoms are hallucinations and delusions. Bleuler emphasizes what an important role these accessory symptoms play in the life of the afflicted individual when he writes:

> It is not often that the fundamental symptoms are so markedly exhibited as to cause the patient to be hospitalized in a mental institution. It is primarily the accessory phenomena which makes his retention at home impossible, or it is they which make the psychosis manifest and give occasion to require psychiatric help. These accessory symptoms may be present throughout the whole course of this disease, or only in entirely arbitrary periods of illness.

Bleuler, E., *Dementia Praecox, Or the Group of Schizophrenias,* J. Zinkin. New York: International Universities Press, 1950; first published, 1911.

acedia   Also spelled "accidia," it is a word that originated in the Middle Ages to refer to the apathetic self-neglect or uncaring behavior of those who are melancholic (depressed) or otherwise mentally ill. In medieval Europe, the church designated "Accidia" (or "sloth") as the fourth of the Seven Cardinal (Deadly) Sins. Acedia also described an impoverishment of mental energy, which, it was felt, could be reversed in an individual through an experience of "conversion," in which lost faith is recovered and psychological revitalization occurs. Thus, acedia was related to "melancholia" or "depression." This term was used in the 19th century but is now considered obsolete.

Jackson, S.W., *Melancholia and Depression: From Hippocratic Times to Modern Times.* New Haven: Yale University Press, 1986.

acromania   A diagnostic term used in the 18th and 19th centuries to label a "confirmed" or "incurable madness."

acting-out   A common bit of jargon in the day-to-day conversation of mental health professionals today; it refers to the expression of socially inappropriate sexual and aggressive behaviors. It has its origins in psychoanalytic theory, in that sexual and aggressive instinctual impulses, which we normally repress, inhibit or sublimate, are not held back (either unconsciously or in fantasy) and are instead "acted-out" in behavior. More often than not it refers to violent behavior, and if a psychiatric patient is engaged in acting-out behavior it is said that he or she is "going-off" (i.e., like the firing of a rocket or an explosion).

active phase of schizophrenia   The most recent (1987) edition of the diagnostic manual most commonly used in North America, DSM-III-R, identifies three major phases in the course of the schizophrenia disease process: the PRODROMAL PHASE, the active phase and the RESIDUAL PHASE. Of these, the active phase is the most critical, for "during the active phase, psychotic symptoms—e.g., delusions, hallucinations, loosening of associations, incoherence, and catatonic behavior—are prominent." *DSM-III-R* further notes that the "onset of the active phase . . . may be associated with a psychosocial stressor." The diagnosis of schizophrenia can be made only during this active phase, and it must be in evidence for a minimum of one week.

acute   In reference to diseases, "acute" refers to those that are sudden in onset and generally rather short-lived. However, acute phases of a disease are those periods when symptoms that are generally dormant can flare up.

acute-chronic distinction   The criterion in schizophrenia research that traditionally explores cognitive, perceptual and behavioral differences in schizophrenics based on the amount of time they have been diagnosed with the disorder and have been hospitalized. Generally, acute schizophrenics are those who have not been institutionalized for more than 3.5 years, and chronic schizophrenics are those whose total time spent in institutions has been six years or more. Acute schizophrenics have been found to differ from chronic schizophrenics across many neurophysiological and neuropsychological variables. (See also CHRONIC SCHIZOPHRENIA.)

acute delirius mania   A late-19th-century term for the acute forms of CATATONIC EXCITEMENT. The syndrome was often described as an acute mental disorder with a rapid onset and course, resembling delirium caused by fever, during which the patient would experience a rise in temperature, rapidly reach exhaustion and then possibly death. Other names for this syndrome were Bell's syndrome or disease, typhomania, *Délire aigu,* delirius mania, acute delirium, delirium grave, mania gravis and delirium acutum.

Fürstner, C., "Über delirium acutum," *Archiv für psychiatrie,* 11(1881), 517–538.

acute recoverable psychosis   Limited psychotic episode for which complete remission can occur. Acute recoverable psychoses (ARPs) is a generic term proposed for the psychotic diagnoses listed in ICD-9 and DSM-III-R that generally last only from two weeks up to six months. These disorders may be predominantly affective, confusional (resembling organic mental disorders) or schizophrenia-like (usually distinguished by paranoid and nonparanoid varieties). The schizophrenia-like ARPs listed in *DSM-III-R* are acute paranoid psychosis, SCHIZOPHRENIFORM DISORDER and BRIEF REACTIVE PSYCHOSIS, and those in *ICD-9* are psychogenic paranoid psychosis, hysterical psychosis and psychogenic psychosis. It has been suggested that the shared core symptoms and characteristic natural history of the schizophrenia-like ARPs indicate they are variants of the same underlying disorder, despite the many diagnostic labels.

Munro, A., "Schizophrenia-like Illnesses," in M.N. Menuck & M.V. Seeman (eds.), *New Perspectives in Schizophrenia.* New York: Macmillan, 1985.

acute schizophrenia   The acute phase of schizophrenia is when the symptoms first flare up into a full psychosis. However, "acute" can also refer to the length of time that active schizophrenic symptoms are evident or refer to a hypothesized variant of schizophrenia that has a better prognosis than CHRONIC SCHIZOPHRENIA. The ACUTE/CHRONIC DISTINCTION in studies of schizophrenia refers to the amount of time that has elapsed since the clear diagnosis of schizophrenia has been made. Many studies have shown psychological and behavioral differences between those patients in the early or acute stages of the illness versus those in the later or chronic stages of schizophrenia. For research purposes, acute schizophrenics are those who have had less than a total of 3.5 years' hospitalization. Studies have shown that chronic schizophrenics have more severe thought disorder and other cognitive deficits than acute schizophrenics, but many have argued that this deterioration may be due to the debilitating effects of institutionalization rather than being a result of the illness itself. Acute schizophrenia is often conceptually confused with REACTIVE SCHIZOPHRENIA, the type of schizophrenia in which patients are found to have a better pre-breakdown history and eventually improve, versus those who follow a lifelong chronic course.

ADD psychosis The acronym for "attention deficit disorder," a clinical diagnostic entity proposed by Leopold Bellak in 1985. Bellak claims that many cases of schizophrenia (perhaps as many as 10%) are misdiagnosed and are instead examples of "ADD psychosis." ADD psychosis is organic in origin, and it is thought to constitute the end result of a particular neurological deficit (attention deficit disorder) on personality organization. Attention deficit disorder (a common childhood diagnosis given to children who are hyperactive and dyslexic, among other attributes) was formerly called "minimal brain dysfunction," and the concept of ADD psychosis is the lifelong extension of these neurological deficits into adulthood. Many of Bellak's proposed symptoms (primarily NEGATIVE SYMPTOMS) and associated neurological findings for ADD psychosis seem to be similar to Crow's Type II schizophrenia and Carpenter's "deficit syndrome." (See also CROW'S HYPOTHESIS; DEFICIT SYMPTOMS/SYNDROME.)

Bellak, L., "ADD Psychosis as a Separate Entity," *Schizophrenia Bulletin,* 11(1985), 523–527.

adoption method and studies One of the research strategies to resolve the "nature versus nurture" controversy in the investigation of the causes of mental disorders. Adoption studies have tended to strongly support the argument for the genetic basis for many psychiatric disorders, including schizophrenia, bipolar disorder (manic-depressive disorder) and even alcoholism.

Adoption studies have been carried out in two ways: In the first method, children separated at birth from parents with a psychiatric disorder, and then raised by adoptive parents, are located. If these offspring show a prevalence for, say, schizophrenia that is the same as might be expected if they had been raised at home by their schizophrenic parent(s), then the argument is supported that genetics rather than environment is the primary cause of schizophrenia. A second method used in adoption studies is to look at all children who have been adopted, matching those in a group who develop schizophrenia (or another mental disorder) and then matching other adoptees in a control group who have not developed schizophrenia. Research is then conducted on both the biological and adoptive relatives of these individuals in these two groups. If the schizophrenia adoptees show a higher prevalence of schizophrenia in their biological relatives but not their adoptive ones, then the genetic explanation for schizophrenia is supported.

The very first published study using these adoptive methods in schizophrenia research was reported by L.L. Heston in the *British Journal of Psychiatry* in 1966. In the late 1960s, a famous series of adoption studies using these two methods was conducted in Denmark by David Rosenthal and Seymour Kety. All of these studies have consistently shown that adopted children who develop schizophrenia are many times more likely to have biological relatives who have developed schizophrenia rather than adoptive relatives who have done so. In the 1980s Rosenthal and Kety and their associates published reviews of clinical studies using the adoptive methods that support this genetic hypothesis in affective disorders (such as bipolar disorder) as well.

Heston, L.L., "Psychiatric Disorders in Foster Home Reared Children of Schizophrenic Mothers," *British Journal of Psychiatry,* 112(1966), 819–825.

Rosenthal, D. and Kety, S., *The Transmission of Schizophrenia.* Oxford: Pergamon Press, 1968.

Wender P. H., Kety, S.S., Rosenthal D. et al., "Psychiatric Disorders in the Biological and Adoptive Families of Adopted Individuals with Affective Disorders," *Archives of General Psychiatry,* 43(1986), 923–929.

affect The behavioral expression of a subjectively experienced feeling or emotion. Euphoria, anger and sadness are very commonly expressed examples of affect. In clinical terms, affect is different from mood in that affect changes over time in response to changing emotional states, whereas mood refers to an emotion that grips a person for a long period of time, coloring the individual's entire perception of his or her world. (See also AFFECTIVE DISORDERS.)

affective disorders Renamed "mood disorders" in 1987 in DSM-III-R, these are a group of mental disorders in which there is a disturbance of mood, accompanied by a full or partial manic or depressive syndrome, which is not due to any other physical or mental disorder. These disorders are usually characterized by a consistent pattern of mood episodes, usually manic episodes or depressive episodes. Studies indicate that almost 20% of persons with major affective disorders (such as BIPOLAR DISORDER) will never completely recover from their illness and will follow a chronic course.

These disorders are now divided into bipolar disorders and depressive disorders. Although the term bipolar disorder is commonly thought to be a mental disorder that includes both manic and depressive episodes, it actually refers only to a mood disorder in which there are manic episodes; depressive episodes need not be present in some mood disorders to be labeled "bipolar." Unipolar disorder always refers to depressive disorders. Bipolar disorders can sometimes develop into a psychosis and can sometimes be difficult to distinguish from paranoid schizophrenia. The distinction between unipolar and bipolar variants of affective (or mood) disorders was first proposed by German psychiatrist K. Leonard and his associates in 1962. Seasonal patterns have been documented in patients with bipolar disorder or recurrent major depression in which regular 60-day periods of the year are marked by the onset and full remission of the disorder.

As with many other psychiatric disorders, affective (or mood) disorders are likely to have a genetic basis. Affective disorders

such as mania and melancholy (depression) have been described since the beginning of recorded history. Emil Kraepelin first separated dementia praecox (schizophrenia) from "periodic psychoses" in 1896, but in 1899 he included almost all affective disorders under the class heading of manic-depressive psychosis while continuing to define dementia praecox very narrowly. This major distinction between these two major groups of psychiatric disorders is still used today. (See also CHROMOSOME ABNORMALITIES; GENETICS STUDIES.)

affective disturbances One of the "Four As" (autism, affective disturbances, association disturbances, ambivalence) that Eugen Bleuler proposed as the fundamental symptoms of schizophrenia. Since then, this disturbance in the ability of schizophrenics to feel and/or express the full range of human emotions has been included in most definitions of schizophrenia. In *Dementia Praecox, Or The Group of Schizophrenias* (1911), Bleuler writes:

> Patients with schizophrenia react differently to their affective disturbances. The majority are not aware of them and consider their reaction as normal. The more intelligent, however, may reason about it quite acutely. At the beginning they sense the emotional emptiness as rather painful, so that they may be easily mistaken for melancholics. One of our catatonics considered himself as "insensitized"; one of Jung's patients could not pray any more because of "hardening of her feelings." Later, they tend to displace the changes in themselves to the outer world which itself becomes hollow, empty, strange, because of these affective changes. Often the element of strangeness has a touch of the uncanny and the hostile.

Bleuler, E., *Dementia Praecox, Or the Group of Schizophrenias*. New York: International Universities Press, 1950; first published, 1911.

Africa Many studies have been done in Africa since the 1930s to determine how prevalent schizophrenia is on this continent. The majority of impressions from around

Africa is that the prevalence of schizophrenia is quite low. Most of the disorders described in these reports resemble an ACUTE RECOVERABLE PSYCHOSIS rather than schizophrenia. Unfortunately, there is as yet no conclusive study that can give a reasonable estimate of the prevalence of schizophrenia in Africa.

after-care movement   the original name for the organized efforts of mental health professionals in Europe (and later the United States) to provide support services for deinstitutionalized mental patients so that they will not relapse and require readmission. A physician by the name of Lindpainter initiated this movement in Nassau, Germany, in 1829. It became so popular that it was advocated by psychiatrist Jean Falret in France in 1841 and instituted in England in 1871, by an organization called the Guild of Friends of the Infirm in Mind.

The first outpatient clinic devoted to the prevention of mental disorders was founded at the Pennsylvania Hospital in Philadelphia in 1885, and other organized efforts to provide financial and social assistance to discharged mental patients were started in America at around this time. Forms of HYDROTHERAPY, various emetics and some pharmacological substances were administered. Due to the excessive amount of psychiatric patients "deinstitutionalized" in the United States in the 1950s (estimated to be about 200,000 between 1955 and 1967), the United States government began to provide federal funds for Community Mental Health Centers (CMHCs) in 1963 to provide aftercare for these people. However, studies have shown that only a small percentage of discharged psychiatric patients have received consistent care from the CMHCs. The lack of a major effort to provide housing for these individuals led to the phenomenon in the U.S. of the tens (and perhaps hundreds) of thousands of "mentally ill homeless" on American streets by the late 1980s.

age at onset   The general age range at which a particular disorder is thought to begin. Some disorders can begin to afflict a person at any age, but most have particular critical periods in the life cycle during which they are more likely to appear. However, the insidious nature of many psychiatric symptoms often makes it difficult to pinpoint exactly when a particular mental disorder is thought to begin.

In schizophrenia it has been commonly observed that the first major signs of this psychotic disorder occur during adolescence or early adulthood. However, cases of LATE-ONSET SCHIZOPHRENIA occurring after the age of 45 have been reported in the literature. Early-onset schizophrenia is more characteristic of males than females, with 1980s studies of late-onset schizophrenia indicating a high female-to-male ratio and a predominance of paranoid symptoms. The average age of onset for bipolar disorders has been found to be about 30 (average range, ages 20 to 40), with occurrences of brief manic or hypomanic episodes in early adulthood leading up to the development of a psychotic disorder at about this time.

It has long been known that many physical illnesses (such as multiple sclerosis or Alzheimer's disease) have typical age ranges of onset, and the establishment of similar patterns in many mental disorders supports the belief that they are essentially biological in nature and not caused by supernatural forces or psychoanalytic demons such as "unresolved conflicts" or "schizophrenogenic mothers." Schizophrenia and bipolar disorder are thought to be disorders characterized by incomplete age-dependent penetrance, which is a term in genetics research that refers to the likelihood that someone with a particular genetic predisposition will develop a corresponding disorder at a particular time in the life cycle. (See also INCOMPLETE PENETRANCE.)

Keith, S.J., and Matthews, S.M., "The Diagnosis of Schizophrenia: A Review of Onset and Duration Issues," *Schizophrenia Bulletin*, 17 (1991), 51–67.

AIDS dementia complex Since 1981, when AIDS was first observed to occur in the United States in homosexual males, there has been an intense effort to identify the signs and symptoms of the disorder. One of the features that has been observed in many persons who have developed AIDS is a marked mental deterioration. It is now known that HIV-positive persons also develop symptoms of an ORGANIC MENTAL DISORDER—namely, DEMENTIA—which is due to the direct infection of the brain by HIV (the "human immunodeficiency virus"). In fact, the syndrome that was first described in a 1986 publication by researcher B.A. Navia and colleagues as the "AIDS dementia complex" has been found to be the initial clinical presentation of AIDS in as many as one-fourth of all patients. Based on this work, the diagnostic criteria for AIDS formed by the Centers for Disease Control in the United States has modified the criteria to allow the diagnosis of AIDS solely on the basis of dementia in a seropositive (that is, tested positive for the HIV in the blood) individual without any other evidence of an opportunistic infection or Karposi's sarcoma. Besides the usual signs of dementia—forgetfulness, poor concentration, confusion, slowed thinking—there are movement problems (loss of balance, leg weakness) and more serious psychiatric symptoms, such as depression, apathy and even the thought disorder or mania of psychosis. The later stages of the disorder are marked by the most severe forms of these symptoms.

There has been some concern that the early stages of AIDS dementia complex may be misdiagnosed as schizophrenia, although a routine HIV test should help to clear up the issue. Research on the retroviruses stimulated by AIDS may lead to a better understanding of the causes of the psychotic disorders. VIRAL THEORIES OF SCHIZOPHRENIA have long been suggested. Some hope may arise from the 1989 announcement of the discovery of traces of a retrovirus (HTLV-1) in the blood cells of persons with multiple sclerosis—a disease that has been compared to schizophrenia. (See also MULTIPLE SCLEROSIS AND SCHIZOPHRENIA.)

Jones, G.H., "HIV and the Onset of Schizophrenia," *The Lancet*, 1(1987), 982.
Navia, B.A. et al., "The AIDS Dementia Complex. I. Clinical Features," *Annals of Neurology*, 19(1986) 517–524.
Navia, B.A. et al., "AIDS Dementia Complex as the Presenting Sole Manifestation of HIV Infection," *Annals of Neurology*. 44(1987), 65–69.

AIDS and psychiatric patients Although no studies of the incidence and prevalence of Acquired Immune Deficiency Syndrome (AIDS) in psychiatric patients have been conducted (as of early 1989), the institutionalized populations and deinstitutionalized "street people" are at high risk for contracting this disorder. This will no doubt be an important issue in the future. As many institutionalized patients contract and develop AIDS, the need will arise for special psychiatric inpatient units designed for those that need to be placed on body fluid precautions. State hospitals in particular are believed to be fertile breeding ground for the spread of this disorder; several high-risk populations (IV drug abusers, prisoners, promiscuous patients with impulse control disorders) are combined together on the wards of these institutions and freely engage in high-risk sexual behaviors. Male wards in psychiatric hospitals—as in prisons—are known for their promotion of homosexual practices, and sometimes these same patients engage in sexual activities with members of the opposite sex when given free hours on the grounds during the day.

Recognizing this danger, and the ethical problems AIDS poses for psychiatrists, the American Psychiatric Association's Ad Hoc Committee on AIDS Policy issued AIDS policy guidelines, which were published in full in the *American Journal of Psychiatry* in April 1988. The APA's "Guidelines for Inpatient Psychiatric Units" recommends to psychiatrists that, "Regardless of HIV serologic status, all inpatients should be considered potentially at risk for transmitting or receiving HIV infection."

During the early years of the AIDS epidemic, there was some concern that the confusion and other signs of mental deterioration documented in AIDS patients might be misdiagnosed as signs of schizophrenia or other mental disorders. But a major study released by the World Health Organization in 1988 indicates that mental deterioration is evident only in the later, more serious stages of the illness, when the diagnosis of AIDS has already become evident through the detectable presence of human immunodeficiency virus (HIV) antibodies in the blood.

American Psychiatric Association, "AIDS Policy: Guidelines for Inpatient Psychiatric Units," *American Journal of Psychiatry*, 145(1988), 4.

akathesia   A symptom found in many psychiatric patients treated with antipsychotic drugs. It is usually defined as the compulsion to be in motion. Patients with akathesia report feeling restless, uncomfortable with remaining still, and needing to pace or fidget continually. The neurological mechanism for this behavior is not well understood. Akathesia seems to be a symptom that appears in patients who are treated with high-potency antipsychotic medication. Sometimes this symptom can be alleviated by lowering the dosage, switching to a lower-potency drug or by administering a contra-active drug such as the ones used to treat acute dystonic reactions (namely, anticholinergic and antiparkinsonian agents, antihistamines and benzodiazepines).

akinesia   See BRADYKINESIA.

Akineton   The trade name for biperiden, an anticholinergic drug that is used to treat the sometimes severe side effects that patients can experience after the initiation of antipsychotic drug therapy or after a significant increase in dosage. These side effects (stiffness, tremors, lockjaw, involuntary motions of the mouth, tongue and hands, involuntary eye rolls), which usually happen within hours or days of administering antipsychotic drugs, are acute dystonic reactions that can be reversed with antiparkinsonian agents such as Akineton, Benadryl or Cogentin. These side effects are acute and are not to be confused with chronic reactions to years of treatment with antipsychotic drugs; these chronic reactions are known as TARDIVE DYSKINESIA and are treated with drugs other than Akineton.

alcohol amnestic disorder   See KORSAKOV'S PSYCHOSIS.

Alexis of Piedmont   (ca. 1471–1565) An Italian physician born in Piedmont who may have been one of the earliest to document instances of childhood psychosis. He referred to this as the "lunatic disease" in children. However, his speculations as to the cause of this disorder were less prophetic, as he attributed it to the presence of a double-headed worm within the body. (See also CHILDHOOD SCHIZOPHRENIA.)

alienation mentale   See MENTAL ALIENATION.

alienism   An obsolete 19th-century term for the study and treatment of mental diseases. In France this medical discipline was referred to as MÈDECINE MENTALE. It predates "psychiatry" as a conventional label for this profession. The word "psychiatry" was first used in English to describe this profession in 1846, following the coining of the word "psychiatrics" by FEUCHTERSLEBEN in 1845. From about the mid-1800s this profession was also called "medical psychology" or "mental science."

alienist An archaic, obsolete term for a psychiatrist that was commonly used in the 1800s. The French term for this professional was *aliéniste*. Other commonly used terms for psychiatrists, especially in England, were "mental pathologist" and "psychiater" (from the German word of the same spelling). "Lunatic doctor" and "mad-doctor" were terms more commonly employed in the 17th and 18th centuries. These men frequently worked in "mad-houses" and later "lunatic asylums." MENTAL ALIENATION—first used in the 15th century as a term for mental illness—became the standard term for mental illness in the late 18th and early 19th centuries, hence the derivation of the label for this type of professional. "Alienists" also referred to those psychiatric experts who were requested to make legal competency determinations in court, especially at LUNACY TRIALS.

allele One of several alternative forms of a GENE. Alleles always occupy the same place ("locus") on a chromosome. Different enzymes produced by them perform similar gene functions.

Allen, Matthew (?–1845) A physician in Britain who studied the patients in many mental institutions and who gave a series of lecture tours to report on his findings. His lectures, entitled "The Mind and Its Diseases," were delivered in many places between 1816 and 1819. He became the resident medical officer of the York Lunatic Asylum in 1819. Allen is important for two reasons: He was apparently the first to cite family problems as the cause of psychotic breakdowns and other mental illnesses, referring to this causative agent as "the demon of domestic strife"; and secondly, he was the first to admit voluntary patients to his "madhouse," and the practice of voluntary commitment is still continued today.

Hunter, R. and Macalpine, I., *Three Hundred Years of Psychiatry, 1535–1835*. London: Oxford University Press, 1963.

Allen, Thomas (?–1684) Thomas Allen was a royal physician to Charles II of England and was an officer of the BETHLEM ROYAL HOSPITAL ("BEDLAM"). He is remembered as a precursor to the practitioners of "moral medicine" in that he strongly opposed a series of experiments on psychiatric patients in the Bethlem Royal Hospital that involved submitting them to BLOOD TRANSFUSIONS with sheep's blood in order to cure them. Not surprisingly, this practice led to many deaths. (See also BLEEDING.)

alms houses Houses founded by private charities for the reception and support of the (usually) poor. These are the famous "poor houses" that provided "indoor relief." Mentally ill individuals were frequently guests at alms houses. The word dates back to medieval times when it referred to the house where the alms of the monastery were dispensed to the needy. Many such institutions were built in the United States during the "Age of Reform" from the 1820s to the 1840s, as were many penitentiaries and asylums for the mentally ill. In Pennsylvania, the famous Philadelphia Poorhouse was utilized by the many medical schools for the training of new physicians. Today's rough equivalent of alms houses are rescue missions and halfway houses. Perhaps the best historical description of these institutions can be found in the chapter entitled "The Almshouse Experience," in David J. Rothman's book on the rise of institutions in America.

Rothman, D.J., *The Discovery of the Asylum: Social Order and Disorder in the New Republic*. Boston: Little, Brown, 1971.

altered state of consciousness Psychologist Charles Tart, who is commonly regarded as a leading authority on altered states of consciousness (ASCs), often defines an ASC as a "qualitative alteration in the overall patterning of mental functioning, such that the experiencer feels his consciousness is radically different from the way it functions ordinarily."

In an effort to understand the phenomenology of schizophrenia, the subjective reports of schizophrenic experience began to be collected in the 1960s and compared with other unusual ASCs—such as those reported in "mystical" experience or in the psychedelic experiences of those who have ingested hallucinogenic substances. A famous paper was published in 1966 by Malcom Bowers and D.X. Freedman, which suggested that some schizophrenics have "psychedelic experiences" during the onset of their psychosis. However, further phenomenological studies of the ASCs of schizophrenics in the 1970s and 1980s have not supported the contention that they are similar to mystical or drug-induced ASCs. In the early 1960s hallucinogens were called psychotomimetic or "psychosis-mimicking" drugs, but this term has fallen out of conventional usage.

In 1961 psychiatrists Humphrey Osmond (who coined the word "psychedelic") and Abraham Hoffer designed a diagnostic test for schizophrenia, the Hoffer-Osmond Diagnostic Test, the first to be based on the subjective reports of schizophrenic experiences of perceptual distortions. It was believed that this test distinguished schizophrenia from other psychiatric disorders based on the uniqueness of the phenomenology of the ASCs experienced by schizophrenics. A later scale whose items were also derived from autobiographical accounts of schizophrenics was devised in 1970 by Osmond and psychologist A. Moneim El-Meligi— the Experiential World Inventory. This self-report inventory of 400 items purported to measure subjective changes with scales for five major phenomenological categories: sensory perception, time perception, body perception, self perception and perception of others. Neither of these phenomenologically-based measures ever became popular, and they have not been used in research since the early 1970s.

Bowers, M. and Freedman, D.X., "Psychedelic Experiences in Acute Psychosis," *Archives of General Psychiatry,* 15(1966), 240–248.

El-Meligi, A.M. and Osmond, H., *EWI: Manual for the Clinical Use of the Experiential World Inventory.* New York: Mens Sana Press, 1970.

Alzheimer, Alois (1864–1915) German neurologist who is best remembered for identifying Alzheimer's disease (a form of presenile dementia), but who also published research on schizophrenia and manic-depressive psychosis. In the early part of the 20th century he worked under Emil KRAEPELIN in the research laboratory at the Psychological Clinic of the University of Munich. Along with German neurologist Franz Nissl (1860–1919), these three men conducted research on the underlying disease processes in the nervous system that caused mental disorders such as DEMENTIA PRAECOX; they made major contributions to the field of neuropathology. Nissl invented new staining techniques that allowed for the study of nerve cells, and Alzheimer discovered the organic disease process in the ailment that is still known by his name. Alzheimer considered dementia praecox an essentially organic disease of the brain. Furthermore, somewhat contrary to the earlier opinions of his supervisor Kraepelin, Alzheimer identified certain forms of manic-depressive psychosis that seemed to have a degenerative course (only dementia praecox was thought to have this). He held a professorship at Breslau University in Poland and taught there from 1912 until his death in 1915.

Alzheimer, A., *Contributions to the Pathological Anatomy of Dementia Praecox.* Breslau: Deutsche Ver. f. Psych., 1913.

ambivalence The presence of two contradictory drives, tendencies, emotions or thoughts that are aimed at the same person, object or goal. These contradictory urges may be unconscious, conscious or only partly conscious, but in schizophrenia they are a very common phenomenon that tends to paralyze the willful, volitional actions of the afflicted. For example, a commonly reported experience of people with schizophrenia is that, when they try to express a thought or feeling or attempt an action, their minds suddenly become flooded with many different and often contradictory choices, and they are unable to focus on only one. One of Eugen Bleuler's higher-functioning patients once told him that, "When one expresses a thought, one always sees the counter thought. This intensifies itself and becomes so rapid that one doesn't really know which was the first." Another of his patients expressed the ambivalence so characteristic of schizophrenia by telling Bleuler, "I am a human being like yourself, even though I am not a human being." Bleuler reports that example in his classic 1911 book, *Dementia Praecox, Or the Group of Schizophrenias,* in which "ambivalence" is described as one of the "fundamental symptoms" of schizophrenia. Ambivalence is one of Bleuler's famous "Four As" (autism, associations disturbances, affective disturbances, ambivalence), which he felt were the central identifying symptoms of schizophrenia that differentiated it from other mental disorders. Bleuler identified three types of ambivalence in schizophrenia: affective ambivalence, ambivalence of will, and intellectual ambivalence. Modern theorists think that schizophrenic ambivalence may be due to disorders in attention that disable the individual's ability to focus attention on one goal or thought and screen out all other contradictory "noise" that might otherwise flood the mind. (See also ATTENTION, DISORDERS IN.)

Bleuler, E., *Dementia Praecox, Or the Group of Schizophrenias.* New York: International Universities Press, 1950; first published, 1911.

ambulatory schizophrenic This is a term for a person with schizophrenia whose level of functioning is high enough that inpatient care is not generally required. It is also applied to schizophrenic patients within psychiatric institutions who can be trusted to reside on open wards or be allowed frequent brief visits into the surrounding community. The term seems to be slowly falling out of conventional usage, with the synonym "high-functioning" replacing "ambulatory" as a label for these schizophrenics. (See also BORDERLINE SCHIZOPHRENIA.)

amenomania In his 1812 psychiatric manual, *Medical Inquiries and Observations Upon the Diseases of the Mind,* American alienist Benjamin Rush claimed that, "Amenomania is a common form of partial insanity." By the examples he gives, it seems that Rush used this term to describe what we might now call a DELUSIONAL DISORDER in people who may not be paralyzed by mental illness, but who have fixed delusions or eccentric beliefs on certain topics that may be quite bizarre.

In particular, Rush believed this disorder was found "most frequently in the enthusiasts in religion," which explains his derivation of the word. The grandiose religious delusions that characterize amenomania, Rush claims, may also be indicative of what we now call bipolar disorder or paranoid schizophrenia, for people with amenomania believe they are "the peculiar favourites of heaven." They converse with angels and with spirits of the dead, they see visions and they believe they are "exalted into beings of the highest order." Rush describes a familiar psychotic delusion still encountered in a few patients today when he reports, "I have seen two instances of persons, who believed themselves to be the Messiah."

Psychologist Milton Rokeach experimentally grouped three such schizophrenic patients together in the same environment and described the results in 1964 in his unique book, *The Three Christs of Ypsilanti.*

Rokeach, M., *The Three Christs of Ypsilanti.* New York: Alfred A. Knopf, 1964.
Rush, B., *Medical Inquiries and Observations On the Diseases of the Mind.* Philadelphia: Kimber & Richardson, 1812.

American Psychiatric Association The professional organization of physicians who specialize in the practice of psychiatry. The APA was founded at a meeting in Philadelphia on October 16, 1844, by "the original thirteen" physicians: Francis T. Stribling, Samuel B. Woodward, Samuel White, Isaac Ray, Pliny Earle, Thomas Kirkbride, Aramiah Brigham, Luther Bell, William Awl, John Galt, Nehemia Cuter, John Butler and Charles H. Steadman. The original name decided upon by these men was the Association of Medical Superintendents of American Institutions for the Insane. Benjamin Rush—the "father of American psychiatry"—was a physician at the Pennsylvania Hospital in Philadelphia in the early 1800s and his image appears on the modern logo for this organization. In that founding year the association also published the first English-language psychiatric journal, the *American Journal of Insanity,* which in 1921, under the urging of then-APA President William Alanson White, changed its name to the *American Journal of Psychiatry.* The association changed its name to the American Medico-Psychological Association in 1893 and then to its present title, the American Psychiatric Association, in 1921.

The American Psychiatric Association is responsible for the continually revised editions of the *Diagnostic and Statistical Manual of Mental Disorders,* which is the most widely accepted diagnostic manual used in North America. The most recent edition, a revision of the third edition of 1980, appeared in 1987. *DSM-IV,* the next scheduled revised edition, will be published in 1992.

McGovern, C.M., *Masters of Madness: Social Origins of the American Psychiatric Profession.* Hanover and London: University Press of New England, 1985.

American Psychological Association

The professional society of American psychologists. It was founded in July 1892 by G. Stanley Hall (1844–1924), a professor of psychology at Clark University in Worcester, Massachusetts.

amine   The name for a type of organic compound that contains nitrogen. Amines function as NEUROTRANSMITTERS in the brain. CATECHOLAMINES are a type of amine. (See also DOPAMINE HYPOTHESIS.)

amphetamine psychosis   An obsolete diagnostic term for the psychotic episodes brought on in some people by the ingestion of amphetamine (usually in the form of the "street drug" methamphetamine, or "speed") or similarly acting substances. Irritability, paranoid delusions and even violent behavior may be exhibited during these acute psychotic episodes. The main pharmacological effect of amphetamine is believed to be the release of CATECHOLAMINES, one of which, dopamine, is hypothesized to cause schizophrenic symptoms when there is an excess of it. Amphetamine activates or worsens preexisting psychotic symptoms, and ANTI-PSYCHOTIC DRUGS work as a potent antidote to the psychosis produced by extreme amphetamine intoxication. Thus, the biochemical properties and effects of amphetamine have been studied as a model for understanding the underlying biochemical processes in schizophrenia. (See also BIOCHEMICAL THEORIES OF SCHIZOPHRENIA; DOPAMINE HYPOTHESIS.)

anhedonia   The chronic inability to experience pleasure. It is often a sign of a MOOD DISORDER, such as a depressive episode, but can also be found in schizophrenics as a form of their AFFECTIVE DISTURBANCES.

animal spirits   A prescientific concept used to explain the cause of mental disorders, particularly mania. A 17th-century treatise by Thomas Willis, *De anima brutorum* (1672), claims that "animal spirits" were distillations from the blood contained in the brain. Their production in the brain was thought to irritate the nervous system and stimulate intellectual functioning so severely that mania would be the result.

anticholinergic effects The effect of some drugs that act as antagonists to the actions of cholinergic nerve fibers, usually of the parasympathetic nervous system. Such cholinergic nerve cells or fibers are those that use acetylcholine as their NEUROTRANS-MITTERS. Drugs that have anticholinergic effects block the transmission of this neurotransmitter, thus preventing the communication between nerve cells and thereby altering behavior.

Most psychoactive drugs have anticholinergic effects in both the central and the peripheral nervous systems. The types of drugs that have anticholinergic effects are heterocyclic antidepressants, antipsychotics, antihistamines, antiparkinsonian drugs and some hypnotics. If a patient is taking a combination of these drugs (such as an antipsychotic drug with an antidepressant—a common combination) or if an overdose of these drugs is taken, the additive anticholinergic effects can cause a crisis. The combination of signs and symptoms that indicate there is too much of an effect is called the "anticholinergic syndrome." At its worst, a patient suffering from an anticholinergic syndrome will have confusion, delirium with disorientation, agitation, visual and auditory hallucinations, anxiety, restlessness, pseudoseizures and perhaps even thought disorder (e.g., delusions). Dry mouth, constipation, urinary retention, decreased sweating, increased body temperature, flushing, discoordination and tachycardia are common but far less serious side effects due to anticholinergic syndrome. The treatment for the anticholinergic syndrome is anticholinesterase drug therapy.

antidepressant drugs The class of psychoactive drugs that alleviate the symptoms of DEPRESSION. They were discovered and developed in the 1950s and early 1960s. The earliest discoveries were for monoamine oxidase inhibitors (often called "MAO inhibitors") and tricyclic antidepressants. Today, the two major classes of antidepressant drugs are *heterocyclic antidepressants,* such as imipramine (trade name Tofranil), amitriptyline (Elavil), amoxapine (Asendin), maprotiline (Ludiomil), trimipramine (Surmontil), trazodone (Desyrel), doxepin (Sinequan) and nortryptyline (Pamelor), and the *monoamine oxidase inhibitors,* such as isocarboxazid (Marplan), phenelzine (Nardil), and tranylcypromine (Parnate). However, due to the many serious adverse reactions that can result from MAO inhibitors, the heterocyclic antidepressants are far more commonly prescribed. A limitation to the use of antidepressant drugs is the fact that it usually takes at least two to three weeks of therapeutic doses before the patient responds and the depression alleviates. Therefore, antidepressant drugs alone are not usually the best form of treatment, with psychotherapy recommended as an adjunct to the medication. Since an overdose of antidepressant drugs is lethal, and suicide may be a risk for those patients suffering from a severe depression (especially schizophrenic or bipolar patients), only nonlethal amounts of the drug should be allowed in the patient's possession, or prescriptions should be entrusted to responsible family members.

antiparkinsonian drugs These are drugs that are administered to relieve PARKINSON'S SYNDROME, the side effects of antipsychotic drugs that will usually appear within weeks or a few months after beginning antipsychotic drug therapy. Patients who suffer from this side effect exhibit a triad of signs: tremors (usually in the hands but also in the wrists and elbows), rigidity (extreme tension in muscles that make the body actually feel rigid) and akinesia or bradykinesia (an absence or a slowness of body or facial muscle motion). Common antiparkinsonian drugs are amantadine (trade name Symmetrel), benztropine (Cogentin), biperiden (Akineton) and diphenhydramine (Benadryl). Parkinson's syndrome, which is induced by antipsychotic drugs, should not be confused with Parkinson's disease, which is a progressive neurological disorder that is not reversible.

antipsychiatry See LAING, RONALD DAVID.

anti-psychosis A curative substance that the prescient Daniel H. Tuke hypothesized, in 1881, would one day be created to reverse the symptoms of mental disorders. His prophetic remarks were delivered on August 2 in London in his presidential address to the Medico-Psychological Association in which he lamented the special problems of "psychological" medicine as opposed to the more forthright "organic" medicine:

> It must be frankly granted that Psychological Medicine can boast, as yet, of no specifics, nor is it likely, perhaps, that such a boast will ever be made. It may be difficult to suppress the hope, but we cannot entertain the expectation that some future Sydenham will discover an *anti-psychosis* which will as safely and speedily cut short an attack of mania or melancholia as bark an attack of ague.

Today's ANTIPSYCHOTIC DRUGS are named, in part, as a memorial to Tuke's farsightedness.

Tuke, D.H., *Chapters in the History of the Insane in the British Isles.* London: Keegan, Paul, Trench & Co., 1882.

antipsychotic drugs The class of drugs that suppress or alleviate psychotic symptoms (such as hallucinations and delusions). They are also commonly referred to as neuroleptics, antischizophrenic agents and major tranquilizers (which is a misnomer). Antipsychotic drugs are the treatment of choice for schizophrenia and the schizophrenia-like ACUTE RECOVERABLE PSYCHOSES. Most antipsychotic drugs work by blocking the receptor-sites for the neurotransmitter DOPAMINE in various pathways within the brain. By inhibiting the firing of certain nerve cells in the brain with these drugs, psychotic symptoms can be alleviated or suppressed and desired behavioral changes can occur.

The very first antipsychotic drugs were reserpine and the PHENOTHIAZINES (such as CHLORPROMAZINE), and they were developed in the early 1950s. Chlorpromazine was approved for use in the United States in March 1954 under the trade name Thorazine, named after the Norse god of thunder, Thor.

The five major chemical classes of antipsychotic drugs (and representative brand names of drugs in each class) are as follows: The phenothiazines, which have the three subclasses aliphatic (Thorazine, Vesprin), piperidine (Mellaril, Serentil) and piperazine (Stelazine, Prolixin, Trilafon); the thioxanthenes (Navane); the butyrophenomes (Haldol); the dibenzoxazepines (Daxolin, Loxitane); and the dihydroindolones (Lidone, Moban).

If a psychotic patient has responded well to a drug in the past, it is usually the case that the attending psychiatrist will represcribe the same drug, or another in its chemical class. If a patient is not responding well to a particular phenothiazine, then the psychiatrist will generally choose a drug from another category of phenothiazines, or from one of the other four chemical classes of antipsychotic drugs. Dosage levels can then be adjusted according to the individual needs of the patient. Two of the earliest antipsychotic drugs ever discovered, the Rauwolfia alkaloids known as reserpine and tetrabenazine, are used very infrequently at present.

New types of antipsychotic drugs are continually being researched and developed. Perhaps the most notable new antipsychotic agent (at least in the United States as of February 1990) is CLOZAPINE. Other new antipsychotic agents that are in development are discussed in a 1991 article in *Schizophrenia Bulletin* by Jes Gerlach, including some, such as serotonin agonists, which do not act on dopamine activity in the brain.

Antipsychotic drugs may cause several types of syndromes as serious side effects, namely acute dystonic reactions, AKA-THESIA, PARKINSON'S SYNDROME, TARDIVE DYSKINESIA (after long-term use) and NEU-ROLEPTIC MALIGNANT SYNDROME. Except for tardive dyskinesia, the other syndromes are usually completely reversible through lowering the dosage of antipsychotic drugs or withdrawing them entirely from use (''drug holidays''). Common side effects experienced by many patients are due to the anticholinergic effects of antipsychotic drugs: dry mouth; dilated pupils and blurred vision; increased heart rate; constipation; urinary retention; dizziness; and drying of lung secretions. The new antipsychotic drug clozapine is estimated to cause seizures in about 3% of patients and agranulocytosis in about 1% of cases, although at present it is not believed that clozapine will lead to the development of tardive dyskinesia.

Although most antipsychotic drugs are taken orally in pill or liquid form, in recent years long-acting injectable forms of some drugs (e.g., Prolixin) have been developed that, depending on the dose, can last for two weeks to a month before requiring the next injection. These have been developed for the chronic schizophrenic patients who are often negligent about taking regular doses of their medication when they are in the community, and thus often bring about their own relapse. The use of the current classes of antipsychotic drugs seems to be the treatment of choice for schizophrenia for the foreseeable future.

Several studies have shown that, on the average, if a group of schizophrenics in remission is switched from antipsychotic medication to placebo medication around 65% to 85% of them will completely relapse within one year. A variety of studies estimate that between 5% and 25% of people with schizophrenia exhibit TREATMENT RE-FRACTORINESS to standard antipsychotic drugs and that an additional number, about 15%, experience an alleviation of symptoms with placebo treatment alone in double-blind studies. Clozapine has been found to be effective with about 30% of the portion of schizophrenics who are treatment refractory.

Antipsychotic drugs do not ''cure'' schizophrenia; their main function is to significantly lower the probability of total relapse into psychosis by reducing primarily the POSITIVE SYMPTOMS (hallucinations and delusions). Clozapine has been touted as the first drug that is actually able to alleviate some NEGATIVE SYMPTOMS, but a recent (1991) informed review of the drug by Allan Safferman and colleagues in *Schizophrenia Bulletin* instead concludes, ''To our knowledge, there is no direct proof that CLOZ is superior to other antipsychotics when negative symptoms are the sole or predominant psychopathology.'' However, it is also true, as some analysts have suggested based on the long-term follow-up studies, that antipsychotic drugs do not seem to ''arrest'' the disease process or have any appreciable effect on the COURSE OF SCHIZOPHRENIA. However, one literature review by the noted schizophrenia researcher Richard Jed Wyatt involving the re-analysis of 22 studies disputes this conclusion (at least in part) and indicates that early intervention with antipsychotic drugs in first-break schizophrenia patients increases the likelihood of an improved long-term course.

A special 1991 issue of *Schizophrenia Bulletin* (Volume 17, Number 2) was devoted to ''New Developments in the Pharmacologic Treatment of Schizophrenia.'' The articles by Gerlach, Wyatt and Safferman cited above can be found in this issue.

Baldessarini, R.J., *Chemotherapy in Psychiatry: Principles and Practice*. Cambridge: Harvard University Press, 1985.

antisocial behavior   Behavior that is disrupting or harmful to society as a whole. Persons who are experiencing a psychotic disorder may, due to their lack of full contact with reality, commit antisocial acts against others or against property. Sometimes extreme violence—such as assaults or even homicides—have been known to result. If such persons are legally judged insane, then they are generally not considered responsible for the antisocial behavior committed while under the influence of the psychotic disorder. Particularly dangerous diagnostic categories include those afflicted with the psychotic hostility and delusional beliefs characteristic of some people with paranoid schizophrenia or the manic episodes of bipolar disorder.

anxiety   A symptom of most mental disorders that is usually described as a feeling of uneasiness, apprehension or dread. Anxiety can be a pervasive feeling that is not associated with any one person or thing in particular, which is generally how most definitions distinguish it from fear, which usually does have an object. Anxiety can be overwhelming in the ACUTE RECOVERABLE PSYCHOSES and in active phases of bipolar disorder. Schizophrenics commonly report anxiety, especially during the PRODROMAL PHASE when the awareness of frighteningly new psychotic symptoms causes anxiety, and during periods in chronic schizophrenia when exacerbations of psychotic symptoms occur. From a psychoanalytic point of view, anxiety is a sign that the ego has not been able to successfully keep unpleasant or threatening thoughts or feelings entirely out of awareness, so that, even though the actual content of the threatening thought or feeling may be unconscious, the unpleasant effects are still experienced as anxiety.

APA nomenclature   The terminology and diagnostic schemata devised and continually revised by the American Psychiatric Association in its continuing editions of the *Diagnostic and Statistical Manual of Mental Disorders*. This term is often used in contradistinction to ICD nomenclature, the diagnostic schemata for mental disorders found in the World Health Organization's continuing revisions of the *International Classification of Diseases*. (See also ICD-9.)

apathy   A symptom present in many mental disorders but especially in depression, organic mental disorders (due to brain damage) and in schizophrenia. This symptom of "uncaring" or of "lack of interest in the self or in the world" is pervasive, like a MOOD DISORDER, and is indicative of the AFFECTIVE DISTURBANCES of schizophrenia.

Argentina   The only prevalence study of schizophrenia conducted in Argentina found a low rate of 1.1 per thousand.

Torrey, E.F., *Schizophrenia and Civilization*. New York: Jason Aronson, 1980.

Arieti,   Silvano   (1914–1981)   An American psychiatrist and psychoanalyst long recognized as a leading authority on schizophrenia. He was a professor of clinical psychiatry at the New York Medical College and was a training analyst and supervisor at the William Alanson White Institute for Psychoanalysis. For many years he was editor-in-chief of *The American Handbook of Psychiatry*. His most significant contribution to the study of schizophrenia was his comprehensive volume, *Interpretation of Schizophrenia*, which was hailed soon after the appearance of the first edition in 1955 as the most complete presentation on the disorder since Eugen Bleuler's in 1911. A significantly revised and expanded second edition appeared in 1974. His psychoanalytic orientation is evident throughout the volume, particularly in the sections concerning psychotherapy and schizophrenics, which contain many practical insights.

Arieti, S., *Interpretation of Schizophrenia*, rev. 2nd ed. New York: Basic Books, 1974.

Aristotelian thinking   A concept used by Silvano Arieti to denote the usual rational, logical processes employed by "normal" human beings. In his book *Interpretation of Schizophrenia*, Arieti contrasts Aristotelian thinking in normals with the more "primitive" and irrational logic that he calls PALEOLOGIC THOUGHT and that, he argues, characterizes schizophrenics. This idea fit in well with psychoanalytic notions of schizophrenia being an expression of REGRESSION to a more primitive and infantile mode of reasoning and experiencing the world. Arieti writes in the 1974 revised edition of his classic volume: "The paleo-logic type of organization is archaic or incomplete in comparison to the Aristotelian. The schizophrenic patient, when he thinks in a typically schizophrenic way, uses non-Aristotelian cognitive organizations."

Arnold, Thomas (1742–1816) The author of *Observations on the Nature, Kinds, Causes, and Prevention of Insanity, Lunacy or Madness* (1782), an important achievement in the development of modern psychiatry. Arnold was an Edinburgh-trained English physician who had studied under William Cullen. After completing his medical training, he opened a private mad-house in Leicester, which provided him with the important observations on mental disorders that he then used to create the classification system outlined in his 1782 book. He classified mental disorders according to their symptom clusters, as it is still done today, and he divided them into two main classes: "ideal insanity," which referred to disorders of perception such as hallucinations and illusions; and "notional insanity," those disorders characterized by delusions. This system influenced later authors of psychiatric works. Two other influential books by Arnold are *A Case of Hydrophobia Successfully Treated* (1793) and *Observations on the Management of the Insane* (1809).

art, schizophrenic The relationship between "madness" and "creativity" has been the subject of speculation for at least 2,000 years. Master artists such as Vincent Van Gogh (1853–90), who clearly suffered from a mental illness that led to his incarceration in an asylum and eventual suicide, or abstract expressionist Jackson Pollock (1912–

1956), who was hospitalized for severe alcoholism in 1938 and whose psychotic-like drawings were later published by his analyst, have stimulated the argument over whether madmen and artists draw from the same unconscious well for their inspiration.

Psychiatrists and psychologists have studied the artwork of schizophrenics in particular for more than a century. The very first psychiatrist to study the artwork of mental patients was Max Simon, whose groundbreaking paper, *"L'Imagination dans la folie: Étude sur les dessins, plans, descriptions, et costumes des aliénés,"* was published in the French psychiatric journal *Annales Médico-Psychologiques* in 1876. Simon correlated five major classifications of artistic style with five different classes of mental disorders. As have most subsequent psychiatric commentators, Simon noted the similarities in style of psychotic art with the creations of small children and of people in primitive societies. In 1880 the famous Italian criminologist and psychopathologist Cesare Lombroso (1836–1909) wrote a paper, "On the Art of the Insane," which was published as a chapter in his book *The Man of Genius* in 1888. In addition to reaffirming Simon's observations, Lombroso remarked on the prevalence of sexual symbolism in the artwork of psychotics. German psychiatrist Fritz Mohr constructed the first diagnostic tests based on the drawings of mental patients in 1906.

Perhaps the most famous book on schizophrenic art was published in German in 1922 (and translated into English and published in 1972)—the classic work *Bildnerei der Geisteskranken (Artistry of the Mentally Ill)* by Hans Prinzhorn (1886–1933). Prinzhorn was a psychiatrist at the Heidelberg Psychiatric Clinic and amassed a unique collection of 5,000 pieces of artwork produced by psychiatric patients from institutions in Germany, Austria, Switzerland, Italy and the Netherlands between 1890 and 1920. Prinzhorn detailed the case histories of "ten schizophrenic artists" along with reproductions of their artwork. His approach to schizophrenic art was essentially aesthetic, and he concluded that the content of the artwork had no value as a diagnostic tool. Prinzhorn made the interesting observation that hallucinations were rarely depicted in the art of schizophrenics. He identified the "components" of the "schizophrenic configuration" that distinguish schizophrenic art from other styles (such as similar productions by children and "primitives"), and argues that the "schizophrenic outlook" is most closely mirrored by the abstract art of the 20th century. Prinzhorn concludes: "Existing artistic abilities are therefore not necessarily destroyed by the schizophrenic process but can in fact maintain themselves unchanged over long periods . . . We have also demonstrated that during the progress of schizophrenia, while the patient declines into a highly confused, unapproachable final state with all the typical symptoms in their greatest extremes, his superficial, craftsman-like dexterity develops great configurative power which allows him to produce pictures of undoubted artistic quality."

Many psychoanalytic papers have been published on schizophrenic art since 1918, perhaps the most notable being Ernst Kris' paper, "Comments on Spontaneous Artistic Creations by Psychotics," which was included in his chapter on "The Art of the Insane" in his famous book, *Psychoanalytic Explorations in Art* (1952). Sexual and aggressive expressions of the id that characterize primitive and infantile PRIMARY PROCESS thinking are examined in the art of schizophrenics in these writings. The practical use of artistic creations as a tool in the psychotherapy of schizophrenics was described by Margaret Naumberg in 1950 in her book, *Schizophrenic Art: Its Meaning in Psychotherapy*. In the second edition (1974) of Silvano Arieti's *Interpretation of Schizophrenia* more examples of this form of art therapy with psychotics are provided, with a psychoanalytic interpretation of these productions.

The use of creative techniques in psychotherapy (such as drawing, painting, sculpture, dance) was pioneered by Swiss psychiatrist C.G. Jung (1875–1961), who interpreted such material as if it gave a snapshot or X ray of the patient's internal world. Although not technically schizophrenic, but apparently often on the brink of psychosis, artist Jackson Pollock spent several years in analysis with Jungian analyst Dr. Joseph Henderson, who eventually allowed the publication of many of the drawings that Pollock did during therapy in *Jackson Pollock: Psychoanalytic Drawings (1970)*. In excerpts from a previously unpublished lecture on his former patient (but reproduced in the Pollock biography by B.H. Friedman, *Jackson Pollock: Energy Made Visible* [1972]), Henderson makes the following observations that are typical of many Jungian psychoanalytic interpretations: "Following a prolonged period of representing human figures and animals in an anguished, dismembered or lamed condition, there came a new development in the drawings Pollock made during therapy. This was not merely the dissociation of schizophrenia, though he was frequently close to it. It has seemed to me a parallel with similar states of mind ritually induced among tribal societies or in shamanistic trance states. In this light the patient appears to have been in a state similar to the novice in a tribal initiation rite during which he is ritually dismembered at the onset of an ordeal whose goal is to change him from a boy into a man." Similar Jungian interpretations of schizophrenic experience and art are found in the writings of the Jungian analyst John Weir Perry.

Honoring the long tradition of schizophrenic art, the quarterly research review publication of the National Institute of Mental Health, *Schizophrenia Bulletin*, continues to feature on its cover the artwork created by current and former mental patients, with a description of the piece by its author included in the "About the Cover" section following the table of contents.

Friedman, B.H., *Jackson Pollock: Energy Made Visible*. New York: McGraw-Hill, 1972.

Kris, E., *Psychoanalytic Explorations in Art*. New York: International Universities Press, 1952.

Lombroso, C., *The Man of Genius*. London: Scott, 1895; first published, 1880.

Naumberg, M., *Schizophrenic Art: Its Meaning in Psychotherapy*. New York: Grune & Stratton, 1950.

Prinzhorn, H., *Artistry of the Mentally Ill: A Contribution to the Psychology and Psychopathology of Configuration*, tr. E. v. Brockdorff from the 2nd German ed. (1922). New York: Springer-Verlag, 1972.

Simon, M., "L'Imagination dans le folie: Étude sur les dessins, plans, descriptions, et costumes des aliénés," *Annales Médico-Psychologiques*, 16(1876), 358–390.

Wysuph, C.I., *Jackson Pollock: Psychoanalytic Drawings*. New York: Horizon Press, 1970.

"as-if" personality   See BORDERLINE CASES; BORDERLINE SCHIZOPHRENIA.

association disturbances   One of the "Four As" (association disturbances, affective disturbances, ambivalence, autism) that Eugene Bleuler identified as the "fundamental symptoms" that uniquely characterize schizophrenia. Bleuler devoted a large section of his 1911 classic, *Dementia Praecox, Or the Group of Schizophrenias*, to the description of these association disturbances in schizophrenia. In one paragraph he summarizes his basic observations on association disturbances in schizophrenia:

> In the normal thinking process, the numerous actual and latent images combine to determine each association. In schizophrenia, however, single images or whole combinations may be rendered ineffective, in an apparently haphazard fashion. Instead, thinking operates with ideas and concepts which have no, or a completely insufficient, connection with the main idea and should therefore be excluded from the thought-process. The result is that thinking becomes confused, bizarre, incorrect, abrupt. Sometimes, all the associative threads fail and the thought chain is totally interrupted; after

such "blocking," ideas may emerge which have no recognizable connection with preceding ones.

Today this association disturbance in schizophrenia is referred to as a form of FORMAL THOUGHT DISORDER. (See also LOOSENING OF ASSOCIATIONS.)

Bleuler, E., *Dementia Praecox, Or the Group of Schizophrenias*. New York: International Universities Press, 1950; first published, 1911.

Association of Medical Officers of Asylums and Hospitals for the Insane   The first and oldest professional psychiatric association in the world, it was founded in Great Britain in 1841. In 1865, its name was changed to the Medico-Psychological Association of Great Britain and Ireland. It became the Royal Medico-Psychological Association in 1926 and eventually changed to its present title, the Royal College of Psychiatrists, in 1971. The association began publication of a professional journal, *The Asylum Journal*, in 1842 but later changed its name to the *Journal of Mental Science*. It is now published by the Royal College of Psychiatrists as the *British Journal of Psychiatry*.

Association of Medical Superintendents of American Institutions for the Insane   The initial name for the professional society of American psychiatrists, founded in 1844, that is known today as the AMERICAN PSYCHIATRIC ASSOCIATION.

asthenic type   One of the types of physique that psychiatrist and neurologist Ernst Kretschmer claimed to be representative of schizophrenics ("schizophrenes") in his 1921 book, *Körperbau und Charakter (Physique and Character)*. Asthenic types were excessively thin and looked taller than they truly were. Other physical types, such as the ATHLETIC TYPE and the dysplastic type, were also thought by Kretschmer to be prevalent among schizophrenics. Kretschmer concludes: "There is a clear biological affinity between the psychic disposition of the schiz-ophrenes and the bodily disposition charac-teristic of the asthenics, athletics, and certain dysplastics.'' Although Kretschmer's theory of how certain temperaments were related to specific types of physique has not been taken seriously for many decades, he nonetheless deserves credit as one of the pioneers in the search for the BIOLOGICAL MARKERS OF SCHIZOPHRENIA.

Kretschmer, E., *Physique and Character: An Investigation of the Nature of Constitution and of the Theory of Temperament*. New York: The Humanities Press, 1951; first published, 1922.

asylums A word that originally meant a place of sanctuary—such as a church or monastery—''asylum'' later became the word of choice to designate institutions for the insane, particularly in the very-late-18th and throughout the 19th centuries. Using the word ''hospital'' as the official name for institutions for the mentally disordered did not come into vogue in the United States until the State Care Act was passed into law in 1890, officially replacing the term ''asy-lum'' with ''hospital'' in the system of state mental hospitals that this legislation man-dated. A similar official shift in terminology followed suit in Great Britain shortly there-after.

For centuries the mentally ill were treated in general hospitals, but more often than not they were relegated to the streets, poor-houses and prisons. Sometimes small houses or ''one-man asylums'' were built to contain particularly troublesome psychotics. In the 17th and 18th centuries, especially in En-gland, hospitals and private ''mad-houses'' were created to incarcerate the mentally ill, although the royal hospitals also treated the general medical problems of the community. With the humanistic movement toward the adoption of moral medicine in the early 1800s, much legislation in England (and subsequently the United States) was passed regulating the care of the mentally ill by setting up national programs of institutions and licensing the operators of private mad-houses. Private psychiatric facilities pres-ently refer to themselves as ''clinics'' or ''institutes.'' Now there is a trend, particu-larly in the United States, to change the names of public institutions for the mentally ill from ''hospitals'' to ''psychiatric cen-ters.''

The first institution in the United States built solely for the care of the insane was opened in Williamsburg, Virginia, in 1769. By 1830, only 13 hospitals and asylums existed in the United States, mostly in the Atlantic states but also as far west as Ohio and Kentucky. Generally their patient pop-ulation was relatively small, no more than 50 or so for most of them, but a few had a capacity of 200 or more. However, in the 1830s and 1840s, a definite shift in public opinion toward the ''deviant and dependant'' led to the notion that institutions should be built and utilized as places of first resort for intervention. Not only were asylums con-structed in record numbers for the insane, but also penitentiaries for the criminal, or-phan asylums for homeless children, alms-houses for the poor and reformatories for delinquents. It was not that overwhelming new numbers of these people were suddenly appearing, but simply that the general public and government's philosophy of dealing with these social problems changed. By 1860, of the 33 states then in existence, 28 had asy-lums for the insane. Incredibly, between 1840 and 1870 the number of people invol-untarily committed to state-run institutions in the United States increased from 2,500 to more than 74,000—far higher than the rate of growth for the population of the United States in that period (only three-and-one-half times). By 1955, just prior to the largest waves in the deinstitutionalization of psy-chiatric patients, that number had swollen to 559,000 patients in psychiatric hospitals. (See also COMMITMENT.)

Deutsch, A., *The Mentally Ill in America: A History of Their Care and Treatment from*

Colonial Times, 2nd ed. New York: Columbia University Press, 1949.

Rothman, D.J., *The Discovery of the Asylum: Social Order and Disorder in the New Republic.* Boston: Little, Brown, 1971.

asyndetic thinking   A term coined by psychiatrist Norman Cameron to describe the apparent lack of causal linkage or connectedness between elements in the language of schizophrenics. Cameron contributed to the study of the unique structure of schizophrenic language in two noted papers written in the 1930s and listed below. (See also COGNITIVE STUDIES OF SCHIZOPHRENIA.)

Cameron, N., "Reasoning, Regression and Communication in Schizophrenics," *Psychological Monographs,* 50:1(1938).

———, "Deterioration and Regression in Schizophrenic Thinking," *Journal of Abnormal and Social Psychology,* 34(1939), 265.

athletic type   One of the three main "types of physique" that Ernst Kretschmer proposed were characteristic of "schizophrenes" in his 1921 book *Körperbau und Charakter (Physique and Character).* The ASTHENIC TYPE was the most clearly associated with schizophrenics; also the dysplastic type was common. The athletic type, according to Kretschmer, "is recognized by the strong development of the skeleton, the musculature and also the skin." Kretschmer attempted to devise a taxonomic system of body-types that correlated with particular psychological types, in particular those with the psychotic disorders of schizophrenia (whom he referred to as "schizophrenes") and manic-depressive psychosis (whom, following FALRET, he referred to as "circulars").

atropine intoxication therapy   A little-used form of treatment for schizophrenia introduced by G.R. Forrer in the late 1940s in which a coma would be induced in patients through the toxic state produced by injections of atropine. Never very popular, this procedure was discontinued in light of the ostensible effectiveness of INSULIN COMA THERAPY. (See also COMA THERAPY; NITROGEN INHALATION THERAPY.)

Forrer, G.R., "Atropine Toxicity in the Treatment of Schizophrenia," *Journal of the Michigan Medical Society,* 49(1950), 184–185.

attention, disorders in   An almost universal characteristic of schizophrenia that has been observed since earliest times is the inability of an individual with the disorder to willfully focus his or her attention on a thought, feeling, object or activity for any great length of time before it is disrupted. Since the late 1950s, this problem in functioning has been referred to as attentional deficits or disorders of attention.

Schizophrenics have been observed to have extreme difficulty in sustaining and selectively focusing their attention. This has been true not only in the earliest clinical descriptions of the disorder, but also in many experimental studies of schizophrenic cognition conducted since 1961. In the 1913 English translation of his papers on *Dementia Praecox and Paraphrenia,* Emil Kraepelin observed in his schizophrenic patients that "it is quite common for them to lose both inclination and ability on their own initiative to keep their attention fixed for any length of time." Oftentimes unsophisticated family members or other caretakers of schizophrenics tragically mistake these "gaps" in attention that disrupt activity as signs that the afflicted person is "lazy" or "being difficult." These short-circuits in the willful activities of schizophrenics are instead almost universal characteristics of the disease, particularly in the nonparanoid subtypes of schizophrenia.

In 1961, Andrew McGhie and James Chapman published a classic paper on this topic that influenced the next several decades of the experimental study of schizophrenia. In their published report, the authors collected representative statements from schizophrenics about their own inner experiences and concluded that in schizophrenia "a primary disorder is that of a decrease in the selective and inhibitory functions of attention." In other words, McGhie and Chapman were arguing that the selective "filtering" mechanism that we all use to screen out unwanted ideas and feelings, when we are focusing our attention on something else, is not functioning properly in schizophrenics. They find it difficult to screen out all of these unwanted stimuli from inside themselves and from the outside world, and this disrupts not only their ability to think and communicate, but it also distorts their perceptions and sensations.

Reports by McGhie and Chapman's patients illustrate the disorders in attention characteristic of schizophrenia:

"It's as if I am too wide awake—very, very alert. I can't relax at all. Everything seems to go through me. I just can't shut things out."

"My concentration is very poor. I jump from one thing to another. If I am talking to someone they only need to cross their legs or scratch their heads and I am distracted and I forget what I am saying."

"I can't concentrate on television because I can't watch the screen and listen to what is being said at the same time. I can't seem to take in two things like this at the same time, especially when one of them means watching and the other means listening. On the other hand I always seem to be taking in too much at the one time and then I can't handle it and can't make sense of it."

"Sometimes when people speak to me my head is overloaded. It's too much to hold at once. It goes out as quickly as it goes in. It makes you forget what you just heard because you can't get hearing it long enough. It's just words in the air unless you can figure it out from their faces."

Since McGhie and Chapman's paper was published, many experimental studies have been conducted to understand the disorders of attention in schizophrenia. This research has been a trend in COGNITIVE STUDIES OF SCHIZOPHRENIA, which use metaphors of the mind derived from the computer sciences to examine INFORMATION PROCESSING IN SCHIZOPHRENIA. Some of this research has

attempted to correlate certain attention deficits with deficits in the specific information processing abilities of the two cerebral hemispheres of the brain.

In the search for childhood predictors of later adult schizophrenia, research has focused on disturbances in attention in children as one possible way to predict the later development of schizophrenia. In an ongoing LONGITUDINAL STUDY, psychologists Barbara A. Cornblatt and L. Erlenmeyer-Kimling of the New York State Psychiatric Institute are following a group of children evaluated for "global attention deficits" that may prove to be a "marker of risk" for schizophrenia. (See also HIGH-RISK STUDIES; NON-PARANOID SCHIZOPHRENIA.)

Cornblatt, B.A. and Erlenmeyer-Kimling, L., "Global Attentional Deviance as a Marker of Risk for Schizophrenia: Specificity and Predictive Validity," *Journal of Abnormal Psychology*, 1985, 470–486.

McGhie, A. and Chapman, J., "Disorders of Attention and Perception in Early Schizophrenia," *British Journal of Medical Psychology*, 34(1961), 103–117.

attention-deficit hyperactivity disorder (ADHD)   See HYPERKINESIA.

auditory hallucinations   Perhaps the most common type of HALLUCINATION found in the psychotic disorders. These are hallucinations of sound, and they are found across many diagnostic categories and are even experienced in rare instances by "normals" who do not exhibit signs of a mental disorder. Strictly speaking, auditory hallucinations may indicate a psychotic disorder only when they are accompanied by gross impairment in REALITY TESTING.

The hearing of "voices" is the most common type of auditory hallucination reported, but individuals have also reported hallucinations of "clicks," "rushing noises" and "music." A common misconception, which is no longer supported by recent research on the psychotic disorders, is that the hearing of "voices" is a definite sign of schizophrenia. Indeed, even in conventional clinical practice today one of the most common (and usually one of the first) questions asked of a patient upon admission to a psychiatric crisis center or a psychiatric hospital is, "Have you been hearing voices?" If the answer is "yes," then the patient is usually diagnosed as schizophrenic. To illustrate how clinicians place too much emphasis on "hearing voices" as a symptom of schizophrenia, Stanford University psychologist David L. Rosenhan had normal volunteers go to psychiatric hospitals and report that they had been hearing voices for about three weeks. This was their only reported symptom. Not only were most of them admitted, but they were also given schizophrenic diagnoses. Rosenhan's remarkable report of this experiment, "On Being Sane in Insane Places," was published in *Science* in 1973 and received much publicity.

In the 1919 English translation of the eighth edition of his famous textbook of psychiatry, *Dementia Praecox and Paraphrenia,* Emil Kraepelin observes that "the hearing of voices" was "the symptom peculiarly characteristic of dementia praecox." He noted that, as a rule, what the voices say is "unpleasant and disturbing." These voices tease, mock, threaten and abuse the suffering patient. However, Kraepelin also reports that some of his patients heard "good voices" at times. A common characteristic of these auditory hallucinations is that, "Many of the voices make remarks about the thoughts and doings of the patient." Another quality that Kraepelin thought was specific to the auditory hallucinations of schizophrenics was that "the patient's own thoughts appear to them to be spoken aloud." One of Kraepelin's patients told him, "I have the feeling as if someone beside me said out loud what I think."

In *Dementia Praecox, Or the Group of Schizophrenias* (1911), Eugen Bleuler argued that hallucinations were one of the accessory symptoms of schizophrenia that could be found in other disorders (such as manic-depressive psychosis) as well. However, Bleuler thought that auditory hallucinations were more common in schizophrenia than in other disorders. "Almost every schizophrenic who is hospitalized hears 'voices,' occasionally or continually." Bleuler adds that,

The most common auditory hallucination is that of speech. The "voices" of our patients embody all their strivings and fears, and their entire transformed relationship to the external world . . . For the patient, as for his attendant, the "voices" become, above all, the representatives of the pathological or hostile powers. The voices not only speak to the patient, but they pass electricity through his body, beat him, paralyze him, take his thoughts away.

Different types of auditory hallucinations were among the 11 FIRST-RANK SYMPTOMS of schizophrenia proposed by the German psychiatrist Kurt Schneider in his phenomenologically-based textbook, *Clinical Psychopathology* (1959). The presence of any one of these 11 symptoms was proposed as sufficient to make the diagnosis of schizophrenia. In this sense, it is said that each of these symptoms—including the auditory hallucinations of voices—is PATHOGNOMONIC of schizophrenia, at least according to Schneider.

The psychoanalytic interpretation of auditory hallucinations was only briefly discussed by Sigmund Freud (1857–1939). In his essay "Metapsychological Supplement to the Theory of Dreams" (1916), Freud made reference to the "dream hallucination" and compared it to schizophrenic auditory hallucinations. Although he noted that both of these were examples of REGRESSION, he suggested that an additional factor in schizophrenia was a disturbance in "that institution of the ego" concerned with the "testing of reality." In his famous 1914 paper "On Narcissism," Freud makes it clear that the "voices" heard in schizophrenic auditory hallucinations do not represent the *superego* itself, as might be thought, given the critical, moralistic judgments and threats made by the voices, but instead Freud thought that these voices represent the regressive undoing or deterioration of the superego. Freud writes: "The voices as well as the indefinite number of speakers, are brought into the foreground again by the disease, and so the evolution of conscience is regressively reproduced."

Later psychoanalytic writers mostly agree with psychoanalyst Otto Fenichel, who, in his textbook *The Psychoanalytic Theory of the Neuroses* (1945), believes that schizophrenic auditory hallucinations serve as a defense: They are "substitutes for perception" after a break with reality. "Inner conflicts are projected and experienced as if they were external perceptions," Fenichel explains.

Surprisingly, there have been few comprehensive theories of auditory hallucinations that have been testable through experimental research. Perhaps the best effort so far has been P.D. Slade's "A Four-Factor Theory of Auditory Hallucinations," published in 1976. Slade's model envisions auditory hallucinations as stemming from the interaction of "psychological stress" (the first factor) with an underlying, genetically determined predisposition to hallucinatory experience (the second factor). This genetic predisposition is supposedly a "critical threshold level," and when the hallucinatory tendency is raised above a certain level, an auditory hallucination is triggered. Slade says this is an "all-or-none" phenomenon. Another aspect to consider is the "level of external stimulation" (the third factor), which might have an inhibitory effect on the conscious experience of a hallucination. For example, it has commonly been reported that schizophrenic "voices" can be made to stop through the introduction of loud noises or by having the patient shout. External sounds can sometimes drown out the internal ones. Finally, Slade says there is also a "positive reinforcement effect" (the fourth factor). If a hallucinatory experience does occur, and the patient's mood state improves because

of it, through a positive reinforcement effect it may become easier and easier for the patient to experience auditory hallucination with weaker and weaker "stress events" because the "critical threshold level" for the individual may be lowered to increase the likelihood of reexperiencing the positive effect. Despite the apparent testability of this model, very little experimental support has emerged for it.

The very few other clinical studies of auditory hallucinations have generally been in phenomenological research on the relationship of certain types of hallucinations with certain diagnostic categories. Auditory hallucinations have been found to occur across diagnostic categories, including in psychotic depressions and bipolar disorder, but the auditory hallucination of "voices" may be most common in the paranoid subtype of schizophrenia.

The most recent review of the considerable psychiatric literature on auditory and other types of hallucinations is by psychiatrists G. Asaad and B. Shapiro.

Asaad, G. and Shapiro, B., "Hallucinations: Theoretical and Clinical Overview," *American Journal of Psychiatry*, 1986, 143(1986), 1088–1097.
Slade, P.D., "Toward a Theory of Auditory Hallucinations: Outline of an Hypothetical Four-factor Model," *British Journal of Social and Clinical Psychology*, 15(1976), 415–423.

Australia   Several studies have been done on the Australian aborigines to determine their prevalence rates for schizophrenia; two of the better ones both came up with a rate of 4.4 per thousand. Schizophrenia prevalence rates for the rest of the continent as a whole still need to be determined.

Autenreith, Ferdinand (1772–1835) A German physician who believed in the curability of acute psychotic disorders. He is remembered as the inventor of the "padded room." A more sinister invention of Autenreith's was a metal mask that would fit over the faces of mental patients, preventing them from making too much noise by limiting the amount of movement of their jaws. He also devised bulb-like gags to perform the same function. (See also MECHANICAL RESTRAINT.)

autism One of the "Four As" (association disturbances, affective disturbances, ambivalence, autism) that Eugen Bleuler proposed as the FUNDAMENTAL SYMPTOMS that uniquely distinguish schizophrenia from other mental disorders. It refers to the unresponsiveness of many schizophrenics to their environment, thus seeming like they're in a "world of their own." In *Dementia Praecox, Or The Group Of Schizophrenias* (1911), Bleuler makes the following observations on autism:

> The most severe schizophrenics, who have no more contact with the outside world, live in a world of their own. They have encased themselves with their desires and wishes (which they consider fulfilled) or occupy themselves with the trials and tribulations of their precursory ideas; they have cut themselves off as much as possible from any contact with the external world.

Bleuler then concludes, "This detachment from reality, together with the relative and absolute predominance of the inner life, we term autism." This symptom in children has led to the identification of infantile autism.

Bleuler, E., *Dementia Praecox, Or the Group of Schizophrenias*. New York: International Universities Press, 1950; first published, 1911.

autism, infantile A brain disease of infancy and childhood first described by psychiatrist Leo Kanner in 1943. It was formerly called Kanner's syndrome but is now known as autistic disorder, the most severe and prototypical form of the general diagnostic category known as pervasive developmental disorders in DSM-III-R. Through the years, many other diagnostic terms have been used for this class of disorders, including atypical development, symbiotic psychosis, childhood psychosis and childhood schizophrenia, but all of these terms are now obsolete.

Autistic disorder is usually apparent in a child's behavior within the first two to three years of life. The child generally does not respond well to touching or other forms of social interaction, is slow to develop language, develops many unusual stereotyped and repetitive behaviors and can become fascinated with certain inanimate objects (such as a spinning fan or faucets). Although some children can experience improvements in language, social and other skills around the ages of five or six, this is not true in every case. Puberty can bring about marked changes either for the better or worse. The disease has lifelong manifestation, although a small minority of these children go on to live relatively independent lives. The majority remain handicapped, with about 25% experiencing epileptic seizures before adulthood. About 50% remain within the mentally retarded range of intellectual functioning.

Studies in England and the United States have found that the prevalence of autistic disorder in the population is about four to five children out of every 10,000. Males are three to four times more likely to be afflicted with this disorder than females.

It is now known that autistic disorder is a brain disease that has nothing to do with child-rearing practices—especially the supposedly monstrous REFRIGERATOR MOTHER of autistic children, who Kanner believed was the cause of the disorder. Autistic disorder has been associated with maternal rubella, anoxia during birth, encephalitis, infantile spasms, tuberous sclerosis, untreated phenylketonuria and the fragile X syndrome. A genetic basis is weakly indicated by studies that show that autistic disorder is more common in siblings than in the general population.

It was formerly thought that autism was a form of a childhood psychosis that would eventually develop into schizophrenia, but most recent research seems to indicate that they are two different disorders. Sancte de Santis described a childhood psychotic disorder in 1906, *dementia praecoxissima,* which he thought was related to dementia praecox in adults. There was much confusion over whether infantile autism was a form of CHILDHOOD SCHIZOPHRENIA, until Kanner separated the two in 1943. Autism was officially removed from the diagnostic class of schizophrenic disorders in the 1970s, primarily as a result of the six published studies on the childhood psychoses published by Kolvin and his colleagues in 1971.

DeMyer, M.K., Hingtgen, J.N. and Jackson, R.K., "Infantile Autism Reviewed: A Decade of Research," *Schizophrenia Bulletin,* 7(1981), 388–451.

Kolvin, J. et al., "Studies in the Childhood Psychoses. II. The Phenomenology of Childhood Psychosis," *British Journal of Psychiatry,* 118(1971), 385–395.

autistic savants   Formerly called "idiot savants," a term coined in 1887 by the pioneer in the study of mental retardation, J. Langdon Down, for "children who, while feebleminded, exhibit special faculties which are capable of being cultivated to a very great extent." Autistic savants, though often mentally retarded, almost invariably develop from an early history of autistic disorder. Psychiatrist Darold Treffert proposes that this phenomenon be renamed the "savant syndrome" in his book, *Extraordinary People: Understanding "Idiot Savants"* (1989). He identifies two subtypes: "talented savants" or "Savant I," who have "skills that are remarkable simply in contrast to the handicap"; and "prodigious savants" or "Savant II," which is a much rarer form of the condition in which "the ability or brilliance is not only spectacular in contrast to the handicap, but would be spectacular even if viewed in a normal person."

The savant syndrome is six times more likely to occur in males than females. Although the condition is rare, some estimates indicate that as many as 9.8% of those children diagnosed with autistic disorder may exhibit this syndrome. And even more rare are the cases of the "prodigious savants," or "Savant II," with less than 100 cases on record in the past 150 years.

The common talent of all children and adults with the savant syndrome is phenomenal memory ability. This enables the sometimes spectacular performance of skills in the following areas: calendar calculating, music (usually the piano), rapid numbers calculating and mathematics, art (painting, drawing and sculpting) and sometimes mechanical ability. The memorization of enormous amounts of information has been documented in some prodigious savants.

Treffert has found that one of the more common patterns is a "triad" of blindness, mental retardation and musical ability.

In 1988 a movie, *Rain Man,* won the Academy Award for best picture for its depiction of a prodigious savant, or "Savant II." The many remarkable feats of memory ability and calculating ability dramatized in the film were all based on actual anecdotes reported in the clinical literature and are generally accurate recreations.

Treffert, D., "The Idiot Savant: A Review of the Syndrome," *American Journal of Psychiatry,* 145(1988), 563–572.

autoimmune hypothesis   This is one of the biological theories of schizophrenia that proposes it is an autoimmune disease. The basic idea is that schizophrenia may be due to an abnormality of the immune system that causes an allergic reaction to the body's own brain proteins. This "fight" of the immune system against its own nervous system might alter brain functioning so severely that it produces the behavioral manifestations that we have labeled as the mental disorder "schizophrenia." Most of the research has focused on lymphocytes and immunoglobulins. Many research studies conducted in the 1980s have found slightly suggestive evidence of disturbances in immuno-function in schizophrenics. However, this has not yet been linked to specific brain antigens or to specific clinical populations. Another confounding factor in these studies is that antipsychotic medication and lithium have effects on the immune system, which may have altered the results.

The immunological hypotheses, such as the autoimmune hypothesis, will be the source of much future research as medical technology enhances the investigation of these subtle neurobiochemical processes. These hypotheses are consistent with theories of the genetic transmission of schizophrenia, as well as with viral theories. For example, it may be found that viral infections in schizophrenia are the cause of immunological disturbances, or the reverse, that immunological disturbances may predispose individuals to the virus (or combination of viruses) that cause schizophrenia.

An excellent review of the research studies of the autoimmune hypothesis was published in 1984 by J. G. Knight.

Knight, J.G., "Is Schizophrenia an Autoimmune Disease? A Review," *Methods and Findings of Experimental Clinical Pharmacology*, 6 (1984), 395–403.

Meltzer, H.Y., "Biological Studies of Schizophrenia," *Schizophrenia Bulletin*, 13(1986), 77–114.

Awl, William See "CURE-AWL, DR."

axonal pruning See CORTICAL PRUNING AS A CAUSE OF SCHIZOPHRENIA.

B

bad news technique Perhaps one of the earliest "cognitive" psychotherapeutic techniques on record is the practice of inventing false "bad news" to tell patients in order to quell their manic mood states. There is evidence that this rather sadistic "counter-cognitions" technique was used in the Bethlem Royal Hospital in England as early as the 1500s to change the behavior of unmanageable patients.

Baillarger, Jules (1809–1890) One of the most eminent of the French psychopathologists of the 19th century. Baillarger was a student of ESQUIROL and founded the famous *Annales Mèdico-Psychologiques* in 1843, the very first French professional publication devoted to the study of psychological medicine. His research contributions include one of the first descriptions (in 1854) of MANIC-DEPRESSIVE PSYCHOSIS, which he called *folie à double forme*. Baillarger's revolutionary connection between alternating melancholic and manic phases, which he hypothesized to be of a single disorder and independent of mental disorders characterized solely by depression or solely by mania, is a concept later used by KRAEPELIN in his definition of manic-depressive psychosis and is still employed today in modern diagnostic systems. A mere two weeks after Baillarger presented his new diagnostic entity another student of Esquirol's, Pierre FALRET, claimed instead that it was he who had first described such a condition in a paper published in 1851—but only in 1854 did he call it *la folie circulaire*, the term historically associated with Falret. Both Baillarger and Falret are thus given the distinction of being the first clinicians to describe manic-depressive psychosis or bipolar disorder, but due to his more complete description and role in drawing attention to the new clinical entity, Baillarger is most often credited with the initial discovery. (See also BIPOLAR DISORDER.)

balderdash syndrome Another name for GANSER'S SYNDROME.

balmy Slang for "eccentric" or "mad." Some scholars have suggested that the term is derived from a 17th-century private madhouse in London known as Balmes House.

It was later known as the Whitmore House or Warburton's madhouse.

Barison, Ferdinando An influential theorist—particularly in Italy—of schizophrenic thinking styles. Differing from those theorists who held that schizophrenics tended to be more concrete in their thinking than normals, Barison argued that schizophrenics become overly abstract in their ideas and speech. Barison thought that schizophrenics employed abstractions in order to cover up the gaps in their thought processes caused by the disease process, thus repairing the "dissociative" breaks in the organization of the typical schizophrenic mind. This viewpoint was largely adopted by psychiatrist Silvano ARIETI in his discussion of the "pseudoabstract form and content" of schizophrenic thought and language in his *Interpretation of Schizophrenia* (1974).

Barison, F., "L'Astrazione formale de; pensiero quale sintomo di schizofrenia," *Schizophrenie*, 3(1934).

basket men The colloquial term used to refer to the male attendants of the Bethlem Royal Hospital in London as late as the 17th century. It was a holdover from medieval times when the hospital was a monastery. "Basket men" was a term for the hospitallers (usually monks or nuns) who would go out into the community—baskets in hand—begging for alms and food, which would then be carried back to the hospital for the care of the hospitallers, their patients and prisoners in the public gaols. Such "alms-baskets" held a highly symbolic significance, for the phrase "to go to the basket" meant to go to prison—a common place to find the mentally ill prior to the reforms of the 19th century. Along with other unfortunate individuals, the mentally ill person might also be termed a "basket-scrambler," meaning one who scrambles for the dole from a basket (i.e., who lives on charity).

Bassett, Anne S. See CHROMOSOME ABNORMALITIES.

Bateson, Gregory (1904–1985) An anthropologist by training, Bateson (and his associates) in 1956 formulated the famous DOUBLE-BIND THEORY of communication patterns in the families of schizophrenics. Bateson was the son of the famous British biologist William Bateson, who coined the word "genetics"; his father named him after Gregor Mendel. After completing his M.A. in anthropology at Cambridge, Bateson conducted fieldwork in New Guinea. He met and married Margaret Mead, a pioneer in cultural anthropology, with whom he conducted important fieldwork in Bali. Their marriage lasted fourteen years. Bateson is noted for his broad theoretical concerns in cybernetics, communications theory (which has influenced family therapy theorists), the family dynamics of schizophrenia, and his work with John Lilly on man-dolphin communication at the Oceanographic Institute in Hawaii. Until his death in 1985, Bateson was a frequent lecturer and scholar-in-residence at the Esalen Institute in Big Sur, California.

Lipset, D., *Gregory Bateson: The Legacy of a Scientist*. Englewood Cliffs, N.J.: Prentice-Hall, 1980.

bath of surprise A type of immersion therapy, used until the 19th century, in which the mentally ill person was plunged without warning into cold water. ESQUIROL, in his *Mental Maladies: A Treatise on Insanity* (first English translation, 1845), lists several forms of cold water treatment for patients, but the bath of surprise "consists of plunging the patient into water when he least expects it." Esquirol goes on to say that, "We administer it, by precipitating him into a reservoir, a river, or the sea. It is the fright which renders this means efficacious in overcoming sensibility. We can conceive the vivid impression that a patient experiences, who falls unexpectedly into the water, with the fear of being drowned.'' However, Esquirol admits that he has no data supporting the usefulness of this form of therapy, and confesses, ''I have never made use of it, but am certain it has been fatal.'' Incredibly, instead of the bath of surprise, Esquirol recommends throwing the patient out of a third-story window in order to effect a cure: ''When I hear of it (the bath of surprise) being prescribed, I should prefer rather, that they advised to precipitate the patient from the third story, because we have known some insane persons cured by falling upon the head.''

Esquirol, J.E.D., *Mental Maladies: A Treatise on Insanity*. Philadelphia: Lea and Blanchard, 1845; first published, 1838.

baths   One of the most ancient forms of treatment for mental illness. It is included by Philippe PINEL as one of the three forms of the ''usual treatment'' (''bleeding, bathing and pumping'') for the mentally ill in asylums circa 1801. Various pseudoscientific theories were put forth at the time to account for the calming or shocking effect of baths that seemed to temporarily reduce active psychotic symptoms. In Daniel Hack Tuke's *A Dictionary of Psychological Medicine* of 1892 a full 10 pages is devoted to the variations on this basic form of treatment for the mentally ill. Indeed, 15 different categories of ''baths'' are listed in that reference work, as follows:

1. Prolonged warm or hot baths.
2. Prolonged warm baths with the addition of cold to the head.
3. Prolonged warm sitz baths.
4. Prolonged warm baths medicated with mustard.
5. Prolonged cold baths.
6. Dip baths.
7. Baths of surprise.
8. Suffusion of tepid and cold water from pails.

9. Douches.
10. Showers.
11. Packing in the wet sheets.
12. Packing in the dry sheets.
13. Packing in mustard and water sheets.
14. Hot air (Turkish) baths.
15. Vapour (Russian) baths.

Many of these types of ''bath treatments'' survived until well into the 20th century. (See also HYDROTHERAPY.)

Williams, D., ''Baths,'' in D.H. Tuke (ed.), *A Dictionary of Psychological Medicine*, Vol. 1. London: J. & A. Churchill, 1892.

Battie, William (1703–1776)   An English physician and anatomist who was the first (and only) psyciatrist ever to be elected president of the Royal College of Physicians, a distinction he earned in 1764. Beginning in 1742, he served on the board of governors of the BETHLEM ROYAL HOSPITAL. However, due to the abusive conditions for patients at ''Bedlam,'' in 1751 Battie founded Saint Luke's Hospital for Lunatics and later acquired two private madhouses. Battie instituted important reforms for the treatment of the mentally ill, many of which were outlined in his classic *Treatise on Madness* (1758), which is a milestone in the history of psychiatry. He advocated the training of the caretakers of the insane, and called for research into the causes of insanity for the purposes of prevention. Battie is also remembered for his vicious battles fought with John Munro, who ran ''Bedlam,'' over administrative and treatment philosophies for the care of the insane. The slang expression that a mentally ill person is ''batty'' or has ''gone batty'' may have originated in England with the expression that a person has ''gone to Battie's,'' i.e., to Battie's private madhouse.

Beck, Samuel Jacob (1896–   )   A Romanian-born psychologist, later educated at Harvard and Columbia, who eventually headed the psychology laboratory at the Michael Reese Hospital in Chicago, Illinois. After psychologist David Levy imported the RORSCHACH TEST from Switzerland around 1925, Beck was the first American psychologist to publish research using the test; he also published the first Rorschach manual in English in 1937. Beck pioneered the use of the Rorschach as a diagnostic test for schizophrenia.

bedlam A well-known euphemism, even today, for pandemonium or chaos—like that found in "mad-houses." There was never a place officially named "Bedlam." Instead, the word was a colloquial corruption of "Bethlem," from the BETHLEM ROYAL HOSPITAL in London. An arresting portrayal of what the real "Bedlam" may have been like is to be found in certain scenes in the motion picture *Bedlam* (RKO, 1946), produced by Val Lewton, in which the chilling chiaroscuro suggests horrors of the asylum that the camera itself doesn't fully depict for the audience. However, the asylum images of life in "Bedlam" that are explicitly revealed bear a striking resemblance to those in the famous painting *Courtyard with Lunatics,* completed by Spanish artist Francisco Goya in 1793, which gives a graphic portrayal of asylum life in the 18th century. Since Lewton was known for the many literary and artistic allusions in his films (including many to Goya), he probably drew upon this painting (as well as Goya's etchings) for his motion picture conception of "Bedlam."

bed saddle A severe form of MECHANICAL RESTRAINT for patients that survived into the 20th century. For example, the "bed-saddle" was reported in use at St. Elizabeth's Hospital in Washington, D.C., until removed from use by William Alanson White after he became superintendent of that institution in October 1903. In his memoirs, White describes the "bed saddle:"

> One day in my first month at the hospital. In going through the wards of the institution I found a colored patient strapped to the bed by means of what was known as a "bed saddle." This bed saddle was made of thin strips of metal in the form of a cross strapped to the bed, and the patient was strapped to it with his arms extended in the position of crucifixion. I had never seen such an apparatus before and immediately issued an order discontinuing its use. I had been trained in the belief that physical restraint was unnecessary, yet in the very hospital where this was a fundamental principle a certain amount of physical restraint had actually been used. I had never seen such a cruel apparatus as this, so I felt justified in ordering its discontinuance.

A standing form of this device was known as the CRUCIFORM STANCE or harness.

White, W.A., *William Alanson White: An Autobiography of a Purpose*. Garden City, N.Y.: Doubleday, Doran, 1938.

Beers, Clifford W. (1876–1943) Beers, an American businessman, underwent a mental breakdown and attempted to commit suicide by jumping out of a window in June 1900, at the age of 24. Paranoia, auditory hallucinations and continual thoughts of suicide had plagued him for several years. After regaining his sanity and his eventual release, Beers wrote an autobiography, *A Mind That Found Itself* (1908), which detailed his treatment—and abuse—in mental institutions. The horrors of these institutions as depicted by Beers shocked the public of his day and helped to win him supporters for his National Committee for Mental Health (later called the National Association for Mental Health), the first major psychiatric patient-advocacy organization in the United States. Beers relates in his book how he would deliberately get himself transferred to the worst wards of the hospital—the "violent wards"—so that he could thoroughly investigate the institution for his later reform efforts. The sad fact is that the reader of Beers' book today who has worked any significant amount of time in psychiatric hospitals will find many of Beers' experiences familiar—suggesting that more than 80 years after the publication of this book many ugly conditions have still not changed in public institutions for the care of the mentally ill. (See also ABUSE OF PSYCHIATRIC PATIENTS).

Beers, C., *A Mind That Found Itself*. Garden City, N.Y.: Doubleday, 1908.

behavior therapy   The behavioral model of mental disorders holds that schizophrenia should not be considered the expression of an underlying mental "disease," but instead reflects the learning of a repertoire of "maladaptive behaviors" that can be corrected through using the operant conditioning techniques of behavior therapy. However, behaviorists have never constructed a complete theory about the recalcitrant maladaptive behaviors of schizophrenics, and long-term success, with behavioral techniques, of patients with schizophrenia has not been demonstrated. Behavior therapists focus on changing selected target behaviors of a patient (e.g., bizarre dressing, excessive smoking or coffee drinking, auditory hallucinations) and try to systematically eliminate them through the manipulation of "reinforcement contingencies" based on the general principles of learning that have been found to be effective in changing the behavior of animals and "normals."

The studies of psychologist T. Ayllon and his colleagues in the 1960s were some of the first applying behavior therapy to institutionalized schizophrenics. A much-publicized behavioral technique that was designed to shape the behavior of entire wards of patients was the "token economy programs" that were popular in the late 1960s and early 1970s. Tokens were introduced on wards as a money substitute that could reward adaptive behaviors and help extinguish or reduce maladaptive ones. The problem with such programs was that they could only work in small environments where there was a highly motivated and highly trained staff on all

three shifts of a 24-hour day—committed to following the rules of the behavioral program to the letter without "giving-in" to the immediate maladaptive demands of the patients. Currently, social skills training programs based on learning theory and behavior therapy paradigms are gaining attention. Modeling, problem solving and reinforcement techniques are used to improve the ability of schizophrenics to hold a conversation, be assertive, etc.

Whether any of the above forms of behavior therapy techniques for individuals or groups has long-lasting effects is questionable. Schizophrenics who do well in such programs in the highly structured environment of an institution lose such skills as soon as they are back in the community and without constant support and reminders as environmental cues. The evidence suggests that the newly learned behaviors instituted by these programs are thus not generalizable. Furthermore, the disease process itself—as schizophrenia is more and more viewed as a brain disease of as yet unknown etiology —seems to sabotage the ability of the nervous system to allow psychosocially induced changes in thinking and behavior to remain permanently and lead to long-term improvements in the level of social and occupational functioning. Behavior therapy—and social skills training programs based on these principles—is thus of limited value in the treatment of schizophrenia.

Ayllon, T., "Some Behavioral Problems Associated with Eating in Chronic Schizophrenic Patients," in *Case Studies in Behavior Modification*, ed. L. Ullman and L. Krasner. New York: Holt, Rinehart & Winston, 1965.

Kazdin, A.E., "The Failure of Some Patients to Respond to Token Programs," *Journal of Behavior Therapy and Experimental Psychiatry*, 4(1973), 7–14.

Kane, J.M., "Treatment of Schizophrenia," in *Special Report: Schizophrenia 1987*. Rockville, Md.: National Institute of Mental Health, n.d.

Belgian cage A wooden cage for the restraint of individuals with severe mental disorders. It stood on short posts. Such a cage was on display at a national exhibition in Brussels in 1880. Older names for such forms of MECHANICAL RESTRAINT, were the "idiot's cage" or "lunatic's cage."

Bellevue Hospital A hospital in New York City whose psychiatric ward achieved the notoriety in the United States that "Bedlam" had earned in England. Special wards reserved specifically for the mentally ill, called "insane pavilions," were first instituted at Bellevue Hospital in 1826. In 1839, a city "Mad House" was constructed and opened on Blackwell's Island (now Roosevelt Island) in the East River of New York City to handle the overwhelming population of the mentally ill that Bellevue was unable to confine. In the mid-20th century, saying that someone "belongs in Bellevue" was equivalent to saying that they were insane. By 1990, such references to Bellevue in popular culture and in everyday conversation had virtually disappeared on a national level, although it maintains a diminishing reputation as a "mad-house" to locals.

Bell's mania or disease A late-19th-century term for CATATONIC EXCITEMENT.

Benadryl The trade name for diphenhydramine, an antihistamine and anticholinergic drug that is used to treat the sometimes severe side effects that patients can experience after the initiation of antipsychotic drug therapy or after a significant increase in dosage. These side effects (stiffness, tremors, lockjaw, involuntary motions of the mouth, tongue and hands, involuntary eye rolls), which usually occur within hours or days of administering antipsychotic drugs, are acute dystonic reactions that can be reversed with antiparkinsonian agents such as Benadryl, Cogentin or Akineton. These side effects are acute, and are not to be confused with chronic reactions (to years of treatment with antipsychotic drugs) that are known as TARDIVE DYSKINESIA, which is treated with drugs other than Benadryl.

benign stupors This term refers to certain forms of MANIC-DEPRESSIVE PSYCHOSIS, as named and identified by psychiatrist August Hoch (1868–1919). Hoch is primarily remembered for his work on the MOOD DISORDERS, especially depression. The term "benign stupors" never became popular and is no longer in use.

Hoch, A., *Benign Stupors*. New York: Macmillan, 1924.

Bethel Hospital Founded in 1713, the Bethel Hospital of Norwich is the second oldest mental hospital in England (after the Bethlem Royal Hospital in London) and is the oldest still standing in its original structure. The hospital was formed, for those persons suffering from "lunacy or madness," by Mary Chapman, in accordance with the wishes of her deceased husband, a rector from Norfolk, England. Bethel's census never totalled more than 75 patients. It is presently a branch of one of the regional mental hospitals.

Bethlem Royal Hospital ("Bedlam") The oldest mental hospital in England, which stood at the present site of the Liverpool Street Railway Station in London. Originally established as a priory in 1247, by 1329 records show that it was functioning as a hospital. The patients were serviced by a religious order of Hospitallers founded in the 13th century and called the "Bethlehemites." The insignia on their habits was a red star with a dark blue center. In 1346 the City of London took control of the priory and hospital from the bishop of Bethlehem, and by 1403 it is recorded that six mentally ill patients resided there.

The person who was brought to the Bethlem Hospital for incarceration when it was relocated in Moorfields entered gates that were topped, on either side, with sculptures of reclining but manacled male nudes, created by Caius Gabriel Cibber in 1677. Such a person may very well have felt that he or she were crossing through the gates of Hell and into the netherworld. These depicted "Raving Madness" (a heavily chained, taut-muscled and -fisted madman whose mouth is opened in an anguishing grimace) and "Melancholy Madness" (a more passive figure, lying on his stomach, a stuporous expression on his face). Noted English poet Alexander Pope referred to them as the "brazen brainless brothers" in his work *The Dunciad*. They are now in the collection of the Victoria and Albert Museum in England.

Financial scandals and stories of abuse and torture in the public media marked the next several centuries of the institution's existence—until the 1870s when official investigations finally reported nothing out of the ordinary at the hospital. Probably not without coincidence, this change followed a period of over a century (from 1728 to 1852) in which the Bethlem Royal Hospital was directed by physician members of the Monro family for four generations (James, John, Thomas, Edward Thomas). In an investigative report of the Committee on Madhouses presented to the House of Commons in 1815 it was noted that many patients were chained and manacled with heavy irons. An American Marine named James Norris had been chained continually for 12 years (since 1804), and a female patient was found to have been restrained in such a manner for eight years. Due to these abuses, particularly of Norris, superintendant Thomas Monro and apothecary John HASLAM were fired from the Bethlem Royal Hospital (Monro through forced retirement). Surgeon Bryan CROWTHER, who was responsible for routinely bleeding all the patients at Bethlem every spring regardless of the type or severity of illness, escaped a similar fate when he died shortly before the committee began its hearings. Monro's only defense against the charges of abusive treatment of patients made by the investi-

gative commission was a weak one: "It was handed down to me by my father, and I do not know any better practice."

An autobiographical account of confinement in "Bedlam" was circulated in 1818 by a former patient, Urbane Metcalf. He describes the hospital as having four main "galleries" (more like cell-blocks than wards), with the worst, the "basement gallery," described as follows:

> It is to be observed that the basement is appropriated for those patients who are not cleanly in their persons, and who, on that account have no beds, but lay on straw with blankets and a rug; but I am sorry to say, it is too often made a place of punishment, to gratify the unbounded cruelties of the keepers.

The hospital was first made into a royal institution in 1547, and the official name became the Hospital of St. Mary of Bethlehem. Later this was shortened to Bethlehem Hospital and then to the Bethlem Royal Hospital. The institution moved several times over the years, with the final move occurring in 1920, to its present location in Monks Orchard, Eden Park, Beckenham. In 1948 it formed an association with Maudsley Hospital and now serves as a postgraduate teaching hospital for psychiatry.

Recent scholarship by the archivist at the Bethlehem Royal Hospital, Patricia Allderidge, questions the "house of horrors" image of "Bedlam" that has been perpetuated for the past 200 years. While noting in a paper published in 1985 that some patients were chained at the hospital, this was standard practice in asylums at the time (see BICÊTRE). After examining the original hospital records in the famous case of Norris (whose real first name is James and not William, as is often reported), she notes that he was quite possibly the most dangerous patient that the hospital staff had ever encountered. A large, strong seaman, Norris was continually making murderous assaults on staff until finally, in 1804, he was cuffed in an iron harness and chained to a post for good (as he is often pictured in drawings). The media attention to the Committee on Madhouses enquiry into this case truly helped to develop the stereotype of the hellish Bedlam, although Allderidge claims that the primary source materials (which have only been open since 1967) do not reveal much else that was extraordinary about the treatment at Bedlam vis-a-vis other asylums at that time. (See also BEDLAM.)

Allderidge, P., *Cibber's Figures From the Gates of Bedlam*. London: Victoria and Albert Museum Masterpieces, No. 14, 1977.

Allderidge, P., "Bedlam: Fact or Fantasy?" in W. Byrnum, R. Porter & M. Shephard (eds), *The Anatomy of Madness: Essays in the History of Psychiatry*, vol. 1. London: Tavistock, 1985.

Metcalf, U., *The Interior of Bethlehem Hospital*. London: 1818.

Metcalf, U., *Report of the Committee for Better Regulation of Madhouses*. London: Baldwin, Craddock, & Joy, 1815.

Tuke, D.H., *Chapters in the History of the Insane in the British Isles*. London: Kegan Paul, Trench, 1882.

bibliotherapy   The reading of books as a therapeutic activity for the mentally ill. Such an activity can help focus the mind of some afflicted persons and give them a sense of structure and organization to help combat chaotic thought processes. For psychotic patients the value is extremely limited, but some patients—particularly those who have paranoid schizophrenia or bipolar disorder—seem to get satisfaction from the activity. Due to the religious preoccupations of many psychotic patients, the Bible remains one of the most common books read and reread by patients in today's psychiatric hospitals, as has been the case for almost two centuries.

In his *Medical Inquiries and Observations on the Diseases of the Mind* (1812), American psychiatrist Benjamin RUSH recommended that the person responsible for the care of the mentally ill should engage them in bibliotherapy: "His business should be, to divert them from conversing upon all the subjects upon which they had been de-

ranged, to tell them pleasant stories, to read to them select passages from entertaining books, and to oblige them to read to him." A pioneer in the psychotherapy of schizophrenia, Swiss psychiatrist and psychoanalyst C.G. JUNG reports in his autobiography the case of a "schizophrenic old woman" whose auditory hallucinations of "voices" told her to let Jung test her knowledge of the Bible. As Jung (1961) tells it,

> She brought along an old, tattered, much-read Bible, and at each visit I had to assign her a chapter to read. The next time I had to test her on it. I did this for about seven years, once every two weeks. At first I felt very odd in this role, but after a while I realized what the lessons signified. In this way her attention was kept alert, so that she did not sink deeper into the disintegrating dream.

Jung reports a partial cure with this bibliotherapy method, admitting that "I would not have imagined that these memory exercises could have a therapeutic effect."

Jung, C.G., *Memories, Dreams, Reflections*. New York: Pantheon, 1961.

Rush, Benjamin, *Medical Inquiries and Observations Upon the Diseases of the Mind*. Philadelphia: Kimber & Richardson, 1812.

Bicêtre   In 1793, following the French Revolution, Philippe PINEL was appointed as physician in charge of this mental institution in Paris, renowned as one of the worst in the world. The Bicêtre became a hospital in 1656 but was essentially a holding tank for all of the undesirables of society. By the time Pinel took charge of the institution, it contained only insane males, whereas the females were kept at the Salpêtrière, also in Paris. Scores of patients, regardless of their illness, were heavily chained and often beaten by sadistic attendants. Records show that riots by the patients were not infrequent and led to the injuries and deaths of many of the attendants—often convicted criminals themselves. Pinel is frequently depicted as stunning the world by unchaining scores of these patients and by instituting policies for the minimum mechanical restraint necessary for maintaining order. Etchings and an 1876 painting by Tony Robert-Fleury depicting Pinel singlehandedly unchaining the mentally ill helped perpetuate this myth, although in the 1809 second edition of his famous textbook Pinel gives credit to the chief male nurse of the Bicêtre, Jean-Baptiste Pussin (1746–1809), for freeing the first 40 patients on May 23, 1789.

In his 1801 classic, *A Treatise on Insanity* (tr., 1806), Pinel argues that "coercion must always appear to be the result of necessity," and that with the changes he brought about at the *Asylum de Bicêtre* with his philosophy of "moral treatment:"

I can assert, from accurate personal knowledge, that the maxims of enlightened humanity prevail throughout every department of its management; that the domestics and keepers are not allowed, on any pretext whatever, to strike a madman; and that straight waistcoats, superior force, and seclusion for a limited time, are the only punishments inflicted.

Pinel, P., *A Treatise on Insanity* (1801), tr. from the French by D.D. Davis, M.D. Sheffield. England: W. Todd, 1806.

biochemical theories of schizophrenia
Biochemical theories of the causes of schizophrenia are among the most promising to date. Almost all of the biochemical theories assume that schizophrenia is caused by abnormal metabolic or enzymatic processes in the chemistry of the brain. Thus, when present-day mental health professionals explain to the family member of a schizophrenic that the brain disease is caused by a "chemical imbalance," it is because of the suggestive evidence for certain aberrant "autointoxicating" chemical processes in the brain. However, there are many different theories involving many different chemicals and biochemical processes in the nervous system, and no one biochemical theory can as yet be targeted as the best explanation for the sole cause of schizophrenia (or of all of its subtypes).

The idea that schizophrenia was perhaps caused by such an "autointoxicating" process in the brain was proposed from the very first by Emil KRAEPELIN in his initial description of dementia praecox in 1896. He writes:

For these reasons I consider it more likely that what we have here is a tangible morbid process occurring in the brain. Only in this way does the quick descent into severe dementia become at all comprehensible. It is true that morbid anatomy has so far been quite unable to help us here, but we should not forget that reliable methods have not yet been employed in a serious search for morbid changes. In the light of our current experience, I would assume that we are dealing with an auto-intoxication, whose immediate causes lie somewhere in the body.

Another early theorist to propose a metabolic disturbance as the cause of schizophrenia was the Swiss psychiatrist C.G. JUNG. In his 1907 classic, *The Psychology of Dementia Praecox*, Jung proposes that purely psychological causes (COMPLEXES) may be primary but are not enough to explain the devastating effects of schizophrenia. He proposed in addition the presence of a mysterious "hypothetical X, or metabolic toxin (?)" as perhaps the organic cause of this mental disorder. "Dementia praecox favors the appearance of anomalies in the metabolism—toxins, perhaps, which injure the brain in a more or less irreparable manner, so that the highest psychic functions become paralyzed," Jung writes early in his monograph. Furthermore, he presciently expresses the hope in 1907 that "a more perfect chemistry or anatomy of the future will perhaps demonstrate the objective metabolic anomalies or toxic effects associated (with dementia praecox)."

The most promising of the various biochemical theories involves the activity of dopamine, a major neurotransmitter in the brain. The DOPAMINE HYPOTHESIS holds that certain dopaminergic pathways in the brain are overactive, with the resulting chemical imbalance (an excess of dopamine, with which the brain "self-intoxicates" itself) causing the symptoms of schizophrenia. Scientists became interested in this hypothesis when it was discovered that most NEUROLEPTIC or ANTIPSYCHOTIC DRUGS stopped the POSITIVE SYMPTOMS of schizophrenia (delusions and hallucinations) by blocking the neurotransmitter dopamine at its receptor sites in the brain. However, it has been suggested that dopamine abnormalities may be implicated only in some types of schizophrenia, particularly the Type I variety identified by Crow (see CROW'S HYPOTHESIS), which is characterized by delusions and hallucinations that seem to respond to treatment with neuroleptic drugs.

The other major biochemical theories of schizophrenia are discussed under their respective entries: NITROGEN METABOLISM DISORDER HYPOTHESIS, TRANSMETHYLATION HYPOTHESIS, CERULOPLASMIN HYPOTHESIS, NEUROTRANSMITTERS, ENZYME DISORDER HYPOTHESIS, ORTHOMOLECULAR THEORY. Scientists still must use a hit-or-miss approach when looking for which bodily processes to target in their research. In addition, when something as suggestive as the dopamine hypothesis is discovered, it is still not known whether this process or any other acts independently or is dependent upon other, perhaps undiscovered factors.

With the promising findings in genetics regarding schizophrenia, biochemical theories have been linked to genetic theories of the causes of schizophrenia. The assumption is that a particular genetic abnormality predisposes an individual to developing a metabolic disorder in the brain. However, while this linkage is suggestive based on our knowledge of the genetic causes of other types of diseases, concrete evidence linking the two in the causes of schizophrenia is still lacking. Furthermore, it must be remembered that, other than through genetic causes, biochemical imbalances may derive from such things as environmental stress, infectious diseases and trauma—all of which have historically been implicated in various theories of the cause of schizophrenia.

Jung, C.G., *The Psychology of Dementia Praecox*, in *The Collected Works of C.G. Jung, vol. 3*. Princeton: Princeton University Press, 1960; first published, 1907.

Kraepelin, E., "Dementia praecox," from *Psychiatrie*, in Cutting, J. & M. Shepherd, *The Clinical Roots of the Schizophrenia Concept: Translations of Seminal European Contributions on Schizophrenia*. Cambridge: Cambridge University Press, 1987; first published, 1896.

Meltzer, H.Y., "Biological Studies in Schizophrenia," *Schizophrenia Bulletin*, 13(1987), 77–114.

biogenic amine hypothesis   The hypothesis that abnormalities in the structure, production and transmission of the biogenic amines are the cause of many mental disorders, especially psychotic disorders. The three primary groups of biogenic amines that are suspected to play this role are the CATECHOLAMINES (such as the neurotransmitter dopamine), the INDOLAMINES (such as the neurotransmitter serotonin) and the HISTAMINES.

biological markers of schizophrenia   The search for certain biological "signs" or "markers" in the biochemistry and neurophysiology of schizophrenia is one of the most important searches presently underway in schizophrenia research laboratories. If it can be shown that certain biochemical or neurophysiological processes are different in schizophrenics than in normals, then further tests can be devised to determine why this is so, perhaps giving scientific clues to the causes of schizophrenia. Furthermore, certain measurable differences found in schizophrenics may then be developed into a useful physiological method for making the diagnosis of schizophrenia (much as we now have tests for many other physical diseases).

Ideally, such tests could then be used in GENETIC COUNSELING (if genetics tests are developed) or in prenatal screening by determining the liability to schizophrenia. At present, although it is almost certain that schizophrenia is a brain disease with a physiological cause, there are no certain biological markers that can be looked for through medical tests in the same way that, for example, diabetes can be diagnosed.

Biological markers for schizophrenia are sought in research on the following areas: neuroanatomy, both gross and histologic (neuropathology, computed tomography, magnetic resonance imaging); dynamic brain functioning (positron emission tomography, mapping of the brain's electrical activity); neuroendocrine measures; neurophysiological measures (tracking of eye movements, electroencephalogram); molecular genetics; biochemical measures; and the biochemical response to the administration of various psychoactive drugs. (See also BRAIN ABNORMALITIES IN SCHIZOPHRENIA; BRAIN IMAGING TECHNIQUES; BIOCHEMICAL THEORIES OF SCHIZOPHRENIA; CARDIOVASCULAR HYPOPLASIA; ENDOCRINE DISORDER HYPOTHESIS; EYE-MOVEMENT ABNORMALITIES; PLATELET MONOAMINE OXIDASE ACTIVITY HYPOTHESIS.)

bipolar disorder "Bipolar disorder" is the most recent clinical name for the psychotic disorder identified in the 1850s in which one or more manic episodes are usually followed by one or more depressive episodes, intermixed or rapidly switching every few days. Usually it is the manic phase of the illness that results in the first hospitalization, and it can be accompanied by psychotic features (delusions, hallucinations, poor reality-testing). Usually a manic or major depressive episode is quickly followed by a mood shift of the opposite type. It is not uncommon for "rapid cycling" to occur, i.e., two or more complete cycles of a manic and major depressive episode that follow one another in less than a year. People who experience this "rapid cycling" are thought to have a more chronic form of the disease than those with other patterns.

The first significant description of bipolar disorder is credited to Jules BAILLARGER in 1854, who called it *la folie à double forme*. Pierre FALRET, another French psychopathologist who claimed priority for describing the illness just two weeks after Baillarger made his findings known (citing an 1851 publication), nonetheless gave it the name *la folie circulaire* in 1854. For many decades thereafter this disorder was called the "circular insanity" in English. In the sixth edition (1899) of his famous (and frequently revised) textbook *Psychiatrie*, Emil KRAEPELIN revised his nosology and renamed this type of "periodic psychosis" *das manisch-depressive Irresein*, or MANIC-DEPRESSIVE PSYCHOSIS, as it is still commonly called. Kraepelin thus separated the FUNCTIONAL PSYCHOSES into the two major groupings still used today: dementia praecox (schizophrenia), which he thought always had a poor prognosis, and manic-depressive psychosis, which he felt was less chronic in nature. The term "bipolar disorder" (and the separate "unipolar disorder") was used for the first time by German psychiatrist and phenomenologist Karl Leonard and his associates in 1962.

Estimates of the prevalence of bipolar disorder in adults range from .4% to 1.2% of the population. Thus, in 1990, there was an estimated two million people suffering from diagnosed manic-depressive illness in the United States alone. Epidemiological studies in the United States have also found that both males and females are equally likely to develop the disorder.

Like schizophrenia, bipolar disorder is thought to be related to genetic abnormalities. In the late 1980s the hope that genetic abnormalities could be found for these mental disorders was raised by the discovery of genetic abnormalities for other diseases, such as Huntington's disease in 1983 (on chromosome 4) and familial Alzheimer's disease (chromosome 21). However, in 1987 two different studies of bipolar disorder produced by two different teams of researchers found abnormalities on two different genes. In a study of an Amish community in Pennsylvania, an inherited gene was positioned near the gene for insulin on chromosome 11. A study of a community in Israel instead found the abnormality on the X chromosome near the gene for color vision. Thus, it may be that in bipolar illness, the symptoms may be similar across some afflicted individuals but with different genes affected in different individuals. This complex causal phenomenon is known as NONALLELIC GENETIC HETEROGENEITY and is most probably implicated in schizophrenia as well.

Bipolar or manic-depressive illness has been suspected in the tempestuous lives of some very famous and highly creative people down through history, thus earning its unfortunate nickname in the popular media as "the genius disease." Some historical figures who are thought to have been stricken with bipolar disorder are artist Vincent Van Gogh, composers Gustav Mahler and Hector Berlioz, political leaders such as Winston Churchill and Oliver Cromwell, and writers such as Lord Byron, Edger Allan Poe, Virginia Woolf and F. Scott Fitzgerald. More contemporary manic-depressives include actress Patty Duke, former activist Abbie Hoffman and statesmen Muammer el-Qaddafi of Libya and former Israeli Prime Minister Menachem Begin.

Suicide is a major risk factor during the depressive phases following manic phases of this disorder.

Since 1970, bipolar disorder has generally been treated with LITHIUM carbonate, particularly for the sometimes psychotic manic phase, and has proven very successful as a preventive measure against the intense ups and downs experienced by people with this disorder. Indeed, the "high" of the manic phase is sometimes so alluring that a common cause of relapse is the deliberate cessation or reduction of dosages of lithium.

(See also CHROMOSOME ABNORMALITIES; EPIDEMIOLOGY; GENETICS STUDIES.)

Baillarger, J., "Note sur un genre de folie dont les accés sont caractérisés par deux périodes réguliéres, l'une de dépression et l'autre d'excitation," *Bulletin de l'Académie Impériale de Médecine*, 19(Jan. 31, 1854), 340–352.

Falret, J.P., "Marche de la folie," *Gazette des Hôpitaux*, Jan. 14, 1851.

Falret, J.P., "Moire sur la folie circulaire, forme de maladie mentale caractériseé par la reproduction successive et réguliére de l'état manique, de l'état mélancolique, et d'un intervalle lucide plus ou moins prolongé," *Bulletin de l'Académie Impériale de Médecine*, 19(Feb. 14, 1854), 382–400.

Goodwin, F.K. and Jamison, K.R., *Manic-Depressive Illness*. New York: Oxford University Press, 1990.

Kraepelin, E., *Psychiatrie: Ein Lehrbuch für Studirende und Aerzte*, 6th ed., 2 vol. Leipzig: Johann Ambrosias Barth, 1899.

Leonhard, K., Korff, I. and Shulz, H., "Die Temperamente in den Familien der monopolaren und bipolaren phasichen Psychosen," *Psychiat.Neurol.*, 143(1962), 416–434.

Birch, John (1745–1815) Birch was a British surgeon and is perhaps the first to use electroshock therapy for mental illness. In the late 1700s Birch founded an "electric department" at London's St. Thomas Hospital and used electricity to treat his patients stricken with melancholia and other assumed mental disorders. He "passed shocks through the brain," as is reported in a book by George Adams (the man who made Birch's special electrical instrument), *An Essay On Electricity, Explaining the Principles of That Useful Science, and Describing the Instruments* (London, 1799).

birth order and schizophrenia In the late 1950s and early 1960s many studies were conducted to determine whether a person's rank in birth order among his or her siblings was correlated to the later development of schizophrenia. This research was partially conducted to test hypotheses generated by psychoanalytic theory, which predicted that the extraordinary oedipal demands made upon the first-born male child might (in combination with a "schizophrenogenic mother") produce adult schizophrenia. The make-up or "constellation" of schizophrenic families, determined by such things as the sex and birth order rank of children, was also of interest to "family systems" theorists who practice family therapy. However, major reviews of these studies have almost uniformly concluded that there is no association between birth order and the development of schizophrenia.

Erlenmeyer-Kimling, L., Van Den Bosch, E. and Denham, B. "The Problem of Birth Order and Schizophrenia: A Negative Conclusion," *British Journal of Psychiatry*, 115(1969), 659–678.

bizarre ideation   A common descriptive term found in the diagnostic assessments of clinicians examining psychotic patients. It refers to the grossly aberrant expressed thoughts of someone with a psychotic mental disorder. It is often used as a more colorful euphemism for the more clinical term, DELUSION.

blacks, incidence of schizophrenia in In the United States, blacks are given the diagnosis of schizophrenia at a greater rate than whites. The most conservative studies indicate that the rate for blacks is at least one-and-a-half times that for whites. There are several reasons suggested for this discrepancy. One is that most clinicians in the United States are white, and that the labeling of blacks with such a serious diagnosis is an expression, consciously or unconsciously, of racism. Others have suggested reasons based on epidemiological grounds, namely that there is a strong association between schizophrenia and lower socioeconomic status—regardless of race—in large cities. This association does not seem to be as strong for smaller cities or rural areas. Demographic studies show that blacks tend to be clustered in major metropolitan areas and less so in smaller cities or rural areas. Studies of schizophrenia rates in rural American areas show no difference between whites and blacks. Thus, those who cite such epidemiological data suggest that the higher schizophrenia rates among black Americans are due to environmental factors—the harsh life of poverty in large urban areas—rather than racial factors.

Kramer, M., "Population Changes and Schizophrenia, 1970–1985," in L. Wynne, et al. (eds.), *The Nature of Schizophrenia*. New York: Wiley, 1978.

bleeding   The deliberate opening of a blood vessel (venesection) or the more localized use of cupping glasses and leeches to draw blood was one of the most common forms of medical treatment for both physical and mental disorders for thousands of years. It gained in popularity as a psychiatric treatment after William Harvey's discovery of the circulation of blood in 1628 and was extensively employed for many physical and mental diseases until the 19th century. Galen, in the second century A.D., recommends it as a treatment for fevers. Due to the HUMORAL THEORY OF MENTAL ILLNESS of Hippocrates (5th century B.C.) it was thought that insanity was caused by an excess of "hot blood" or of particular humors, which thus needed to be drawn off from the body. The word for this condition of excess—the Greek *plethora*—is still used today, although not in its original, humoral sense.

Bloodletting was a common medical practice for centuries, although in the 12th century priests and monks (who were long involved in the medical treatment of the sick and poor) were forbidden to use it or other physical treatments by Pope Innocent II and instead were ordered to concentrate on religious matters of the soul. To compensate for this loss of medical specialists, a group of lay specialists known as "barbers" or "barber-surgeons" arose to meet the demand for bloodletting services. In England, a subspecialty group known as "Lay-Barbers" or "Surgeons of the Short Robe" was one of the groups represented in the Guild of the Barber-Surgeons, which was formed in 1210. Later legislation restricted the Lay-Barbers to bloodletting, wound surgery, cupping leeching, the extraction of teeth, the giving of enemas and—the only service that the "barbers" of today still perform—shaving. To distinguish themselves from the Surgeons of the Long Robe, who performed amputations and other services that the surgeons of today still provide, the Lay-Barbers placed a striped pole or sign outside their doors, under which was attached a "bleeding bowl" to advertise the nature of their services. The barber-pole represented the stick held and squeezed in the patient's hand to help increase the flow of blood from a wound produced on a vein in the arm (the same place where blood is most commonly drawn today), with the white stripe on the pole symbolizing the tourniquet tied around the arm above the opened vein and the red stripe, of course, symbolizing the blood. This is the way barber poles still appear today. Sometimes on the older poles a blue line might appear, which symbolized the appearance of the veins in the body.

There were three main bloodletting techniques. In venesection, sometimes called "breathing a vein," a vein (usually on the arm or foot) was opened with a sharp-pointed, double-edged and straight-bladed cutting instrument known in ancient Greece and Rome as a "phlebotome" (from the Greek words for "a vein" and "to cut") or later as a "lancet." The noted British medical journal *The Lancet* is named after this bloodletting instrument. A practitioner would be advised to carry a variety of lancets of various sizes for different-sized veins. They could be either the manually-applied type or, later, a "spring-lancet," in which a spring-propelled device could be released to mechanically push into and puncture a vein. Special "bleeding bowls" with internal gradations marked to measure the amount of blood collected were

used, with some of the finer ones made of pewter. It was considered an art not to spill a drop of blood anywhere but in these bowls.

A second method, "wet cupping," involved the application to the surface of the skin of a glass (usually) cup that had first been exhausted of air inside (usually through holding it over a flame until the flame expired), causing the skin to puff up (tumefy). After the skin responded in this manner, the cup was lifted and several incisions were made (sometimes with special devices, with multiple, razor-sharp blades, known as "scarificators"), and the cup reapplied to collect the blood.

The third method, "leeching," involved applying the freshwater parasitic invertebrate still known as *Hirudo medicinalis* to various parts of the body. The animal would then attach itself to the skin through its three-pronged bite and would engorge itself until full (in the largest leeches, about an ounce of blood). Cupping the wound after the leech was removed would then obtain much more blood, since leeches inject an anti-coagulant substance into the blood and such wounds would not readily clot or heal. The word "leech" is actually an old Anglo-Saxon word for a "healer" or "to heal," and for many centuries the animal was more commonly known by its ancient Latin name, *hirudo*. With the popularity of the medical practice of bloodletting, the word "leech" only later began to refer to the animal itself.

That the anemia caused by an excessive loss of blood could weaken anyone—and thus diminish their symptoms of mental illness—is no surprise. Many individuals lost their lives through this misguided form of treatment based on an incorrect theory. The history of psychiatry seems to be particularly prone to such tragic treatments, usually based upon some new scientific discovery (as the treatment of bleeding followed the discovery of the circulation of the blood), particularly since there are also modern examples of dangerous treatments based on little or no scientific theory—20th-century equivalents of "bleeding," such as PSYCHOSURGERY, the COMA THERAPIES, and the CONVULSIVE THERAPIES for schizophrenics.

Up until the 19th century, all of the patients in the BETHLEM ROYAL HOSPITAL in London were bled several times every summer, regardless of the severity or type of disorder, and as a commonly reported form of punishment. In 18th-century France, prior to their transfer to the care of Philippe PINEL at the Bicêtre Asylum in the 1790s, the mentally ill patients of Paris' oldest hospital were bled so often that the general public referred to bleeding as the *"traitement de l'Hôtel-Dieu."* French mental patients were usually bled once or twice in the spring and autumn and then bathed (or simply cast) into cold water. Pinel did not advocate bleeding, nor did J.E.D. ESQUIROL, who bluntly stated in his 1838 psychiatric manual that "I do not believe it necessary to proscribe bloodletting in the treatment of insanity."

Perhaps the greatest advocate of bleeding among the fathers of modern psychiatry was the American Benjamin RUSH of Philadelphia. In his 1812 textbook, *Medical Inquiries and Observations on the Diseases of the Mind,* he gives modern readers a glimpse into this long-rejected practice as a treatment for "mania":

Blood-letting is indicated by the extraordinary success which has attended its artificial use in the United States, and particularly in the Pennsylvania Hospital. In the use of bleeding in this state of madness, the following rules should be observed:
It should be copious on the first attack of the disease. From 20 to 30 ounces of blood may be taken at once, unless fainting be induced before that quantity be drawn. It will do most service if the patient be bled in a standing posture. The effects of this early and copious bleeding are wonderful in calming mad people. It often prevents the necessity of using any other remedy, and sometimes it cures in a few hours.

Rush's treatment of choice (which he picked up during his training in Edinburgh

and London, where he witnessed the regime at Bedlam and St. Luke's) did not meet with widespread approval in the United States, and by 1832 was no longer in use in American asylums. By the mid-1800s, the use of bleeding as a treatment for mental illness had almost entirely disappeared in Europe as well, leading the noted German psychiatrist Wilhelm GRIESINGER to write in 1845 that, "The use of bleeding . . . has in recent times been considerably restricted, and all are agreed that the necessity for venesection is not to be inferred from delirium, or any of its forms, even the most active, excited, and furious."

The best source of information on the medical practice of bleeding for modern readers is the essay and illustrations in a catalog of "bloodletting instruments" in the collection of the Smithsonian Institution in Washington, D.C., published in 1979 by Audrey Davis and Toby Appel.

Brain, P., *Galen On Bloodletting: A Study of the Origins, Development and Validity of His Opinions, With a Translation of the Three Works.* Cambridge: Cambridge University Press, 1986.

Davis, A. and Appel, T., *Bloodletting Instruments in the National Museum of History and Technology,* Smithsonian Studies in History and Technology, Number 41. Washington, D.C.: Smithsonian Institution Press, 1979.

Earle, P., "Bloodletting in Mental Disorder," *American Journal of Insanity,* 10(1854), 387–405.

Esquirol, J. E. D., *Mental Maladies, A Treatise On Insanity,* tr. E. K. Hunt. Philadelphia: Lea & Blanchard, 1845; first published, 1838.

Griesinger, W., *Mental Pathology and Therapeutics,* tr. C. L. Robertson of 2nd ed. New York: William Wood & Co., 1882; first published, 1845.

Rush, B., *Medical Inquiries and Observations Upon the Diseases of the Mind.* Philadelphia: Kimber & Richardson, 1812.

Bleuler, Eugen (1857–1939) An empathetic healer and prominent Swiss psychiatrist who coined the term "SCHIZOPHRE-

NIA" in a 1908 paper and who gave its clearest and unsurpassed description in his classic book, *Dementia Praecox, Or the Group of Schizophrenias* in 1911. Bleuler was born in Zollikon, near Zürich, where his ancestors were largely farmers. After earning his diploma, he served his medical residency at the Waldau mental hospital near Bern. He then left to study in Paris with such noted French psychiatrists as Jean Martin Charcot and Victor Magnon. In 1885 he returned to Zürich to serve as assistant to August Forel, the chief of the BURGHÖLZLI HOSPITAL. The following year, Bleuler at the age of 29 became the director of a mental hospital, the Reinau, located in a former monastery on an island in the Rhine River.

Bleuler's next 12 years were spent at Reinau and provided him the intimate experience of the everyday life of schizophrenics that he based his later theoretical work on. Bleuler lived in the same building with 800-plus patients (considered some of the worst and most chronic in this "backwater" institution) and devoted himself selflessly to every aspect of their care. Still a bachelor, Bleuler spent almost all of his waking hours with his patients and succeeded in his goal of attaining a close emotional rapport *(affektiver Rapport)* with each of them. Despite his relative youthfulness, the patients and the attendants addressed him as "Father" out of reverence.

This devotion to understanding the inner world of the schizophrenic patient he carried with him to the Burghölzli Mental Hospital when he succeeded his mentor Forel as the director in 1896. His lectures to his new staff, based on his observations made during his 12 years at Reinau, were the basis of his later book on schizophrenia. He organized work therapy programs *(Arbeitstherapie)* for the patients and would visit the wards several times at any hour during the day. He was also insistent that his staff demonstrate the same devotion as Bleuler himself to understanding the patients—a revolutionary approach in the days when physicians were

rarely seen by the patients at all, let alone involved in discussions with them. Over the years his staff contained individuals who would later become famous for their own contributions to psychiatry and psychoanalysis: C. G. Jung, Karl Abraham, A. A. Brill, Ernest Jones and Ludwig Binswanger. Alphonse Maeder (cited in Ellenberger's book, *The Discovery of the Unconscious*), who also became well known, described what life was like with Eugen Bleuler in those legendary days at the Burghölzli:

> The patient was the focus of interest. The student learned how to talk with him. Burghölzli was in that time a kind of factory where you worked very much and were poorly paid. Everyone from the professor to the young resident was totally absorbed by his work. Abstinence from alcoholic drinks was imposed on everyone. Bleuler was kind to all and never played the role of the chief.

Bleuler was briefly associated with Sigmund Freud's psychoanalytic movement but broke with Freud in 1910. He is credited with coining the word "depth psychology," which refers to the psychology of the unconscious mind made famous by Freud and Jung.

Bleuler, E., *Dementia Praecox, Or the Group of Schizophrenias,* tr. J. Zinkin. New York: International Universities Press, 1950; first published, 1911.
Ellenberger, H., *The Discovery of the Unconscious.* New York: Basic Books, 1970.

Bleuler, Manfred (1903–) Son of Eugen Bleuler and a major contributor to the study of schizophrenia in his own right. Manfred assumed his father's former position as the director of the Zürich Psychiatric University Clinic at the Burghölzli in 1942. He remained in this position for 27 years and is known for his long-term studies of schizophrenic patients and their families. Like his father, Manfred also placed a great importance on understanding the inner world of those afflicted with schizophrenia. In 1979 he wrote:

A healthy life exists buried beneath this confusion. Somewhere deep within himself the schizophrenic is in touch with reality despite his hallucinations. He has common sense in spite of his delusions and confused thinking. He hides a warm and human heart behind his sometimes shocking affective behavior. We must know how to approach the schizophrenic. We must enter and feel with him his vision of reality. We must never relinquish this endeavor.

Bleuler, M., *The Schizophrenic Disorders: Long-Term Patient and Family Studies*, S. M. Clemens. New Haven: Yale University Press, 1978; first published, 1972.

Bleuler, M., "My Sixty Years with Schizophrenics," in L. Bellak (ed.), *Disorders of the Schizophrenic Syndrome*. New York: Basic Books, 1979.

Bleuler's syndrome

The eponymous label given by British psychiatric researcher Timothy Crow to his proposed "Type I" schizophrenia, which is the variety characterized by positive symptoms, good response to psychotropic medication, and a relative lack of intellectual impairment. This last characteristic is why Crow named Type I schizophrenia after Eugen BLEULER, whose contribution to the study of schizophrenia was his recognition that there were forms of schizophrenia that did not necessarily follow the strict degenerative course that Emil KRAEPELIN thought characterized all dementia praecox. Kraepelin's concept of dementia praecox more closely fits Crow's Type II schizophrenia, which he named the PINEL-HASLAM SYNDROME after the two famous alienists who each, apparently, provided the first clinical descriptions of this disorder in books that they published in 1809. (See also CROW'S HYPOTHESIS.)

Crow, T. J., "The Two-syndrome Concept: Origins and Current Status," *Schizophrenia Bulletin*, 11(1985), 471–485.

blocking

A very common symptom of schizophrenia wherein a person has an abrupt loss of their train of thought, feeling as though he or she is suddenly "blanking out" in mid-sentence. Many schizophrenics describe this experience as a sudden loss of all thoughts and feelings, leaving awareness "empty" or filled with "nothingness." Often they cannot remember what they were previously saying or thinking when asked after such an experience. One paranoid schizophrenic patient that the author knew would scream out, "They just killed me right now!" to describe his anxiety over the frequent, sudden loss of his inner world. The term was used by Eugen Bleuler as early as 1911.

bloodletting See BLEEDING.

blood transfusion

Down through the centuries the idea has persisted that mental illness might be caused by abnormalities in the blood. The practice of BLEEDING attempted to cure the mentally ill by drawing significant quantities of blood from the afflicted until a change in symptoms could be noted. Similarly, the idea of blood transfusions as a possible treatment of mental illness developed in Europe in the 1660s. A French physician, Jean Baptiste Denis, performed the first recorded transfusion of blood in a 34-year-old melancholic man. Denis replaced the man's blood with calf's blood. Later the same year Sir George Ent convened a meeting of the Royal Society on November 23, 1667, and demonstrated the transfusion of sheep's blood into a patient from the Bethlem Royal Hospital in London. This event was recorded by Samuel Pepys in his famous diary. Besides France and England, these transfusion treatments were recommended in Germany by physicians Klein and Ettmüller, the latter of which suggested this form of treatment in his 1682 *Chirurgia Transfusoria*.

A 20th-century resurrection of this "bad blood" theory of the cause of mental illness was made in 1977 by psychiatrists J. Wagemaker and R. Cade, who noticed a significant improvement in a paranoid schizophrenic patient following hemodialysis for kidney disease. They hypothesized that an unknown "toxin," which caused schizophrenic symptoms, may have been removed through hemodialysis. Although a further study using hemodialysis on schizophrenics with no kidney disease proved promising and attracted media attention, replications of this study by others have not found the same results. (See also HEMODIALYSIS TREATMENT OF SCHIZOPHRENIA.)

blunted affect A commonly used descriptive term for a significant reduction in the (normal) intensity of the expressed emotions of a person. This is one of the major symptomatic expressions of schizophrenia but can also be witnessed in those persons who are depressed. A related term, FLAT AFFECT, refers to the nearly complete absence of any emotions whatsoever, with the voice sounding monotonous and the face rigid.

Bly, Nellie (1867–1922) The pseudonym of an American journalist for the *New York World*, Elizabeth Seaman (*née* Cochrane), who faked insanity and gained admittance to the New York City Lunatic Asylum (formerly "Mad House") on Blackwell's Island (now Roosevelt Island). Her serialized exposé was entitled "Ten Days in a Mad House," with the engaging subtitle "Feigning insanity in order to reveal asylum horrors. The trying ordeal of the *New York World*'s girl correspondent." Her articles were published in book form the following year.

Bly detailed abuses involving the unnecessary use of restraints, cruelty to patients by attendants, and unsanitary conditions. These were the same kinds of maltreatment documented by Charles Dickens when he went to the asylum on Blackwell's Island during his trip to America in 1842.

Bly, N., *Ten Days in a Mad House.* New York: 1888.

boarding homes The mentally ill have long resided in boarding homes in the United States, but this type of residence has proliferated since the DEINSTITUTIONALIZATION of psychiatric patients from state hospitals, which began in the 1950s. The idea was that it would be more "normal" for patients to live in the community in such homes. However, in the United States such homes are often found to be under-supervised, with their high turnover rates not infringing upon their profitability to the private owners, who generally have no professional training for supervising such patients. Many psychiatric patients actually prefer the relatively close supervision of the psychiatric hospital where there are always other people around in case of danger. A cogent critique of the problem of the "homeless mentally ill" in the 1980s is provided in a book by psychiatrist E. Fuller Torrey.

Torrey, E. F., *Nowhere To Go: The Tragic Odyssey of the Homeless Mentally Ill.* New York: Harper/Perennial, 1988.

body image in schizophrenia A commonly reported phenomenon in schizophrenia is the experience of distortions in body image. The afflicted person feels, fears or believes that the physical body itself is changing and will look different to others. Such body distortions can take bizarre forms in people with schizophrenia and are fully experienced as "real" by them. A former patient of the author's was fully experiencing the feeling that his face had turned into that of a dog's, and that this was how people were actually perceiving him. Others may believe that they have huge, gaping holes in the middle of their torsos through which they experience the wind passing, or feel much thinner or fatter than they really are. The issue of a person's body image has been much discussed in recent years, with the phenomenon of females with anorexia nervosa having the delusional belief that they are being perceived as fat when, in fact, they are emaciated. The concept of "body image" was first proposed by the psychoanalyst Paul Schilder in 1935 in his book, *The Image and Appearance of the Human Body: Studies in the Constructive Energies of the Psyche.*

Boerhaave, Hermann (1668–1738) A Dutch physician, known for his psychiatric interests. He is acknowledged as the inventor of the "spinning chair," a device of mechanical restraint that was designed to render patients unconscious. (See also CIRCULATING SWING.)

borderline cases No diagnostic system is perfect, especially when it comes to identifying mental disorders, and so over the years they must constantly be revised. New categories must be added and others discarded. In the 20th century, the concept that there could be cases that fall between "neurosis" and "psychosis" because they have the features of each, began to take hold when it was discovered that more and more patients could not be evenly classified by this simple dichotomy. These have been called "borderline cases." However, following the dichotomy of psychotic disorders identified by KRAEPELIN in the late 1890s, it has generally been found that these so-called borderline cases seemed to be related either to schizophrenia (dementia praecox) or to bipolar disorder (manic-depressive psychosis). Those borderline cases that seemed to more closely resemble schizophrenia are now labeled SCHIZOTYPAL PERSONALITY DISORDER (see BORDERLINE SCHIZOPHRENIA), and those that are allied with manic-depressive psychosis are now called BORDERLINE PERSONALITY DISORDER. However, this distinction is also reflected in the clustering of other types of similar personality disorders in the *Diagnostic and Statistical Manual of Mental Disorders, Third Edition, Revised* (1987), with "Cluster A" consisting of schizotypal, paranoid and schizoid personality disorders. These people are said to appear "odd or eccentric." "Cluster B" is grouped into borderline, antisocial, histrionic and narcissistic personality disorders, in all of which an individual's behavior appears "dramatic, emotional or erratic."

Spitzer, R. L., Endicott, J. and Gibbon, M., "Crossing the Border into Borderline Personality and Borderline Schizophrenia," *Archives of General Psychiatry,* 36(1979), 17–24.

borderline neuroses See BORDERLINE SCHIZOPHRENIA.

borderline personality disorder Although the descriptions of this disorder differ, the most widely accepted diagnostic description is an erratic pattern of interpersonal relationships characterized by extremes of overidealization and devaluation, problems with self-identity, emotional instability (usually depicted as vaccillating between intense feelings and displays of anger and an "emptiness" depression), and, in the most severe forms of the disorder, self-mutilation and suicide threats and attempts. During stressful periods, psychotic symptoms (such as bizarre delusions or hallucinations) can appear. For example, a woman whose daily occupation requires a significant amount of reasoning ability and responsibility (e.g., as a social worker) may nonetheless suddenly be afraid to open the door of her apartment to pay for the pizza she ordered over the telephone, for fear that the delivery boy had poisoned it.

Borderline personality disorder is apparently becoming more common than in the past and is generally diagnosed more in females than in males. Males with similar symptoms tend to be involved in antisocial activities (e.g., stealing, violence, substance abuse) acted-out against others and thus are usually given the diagnosis of antisocial personality disorder (see ANTISOCIAL BEHAVIOR). Since this disorder is often difficult for most people to identify, fictional examples from motion pictures or television are sometimes referred to in the training of mental health professionals. Some recent, fiction-alized examples of extreme forms of the disorder are the roles of actresses Glenn Close in the movie *Fatal Attraction* (1987) and Meryl Streep in the movie *Plenty* (1985).

Borderline personality disorder is the best example of the types of BORDERLINE CASES that resemble affective disorders, such as BIPOLAR DISORDER, rather than those that resemble schizophrenia.

borderline schizophrenia   A term that became popular in the 1920s but is no longer in use for the type of disorder in which a person has what resembles schizophrenia across many traits, but is not fully psychotic and does not have all of the symptoms of schizophrenia. Such individuals might now be commonly diagnosed as having a SCHIZO-TYPAL PERSONALITY DISORDER. The concept that some patients fall between "neurosis" and "psychosis" with their mental illness is expressed in the use of the world "border-line." In psychoanalytic publications, this concept formerly meant patients who were intermediate between the groups that were clearly "analyzable" (such as those with neurotic disorders) and "nonanalyzable" (those who are psychotic).

Other clinical terms used over the years that overlap with borderline schizophrenia (with the person who coined them and in what year) are as follows: borderline neu-rosis (L. P. Clark, 1919); impulsive char-acter (W. Reich, 1925); INCIPIENT SCHIZO-PHRENIA (Glover, 1932); SCHIZOAFFECTIVE DISORDER (Kasanin, 1933); AMBULATORY SCHIZOPHRENIA (Zilboorg, 1941); "as-if" personality (H. Deutsch, 1942); LATENT PSYCHOSIS (Federn, 1947); pseudoneurotic schizophrenia (Hoch & Polatin, 1949); and LATENT SCHIZOPHRENIA (Bychowski, 1953). It is also thought that Eugen Bleuler at-tempted to identify this type of "borderline" person with the term "compensated schizo-phrenic" in 1911.

Stone, M. H., "The Borderline Syndrome: Evo-lution of the Term, Genetic Aspects, and Prog-nosis," in M. H. Stone (ed.), *Essential Papers on Borderline Disorders: One Hundred Years at the Border*. New York: New York Univer-sity Press, 1986.

Bose, Katrick   Together with Ganneth Sen, these two Indian scientists published research in 1931 detailing the use of a drug, *Rauwolfia serpentina*, in the treatment of high blood pressure and psychosis. *Rauwol-fia's* ability to calm excited persons had been known for centuries in India, where it had been used for madness and other ailments. The work of Bose and Sen stimulated inter-est in new research aimed at finding phar-macological treatments for schizophrenia and the psychotic disorders. However, it was not until 1954 that *Rauwolfia's* active ingredi-ent—reserpine—was chemically isolated and refined for treatment. The first published research on the use of reserpine with psy-chotic patients was by N. S. Klein and A. M. Stanley in 1955. Today it is more commonly used for the treatment of essential hypertension than for psychosis.

Sen, G. and Bose, K., "Rauwolfia Serpentina, a New Indian Drug for Insanity and High Blood Pressure," *Indian Medical World*, 2(1931), 194–201.
Klein, N. S. and Stanley, A. M., "Use of Re-serpine in a Neuropsychiatric Hospital," *An-nals of the New York Academy of Sciences*, 61(1955), 85–91.

bouffée délirante aigüe   A term com-monly used in Haiti to refer to a "culture-bound syndrome"; characterized by a sud-den, transient delusional episode, sometimes with visual and auditory hallucinations, which are often recurrent. Delusions might be per-secutory, grandiose or sexual. Beliefs of being possessed or of having special magical powers are also associated with this disorder. Native Haitian Vodun priests, the houngans, ascribe such an illness to possession by var-ious spirits, which results from the afflicted person's unwillingness to heed the call of Vodun deities to participate in that religion's rituals. Participation in Vodun rituals is prescribed by the houngans as a cure for the disorder. Many French psychiatrists have used this term to refer generally to the cultural phenomenon of "spirit possession" in Haitian society. In the United States and Canada, such a disorder would probably be diagnosed as a BRIEF REACTIVE PSYCHOSIS, a DELUSIONAL DISORDER or an atypical DISSOCIATIVE DISORDER.

boundary disturbances in schizophrenia   This is a type of perceptual distortion that many schizophrenics report in which they feel they are merging or blending into or are part of another person. Such persons may describe the anxiety felt when in the presence of others as being due to the frightening feeling that they are "sliding into" another person and thus losing the sense of individual identity. Such experiences—although terrifying for most psychotics—have been reported by "normals" who have ingested certain hallucinogens, thus giving rise to the research in the experiential similarities between schizophrenia and hallucinogenic states.

bradykinesia   One of the triad of signs of PARKINSON'S SYNDROME that is an adverse effect of the administration of ANTIPSYCHOTIC DRUGS. Along with tremor and rigidity, bradykinesia (or akinesia) can occur in patients within weeks to months after the beginning of antipsychotic drug therapy. Bradykinesia is a slowness of motion, whereas akinesia (less common and more severe) is an absence of motion that is not caused by a general paralysis. The person with bradykinesia will frequently seem to have a masklike face, with little expressiveness and infrequent and slow eye blinking. The motions of such a patient can seem "zombie-like." The bradykinetic patient is said to turn his or her body "en bloc," as if rigidly frozen into a body without joints. Drooling is a common associated phenomenon with the triad of Parkinsonian symptoms.

Brady- is a prefix that means "slow" and is used in many other clinical behavioral terms. (See also ANTIPARKINSONIAN DRUGS.)

brain abnormalities in schizophrenia
The search for abnormal structures in the brains of schizophrenia patients has a long history, beginning with the 19th-century ABLATION STUDIES and continuing with the sophisticated technology of BRAIN IMAGING TECHNIQUES today. It is known that autopsies were performed on the deceased patients at the BETHLEM ROYAL HOSPITAL in London, England, in the early 1800s as well as in Paris, France, by PINEL and ESQUIROL at about the same time. Between 1802 and 1804, Pinel conducted over 250 autopsies or "openings" *(ouvertures)* of corpses of deceased mental patients. Only about one-fourth of these patients showed cerebral lesions, thus confirming the belief of Pinel and his student Esquirol after their *recherches cadavériques* that insanity was more likely to be caused by visceral lesions rather than brain abnormalities.

Studies conducted on the brains of the deceased (such as the ablation studies) are commonly referred to as neuropathology, whereas studies on the living are called neuroimaging studies. Modern imaging techniques give clues not only to how the brains of some schizophrenics may differ from normals, but also how the dynamic functioning of the brian may be unusual. Until the mid-1970s investigations into the structural brain abnormalities of schizophrenics were discouraged by negative or inconclusive results, but these were due to the inexact technology used to conduct these studies. Brain imaging techniques, however, have found *some* structural abnormalities in *some* schizophrenics in several major areas of the brian. It must be remembered, however, that studies show that most areas of the schizophrenic brain are normal.

The Frontal Lobe   This area of the brian is known to be involved in "higher cortical functions" such as thinking and purposeful action (volition). In the late 1980s studies using CT scans found reduced numbers of cells in the prefrontal cortex of schizophrenics, as well as smaller sizes for the prefrontal area as a whole in studies using magnetic resonance imaging (MRI) techniques. This corresponds to PET-scan studies that have indicated "hypofrontality" and functional deficits of the frontal lobes of schizophrenics.

The Limbic System This area of the brain consists of clusters of nerve cells (nuclei) that are highly integrated and are connected to the cortex. This is commonly portrayed as the "instinctual" area of the brain, as feelings, sex, aggression, memory and certain hormonal functions are regulated by this network of nuclei. Studies have found abnormal shrinkage in the number, size and organization of cells in the limbic areas, as well as a reduction for the area as a whole in some schizophrenics. Left-hemisphere abnormalities have been suggested by these studies.

The Extrapyramidal Motor System This area of the brain coordinates muscle activity and movement. The basal ganglia in particular seems to be an area that also evidences reductions in size and number of cells in schizophrenic brains as compared to normal brains.

Ventricles These "spaces" between the lobes of the brain through which the cerebrospinal fluid passes have been found to be enlarged in about 30% to 40% of schizophrenics across numerous studies. The clinical significance of enlarged ventricles in some schizophrenics is not known, although since it is not universal it cannot be used as a BIOLOGICAL MARKER for schizophrenia.

Hemispheres With so much interest in the different functions of the left and right hemispheres of the brain, many researchers have sought left-hemisphere abnormalities in schizophrenics because of the extreme language and thought disorder that they exhibit. Neuropsychological studies suggest evidence for the role of abnormal functional

cerebral asymmetry in schizophrenia. However, while some evidence of structural abnormalities, particularly in the temporal and frontal regions, is suggestive, as of yet there is no conclusive evidence for the theory that schizophrenia may be a "left-hemisphere disease" whereas affective disorders (such as bipolar disorder) might be indicative of "right-hemisphere disease." (See also NEUROHISTOPATHIC HYPOTHESIS; NEUROPSYCHOLOGICAL STUDIES OF SCHIZOPHRENIA.)

Meltzer, H. Y., "Biological Studies in Schizophrenia," *Schizophrenia Bulletin,* 13(1987), 77–114.

Weinberger, D. R., Wagner, R. L. and Wyatt, R. J., "Neuropathological Studies of Schizophrenia: A Selective Review," *Schizophrenia Bulletin,* 9(1983), 193–212.

brain imaging techniques Also called neuroimaging techniques, these are technologically sophisticated methods for studying the structure and functioning of the brains of living human beings by generating "pictures" or "images" that can then be studied and compared with images from the brains of others. These techniques have revolutionized the neurosciences. The first such techniques was the CT SCAN, pioneered for use by G. N. Hounsfield in 1973. The first report of the use of brain imaging techniques to study schizophrenic brains was the classic report by E. D. Johnstone and his colleagues published in the British medical journal *Lancet* in 1976. Many other types of brain imaging techniques have been developed and used in schizophrenia research since then.

CT scan (computerized tomography) and nuclear magnetic resonance (NMR), also called MAGNETIC RESONANCE IMAGING (MRI), generate images of the structure of the brain. MRI images are considered to be clearer and of more value. The dynamics of brain functioning, however, are studied with brain imaging techniques such as brain electrical activity mapping (BEAM), cerebral blood flow imaging (also known as regional cerebral blood flow, or RCBF), positron emission tomography (PET SCANS), single photon emission computed tomography (SPECT) and magnetoencephalography (MEG).

Brain imaging techniques are considered to be among the most promising avenues of schizophrenia research for decades to come.

Hounsfield, G. N., "Computerized Transverse Axial Scanning (Tomography)," *British Journal of Radiology*, 46(1973), 1016–1022.

Johnstone, E. D. et al., "Cerebral Ventricular Size and Cognitive Impairment in Chronic Schizophrenia," *Lancet*, 2(1976), 924–926.

Wagner, H. N. et al., "Neuroimaging and Neuropathology," *Schizophrenia Bulletin*, 14(1988), 383–398.

brief reactive psychosis

brief reactive psychosis   This is a psychotic episode of only a few hours to less than one month in duration, after which there is a full return to previous levels of functioning. This is generally in response to an event or events that are considered highly stressful by the person (and by most people in that person's culture), such as the sudden loss of a loved one, or the traumatic experience of violence or war. Such a man or woman may become incoherent, screaming or babbling inarticulate gibberish. Some delusions and hallucinations are not uncommon, and catatonic or disorganized behavior may be observed. Rapid shifts in emotional states are common (e.g., periods of crying followed by hyperactivity) and are indicative of the inner confusion such people experience with the rapid onset of psychotic symptoms. The usual duration of such symptoms is only a day or two before the individual recovers, although depression may then be present. Epidemiological studies show it is more common in adolescence and early adulthood. It is thought that some people with a preexisting mental disorder (such as borderline personality disorder, schizotypal personality disorder or others) may be more likely to have brief psychotic reactions under situations of extreme stress.

Brierre de Boismont, Alexander

Brierre de Boismont, Alexander (1798–1881)   A noted French *aliéniste* who is most remembered for his comprehensive study of hallucinations published in 1853. This study examined the phenomenon of hallucinations not only in the mentally ill, but also in hypnosis ("magnetic visions"), religious experience and in other ALTERED STATES OF CONSCIOUSNESS. Brierre de Boismont was a disciple of ESQUIROL and was a member of the famous "Esquirol Circle."

Brierre de Boismont, A., *Hallucinations: Or, the rational history of apparitions, visions, dreams, ecstasy, magnetism and somnambulism*. Philadelphia: Lindsay & Blakiston, 1853.

Brigham, Amariah

Brigham, Amariah (1798–1848)   One of the original 13 founders of the American Psychiatric Association in 1844 (then called the Association of Medical Superintendents of American Institutions for the Insane). In 1843 he became the superintendent of the newly opened Utica State Hospital in New York. The following year, in 1844, he started the *American Journal of Insanity*, which later became the *American Journal of Psychiatry*, as it is known today. He printed it in the hospital with the assistance of patients in work programs.

Broadmoor Hospital

Broadmoor Hospital   Broadmoor has achieved notoriety in the British Isles as the place where the most homicidal of "homicidal maniacs" are kept. Since it opened its doors in 1863, Broadmoor has been where the most dangerous or violent mentally ill criminals have been placed. Prior to its construction in Crowthorne, Berkshire, such dangerous patients were kept in a special "gallery" at the BETHLEM ROYAL HOSPITAL in London.

Brosius, C. M.

Brosius, C. M. (1825–1910)   A German psychiatrist who, along with Wilhelm GRIESINGER, is noted for quickly and successfully instituting policies of nonrestraint for the patients in German asylums and hospitals in the mid-1800s. German institutions took the lead in this more humane treatment of the mentally ill, whereas hospitals in the rest of Europe, notably England and France, only significantly improved near the end of the 1800s.

Broussais, Francois Joseph Victor (1772–1838) A French physician, army surgeon and professor of general pathology of the University of Paris who was a bitter enemy of Philippe PINEL. Broussais entertained a rather unusual—and not well received—theory that mental illness was caused by gastrointestinal "irritation." BLEEDING, PURGING and diets were suggested as treatments for this irritation.

Broussais, F. J. V., *De l'irritation et de la folie.* Paris: 1828.

Bucknill, Sir John Charles (1817–1897) A major figure in 19th-century British psychiatry, Bucknill was an important advocate of nonrestraint policies and the boarding-out of mental patients from the hospitals to community placements. Superintendent of the Devon Asylum from 1844 to 1862, he also became the first president of the Association of Medical Officers of Asylums and Hospitals for the Insane (now the Royal College of Psychiatrists), and in 1862 he rose to the prominent position of Lord Chancellor's Visitor in Lunacy. Bucknill was also the first honorary member of the American Psychiatric Association; together with D. H. Tuke he wrote a standard textbook, *A Manual of Psychological Medicine,* in 1858 (2nd ed., 1882) that was widely used for many years.

Burghölzli Hospital The famous psychiatric hospital and clinic that is associated with the University of Zürich in Switzerland. After accepting a position as professor of medicine at the university in 1860, Wilhelm GRIESINGER assisted in planning and overseeing the construction of the new hospital. Griesinger also became its first director upon

opening. Other famous directors of the Burghölzli over the years have been August Forel, Eugen BLEULER and Manfred BLEULER. Burghölzli holds a special significance for the history of the scientific study of schizophrenia and the psychotic disorders because it was while they worked together there that Eugen Bleuler and C. G. JUNG wrote their famous monographs on "dementia praecox," and it is the place where the term "schizophrenia" was first coined and used. Jung also carried out his famous diagnostic "word-association" experiments at Burghölzli in the early 20th century. In the last several decades, the Burghölzli has been the site of a noted longitudinal study of schizophrenia, carried out by Manfred Bleuler. (See also COURSE OF SCHIZOPHRENIA.)

butyrophenome A chemical class of ANTIPSYCHOTIC DRUGS, of which haloperidol (trade name Haldol) is the only one presently approved for antipsychotic use in the United States.

C

cacodemonomania This is one of the two types of DEMONOMANIA identified by ESQUIROL in his chapter on the topic in his 1838 textbook, *Des Maladies Mentales.* The word is used to refer to those mentally ill persons who believe they are possessed by, or in contact with, evil spirits or Satan himself. It is derived from two Greek words, *kakos* and *daimon,* for "bad" and "demon." The word *daimon* in the classical world did not have a bad connotation, as Esquirol notes, but had more of the meaning of a "guardian spirit" or "spiritual guide," which a person could consult. Esquirol asserts the diagnosis of cacodemonomania should be applied to "all those unfortunate beings who fancied that they were possessed by the devil, and in his power; who were convinced that they has been present at the imaginary assemblies of evil spirits, or who feared damnation, and the misery of eternal fire.''

Possession by ''evil spirits'' has been attributed as a cause of mental illness for thousands of years. Cacodemonomania can still be witnessed from time to time in certain individuals even today, and a modern case of this disorder, reported in the psychiatric literature as recently as 1987, can be found reprinted in the volume by Richard Noll listed below.

Esquirol, J. E. D., *Mental Maladies, A Treatise On Insanity.* Philadelphia: Lea & Blanchard, 1845; first published, 1838.
Kemp, S. and Williams, K., ''Demonic Possession and Mental Disorder in Medieval and Early Modern Europe,'' *Psychological Medicine*, 17(1987), 21–29.
Noll, R., *Vampires, Werewolves and Demons: Twentieth Century Reports in the Psychiatric Literature.* New York: Brunner/Mazel, 1991.
Salmons, P. H. and Clarke, D. J., ''Cacodemonomania,'' *Psychiatry*, 50(1987), 50–54.

Cameron, Donald (1901–1967) A British psychiatrist who became the first president of the World Psychiatric Association. While a professor of psychiatry at McGill University in Montreal, Canada, in the 1940s, Cameron helped popularize the form of treatment of schizophrenia known as INSULIN COMA THERAPY in North America.

camisole A heavy-canvas coat, reaching from neck to waist, with long, closed sleeves that are designed to wrap the wearer's arms across the chest and are tied with cords behind the wearer's back. Apparently, the 19th-century term ''camisole'' was merely a euphemism for a type of STRAIGHTJACKET, a term that had taken on a negative connotation by the end of the 1800s. In *A Mind That Found Itself,* Clifford BEERS graphically describes his torturous experience of being placed in a camisole in 1902, and describes this type of mechanical restraint as follows:

''A camisole is a type of straight-jacket; and a very convenient type it is for those who resort to such methods of restraint, for it enables them to deny the use of a straight-jacket all. A straight-jacket, indeed, is not a camisole, just as electrocution is not hanging.''

Beers, C., *A Mind That Found Itself.* New York: Doubleday, 1908.

Canada The only major study of prevalence rates for schizophrenia in Canada was carried out by research psychiatrist H. M. B. Murphy and his colleagues in the 1960s. In a survey of 14 Canadian villages with different ethnic compositions he found an overall age-corrected prevalence rate of 4.6 per thousand in Canada. However, considering that he used a much narrower (at the time) definition of schizophrenia than was accepted in the United States, the Canadian rate would have been much higher if the broader, American criteria had been used. Murphy found that traditional, ''Old French'' villages had a much higher rate of schizophrenia than other types, measuring twice as high as Anglo-Protestant villages. Furthermore, Canadian Catholics as a whole had a much higher rate of schizophrenia than Canadian Protestants.

Many studies have also been conducted in Canada on the native Canadian Inuit populations. Hudson Bay Inuit groups were found to have higher prevalence rates for schizophrenia, with studies ranging from 12.7 to 30.4 per thousand.

Schizophrenia may also be especially prevalent among Canadian Indians, particularly the Cree and Salteaux Indians of northern Saskatchewan, where the age-corrected prevalence rate was 11.0 in one study. The same study looked at the non-Indian population in the area and found that the age-corrected prevalence rate for schizophrenia was only 2.4 per thousand.

Murphy, H.B.M. and Lemieux, M., ''The Problem of High Schizophrenic Prevalence in One

Type of French-Canadian Rural Community,''
Canadian Psychiatric Association Journal,
12(1967), 72–81.

Sampath, H., ''Prevalence of Psychiatric Disorders in a Southern Baffin Island Eskimo Settlement,'' *Canadian Psychiatric Association Journal,* 19(1974), 363-367.

Roy, C. et al., ''The Prevalence of Mental Disorders among Saskatchewan Indians,'' *Journal of Cross-Cultural Psychiatry,* 1(1970), 383–392.

candidate genes   Genes that are believed to be implicated in the cause of a particular disease (pathogenesis). Essentially, if a biological marker of a particular disease (such as schizophrenia) is also shared by another disease, and if the location of the disease-causing gene or genes are known for this other disease, a directed search of candidate genes that cause the disorder under question can be conducted in that region. For example, the gene underlying familial Alzheimer's disease was found near a gene that produced a protein abnormality that was known to exist in Down's syndrome as well as in Alzheimer's disease. Since chromosome 21 had long been discovered to be the place where abnormalities existed that caused Down's syndrome, geneticists conducted a directed search of candidate genes in that area in Alzheimer's patients and located the pathogenic gene for that disease. Using the known biological markers of schizophrenia and affective disorders, such as bipolar disorder, is enabling researchers to conduct directed genetic searches in this manner. In schizophrenia research, candidate genes of potentially great importance are those that encode the receptors for dopamine in the brain, since abnormalities in these receptors have been linked to the development of some variants of schizophrenia. (See also BIOLOGICAL MARKERS OF SCHIZOPHRENIA; GENETICS STUDIES; GENOME; DOPAMINE HYPOTHESIS.)

Capgras, Jean Marie Joseph (1873–1950)   An eminent French psychopathologist who first identified a type of delusional

syndrome in psychotic patients known as CAPGRAS SYNDROME, for which he is most remembered.

Capgras syndrome   A delusional condition that some psychotic individuals develop in which they believe that a person, usually closely related in some way, has been replaced by an impostor or a ''double.'' The delusion is often quite fixed and can be very distressing for the concerned family member, friend or caretaker whose identity is constantly denied even when confronted with the absurdity of the notion. Usually the person accused of being an ''impostor'' or a ''replacement'' is also thought to bear bad intentions toward the delusional person.

The very first case was described by J. M. CAPGRAS and J. Reboul-Lachaux in 1923: a woman with a chronic paranoid psychosis who insisted that various individuals involved in her life had been replaced by ''doubles.'' Their name for the condition was *l'illusion des sosies,* or ''the illusion of doubles,'' but it is now almost universally known as the Capgras syndrome.

Capgras syndrome is one of the MISIDENTIFICATION SYNDROMES that are sometimes witnessed in psychotic individuals. As is the case with many fictional works of horror or science fiction that exploit common human fears, the 1956 motion picture *Invasion of the Body Snatchers* is based on a premise very similar to the fearful experience of persons suffering from Capgras syndrome.

Capgras, J. and Reboul-Lachaux, J., ''L'illusion des soises dans un délire systématisé chronique,'' *Soc.Clin.Med.Psychol.,* 81(1923), 186.

Enoch, M. D. and W. H. Trethowan, *Uncommon Psychiatric Syndromes,* 2nd ed. Bristol, U.K.: John Wright & Sons, 1979.

carbamazepine   A drug generally known by its trade name, Tegretol, that is used to treat seizure disorders. However, it has come into use in psychiatric centers as a treatment for certain psychotic patients who tend toward violence. It is structurally related to the heterocyclic antidepressants (such as imipramine and others) and to another anticonvulsant, phenytoin (trade name, Dilantin). A further use of tegretol was reported in 1989 when research was reported that suggested it could quell the craving for cocaine in cocaine addicts, thus indicating its use as an adjunct to the rehabilitation of such individuals.

cardiazol therapy   See METRAZOL SHOCK THERAPY.

cardiovascular hypoplasia   One of the early hypothesized BIOLOGICAL MARKERS OF SCHIZOPHRENIA. Between 1923 and 1925, pathologist N.D.C. Lewis performed autopsies on 4,800 mental patients, of which 601 were diagnosed with dementia praecox (schizophrenia). Lewis concluded that a biological marker of schizophrenia was a primary hypoplasia (underdevelopment or atrophy of tissue or an organ) of the cardiovascular system. Dementia praecox patients, it was found, were marked by small hearts and a hypoplasia throughout the vascular system. This, it was hypothesized, led to a general reduction of oxygen to the brain (cerebral hypoxemia), thus, perhaps, leading to the development of dementia praecox. Several confirmatory replications of Lewis' study were performed by others and reported until about 1940. Since that time, however, there has been little interest in cardiovascular hypoplasia as a biological marker of schizophrenia. Lewis' original report of his findings was published in a special monograph in 1923.

Lewis, N.D.C., "Pathology of Dementia Praecox," *Journal of Nervous and Mental Disease*, 62(1925), 225–260.

catalepsy   Another name for CATATONIC WAXY FLEXIBILITY, or *flexibilitas cera*.

catathymic crisis   The crisis state induced in a person who is aware that he or she is developing a psychosis, or for whom an existing psychotic state is worsening. The terrible fear and anxiety caused by this awareness of a loss of control and a degeneration into mental chaos somehow leads the person to commit a violent or other antisocial act. As first described by Wertham in 1937, the crisis-provoked act is intended as a cry for help by the afflicted person. Wertham writes: "One gains the impression that the violent act in these cases prevents the developments that would be far more serious for the patient's health. The overt act seems to be a rallying point for the constructive forces of the personality."

Wertham, F., "The Catathymic Crisis," *Archives of Neurology and Psychiatry*, 37(1937), 974.

catatonia   An abnormal motor behavior, not caused by any known organic disease, in which a person assumes an unusual posture and then remains practically "frozen" in that posture for a long period in a somewhat stuporous state. The condition was first named by German psychiatrist Karl KAHLBAUM in 1869 (first written about in 1874) and was apparently much more commonly seen in the mental hospitals of that time than it is today, when it is only rarely encountered. CATATONIC TYPES were later included in Emil KRAEPELIN's diagnostic category of dementia praecox and were kept by Eugen BLEULER in his definition of schizophrenia.

Kahlbaum, K., *Die Katatonie oder das Spannungsirresein*. Berlin: Hirschwald, 1874.

catatonic excitement   A behavior that occurs intermittently in catatonic persons in which they move about in a very active fashion without any apparent purpose and seemingly unguided by environmental cues. This excited motor behavior can occur between periods of other types of less mobile catatonic behavior. In the late 19th century, catatonic excitement was sometimes thought to result in death from exhaustion, and other names for it included "acute delirius mania," "Bell's mania" and "Bell's disease."

catatonic negativism   A seemingly purposeless resistance to all attempts, whether physical or verbal, to being moved. If the person is passive, he or she may simply be unresponsive. When in a more active state, the person may be oppositional and do the opposite of what is asked.

catatonic posturing   The bizarre or unusual postures that catatonic persons can maintain for a long period of time.

catatonic rigidity   The maintenance of a muscularly tense, rigid position by a catatonic person, despite the forceful efforts of others to move him or her.

catatonic stupor   The common image of a catatonic person's behavior. The person behaves as if in a stupor, hardly moving and relatively unresponsive to his or her environment.

catatonic type   In defining the group of disorders he termed "dementia praecox" in 1896, Emil KRAEPELIN included Kahlbaum's CATATONIA as one of its three subtypes. Eugen BLEULER also included it as one of the "schizophrenias" in his 1911 text. Even today the "catatonic type" remains as one of the four major subtypes of schizophrenia identified in DSM-III-R (1987). It is rarely diagnosed any more but was apparently much more commonly observed in the days of Kraepelin and Bleuler. The current *DSM-III-R* diagnostic description is as follows: "The essential feature of this type is marked psychomotor disturbance, which may involve stupor, negativism, rigidity, excitement or posturing. Sometimes there is a rapid alternation between the extremes of excitement and stupor."

catatonic waxy flexibility   This is a behavior found in persons with the rare catatonic subtype of schizophrenia in which a person's body or limbs can be molded into a particular position and will remain passively in place, as if the person were a doll or made of wax. An older medical term for waxy flexibility is *cera flexibilitas*.

catecholamines   A class of biogenic amines that includes the neurotransmitters dopamine, epinephrine and norepinephrine. (See also BIOGENIC AMINE HYPOTHESIS; DOPAMINE HYPOTHESIS; INDOLAMINES; HISTAMINES.)

CAT scan   See CT SCAN.

causality, teleologic   An aspect of the thinking of schizophrenics, as identified by Silvano ARIETI, in which events in the world are interpreted as purposeful and due to somebody's will. Arieti compares this aspect of schizophrenic cognition to the thought patterns of children and people in primitive societies. Teleologic causality is contrasted with "deterministic causality," the more rational and scientific way in which most "civilized" normal adults attribute causes to events that they experience.

cautery treatment   A rather primitive form of "shock treatment" used on the mentally ill in the 18th and early 19th centuries in which they would be touched on the head or neck with a hot iron poker. Alternatively, the ancient technique of igniting moxa (small combustible cones from a plant that was introduced into Europe from Asia) on the skin to cauterize it. A treatment manual advocating the use of this method was written by French psychiatrist L. Valentin and published in 1815. ESQUIROL was greatly influenced by this book and successfully applied the treatment himself. This is how he described its use:

> I cannot omit making some remarks respecting the use of fire and moxa, applied to the top of the head, and over the occiput or neck in mania.

Doctor L. Valentin has published some valuable observations concerning the cure of mania by the application of fire. I have many times applied the iron at a red heat to the neck, in mania complicated with fury, and sometimes with success.

Esquirol, J.E.D., *Mental Maladies, A Treatise on Insanity* (1838). Philadelphia: Lea & Blanchard, 1845; first published, 1838.

Valentin, L., *An Essay and Observations Concerning the Good Effects of the Actual Cautery, Applied to the Head in Various Disorders*, 8 vols. Nancy: 1815.

centimorgan   In genetics research, this is a unit of measurement. It refers to the genetic distance in which the probability of a recombination occurring is 1%.

cera flexibilitas   See CATATONIC WAVY FLEXIBILITY.

Cerletti, Ugo (1877–1963)   Italian psychiatrist and inventor of ELECTROSHOCK (or "electroconvulsive") THERAPY. Cerletti was inspired to invent this treatment in a rather macabre way—by observing the reactions of pigs who were given electrical shocks just before slaughter. Together with his colleague, Lucio Bini, Cerletti perfected his new treatment, and the very first schizophrenic to receive this treatment did so on April 15, 1938. Electroconvulsive therapy, or ECT as it is commonly referred to, was considered a safer and more humane type of CONVULSIVE THERAPY than the one invented by Hungarian psychiatrist von MEDUNA, in which convulsions were induced by pharmacological means.

Cerletti had a varied medical career, undergoing training in Turin, Rome, Paris, and Heidelberg, where he was exposed to Emil KRAEPELIN and his associates. Cerletti seems to have always been attracted to unconventional ideas about medical treatments for mental disorders. Near the end of his life, he attempted to find a chemical alternative to his own electroshock therapy, which would have none of the harsh side effects of the convulsive therapies. He concocted a serum, from the brains of animals that had been subjected to repeated electroshock sessions, that he thought would have the same therapeutic effect as electroshock therapy. This serum was alleged to contain a special chemical created in these animal brains from the treatments—vitalizing substances that Cerletti called *aeroagomines*—which he believed he could inject into schizophrenics and obtain similar results. However, Cerletti's work in this area has been discounted.

Cerletti, U. and Bini, L., "L'Electroshock," *Arch. Gen. Neurol. Psichiatr. Psicoanal.*, 19(1938), 266.

Cerletti, U., "Old and New Information about Electroshock," *American Journal of Psychiatry*, 107(1950), 87–94.

ceruloplasmin hypothesis   In 1957, Swiss biochemist S. Akerfeldt announced research findings that suggested that an increased level of the copper-containing substance ceruloplasmin might be related to the development of schizophrenia. He developed a relatively simple test, which he thought could discriminate between the BIOLOGICAL MARKERS OF SCHIZOPHRENIA and other mental diseases. Despite media attention, his theory was soon disproved when it was found that the level of ceruloplasmin depended on the amount of ascorbic acid (vitamin C) in the blood, and institutionalized psychiatric patients have been known to have low serum ascorbic acid levels.

Akerfeldt, S., "Oxidation of N_1N-Dimethyl-p-phenylenediamine by Serum from Patients with Mental Disease," *Science*, 125(1957), 117–123.

Ceylon   (Sri Lanka) A 1974 study of the prevalence rate for schizophrenia in Ceylon (now Sri Lanka) found a rate of 3.7 per thousand.

Wijesinghe, C.P. et al., "Survey of Psychiatric Morbidity in a Semi-urban Population in Sri

Lanka,'' *Acta Psychiatrica Scandinavica*, 58(1978), 413–441.

chemical restraint   The use of drugs, as opposed to MECHANICAL RESTRAINTS (such as straps, STRAIGHTJACKETS, MUFFS) to subdue psychiatric patients. Although ANTI-PSYCHOTIC DRUGS were only brought into use in the 1950s to treat psychotic disorders by reducing their symptoms, many different types of drugs have been used for centuries to restrain patients engaged in undesirable behaviors. Often such pharmacological agents were used as punishment. In the 18th and 19th centuries such drugs may have been administered as a daily "physic" said to improve the health of a patient. Camphor and opiates in particular are mentioned in these early accounts. By the end of the 19th century many sedatives had been created that were then widely used (often to the point of excess) in mental hospitals. In his autobiography of his life as a mental patient, Clifford BEERS makes the following remarks about chemical restraint:

> Chemical restraint (sometimes called medical restraint) consists in the use of temporarily paralyzing drugs—hyoscine being the popular "dose." By the use of such drugs a troublesome patient may be rendered unconscious and kept so for hours at a time. Indeed, very troublesome patients (especially when attendants are scarce) are not infrequently kept in a stupefied condition for days, or even for weeks—but only in institutions where the welfare of the patients is lightly regarded.

Chemical restraint is one of the main instruments of psychiatric abuse in many countries, particularly the Soviet Union. (See also ABUSE OF PSYCHIATRIC PATIENTS; SLUGGISH SCHIZOPHRENIA.)

Beers, C., *A Mind That Found Itself*. New York: Doubleday, 1908.

chemistry of the brain   See BIOCHEMICAL THEORIES OF SCHIZOPHRENIA.

cheromania   A term used in the Middle Ages to describe the unnatural euphoric reaction to epidemics (such as the plague) and other disasters. It is equivalent to the elation reported in "maniacs" in archaic psychiatric textbooks, and to the same behavior in persons undergoing a "manic episode" in today's nomenclature.

Chevigné   The massive bodyguard of Philippe PINEL. He was one of the patients freed from his shackles after Pinel assumed control of the institution in the 1790s. Chevigné had been incarcerated at the BICÊTRE for 10 years; afterwards he apparently saved Pinel's life on many occasions.

Chiarugi,   Vincenzo   (1759–1820) Sometimes referred to as the "Pinel of Italy." Chiarugi was an Italian physician appointed in 1789 by the Grand Duke Pietro Leopoldo of Tuscany to head the Hospital of Bonifacio in Florence. His work with the mentally ill at that hospital led to his publishing several works regarding mental illness, including a volume of 100 observations on mental illness. He believed that psychoses were the result of a deterioration of the brain, thus linking him with modern theories of the organic etiology of mental illness. He was also an early reformer and an opponent of cruel or unnecessary forms of restraint, and he shares an historic distinction as one of the earliest proponents of non-restraint policies, with Pinel in France and William Tuke of the YORK RETREAT in England. A translatioin of an indicative passage from one of Chiarugi's works is provided by historian of psychiatry George Mora:

> It is a supreme moral duty and medical obligation to respect the insane individual as a person. It is especially necessary for the person who treats the mental patient to gain his confidence and trust. It is best, therefore, to be tactful and understanding and try to lead the patient to the truth and to instill reason in him little by little in a kind way . . . The attitude of doctors and nurses must be authori-

tative and impressive, but at the same time pleasant and adapted to the impaired mind of the patient . . . Generally it is better to follow the patient's inclinations and give him as many comforts as is advisable from a medical and practical standpoint.

Chiarugi, V., *Della pazzia in genere e in specie trattato medico analitico con una centuria di observazioni.* Florence: 1793–1794.
———, *On Insanity and Its Classification,* ed. and tr. G. Mora. Canton, Mass.: Science History Publications, 1987.
Mora, G. Vincenzo, "Chiarugi (1759–1820) and His Psychiatric Reform in Florence in the Late 18th Century," *Journal of the History of Medicine,* 14(1959), 431.

childhood psychosis See CHILDHOOD SCHIZOPHRENIA.

childhood schizophrenia A disorder of childhood thought to be the very early onset of schizophrenia. Other names for this childhood disorder have been childhood psychosis, symbiotic psychosis and atypical development. However, in 1980 the term "childhood schizophrenia" was replaced with the diagnostic category of "pervasive development disorders." This was due to evidence that shows that children who develop infantile autism do not go on to develop a psychotic disorder in adulthood. Since no other clearly defined subtype of pervasive developmental disorders has yet been identified to account for the other cases that are not related to infantile autism, especially one that clearly seems to be the very early onset of schizophrenia, the term "childhood schizophrenia" is no longer in official psychiatric use. The general diagnosis of a pervasive developmental disorder can then be applied to these cases. (See also AUTISM, INFANTILE.)

Howells, J.G. and Guirguis, W.R., "Childhood Schizophrenia 20 Years Later," *American Journal of Psychiatry,* 41(1984), 123–128.

children at risk for schizophrenia See HIGH-RISK STUDIES.

chiromania An archaic term for madness caused by MASTURBATION, a common belief of psychiatrists throughout the 19th century and earlier. It is derived from the Greek words for "hand" and "insanity."

chlorpromazine The first true ANTIPSYCHOTIC DRUG, approved for use in the United States in March 1954. It was discovered in France in 1949 by Charpentier, and its first documented use for the alleviation of psychotic symptoms was reported by French psychiatrists Delay, Deniker and Harl in 1952. The drug is a phenothiazine and is more commonly known by its trade name, Thorazine; it was named by the manufacturer, Smith, Kline and French, after the Norse god of thunder, Thor. Like most of the first antipsychotic drugs, chlorpromazine was discovered serendipitously.

Delay, J., Deniker, P. and Harl, J., "Utilization en thérapeutique psychiatrique d'une phenothiazine d'action centrale élective," *Annales medico-psychologique,* 1952, 110–112.
Lehmann, H.E. and Hanaran, G.E., "Chlorpromazine, a New Inhibiting Agent for Psychomotor Excitement and Manic States," *AMA Archives of Neurology and Psychiatry,* 71(1954), 227–237.

cholinergic nerve fibers See ANTICHOLINERGIC EFFECTS.

choromania An archaic term for the uncontrollable impulse to dance or sway. The famous "dancing-manias" that were epidemic in the Middle Ages are another example of this. Perhaps the classic reference to "dancing manias" or "frenzies" is the work of the 19th-century German scholar J.F.C. Hecker, and translations of representative excerpts of his writings can be found in the appendix to a book by psychiatrist Harold Mersky of the London Psychiatric Hospital, London, Ontario, Canada.

Hecker, J.F.C., *Die grossen Volkskrankheiten des Mittelalters, Historisch-pathologische Un-*

tersuchungen. . . , ed. August Hirsch. Berlin: Th.Chr.Fr.Enslin, 1865.

Mersky, H., *The Analysis of Hysteria.* London: Baillière Tindall, 1979.

chromosome Within the nucleus of each cell in the human body there are rod-like organic bodies (normally 46 in humans) called chromosomes, which are the bearers of GENES. Each chromosome is made up of an extended double helix of DNA and associated proteins. Chromosomes are arranged in 23 different pairs. One pair, made up of the X and Y chromosomes, is called the sex chromosomes and is responsible for the transmission of genetic information regarding sex differentiation. The other 22 pairs (numbered from 1 to 22) are called autosomes. The 46 chromosomes in humans were first observed directly by scientists when new techniques were developed by Tijo and Levan in 1956. Since that time, a series of studies have been conducted on large samples of psychiatric patients of varying diagnoses—especially schizophrenics—with little success in detecting specific abnormalities. This has changed with the development of clearer research diagnostic criteria for schizophrenia and the more advanced research technologies of molecular genetics.

A series of techniques known as "chromosome mapping" attempt to determine the position of specific genes on specific chromosomes and then construct a diagram of each chromosome showing the relative position of genes. There are estimated to be between 50,000 and 100,000 human genes, most of which are yet to be identified. A multinational project to map the entire human GENOME was proposed by teams of geneticists from around the world (led by Dr. James D. Watson, director of the Cold Spring Harbor Laboratory in New York) in their announcement of the foundation of the Human Genome Organization in April 1989. (See also CHROMOSOME ABNORMALITIES; GENETICS STUDIES; KARYOTYPE.)

Tijo, H. and Levan, A., "The Chromosome Number of Man," *Hereditas,* 42(1956), 1–6.

chromosome abnormalities The search for specific BIOLOGICAL MARKERS of the psychotic disorders has been rewarded by the discovery of chromosomal abnormalities that may very well prove to be the true GENETIC MARKERS of schizophrenia and bipolar disorder. The implications of such discoveries are mind-boggling. As yet unthought-of technologies for the early detection, prevention and treatment of these disorders may one day make today's pharmacological treatments look to future generations as arcane and ridiculous as bleeding and purging patients in the 19th century look to ours.

The credit for the first announcement of the discovery of a chromosomal abnormality in schizophrenia belongs to molecular geneticist Anne S. Bassett and her colleagues at the University of British Columbia, who made the announcement at the annual meeting of the American Psychiatric Association in Chicago in May 1987. This first study was published in the British medical journal *The Lancet* in April 1988. In Bassett's study of an Asian family living in Vancouver, Canada, abnormalities were found on CHROMOSOME 5. Later the same year, an issue of the British scientific journal *Nature* published two further studies concerning the linkage of schizophrenia to abnormalities on chromosome 5, one confirming the association and another finding no relationship. Such contradictory findings do not necessarily rule out an association to chromosome 5, since there are thought to be different types of schizophrenia (making it a heterogeneous disorder), and only some varieties of schizophrenia may be connected to this chromosome.

Besides chromosome 5, another suspected area of abnormalities that is linked to schizophrenia (and affective psychoses) are the X and Y sex chromosomes. The X chromosome is singled out as the genetic locus for schizophrenia in a report by DeLisi and

Crow (1989). The specifically hypothesize that there is a locus for psychosis within the pseudoautosomal region on the short arm of the sex chromosomes (the X chromosome). Crow (1986) in particular proposes that this single genetic locus is where significant variation occurs that results in psychotic illness, which is distributed along a continuum that extends from unipolar depression through bipolar (manic-depressive) and schizoaffective psychosis to schizophrenia. His theory is a 20th-century version of the 19th-century idea of the EINHEITSPSYCHOSE—that all mental disorders are progressively degenerative stages of the same underlying disease process. Crow's progression matches exactly the series of successive stages proposed in 1845 by Wilhelm GRIESINGER, the "father of biological psychiatry."

Evidence that bipolar disorder (manic-depressive psychosis) may be related to chromosomal abnormalities has also been reported. Two different studies published in 1987 have implicated two different chromosomes in the development of bipolar disorder. One study, involving the Amish community in Pennsylvania, found a CANDIDATE GENE on chromosome 11, near the gene for insulin. Another study done in Israel found that the chromosomal abnormality was a defect on the X chromosome, located near the genes for color vision and an important enzyme. Again, these studies may not really be contradicting one another, but instead may be biological evidence for the heterogeneity of bipolar disorder.

An entire issue devoted to advances in the genetics of schizophrenia, which summarizes this new research on chromosomal abnormalities, was published by *Schizophrenia Bulletin* (15:3) in 1989. (See also GENETICS STUDIES; GENETIC TRANSMISSION.)

Baron, M. et al., "Genetic Linkage between X-chromosome Markers and Bipolar Affective Illness," *Nature*, 326(1987), 289–292.

Bassett, A.S. et al., "Partial Trisomy Chromosome 5 Cosegregating with Schizophrenia," *The Lancet*, April 9, 1988, 799–801.

Crow, T.J., "The Continuum of Psychosis and Its Implication for the Structure of the Gene," *British Journal of Psychiatry*, 149(1986), 419–429.

DeLisi, L.E. and Crow, T.J., "Evidence for a Sex Chromosome Locus for Schizophrenia," *Schizophrenia Bulletin*, 15(1989), 431–440.

Egeland, J.A. et al., "Bipolar Affective Disorders Linked to DNA Markers on Chromosome 11," *Nature*, 325(1987), 783–787.

Kennedy, J.L. et al., "Evidence Against Linkage of Schizophrenia to Markers on Chromosome 5 in a Northern Swedish Pedigree," *Nature*, 336(1988), 167–170.

Sherrington, R. et al., "Localization of a Susceptibility Locus for Schizophrenia on Chromosome 5," *Nature*, 336(1988), 164–167.

chronic schizophrenia   The idea that some forms of schizophrenia seem to follow a chronic lifetime course without improvement is as old as the concept of schizophrenia itself. It has always been observed throughout the history of psychiatry that there were some psychotic disorders that improved and some that ended in permanent deterioration or "dementia." Indeed, KRAEPELIN's concept of "dementia praecox," which he formed in 1896, was based entirely on the idea that it was a progressively degenerative disorder with a poor prognosis. He called this mental deterioration the *Verblodung-sprocess*. However, his definition of the MANIC-DEPRESSIVE PSYCHOSES (see also BIPOLAR DISORDER) was of a group of psychotic disorders with a relatively good prognosis for improvement. Eugen BLEULER produced the still prevalent picture of schizophrenia as having acute and chronic forms in his 1911 *Dementia Praecox, Or The Group of Schizophrenias*.

Schizophrenia has long been conceptualized as pairs of opposites across many different dimensions. The acute/chronic distinction and the reactive/process distinction are essentially equivalent, expressing the idea that there is a form of schizophrenia with a sudden onset and a better prognosis (acute or reactive) and a form that has an insidious onset that gradually develops from early in life and does not seem to get any better (chronic or process). In recent years the term "chronic schizophrenia" has been falling out of use in the clinical research literature (although it is still part of the everyday jargon of mental health professionals) due to the appearance of more descriptive terms for this apparent strain of schizophrenia.

The traditional notion of "chronic schizophrenia" is now being redefined by (a) its unique symptoms and (b) its unique neurophysiological and neuropsychological functioning. In terms of its symptoms, in the psychiatric research literature chronic schizophrenia is characterized by its NEGATIVE SYMPTOMS, such as restricted emotional range, poverty of speech, reduction of curiosity in the immediate environment around a person, an apathetic or diminished sense of "purpose" in the afflicted person, and a reduced need to engage in social interactions. Negative symptoms are based on the idea that something is "taken away" from a person. When they endure, they have been called "deficit symptoms." There is a vast amount of research that also shows that chronic schizophrenics also show certain "soft neurological signs" and sometimes structural abnormalities in the brain that make them resemble brain-damaged patients more than the other type of schizophrenics, who do not have such deficits. It has been said that perhaps the best evidence that schizophrenia is a "brain disease" is provided by the many scientific studies of the traditional "chronic schizophrenics." (See also POSITIVE SYMPTOMS; CROW'S HYPOTHESIS; DEFICIT SYMPTOMS; DEGENERATION, PINEL-HASLAM SYNDROME; ACUTE-CHRONIC DISTINCTION.)

circular insanity   The name given in 1854 by FALRET to what we now call BIPOLAR DISORDER. The term was widely used in English-language literature until KRAEPELIN's new definition of the disorder and invention of the term manic-depressive psychosis. People stricken with this mental disorder were often referred to as "circulars," much in the same way that we presently refer to them as "manic-depressives."

Ritti, A., "Circular Insanity," in D.H. Tuke (ed.), *A Dictionary of Psychological Medicine*, 2 vols. Philadelphia: P. Blakiston & Son, 1892.

circulating swing   A form of treatment for the mentally ill that was popular throughout the 18th and into the early 19th centuries in which patients would be rapidly spun around in a circular motion. Although Dutch physician Herman Boerhaave (1668–1738) may have been the first to use such a device, the first working model of a circulating swing is credited to English physician John Mason Cox, who describes the device in his 1806 book, *Practical Observations on Insanity:*

His *swing* formed by suspending a Windsor chair to a hook in the ceiling, by two ropes to hind legs and two to fore, joined by a sliding knot to regulate elevation: patient in a straight waistcoat, and a leathern strap around his waist, buckled to the bars behind; legs fastened by straps to the front ones of the chair; then turned around.

Reflecting the many mechanical variations of this basic concept by innovative physicians in other asylums, it was also called the "GYRATOR" or "gyrating chair," "rotary machine," "spinning chair," "rotating swing" or "chair" and also "Darwin's chair" or "machine," since it was suggested by Erasmus Darwin (1731–1802), the physician grandfather of Charles Darwin, as a form of treatment for patients with many different types of ailment. The device attributed to Darwin consisted of a box-like chair (or bed, apparently), which was suspended by an iron rod from the ceiling. The patient would be tightly strapped into this seat. A small wooden platform was built next to the chair on which another person could push another rod back and forth, which generated the rotation of the rod on which the chair was suspended. Psychiatrists Alexander and Selesnick reproduce an 18th-century illustration of this machine in their book on the history of psychiatry.

It is said that the curculating swing could be driven up to 100 rotations per minute, causing considerable disorientation, vomiting, purging, bleeding from the eyes and eventual unconsciousness in patients. Needless to say, treatment sessions lasted only a matter of minutes. ESQUIROL, who called it "the machine of Darwin" in 1838, was apparently the first to introduce this rotary machine to France, but he discourages its use along with the following report:

Doctor Martin, physician of the hospital at Antiquaille, where to this day the insane of Lyons are treated, has informed me that he has been frightened at the accidents which the insane had met with, who had been submitted to the influence of this machine. They fall into a state of syncope, and had also copious evacuations both by vomiting and purging, which prostrated them extremely.

Esquirol notes at the bottom of the page of his *Mental Maladies* in 1838 that, "Since the first edition of this article was published, the rotary machine has been every where abandoned."

American psychiatrist Benjamin RUSH was an enthusiastic advocate of his "gyrater,"' as well as a stationary "coercion chair," which he referred to as his "TRANQUILLIZER." However, he utilized a form of the circulating swing and had suggestions for technical improvements on the machine. The circulating swing was also part of the regimen recommended by 18th-century Englishman John HASLAM (of "Bedlam"). (See also HAYNER'S WHEEL; MECHANICAL RESTRAINT.)

Alexander, F.G. and Selesnick, S.T., *The History of Psychiatry*, New York: Harper & Row, 1966.

Esquirol, J.E.D., *Mental Maladies, A Treatise on Insanity*. Philadelphia: Lea and Blanchard, 1845; first published, 1838.

Scull, A., "The Domestication of Madness," *Medical History*, 27(1983), 233–248.

clanging A frequently observed speech anomaly, in persons with psychotic disorders, in which words are spoken for the way they sound, rather than for what they mean. This can sometimes appear like bizarre punning or attempts at rhyming. "I am the needle-nose who knows. Like the rose in his hair, OK?" is an example of the clanging found in psychotic speech patterns. BLEULER (in 1911) referred to these language anomalies as "clang associations." (See also LANGUAGE ABNORMALITIES IN SCHIZOPHRENIA.)

Clérambault, Gaétan de (1872–1934) A French psychiatrist remembered most for his work in identifying delusional patterns in psychotic individuals. Among the syndromes he identified are the de Clérambault-Kandinsky syndrome, a psychotic mental state in which a person feels that his mind is being controlled by another person or by outside influences (e.g., "The man on TV is controlling my thoughts."). This is now included among the primary symptoms of schizophrenia in contemporary diagnostic manuals. He is probably best known for his clinical descriptions of de Clérambault's syndrome, which is also known as EROTOMANIA.

climate as a cause of insanity Many early authorities on mental illness claimed that the nature of a particular climate could cause such disorders. Both Benjamin RUSH and J.E.D. ESQUIROL agreed that temperate climates, which had frequent alterations of hot and cold, were the most likely to cause insanity. These ideas exist in a modern form in studies of the EPIDEMIOLOGY of mental disorders, which show that incidence and prevalence rates are different in different parts of the world—particularly for schizophrenia. (See also VIRAL THEORIES OF SCHIZOPHRENIA.)

clown syndrome See FAXENSYNDROM.

clozapine An example from the chemical class of ANTIPSYCHOTIC DRUGS known as dibenzodiazepines that were first used in treatment in the 1970s. Clozapine (CLOZ) is significant because it appears to produce few (or perhaps no) EXTRAPYRAMIDAL SYMPTOMS as side effects, such as PARKINSON'S SYNDROME or TARDIVE DYSKINESIA. Other antipsychotic drugs that also appear to have this added benefit are LITHIUM and reserpine. However, due to its other serious side effects—producing abnormally low white blood cell counts (leukopenia or agranulocytosis), hypotension and hyperthermia—its manufacturer, Sandoz, Inc., removed clozapine from general distribution in the early 1980s. It has since been available in at least 30 countries, mainly in Europe, although on a restricted basis. There has been an active search by many pharmaceutical laboratories to find clozapine-like compounds that do not have its toxic effect. However, psychiatrists can still order it through a special program set up by Sandoz, Inc., for "treatment-resistant patients."

In the 1988, revised edition of his book *Surviving Schizophrenia: A Family Manual,* psychiatrist E. Fuller Torrey asserts that "clozapine is potentially the most exciting drug for schizophrenia to come along in several years." After rejecting an application to market the drug in the United States in 1984, on October 3, 1989, the U.S. Food and Drug Administration reversed its prior judgment and approved the use of clozapine for severe schizophrenia after other forms of treatment have failed. The FDA press release stated that, "Clozapine is not a cure, but it may help previously unresponsive patients to live more satisfying and productive lives." The drug was first released in the United States for use in February 1990, the first new antipsychotic drug to be released in that country in 15 years. The drug is marketed in the United States under the brand name Clozaril.

Clozapine has been found to be effective in treating about 30% of those schizophrenics who exhibit TREATMENT REFRACTORINESS.

Clozapine is often touted as being the first antipsychotic agent to alleviate the NEGATIVE SYMPTOMS of schizophrenia, which are considered the most organic in origin and hence the most treatment-refractory. However, as a recent review by Allan Safferman and his colleagues concludes, "This advantage in treating negative symptoms has been conclusively demonstrated only within the context of 'coexisting' positive symptomatology . . . To our knowledge, there is no direct proof that CLOZ is superior to other antipsychotics when negative symptoms are the sole or predominant psychopathology."

Safferman, A. et al., "Update on the Clinical Efficacy and Side Effects of Clozapine," *Schizophrenia Bulletin,* 17(1991), 247–261.

CNS The acronym for "central nervous system," essentially designating the brain, the spinal cord and their associated processes. The "peripheral nervous system" refers to the sensory (afferent) and motor (efferent) nerve cells that connect the remainder of the body with the central nervous system.

Cogentin The trade name for benztropine, an antihistamine and ANTICHOLINERGIC DRUG that is used to treat the sometimes severe side effects that patients can experience after the initiation of antipsychotic drug therapy or after a significant increase in dosage. These side effects (stiffness, tremors, lockjaw, involuntary motions of the mouth, tongue and hands, involuntary eye rolls), which usually happen within hours or days of administering antipsychotic drugs, are acute dystonic reactions that can be reversed with antiparkinsonian agents such as Cogentin, Benadryl or Akineton. These side effects are acture and are not to be confused with chronic reactions to years of treatment with antipsychotic drugs, which is known as TARDIVE DYSKINESIA and is treated with drugs other than Cogentin.

cognitive studies of schizophrenia In the late 1950s a revolution began in the way experimental studies in psychology were conducted. Advances in cybernetics, linguistics (particularly the work of Noam Chomsky) and the computer sciences gave rise to a new type of psychology. Called "cognitive psychology," it borrowed the metaphors of information processing from the computer sciences to approach the study of human thought and experience in a new way—by examining the human mind's processes of encoding, transforming, storing and using information for regulating behavior. Thought and language abnormalities had long been noted by schizophrenia researchers, but cognitive psychology extended the study of schizophrenia to find patterns of information processing in sensation, perception, memory, motor (movement) processes and, in particular, the ability to focus one's attention. Studies comparing schizophrenic and normal information processing almost always find significant differences between these two groups. One line of evidence tends to indicate that some schizophrenics have information processing problems associated with the left hemisphere of the brain when compared to normals. Furthermore, cognitive studies have helped document evidence for distinct subdivisions within schizophrenics, thus giving more suggestive evidence for subtype differences than had hitherto been possible with strictly behavioral or biological approaches. An example of this is the highly successful demonstration across numerous studies that there are distinct differences between the paranoid subtype of schizophrenia and the nonparanoid subtypes. Indeed, a special issue of *Schizophrenia Bulletin,* edited by experimental psychologist Peter Magaro, was devoted to this evidence in 1981. An excellent review of the experimental studies of "schizophrenic cognition" was published by Canadian psychologist Leonard George in 1985. (See also ATTENTION, DISORDERS IN.)

George, L., and Neufeld, R. "Cognitioin and Symptomatology in Schizophrenia," *Schizophrenia Bulletin,* 11(1985), 264–285.

Magaro, P.A. (ed.), "Special Issue: Paranoia," *Schizophrenia Bulletin,* 7:4(1981).

collective insanity See FOLIE À DEUX.

Columbia-Greystone Project A PSYCHOSURGERY research project initiated in 1947 combining the psychiatric research scientists of Columbia University Medical Center in New York City and the psychiatric patients of the New Jersey State Hospital at Greystone Park. The goal was to refine the methods of psychosurgery as a treatment for mental disorders, specifically to find the critical locations in the frontal lobes where more limited incisions could maximize the benefits and minimize the sometimes terrible aftereffects. A review of this research was published in 1949. The group called itself the "Columbia-Greystone Associates" and was co-led by Fred Mettler, a professor of anatomy at Columbia University, and Marcus Currey, the medical superintendent and CEO of the Greystone Park State Hospital. Mettler was also a board member of the National Institute of Mental Health at the time, and his influence led to the large supporting grant from the NIMH, totaling hundreds of thousands of dollars, that funded the project.

The project had two phases: a 1947–48 study and a 1951–52 study. In the first study, the more important of the two, a series of 19 patients underwent a psychosurgical procedure known as a TOPECTOMY, a more localized and focal procedure than the tradtional "ice pick" lobotomies performed by Walter FREEMAN, the world's leading authority on psychosurgery. They also explored other "open" methods (i.e., procedures that required the surgical opening of the skull), but their results were all rather inconclusive. Realizing the less than spectacular results they were getting with their methods, the associates then invited Freeman to perform a series of his famous TRANS-

ORBITAL LOBOTOMIES on a series of patients at Greystone Park in October 1948. Of this tragic failure, which led him to abandon the hope of an assembly-line approach to treating chronic psychiatric patients (largely schizophrenics) with transorbital lobotomies, Freeman later wrote:

> Of the 18 patients operated upon . . . there was not a single one that I would have chosen from my own practice. The results were as bad as I anticipated. Furthermore, in one patient the icepick broke, leaving a small bit embedded in the base of the brain. Fortunately, there was no unfavorable effects, but the embarrassment was mine [cited in Shutts, 1982].

Mettler, F.A. (ed.), *Selective Partial Ablation of the Frontal Cortex*. New York: Hoeber, 1949.
Shutts, D., *Lobotomy: Resort to the Knife*. New York: Van Nostrand-Reinhold, 1982).

coma therapy In the 20th century several biological treatments were developed for schizophrenia that were based on the deliberate induction of a comatose state in the patient, with the assumption that the patient would reawaken in a much improved state. The most famous variety of coma therapy was INSULIN COMA THERAPY, developed by psychiatrist M. SAKEL and his associates in Austria in 1936, in which a deep hypoglycemic coma was induced in schizophrenics as a sort of "shock" to their system. While coma therapy was widely used (along with PSYCHOSURGERY and ELECTROSHOCK THERAPY) throughout the 1940s and 1950s, it disappeared after the introduction of ANTIPSYCHOTIC DRUGS for the treatment of schizophrenia. Other forms of coma therapy for schizophrenia involved inducing a comatose state through inhaling pure nitrogen or by injections of atropine, but neither of these forms were widely utilized. No rational theory explaining why coma therapy worked for some patients was ever formulated. (See also NITROGEN INHALATION THERAPY.)

command hallucination Despite media depictions of "psychotic killers" who carry out murderous crimes "because God told me to," the phenomenon of command hallucinations is relatively uncommon in psychotics. When such hallucinations are present, they tend to be in the form of a "voice" telling the person to do various acts, some of which may be harmful to self or others. Many patients resist the commands and experience great fear and anxiety because of them. For example, a patient once cried out to the author in the middle of a conversation, "They're trying to get me to kill myself, but I won't do it!" He apparently had just then experienced a command-type auditory hallucination urging him to commit suicide. Sometimes, however, psychotic individuals *do* give in to the commands, and suicide and/or acts of violence can be carried out against others.

Commissioners in Lunacy Commissioned by the British government in 1845, this committee of 15 individuals was endowed with the power to inspect existing madhouses and asylums and refuse or approve the licensure of new ones. The commissioners' jurisdiction extended over England and Wales, unlike previous regulatory boards, which had jurisdiction just over London and a seven mile radius around it. The direct precursors to the Commissioners in Lunacy were the committee of five medical commissioners from the College of Physicians empowered in 1774, and its successor, the Metropolitan Commissioners in Lunacy, established in 1828.

commitment One of the most frightening experiences anyone can imagine is being involuntarily committed to a mental hospital. The many autobiographical accounts of such traumatic events by ex-mental patients have served only to stimulate the public's imagination, and they have been depicted frequently in fictional accounts in literature, motion pictures and on television. There have been many critics of the role of psychiatrists, which gives them extraordinary power over others usually granted only to judges or the police, and many of these critics have been psychiatrists themselves, notably Thomas Szaz and R.D. LAING (1927–1989). Szaz caused a stir in 1963 with his book, *Law, Liberty and Psychiatry,* because he called for eliminating all forms of involuntary commitment. In his 1985 autobiography, Laing bluntly expresses his view of the powers of psychiatry when he writes:

Thus, society expects psychiatry to perform two very special functions. To lock certain people up, and to stop and, if possible, change certain states of mind and types of conduct in the name of curing mental illnesses . . . These two tasks are placed on psychiatry. It is ensured that psychiatrists carry out these tasks by giving them the *power* to do so, a power *they* can't refuse, if they want to practice psychiatry.

In the United States, each state is responsible for making its own commitment laws. In most cases, they are understandably vague (given the great variety of symptoms and behaviors exhibited in persons with severe mental disorders), but since the 1970s states have generally focused narrowly on the issue of dangerousness, specifically whether the person is a danger to himself or others. Generally it takes the written approval of only one or two psychiatrists to commit someone involuntarily to a mental hospital. That such a process is needed in the treatment of severe mental illness is largely unquestioned, since in floridly psychotic states of mind people can—and do—engage in harmful acts against themselves or others. Judgment is impaired during such episodes, and a person who is indeed suffering from a severe mental illness may not know that he or she requires help.

Most of the laws governing commitment have been transformed over the years to become more humane, largely due to the lobbying efforts of patient advocacy groups since the end of the 1800s. It has become progressively more difficult to commit someone to a psychiatric hospital, and laws have been changed to require frequent psychiatric and judicial review to expedite the earliest possible release.

One of the abuses of the power of commitment held by psychiatrists was the commitment of married women to "insane asylums" at their husband's request even though they were not truly insane. Such power was granted to the superintendents of asylums by some state legislatures, notably in Illinois, whose 1851 commitment law declared: "married women . . . may be entered or detained in the hospital (the state asylum at Jacksonville, Illinois) at the request of the husband of the woman . . . without evidence of insanity required in other cases." These laws were eventually changed after the intense lobbying efforts of one such woman, Elizabeth Parsons Ware Packard, who in 1860 was committed by her husband (the Reverend Theophilus Packard) to the Illinois State Asylum at Jacksonville and was incarcerated there for three years. She apparently drew her husband's ire for expressing philosophical differences on religious matters. The commitment was carried out by two doctors who were members of her husband's church, and judged her insane by merely feeling her pulse. She kept a diary while in the asylum, and produced many publications based on it over the years. An 1867 investigation of the Jacksonville asylum found 148 such women committed there. Packard persuaded the Illinois state legislature to change the commitment law that year, and she persuaded Iowa to do the same in 1872. Efforts by groups in the Mental Hygiene Movement working with the American Psychiatric Association helped to abolish such inhumane laws in the United States by the 1930s.

Changes in current laws regarding commitment can be found in the *Mental Disability Law Reporter,* a bimonthly publication of the American Bar Association. A survey of individual state commitment laws can be found in an appendix of the 1988 edition to E. Fuller Torrey's book, *Sur-*

viving Schizophrenia. (See also LUNACY TRIALS.)

Laing, R.D., *Wisdom, Madness, and Folly: The Making of a Psychiatrist.* New York: McGraw-Hill, 1985.

Packard, E.P.W., *Marital Power Exemplified in Mrs. Packard's Trial, and Self-Defense From the Charge of Insanity; or, Three Year's Imprisonment for Religious Belief, by the Arbitrary Will of a Husband, with an Appeal to the Government to so Change the Laws so as to Afford Legal Protection to Married Women.* Hartford: Case, Lockwood, 1866.

Szaz, T., *Law, Liberty and Psychiatry.* New York: Macmillan, 1963.

communicated insanity   See FOLIE À DEUX.

community mental health centers
Following the pattern of the DEINSTITUTION-ALIZATION of the mentally ill from psychiatric institutions in the United States in the 1950s, it soon became clear that these discharged patients were not receiving the proper care in the community. In a 1961 report entitled, *Action for Mental Health,* the Joint Commission on Mental Illness and Health recommended the establishment of federally-funded community-based mental health centers so that seriously ill patients could be treated closer to home and be kept out of psychiatric hospitals. In a special message to Congress in February 1963, President John F. Kennedy proposed a system of "Community Mental Health Centers" to be set up around the United States. President Kennedy optimistically argued that, "when carried out, reliance on the cold mercy of custodial isolation will be supplanted by the open warmth of community concern and capability." Community care was designed to be a replacement for confinement in state hospitals.

Unfortunately, as many studies have shown, right from the start CMHCs have treated only a small percentage of discharged psychiatric patients—at most, only 10% to 15% of the new cases admitted to the CMHCs were for people with serious psychiatric diagnoses such as schizophrenia. Instead of providing services to the seriously mentally ill—as was the idea behind the plan—CMHCs have overwhelmingly provided counseling and psychotherapy for people with marital problems, family problems, relationship problems and other interpersonal problems. In many settings valuable treatment resources are being drained by court-mandated "therapy" for individuals as a form of "pretrial intervention" so that they do not have to schedule full trials and be sent to already overcrowded jails. Such individuals often include sociopaths (especially juveniles) who are poorly motivated to change their behavior and see their weekly appointments with a therapist at the local CMHC as merely a way of staying out of jail.

It is estimated that, by 1987, over 800 CMHCs have been granted over $3 billion in federal funds to maintain this system, but without any appreciable improvement in the care of the seriously mentally ill. An illuminating critique of the CMHC system in the United States and its almost exclusive treatment of the "worried well" is provided by psychiatrist E. Fuller Torrey in his section on "The Failure of the Community Health Centers" in his book, *Surviving Schizophrenia.*

Goldman, H.H. et al., "Community Mental Health Centers and the Treatment of Severe Mental Disorder," *American Journal of Psychiatry,* 137(1980) 83–86.

Torrey, E.F., *Surviving Schizophrenia: A Family Manual,* 2nd ed. New York: Harper & Row, 1988.

complex   A term used by C.G. JUNG to describe organized clusters of feelings that take on a life of their own and that exist in all of us. The term was first used by the German philosopher and psychiatrist Theodor Ziehen (1862–1950) as "emotionally charged complex of representations" *(gefühlsbetonter Vorstellungskomplex)* to explain the underlying cluster of feelings that caused delayed reactions in the course of his experiments with the word association test, later made famous by Jung. Jung thought that the mind's basic structure is made up of autonomous "feeling-toned complexes" (gefühlsbetonter Komplex), nodal points or clusters of affect whose dynamics are observed in the phenomenon we call "personality." Jung felt that the "ego" was essentially a complex, and although it was the most important one, it was only one among many. The ego could be influenced and even paralyzed by other such clusters of feelings, which we experience when we suddenly feel we are losing control when mad, joyful, etc. in everyday life. Everyone has complexes, but in normals they work together within a functional system that is adaptive for the survival of the individual. In mental disorders, particularly severe ones such as schizophrenia or multiple personality disorder, their strength is greater and their autonomy from the ego more extreme due to DISSOCIA-TION, thus disabling the personality, as Jung observes, with "a multiplication of its centers of gravity."

In schizophrenia, Jung thought that the disturbances in the will of the individual, and his or her hallucinations and delusions, represented the pathological work of complexes. In his famous monograph, *The Psychology of Dementia Praecox* (1907), he demonstrated how the nature of complexes in schizophrenia fits in with descriptions of similar phenomena in the psychoanalytic theories of Sigmund FREUD. Although Jung recognized that dementia praecox was caused by a "toxin" that led to an irreversible disease process in the brain, he was largely under the influence of the psychological approach of Freud at this time and felt that it was possible for the "feeling-toned complex" to make the changes in the chemistry of the brain to produce the toxin. In this respect he differed significantly from his supervisor Eugen BLEULER, who felt that the organic disease process in the brain came

first and that the complexes only gave the psychotic symptoms their form, but did not cause them. In 1908, Bleuler and Jung published a paper together that contrasted their views on this issue. After his break with Freud, Jung returned much later to a more organic view of the causes of schizophrenia.

Jung thought that ancient reports of demoniacal possession (see DEMONOMANIA) were simply due to the work of complexes that had become too strong and had begun to form alternate egos in the personality of the afflicted. Jung's "complex theory" is at the center of his entire psychology, which was briefly referred to as "complex psychology" but is now more widely known as "analytical psychology." (See also ABAISSE-MENT DU NIVEAU MENTAL; MULTIPLE PERSONALITY AND SCHIZOPHRENIA.)

Bleuler, E. and Jung, C.G., "Komplexe und Krankheitsursachen bei Dementia Praecox," *Zentralblatt für Nervenheilkunde und Psychiatrie,* 31:19(1908), 220–227.
Jung, C.G., "The Psychology of Dementia Praecox," in *The Collected Works of C.G. Jung,* vol. 3. Princeton: Princeton University Press, 1960; first published, 1907.
Jung, C.G., "The Psychogenesis of Schizophrenia," *Journal of Mental Science,* 85(1939), 999–1011.
Noll, R., "Multiple Personality, Dissociation, and C.G. Jung's 'Complex Theory,'" *Journal of Analytical Psychology,* 34(1989), 353–370.

compos mentis   A Latin term for "sanity" that has found its way into jurisprudence over the centuries. *Non compos mentis* is its opposite, meaning "not in full possession of mental faculties." The expression apparently is derived from the Roman author Tacitus, who uses it in his *Annals.* (See also INSANITY.)

concordance rate   The rate of agreement, association or correlation between two individuals (or types of individuals) and a given trait. Concordance rates are most often encountered in discussions of twins studies of schizophrenia and BIPOLAR DISORDER that have sought evidence for the genetic transmission of these diseases. For example, since we known that MONOZYGOTIC TWINS (also known as identical twins) share all the same genes, we known that they must be highly concordant for traits like eye and hair color, blood type and most physical characteristics. DIZYGOTIC TWINS, on the other hand, who have on the average only half their genes in common, will resemble each other no more than other siblings, making them discordant across many traits. Concordance rates are often presented as decimaled numbers that represent a correlation coefficient, and the closer the number is to 1.0 the more concordant two individuals or groups are for a given trait. If schizophrenia (or bipolar disorder) is the result of genetic inheritance, then the assumption in research studies is that monozygotic twins should *both* develop the disease at higher rates (that is, with concordance rates closer to 1.0) than dizygotic twins, where perhaps only one member is likely to develop the disorder.

Almost all research studies have shown that monozygotic twins do indeed have a higher concordance for schizophrenia and for bipolar disorder than dizygotic twins. On the average, most studies show that the concordance rate for schizophrenia is three times higher in monozygotic twins than in dizygotic twins. Furthermore, the risk for schizophrenia is 40 to 60 times higher in monozygotic twins than in the general population. In patients with bipolar disorder, the concordance rate is four times higher for monozygotic twins (.79) than dizygotic twins (.19).

Also supporting the hypothesis of the genetic transmission of schizophrenia are recent re-analyses of these twin studies data, in which it is found not only that monozygotic twins are more concordant for schizophrenia than dizygotic twins, but also that within these pairs of monozygotic twins, those that have a greater presence of NEGATIVE SYMPTOMS (which have been associated

with a more degenerative, more "genetic" variety of schizophrenia) have a higher concordance rate (.52) than those monozygotic twins who have a lesser presence of such symptoms (.36). (See also CHRONIC SCHIZOPHRENIA; CONSANGUINITY METHOD; CROW'S HYPOTHESIS; DEFICIT SYMPTOMS; GENETICS STUDIES; TWINS METHOD AND STUDIES.)

Bertelsen, A. et al., "A Danish Twin Study of Manic-depressive Disorders," *British Journal of Psychiatry*, 130(1977), 330–351.

Dworkin, R.H. & Lenzenweger, M.F., "Symptoms and the Genetics of Schizophrenia: Implications for Diagnosis," *American Journal of Psychiatry*, 141(1984), 1541–1546.

Kendler, K.S., "Genetics of Schizophrenia," in *Psychiatry Update: American Psychiatric Association Annual Review*, vol. 5. Washington, D.C.: American Psychiatric Press, 1986.

concretization   An aspect of schizophrenic thought patterns in which abstract thoughts or feelings are "concretized," usually in bizarre ways. For example, during an exacerbation of the psychosis a schizophrenic may feel a loss of control, which causes considerable anxiety. If paranoid, the individual may attribute this distress to the effect of a particular facial expression someone in his immediate environment may just have manifested—perhaps without any awareness of or conscious interaction with the paranoid patient. The notion that humans tend to think in two broad modes—the concrete and the abstract—was first proposed by the psychologist Kurt GOLDSTEIN in 1939. Goldstein noticed that concrete thinking was particularly found in brain-damaged patients and, to a lesser degree, in schizophrenics. Psychologist and psychoanalyst Silvano ARIETI picked up on this idea and asserted that the "process of active concretization" formed the essential basis of the way in which the thinking of people is changed by schizophrenia when compared to normal thinking processes.

Arieti, S. *Interpretation of Schizophrenia*, 2nd ed. New York: Basic Books, 1974.

Goldstein, K., *The Organism*. New York: American Books, 1939.

confabulation This is the unconscious fabrication of facts or events that is often noted in brain-damaged individuals and in those persons with amnestic disorders. They confabulate due to gaps in memory, and the fabricated response to questions are facile attempts to fill in these gaps, but without any awareness of the person that he or she is confabulating. This is different than lying or DELUSIONS, which are found in the psychotic disorders and are not the response to memory impairment.

confidentiality Individuals have the right to privacy. Special relationships between a person and certain specific medical, mental health or legal representatives are protected by this right of privacy, and many statutes have established the privileged nature of communications made during the course of professional relationships. A breach of confidentiality by a practitioner is a basis of malpractice actions against that person. Patients of mental health professionals should expect that what is discussed or included as part of treatment is private information, to be released to others only by the patient's (ideally, written) consent. (See also LEGAL ISSUES IN SCHIZOPHRENIA.)

confusion A psychological state of disorientation that is found across many different types of mental disorders (including ORGANIC MENTAL DISORDERS), but in particular is evident in the psychotic disorders. It is usually evident during exacerbations of a psychosis.

conjugal insanity See FOLIE À DEUX.

Conolly, John (1794–1866) An English psychiatrist and reformer. After graduating from Edinburgh University, Conolly studied in France where he was influenced by the "moral treatment" of Philippe PINEL.

Returning to England, in 1839 he became the chief physician to the Hanwell Asylum in Middlesex and there began to practice his own moral treatment of the mentally ill, including the abolition of MECHANICAL RESTRAINTS. He remained there for four years. He wrote many books on his philosophy of treatment; although they were controversial for their time, they were also highly influential. As the guiding leader of the NONRESTRAINT MOVEMENT, Conolly's ideas spread throughout Europe and America. Indeed, his ideas were held in very high regard in the United States and were partially the inspiration that brought together the 13 founders of the AMERICAN PSYCHIATRIC ASSOCIATION in 1844.

Conolly, J., *An Inquiry Concerning the Indications of Insanity With Suggestions for the Better Protection and Cure of the Insane*. London: 1830.
———, *The Treatment of the Insane Without the Use of Mechanical Restraints*. London: Smith, Elder, 1856.

consanguinity method One of the methods of conducting GENETICS STUDIES of schizophrenia and other mental disorders (such as BIPOLAR DISORDER), which are assumed to have a genetic basis. The consanguinity method is based on a simple idea: If a particular disease is assumed to be genetic in origin, then the disease will be more prevalent in relatives of an afflicted person than in the general population as a whole. The afflicted person is known in these studies as the "index case." The assumption in consanguinity studies is that the closer a relative is biologically to the index case, the more likely he or she is to develop the disorder. Twins studies are based on this principle but for many reasons are considered more scientifically powerful evidence than traditional consanguinity studies.

The very first published study on the genetics of schizophrenia was the consanguinity study conducted by Ernst Rüdin in 1916. He apparently carried out this study at the urging of Emil KRAEPELIN. Rüdin, as expected, found a significant increase in the prevalence rate of schizophrenia in the biological relatives of his index cases. He also recognized that the gene seemed to be passed on in NON-MENDELIAN PATTERNS OF TRANSMISSION. Further studies were conducted in Europe by Schultz in 1932 and in the United States by Kallmann in 1938.

The results of just about every published study since Rüdin's in 1916 show that first-degree relatives (parents, children, siblings) of the index case are 10 times more likely than people in the general population to develop schizophrenia. The prevalence rate in the general population is 1% (allowing for approximately 2.0 million schizophrenics in the United States in 1990) and 10% for the first-degree relatives of the index case. In second-degree relatives (uncles, aunts, nieces, nephews, grandparents) the prevalence rate for schizophrenia is five or six times that for the general population. Thus, as the degree of consanguinity diminishes (the further away biologically the index case is from his or her relatives), so does the prevalence of the disorder in the family, until in the extended family the rate approaches that expected in the general population.

The consanguinity studies have been criticized because many argue that environmental factors may play as large a role as genetics in the development of schizophrenia. Families share more than just genes: They share patterns of interaction that may also lead to the development of serious mental illnesses such as schizophrenia. While the consanguinity studies suggest the role of genetics in schizophrenia, the evidence they provide is not sufficient proof for this hypothesis. (See also TWINS METHOD AND STUDIES.)

Rüdin, E., *Zur Vererbung und Neuentstehung der Dementia Praecox*. Berlin: Springer-Verlag, 1916.

Slater, E., "A Review of Earlier Evidence on Genetic Factors in Schizophrenia," in D. Rosenthal and S. Kety (eds.), *The Transmission of Schizophrenia*. Oxford: Pergamon Press, 1968.

contagious insanity   See FOLIE À DEUX.

continuous sleep therapy   Swiss psychiatrist Jacob Kläsi developed this form of therapy for schizophrenics in the early 1920s. It is perhaps the first true physical treatment for schizophrenia. Kläsi induced a prolonged sleep in his patients with the use of barbiturates. These periods of sleep lasted a week or more, and the patient was only allowed to eat or perform bodily functions upon wakings, after which more barbiturates would be administered and the patient would be put back to sleep. His only theory to rationalize this treatment was that schizophrenia was the result of a pathological excitement that resulted from an inflammatory process in the brain that could be alleviated through rest, as other inflammatory conditions could be. However, the complications of the procedure (toxicity, the development of respiratory problems and pneumonia) outweighed the apparent therapeutic benefits, and thus the treatment was not widely used. (See also SLEEP TREATMENT.)

Diethelm, O., "An Historical View of Somatic Treatment in Psychiatry," *American Journal of Psychiatry*, 95(1938) 1165–1179.

Kläsi, J., "Über die therapeutische Anwendung der 'Dauernarkose' mittels sominifens bei Schizophrenen," *Z. Neurol. Psychiatr.*, 74 (1922), 557–592.

continuum of psychosis   See EINHEITS-PSYCHOSE.

convulsive therapies   Although no sound scientific theories have ever supported their use, the convulsive therapies have been among the most widely used somatic treatments for schizophrenia in this century. The basic idea is that deliberately inducing a convulsion or seizure—either by drugs or electricity—somehow has a therapeutic effect in schizophrenia.

The first report of a convulsive therapy was by the Hungarian psychiatrist L. von MEDUNA in 1935. Von Meduna apparently believed (without any supporting scientific evidence) that epilepsy and schizophrenia were biologically incompatible, and that, therefore, inducing a convulsive seizure in schizophrenics would be therapeutic. He used camphor and metrazol to induce these convulsions and reported successful results. However, his relapse rate was high, and his "convulsive therapy" was found to be more effective with patients with affective disorders (such as depression) than with schizophrenics. This similar beneficial result with people with severe affective disorders has also been found to be true for ELECTROSHOCK THERAPY (now commonly referred to as ECT, or "electroconvulsive therapy") which was first used by CERLETTI and Bini in 1938. Since the 1970s ECT has been infrequently used for schizophrenia in the United States.

von Meduna, L., "Versuche über die biologische Beinflussung des Ablaufes der Schizophrenic," *Z. Neurol. Psychiatr.*, 152(1935), 235–262.

———, *Die Konvulsionstherapie der Schizophrenie*. Halle: Marhold, 1937.

copro-psychiatrie   A 19th-century "school" of psychiatry that claimed that mental illnesses, and particularly the psychotic disorders, were caused by diseases of the digestive tract, particularly the intestines and bowels. These physicians primarily studied the feces, urine and other bodily "secretions of the insane." In the second (1861) edition of his famous textbook, *Die Pathologie und Therapie der Psychische Krankheit* (the first was in 1845), German psychiatrist Wilhelm GRIESINGER notes that this "peculiar bud from the stem of the 'Somatic School' has . . . gone out of fashion."

cortical pruning as a cause of schizophrenia   This is a theory that proposes a developmental process ("cortical" or "axonal pruning") that is extended past its normal point of termination (at about age 16) and goes on to cause schizophrenia. In the brain, neurons ("brain cells") pass messages back and forth to one another through a vast web of interconnections. From the nucleus of the neuron, a "message" travels down a branch-like structure called the "axon." The point at which information from one cell passes to another is a gap separating the axons called a "synapse." Biochemical neurotransmitters such as dopamine, serotonin, norepinepherine, all cross this gap to affect the adjoining neuron.

Starting with the postmortem studies of P. R. Huttenlocher, published in 1979, it was discovered that there are major changes in the number of synapses (especially in the prefrontal cortex) throughout childhood and adolescence. "Synaptic density" (think of this as the thick branches of a tree or bush— the axons—intercrossing one another) increases in this cortical area until about ages 5 to 7, and then it begins a gradual decline until about age 16, when the density of synapses seems to level off to average adult levels. It is estimated that as much as 30% to 40% of these interconnections between brain cells disappear or "fall off" or are "pruned" (as one would a tree or shrub), and as a result the brain is measured to be less "active" or have less "energy" ("reduced cerebral metabolism"), particularly in the prefrontal cortical regions. This process is called axonal pruning.

A recent theory for a possible contributing cause of schizophrenia based on this normal process of "cortical" or "axonal pruning" was first put forth by Irving Feinberg in 1982, and developed by researchers Ralph Hoffman and Steven Dobscha in a paper published in 1989. In that paper, they hypothesize that the normal developmental process of cortical pruning that happens to us all in childhood and adolescence, and especially its measured reduction of cerebral metabolism in the prefrontal cortex, may actually cause schizophrenia if the process continues into late adolescence and early adulthood. In the studies of BRAIN ABNOR-MALITIES IN SCHIZOPHRENIA, "hypofrontality," or the atrophy of neural tissue in the prefrontal cortical regions of the brain, has been found in some schizophrenics. As they put it:

Hypofrontality reflects a longstanding developmental process run amok. Moreover, the fact that the onset of schizophrenia generally occurs in late adolescence or early adulthood is account for—this would be the time when the cumulative effects of axonal overpruning would first be fully felt.

A computer model simulation of what the effect of cortical pruning would be in normals was conducted by Hoffman and Dobscha, and it was found that such experiences as delusions and hallucinations and other psychotic symptoms might be experienced by humans. Another prominent schizophrenia researcher, Letten Saugstad of Norway, proposes that the cortical pruning process is implicated in the development of manic-depressive psychosis as well, with the hypothesis being that very early puberty is the necessary factor in the development of manic-depressive psychosis, and extremely late puberty the necessary factor in the development of schizophrenia. If the onset of puberty is viewed as coinciding with the last major step in brain development (the end of the cortical pruning process), then manic-depressiveness may result from the earlier than normal termination of the cortical pruning process. However, as of 1990, no empirical test of this theory of cortical pruning as the cause of schizophrenia or manic-depressive psychosis has been published. (See also HYPO-FRONTALITY.)

Feinberg, I., "Schizophrenia and Late Maturational Brain Changes in Man," *Psychopharmacology Bulletin*, 18(1982), 29–31.
———, "Schizophrenia: Caused By A Fault in Programmed Synaptic Elimination During Adolescence?" *Journal of Psychiatric Research*, 4(1982/1983), 319–334.
Hoffman, R.E. and Dobscha, S.K., "Cortical Pruning and the Development of Schizophrenia: A Computer Model," *Schizophrenia Bulletin*, 15(1989) 477–490.
Huttenlocher, P.R., "Synaptic Density in Human Frontal Cortex—Evidence for Synaptic Elimination During Normal Development," *Neuroscience Letters*, 33(1979), 247–252.
Saugstad, L. F., "Social Class, Marriage, and Fertility in Schizophrenia," *Schizophrenia Bulletin*, 15(1989), 9–43.

Cotard's syndrome A relatively uncommon delusional syndrome, usually found in people with a psychotic disorder (usually, paranoid schizophrenia) or with an organic mental disorder, in which he or she denies his or her own existence or the existence of the external world. For this reason, French psychiatrist Cotard introduced this idea in 1880 at a meeting in Paris of the Societé Médico-Psychologique by calling it *le délire de négation* (delusions of negation). Cotard first published his ideas on this newly identified syndrome in 1882. Another French psychiatrist, Séglas, named this condition the "Cotard Syndrome" in 1897. Schizophrenics who exhibit Cotard's syndrome may make statements such as "I'm dead" or "I'm not here or anywhere. I'm a ghost." Nonpsychotic conditions that are probably related to Cotard's syndrome are feelings of DEREALIZATION or DEPERSONALIZATION.

Cotard, J., *Maladies cebrales et mentales*. Paris: Bailliére, 1891.
Séglas, J., *La Délire de Négation*, vol. 1. Paris: Masson, 1897.

cottage system Another name for the centuries-old system of caring for the mentally ill in which they are maintained in the community rather than in institutions. Belgium's Gheel Colony, which is almost 1,000 years old, is an example of how long this system has been maintained.

Cotton, Henry A. See FOCAL INFECTION AS CAUSE OF PSYCHOTIC DISORDERS.

countertransference A concept from psychoanalytic theory that refers to the unconscious or conscious, biased emotional reaction that a therapist experiences toward the patient in treatment. According to psychoanalytic theory, these emotions come from the early interpersonal experiences of the therapist and the significant people from the therapist's infancy and childhood. Such attitudes and emotions with early origins of the patient are considered to be projected onto therapists by patients and the term for this is TRANSFERENCE. The countertransference toward schizophrenic patients in treatment is often described as one of the most difficult for the therapist to overcome since it is usually a negative one. In her essay on "The Basic Problems of Psychotherapy of Schizophrenia" (1957), psychoanalyst Frieda Fromm-Reichmann writes that the countertransference problems of the therapist "are greater and of more consequence in working with the schizophrenic patient than they are in work with neurotic patients." Fromm-Reichman then outlines a few of the specific countertransference difficulties:

First, I should like to consider the negative countertransference reactions. Severe anxiety states of the patient may be contagious to some psychotherapists. Schizophrenic loneliness, as evidenced by the mute, stuporous catatonic or the withdrawn hebephrenic, may arouse severe anxiety in other therapists. Some may become quite anxious in the face of marked schizophrenic dependency needs, and, for almost all psychotherapists, schizophrenic hatred and threatened or actual violence constitute a source of anxiety. Negative countertransference may also occur if the patient does not show marked signs of improvement after the therapist has invested much interest and effort.

Fromm-Reichmann, F., *Psychoanalysis and Psychotherapy: Selected Papers*. Chicago: University of Chicago Press, 1959.

course of schizophrenia   Since the beginning of the century, there has been much interest in the "natural history of schizophrenia," that is, the typical pattern or patterns the disease demonstrates in people over

long periods of time. Ideally, people with schizophrenia should be studied over the course of a lifetime, with careful research criteria for the type of onset (sudden or insidious), pattern of exacerbations and remissions of psychotic symptoms (which can be graphically demonstrated as "simple" [chronic] or "undulating" [isodic] patterns over time) and the end state (generally the end of the long-term period under study, but ideally a lifetime). There have been many studies of the course of schizophrenia since the beginning of the century, and all of them have challenged Emil KRAEPELIN's fatalistic definition of "dementia praecox" as always ending in a state of chronic deterioration.

The earliest studies of the course of schizophrenia seemed to indicate a rule of "thirds"—a third completely recovered, a third improved and a third progressively worsened. In his book, *Surviving Schizophrenia* (1988), psychiatrist E. Fuller Torrey cites evidence that after 10 years the disease seems to follow a rule of "quarters" rather than of "thirds"—completely recovered (25%); much improved, relatively independent (25%); improved but require extensive support network (25%); hospitalized, unimproved (15%); dead, mostly by SUICIDE (10%). After 30 years, according to Torrey, the long-term studies of schizophrenics reveal the following basic pattern: completely recovered (25%); much improved, relatively independent (35%); improved but require extensive support network (15%); hospitalized, unimproved (10%); dead (15%).

The three very-long-term studies of the course of schizophrenia that are considered among the most definitive are known as the Lausanne Investigations (by Luc Ciompi in Switzerland), the Burghölzli Hospital Study (by Manfred Bleuler in Zurich, Switzerland) and the Vermont Longitudinal Research Project (by Courtenay Harding at Vermont's only state hospital). A study comparing the results of the three longitudinal studies was published by Harding in 1988 and showed that the studies agreed on eight different patterns or "course types" of schizophrenia. These possibly comprise the "group of schizophrenias," with schizophrenia once again demonstrating the heterogeneity that Eugen BLEULER suggested in 1911. Each of these eight course types differed according to type of onset (acute or chronic), course type (simple or undulating) and end state (recovery or mild, moderate or severe). A chart classifying these same eight patterns of course of schizophrenia (but using slightly different terms) was included in a 1988 paper by Carpenter and Kirkpatrick and is reproduced here in a modified form:

Pattern	Onset	Nature of Psychotic Episodes	Improvement Late in Life?
1.	Insidious	Chronic	Yes
2.	Insidious	Chronic	No
3.	Insidious	Episodic	Yes
4.	Insidious	Episodic	No
5.	Acute	Chronic	Yes
6.	Acute	Chronic	No
7.	Acute	Episodic	Yes
8.	Acute	Episodic	No

Also in 1988, a review of 10 North American long-term follow-up studies of the course of schizophrenia (minimum of 10 years of study) was published by T.H. McGlashan, who reached the following conclusions about the natural history of schizophrenia as a result of analyzing these studies:

1. Schizophrenia is a chronic disease, frequently disabling for a lifetime.
2. The average number of bad outcomes for schizophrenia is worse than that of other major mental disorders. In general, the studies support Kraepelin's 1896 bifurcation of the psychotic disorders into those that have a good prognosis (manic-depressive psychosis) and those that have a bad prognosis (dementia praecox). People with bipolar disorder fare better than those with schizophrenia.
3. Schizophrenia is associated with an increased risk for suicide, physical illness and mortality.
4. The schizophrenic process, while disabling and chronic, does not get progressively worse over the long term. In fact, people with schizophrenia who seem to be following a "chronic" course seem to reach a "plateau" after five or 10 years, after which their symptoms either do not get any worse or go into partial remission. This evidence also defies Kraepelin's notion that schizophrenia is always a progressively degenerative process that ends in "dementia."
5. A lot of patients recover from schizophrenia, but the outcome generally follows many different patterns (see chart above).
6. The long-term follow-up studies have not demonstrated that treatment—of any type—has any effect on the natural history of schizophrenia. This means that treatment with ANTIPSYCHOTIC DRUGS may be fine for reducing the transient psychotic symptoms of some schizophrenics, but that they do not directly inhibit the disease itself.

A special issue of *Schizophrenia Bulletin* devoted to "Long-Term Followup Studies of Schizophrenia" was published in 1988. (See also ACUTE SCHIZOPHRENIA; CHRONIC SCHIZOPHRENIA; PROGNOSIS.)

Carpenter W.T. and Kirkpatrick, B. "The Heterogeneity of the Long-term Course of Schizophrenia," *Schizophrenia Bulletin,* 14:4(1988), 645–652.

Harding, C.M., "Course Types in Schizophrenia: An Analysis of European and American Studies," *Schizophrenia Bulletin,* 14(1988), 633–644.

McGlashan, T.H., "A Selective Review of Recent North American Long-term Followup Studies of Schizophrenia," *Schizophrenia Bulletin,* 14(1988), 515–542.

Torrey, E.F., *Surviving Schizophrenia: A Family Manual,* 2nd ed. New York: Harper & Row, 1988.

creativity and psychosis   Is there a relationship between "madness" and creativity? Thousands of years of popular speculation have thought so. The first of the now familiar "pathographies" of famous creative individuals began to appear in the mid-1800s, led by the works of French alienist J.J. Moreau de Tours (1804–1884) and German psychiatrist P.J. Möbius (1853–1907), who wrote psychiatric interpretations of the creative lives of Rousseau, Goethe, Schopenhauer and Nietzsche. In the 20th century, psychologists have tried to answer this question experimentally by comparing the thought processes of schizophrenics with those of highly creative nonschizophrenic individuals. It has long been reported that when highly creative nonschizophrenics are given traditional diagnostic tests, they tend to score higher on psychopathology than "normals." However, there is no evidence that these people or other highly creative individuals are more susceptible to schizophrenia than the general population.

A review of these studies on creativity and schizophrenia was published by J.A. Keefe and P.A. Magaro in 1980. Although there was no direct evidence of a link between the two, schizophrenics and creative nonschizophrenics did share several qualities in the styles of their thinking: Both used language in very unusual ways, both had deviant, idiosyncratic views of reality when compared to other people, and both tended to be perceived as "eccentric" by others. An important distinction to be made is that one of the hallmarks of a schizophrenic is the inability to focus attention in a normal, sustained manner, and such attention is necessary for planning and carrying out all activities of life—including creative ones. Thus, being "schizophrenic" does not make one creative, nor vice versa.

However, there has been much speculation that many highly creative people throughout history may have been afflicted (or blessed, as the case may be) with BIPOLAR DISORDER. The thought disorder of schizophrenia is generally absent in manic-depressives, but there is an incredible rush of energy due to the manic phase of the illness that can keep creative people working on projects literally for days with little or no sleep. Such persons may have been Vincent Van Gogh, Edgar Allan Poe, Handel, Berlioz, F. Scott Fitzgerald, Eugene O'Neill and Virginia Woolf. The anecdotal evidence for a connection between manic-depressive illness and creativity is quite strong.

Alcoholism, either in connection with bipolar illness or alone, is prominently represented in creative individuals. Writers in particular seem to be prone to alcoholism, and the first five American Nobel laureates for literature (Lewis, O'Neill, Faulkner, Hemingway and Steinbeck) were all alcoholics.

There has also been some speculation, based on anecdotal evidence, that relatives of highly creative people are often schizophrenic or manic-depressives. For example, Albert Einstein's son Edward (born in 1910) was afflicted with schizophrenia. James Joyce's daughter Lucia was a diagnosed schizophrenic who spent most of her life in mental institutions. British horror writer Ramsey Campbell's mother was schizophrenic, and Jane Fonda's mother (Frances Seymour Brokow) committed suicide in a mental hospital in 1950 by slitting her own throat. The exact nature of her severe illness is not known. Even famous psychiatrists have not been exempt, for the mothers of both Harry Stack Sullivan and C.G. Jung are known to have had serious mental disorders that may have resulted in psychiatric hospitalization. Indeed, both Stack and Jung themselves are known to have had periods in their lives when psychotic-like symptoms and a general functional breakdown were known to occur. Thus, the question of madness and creativity is an intriguing one that will continue to generate endless speculation. (See also ART, SCHIZOPHRENIC.)

Dykes, M. and McGhie, A., "A Comparative Study of Attentional Strategies of Schizophrenic and Highly Creative Normal Subjects," *British Journal of Psychiatry*, 128(1976) 50–56.

Goodwin, D.W., *Alcohol and the Writer*. Kansas City: Andrews & McMeel, 1988.

Keefe, J.A. and Magaro, P.A., "Creativity and Schizophrenia: An Equivalence of Cognitive Processing," *Journal of Abnormal Psychology*, 89(1980), 390–398.

Croatia   Some parts of Croatia, which is in Yugoslavia, have some of the highest prevalence rates for schizophrenia in the world; the northwestern coastal area has a prevalence rate twice as high as that of the rest of Yugoslavia. Rates for manic depression are also high in Croatia. The Istrian Peninsula in Croatia has a particularly high rate (about 7.4 per thousand) when compared to other areas of Croatia (from 2.9 to 4.2 per thousand).

Lemkau, P.V., "Selected Aspects of the Epidemiology of Psychoses in Croatia," *American Journal of Epidemiology*, 94(1971), 112–117.

cross-cultural studies   It has long been reported that severe mental disorders such as schizophrenia and manic-depressive illness seem to be more prevalent in technologically developed Western countries than in developing countries in the Third World. This is a very old observation. As early as 1835 British psychiatrist J.C. Prichard (1786–1848) noted in his text, *A Treatise On Insanity*, that "insanity belongs almost exclusively to civilized races of man: it scarcely exists among savages, and is rare in barbarous countries." Other prominent figures in psychiatry in the 19th century who expressed these views were Isaac Ray, Dorothea Dix, Edward Jarvis and Pliny Earle.

In the 19th and early 20th century, many anecdotal reports by psychiatrists and anthropologists about mental disorders in "primitive" societies supported the view that schizophrenia in particular seemed to be uncommon. The more scientific epidemiological studies of the prevalence of schizophrenia show that it is found in different amounts in different parts of the world. In reviewing all of this data, psychiatrist E. Fuller Torrey published a fascinating book in 1980 on *Schizophrenia and Civilization* in which he argues that, "schizophrenia appears to be a disease of civilization, with a close correlation between its prevalence and the degree of civilization."

However, diagnostic criteria can be very different from culture to culture, and many diseases that look like schizophrenia (such as manic-depressive psychosis in its earliest stage, certain metabolic disorders, or organic mental disorders caused by strokes, tumors or lesions induced by head trauma) may not in fact be so. To correct these problems and to construct a true picture of schizophrenia worldwide, many rigorous, scientific, long-term follow-up studies have been conducted in many areas of the world. The two most important studies have been major projects of the World Health Organization: the International Pilot Study of Schizophrenia (IPSS), which was carried out in nine countries (Denmark, India, Colombia, Nigeria, United Kingdom, Soviet Union, Czechoslovakia, Taiwan and the United States) between 1968 and the early 1970s; and the Determinants of Outcome Study, conducted between 1983 and 1985 in 10 countries, using methods that were improvements over the IPSS study of a decade earlier. Both of these studies have shown that schizophrenic patients in less-industrialized societies (as in the Third World) have a significantly better prognosis than do those schizophrenics in industrialized nations. However, both of these studies also show a core of "worst outcome" schizophrenics, and these groups seem to match the familiar descriptions of CHRONIC SCHIZOPHRENIA known in Western societies, where it is thought to be more genetically based and more "organic" and degenerative in nature than the "acute-onset" types. "Acute onset psychoses" were found, instead, to predominate in the non-Western world.

Whether these cross-cultural differences are due to sociocultural differences (Third World countries being more "sociocentric", Western societies more "egocentric") or to the prevalence of different, less chronic strains of schizophrenia in Third World countries is presently unknown.

Lin, K.M. and Kleinman, A.M., "Psychopathology and Clinical Course of Schizophrenia: A Cross-Cultural Perspective," *Schizophrenia Bulletin*, 14(1988), 555–567.
Torrey, E.F., *Schizophrenia and Civilization*. New York: Jason Aronson, 1980.

Crow's hypothesis   For many years researchers sought to combine all of the highly diversified studies of schizophrenia into a single theory that could account for all of the new findings that advances in technology had brought. In essence, the desire was for a theory that could account for the symptoms of schizophrenia and relate them to specific biological processes. Furthermore, such a theory would have to be testable. In 1980, psychiatrist T.J. Crow did just that. He published his concept of schizophrenia as essentially a "two-syndrome" disease, and connected findings on the symptomatology of schizophrenia with the biochemical and neurophysiological qualities of the disease. He named these two subtypes of schizophrenia "Type I" and "Type II"; because it has been so popular with those who carry out schizophrenia research, the theory is commonly referred to as "Crow's hypothesis" or "two-syndrome paradigm."

Type I schizophrenia is thought by Crow to be characterized by an acute onset, generally normal intellectual functioning, no discernible abnormalities in the structure of the brain, a good response to antipsychotic drugs. It is thought to be caused by an excess of dopamine production in the brain and is generally associated with POSITIVE SYMP-

TOMS (symptoms that seem to be "additions" to the personality, such as hallucinations and delusions). Most importantly, it is associated with the absence of NEGATIVE SYMPTOMS (those symptoms that represent something "taken away" from the personality, such as poverty of speech, poverty of content of speech, restricted affect, psychomotor retardation, reduced desire for social interaction, constricted thought process).

In Type II schizophrenia, characteristics include insidious onset (i.e., it develops slowly, like a chronic illness), intellectual deterioration, enlarged ventricles in the brain, poor response to antipsychotic drugs and prominent negative symptoms. Thus, the difference in Type I versus Type II schizophrenia is based not only on the predominance of unrelated symptoms (positive versus negative) but also the fact that Type II schizophrenia is clearly characterized by structural BRAIN ABNORMALITIES. Type II, therefore, is the subtype of schizophrenia that most resembles traditional brain diseases. (See also DEFICIT SYMPTOMS/SYNDROME; DOPAMINE HYPOTHESIS.)

Crow, T.J., "Molecular Pathology of Schizophrenia: More Than One Disease Process?" *British Medical Journal*, 280(1980), 66–86.
———, "The Two-syndrome Concept: Origins and Current Status," *Schizophrenia Bulletin*, 11(1985), 471–486.

Crowther, Bryan (1765–1814)   A surgeon of the BETHLEM ROYAL HOSPITAL who wrote a book in 1811 of his observations made during the dissections of the brains of deceased "Bedlam" patients. He was assisted by apothecary John HASLAM in these autopsies, who also incorporated his observations in a book. He is thus one of the early investigators to use neuropathological methods to look for BRAIN ABNORMALITIES in the severely mentally ill. In his book, Crowther also mentioned that, as surgeon to the Bethlem Royal Hospital, he routinely practiced the BLEEDING of patients every spring regardless of the type or severity of their illness.

When John Haslam was interrogated in 1815 by a committee of the House of Commons about alleged abuses at "Bedlam," it came up in his testimony that Crowther was a raging alcoholic who needed to be put in MECHANICAL RESTRAINT at times. Haslam told the committee: "Mr. Crowther was generally insane, and mostly drunk. He was so insane as to have a straight-waistcoat." Haslam and the superintendent of Bethlem, Thomas Monro, were dismissed as a result of the committee's findings, but Crowther died shortly before the committee opened its hearings—escaping, no doubt, a similar fate.

Crowther, B., *Practical Remarks On Insanity, To Which Is Added A Commentary On the Dissection of the Brains of Maniacs, With Some Account of Diseases Incident To The Insane.* London: 1811.

Report of the Committee for Better Regulation of Madhouses. London: Baldwin, Craddock, & Joy, 1815.

cruciform stance A form of MECHANICAL RESTRAINT in which a disobedient patient was harnessed and tied in a standing position to a cross-shaped metal structure. Patients were then left on this structure for many hours or days at a time. An eminent 19th-century German psychiatrist, Heinrich Wilhelm Neumann (1814–1884), recommended the cruciform stance or harness as "the best possible punishment for the worst transgressions of the insane." The horizontal form of this mode of mechanical restraint was known as the BED SADDLE and survived into the 20th century.

Kreapelin, E., *One Hundred Years of Psychiatry,* tr. W. Baskin. New York: Philosophical Library, 1962; first published, 1917.

CT scan Abbreviation for "computed tomography," a BRAIN IMAGING TECHNIQUE used to study the structure of the brain. It is the same as the more commonly known term

"CAT scan" or "computerized axial tomography." Information is gathered from the body in cross-sectional planes, as if examining the body with X rays slice by slice. An image is created by a computer synthesis of X-ray transmission data obtained from many different directions through each plane. Image by image (or "slice" by "slice") the body is studied, and abnormalities are searched for in the computer-generated images. CT scans and other brain imaging techniques are now commonly being used to study brain abnormalities in schizophrenia and have led to discoveries about how the brains of people with schizophrenia are different from the brains of normals. It is the first of the many new brain-imaging techniques developed since the first published report of the use of a CT scan in 1973; its first use in schizophrenia research was reported in 1976. (See also BRAIN ABNORMALITIES IN SCHIZOPHRENIA.)

Cullen, William (1710–1790) A noted British physician and one of the influential instructors of Benjamin RUSH. He is remembered for founding the Glasgow Medical School in Scotland, and for a system of classifying mental disorders that influenced later psychiatrists, notably Philippe PINEL and Rush. Cullen is also remembered for coining the term NEUROSIS, a class of diseases with a physiological basis in the nervous system. One of these, Vesania, was an ancient Latin term for "insanity," used until the end of the 18th century. His treatment recommendations for mental illness were largely those also used for other physical disorders: bleeding, purging, bathing and changes in diet.

Cullen, William, *First Lines of the Practice of Physic, with practical and explanatory notes by John Rotheram.* Edinburgh: Bell, Bradfute, etc., 1796.

"Cure-Awl, Dr." This was the derisive nickname of physician William Awl, the first superintendent (in 1838) of the Ohio State

Asylum for the Insane and one of the 13 founders of the AMERICAN PSYCHIATRIC ASSOCIATION. The nickname derives from his incredible claim in 1842 that under his direction the Ohio Asylum had achieved a 100% cure rate for insanity.

Exaggerated claims of the curability of severe mental illness were not uncommon in the mid-19th century in the young United States, and such claims were considered a source of national pride. In fact, the preponderance of such claims in the 1830s and 1840s led to a "cult of the asylum" in the United States, led by Dorothea DIX, who cited this evidence in her lobbying efforts to state legislators to build more asylums. Without evidence to the contrary, state after state mandated the construction of state asylums for the insane, and Dix was credited for being personally responsible for 32 of them. It wasn't until 1877 that these fabricated statistics were finally shown to be false in an influential book by Pliny EARLE, another of the 13 founders of the American Psychiatric Association.

Earle, P., *The Curability of the Insane*. Philadelphia: Blakiston, 1877.
Rothman, D.J., *The Discovery of the Asylum: Social Order and Disorder in the New Republic*, Boston: Little, Brown, 1971.

cycloid psychoses   A variety of ACUTE RECOVERABLE PSYCHOSIS that is more often described in German psychiatry. It refers to a group of disorders that resemble an acute episode of PARANOID SCHIZOPHRENIA but with a periodic course that resembles major AFFECTIVE DISORDERS. However, they are neither fully schizophrenia or bipolar disorder. In Leonhard's original clinical description of the cycloid psychoses, he identified three major types, each of which was "bipolar" in nature: motility psychoses; confusion psychoses; and anxiety-elation psychoses. More recent comparisons of the cycloid psychoses with other mental disorders seems to relate them more closely to BIPOLAR DISORDER than to schizophrenia. (See also BORDERLINE SCHIZOPHRENIA.)

Fish, F.J., "The Cycloid Psychoses," *Comprehensive Psychiatry*, 5(1964) 155–169.
Leonhard, K., "Cycloid Psychoses—Endogenous Psychoses which Are Neither Schizophrenic nor Manic-depressive," *Journal of Mental Science*, 107(1961), 633.

cytogenetics   This is the area of specialization within genetics that is concerned with the study of the structure and function of the cell, and especially the study of the CHROMOSOMES.

D

Darwin's chair (or machine)   See CIRCULATING SWING.

daseinanalyse   Literally, the "analysis of existence," a method and mode of treatment formulated by Ludwig Binswanger (1881–1966) in the 1950s that was based on understanding the experiential structures of the inner worlds of mentally ill persons. Binswanger had worked at the BURGHÖLZLI HOSPITAL under Eugen Bleuler and C.G. Jung in the first years of the 20th century. He constructed this revision of Freud's psychoanalysis with the ideas of phenomenological philosophers Heidegger and Husserl. His emphasis on carefully describing the inner experiences of schizophrenics (the phenomenology of schizophrenic experience) had great influence on subsequent studies of the afflicted individual's experience of his or her own disease process. It influenced British psychiatry, in particular in the 1950s and 1960s and especially the work of R.D. LAING.

Binswanger thought that the experiential world of schizophrenics was characterized by four qualities:

1. A breakdown in the consistency of natural experience. To get out of this situation, they construct delusions to minimize the anxiety felt about the inner chaos and to reestablish order in the world.
2. A splitting-off of experiential consistency into rigid pairs of alternatives. The world is seen as good/bad, pure/evil, yes/no. These alternatives are often grandiose, inflated, "exaggerated ideals." When choices in the world are limited in this dualistic way, the schizophrenic cannot help but to sometimes fall into the darkness of making the negative choice, therefore viewing him- or herself only in terms of deficiency, imperfection or "sin."
3. A process of "covering." The schizophrenic tries to "cover-up" through thoughts, words and behaviors the awful negative aspect of existence (the *Dasein*, in Binswanger's terminology) that is unbearable to the schizophrenic. This naturally leads to an inflated notion of the preferred alternative for viewing existence.
4. An experience of existence as being "worn away," as though by friction. No longer can the person find a way in or out of his way of being, and this eventually fatigues him and leads to a renunication or resignation of the world, what Binswanger calls an "existential retreat."

In 1957, Binswanger published a series of five case histories of schizophrenics that he treated using his *daseinanalyse*. Despite a significant amount of interest in its philosophy and its phenomenological approach to clinical situations, daseinanalysis never was a widely accepted treatment for schizophrenics and is today an uncommon treatment mode in general.

Binswanger, L., *Schizophrenie*. Pfullingen: Gunther Neske Verlag, 1957.
———, *Being-in the-World: Selected Papers of Ludwig Binswanger*, tr. and ed. J. Needleman. New York: Basic Books, 1963.

day hospitals   An alternative to commitment to psychiatric institutions, day hospitals provide care for severely mentally ill people during the day, after which they are allowed to go home at night. This is generally viewed as a cheaper and more humane alternative to full-time care in institutions, which are usually the sponsors of such programs. A rarer version of this idea involves "night hospitals," where patients return at night after spending the day in a community setting. Both are forms of what is commonly referred to as "partial hospitalization." The earliest recorded operating day hospital was opened in the Soviet Union in the 1930s. It was not until 1946 that the movement began in Britain with the opening of a day hospital in London by a British psychiatrist by the name of Bierer. Day hospitals were introduced in North America in 1947 by Donald Cameron, a psychiatrist from McGill University in Montreal, Canada. (See also COMMUNITY MENTAL HEALTH CENTERS.)

Vaughan, P.J., "Developments in Psychiatric Day Care," *British Journal of Psychiatry*, 147 (1985), 1–4.

de Clerambault-Kandinsky syndrome
See CLERAMBAULT, GAETAN DE.

de Clerambault's syndrome   See EROTOMANIA.

defense mechanisms   A psychoanalytic term coined by Sigmund FREUD for those involuntary (and unconsciously produced) patterns of feelings, thoughts or behaviors that are automatically enacted to provide relief from perceived dangers. These dangers can arise from within the person or from without. They help keep out of awareness those conflicts that the ego finds threatening. In psychotic individuals, psychoanalytic theory holds that the most "primitive" (meaning, most "infantile") defenses are used, especially PROJECTION, DISSOCIATION and

ACTING-OUT. These defense mechanisms are generally designed to protect the person and enhance his survival, although some of them are almost always maladaptive. Positive defense mechanisms, indicative of the best functioning individuals, are humor and sublimation (the channeling of potentially sexual and aggressive "id impulses" into adaptive and socially-acceptable activities).

deficit symptoms/syndrome These are the primary, enduring NEGATIVE SYMPTOMS of schizophrenia that are not considered secondary to other factors (e.g., depression or anxiety, the effects of antipsychotic drugs, or the environmental deprivation found in institutions). These terms were first proposed in a 1985 paper by W.T. Carpenter and his colleagues on deficit and non-deficit forms of schizophrenia. They are intended as a clarification and an alternative to CROW'S HYPOTHESIS of "Type I" and "Type II" schizophrenia. In Crow's two subtypes, POSITIVE SYMPTOMS (such as delusions and hallucinations) predominate in Type I but can also appear on a transient basis in Type II schizophrenia. The negative symptoms in Type II schizophrenia (restricted affect, diminished social drive, anhedonia, diminished intellectual ability) can also be transient in some cases, due to the secondary factors listed above. Carpenter and his coworkers wish to more closely restrict the two proposed subtypes of schizophrenia to one displaying a "primary enduring core of deficit symptoms" and one that does not. This proposed diagnostic category of "schizophrenia with deficit syndrome" would then most clearly be related to the variety of the disease most associated with neurological deterioration and a chronic course. (See also ADD PSYCHOSIS; CHRONIC SCHIZOPHRENIA; COURSE OF SCHIZOPHRENIA.)

Carpenter, W.T., Heinrichs, D.W. and Wagman, A.M., "Deficit and Nondeficit Forms of Schizophrenia: The Concept," *American Journal of Psychiatry,* 145(1988), 578–583.

Defoe, Daniel (1661–1736) Best remembered as the author of *Robinson Crusoe* (1719), Defoe was prolific writer and social critic who took a particularly keen interest in the humane treatment of the mentally ill. He wrote many articles on the abusive conditions in private madhouses, arguing that they should be inspected and licensed, which they eventually were. He published his own journal, known as the *Review,* and from time to time included articles of his own with themes like the 1706 "Scheme for the Management of Mad-houses."

degeneration The progressive deterioration of mental functioning to a chronically impaired state. The concept was first put forth in psychiatry by Benedict Augustin MOREL in 1857 and was very influential in describing certain disease patterns, including DEMENTIA PRAECOX *(démence précoce),* a term that Morel coined and used as early as 1852. Degenerations were thought to be hereditarily transmitted and to progressively worsen until resulting in death. There was no stopping this degenerative process, and, once developed, a person's fate was thought to be sealed. Morel outlined a series of "stigmata of degeneration" to be found in the mentally ill, signs of physical malformations and intellectual and moral abnormalities. Besides the cases of dementia praecox, degeneration was characteristic of the phenomenon, found in people in mental institutions in the 18th and 19th centuries, called the GENERAL PARALYSIS OF THE INSANE, a condition that was later found to be the result of syphilis. Morel also believed that toxic substances, such as alcohol or narcotics, could also lead to degeneration in an individual, and dependency on these substances would lead to the hereditary transmission of this susceptibility to degeneration.

Genil-Perrin, G., *Historie des origines et de l'évolution de l'idée de dégénérescence en médecine mentale.* Paris: 1913.

Morel, B.A., *Traité des dégénérescences physiques, intellectuelles et morales de l'espèce humaine.* Paris: 1857.

deinstitutionalization With the advent of ANTIPSYCHOTIC DRUGS in the mid-1950s, and with the growing concern over the costs of institutionalizing large numbers of people and the harmful effects such living conditions might have, starting in 1955 literally hundreds of thousands of psychiatric patients were released—all too often to the streets—with little or no support services available to them. In 1955 there were approximately 559,000 patients in public psychiatric facilities in the United States, but by the mid-1980s that number had dwindled to about 110,000. The greatest number were released between 1965 and 1980, when an estimated 358,000 patients were sent back into the community to live. This process, although initially well-intentioned, led to the alarming problem of the homeless mentally ill, the "street people," that characterizes the last quarter of the 20th century.

Talbott, J.A., "Deinstitutionalization: Avoiding the Disasters of the Past," *Hospital and Community Psychiatry,* 30(1979) 621–624.

Torrey, E.F., *Nowhere To Go: The Tragic Odyssey of the Homeless Mentally Ill,* New York: Harper/Perennial, 1989.

délire de négation See COTARD'S SYNDROME.

délire d' énormité Literally the "delusion of enormity," a psychotic delusion that a person has undergone a massive increase in size. Such a person may insist that he or she fills up the entire room or is as large as the Earth or perhaps even the entire universe. In some cases it has been known to alternate with COTARD'S SYNDROME (the "delusion of negation"), and in fact it has been referred to as a "manic" form of Cotard's syndrome.

Enoch, M.D. and Trethowan, W.H., "Cotard's Syndrome," in Enoch and Trethowan (eds.),

Uncommon Psychiatric Syndromes, 2nd ed. Bristol: John Wright & Sons, 1979.

delirium An acute, reversible mental state characterized by clouded consciousness, confusion, extreme mental and motor excitement, defective perception, impaired memory and a rapid flow of disconnected ideas. Delusions and hallucinations can accompany delirious states. Delirium is a symptom of an organic brain disorder, for it has a physiological basis (fevers, toxic effects from drugs or alcohol, exhaustion, etc.). Delirium is reversible, which distinguishes it from dementia, which is not.

From the time of Ancient Greece and Rome, "delirium" has referred to a disturbance in the train of thinking, associated with physical disease. In 19th-century France the term began to be used in reference to such a disturbance in thinking but without any connection to physical disease. For example Philippe PINEL uses the term *délire* to refer both to disturbances in logical reasoning and judgment (delusions) as well as to organic brain disease. In Great Britain and Germany the distinction between "delusion" and "delirium" was largely maintained throughout the 19th century and is the basis of our modern definitions of these terms.

Berrios, G.E., "Delirium and Confusion in the 19th Century: A Conceptual History," *British Journal of Psychiatry,* 139(1981) 439–449.

delusion Historically, one of the primary symptoms of a psychotic disorder. The German philosopher Karl Jaspers states that, "Since time immemorial Delusion has been taken as the basic characteristic of madness." Although there is disagreement in the many different theories and definitions of what exactly a delusion is, a delusion is defined by DSM-III-R as "a false personal belief based on incorrect inference about external reality" and is firmly maintained despite the consensually accepted beliefs of most others. Individuals with delusions will generally hold on to their beliefs even when confronted with strong evidence that contradicts their beliefs. In this sense, delusions are said to be "fixed," as if unchangeably cemented into the mind. Delusions are sometimes referred to as "ideational symptoms," because they involve a disturbance in ideas or cognition, whereas HALLUCINATIONS are sometimes called "perceptual" or "sensational symptoms," since they represent a disturbance in the processes of sensation and perception.

The first use of the word "delusion" in the English language in reference to mental disorder was in 1552, and the word's derivation can be traced back to a form of the Latin verb meaning "to play false." In Great Britain in the first half of the 19th century, the word "delusion" was used in a medical sense to refer to perceptual disorders (similar to our present use of the word "illusion"), but after 1850 it appears to have taken on its present meaning of "wrong belief." (See also DELIRIUM.)

Arthur, A.Z., "Theories and Explanations of Delusions: A Review," *American Journal of Psychiatry*, 121(1964), 105–115.

Garety, P., "Delusions: Problems in Definition and Measurement," *British Journal of Medical Psychology*, 58(1985), 25–34.

Schmidt, G., "A Review of the German Literature on Delusion Between 1914 and 1939," in J. Cutting and M. Shepherd (eds.), *The Clinical Roots of the Schizophrenia Concept*. Cambridge: Cambridge University Press, 1987.

delusional disorder A new classification of psychotic disorder that first appears in the 1987 DSM-III-R. The essential characteristic of delusional disorder is the persistent presence of a delusion that is not "bizarre" and is not due to any other psychotic disorder (such as schizophrenia, schizophreniform disorder or a mood disorder such as bipolar illness). Persons with this disorder do not have obviously odd or peculiar behavior. As *DSM-III-R* states, "A common characteristic of people with Delusional Disorder is the apparent normality of their behavior and appearance when their delusional ideas are not being discussed or acted upon." Yet they secretly (or in some cases, not so secretly) harbor a delusion that profoundly disagrees with reality. Formerly, this type of disorder was called paranoid disorder, but there are many different types of delusions that have nothing to do with "paranoia" (which is commonly interpreted as unfounded suspiciousness). The disorder rarely causes interruptions in intellectual or occupational functioning, and in most studies the average age of onset seems to be between 40 and 55.

There are six different subtypes of delusional disorder: erotomanic (more traditionally known as de Clerambault's syndrome), in which the delusion is that another person, usually of a higher social status, is in love with the subject; the grandiose, in which a person is convinced that he or she is "special" due to an inflated sense of power, identity, wealth or special relationship to a deity or a special person (such as a celebrity); the jealous, in which the delusion is that one's sexual partner is unfaithful; the persecutory, in which the delusion involves a convincing belief that one is being purposely maligned or singled out for harassment in some way; the somatic, in which the person is convinced that he or she has some disease, mental disorder or physical defect; and finally, a category of unspecified type, for other, less common types of delusion. (See also EROTOMANIA; PARANOIA.)

delusional jealousy The false belief that one's sexual partner is engaging in sexual activities with others. This delusion of infidelity is also known as the OTHELLO SYNDROME. Delusional jealousy is considered a psychotic disorder, whereas "obsessional jealousy" is the term used for persons with neurotic disorders.

delusional perception A term for a phenomenon noticed in certain psychotic disorders in which the distinction between a

DELUSION and an HALLUCINATION is not clear. It almost appears as if those individuals who are delusional are also caught in a process that changes their perceptual processes. Thus, when asked about their experiences, it is often difficult to distinguish whether the events described are simply delusions (bizarre ideas) or actual hallucinatory experiences that were "perceived" with the senses. This term (also called "perceptual delusions") is more often described in the German and French psychiatric literature than in the English-language literature.

Matussek, P., "Studies in Delusional Perception," in J. Cutting and M. Shepherd (eds.), *The Clinical Roots of the Schizophrenia Concept: Translations of Seminal European Contributions On Schizophrenia.* Cambridge: Cambridge University Press, 1987.

delusions, bizarre A totally implausible idea or belief that is idiosyncratic and would not be believed as true by anyone. For example, a psychotic individual may believe that singer Diana Ross is the "Antichrist" or that singer Madonna is the Biblical "Whore of Babylon."

delusions, grandiose A common psychotic delusion found particularly in paranoid schizophrenia and in manic-depressive psychosis, in which a person has a highly exaggerated sense of his or her importance, identity, knowledge or influence. For example, a psychotic individual may claim to own IBM and generously offer to write a hospital staff member a check for $5 million if they would only help that person escape or be discharged from the hospital. Many religious delusions are grandiose (e.g., "I'm Jesus Christ").

delusions, mood-congruent A delusion whose content matches the particular manic or depressed mood state that a person is in. For example, the delusion that one has AIDS or cancer when, in fact, one does not is consistent with a depressed mood in an individual. If in a manic mood state, grandiose delusions in particular may be mood-congruent (e.g., claims of owning millions of dollars or of being the most brilliant writer in the world).

delusions, mood-incongruent A delusion whose content does not match the particular mood state that a person is experiencing. These are the opposite of MOOD-CONGRUENT DELUSIONS.

delusions, nihilistic Commonly found in schizophrenia, these delusions involve the conviction that one does not exist, or that external reality does not exist. This is also referred to as COTARD'S SYNDROME.

delusions, persecutory One of the most common types of delusion found in paranoid schizophrenia, and occasionally in other psychotic disorders as well. It is the delusion that the psychotic individual is being singled out, and even pursued for special abuse, by persons or "forces," and that this places the mentally disordered person in a constant state of danger. Delusions of being poisoned are common. Although known since antiquity, and included in Esquirol's descriptions of "monomania," the earliest comprehensive treatment of persecutory delusions was perhaps given by German psychiatrist Carl Wilhelm Ideler (1795–1860) in 1848. These delusions were also referred to as "persecutory delirium" by French psychiatrist Charles Lesèques in 1852.

Ideler, C.W., *Der Wahnsinn*, Bremen: 1848.

delusions, somatic A delusional belief about the structure of functioning of one's body. For example, a male schizophrenic patient may fully believe that he is pregnant, or a psychotic woman may believe that a team of doctors kidnapped her during the night and removed her uterus and genitalia.

delusions, systematized An organized system of delusions that all refer to a similar theme and that form the basis for a psychotic individual's incorrect interpretion of new experiences. For example, a psychotic person who has failed a psychology licensing examination may believe that the members of the licensing board in that state are involved in a conspiracy against the afflicted person and, furthermore, that these board members are responsible for the person's inability to find a parking space.

delusions of being controlled One of the most common types of delusion found in schizophrenia, it involves the idea that a person's thought, feeling and behavior are controlled by some external force (e.g., "Kate Kelley is controlling my thoughts"). This is also known as the de Clerambault-Kandinsky Syndrome. (See also CLERAMBAULT, GAETAN DE.)

delusions of passion See EROTOMANIA.

delusions of poverty The delusion that a person is totally devoid of any material possessions, or that such possessions will soon be taken away from the person, rendering him or her poverty-stricken.

delusions of reference The delusions that people, objects or events in an individual's immediate environment have an unusual or "special" significance. This significance is usually of a negative or threatening quality, but not always. For example, a psychotic individual may believe that the expression on television newsman Dan Rather's face is a secret message that is intended just for that person.

demence A term used by both Philippe PINEL in 1801 and Benjamin RUSH in 1812 to describe what we would now call THOUGHT DISORDER—disconnected and disorganized thoughts that are strung together without any logical order. Pinel describes the "special character of dementia" that is still observed in schizophrenics today:

Rapid succession or uninterrupted alternation of indulated ideas, and evanescent and unconnected emotions. Continually repeated acts of extravagance; complete forgetfulness of every previous state; diminished sensibility to external impressions; abolition of the faculty of judgment; perceptual activity.

Benjamin Rush preferred to rename this condition "Dissociation," as he believed that this constituted its primary symptom. However, Rush's use of this term is different than the more commonly accepted definition of DISSOCIATION by Janet. Dissociation was "an association of unrelated perceptions, or ideas, from the inability of the mind to perform the operations of judgement and reason." Furthermore, "ideas, collected together without order, frequently constitute a paroxysm of the disease." Rush's emphasis on ASSOCIATION DISTURBANCES was later also emphasized by Eugen BLEULER in 1911 as one of the four PRIMARY SYMPTOMS OF SCHIZOPHRENIA.

Pinel, P., *A Treatise On Insanity* Sheffield: W. Todd, 1806; first published, 1801.
Rush, B., *Medical Inquiries and Observations Upon Diseases of the Mind*. Philadelphia: Kimber & Richardson, 1812.

dementia In its present definition, dementia is an ORGANIC MENTAL SYNDROME that is characterized by impairment in short- and long-term memory, disturbances in the ability to think abstractly, impaired judgment and personality changes; there is also evidence of other abnormal brain functioning. In personality changes, a person may not seem him- or herself, may become withdrawn, and a once lively personality may become flat. A once neat person may start to appear sloppy and apathetic. When social judgment is impaired by the organic brain disease process that produced the dementia, some people may become irritable, impulsive or paranoid. They may wander about and become lost. Alzheimer's disease (primary degenerative dementia of the Alzheimer's type) is the picture of extreme dementia that most of us are familiar with.

According to modern definition, dementia may not necessarily be progressively degenerative, and actually may go into remission in some circumstances (as, for example, when chronic alcoholics remain abstinent for six months to a year or more). However, in the 19th century the older idea of dementia was that it referred to chronic insanity or that it was a progressively degenerative brain disease that led to death (see DEGENERATION). With advances in the science of neurology in the second half of the 19th century, specific chronic brain disorders were identified that involved dementia, although conditions that could not be conclusively identified as "organic" were also recognized as "vesanic dementias." The idea of vesanic dementias contributed to the formation of the idea of PSYCHOSIS in the latter half of the 19th century.

Berrios, G.E., "Dementia during the 17th and 18th Centuries," *Psychological Medicine,* 1987.

dementia infantalis   A term first used in 1930 by Austrian psychiatrist Theodore Heller to describe CHILDHOOD SCHIZOPHRENIA. He thought that dementia infantalis was present in children before the age of four. It is sometimes referred to as "Heller's disease." (See also AUTISM, INFANTILE.)

dementia paralytica   See GENERAL PARALYSIS OF THE INSANE.

dementia paranoides   Another term for the paranoid type of Kraepelin's DEMENTIA PRAECOX. Sigmund FREUD's famous interpretation of the autobiography of the psychotic Daniel Paul Schreber, formerly a presiding judge on Saxony's highest court, is where this term figures most prominenty in his writings. Since Schreber was a homosexual, this helped support Freud's theory that homosexual panic was at the root of

paranoia. (See also PARANOID SCHIZOPHRENIA.)

Freud, S., "Psycho-analytic Notes on an Autobiographical Account of a Case of Paranoia (Dementia Paranoides)," in J. Strachey (ed.), *The Standard Edition of the Complete Psychological Works of Sigmund Freud.* New York: Macmillan, 1964, first published, 1911.

dementia praecocissima   This term was first used in 1905 by Italian psychiatrist Sante De Sanctis (1862–1935) to describe a form of dementia praecox that had its onset before puberty. De Sanctis is generally credited for being the first to describe what later became known as CHILDHOOD SCHIZOPHRENIA.

De Sanctis, S., "On Some Varieties of Dementia Praecox," tr. M. Osborn, in J.G. Howells (ed.), *Modern Perspectives in International Child Psychiatry.* Edinburgh: Oliver & Boyd, 1969; first published, 1906.
———, *Neuropsichiatria infantile. Patalogia e diagnostica.* Turin: Lattes, 1925.

dementia praecox   A term that referred to a mental disorder marked by rapid mental disintegration (the original meaning of the term) or an "early" or presenile "degeneration." It was thus a term to describe the type of dementia in younger individuals that is usually found in very old or brain-damaged individuals. Benedict Augustin Morel coined the term and used it in his writings in 1852 as *démence précoce* in his *Etudes cliniques.* In the 1896 fifth edition of his often revised textbook, *Psychiatrie,* Emil KRAEPELIN used this term for the first time to describe the progressively degenerative mental disorder—dementia praecox—that was comprised of three distant disorders described by previous psychiatric authorities: CATATONIA (named by German psychiatrist Karl Ludwig Kahlbaum in 1869, first written about in 1874); HEBEPHRENIA (described by Kahlbaum's student, Ewald Hecker, in 1871); and PARANOIA, an ancient term for a disorder known to Hippocrates. In 1903 a fourth subtype, dementia simplex, was added by psychiatrist Otto Diem. These four subtypes are, with minor revisions, still in use in the most widely accepted diagnostic manual today, DSM-III-R (1987) to describe schizophrenia.

Kraeplin's very first description of dementia praecox from 1896 (translated into English only in 1987) is as follows:

Dementia praecox is the name I have given to the development of a simple, fairly high-grade state of mental impairment accompanied by an acute or subacute mental disturbance.

Kraepelin asserted that dementia praecox began in late adolescence or early adulthood, and that half of his cases (in the 1896, initial description) first became ill between the ages of 16 and 22. He felt that the disease was due not only to "heredity," but that it was also a brain disease because of a "tangible morbid process occurring in the brain." Most importantly, Kraepelin viewed the disease as progressively degenerative with almost no chance of recovery or significant improvement. Although Eugen BLEULER described the same four subtypes of dementia praecox in his 1911 book, *Dementia Praecox, or the Group of Schizophrenias,* his notion of SCHIZOPHRENIA differed from Kraepelin's "dementia praecox" in that he did not agree with Kraepelin's fatalistic view of poor prognosis. Bleuler first used the term "schizophrenia" and differentiated it from Kraepelin's concept in an article published in 1908. (See also DEGENERATION.)

Diem, O., "Die einfach demente Form der Dementia praecox," *Archiv für Psychiatrie und Nervenkrankheiten,* 37(1903), 111–187

Hecker, E., "Die Hebephrenie," *Virchows Archiv für pathologische Anatomie,* 52(1871), 392–449.

Kahlbaum, K., *Die Katatonie oder das Spannungsirresein,* Berlin: Hirschwald, 1874.

Kraepelin, E., "Dementia praecox," in J. Cutting and M. Shepherd (eds.), *The Clinical*

Roots of the Schizophrenia Concept: Translations of Seminal European Contributions On Schizophrenia. Cambridge: Cambridge University Press, 1987; first published, 1896 (5th ed.).

Wender, P., "Dementia Praecox: The Development of the Concept," *American Journal of Psychiatry,* 119(1963) 1143–1151.

demoniac   A person who is "possessed" by demons or evil spirits. In all cultures, whether simple or complex and technological, there is usually a belief that mental illness was caused by such discarnate entities. (See also CACODEMONOMANIA; POSSESSION SYNDROME.)

demonomania   A 19th-century term for a type of mental disorder in which a person believes his or her thoughts, feelings or behaviors are due to the direct influence of, or communication with, "spiritual" entities. ESQUIROL devoted an entire chapter to this disorder in his 1838 *Mental Maladies,* which he said is comprised of "all those forms of delirium which have reference to religious beliefs." He identifies two distinct subtypes of demonomania, depending on whether the person believes he or she is influenced by "good" or "bad" spirits. The first of these, *theomania,* "would have designated that class of the insane, who believe that they are God, who imagine that they have conversations and intimate communications with the Holy spirit, angels and saints, and who pretend to be inspired, and to have received a commission from heaven to convert men." The second type of demonomania, CACODEMONOMANIA, involves such imagined contact with evil spirits or the Devil. Esquirol uses the word "demonomania" to refer to both "good" and "evil" spiritual influences rather than just evil ones since, as he correctly points out, "The word demon among the ancients was not understood in a bad sense. It signified the Divinity, a tutelary Genius, a guardian Spirit . . ." Esquirol suggests he is thus "preserving the primitive significance of this word." (See also POSSESSION SYNDROME.)

Esquirol, J.E.D., *Mental Maladies, A Treatise On Insanity,* tr. E.K. Hunt. Philadelphia: Lea & Blanchard, 1845; first published, 1838.

Noll, R. *Vampires, Werewolves, and Demons: Twentieth Century Reports In The Psychiatric Literature,* New York: Brunner/Mazel, 1991.

denial   A type of DEFENSE MECHANISM in which a person does not seem to be aware of some aspect of external reality or of himself that is obvious to others. This type of behavior is commonly observed in people with psychotic disorders, and in its extreme forms denial can give an individual's statements an almost delusional quality. (See also DELUSION.)

Denis, Jean Baptiste (1643–1704)   A French physician who is credited with performing the first BLOOD TRANSFUSION treatment for mental illness in 1667. He replaced some of the blood of a psychotic man with calf's blood. The patient improved and was less excitable only a day or so later, but died shortly thereafter. Nonetheless, Denis was recognized all over Europe for his "scientific" achievement, and blood transfusions were afterwards performed on the mentally ill in many other countries, particularly England.

Denmark   See SCANDINAVIA.

depersonalization   An aberration of the sense or experience of oneself in which the feeling of the "reality" of one's experience is missing. People experiencing depersonalization claim that they feel distant from their own experience, that it is "dreamlike," or that reality has an uncanny "strangeness" to it. They may feel that they are automatons, or that their experience is "automatic" and not "spontaneous" in any way. Feelings that one's extremities have

changed in size sometimes accompany this syndrome. Depersonalization can occur in normals for temporary periods of time (particularly in adolescents, with estimates that as many as 70% of them experience it at one time or another), but it is also experienced by those individuals who are diagnosed with schizotypal personality disorder, schizophrenia or, when not psychotic, depersonalization disorder, which is one of the DISSOCIATIVE DISORDERS.

depression   When depression is present in an individual afflicted with one of the psychotic disorders it is considered a dangerous sign. Suicide is far more likely to result from depression in psychotic individuals. Indeed, about 10% of all individuals with BIPOLAR DISORDER (manic-depressive psychosis) and an equal amount of those diagnosed as schizophrenic commit suicide. Studies have shown that for schizophrenia, an individual is most likely to commit suicide within the first 10 years of the onset of the disease.

Depression has always been a feature of AFFECTIVE DISORDERS such as bipolar disorder, in some of its forms (mania and manic episodes in various patterns are more characteristic of it), but there has been more recognition that many people who are diagnosed with schizophrenia suffer from depression. This depression may be caused by the underlying schizophrenic disease process, the realization by the person that his or her mental capacities are deteriorating, or as a side effect of antipsychotic medication. Many schizophrenics are thus also given ANTIDEPRESSANT DRUGS along with their antipsychotic medication. Sometimes people who are suffering from a severe depression can hear auditory hallucinations and, in many ways, appear to be schizophrenic. However, clinicians must make the sometimes difficult differential diagnosis between this depression with psychotic features and true schizophrenia. An excellent review of the research on depression and schizophrenia is found in a 1990 book edited by Lynn DeLisi. (See also ANTIPSYCHOTIC DRUGS.)

Breier, A. and Astrachan, B.M., "Characterization of Schizophrenic Patients who Commit Suicide," *American Journal of Psychiatry,* 141 (1984), 206–209.
DeLisi, L.E., *Depression in Schizophrenia.* Washington, D.C.: American Psychiatric Press, 1990.
Roy, A., "Depression, Attempted Suicide, and Suicide in Patients with Chronic Schizophrenia," *Psychiatric Clinics of North America,* 9 (1986), 193–206.

derealization   This is the component of DEPERSONALIZATION in which one's sense of the reality of one's world is disturbed. Depersonalization includes alterations in the sense of identity (e.g., the feeling of being an automaton), in addition to derealization.

dereistic thinking   A word coined by Eugen BLEULER in 1912 to describe a type of intense fantasy activity that totally ignores any contradictions with reality and that may seem quite realistic. Bleuler constructed the term "dereistic" from two Latin words meaning "away from reality." Dereistic thinking sometimes occurs in the daydreams of normal people, but it is found in its clearest (and most reality-free) forms in dreams, the hallucinations and delusions of schizophrenics, and in mythology. Bleuler's concept of dereistic thinking resembles a similar process later referred to by his colleague at the BURGHÖLZLI HOSPITAL in Zurich, C.G. JUNG, as "active imagination." Dereistic thinking also resembles the descriptions of REGRESSION or of "regression in the service of the ego" by Sigmund FREUD and his followers.

Bleuler, E. *Textbook of Psychiatry,* 4th ed., A.A. Brill. New York: Macmillan, 1924.

De Sanctis, Sante (1862–1935)   An Italian physician and a professor of psychiatry at the University of Rome who is perhaps best remembered for his 1905 description of DEMENTIA PRAECOCISSIMA, a childhood form of dementia praecox. He wrote on a wide variety of topics, including dreams, experimental psychiatry and forensic psychiatry. In 1932, he published an autobiography of his life and career in psychiatry.

deteriorating psychoses   A 19th-century term for psychotic disorders marked by their DEGENERATION, such as dementia praecox.

diagnosis, differential   One of the most important determinants of treatment is the diagnosis of the disorder. This is extremely important when it comes to severe mental disorders such as schizophrenia or bipolar disorder, which often require different classes of drugs and which have different courses. Often one of the first diagnostic decisions that a clinician must make is whether the patient is psychotic (out of touch with reality) or not. If so, then: Are the symptoms due to one of the psychotic disorders, or are they due to an organic mental disorder (such as an underlying neurological disease or intoxication)? If a known organic brain disease, or intoxication, can be ruled out, then the clinician must decide which among the various psychotic disorders best fits the history of the person's illness and the types of symptoms that person is displaying. Often a difficult differential diagnosis must be made between schizophrenia (particularly the paranoid subtype) and the manic psychosis in bipolar disorder.

The two most commonly used diagnostic system are the American Psychiatric Association's DSM-III-R (1987) and the World Health Organization's ICD-9 (1978).

American Psychiatric Association, *Diagnostic and Statistical Manual of Mental Disorders,* third edition, revised. Washington, D.C.: American Psychiatric Association, 1987.

World Health Organization, *Mental Disorders: Glossary and Guide to Their Classification in Accordance with the Ninth Revision of the International Classification of Diseases* Geneva, Switzerland: World Health Organization, 1978.

diathesis-stress theories   One of the main categories of genetic theories of schizophrenia. Diathesis-stress theories all posit that it is the interaction between genetic heritage (the "diathesis" or "inherited predisposition," which places the person at "high-risk" for the development of the disease) and stressors in the environment that causes the disease. Diathesis-stress theories are polygenetic ones. The diathesis is often assumed to involve the additive effect of the operation of a large number of genes, sometimes called "schizophrenic polygenes." These theories hold that the more schizophrenic polygenes an individual inherits, the more vulnerable that person is to stressors in the environment that can induce the onset of schizophrenia.

A famous theory of the diathesis-stress causes of schizophrenia was put forth by clinical psychologist Paul Meehl in 1962. Meehl proposed that a genetic predisposition for particular kinds of neurological defects, which he called schizotaxia, must interact with the experiences of environmental social learning to produce a type of person that may be called a schizotype. If the schizotype is subjected to certain stressors that are severe enough, that person will develop schizophrenia. Meehl's theory fits in with the other polygenetic diathesis-stress theories because it accounts for the interaction of heredity and the environment in the production of schizophrenia, and it allows for a wide range of schizophrenia-like disorders that the schizotype can exhibit without experiencing the extreme stressors that could cause schizophrenia. Furthermore, it assumes that the environment may be the source of the development of one over the other type of schizophrenic subtype.

Diathesis-stress theories based on polygenetic assumptions are still among the most widely accepted theories with researchers who are trying to learn the causes of severe mental disorders such as schizophrenia and bipolar disorder. These theories are the latest battleground in the long-standing "nature vs. nurture debate" in science. Yet, with increases in our knowledge of the causes of diseases, it is becoming clearer and clearer that the nature-nurture distinction is becoming more and more blurred. Epidemiologist Brian McMahon succinctly lists the problems in understanding the complexity of gene-environment interactions:

1. It has become clear that there is no disease that is determined entirely by genetic or environmental factors.
2. There is, evidently, more overlap in the time of operation of genetic and environmental factors than was previously suspected.
3. Just as the environment may exert its effect through the genetic mechanism of mutation, so may genetic factors operate by changing the environment.
4. The roles of gene and environment, and the nature of the specific factors involved, may be quite different in individuals with identical manifestations.

(See also HIGH-RISK STUDIES; GENETIC TRANSMISSION.)

MacMahon, B., "Gene-environment Interaction in Human Disease," in D. Rosenthal and S. Kety (eds.), *The Transmission of Schizophrenia*. Oxford: Pergamon Press, 1968.
Meehl, P., "Schizotaxia, Schizotypy, Schizophrenia," *American Psychologist*, 17(1962), 827–828.

dibenzodiazepine   A class of ANTIPSYCHOTIC DRUGS, of which the drug CLOZAPINE is its best known member.

dibenzoxazepine   A class of ANTIPSYCHOTIC DRUGS. The most widely known member is the drug loxapine (trade names Daxolin, Loxitane).

dihydroindolone A class of ANTIPSY-CHOTIC DRUGS. Molindone (trade names Lidone, Moban) is the best known member.

diminished responsibility A legal term in England that has been used since the 13th century as an argument to plea the innocence of mentally ill offenders. Prior to this time insanity was viewed as an affliction from God to punish sinfulness, and therefore criminal activities by such individuals were not viewed with compassion. The concept of "guilty, but insane" was introduced only in 1843. (See also INSANITY DEFENSE; M'NAUGHTEN RULES.)

direct analysis A technique developed by psychiatrist John Rosen in 1946 for the psychoanalysis of people with psychotic disorders. The term "direct analysis" was originally suggested to Rosen by psychoanalyst Paul Federn. Rosen argued that many psychotic individuals, especially those in institutions, cannot be expected to follow the structure of classical psychoanalytic treatment (e.g., lying on a couch for a 50-minute session, understanding the silence of the analyst). Therefore, less formal, or "direct," approaches were deemed necessary for the treatment of psychotics by Rosen. By making "direct interpretations" of the patient's speech or behavior, Rosen thought he was "talking directly to the unconscious" of the patient.

Rosen's direct analysis assumed that psychotics were under the domination of the unconscious and were reduced to an infantile state and, as such, were "fixated" at the "oral stage." This is in opposition to neurotics, who were more advanced and whose mental illness was caused by conflicts arising from the "Oedipus complex" of the "genital stage" of psychosexual development. To cure the psychotic patient, Rosen suggested that direct interpretations should be phrased using infantile "oral" themes, particularly those feelings regarding the mother's breast. Rosen states that, "Psychotics live imme-diately under the shadow of the breast. This is able to tell us two things: first, the presenting aspect of their psychologic life is again the earliest infancy, and second, the nature of the breast upon whom they are so dependent threatens their life."

Rosen believed that psychotic disorders are psychogenic in origin and that psychological techniques could cure them. Although his unorthodox methods attracted wide attention in the 1940s and 1950s and were replicated by some, they seem rather bizarre by today's standards. Neurophysiological theories of the causes of psychotic disorders predominate in the 1990s, whereas psychoanalysis—the dominant theory for the causes and treatment of mental illness in Rosen's day—is almost never utilized for the treatment of these serious disorders. A graphic example of Rosen's idiosyncratic techniques is given in his summary of a female patient's behaviors and his direct interpretations of them in the following case history included in his book, *Direct Analysis* (1953):

A young female patient was brought to my office after many sleepless psychotic nights. She was hallucinating actively, and asked, "What will happen when they discover what I have stolen?" I replied, *"If your mother wouldn't give it to you, you had a perfect right to steal it."* Here again, the genital interpretation would have been, "You have no penis. You have to steal one." But the emphasis that had to be made in this case was that she had to find a way to surmount her mother's ungiving nature (breast). Later we were able to say, *"In struggling to gain mother's love and protection, you stole what you didn't have—something symbolizing a penis, hoping that possessing a penis, perhaps mother would love you."* The patient actually was a kleptomaniac before she became psychotic. During the analytic phase of her therapy, she came to understand that she wished to steal not because of penis envy, but because if she had a penis then perhaps mother would love her.

In the late 1950s, Rosen founded the Institute for Direct Analysis in Philadelphia, Pennsylvania, where he treated individual patients with the use of assistant therapists. His later theories and techniques of direct analysis were reported in a second book in 1962.

Rosen, J., *Direct Analysis: Selected Papers*. New York: Grune & Stratton, 1953.

————, *Direct Psychoanalytic Psychiatry*. New York: Grune & Stratton, 1962.

disintegrative psychosis The current diagnostic label in ICD-9 for Heller's syndrome, or DEMENTIA INFANTALIS. It is a psychotic disorder of childhood that is generally considered to be a form of CHILDHOOD SCHIZOPHRENIA. (See also AUTISM, INFANTILE; HELLER'S DISEASE.)

disorganized type Still regarded in diagnostic manuals as one of the four major subtypes of schizophrenia. The disorganized type is one of the three nonparanoid subtypes of schizophrenia according to DSM-III-R, and it is one of the most familiar forms of schizophrenia. Incoherence, very disorganized behavior, an obvious LOOSENING OF ASSOCIATIONS, and FLAT AFFECT are the main characteristics of people afflicted with this subtype. Sometimes there can be a "silliness" to them, including giggling, strange mannerisms, frequent hypochondriacal complaints and perhaps unusual facial expressions (such as grimaces) or other odd behavior. There may be delusions and hallucinations, but they appear disconnected, fragmented and grossly illogical.

This subtype of schizophrenia was named HEBEPHRENIA by Ewald Hecker in 1871 and was included as one of the three original subtypes of DEMENTIA PRAECOX by Emil KRAEPELIN in 1896. It is still called the "Hebephrenic Type" by the World Health Organization's ICD-9 (1978).

The disorganized subtype is the one that most clearly matches the picture of the type of schizophrenia with an insidious onset and a chronic course with rare episodes of remission. NEGATIVE SYMPTOMS (constricted emotional range and intellectual abilities, poverty of speech, poverty of content of speech, etc.) seem to predominate over POSITIVE SYMPTOMS (delusions and hallucinations) in this subtype, especially in its later stages. It is the subtype of schizophrenia that is probably most similar to schizophrenia research findings on the types of schizophrenia that most closely resemble a degenerative brain disease, such as CHRONIC SCHIZOPHRENIA or "Type II schizophrenia" as defined by CROW'S HYPOTHESIS. (See also BRAIN ABNORMALITIES IN SCHIZOPHRENIA.)

disorientation This is the clinical term most often used for people who have an obvious organic mental disorder (such as DELIRIUM or DEMENTIA) who are confused about who they are, where they are or what day of the week, month or even year it is. A common shorthand notation for this, often seen in clinical progress notes, is "disoriented × 3" (i.e., disoriented in three spheres of normal experience).

dissociation This is literally a splitting of the normally coherent and integrated functions of consciousness, particularly identity and memory. It is the defining characteristic of the DISSOCIATIVE DISORDERS, which include multiple personality disorder, psychogenic fugue, psychogenic amnesia and depersonalization disorder.

The concept of dissociation was apparently introduced by French alienist J.J. Moreau de Tours in 1845. Pierre JANET (1859–1947) provided the first extensive psychological elaboration of this concept in his classic work, *L'Automatisme Psychologique,* in 1889 to describe systems of associated ideas that have been split off from consciousness and exist in a parallel life along with the dominant stream of consciousness. Janet referred to dissociation as *"dèsagrègation."* As this "disaggregation" or "dissociation" (as became the customary translation and use of this word in English) strengthens around its thematic core, referred to by Janet as "subconscious fixed ideas," the gap between these parallel streams of consciousness are widened and *existences* secondes, or "secondary existences," are then created. Janet felt that this was a pathological—not a normal—psychological process, and was to be found in hysteria, hypnosis and in instances of "dual consciousness" or multiple personality.

Joseph Breuer (1842–1925) and Sigmund Freud (1856–1939) also contributed to the study of dissociative phenomena with their interpretation of the famous case of "Anna O." reported in 1895 in their book, *Studies On Hysteria.* Anna O. was treated by Breuer from 1880 to 1882 for a series of psychosomatic problems and peculiar dissociative *absences.* However, Breuer and Freud disagreed as to the fundamental nature of these *absences,* with Breuer interpreting these phenomena as a form of "autohypnosis" and Freud insisting that their basic reason for existing was to serve as a DEFENSE MECHANISM. It is Freud's basic claim that has been accepted by generations of clinicians, although Breuer's autohypnotic hypothesis has been resurrected recently as a major factor in the early childhood creation of multiple personalities. Only Swiss psychoanalyst and psychiatrist C.G. Jung (1875–1961) seems to have included a nonpathological interpretation of dissociation as a major part of his psychological theories. (See also COMPLEX; MULTIPLE PERSONALITY.)

Bliss, E.L., "A Reexamination of Freud's Basic Concepts from Studies of Multiple Personality Disorder," *Dissociation,* 1(1988), 36–40.
Moreau de Tours, J.J., *Du hachisch et de l'aliénation mentale: Etudes psychologiques.* Paris: Fortin, Masson, & Cie, 1845.
Noll, R., "Multiple Personality, Dissociation, and C.G. Jung's Complex Theory," *Journal of Analytical Psychology,* 34(1989), 353–370.
van der Hart, O. and B. Friedman., "A Reader's Guide to Pierre Janet on Dissociation: A Neglected Intellectual Heritage," *Dissociation,* 2(1989), 3–16.

dissociative disorders A category of mental disorders first created in 1980 in DSM-III-R whose primary symptom is DISSOCIATION. Disturbances in identity and memory characterize these disorders, and the four identified in *DSM-III-R* (1987) include multiple personality disorder, psychogenic fugue, psychogenic amnesia and depersonalization disorder. The dissociative disorders can often be mistaken for more serious psychotic disorders such as schizophrenia. Since there is no significant break with reality, persons suffering from dissociative disorders are not considered psychotic. This concept is recognized even by the legal system in the United States, where there have been instances of individuals with multiple personality disorder who have committed serious crimes but who have not been judged "insane" because they were not technically psychotic. An example of this is the sensational case of convicted rapist Billy Milligan in Ohio in the 1970s; he suffered from multiple personality disorder but was not judged legally insane.

A more traditional clinical term for the dissociative disorders is "hysterical neuroses, dissociative type." In ICD-9 (1978), these disorders are included among those subtypes listed for "Hysteria."

Keyes, D., *The Minds of Billy Milligan.* New York: Random House, 1981.
Putnam, F.W., "Dissociation as a Response to Extreme Trauma," in R. Kluft (ed.), *Childhood Antecedents of Multiple Personality.* Washington, D.C.: American Psychiatric Press, 1985.

distractibility A descriptive clinical term for when a person's attention seems to be easily diverted to unimportant or irrelevant events in the person's immediate environment. This is a characteristic found in many people who do not have diagnosable mental disorders, and such people are often referred to as "dreamy," "spacey" or "spaced-out." However, in certain psychotic disorders such as schizophrenia this distractibility can be extreme, and such disturbances in the processes of attention are often said to be one of the primary characteristics of schizophrenia. (See also ATTENTION, DISORDERS IN; COGNITIVE STUDIES OF SCHIZOPHRENIA.)

Dix, Dorothea Lynde (1802–1887) It is said by historian of psychiatry Gregory Zilboorg in his 1941 classic, *A History of Medical Psychology,* that "The history of medical psychology in American during the nineteenth century is the history of the American Psychiatric Association and the life of Dorothea Dix." Dix was a retired schoolteacher who, starting in 1841, became one of the most noted reformers of the care of the mentally ill in the 19th century. Her investigations of the terrible conditions suffered by the mentally ill and the poor in alms houses, prisons and the few institutions that existed fueled her energetic campaign of petitions to state legislatures and the Congress of the United States, and to the Parliament in England, to allocate funds to build more humane institutions for the care of the mentally ill. It is estimated that between the 1840s and 1880s she was directly responsible for the building of 32 new state asylums for the insane in the United States.

In an 1848 "Memorial" address to Congress in Washington, D.C., Dix reported that during her investigations she had seen "more than 9000 idiots, epileptics and insane in the United States, destitute of appropriate care and protection . . . bound with galling chains, bowed beneath fetters and heavy iron balls attached to drag-chains, lacerated with ropes, scourged with rods and terrified beneath storms of execration and cruel blows; now subject to jibes and scorn and torturing tricks; now abandoned to the most outrageous violations."

Dix remained a reformer until late in her life. To honor her achievements in the caretaking of others, she was given a permanent apartment on the grounds of the New Jersey State Hospital at Trenton, where she lived out most of her remaining years. (See also ABUSE OF PSYCHIATRIC PATIENTS; ASYLUMS; BEERS, CLIFFORD.)

Deutsch, A., *The Mentally Ill in America.* Garden City, N.Y.: Doubleday, 1937; chapter 9.

Tiffany, F., *The Life of Dorothea Lynde Dix.* Boston: 1891.
Zilboorg, G., *A History of Medical Psychology.* New York: W.W. Norton, 1941.

dizygotic twins "Fraternal" or "nonidentical" twins. Dizygotic twins are thought to share about 50% of their genes in common, compared to the nearly 100% shared by MONOZYGOTIC TWINS. This makes for an interesting comparison between these two types of twin-pairs in GENETICS STUDIES of schizophrenia and bipolar disorder, and some of the most suggestive evidence that these mental disorders have a genetic basis is the fact that a particular disease is much more likely to appear in both monozygotic twins than in both dizygotic twins. (See also CONCORDANCE RATE; CONSANGUINITY METHOD; TWINS METHOD AND STUDIES.)

DMPEA The acronym for dimethoxphenethylamine, once thought to be one of the BIOLOGICAL MARKERS OF SCHIZOPHRENIA. DMPEA is a product of a chemical process known as transmethylation (in biochemistry, the transference of a methyl group from one compound to another). In 1963, scientists Friedhoff and Van Winkle found increased concentrations (when compared to normal controls) of DMPEA in the urine of 60% of acute schizophrenics who were not treated with ANTIPSYCHOTIC DRUGS. Furthermore, they found the even more suggestive evidence of higher than normal concentrations of DMPEA in the urine of 71% of male paranoid schizophrenics and in 75% of female paranoid schizophrenics. However, further research on the role of this and other compounds produced by the biochemical process of transmethylation found in the body fluids of schizophrenics, has not indicated a specific relationship to this or any other mental disorder. (See also BIOCHEMICAL THEORIES; TRANSMETHYLATION HYPOTHESIS.)

Friedhoff, J.J. and Van Winkle, E., "Conversion of Dopamine to 3,4-dimethoxyphenylacetic Acid in Schizophrenia Patients,'' *Nature*, 199(1963), 1271–1272.

Luchins, D., Ban, T.A. and Lehmann, H.E., ''A Review of Nicotinic Acid, N-methylated Indolamines and Schizophrenia,'' *International Journal of Pharmacopsychiatry*, 13(1978), 16–33.

DNA marker   See MOLECULAR MARKER.

Dollhaus   An old German term for ''madhouse.''

dominant   In genetics, a trait observable in an individual (called the phenotype) and caused by one allele (the term for an alternative form of a gene) is said to be dominant with respect to another trait known to be caused by a second allele, if the individual carrying both alleles shows signs only of the first trait and not the second.

dopamine   A chemical substance in the brain that functions as a NEUROTRANSMITTER, that is, it is involved in the communication between neurons in the brain. Dopamine is one of the CATECHOLAMINES. For the most part, dopamine is thought to play the role of an inhibitor of functions. It has been found to be implicated in the motor (movement) control systems of the brain, and especially in schizophrenia. (See also DOPAMINE HYPOTHESIS.)

dopamine hypothesis   First proposed by researchers Carlsson and Lindqvist in 1963, this has been one of the most researched hypotheses of the causes of schizophrenia and has generated many different theories. The idea is that the neurotransmitter dopamine (DA)—specifically, ''overactive dopaminergic pathways''—is linked to the causes of schizophrenia. An abnormality in the processes of the brain causes an excess of dopamine, with which the brain ''autointoxicates'' itself, thus creating the symptoms of schizophrenia (in particular, the POSITIVE SYMPTOMS such as delusions and hallucina-

tions). This line of scientific inquiry was suggested by the introduction of ANTIPSYCHOTIC DRUGS in the 1950s and early 1960s. Research found that these NEUROLEPTIC drugs work to relieve symptoms by blocking dopamine at its receptor sites in the brain and that—because it is known that amphetamine acts by releasing dopamine in the brain—the positive symptoms often noted in schizophrenia could be brought on by the ingestion of amphetamine (as in AMPHETAMINE PSYCHOSIS) by schizophrenics. Much of the research in this area has been devoted to identifying the dopamine receptor sites in the brain.

Increased dopamine activity is implicated in the production of ''Type I schizophrenia,'' according to British researcher Timothy Crow. However, a critique of CROW'S HYPOTHESIS by Herbert Y. Meltzer and colleagues of Case Western Reserve University argues that more recent research instead indicates that the dopamine hypothesis of schizophrenia should be revised in three respects: (1) some patients with the schizophrenic phenotype may have an entirely nondopamine-dependent disorder; (2) dopaminergic activity may be involved only in the early (acute) stages of the disorder; and (3) some aspects of schizophrenia, particularly NEGATIVE SYMPTOMS (e.g., flat affect, poverty of thought content and social withdrawal) could be due to decreased dopaminergic activity. (See also BIOCHEMICAL THEORIES OF SCHIZOPHRENIA.)

Carlsson, A. and Lindqvist, M., ''Effect of Chlorpromazine or Haloperidol on Formation of 3–Methoxytyramine and Normetanephrine in Mouse Brain,'' *Acta Pharmocologia*, 20(1963), 140–144.

Meltzer, H.Y., ''Dopamine and Negative Symptoms in Schizophrenia: Critique of the Type I-II Hypothesis,'' in M. Alpert (ed.), *Controversies in Schizophrenia*. New York: Guilford, 1985.

Meltzer, H.Y., ''Biological Studies of Schizophrenia,'' *Schizophrenia Bulletin*, 13(1987), 77–114.

Seeman, P., "Brain Dopamine Receptors in Schizophrenia, "in M.N. Menuck and M.V. Seeman (eds.), *New Perspectives in Schizophrenia*. New York: Macmillan, 1985.

double-bind theory One of the most widely discussed theories of the cause of schizophrenia, from the 1950s to the 1970s, although it is now generally regarded as of little scientific significance. This theory was derived from communications and cybernetics research and was first put forth by Gregory BATESON and his colleagues in 1956. Essentially, it places the cause of schizophrenia in the interaction patterns of the family, and this theory was the basis of much later family interaction research.

Essentially, the double-bind theory centers on the incongruence between the basic content of primary communications and the underlying meaning (expressed by tone of voice, gestures or context of the communication), which incongruence is called metacommunications. Bateson and his colleagues purported to find that, in the families of schizophrenics, the schizophrenic member is caught in a double-bind when incongruent messages are communicated and the recipient must respond to the incongruent message without being given the opportunity to clarify the incongruence in the message. For example, the parent of a schizophrenic may say "Of course I love you," while wearing a facial expression of disgust or while doing something intrusive or harmful to the afflicted person. A lifetime of such aberrant communications since early childhood is thus thought to produce schizophrenia. The double-bind theory has remained just that, with no carefully controlled scientific study to validate its claims. (See also FAMILY INTERACTION THEORIES.)

Bateson, G. et al., "Towards a Theory of Schizophrenia," *Behavioral Science,* 1(1956), 251–264.

double conscience or consciousness These are 19th-century terms that refer to MULTIPLE PERSONALITY disorder, in which one or more alternate personalities would coexist with the ego of the "birth personality." The very first complete medical case history of a person with multiple personalities was that of the young American woman Mary Reynolds, first reported in 1817.

Mitchell, S.L., "A Double Consciousness or a Duality of Person in the Same Individual," *Medical Repository,* 3(1817), 185–186.
Mitchell, S.W., "Mary Reynolds: A Case of Double Consciousness," *Transactions of the College of Physicians of Philadelphia,* 10(1888), 366–389.

double insanity See FOLIE À DEUX.

douche One of the primary modes of alleviating the active symptoms of mental illness since antiquity; in particular, in mental institutions in the 18th and 19th centuries the patient would be forced under a shower of (usually) ice-cold water. This was done in many fashions, including: by physically restraining the patient and pouring buckets of cold water over his or her head (as in the SPREAD-EAGLE CURE); or by using a "douching machine" in which a patient would be strapped in a chair beneath an apparatus that forced strong jets of cold water down onto his head. The reproduction of a design drawing of such an apparatus from the 1820s is provided in the first volume of Howells and Osborn's *A Reference Companion to the History of Abnormal Psychology.*

ESQUIROL describes the use of the douche on the mentally ill in his 1838 textbook, *Mental Maladies:*

The douche consists in pouring water upon the head from a greater or less height. It was known to the ancients; and is administered in different ways . . . The patient received the douche, seated in an arm chair; or better, plunged into a bath of tepid or cold water.

The douche produces its effects, both by the action of the cold, and the percussion. It exercises a sympathetic influence upon the epigastrium. It causes cardialgia, and desires to vomit. After its action ceases, the patients are pale, and sometimes sallow. It also acts morally, as a means of repression; a douche often sufficing to calm a raging excitement, to break up dangerous resolutions, or force a patient to obedience . . . The douche ought to be applied with discretion, and never immediately after a repast . . . Its employment ought to be continued but a few minutes at a time, and its administration never left to servants. They may abuse it, and we ought not to be ignorant that the douche is not exempt from grave accidents.

In describing the douche method of BATHS for the mentally ill included in Tuke's *A Dictionary of Psychological Medicine,* 14 other means of administering baths are discussed in detail. One of them sounds like the "Chinese water-torture" of motion picture fame:

> Schneider and Morel shaved their patients' heads, and placed them under an intermittent stream of water, which fell drop by drop on the back of the scalp . . .

(See also HYDROTHERAPY.)

Williams, D., "Baths," in D.H. Tuke (ed.), *A Dictionary of Psychological Medicine,* vol. 1 London: J. & A. Churchill, 1892.

Esquirol, J.E.D., *Mental Maladies, a Treatise On Insanity* Philadelphia: Lea & Blanchard, 1845; first published, 1838.

Howells, J.G. and Osborn, M.L., *A Reference Companion to the History of Abnormal Psychology,* 2 vols. Westport, Conn. Greenwood Press, 1984.

dreams, schizophrenic It has often been noted by many psychiatrists and psychologists that the dreams of people with schizophrenia are different from those of people who are not suffering from a psychotic disorder. This distinction has been discussed in the psychiatric literature since the late 1800s. Many studies have been written about this phenomenon. In his review of this literature in the 1974 edition of his book *Interpretation of Schizophrenia,* psychoanalyst and psychiatrist Silvano ARIETI identifies three distin-

guishing characteristics in the dreams of schizophrenics when compared to other people:

1. The element of bizarreness is more pronounced. More frequently than in dreams of other people there are transformations of persons into animals, plants, flowers, and so on.
2. Secondary process material hides less the latent content. Thus, in spite of their bizarreness, these dreams are easier to interpret than those of neurotics.
3. There is a pervading feeling of despair or a crescendo of anxiety with no resolution.

Arieti, S., *Interpretation of Schizophrenia,* 2nd ed. New York: Basic Books, 1974.

drug holiday A "vacation" from taking ANTIPSYCHOTIC DRUGS that is necessary from time to time so that the psychiatrist can assess the further need of medication for a patient.

drug psychoses A category of organic psychotic conditions, listed in ICD-9 (1978), for those psychoses induced by the ingestion of various drugs (e.g., amphetamines, barbiturates, opiates and hallucinogens). There is a break with reality, and hallucinations and delusions may be present. They can be due to the active intoxicating effects of the substances, or to the effects of withdrawal. (See also AMPHETAMINE PSYCHOSIS.)

DSM-III-R The *Diagnostic and Statistical Manual of Mental Disorders,* Third Edition–Revised, which appeared in 1987 as a revision of *DSM-III.* Since the appearance of *DSM-I* in 1952, the American Psychiatric Association has periodically updated its diagnostic manuals to be consistent with advances in research on mental disorders. The later editions have attempted to be phenomenologically-based (i.e., focused on descriptions of behaviors in various mental disorders) and have attempted to be free of pejorative theoretical assumptions. For example, the word "neurosis" was no longer included when *DSM-III* came out in 1980 since it referred to a concept from psychoanalytic theory that did not always match current research on the various disorders. Teams of psychiatrists are continually working in committees to collect research information and to revise, eliminate or create new diagnostic categories for each revision of the manual.

Originally designed for use in the United States, it is now one of the most widely used diagnostic manuals for mental disorders in the world. For example, *DSM-III* (1980) has been translated into Chinese, Danish, Dutch, Finnish, French, German, Greek, Italian, Japanese, Norwegian, Portuguese, Spanish and Swedish.

Spitzer, R.L. and Williams, J., "Introduction," in *Diagnostic and Statistical Manual of Mental Disorders,* Third Edition–Revised. Washington, D.C.: American Psychiatric Association, 1987.

dual diagnosis   The presence of two existing mental disorders in a person that requires the granting of two different diagnostic labels. This term is most often used to describe those "dually diagnosed" patients who are mentally retarded as well as schizophrenic (or carry some other psychotic diagnosis). One of the growing problems in the post-psychedelic era of the 1960s is the large number of YOUNG ADULT CHRONIC PATIENTS who are abusers of drugs and alcohol and who also seem to have a serious (often psychotic) mental disorder. These patients are also dually diagnosed and in the United States are sometimes referred to as "double trouble" patients.

ducking   See BATHS; BATH OF SURPRISE; HYDROTHERAPY.

duplex personality   See DOUBLE CONSCIENCE OR CONSCIOUSNESS.

E

Earle, Pliny (1809–1892)   Earle was a psychiatrist and one of the 13 founders of the AMERICAN PSYCHOLOGICAL ASSOCIATION in 1844. He had traveled widely in Europe and was knowledgeable about European treatments for mental illness. He held several important positions in his lifetime, including that of medical superintendent of the Bloomingdale Asylum in New York in 1844 and the State Lunatic Hospital at Northampton, Massachusetts, in 1864, where he remained for the next 21 years. He is perhaps best remembered for pioneering the teaching of psychiatry in American medical schools, and for his 1887 book, *The Curability of the Insane,* which sharply contradicted the wildly inflated claims of "curability" of the insane that had been made by various superintendents of ASYLUMS in the United States during the previous 40 years.

ècho de la pensèe   Literally, "echo of the thoughts." This is a characteristic of schizophrenic THOUGHT DISORDER that is commonly called "thought broadcasting." A psychotic individual exhibiting *ècho de la pensèe* believes that his private thoughts are being sent out into the minds of other people, who may then speak them for him. In more-deteriorated psychotic states, the person may not even recognize these thoughts as his or her own and attribute them entirely to other people.

echolalia   The spontaneous (yet persistent) repetition of the words and phrases of others. It is as if the listening person is an "echo" of the speaker's speech. For example, the speaker may ask, "Does that belong to you?" only to be met with the response (usually in a mumbling, mocking or staccato tone) "Belong to you. Belong to you." Informally, it is sometime called "parroting" after the behavior of parrots.

This symptom is found in schizophrenia (particularly the DISORGANIZED TYPE) and especially in autistic children or individuals with certain brain disorders. (See also AUTISM, INFANTILE; LANGUAGE ABNORMALITIES IN SCHIZOPHRENIA.

ECT   The acronym for "electroconvulsive therapy" is the most recent attempt to neutralize the negative connotations most people associate with the method's original name, ELECTROSHOCK THERAPY.

EEG studies of schizophrenia   German psychiatrist Hans Berger (1873–1941) invented the electroencephalogram in 1924 and first published the results of his studies of the electrical activity of the human brain in 1929. The EEG (as it is still known today) employed electrodes, which were attached to the scalp in strategic locations around the head, to map the electrical activity of the different regions of the brain. In the decade that followed this discovery there was great hope that the EEG could be used in psychiatry as a diagnostic tool, the assumption being that the brain wave patterns of people with particular mental disorders would differ from one another and from the patterns of people without diagnosable disorders. Although applications were found in neurology, psychiatry eventually found the EEG was of little diagnostic value.

EEG studies of schizophrenics generally showed more abnormalities than those of nonschizophrenic persons, but no specific brain wave abnormality could be linked to schizophrenia. However, an improvement on the classical EEG methodology has been the use of event-related potentials, also known as "ERPs," which have been a much more promising BIOLOGICAL MARKER OF SCHIZOPHRENIA. Whereas most EEG studies are conducted while the subject is at rest, ERPs involve the presentation of a flash of light, a tone or a very mild electrical stimulus to a subject so that the responding electrical activity in the brain can be recorded. ERPs

are very useful because they are a nonintrusive way (unlike the surgical implantation of electrodes in the brain) of measuring the neural activity in relation to sensory, motor and cognitive processes.

A large literature exists of ERP research that has been conducted with people diagnosed with schizophrenia. Three lines of evidence have been considered to be most promising in the search for biological markers: (1) Certain brain wave abnormalities in schizophrenics (technically, amplitude reductions in middle and late positive components) are thought to be related to dysfunctions in attention, which are found in some schizophrenics and in some individuals at high-risk for schizophrenia; (2) ERP patterns have been found to differ from those of people diagnosed with other mental disorders; and (3) certain aspects of the electrical activity of the brain measured by ERPs seem to be genetically determined (i.e., the brain may be predisposed to react to certain types of stimuli in specific ways). (See also ATTENTION, DISORDERS IN; HIGH-RISK STUDIES.)

Berger, H., "Über das Elektrenkephalogramm des Menschen," *Archiv für Psychiatrie und Nervenkrankheiten*, 98(1933), 231–255.
Erlenmeyer-Kimling, L., "Biological Markers for the Liability to Schizophrenia," in H. Helmchen and F.A. Henn (eds.), *Biological Perspectives of Schizophrenia*. New York: John Wiley, 1987.
Holzman, P.S., "Recent Studies of Psychophysiology in Schizophrenia," *Schizophrenia Bulletin*, 13(1987), 49–76.

egocentricity   Individuals with psychotic disorders are sometimes described as being "egocentric" in the same way that, for example, an infant is egocentric: Impulses are expressed without regard to the context of social situation. Thus, psychotic individuals may engage in activities that are socially repugnant, bizarre or simply inconsiderate. According to psychoanalytic theory, energy ("libido") is withdrawn from the external world and drawn back into the internal world in psychotic individuals. Thus, the person becomes more interested in his or her internal world and its needs rather than the demands of external reality. In this way, the concept of egocentricity is related to descriptions of the AUTISM of some psychotic individuals, particularly schizophrenics.

Einheitspsychose In German, a "unitary psychosis," the idea that all mental illnesses (certainly all of the psychotic disorders) are simply variations of the same underlying disease process (the *Einheitspsychose*) and are not separate mental disorders with no apparent relationship to one another. This idea was first proposed by the Belgian alienist Joseph Guislain (1797–1860).

The eminent German psychiatrist Wilhelm GRIESINGER adopted this concept from this mentor, Ernst Zeller (1804–1877), and utilized it when introducing the "Form of Mental Disease" chapter in his 1845 classic, *Mental Pathology and Therapeutics*. He proposes that there are "two grand groups" or "fundamental states of mental anomalies": (1) those characterized by disturbances in emotional states (what we would call MOOD DISORDERS); and (2) those characterized by "disorders of the intellect and will" (the "thought disorder" characteristic of schizophrenia and related "spectrum" disorders). Furthermore, Griesinger believed that these types of disorder fit a degenerative pattern, with the mood disorders ("states of depression" then "states of exaltation" or manic states) developing eventually into more serious disorders in which thinking functions deteriorate ("states of mental weakness"), leading to the total degeneration of the mind. Griesinger writes:

> Observation shows, further, that in the great majority of cases, those conditions which form the first leading group *precede* those of the second group; that the latter generally appear only as consequences and *terminations* of the first, when the cerebral affection has not been cured. There is, moreover, again presented within the first group, in a great proportion of

cases, a certain definite *succession* of the various forms of emotional states, whence there results a method of viewing insanity which recognizes in the different *forms*, different *stages* of one morbid process; which may, indeed, be modified, interrupted, or transformed by the most varied intercurrent pathological circumstances, but which, on the whole, pursues a constantly progressive course, which may proceed even to complete destruction of the mental life.

The idea of the *Einheitspsychose* has its most modern expression in a theory by the noted British schizophrenia researcher Timothy J. Crow. He postulates in a 1986 article that all of the psychotic disorders are distributed along a continuum that extends from unipolar depression through bipolar (manic-depressive) and schizoaffective psychosis to schizophrenia—a progressive degeneration from bad to worse. This matches Griesinger's observations exactly: that the psychotic disorders characterized by disturbances in emotion degenerate into psychoses characterized by disturbances of will and thought. Crow adds a 20th-century twist to this idea by proposing that this spectrum of disorders is caused by a single gene; in other words, there is a single genetic locus where significant variation occurs in defect that predisposes to all of these psychotic disorders. In a 1989 article he reviews the evidence that the defective gene has a locus on the sex chromosomes, particularly the X chromosome. Crow guesses the "psychosis gene" is located somewhere on the X chromosome. (See also CHROMOSOME ABNORMALITIES; GENETIC TRANSMISSION.)

Crow, T.J., "The Continuum of Psychosis and Its Implications for the Structure of the Gene," *British Journal of Psychiatry*, 149(1986), 419–429.

DeLisi, L.E. and Crow, T.J., "Evidence for a Sex Chromosome Locus for Schizophrenia," *Schizophrenia Bulletin*, 15(1989), 431–440.

Griesinger, W., *Mental Pathology and Therapeutics*, tr. C.L. Robertson and J. Rutherford. New York: William Wood & Co., 1882; first published, 1845; 2nd ed., 1865.

Vleigen, J., *Die Einheitspsychose*. Stuttgart: F. Enke, 1980.

elective mutism   A symptom found in some people who are diagnosed with a psychotic disorder who, for whatever reason, simply refuse to talk. This has been described particularly in connection with CATATONIA.

electroshock therapy   Now more commonly known as electroconvulsive therapy, or "ECT," it is a form of treatment designed by Italian psychiatrist Ugo CERLETTI and his colleagues in Rome to treat severe mental illness by electrically inducing seizures. An alleviation of symptoms followed the deliberate induction of such seizures. It was considered an improvement on other types of CONVULSIVE THERAPIES, which had many toxic side effects associated with the use of drugs to induce such powerful seizures. The very first patient to receive this treatment (a schizophrenic) did so on April 15, 1938. Electroshock therapy then became one of the most widely used forms of treatment for schizophrenia until the 1970s, when it became clear that ANTIPSYCHOTIC DRUGS were a more effective means of controlling psychotic symptoms and that ECT was much more effective with severe depression than with schizophrenia.

Cerletti experimented with pigs before attempting the procedure on humans. Most other psychiatrists were afraid to try this new procedure, but not Cerletti. In a rather macabre account of the very first electroshock treatment ever administered, D.J. Impastato relates the details of this historic (and horrific) event:

> Now came the search for Rome's first patient. For obvious reasons this was not a simple matter. Then, luckily, a patient from North Italy was admitted to the clinic who was a catatonic schizophrenic and who spoke an incomprehensible gibberish. He was unable to give his name or state anything about himself. No one could identify him. Dr. Cerletti decided he should be the historic patient. Following adequate preparations the first treatment was given in 1938. Present were Cerletti, Bini, Longhi, Accornero, Kalinowsky and Fleischer. The patient was brought in, and the machine was set at 1/10 of a second and 70 volts and the shock given. Naturally, the low dosage resulted in a petit mal reaction. After the electric spasm, which lasted a fraction of a second, the patient burst out into song. The Professor suggested that another treatment with a higher voltage be given. The staff objected. They stated that if another treatment were given the patient would probably die and wanted further treatment postponed until the morrow. The Professor knew what that meant. He decided to go ahead right then and there, but before he could say so the patient suddenly sat up and pontifically proclaimed, no longer in a jargon, but in clear Italian: "Non una seconda! Mortifera!" (Not again, it will kill me). This made the Professor think and swallow, but his courage was not lost. He gave the order to proceed at a higher voltage and a longer time: and the first electroconvulsion in man ensued. Thus was born EST out of one man and over the objection of his assistants.

No scientifically satisfying theory has *ever* been put forth to justify or explain the use of electroshock therapy for schizophrenia. Like most treatments for mental illness over the last several centuries, as soon as a new scientific discovery is made it is quickly adapted for use on the mentally ill in the hope that a new treatment or cure can finally be found. When it was discovered that blood circulated in the body, BLEEDING and BLOOD TRANSFUSIONS (often using animal blood) were quickly tried on the insane. When Hungarian psychiatrist Von Meduna put forth the scientifically unsound theory that, since epilepsy and schizophrenia were biologically incompatible, deliberately inducing seizures (by chemical means) in schizophrenics would cure it, such methods were widely tried and efforts were made to improve upon them. Electroshock therapy was such an improvement, despite the fact that the initial theory to explain its beneficial effects was unsound.

Electric shocks that were too weak to produce convulsions were used almost 200 years before Cerletti to treat illness, but it was only around 1804 that a use for psychosis is recorded. A machine that produced electric shocks from weak electric currents was set up in the Middlesex Hospital in England in 1767 to treat various ailments, and shocks were applied to various parts of the body. At about this time American inventor and statesman Benjamin Franklin suffered unconsciousness and retrograde amnesia after a severe electric shock during one of his electricity experiments, and he apparently suggested its use for the treatment of the insane. In the 1790s, British surgeon John BIRCH used his machine to "pass shocks through the brain" of depressed patients at London's Saint Thomas Hospital; this may be the first recorded use of electric shocks applied directly to the brain to treat a mental disorder. In 1838, ESQUIROL reviewed the reports of the use of electricity in the treatment of mental illness, including his own experiments with its use:

Gmelin and Perfect affirm, that they have effected cures by electricity. At the Salpêtrière, during two summers, those of 1823 and 1824, I submitted to the influence of electricity a large number of our insane women. One only was cured, in the course of my experiments. This was a young and very strong girl, who had become a maniac in consequence of a fright, which suppressed her menses. She had been insane for a month, and was electrized for fifteen days. At the menstrual period, the discharge appeared, and she was immediately restored.

Although electroshock therapy is still sometimes used for schizophrenia, this is quickly becoming an outmoded form of treatment for the disease, at least in the United States. Symptomatic relief is often only temporary, and a major review of the bulk of the research published prior to 1980 has concluded that electroshock therapy has not been shown to improve the quality of life of schizophrenic patients.

In June 1985, the National Institute of Mental Health in the United States convened a Consensus Development Conference on Electroconvulsive Therapy and issued a summary statement on the body of scientific evidence about ECT. The panel of experts concluded that, "The evidence for the efficacy of ECT in schizophrenia is not compelling but is strongest for those schizophrenic patients with a shorter duration of illness, a more acute onset, and more intense affective symptoms. ECT has not been useful in chronically ill schizophrenic patients." When is ECT indicated? The expert panel found that, "The efficacy of ECT has been established most convincingly in the treatment of delusional and severe endogenous depressions, which make up a clinically important minority of depressive disorders." However, the panel warns that there are "significant side effects, especially acute confusional states and persistent memory deficits for events during the months surrounding ECT treatment."

Arndt, R., "Electricity," in D.H. Tuke (ed.), *A Dictionary of Psychological Medicine*, vol. 1. London: J. & A. Churchill, 1892.

Esquirol, J.E.D., *Mental Maladies, A Treatise On Insanity*. Philadelphia: Lea and Blanchard, 1845; first published, 1838.

Harms, E., "Origins and Early History of Electrotherapy and Electroshock," *American Journal of Psychiatry*, 12(1955), 933.

Impastato, D.J., "The Story of the First Electroshock Treatment," *American Journal of Psychiatry*, 116(1960), 1113–1114.

National Institutes of Health, *Electroconvulsive therapy*, Consensus Development Conference Statement, 1985, vol. 5, no. 11. Bethesda, Md.: U.S. Dept. of Health and Human Services, National Institutes of Health, Office of Medical Applications of Research.

Salzman, C., "The Use of ECT in the Treatment of Schizophrenia," *American Journal of Psychiatry*, 137(1980), 1032–1041.

EMD   An acronym for "eye movement dysfunction," perhaps one of the most promising candidates for a BIOLOGICAL

MARKER for schizophrenia. (See also EYE MOVEMENT ABNORMALITIES IN SCHIZOPHRENIA.)

endocrine disorder hypothesis With the rise of the science of endocrinology in the 20th century, and its powerful demonstration of the roles that hormones play in our development, it has often been suggested that a predisposition for, or the actual cause of, schizophrenia may be due to endocrine disturbances. This has been hypothesized because schizophrenia's typical age of onset—adolescence and early adulthood—is also known as the time when there are major shifts in the neuroendocrine functioning (i.e., "hormones") of the body. Even Emil KRAEPELIN noticed this typical age of onset and thought it might perhaps have something to do with an "auto-intoxicating" process in the body. In addition, many schizophrenia research reports have found (albeit inconsistently) disturbances of adrenal, thyroid and gonadal functioning in persons afflicted with this disease. Research psychiatrist Herbert Y. Meltzer, M.D., of Case Western Reserve University has published extensive reviews of these complex and highly technical studies. He has identified the following goals of modern neuroendocrine research on schizophrenia: (1) to obtain indirect evidence of the function of neurotransmitters that regulate the secretion of hypothalamic hormones; (2) to assess the effects of drugs, which release hormones in the brain, on neurotransmitter dynamics or receptors; (3) to study the relationship between hormone levels and mental illness; and (4) to predict the clinical response or relapse after treatment with antipsychotic drugs is withdrawn.

Meltzer, H.Y. and Lowy, M.T., "Neuroendocrine Function in Psychiatric Disorders and Behavior," in P. Berger and H. Brodie (eds.), *American Handbook of Psychiatry*, 2nd ed. New York: Basic Books, 1986.

endogenous psychosis See PSYCHOSIS.

endophenotype In genetics research, an endophenotype is perhaps best thought of as a BIOLOGICAL MARKER of a particular mental disorder. It is a biological abnormality that is a much more direct result of the hypothesized genetic defect than the actual symptoms and behaviors of the disorder itself. For example, such an abnormality could be sought as a marker that indicates a person is genetically vulnerable to developing the disorder. It would then be said that the endophenotype demonstrates greater penetrance (i.e., it occurs with greater frequency) than the mental illness itself. The endophenotype may be found in the close relatives of the person with the disorder (known as the INDEX CASE or the PROBAND), but the symptoms of the mental illness itself may be fully evident only in the person in question. (See also CANDIDATE GENES; CONCORDANCE RATE; INCOMPLETE PENETRANCE; GENETICS STUDIES.)

England Studies of the prevalence rates for schizophrenia in England have found substantial differences in different parts of the country, thus producing a mixed picture. Some researchers have suggested that if the diagnostic criteria differences between England and the United States were resolved, England would have a higher prevalence rate than the United States. A 1965 study of a working-class area by South London's Maudsley Institute found a prevalence rate of 3.4 per thousand. One clear fact is that in England schizophrenia occurs much more often in the lower socioeconomic groups. Scotland has a higher rate of schizophrenia than England.

Torrey, E.F., *Schizophrenia and Civilization*. New York: Jason Aronson, 1980.

enzyme In biochemistry, an enzyme is a protein, secreted by cells, that acts as a catalyst to induce chemical changes in other substances, itself remaining largely unchanged by the process. For this reason enzymes are also called "biocatalysts," "biocatalyzers" and "organic catalysts." Most modern enzymes, as they are discovered, are named by adding the suffix "-ase" to the name of the substance on which the enzyme acts or activates, and/or the type of reaction it causes.

enzyme disorder hypothesis One of the BIOCHEMICAL THEORIES OF SCHIZOPHRENIA is that the disease is caused by abnormal enzyme activity. In fact, since the 1970s one of the most active areas in schizophrenia research has been the search for metabolic (i.e., biochemical, neurochemical, neuroendocrinologic) changes in certain substances (neuroenzymes, neurohormones, neuropeptides and their metabolites) in the neurophysiology of people diagnosed with schizophrenia.

Several diverse areas of research have yielded biological markers of uncertain significance. First, there seems to be consistent evidence for elevations in the activity of the enzyme creatine kinase (CK) during acute psychotic phases of schizophrenia and affective disorders. This was first reported by H.Y. Meltzer in 1968, and later work by him has indicated that serum CK activity is genetically regulated.

Second, many studies since 1941 (by Birkhauser) have indicated decreased levels of the enzyme monoamine oxidase, or "MAO," in the blood platelets of psychiatric patients, particularly schizophrenics. Much of the recent interest in this work was stimulated by a series of studies conducted by researchers Murphy and Wyatt and published in 1972. It is thought that this decrease in MAO activity may be a genetic marker of vulnerability to a range of mental disorders, not just schizophrenia. However, decreased MAO activity has been most associated with schizophrenics who experience AUDITORY HALLUCINATIONS and are diagnosed with the paranoid subtype.

Third, some reports have indicated a decrease in the activity of the enzyme dopamine-beta-hydroxylase ("DBH") in the blood and the cerebrospinal fluid ("CSF") of schizophrenics. The first published finding of this DBH abnormality was by scientists Wise and Stein in 1973.

Fourth, many other enzymes (such as choline acetyltransferase and glutamic acid decarboxylase), other neurotransmitters than dopamine (such as GABA, norepinepherine and serotonin), and peptides (such as the endorphins) have also been investigated as possible causal factors in the development of schizophrenia.

The research in this area is often incomprehensible to those not educated in the language of biochemistry, but a 1987 review by Meltzer published in *Schizophrenia Bulletin* provides one of the more accessible sources of information in this important area of schizophrenia research.

Berger, P.A., "Biochemistry and the Schizophrenias: Old Concepts and New Hypotheses," *Journal of Nervous and Mental Disease,* 169(1981), 90–99.

Birkhauser, V.H., "Cholinesterase und monoaminoxydase in zentralen nervensystem," *Schweitzer. Med. Woch.,* 71(1941), 750–752.

Meltzer, H.Y., "Creatin Kinase and Aldolase in Serum: Abnormality Common to Acute Psychoses," *Science,* 159(1968), 1370.

———, "Biological Studies in Schizophrenia," *Schizophrenia Bulletin,* 13(1987), 77–114.

Wise, C.D. and Stein, L., "Dopamine-beta-hydroxylase Deficits in the Brains of Schizophrenic Patients," *Science,* 181(1973), 344–347.

epidemiology Epidemiology is an area of study that combines the methods of many different disciplines (demographic, sociological, psychological and medical) to study diseases. Of particular interest is the incidence and prevalence of a disease in a population, the demographic factors involved (e.g., race, sex, area inhabited), the natural history of the disease (e.g., age of onset, subtypes) and how the disease affects the environment. Most medical phenomena have been studied in this way, including the epidemiology of mental disorders.

Incidence and prevalence rates for a disease are the two most commonly encountered epidemiological statistics in research reports. Incidence refers to how frequently a particular disease occurs in a given population, whereas prevalence refers to the total number of cases of a particular disorder in a population in a given time period. Both incidence and prevalence rates can vary from study to study, depending upon the demographic characteristics of the area. For example, according to DSM-III-R (1987), studies of the prevalence of schizophrenia in Asia and Europe have reported lifetime prevalence rates ranging from .2% percent of 1% of the population. However, since these studies use narrower criteria for schizophrenia and have examined populations less urban than in those studies conducted in the United States, prevalence rates for Americans have been higher for schizophrenia. For bipolar disorder (manic-depressive psychosis), prevalence rates have ranged from .4% to 1.2% of the adult population of the United States. Some research (summarized by L.F. Saugstad in 1989) indicates a marked increase of manic-depressive psychosis over the past 30 years in several countries (mainly Scandinavia).

Perhaps the most readable source of information on the epidemiology of schizophrenia is psychiatrist E. Fuller Torrey's book, *Schizophrenia and Civilization* (1980). Chapter by chapter he reviews the epidemiological evidence collected on schizophrenia. Torrey reaches the following conclusions:

1. Schizophrenia appear to be a disease of civilization, since it appears to be found in more urban and technologically advanced areas of the world than in so-called "Third World" countries.
2. In the United States, prevalence rates for schizophrenia have ranged from 1.1 to 4.7 persons per thousand.
3. Chinese-Americans and Mexican-Americans appear to have low schizophrenia rates. Schizophrenia is more common among the lower socioeconomic groups, among blacks and among urban dwellers.
4. Scandinavian prevalence rates for schizophrenia are two to three times that of the United States. Rates also appear to be higher in the Soviet Union and Eastern European countries, but may be very low in Southern European countries, especially in Italy.
5. The two areas of the world with perhaps the highest prevalence rates for schizophrenia (and for manic-depressive psychosis) are Croatia, in Yugoslavia and—in particular—Western Ireland. In fact, the likelihood that a person will be hospitalized for schizophrenia in certain counties in Ireland is higher than 1 in 25 (4%), the highest of any area in the world. The counties most affected are Mayo, Sligo, Roscommon, Galway, Clare, Kerry, Cork and Waterford. Irish immigrants to the United States and Canada have also traditionally had high rates of psychiatric hospitalization.
6. The prevalence rate for schizophrenia in Japan is about 2.3 per thousand.
7. Schizophrenics may have a typical "season of birth," since, according to Torrey, studies indicate that—for unknown reasons—schizophrenics are disproportionately born in the late winter and early spring months in the Northern Hemisphere. This contention has been criticized on statistical and other methodological grounds by psychologist M.S. Lewis in a paper published in the *Schizophrenia Bulletin* in 1989.
8. There is evidence that there are cultural differences in the response to antipsychotic medication. Europeans have been found to require lower doses of certain drugs than American patients.

Since viruses follow seasonal patterns and have been studied with epidemiological approaches, it has been suggested that some of this data point to the role of viruses in the case of schizophrenia. However, a 1985 comprehensive review of the epidemiological evidence on schizophrenia by William W. Eaton of the Center for Epidemiological Studies at the National Institute of Mental Health concludes that genetics are the most important factor worldwide in the development of this disorder. (See also CROSS-CULTURAL STUDIES; GENETICS STUDIES; VIRAL THEORIES OF SCHIZOPHRENIA.)

Eaton, W.W., "Epidemiology of Schizophrenia," *Epidemiological Review,* 7(1985), 105–126.

Lewis, M.S., "Age Incidence and Schizophrenia: Part I. The Season of Birth Controversy," *Schizophrenia Bulletin,* 15(1989), 59–71.

Rawnsley, K., *Epidemiology of Affective Psychoses.* London: Cambridge University Press, 1982.

Saugstad, L.F., "Social Class, Marriage, and Fertility in Schizophrenia," *Schizophrenia Bulletin,* 15(1989), 11–43.

Torrey, E.F., *Schizophrenia and Civilization.* New York: Jason Aronson, 1980.

Torrey, E.F., "Geographical Distribution of Insanity in America: Evidence for an Urban Factor," *Schizophrenia Bulletin,* 16(1990), 591–604.

epilepsy and schizophrenia   There has been a long controversy as to whether epilepsy and schizophrenia are related in any way. For example, the CONVULSIVE THERAPIES were invented by von MEDUNA in the 1930s and were based on a scientifically unsupported theory that epilepsy and schizophrenia are biologically incompatible; it was thought that inducing a seizure in schizophrenics might "cure" them. Many studies both pro and con have explored this relationship. One finding that seems to be reliable is that the symptoms of one type of seizure disorder, temporal lobe epilepsy, very often resemble schizophrenia in presentation. In fact, evidence presented by K. Davison in 1983 suggest that as much as 17% of people suffering from temporal lobe epilepsy display some symptoms of schizophrenia. In particular, temporal lobe epileptics have been known to have symptoms that resemble paranoid schizophrenia, including grandiose, mystical and religious delusions and hallucinations.

Davison, K., "Schizophrenia-like Psychoses Associated with Organic Cerebral Disorders: A Review," *Psychiatric Developments,* 1(1983), 1–34.

epistaxis   From the Greek, meaning a "nosebleed." Profuse bleeding from the nose was one of the variations of BLEEDING as a treatment for mental illness in the 18th and early 19th centuries. ESQUIROL in 1838 mentions its successful use in the treatment of a young man.

equinoxes   Certain times of the year were thought to cause madness or exacerbate its symptoms more than at other times. For example, the mentally ill were called "lunatics" because of the mistaken belief that the phases of the moon, particularly the full moon, had a role in causing madness. The vernal and autumnal equinoxes, were singled out by many authorities in centuries past as critical periods for the development of "madness." Esquirol notes in 1838 that "a house for the insane is most disturbed, and requires more careful supervision, at the period of the equinoxes." Philippe PINEL, however, differed, writing in 1801 that the critical period of "maniacal paroxysms" "generally being immediately after the summer solstice, are continued with more or less violence during the heat of summer, and commonly terminate towards the decline of autumn."

Esquirol, J.E.D., *Mental Maladies, A Treatise On Insanity.* Philadelphia: Lea and Blanchard, 1845; first published, 1838.

Pinel, P., *A Treatise On Insanity.* Sheffield: W. Todd, 1806; first published, 1801.

erotic jealousy syndrome   See OTHELLO SYNDROME.

erotomania "Love is a madness" *(furor amoris)* the Roman orator and statesman Cicero once wrote, and indeed there are very few human experiences that can generate more delusions than our erotic passions can. Forms of "love-madness" have been called *erotomania* at least since the 17th century. The word first appears in English in 1640 in a book by Jacques Ferrand, which was originally published in French in 1623, entitled *Erotomania or a Cure of Love or Erotique Melancholy.* For the next several centuries different authors defined erotomania in different ways, often confusing what we now know as nymphomania for this essentially delusional phenomenon.

Erotomania is often referred to as De Clérambault's syndrome, since this most recent definition was put forth in 1942 by Gaetan de CLERAMBAULT, a noted French psychiatrist. It had been known by French psychiatrists as the *psychose passionelle,* but de Clérambault identified very specific characteristics of this delusional syndrome: "A conviction of being in amorous communication with a person of much higher rank, who has been the first to fall in love and the first to make advances." De Clérambault thought that women in particular were susceptible to this delusion, and he published supporting case histories of women who had developed delusional beliefs that particularly desirable men (who, in reality, may never have met the women or had any contact with them) had fallen in love with them. This picture of erotomania was termed *pure erotomania* by de Clérambault to distinguish it from the descriptions of other psychiatric authorities, who tended to define it as a form of PARANOIA.

As a type of delusional syndrome, erotomania generally does not appear alone and is usually an aspect of a serious psychotic disorder, such as schizophrenia or bipolar disorder. A tragic modern example of this is potential presidential assassin John Hinckley Jr.'s erotomanic fascination with the actress Jodie Foster, which led him to attempt to assassinate President Ronald Reagan in 1981, in order to forever link their names together in history.

Clérambault, C.G. de, *Les Psychoses Passionelles. Oeuvre Psychiatrique.* Paris: Presses Universitaires, 1942.
Enoch, M.D. and Trethowan, W.H., "De Clérambault's Syndrome," in M.D. Enoch and W.H. Trethowan (eds.), *Uncommon Psychiatric Syndromes,* 2nd ed. Bristol, England: John Wright & Sons, 1979.
Segal, J.H., "Erotomania Revisited! From Kraepelin to *DSM-III-R,*" *American Journal of Psychiatry,* 146(1989), 1261–1266.

erotomania, paranoid type See PARANOIA EROTICA.

erotomania proper The name given in 1882 by J.C. Bucknill and D.H. Tuke to what was later called pure erotomania, as described in 1942 by de Clérambault. Following a similar distinction made in 1838 by ESQUIROL, Bucknill and Tuke distinguished the delusional syndrome of erotomania from those syndromes in which the sexual passions were actually acted out, such as nymphomania. They write:

> Erotomania, in its extended signification, not infrequently follows upon religious melancholy . . . It is not uncommon in the old, and . . . in persons who have been patterns of chastity during life . . . It is more frequent among women than in men, and . . . among the unmarried and widows than the married . . . It may attack any age; but the sentimental form—erotomania proper—more especially affects the young, and those of an ardent, susceptible temperament . . . Erotomania is often complicated with hysteria, and sometimes with hypochondriasis.

Bucknill, J.C. and Tuke, D.H., *A Manual of Psychological Medicine,* 2nd ed. London: J. & A. Churchill, 1882.

erotomanic type One of the variants of DELUSIONAL DISORDER as defined in DSM-III-R (1987). It corresponds to EROTOMANIA as defined by de Clérambault.

ERP The acronym for "event-related potentials." (See also EEG STUDIES OF SCHIZOPHRENIA.)

Esquirol, Jean Étienne Dominique (1772–1840) A student of Philippe PINEL's at the Salpêtrière in Paris and the author of the 1838 book, *Des Maladies Mentales,* a classic textbook in the field of psychiatry, or *médecine mentale* as it was then called. A recent study of the 19th-century French psychiatric profession by Goldstein concludes that until well past the middle of the century approximately 95% of all French *aliénistes* had studied in Paris with either Pinel or Esquirol. Esquirol received his doctorate in 1805 with the completion of his thesis, entitled "Passions Considered as Causes, Symptoms, and Therapeutic Means of Mental Diseases." He won the position of an attending physician at the Salpêtrière in 1811, and in that year instituted the very first official training courses on mental diseases for medical students and other physicians. A select group of young physicians who had trained under Esquirol and had become his disciples formed the "Esquirol Circle," an informal intellectual society that met for Sunday luncheons, which were presided over by Esquirol himself. Many of these "Circle" members became famous in their own right as their careers developed during the 19th century, notably, J.-P. FALRET, A.J.F. BRIERRE DE BOISMONT, J.J. Moreau de Tours and Jules BAILLARGER.

The search for BIOLOGICAL MARKERS of mental disorders has always existed in one form or another, and in Esquirol's day PHYSIOGNOMY was considered an important diagnostic tool. According to an entry for March 22, 1818, in the diary of Sir Alexander Morison, which described his visit to the Salpêtrière, Esquirol showed Morison his large personal collection of plaster casts of the faces of insane persons. The search for physiological markers of insanity also led Esquirol to become involved in the autopsies of deceased patients, referred to at that time as "openings *(ouvertures)* of corpses." Following the lead of his mentor Philippe Pinel, who also conducted *recherches cadavériques* between 1802 and 1804, Esquirol believed that visceral lessions were more likely to cause insanity than brain abnormalities, particularly in melancholics in which, he purported, the transverse colon was displaced.

Esquirol traveled widely in his life and inspected many institutions for the insane throughout Europe. His review of the inhumane conditions in French institutions moved him enough to write a strong report of his experiences to the French minister of the interior in 1818. In 1823 he was named inspector general of the faculty of medicine at the Salpêtrière; he left in 1825 to become the superintendent of the Maison de Charenton, one of France's oldest mental hospitals. The Maison de Charenton was the place where the Marquis de Sade was held for many years until his death. Esquirol spent 15 years working on his famous textbook, which was instantly recognized as a classic and translated into Italian, English and German soon after publication. Esquirol is particularly remembered for providing the first clear description of HALLUCINATIONS and, especially, how they differ form illusions.

Esquirol, J.E.D., *Des Maladies Mentales,* 2 vols. Paris: J.B. Baillière, 1838.
Goldstein, J., *Console and Classify: The French Psychiatric Profession in the Nineteenth Century.* Cambridge: Cambridge University Press, 1987.
Mora, G., "On the Bicentenary of the Birth of Esquirol (1772–1840), the First Complete Psychiatrist," *American Journal of Psychiatry,* 129(1972), 562–566.

etherization After the anesthetic properties of ether were discovered in 1846, it was highly recommended for use in American asylums, from about 1849 to 1860, for acute excitements and for agitated depression. In France it was especially given to those patients suffering from mental DEGEN-

ERATION, most likely those suffering from the general paralysis of the insane and dementia praecox. However, this form of somatic treatment for mental illness fell into decline in the remaining decades of the 19th century.

The discovery of ether's effects also eclipsed the use of hypnosis as anesthesia during surgery. British "Civil-surgeon" James Esdaille had perfected the use of hypnosis anesthesia to perform thousands of minor operations and about 300 major ones (including 19 amputations) between 1846 and 1848, in the experimental "Mesmeric Hospital" that he had been granted permission to establish in Calcutta, India, by the governor of Bengal. Although the medical discipline of anesthesiology evolved from the early surgical use of ether, the use of hypnosis anesthesia during surgery did not come into any significant use again until the 20th century.

Bramwell, J.M., *Hypnotism: Its History, Practice and Theory*. London: Alexander Morning, 1906.
Diethelm, O., "Somatic Treatment in Psychiatry," *American Journal of Psychiatry*, 95 (1938), 1165–1179.

ethnicity and schizophrenia See BLACKS, INCIDENCE OF SCHIZOPHRENIA IN; CROSS-CULTURAL STUDIES; EPIDEMIOLOGY.

etiologic heterogeneity This is essentially a term for expressing the idea that a single disease may have many different causes (etiologies). This idea, which is prominent in GENETICS STUDIES, is derived from the growing body of evidence that several mental disorders—especially schizophrenia and bipolar disorder—are in reality a *spectrum* of disorders, not just a single, homogeneous disease entity. The subtypes of schizophrenia and bipolar disorder, while somehow related, may develop from different causes. Etiologic heterogeneity may result from NONALLELIC GENETIC HETEROGENEITY, PHENOCOPIES or both.

etiology The cause or causes of a disease.

evacuants Now called "laxatives," these were substances that induced defecation in order to "purge" (and therefore "purify") the body. Evacuants and purgatives, especially emetics that caused vomiting, were a popular form of treatment for the mentally ill. The use of these substances continued in one form or another until the late 19th and early 20th centuries. Wilhelm GRIESINGER, the noted German psychiatric authority, writes of the significance of evacuants for the treatment of mental illness in the 1867 second edition of his famous textbook:

> Those medicines which act upon the digestive canal are the oldest, and still those that are most frequently used. Besides their evident indication in constipation—which is common in these diseases–, and very often better obviated by dietetic means and mild clysters than by medicines—they are also given with advantage in all recent cases associated with cerebral congestion, and are the chief remedy in acute inflammatory states of the brain.

Evacuants are no longer used as a treatment for mental illness, although laxatives may be prescribed for a limited time to counteract the constipation that may be one of the side-effects of some types of ANTIPSYCHOTIC DRUGS.

Griesinger, W., *Mental Pathology and Therapeutics*. New York: William Wood & Company, 1882; reprint of 2nd ed., 1867.

exacerbations Those periods when the symptoms of a disease flare up and become worse. They then may go into remission. Many of the psychotic disorders are characterized by exacerbations and remissions. Such is also the case with most other mental and physical diseases (such as multiple sclerosis). These ACUTE episodes may accompany a more chronic course of an illness, such as the POSITIVE SYMPTOMS (delusions and hallucinations) of schizophrenia, which may wax and wane over the lifetime course

of a disease. (See also COURSE OF SCHIZO-
PHRENIA.)

existential analysis   See DASEINANA-
LYSE.

exogenous psychosis   See PSYCHOSIS.

exorcism   Throughout history, many diseases—and mental illnesses in particular—
were thought to be the result of "possession" by malevolent spirits or "demons."
Therefore, the remedy for this, exorcism,
entailed the forceful removal of these entities
by magical means. This spirit possession
theory of disease and exorcism has been
recorded in "primitive" societies worldwide
and is mentioned in historical works dating
back as far as ancient Egypt. In the New
Testament, particularly the Gospel according
to Mark (A.D. 64), one of the defining attributes of Jesus is his magical ability to cast
out "devils" from "demoniacs" and thereby
cure them. As a treatment, formal exorcisms
by practitioners of all sorts, clerical or otherwise, were carried out with regularity in
Europe until the 17th century. (See also
CACODEMONOMANIA; POSSESSION SYN-
DROME.)

Kemp, S. and K. Williams. "Demonic Posses-
sion and Mental Disorder in Medieval and
Early Modern Europe," *Psychological Medi-
cine*, 17(1987), 21–29.
Noll, R., *Vampires, Werewolves and Demons:
Twentieth Century Reports in the Psychiatric
Literature*. New York: Brunner/Malec, 1991.
Smith, M., *Jesus the Magician*. San Francisco:
Harper & Row, 1978.

expressed emotion   It has long been suspected that the behavior of the family has
an influence on the development of mental
illness in afflicted family members. Proponents of most FAMILY INTERACTION THEO-
RIES propose that abnormal communication
patterns actually cause mental illness, and
many theories have been put forth to describe the role of the family in the cause of

schizophrenia. However, the research in this
area has been difficult and so far inconclusive, and many of the older research tends
to disregard entirely the role of biological
factors in the causation of schizophrenia.
Instead, many researchers have turned their
attention to the effect of the family on the
course of an illness. These studies try to
identify family behavior patterns that influence—either positively or negatively—the
mental illness of a particular family member.
The strength of this approach is that it is not
incompatible with the impressive body of
research that points to significant biological
factors in the causation of mental illness
(particularly schizophrenia).

One of the most significant findings is that
the "expressed emotion" or "EE" within a
particular family environment is a suggestive
predictor of relapse in patients after their
discharge from hospital care. EE was measured in families indirectly by analyzing in-
terviews with family members (without the
patient being present). The first published
report on EE appeared in 1962 and was the
result of the work in England of Brown and
colleagues; replications of this work that
consistently support the role of EE in relapse
continued into the 1980s. The consistent
finding is that patients returning to families
with low levels of EE have consistently
lower relapse rates and had less of a need
for antipsychotic medication. The conclusion is that in people with schizophrenia (at
least in its earliest years of manifestation)
there is a lower tolerance for intense environmental stimuli, particularly critical or in-
tensely emotional comments or interactions
involving family members. Thus, a family
environment that is relatively supportive and
emotionally undemanding may help a person
with schizophrenia to reduce dependence on
medication and help prevent relapse. Given
this finding, other research has been conducted that has had trained families of
schizophrenics with high levels of EE (high
emotional overinvolvement of family members and high numbers of critical comments)

monitor their interactions and actually lower their levels of EE. Controlled studies have shown that relapse rates can be significantly reduced for patients whose families can learn to lower their usually high levels of EE.

Some research has examined other variables than EE as the source of important influences on the course of a family member's mental illness. For example, an important study by the UCLA Family Project (reported by Goldstein in 1985) found that instead of EE, which is measured indirectly, other factors, such as a directly measured index of a family's "affective style" or "AS" and a family's "communication deviance" or "CD," had more of an effect either independently or together in the development of schizophrenia.

More research clearly needs to be done in this area. But what is important about these studies is the knowledge that, to some extent, schizophrenia can be managed by reducing or changing emotional interactions within the family.

Brown, G.W., Birley, J.T.L. and Wing, J.K., "Influence of Family Life on the Course of Schizophrenic Disorders: A Replication," *British Journal of Psychiatry*, 121(1972), 241–258.

Campbell, T.L., *Family's Impact on Health: A Critical Review and Annotated Bibliography*, National Institute of Mental Health, Series DN No. 6, DHHS Pub. No. (ADM)87-1461. Washington, D.C.: Supt. of Documents, U.S. Government Printing Office, 1987.

Goldstein, M.J., "Family Factors that Antedate the Onset of Schizophrenia and Related Disorders: The Results of a Fifteen Year Prospective Longitudinal Study," *Acta Psychiatrica Scandinavica*, 71: Supp. 319 (1985), 7–18.

Leff, J. and Vaughn, C., *Expressed Emotion in Families*. New York: Guilford Press, 1985.

expressivity   In genetics, expressivity is the extent to which a given phenotype, or observable trait, is manifest in an individual. It is the extent to which a trait (an observable behavior or a physical characteristic), known to be caused by the influence of a particular gene or genes that predisposes an individual

to that trait, can be observed in the individual.

extrapyramidal symptoms/syndromes
In the human body, the extrapyramidal system encompasses those parts of the central nervous system that are responsible for the coordination and integration of body movements. Perhaps the most serious drawback to the use of ANTIPSYCHOTIC DRUGS in the treatment of the psychotic disorders is their very serious adverse effects on the extrapyramidal system. The symptoms that these side effects produce can include tremors, muscular rigidity, drooling, eyes rolling upwards toward the forehead, odd or jerky movements, blurred vision, dry mouth, odd motions of the tongue and hands, and a shuffling gait. There are four extrapyramidal syndromes: acute dystonic reactions, AKATHESIA, PARKINSON'S SYNDROME and TARDIVE DYSKINESIA. Of these, the first three syndromes can be alleviated with drugs such as BENADRYL or COGENTIN, or through the reduction or cessation of antipsychotic medication. However, the fourth of these syndromes, tardive dyskinesia, is a chronic condition that develops from the prolonged use of antipsychotic medication (usually many years, although sensitivity levels differ from person to person).

eye movement abnormalities in schizophrenia   One of the clearest candidates for being a BIOLOGICAL MARKER OF SCHIZOPHRENIA is certain eye movement dysfunctions. These abnormalities were first detected in schizophrenics in 1908 by researchers Diefendorf and Dodge, and have been studied for their possible link to schizophrenia ever since. The majority of these studies have involved "smooth pursuit eye movements" (SPEM), that is, those eye movements made when following a moving object. With recent advances in technology, scientists have also found that eye movement dysfunctions are detectable even while the eyes are focused on a stationary target.

Overall, smooth pursuit eye movements have been found to be abnormal in about 50% to 85% of schizophrenics in most studies, with the same dysfunctions found in about 8% of the general population. Furthermore, 40% 50% of first-degree relatives of schizophrenics also have smooth pursuit eye movement abnormalities. The rate of abnormalities in persons with bipolar disorder (30% to 50%) is though to be inflated due to LITHIUM treatment, and the number of first-degree relatives of manic-depressives that have these abnormalities is just 10% to 13%—only slightly above the rate for the general population. Thus, smooth pursuit eye movement abnormalities seem to be a genetically transmitted dysfunction and are thus becoming more and more accepted as a solid biological marker for schizophrenia. There is great hope that SPEM dysfunction is, indeed, such a marker, since it could then be used as a predictor for identifying which high-risk individuals are at true genetic risk for one day developing schizophrenia.

Diefendorf, A.R. and Dodge, R., "An Experimental Study of the Ocular Reactions of the Insane from Photographic Records," *Brain, 31* (1908), 451–489.

Erlenmeyer-Kimling, L., "Biological Markers for the Liability to Schizophrenia," in H. Helmchen and F. Hein (eds.), *Biological Perspectives of Schizophrenia.* New York: John Wiley & Sons, 1987.

Holzman, P.S., "Recent Studies of Psychophysiology in Schizophrenia," *Schizophrenia Bulletin,* 13(1987), 49–75.

eyes, subduing patients with   See FIXING.

F

"Factors of Insanities, The"   In 1894 John Hughlings Jackson (1835–1911), a British neurologist who is still considered one of the most important in his field, published a paper on "The Factors of Insanities" in which he proposed some very important ideas that are still used today. In particular, Jackson defined the difference between POSITIVE SYMPTOMS and NEGATIVE SYMPTOMS and their relationship to the nervous system. In the 1980s, these concepts became especially important in schizophrenia research with the work of research psychiatrist T.J. Crow (see CROW'S HYPOTHESIS). Jackson divided the presenting symptoms found in the psychotic disorders according to whether they are the result of the "dissolution" of certain centers in the brain (the negative symptoms), or whether they are caused by the remaining "healthy nervous arrangements" left intact but nonetheless affected in their functioning by the destruction of neural tissue in other parts of the brain (the positive symptoms). The positive symptoms, then, should disrupt the normally complex integrative functions of the higher cortical functions (for example, thoughts and perceptions) and make them caricatures— less differentiated, less complex and more automatic or involuntary variations (such as delusions and hallucinations). Jackson writes:

We must not speak crudely of disease causing the symptoms of insanity. Popularly the expression may pass, but properly speaking disease of the highest centres no more causes positive mental states, however abnormal they may seem, than opening flood gates causes water to flow or cutting the vagi causes the heart to beat more frequently. Disease only causes the negative element of the mental condition: the positive mental element, say a delusion, obviously an elaborate delusion however absurd it may be signifies activities of the healthy nervous arrangements, signifies evolution going on in what remains of the highest cerebral centres.

Jackson's observation that the "disease" or "dissolution" of brain tissue is related to negative symptoms is supported in the evidence for Crow's "type II schizophrenia," in which negative symptoms, such as flat affect, poverty of speech, blocking, are correlated with structural abnormalities in the brain. (See also BRAIN ABNORMALITIES IN SCHIZOPHRENIA.)

Jackson, J.H., "The Factors of Insanities," in *Selected Writings,* vol. 2. New York: Basic Books, 1958; first published, 1894.

Falret, Jean-Pierre (1794–1870) A noted French *aliéniste* who was a member of the "Esquirol Circle," the group of influential physicians to the insane females at the Salpêtrière in Paris (males were kept at another hospital, the Bicêtre), who met regularly for case seminars with their mentor, J.E.D. ESQUIROL. Falret joined the medical staff at this hospital in 1815. After assuming charge of the section for lunatics at the Salpêtrière in 1841, Falret began a program of treatment based on the belief that religion should play a role in psychiatric treatment, a belief that sharply contrasted with his mentors Pinel and Esquirol. He induced a cleric— a certain Abbé Christophe—to come to the hospital and lead group religious activities that included hours of praying, singing and Biblical recitations. He believed that religious practics helped to bring about the cure of mental illness and to avoid relapses. In addition, as he told a journalist in the 1840s, religion played another role in the lives of his female patients at the Salpêtrière because, "Not being able to give them a lover to comfort the solitude of their hearts, I seek to give them God."

Falret is best remembered for his 1854 description of *la folie circulaire,* or the CIRCULAR INSANITY, as it became known in English and which is now known as BIPOLAR DISORDER. However, his linkage of phases of melancholia and mania together into a separate disorder from either of these mental disorders alone had been preceded only two weeks earlier by fellow "Esquirol circle" member Jules BAILLARGER's published description of *la folie à double forme.* Thus, it is Baillarger who is given credit for what

was later named by KRAEPELIN as MANIC-DEPRESSIVE insanity. Falret, however, claimed he had published a description of this disorder in 1851, but did not use the term *la folie circulaire* in that earlier paper. Falret stressed the role of heredity in the transmission of this disorder, and he argued that the disorder was more commonly found in women.

Falret's other contributions include: in 1853, authoritative diagnostic indicators for the GENERAL PARALYSIS OF THE INSANE; and in 1822, the first published study of suicide that used statistical data. He believed that suicide was the result of a combination of predisposing and environmental causal factors.

Falret, J.-P., *De l'hypochondrie et du suicide.* Paris: 1822.
———, "Marche de la folie," *Gazette des Hôpitaux,* Jan. 14, 1851.
———, "Mémoire sur la folie circulaire, forme de maladie mentale caractérisée par la reproduction successive et régulière de l'état manaiaque, de l'état mélancolique, et d'un intervalle lucide plus ou moins prolongé," *Bulletin de l'Académie Impériale de Médecine,* 19(Feb. 14, 1854), 382–400.
———, *Recherches sur la folie paralytique et les diverses paralysies générales.* Paris: 1853.
Goldstein, J., *Console and Classify: The French Psychiatric Profession in the Nineteenth Century.* Cambridge, U.K.: Cambridge University Press, 1987.

Falret, Jules-Philippe-Joseph (1824–1902) A french *aliéniste* and the son of Jean-Pierre FALRET. He continued his father's work in the understanding of the "circular insanity" and of the general paralysis of the insane. However, he is perhaps best remembered for his identification (along with Ernest Lasègue) in 1877 of a form of "communicated" or "shared" delusional disorder, which is still known as FOLIE À DEUX.

Lasègue, E and Falret, J.-Ph.-J., "La folie à deux (ou folie communiquée)," *Annales médico-psychologique,* 18(1877), 321.

family care The placement of mentally ill people in households under the care of unrelated families. In Europe this tradition has persisted since at least the 1300s in Gheel, Belgium, where a shrine to the patron saint of the mentally ill, Saint Dymphna, attracted far too many of the afflicted seeking miracle cures for the local hospital to handle. Thus, a tradition of boarding the mentally ill in private households began and is continued to this day on a reduced scale under the sponsorship of the Belgian government. Foster home care of the mentally ill became more prevalent in Europe only in the 19th century. British psychiatrist Henry MAUDSLEY, who dominated the field in his country in the latter third of the 1800s, strongly advocated the return of the most chronic patients to the care of their own families. In the United States, the very first such formal foster home program was apparently instituted in Massachusetts in 1885.

family interaction theories Popular from the 1950s to the 1970s, this group of theories asserts that severe mental illness (and in particular schizophrenia) is caused by abnormal family communication patterns. The assumption is that the underlying pathological communication patterns of the family create the mental illness in a selected person who is the "scapegoat" or the bearer of the "sick role" for the other members of the family, which acts together in an organized whole usually called a "system." Treating the mentally ill person ("the identified patient") is often depicted by proponents of family interaction as a group "family therapy" during which pathological communication patterns can be pointed out and changed, thus, theoretically, healing or curing the "identified patient." When applied to schizophrenia, most of these theories usually completely ignore biological evidence for the cause of the psychosis.

The family interaction theories were derived from the interest of psychoanalysis in family dynamics as the cause of schizophrenia. For example, psychoanalyst Frieda Fromm-Reichmann first used the term "schizophrenogenic mother" in 1948 to single out the mother as the primary cause of schizophrenia in her children. This concept was later "verified" in a study of 25 mothers of schizophrenics by Trude Tietze in 1949. Also in the 1940s, Leo Kanner wrote about the role of the "refrigerator mother" as the cause of AUTISM in infancy and childhood.

By the 1950s, more sophisticated family interaction theories were proposed that shifted from the focus on the single mother-child relationship to the study of the family as an interactive system that works together as a whole. As early as 1949 Theodore Lidz and his colleagues at Yale University began to publish work on the study of communication patterns in families with schizophrenic members. The family triad of father, mother and schizophrenic child was of particular interest, and two typical patterns of families were discerned, schizmatic and skewed. In the "skewed family," an umempathetic and intrusive mother is the guilty party, and she is paired with an ineffectual male who is passive and perhaps mentally ill or alcoholic himself. The lack of a strong male role model and the over-intrusiveness of the mother tends to produce schizophrenic sons in these families, according to Lidz. In families characterized by a "marital schism," the entire family (rather than just the mother) seems to be at war with one another, with the parents continually threatening separation and undercutting one another. Lidz believed this sort of pattern was more characteristic of the lives of female schizophrenic patients that he and his colleagues studied.

In 1956, Gregory BATESON and his colleagues at Stanford University (the "Palo Alto Group") proposed the theory of the double bind (see DOUBLE-BIND THEORY). The theory is that schizophrenia develops in people from families that engage in "double-bind" communications, i.e., communications in which the content of the verbally expressed message does not match, or is "incongruent," with the underlying message expressed in the tone of voice, gesture, facial expression or context of the message. For example, "I love you" may be said while the parent may have a facial expression of total apathy, or perhaps during a situation in which the parent is being particularly cruel to the child. The double-bind theory was the basis of further elaborations of "family systems theory" by Jay Haley, one of Bateson's original colleagues, and a major influence in the development of "family therapy" as a treatment modality. The essence of the rationale for using family therapy as the treatment for schizophrenia was expressed by Haley in a 1962 article when he notes, "It became apparent that it was not entirely reasonable to have a child driven mad by his family, then hospitalize him and get him on his feet and send him right back into his family to be driven mad again."

Other family interaction theorists have invented other terms for the types of family communications that seem to cause a schizophrenic break in one of the children. For example, in research spanning more than a decade Wynne and various colleagues have identified deviant styles of parental communication that may lead to the development of thought disorder in genetically susceptible children. Communication deviance (CD) is thought to comprise such characteristics as the lack of firm commitment to ideas, unusual language patterns, and problems in bringing closure to ideas or in interactions with others. However, it cannot be as yet determined whether the CD of the parents is the expression of a latent genetic trait, such as deficits in attention that have not fully developed into schizophrenia (but which their child *is* experiencing as schizophrenia) or whether it is the parents' response to daily communication with a psychotic child. Several prospective studies of children at high risk for schizophrenia are currently underway to determine whether family factors such as CD are present prior to the development of schizophrenia.

In the 1988 edition of *Surviving Schizophrenia*, E. Fuller Torrey asserts that,

"Family interaction theories, like psychoanalytic theories, have by now been discarded and for many of the same reasons." He argues that research has been of poor quality or has not held up to replication by others, and that it fails to distinguish between family communication patterns that cause schizophrenia versus those that are caused by it. However, research in this area continues, since at present only a small amount of the "cause" of schizophrenia can be attributed to genetics, suggesting that the environment—specifically, family interaction patterns—may still play a significant role in the development, or at least the severity of the course, of schizophrenia. (See also EXPRESSED EMOTION.)

Bateson, G. et al., "Towards a Theory of Schizophrenia," *Behavioral Science,* 1(1956), 251–264.

Lidz, R. and Lidz, T., "The Family Environment of Schizophrenic Patients," *American Journal of Psychiatry,* 106(1949), 332–345.

Lidz, T., *The Origin and Treatment of Schizophrenic Disorders.* New York: Basic Books, 1973.

Tietze, T., "A Study of Mothers of Schizophrenic Patients," *Psychiatry,* 12(1949), 55–65.

Wynne, L.C. et al., "Schizophrenics and Their Families: Research on Parental Communication," in J.M. Tanner (ed.), *Developments in Psychiatric Research.* London: Hodder & Stoughton, 1977.

family studies (genetics) See CONSANGUINITY METHOD.

family therapy See FAMILY INTERACTION THEORIES.

farming (as treatment) The physical exercise of work has long been employed in the treatment of some mentally ill persons, and well into this century many institutions continued the practice of using patients to help farm or take care of the institutional grounds. However, due to the decline of a farming-based society, most institutions now have pragmatic "occupational therapy" training programs that are designed to help patients gain and maintain skills they will need upon discharge back to an urban community. ESQUIROL in particular recommended farming as the best form of therapeutic physical exercise for the mentally ill, particularly depressed people. In 1838 he writes:

> Corporeal exercises, riding on horseback, the game of tennis, fencing, swimming and traveling, especially in melancholy, should be employed, in aid of other means of treatment. The culture of the earth, with a certain class of the insane, may be advantageously substituted for all other exercises. We know the result to which a Scottish farmer arrived, by the use of labor. He rendered himself celebrated by the cure of certain insane persons, whom he obliged to labor in his fields.

Esquirol, J.E.D., *Mental Maladies. A Treatise On Insanity,* tr. E.K. Hunt. Philadelphia: Lea and Blanchard, 1845; first published, 1838.

Faxensyndrom Also known as the "Clown Syndrome," it is a form of reactive mental disorder, found in prisoners, that simulates a true psychosis. "Childish" or "silly" behavior predominantes in this syndrome as a dissociated reaction to the confines of prison. It was first identified by Eugen BLEULER, and it is related to the more commonly described GANSER'S SYNDROME, also known as "prison psychosis."

Bleuler, E., "Das Faxensyndrom," *Psychiatr.-Neurol. Wochenschrift,* 12(1910–11), S. 375.

Federn, Paul (1871–1950) As associate of Sigmund Freud and a founding member of the Vienna Psychoanalytic Society. Federn applied psychoanalytic treatment to schizophrenia and theorized that the goal of treatment should be the rebuilding of normal defensive boundaries between the ego, which has been weakened, and the id, on the one hand, and the external world, on the other. The healthy part of the person, the remnant of the ego, was to be encouraged and used to combat the sick parts. Federn deviated from classical psychoanalytic techniques to treat schizophrenics, for he believed that free association and the analysis of the positive transference—used in the treatment of neurotics—would only worsen the condition of the patient by creating a "transference psychosis" in which the analyst was viewed as a persecutor. Federn's writings contain many descriptions of the inner experiences of schizophrenics and are concerned with providing new theories about the importance of the ego, following a tradition of "ego-psychologists" of various types who succeeded Freud and deviated from his focus on the unconscious ("id") and its dynamics. He developed bladder cancer in 1949, and in 1950, on the morning of the day he was to undergo an operation for this condition, he committed suicide by shooting himself in the head in his consulting office.

Federn, P., *Ego Psychology and the Psychoses.* New York: Basic Books, 1952.

Feighner research criteria In the 1970s, researchers in the field of schizophrenia began to develop specific criteria for defining schizophrenia that would be universally acceptable and used in all future studies. For many decades, scientists had been conducting research studies on "schizophrenics" without any commonly accepted definition of what a "schizophrenic" was. Furthermore, many studies did not list their criteria for defining schizophrenia, and many studies reported using "schizophrenics" as a single generic group without regard to important differences in the subtypes of schizophrenia. Hence, most of the research prior to the mid-1970s is not cited in scientific journals today, because the patients that were used then might not match the generally accepted definition of the schizophrenic subjects used in research today. The assumption is that the knowledge gained in those earlier studies may not be generalizable to the results of today.

The Feighner research criteria were developed at the Washington University School of Medicine in St. Louis and first proposed in a 1972 publication. They were referred to as the Feighner criteria because of the name of the senior author of the publication. The Feighner criteria consists of suggested diagnostic criteria for 14 mental disorders (including schizophrenia), criteria that would ensure that all future research used subjects with the same characteristics. The Feighner criteria was used extensively in schizophrenia research throughout the 1970s. Other research criteria that were also proposed in the early 1970s were the New Haven Schizophrenia Index and the World Health Organization International Pilot Study of Schizophrenia Criteria, revised by Carpenter, Strauss and Bartko and called the "CSB system" or the "WHO Flexible System." However, in 1975 the RESEARCH DIAGNOSTIC CRITERIA (or RDC) was developed by researchers at the New York State Psychiatric Research Institute, and it is the RDC that has been the most widely accepted research criteria in the study of schizophrenia.

Feighner, J.P. et al., "Diagnostic Criteria for Use in Psychiatric Research," *Archives of General Psychiatry*, 20(1972), 57–63.

Endicott, J. et al., "Diagnostic Criteria for Schizophrenia: Reliabilities and Agreement between Systems," *Archives of General Psychiatry*, 39 (1982), 864–889.

feigned insanity Ever since laws began to accept that some severely mentally ill people could commit criminal acts for which they were not responsible due to their loss of reason, there have been otherwise-normal criminals and selected others who have "feigned" or "simulated" insanity to escape imprisonment or other punishment for criminal acts. In his 1801 classic, *A Treatise on Insanity*, Philippe PINEL devotes an entire section to "Feigned Mania: The Method of Ascertaining It." In this section he provides two illustrative case histories, one being a case of "feigned mania" in a political pris-

oner (whom Pinel humanely does not reveal to the authorities and thus spares the dissident a return to prison) and another exemplifying genuine mental illness. Pinel makes the observation, still all too true today (as anyone who has worked in a state psychiatric facility will admit), that "A guilty prisoner sometimes counterfeits insanity in order to escape the vengeance of the law, preferring confinement in a lunatic hospital to the punishment due to his crime." However, Pinel is honest about the difficulty of identifying simulated insanity.

It may be thought astonishing, that in an object of so much importance as that of ascertaining the actual existence of mental derangement, there is yet no definite rule to guide us in so delicate an examination. In fact, there appears no other method than what is adopted in other departments of natural history: that of ascertaining whether the facts which are observed belong to any one of the established varieties of mental derangement, or to any of its complications with other disorders.

American physician Isaac RAY, whose 1838 book, *A Treatise On the Medical Jurisprudence of Insanity*, was perhaps the greatest contribution made by American psychiatry in the 19th century, devotes several chapters to such topics as "Simulated Insanity," "Concealed Insanity" and "Simulated Somnambulism." He criticizes the practice of using the courtroom testimony of physicians who have no experience working with the mentally ill in distinguishing cases of simulated insanity from genuine ones:

Those who have been longest acquainted with the manners of the insane, and whose practical acquaintance with the disease furnishes the most satisfactory guaranty of the correctness of their opinions, assure us that insanity is not feigned easily, and consequently that no attempt at imposition can long escape the efforts of one properly qualified to expose it.

Ray states that all cases of simulated insanity betray a common characteristic: "The grand fault committed by impostors is, that in their anxiety to produce an imitation that shall deceive, they overdo the character they assume, and present nothing but a clumsy caricature.'' He then describes specific symptoms of ''mania'' that are often clumsily mimicked, and he gives physicians guidelines on how to trick the suspected simulator, urging them to ''contrive some plan for outwitting the pretender, and entrapping him in his own toils.''

Many techniques have been employed through the centuries to detect feigned insanity. Ray relates a tale reported by Benjamin RUSH of Philadelphia in which Rush was called in by the courts to determine whether a man who had just been condemned to execution was ''feigning madness'' or not. Incredibly, Rush based his decision on the man's PULSE, which he found''twenty beats more frequent than in the natural state,'' and therefore, ''he decided, chiefly on the strength of this fact, that the prisoner was really mad.'' With the rise of experimental research on psychology and psychophysiology at the end of the 19th century, objective techniques were eventually sought for use in forensic psychiatric situations. Swiss psychiatrist C.G. JUNG was a pioneer in the creation of a diagnostic device with the famous ''word association'' test, which had already been used in psychiatric research by others. Jung reports the application of his word association tests to forensic issues, including determining cases of ''simulated insanity'' in a series of papers he published between 1903 and 1908.

Today, our knowledge of the psychotic disorders (particularly schizophrenia and bipolar disorder) is so widely distributed that, in most legal situations, it would be highly unlikely for someone to simulate them successfully for any great length of time. However, in non-forensic situations in which it is rarely expected that the presenting patient is lying about his or her symptoms, an impostor can gain admittance to psychiatric facilities by perhaps just claiming to ''hear voices.'' Such was the ruse reported in a famous 1973 article by psychologist David Rosenhan and his associates at Standford University, who sent normal impostors to a psychiatric facility and who instructed them to report only such auditory hallucinations. Most of them were admitted to the facility with a diagnosis of schizophrenia. Rosenhan's criticisms of psychiatric diagnostic practices have, in turn, been criticized by many others (see Spitzer's 1976 article) who defend the actions of the admitting psychiatrists in the Rosenhan study as rational decisions based on the context in which the claims of psychotic symptoms were made.

Jung, C.G., ''On simulated insanity,'' in H. Read, M. Fordham, G. Adler (eds.), *The Collected Works of C.G. Jung, Volume 1: Psychiatric Studies*. Princeton: Princeton University Press, 1970; first published, 1903.

Pinel, P., *A Treatise On Insanity*, tr. D.D. Davis. Sheffield, England: W. Todd, 1806; first published, 1801.

Ray, I., *A Treatise On the Medical Jurisprudence of Insanity*. Boston: Charles C. Little and James Brown, 1838.

Rosenhan, D.L., ''On Being Sane in Insane Places,'' *Science*, 179(1973), 250–258.

Spitzer, R.L., ''More on Pseudoscience in Science and the Case for Psychiatric Diagnosis,'' *Archives of General Psychiatry*, 33(1976), 459–470.

Ferriar, John (1761–1815)   A Scottish physician who served at the Manchester Lunatic Asylum in England. He is remembered for his careful empirical observations and case histories of mental illness, provided in his 1792 book, *Medical Histories and Reflections*. He criticized BLEEDING and PURGING as treatments for mental illness and was one of the first to recommend isolation rather than mechanical restraints for violent patients. He is credited for introducing the term ''hysterical conversion'' into the psychiatric vocabulary.

Ferriar, J., *Medical Histories and Reflections*. London: 1792.

fertility The ability to reproduce children. Fertility rates for people diagnosed with the psychotic disorders have been determined on various populations in many countries over many decades. Many studies have found that the highest rates of childlessness occur among nonparanoid schizophrenics (Type II schizophrenics). The low marriage rates for schizophrenic patients (particularly males) also contribute to low rates of marital fertility (the rate of children per marriage). When census data is used, marital fertility rates for schizophrenia and for manic-depressive psychosis (bipolar disorder) are lower than the norm for the population as a whole. On the whole, no studies have found evidence of any physiological dysfunction that might impair fertility in those people diagnosed with schizophrenia. Therefore the lower rates of fertility are probably due to the severe disruption in the ability to form and maintain social relationships with others.

Saugstad, L.F., "Social Class, Marriage, and Fertility in Schizophrenia," *Schizophrenia Bulletin,* 15(1989), 9–43.

fetal neural development and schizophrenia There is growing evidence for BRAIN ABNORMALITIES IN SCHIZOPHRENIA, particularly "Type II" schizophrenia (see CROW'S HYPOTHESIS) with its NEGATIVE SYMPTOMS. The evidence that now exists suggests that these brain abnormalities develop early in the lives of people later diagnosed with schizophrenia and are already in existence before the full onset of the disease occurs. In many areas of the brain that demonstrate structural abnormalities, particularly those involving the subcortical structures of the LIMBIC SYSTEM (e.g., the hippocampus and parahippocampal areas, amygdala, dorsolateral frontal cortex, and the globus pallidus), the damage is thought to arise during the development of the nervous system in the fetus during gestation.

During fetal neural development, certain nerve cells (neurons) seem to actually travel to specific spots (a process called neuronal migration) and form very specific connections with one another to create distinct structures in the brain (a process called the specification of cerebral cortical areas). In fact, some researchers have argued that there is a strong possibility that the development of schizophrenia later in life is related to a defect in the gene controlling the migration and interconnection of these young neurons during fetal neural development.

A conference on fetal neural development and schizophrenia was held in Washington, D.C., from May 31 to June 1, 1988, and included many of the major researchers in schizophrenia and experts in brain imaging and neuropathology. A summary of the conference proceedings published in *Schizophrenia Bulletin* in 1989 listed the following findings as possible evidence that disturbances in the development of the nervous system of the fetus may be the source of the brain anomalies found in schizophrenia:

1. Recent neuropathological studies have found structural deviance that has been interpreted as evidence of fetal neural development, most likely in the second trimester.

2. Helsinki residents whose *second trimester* of gestation overlapped a particularly severe viral epidemic evidenced an increased rate of hospital diagnoses of schizophrenia. First or third trimester exposure was not associated with an elevation of rates of schizophrenia. A recent study by (E. Fuller) Torrey has found support for these results in the United States.

3. Two clinical studies have found that disturbances of gestation during the second trimester are linked to childhood and adult psychoses.

4. McNeil (1987) has reviewed the now extensive literature on the prenatal and

perinatal experiences of schizophrenic patients; he presents convincing evidence that schizophrenic patients tend to have suffered considerably more prenatal and perinatal complications than controls. Indeed, some perinatal complications may actually be the result of a prenatal insult.

5. Minor physical anomalies are benign congenital abnormalities associated with the disruptions of fetal development. These external signs have been used as indices of otherwise cryptic fetal neural maldevelopment. Several investigators have reported that schizophrenic patients have a significantly elevated incidence of these anomalies.

6. Several investigators have found that the brains of schizophrenic patients are significantly reduced in volume. Such findings could reflect a failure in fetal neural development.

It is hoped that by studying the role of fetal neural development in schizophrenia the interaction of both genetic (neuronal migration and specification of areas) and environmental (viruses, birth complications) factors can be better understood. (See also PERINATAL FACTORS HYPOTHESIS.)

Lyon, M. et al., "Fetal Neural Development and Schizophrenia," *Schizophrenia Bulletin,* 15 (1989), 149–161.

Rakic, P., Specification of Cerebral Cortical Areas," *Science,* 241(1988), 170–176.

Feuchtersleben, Ernst von (1806–1849) Feuchtersleben was an influential Austrian physician whose primary contribution was the invention of many clinical terms still used today. For example, in 1845 Feuchtersleben coined the word "PSY-CHOSIS" to refer to mental illness that was not due to identifiable diseases in the tissue of the nervous system. He proposed this term as a counterpart to "NEUROSIS," already long in use to refer to a mental disorder that is due to the pathology of nervous tissue (unlike today's colloquial usage, which does not carry that emphasis on physiological causes of the disorder). Feuchtersleben also coined or popularized many other terms still in use today, most importantly "psycho-pathology," "psychopathy" and "psychiatrics."

Feuchtersleben, E.v., *Lehrbuch der ärztlichen Seelenkunde.* Vienna: 1845.

fever therapy   Throughout the centuries there have been many anecdotal reports of improvements in the mentally ill following physical illnesses that were accompanied by fever. For example, in the mid-1700s Malcolm Flemyng (?–1764), an English physician, made the observation that "intermittent fevers strengthen the nerves." In a chapter on "The Causes of the Disease" in his 1911 text *Dementia Praecox, Of the Group Of Schizophrenias,* Eugen BLEULER also notes, "yet we often see that mentally ill patients improve extensively after having had fever."

In 1887, Austrian neurologist and psychiatrist Julius Wagner von Jaureg (1857–1940) first proposed the idea that the introduction of fevers might be therapeutic for patients with certain mental illnesses, specifically those with the disorder known as the GENERAL PARALYSIS OF THE INSANE, which was later found conclusively to be the result of syphilis. His first experiments, in which he inoculated these "paretics" with malarial organisms, were conducted in 1917. He achieved significantly beneficial results with this malarial fever treatment, and in 1927 he won a Nobel Prize for this work.

"Malaria treatment" was first used in the United States on the patients at St. Elizabeth's Hospital in Washington, D.C., in 1922, at the initiative of its superintendent, William Alanson White, who ordered from Puerto Rico a supply of 12 mosquitoes contaminated with benign tertian malaria. Eleven of the mosquitoes died in transit, but the sole surviving insect was placed in a small cage and then strapped to the arm of a schizophrenic. After being bitten through the wire mesh of the cage, blood continued to be drawn from this schizophrenic so as to infect 12 other syphilitics and induce the curative fevers in them. The first published report of this syphilotherapy appeared in 1924. Also in 1924, the then-29-year-old Walter FREEMAN, of later "psychosurgery" fame, was made director of the research laboratories (bacteriology, psychology, pathology and roentgenology) at St. Elizabeth's and subsequently continued this research. Prior to "malaria therapy," fevers were induced in patients with substances such as sterile milk and other proteins, with the intention of alleviating symptoms or producing a cure.

Lewis, N.D.C. et al., "Malaria Treatment of Paretic Neuro-syphilis," *American Journal of Psychiatry*, 4(1924), 175–188.

Finland   See SCANDINAVIA.

fire and moxa treatment   See CAUTERY TREATMENT.

first break   The first clear onset of the schizophrenic illness in a person's life. It is an old term in the schizophrenia literature that is derived from the notion of a "first (nervous) breakdown." The term "first-break schizophrenics" is still used to designate those people who come to the attention of mental health professionals for the very first time with the clear psychotic symptoms of schizophrenia.

first-degree relatives   In the search for the genetic basis of mental disorders, it is assumed that the closer the relationship between an afflicted person and his blood-relatives, the more likely these blood relatives will also manifest signs of the disorder. The parents, siblings (brothers and sisters) and children of an afflicted person are known as "first-degree relatives," whereas grandparents, cousins, aunts and uncles, and nieces and nephews are known as "second-degree

relatives." In studies of the transmission of schizophrenia using the CONSANGUINITY METHOD, it has generally been concluded, since the first studies were completed in 1916, that the first-degree relatives of an afflicted person (the "index case") are ten times more likely than people in the general population to develop this disorder. Second-degree relatives are five to six times more likely to develop schizophrenia than the general population.

first-rank symptoms   Due to the extremely complex nature of schizophrenia, many different systems using different criteria have been proposed for its diagnosis. Some systems are based on theory, whereas others are based primarily on phenomenology, i.e., the presence (or absence) of certain carefully described symptoms that are commonly observed in schizophrenic patients in clinical practice. This pragmatic approach to psychiatric diagnosis was characteristic of the "phenomenological school" of German psychiatry, which included such representatives as Jaspers, Mayer-Gross, Kleist, Leonhard and, especially, Kurt Schneider. A phenomenological approach developed by Schneider in the 1939 book *Psychischer Befund und Psychiatrische Diagnose* (published in subsequent editions as *Klinische Psychopathologie*) was to identify only those symptoms that he thought would discriminate schizophrenia from other forms of mental illness. The identified symptoms would be considered "pathognomonic" of schizophrenia.

Schneider identified 11 characteristic symptoms of schizophrenia, which he called "first-rank symptoms," the presence of any one of which would be sufficient for diagnosing a person with schizophrenia. The first three of Schneider's first-rank symptoms are forms of auditory hallucinations: (1) the patient hears voices speaking his or her thought out loud; (2) the patient experiences himself or herself as the subject about which the voices are discussing or arguing; and (3) the patient hears voices commenting on his or her actions as they are performed. The fourth symptom is a delusional percept, a two-stage process in which a patient's normal perception is followed by a highly personalized delusional interpretation of the perception.

The fifth through eleventh symptoms on Schneider's list are best characterized as serious defects in the experience of the normal boundaries that separate the self from the environment: (5) in somatic passivity, the patient experiences him- or herself as the passive and reluctant recipient of body sensations that are imposed from the outside; (6) in thought withdrawal, the patient believes his thoughts are being taken out of his mind by some external force; (7) in thought broadcast, the private thoughts in the mind of the patient are experienced as being magically transferred into the minds of others; and (8) in thought insertion, the patients experience certain thoughts as being inserted into their head by others. First-rank symptoms 9 through 11 consist of affect, impulses and motor activity that are experienced as imposed and controlled from outside the patient's body.

Schneider's first-rank symptoms were adopted in Europe and in many other parts of the world as a primary method of diagnosing schizophrenia. The first-rank symptoms became familiar to American psychiatrists only in the 1970s, and although many of the individual symptoms are mentioned in *DSM-III* (1980), they did not achieve the prominence attributed to them in other parts of the world. Many research studies have been conducted that show that the first-rank symptoms are not pathognomonic of schizophrenia, that the mere presence of any one of the 11 is *not* sufficient for giving someone a diagnosis of schizophrenia. For example, auditory hallucinations can occur in other mental disorders, such as bipolar disorder or in depression with psychotic features. Furthermore, Schneider's first-rank symptoms seem to represent only the POSITIVE SYMPTOMS of schizophrenia (delusions and hal-

lucinations) and do not take into account the presence of NEGATIVE SYMPTOMS (flat affect, poverty of speech, etc.) in some forms of schizophrenia. (See also AUDITORY HALLUCINATIONS; CROW'S HYPOTHESIS.)

Carpenter, W.T., Strauss, J.S. and Muleh, S., "Are There Pathognomonic Symptoms of Schizophrenia?," *Archives of General Psychiatry*, 28(1973), 847–852.

Schneider, K., *Clinical Psychopathology*, tr. M.W. Hamilton. New York: Grune & Stratton, 1959.

five-point restraints   The label given to a technique of restraining violent patients in a psychiatric setting. It refers to the practice of tying a violent patient to a bed, usually with thick cotton cords. Each ankle is tied to a leg of the bed as the patient either lies or is restrained physically on the bed, and the wrists are tied to portions of the bed frame on either side of the patient's body. This technique is called FOUR-POINT RESTRAINTS. For particularly violent patients, a bed sheet or another restraint cord is wrapped across the chest and under the arms and tied under the bed to keep the patient restrained flat on his or her back. (See also MECHANICAL RESTRAINT.)

fixing   A technique recommended by some 18th- and early 19th-century physicians who worked with "lunatics" or "madmen" to subdue unmanageable patients by "fixing," "setting" or "catching the patients by the eye." Although it is unclear whether this practice was derived from the hypnotic induction techniques of practitioners of the "animal magnetism" of Franz Anton Mesmer (1734–1815), which was popular at the time, this willful gazing or staring into the eyes of patients in order to quiet them was recommended by English physician William Pargeter (1760–1810) in his 1792 book, *Observations on Manaical Disorders*. However, this practice was ridiculed by John HASLAM in his 1798 manual, *Observations On Insanity*. Nonetheless, American physician Benjamin RUSH of Philadelphia's Pennsylvania Hospital recommended this practice as an effective "Remedie for Mania" in his 1812 textbook, *Medical Inquiries and Observations Upon the Diseases of the Mind*. After isolating the violent patient from his family and placing him in a private chamber in either "a public or private madhouse," Rush then gives physicians the following advice:

This preliminary measure being taken, the first object of the physician, when he enters the cell, or chamber, of his deranged patient, should be to catch his EYE, and look him out of countenance. The dread of the eye was early imposed upon every beast of the field. The tyger, the mad bull, and the enraged dog, all fly from it: now a man deprived of his reason partakes so much of the nature of those animals, that he is for the most part easily terrified, or composed, by the eye of a man who possesses his reason. I know this dominion of the eye over mad people is denied by Mr. Haslam, from his supposing that it consists simply in imparting to the eye a stern or ferocious look. This may sometimes be necessary; but a much greater effect is produced, by looking the patient out of countenance with a mild and steady eye, and varying its aspect from the highest degree of sternness, down to the mildest degree of benignity; for there are keys in the eye, if I may be allowed the expression, which should be suited to the state of the patient's mind, with the same exactness that musical tones should be suited to the depression of spirits in hypochondriasis. Mr. Haslam again asks, "Where is the man that would trust himself alone with a madman, with no other means of subduing him than by his eye?" This may be, and yet the efficacy of the eye as a calming remedy may not be called in question. It is but one of several other remedies that are proper to tranquilize him, and, when used alone, may not be sufficient to that purpose. Who will deny the efficacy of bleeding for the cure of madness? and yet who would rely upon it exclusively, without the aid of other remedies? In favour of the power of the eye, in conjunction with other means, in composing mad people, I can speak from the experience of many years. It has been witnessed by several hundred students of medicine in our hospital, and once by several of the managers of the hospital, in the case of a man recently brought into their room, and whose conduct for a considerable time resisted its efficacy.

The most famous case of a "cure" using the technique of "fixing" by a physician was the successful treatment of King George III of England for an attack of "mania" in 1788 by mad-doctor Francis Willis, who demonstrated his use of "the EYE" to a parliamentary committee inquiring into the physician's activities.

Rush, B., *Medical Inquiries and Observations Upon the Diseases of the Mind*. Philadelphia: Kimber & Richardson, 1812.
Scull, A., "The Domestication of Madness," *Medical History*, 27(1983), 233–248.

flat affect One of the NEGATIVE SYMPTOMS of schizophrenia. In flat affect there is virtually no expression of affect, and in behavior this may mean that the person speaks in a monotone and that the face is relatively immobile and without expression. Although some contemporary critics of the use of ANTIPSYCHOTIC DRUGS point to such behavior as evidence that these substances reduce people suffering with schizophrenia to "zombies," in fact, such behavioral qualities have been described for more than a century, long before the widespread use of antipsychotic drugs in the 1950s.

flexibilitas cerea See CATATONIC WAXY FLEXIBILITY.

flight of ideas This term refers to the rapid, continuous flow of a person's speech in which there are quick jumps form topic to topic. These rapid shifts are usually based on common associations, plays on words, or are in response to events happening in the immediate invironment. "Ideas" literally "fly" rapidly from the mouth of the person speaking, and this is a very characteristic symptom of someone experiencing a MANIC EPISODE. This can be a sign of BIPOLAR

DISORDER, as well as a sign of ORGANIC MENTAL DISORDERS, SCHIZOPHRENIA or acute reactive psychoses. Flight of ideas may also appear in non-psychotic conditions, such as an acute reaction to stress. (See also LANGUAGE ABNORMALITIES IN SCHIZOPHRENIA.)

flogging In the Middle Ages, a common practice in Europe (especially in German-speaking areas) was the ritual beating or "flogging" of wandering, mentally ill people before escorting them back to the towns from which they originated. At other times, public flogging (sometimes at a whipping post) was the prescribed treatment for the inappropriate behavior of the mentally ill. In his *Dialogue of Cumfort* of 1533, Sir Thomas More of England relates the story of an instance when he ordered the public flogging of "a lunatic" for disruptive behavior in church during the Mass. Apparently the mentally ill person in question would lift the skirts of praying women just as the Host was elevated by the priest during the ceremony. More ordered his seizure and he was flogged until the lesson "was beaten home. For he could then very well rehearse his faults himself, and speak and treat very well, and promise to do afterward as well" (cited in Tuke).

Formally prescribed beatings were common even in institutions for the insane until the early 1800s. Although the practice had disappeared in English and French institutions by the 1820s, it was still a part of the treatment regime in German asylums. Reviewing primarily rare German-language texts from the 18th and early 19th centuries, Emil KRAEPELIN documents this form of "treatment" in his 1917 historical sketch, *Hundert Jahre Psychiatrie (One Hundred Years of Psychiatry)*:

> Rivaling chains in popularity was the lash. Müller (in 1700) related that in the Juliusspital attendants were generously provided with many restraining and punitive devices—chains, manacles, shackles, and efficient, leather-encased bullwhips. They made ample use of these instruments whenever a patient complained, littered his quarters, or became recalcitrant or abusive. "Thrashing was almost part of the daily routine," he concluded. Lichtenberg explained that thrashings were often better for lunatics than anything else, and that they helped them to adjust to the harsh realities of daily life. Even Reil, the enthusiastic champion of mental care for the insane, noted that the straight jacket, confinement, hunger, and a few lashes with the bullwhip would readily bring patients into line. Frank was also of the opinion that a "light blow" was "effective in dealing with malicious or unreasonable patients." Autenreith found that women who persisted in going around naked quickly dressed in response to a few applications of the lash . . .

(See also ABUSE OF PSYCHIATRIC PATIENTS.)

Kraepelin, E., *One Hundred Years of Psychiatry*, tr. W. Baskin. New York: Philosophical Library, 1962; first published 1917.

Marx, O., "Descriptions of Psychiatric Care in Some Hospitals During the First Half of the 19th Century," *Bulletin of the History of Medicine*, 1967, 208–214.

Tuke, D.H., *Chapters in the History of the Insane in the British Isles*. London: Kegan, Paul, Trench, 1882.

focal infection as cause of psychotic disorders A disputed theory of the cause of mental illness that has not been seriously considered since the 1920s. The short-lived "focal infection" theory of American psychiatrist Henry A. Cotton, which he first formulated and investigated in 1916, held that the "functional psychoses" were due to chronic infections in specific areas of the body that nonetheless had an effect on the entire physiological system. It was proposed by Cotton that the weakest infections would result only in "psychoneuroses" in people, but the stronger the infection the more severe the disorder it produced, with dementia praecox (schizophrenia) apparently the result of the most severe systemic focal infections. These infected areas may not appear to be infected nor give the patient any unusual distress, but they were verified as being infected through laboratory tests. The primary areas of focal infection were thought to be the teeth and tonsils. From these areas infections then spread (by constantly swallowing the bacteria originating in the mouth) to the stomach and lower intestinal tract (including the duodenum, small intestine, gall bladder, appendix and colon) and the genitourinary tract. In mentally ill women, Cotton claimed in 1922, the cervix was infected in about 80% of the cases—even in virgins.

From 1916 to 1918, Cotton investigated the suspected foci of infection on the patients of the New Jersey State Hospital at Trenton, where he was the superintendent. By 1918, Cotton decided to take his bizarre theory one step further and actually devised a surgical procedure of treatment based on the theory that this would cure psychosis. In an October 1922 article that summarizes his work, Cotton explains his rationale with the following claim: "For the general practitioner can, not only arrest many cases after a psychosis has developed, but, better still, by eliminating the foci of infection can easily prevent the occurrence of a psychosis." Thus, between 1918 and 1922, Cotton and medical and surgical colleagues from other disciplines performed "detoxication" surgery on some 1,400 patients, removing teeth, tonsils, colons, parts of the stomach and intestines, and glandular tissue form the cervix. In 38 women full hysterectomies were performed, and some patients—both male and female—also lost their thyroid glands. Cotton claimed that, because of this "detoxication" surgery, the recovery rate from psychosis from 1918 to 1922 jumped to 80% of all cases, up from an average of 37% for the 10-year period prior to 1918.

Even in Cotton's time this theory and his surgical techniques for "arresting" psychosis were considered bizarre by many of his contemporaries. In a publication of the remarks of other prominent psychiatrists following Cotton's research summary article in the *American Journal of Psychiatry* in 1922, one critic made the following remarks to Cotton:

> Now, to my mind a colostomy or a colectomy is a somewhat serious operation. Mr. Cotton speaks of them in a way that would almost lead one to think the operation as simple and as devoid of danger as the extraction of a tooth . . . we find ourselves told by the friends of patients, people who have heard of these activities and this theory, not through medical publications, seldom through their family physicians, but through lay journals and the daily press, that something is being done at Trenton by Dr. Cotton and his associates which the rest of us are not doing, and they are demanding that we shall adopt these theories and follow the methods pursued at Trenton.
> We should study this matter so carefully and so thoroughly, not being carried away by the enthusiasm of Dr. Cotton . . . Shall we have our daughter's uterine cervix enucleated, or the tonsils cut out, or the colon removed in whole or part, or my son's teeth extracted with a hope of recovery from dementia praecox or some other bad mental state (?) . . .

The support of the popular media, however, was not enough to keep Cotton in good scientific standing. A carefully designed study to test Cotton's theory was conducted in 120 patients at the New York State Psychiatric Institute on Ward's Island in New York City by the medical director (George Kirby) and a bacteriologist (Nicholas Kopeloff). They found that the removal of focal infections in 58 of the cases did not result in a higher improvement rate than that of the other 62. Surgical work was done on infected teeth, tonsils, sinuses and genitals, but not on the intestinal tract. Furthermore, the study strongly criticized as "unsatisfactory" from a scientific point of view Cotton's methods for establishing focal infection. Thus, the study conclusively rejected Cotton's claim that focal infection is the cause of functional psychoses.

Cotton, H.A., "The Etiology and Treatment of the So-called Functional Psychoses. Summary of Results Based on the Experience of Four Years,'' *American Journal of Psychiatry,* 2(1922), 157–210.

Kopeloff, N. and Kirby, G.H., ''Focal Infection and Mental Disease,'' *American Journal of Psychiatry,* 3(1923), 149–199.

folie à deux   Literally a ''psychosis of two.'' Folie à deux is a mental disorder afflicting at least two closely related persons in which identical delusions and sometimes psychotic behavior are shared and, indeed, strongly supported by each of the partners. Although this disorder is most commonly found in relationships between two people, case histories have been published that show that it can afflict as many as 12 persons in a family *(folie à familie).* In DSM-III-R (1987), the diagnosis of induced psychotic disorder is to be given to those people who were initially not psychotic (the second person or persons), but in whom a delusion or delusions develop as the result of a close relationship with another person (''the primary case''), who already had the delusion prior to the relationship. The many case histories that have been recorded indicate that the ''primary case'' individual may have a higher IQ or some other elevated social status when compared to the person or persons in whom the psychosis is induced. Because this disorder occurs in the context of close and longlasting relationships, folie à deux seems to follow a chronic course that can be eliminated only partially by treatment.

French alienists Lasèuge and Falret first described and named this disorder in a famous paper published in 1877 (translated into English and published in 1964) in which they provide seven case history examples of folie à deux. Prior to this time and as early as 1838, similar disorders had been called ''infectiousness of insanity'' (Ideler) or ''psychic infection'' (Hoffbauer), but the conditions under which they occurred were not described. Lasègue and Falret describe these conditions that lead to the ''contagion on insanity'' in the following way:

In ''folie à deux,'' one individual is the active element; being more intelligent than the other he creates the delusion and gradually imposes it upon the second or passive one; little by little the latter resists the pressure of his associate, continuously reacting to correct, modify, and coordinate the delusional material. The delusion soon becomes their common cause to be repeated to all in almost identical fashion.

Other names given to folie à deux after the time of Lasègue and Falret have been as follows: ''contagious insanity'' (Seguin); ''reciprocal insanity'' (Parsons); ''psychosis of association'' (Gralnick); ''insanity by contagion'' (Carrier); ''double insanity'' (Tuke); ''collective insanity'' (Ireland); ''conjugal insanity'' (Rhein); ''influenced psychosis'' (Gordon); ''mystic paranoia'' (Pike). *DSM-III* (1980) referred to this syndrome as shared paraonid disorder.

At least four different subtypes of folie à deux have been suggested over the years:

1. *Folie imposèe,* in which the psychotic delusions of the psychotic ''primary case'' are induced in a mentally healthy person and disappear in the healthy person after the individuals are separated.
2. *Folie simultanèe,* in which two related persons who are morbidly predisposed in some way simultaneously develop a paranoid and depressive psychosis.
3. *Folie communiquèe,* in which the delusional ideas are induced in a second person, after that person had initially resisted them for a long period of time, and are maintained in the second person even when the related persons are separated.
4. *Folie induite,* in which a relationship between two psychotic persons results in the weaker person's adoption of new delusions that initially belonged only to the stronger one—a commonly observed phenomenon in many psychiatric hospitals even today.

When a group of people (such as a family) succumbs to the delusional beliefs of a stronger personality within the group, this has been termed *folie à plusieurs* or *folie partagèe* ("shared madness"). The famous "Manson family" case of the late 1960s would be a good example of this phenomenon.

Dewhurst, K. and Todd, J., "The Psychosis of Association—Folie à Deux," *Journal of Nervous and Mental Disease,* 124(1956), 451.

Enoch, M.D. and Trethowan, W.H., *Uncommon Psychiatric Disorders,* 2nd ed. Bristol, U.K.: John Wright & Sons, 1979.

Lasègue, C. and Falret, J., "La folie à deux (ou folie communiquèe)," *Annales Medico-psychologique,* 18(1877), 321. English translation by R. Michaud in *American Journal of Psychiatry,* 121:Supplement, 1964.

folie à double forme   This is the very first name given by BAILLARGER in 1854 to the mental disorder we know as manic-depressive psychosis. (See also BIPOLAR DISORDER.)

folie à familie   See FOLIE À DEUX.

folie circulaire   The name given to manic-depressive psychosis by FALRET in 1854—but two weeks after BAILLARGER's publication of a description of this syndrome. Although the two famous French alienists argued over who was first in describing this disorder, Falret's term was more widely used in the English psychiatric literature of the late 1800s, and as a result, people whom we would now call "manic-depressives" were referred to as "circulars" until the early 1900s. (See also BIPOLAR DISORDER.)

food allergies as a cause of psychosis
With the rise in interest in the effects of nutrition on the mind and the emotions in the 1960s, many have suggested that even such serious mental disorders as schizophrenia and bipolar disorder may be due to imbalances in nutrition. In particular, a commonly discussed theory is that these psychotic disorders may be due to the effects of allergic reactions to certain substances in various foods. Since the list of possible allergens in food is gigantic, it has been difficult to support this hypothesis in controlled research studies, although many researchers who hold to the principles of "orthomolecular psychiatry" have continued the search. Most adequately controlled studies have not been able to find evidence of antibodies in the bodies of schizophrenics that would support the notion that the physical system was fighting a substance that it was allergic to. However, it is probable that nutrition does, in some way, contribute either to the development of some psychotic disorders or at least affects the course of the disease. (See also MEGAVITAMIN THERAPY.)

Kinnell, H.G. et al., "Food Antibodies in Schizophrenia," *Psychological Medicine,* 12(1982), 85–89.

formal thought disorder   A central characteristic of many psychotic disorders, and schizophrenia in particular, in which the form of thought processes is disturbed. This is distinguished from disturbances in the content of thought (such as BIZARRE IDEATION). Formal thought disorder may include such commonly observed phenomena in the psychotic disorders as LOOSENING OF ASSOCIATION, INCOHERENCE, BLOCKING, CLANGING, ECHOLALIA, NEOLOGISMS, PERSEVERATION and POVERTY OF CONTENT OF SPEECH. However, DSM-III-R (1987) does not see formal thought disorder as a specific descriptive term due to a lack of clear boundaries of the concept, as there is some controversy as to which disturbances in thought and speech to include as part of this concept and which to exclude. Nonetheless, in practice, and in much of the published literature, formal thought disorder is a commonly used term.

formication   This is the term for a tactile hallucination (a hallucination of touch) in which a person believes insects or other living creatures are crawling around under the person's skin. Although it is rare among the psychotic disorders, it can be more commonly found in people who may exhibit signs of an ORGANIC PSYCHOSIS induced by substance abuse, particularly cocaine intoxication, or may be a part of delirium tremens in alcoholism. In Europe, formication may be one of the defining symptoms of a delusional syndrome known as the MONOSYMPTOMATIC HYPOCHONDRIACAL PSYCHOSIS.

Four As, the   A useful mnemonic term invented by later generations of scholars to refer to the four FUNDAMENTAL SYMPTOMS OF SCHIZOPHRENIA proposed by Eugen BLEULER in 1911. The "Four As" are AUTISM, AFFECTIVE DISTURBANCES, ASSOCIATION DISTURBANCES and AMBIVALENCE.

four-point restraints   See FIVE-POINT RESTRAINTS.

Franklin, Benjamin   (1706–1790) Early American statesman and scientist. He founded the Pennsylvania Hospital in Philadelphia in 1752, the first hospital in the United States and the place where Benjamin RUSH served (starting in 1785) and made his observations of the mentally ill (who had been allowed admission since the hospital first opened its doors). The original buildings are still used today, at their location on Pine Street in Philadelphia. Franklin and Rush were political as well as scientific contemporaries, and Franklin's signature can be seen just below Rush's on the Declaration of Independence. Franklin's experiments in electricity led to the development of treatments by physicians that consisted of passing weak electrical currents into patients to cure a variety of ills—including mental illness. Franklin was chosen by King Louis XVI of France to chair the famous royal commission to investigate "animal magnetism" in March 1784. The eight other members included the distinguished scientist Lavoisier and Guillotin, the inventor of the famous device of execution used extensively during the Reign of Terror following the French Revolution. The committee essentially debunked Franz

Anton Mesmer's claims about the special "fluids" that were supposedly transferred from the operator to the patient and that supposedly caused the sometimes wondrous manifestations. In its report, the committee did not deny that healing and curing was effected by the use of animal magnetism, but asserted that the mechanism at work was simply "imagination." (See also ELECTROSHOCK THERAPY.)

Laurence, J.-R. and Perry, C., *Hypnosis, Will and Memory: A Psycho-Legal History*. New York: Guilfrod, 1988.

McComnkey, K.M. and Perry, C., "Benjamin Franklin and Mesmerism," *International Journal of Clinical and Experimental Hypnosis*, 33 (1985), 122–130.

Freeman, Walter   (1895–1972) The "father of lobotomy." Freeman was born into a prominent Philadelphia medical family and studied neurology in Philadelphia and in Europe. Upon the recommendation of former mentors, in 1924, at the age of 29, Freeman was hired by William Alanson White to direct the research laboratories of St. Elizabeth's Hospital in Washington, D.C. His influential contact in Europe with Wagner-Jauregg, who invented the "malaria treatment" for syphilis, led to Freeman's continuation of this FEVER THERAPY work at St. Elizabeth's in the 1920s. He remained at St. Elizabeth's until 1933, when he required recuperation for a "nervous breakdown" caused by overwork and the ingestion of the barbiturate Nembutal, which he had taken every night for many years. At a neurological conference in London in August 1935, Freeman met Antonio Egas MONIZ, a Portuguese neurosurgeon who had been conducting PSYCHOSURGERY experiments with animals. Moniz excited Freeman with his theories about behavior change through psychosurgery; after returning to Portugal, Moniz performed the first psychosurgery on a human subject (a chronic, severely depressed female patient from a local mental hospital) on November 15, 1935. Moniz published his classic book on the subject in the spring of 1936 and sent a copy to Freeman.

Freeman and his colleague James Watts studied Moniz's book; after procuring the "Moniz leucotome"—the surgical instrument designed by Moniz for psychosurgery—they practiced these techniques on the brains of cadavers. Finally, on September 14, 1936, Freeman and Watts performed the first American leucotomy (psychosurgery on the white fibers that connect the frontal lobe to the rest of the brain) on a 63-year-old woman who had been admitted to George Washington University Hospital in Washington, D.C., with "agitated depression." In November 1936, Freeman used the term "lobotomy" for the first time to describe these operations instead of Moniz's term, leucotomy. Lobotomy simply referred to the severing of the nerve fibers of a lobe of the brain. However, Freeman streamlined psychosurgery with the invention of the technique of trans-orbital lobotomies, in which a gold-plated icepick was inserted directly into the frontal lobes of the brain through the corner of each eye socket (the orbit of the eye) rather than drilling through the skull, as was Moniz's technique. This allowed for the "assembly-line" approach to psychosurgery that enabled the procedure to be performed quickly and with a minimum of preparation on large numbers of patients. In January 1946, Freeman performed the first transorbital lobotomies, assembly-line-style "icepick surgery," on 10 patients in his consulting office. Since the "leucotome" was too fragile for such a procedure, on this historic occasion Freeman used an ordinary icepick found in his kitchen drawer at home.

Based on their lobotomies of 80 patients, Freeman and Watts published their famous textbook, *Psychosurgery,* in 1942, and became world-renowned. Although later discontinued as a dangerous and inhumane technique, it is estimated that, due to the influence of Freeman and Watts, as many as 40,000 lobotomies were performed in the United States in the 1940s and the 1950s. Freeman had high hopes for psychosurgery as a treatment for the psychotic disorders, in particular, schizophrenia. In the preface to the 1950 second edition of *Psychosurgery,* Freeman and Watts argue, "Even more important from the strictly psychiatric point of view is the recognition that some chronically disturbed schizophrenic patients may become completely restored to effective citizenship." On a personal mission to make state hospitals obsolete with psychosurgery, Freeman made dozens of road trips to a dozen or more states in the early 1950s and performed rapid transorbital lobotomies on thousands of mental patients in V.A. and state hospitals. Freeman informally dubbed his missionary travels "Operation Icepick." Many patients still exist in psychiatric hospitals today who were subjected to surgery, their condition either unchanged or worse.

When the U.S. Food and Drug Administration approved the use of chlorpromazine in March 1954, psychosurgery and the chemical CONVULSIVE THERAPIES gradually fell into disuse. Treatment with antipsychotic drugs began to be viewed as the most humane treatment for the psychotic disorders, and there was a public and scientific backlash directed at Freeman and his psychosurgery work. Freeman moved from Washington to California in 1954 and never again performed lobotomies on such a grand scale. He performed his last lobotomy on a previously-lobotomized woman at Herrick Memorial Hospital in Berkley, California, in February 1967, when he was 72. Freeman died of cancer in May 1972. (See also CO-LUMBIA-GREYSTONE PROJECT.)

Freeman, W. and Watts, J., *Psychosurgery.* Springfield, Ill.: Charles C. Thomas, 1942; 2nd ed., 1950.

Moniz, E., *Tentatives Opératoires dans le Traitement de Certaines Psychoses.* Paris: Masson, 1936.

Shutts, D., *Lobotomy: Resort to the Knife.* New York: Van Nostrand Reinhold, 1982.

Fregoli's syndrome One of the delusional MISIDENTIFICATION SYNDROMES of the psychotic disorders (along with the CAPGRAS SYNDROME and the INTERMETAMORPHOSIS SYNDROME. In this delusion, a familiar person, who is seen as a persecutor, exists in the bodies of various others in the immediate environment, who are unknown to the delusional person. The afflicated person recognizes that physical differences exist between the body of the persecutor and the bodies of the people in which the persecutor is thought to exist. This distinguishes Fregoli's syndrome from Capgras syndrome, in which the physical body of the "impostor" is transformed to match the delusion as well. This syndrome was first reported by French psychiatrists Courbon and Fail in 1927, in the case of a woman who felt that a famous actor of that time, Fregoli, was making himself known to her by occupying the bodies of various persons in her environment. The actor Fregoli was known for his effectiveness at changing facial expression on stage, and was in this regard similar to the famous American silent screen actor Lon Chaney—"The Man of a Thousand Faces." Cases of Fregoli's syndrome are extremely rare and may involve an organic component.

Courbon, P. and Fail, G., "Syndrome d'illusion de Fregoli et schizophrénie," *Bull. Soc. Clin, Med. Ment.*, 15(1927), 121.

Christodoulou, G.N., "Delusional Hyper-identification of the Fregoli-type: Organic Pathogenic Contributors," *Acta Psychiatrica Scandanavica*, 54(1977), 305.

Freud, Sigmund (1856–1939) An Austrian neurologist and the creator of psychoanalysis, the famous "talking cure," which has had a profound influence on the treatment of mental illness in this century. Today's various psychotherapies all owe a major debt to Freud and pyschoanalysis for demonstrating that certain mental disorders can be treated or even cured through the use of psychotherapeutic techniques that were not physical (such as drugs or baths). Al-

though the bulk of Freud's clinical experience was not with patients suffering from severe psychotic disorders (unlike that of his one-time disciple, C.G. JUNG), Freud proposed and revised several theories about psychosis during the course of his lifetime.

Due largely to the influence of the German psychiatric literature in the latter half of the 19th century, by Freud's time the terms "neurosis" and "psychosis" had become mutually exclusive categories, and Freud's earliest writings reflect this distinction. As early as 1894, in a letter to his mentor Wilhelm Fliess ("Draft H," dated January 24), Freud speaks of the psychoses as being comprised of "hallucinatory confusion," "paranoia" and "hysterical psychosis." From the earliest, Freud considered the psychoses as disruptions in the way in which a person relates to the outside world. Since Freud determined that many of the psychological and psychosomatic symptoms found in his neurotic consulting-room patients were due to an inner "defensive" conflict between the drive to express sexuality and the efforts to "repress" these feelings and ideas, in his earliest work he mentions "defense psychoses" that are likewise the result of a defensive conflict against sexuality. In other words, people with psychotic disorders defended against their sexual drives by "projecting" the source of their problems on the outside world (e.g., "hallucinations" are internal images or thoughts experienced as "external"; paranoid delusions are the projection of internal strife on the outside world). In fact, their problems are internal in origin. Psychotic people thus withdraw from the external social world because it is mistakenly perceived as a threat.

Between 1911 and 1914, Freud developed his first detailed model of the mind ("the psychical apparatus"). His interpretation of the case history of the paranoid psychosis of Schreber, and his famous 1914 essay "On Narcissism," both led to an interpretation of psychosis as a withdrawal of libido (the energy of the sexual instinct) from its normal attachment to objects and people of the external world (object-love) and a return to an infantile attachment on the self ("infantile auto-eroticism"). This withdrawal of energy to an infantile state was a process of "regression" to a state of "primary narcissism." In practical terms, this means that Freud thought that psychotics "regressed" to an egocentric mental state akin to that experienced by pre-verbal infants, as evidenced by the loss of connection to the "real world" ("abandonment of object-love") that is observed in people with psychotic disorders. After this withdrawal of libido, there is an ineffective attempt to reestablish a connection with the "object world" of external reality, but this is instead done with the projection of delusions and hallucinations, which take the place of reality. Psychotic symptoms were thus seen by Freud as a defense, a way of shutting out the demands of the external world.

In the early 1920s, Freud developed his second theory of the psychical apparatus—the famous structural theory of the interplay of the ego, id and superego in psychic life. While convalescing from the first of many major surgical operations for cancer during the last 16 years of his life, Freud wrote a short paper in 1923 on "Neurosis and Psychosis," which described how these two clinical classes of disorders could be caused by specific disturbed relationships among the three parts of the human mind. In this paper, Freud distinguishes among "transference neuroses" (the type of distorted relationship that arises in a patient in psychoanalysis in which the patient transfers to the analyst infantile thoughts and feelings that were originally "projected" onto the parents), "narcissistic neuroses" and the "psychoses" based on the following formulas: "Transference neuroses correspond to a conflict between the ego and the id; narcissistic neuroses, to a conflict between the ego and the superego; and psychoses, to one between the ego and the external world." Furthermore, in psychosis, the ego was thought to be in

the service of the id, and the main defense mechanism it employed was denial or disavowal.

Even after Freud was forced by the Nazis into exile in England from his native Vienna in June 1938, he continued to write about the psychoanalytic theory of psychosis. In his very last major piece of writing, the unfinished book, *An Outline of Psycho-Analysis* (1940), Freud explained that "the precipitating cause of the outbreak of a psychosis is either that reality has become intolerably painful or that the instincts have become extraordinarily intensified." Yet, as is commonly observed in people afflicted with the psychotic disorders, no one is ever completely out of touch with reality when in a psychotic state and there are "healthy" parts of the mind that are always intact. Freud graphically describes this phenomenon in the following passage from the same paragraph of the *Outline:*

> The problem of psychoses would be simple and perspicuous if the ego's detachment from reality could be carried through completely. But that seems to happen only rarely or perhaps never. Even in a state so far removed from the reality of the external world as one of hallucinatory confusion, one learns from patients after their recovery that at the time in some corner of their mind (as they put it) there was a normal person hidden, who, like a detached spectator, watched the hubbub of illness go past him.

Although true psychotics were generally considered "unanalyzable," Freud's psychoanalysis was used by some of his later followers to treat dementia praecox (schizophrenia). Notable analysts include Abraham, Federn, Sullivan, Fromm-Reichmann, Searles and Rosen, who developed a hybrid treatment ("direct analysis") that he used with institutionalized patients. Although claims of success abound in this literature, with our present knowledge of the course of schizophrenia and the strong biological basis for the disease process, there is much skepticism of claims of lasting therapeutic suc-

cess using this modality of treatment. Indeed, by 1980 the use of psychoanalysis for
the treatment of the psychotic disorders had
virtually disappeared in practice.

Freud, S., "Psychoanalytic Notes on an Auto-
biographical Account of a Case of Paranoia
(Dementia Paranoides)," *Standard Edition of
the Complete Works of Sigmund Freud*, vol.
12, J. Strachey (ed.). New York: Macmillan,
1964– ; first published, 1911.
———, "On Narcissism," *Standard Edition*,
vol. 14. First published, 1914.
———, "Neurosis and Psychosis," *Standard
Edition*, vol. 19. First published, 1924.
———, "The Loss of Reality in Neurosis and
Psychosis," *Standard Edition*, vol. 19.
———, *An Outline of Psycho-analysis*, in *Stan-
dard Edition*, vol. 23.

Fromm-Reichmann, F. (1890–1957).

A German psychoanalyst and a student of
Harry Stack Sullivan at the Chestnut Lodge
sanitarium in Rockville, Maryland. Sullivan
was another psychoanalyst known for his
psychotherapeutic efforts with schizophrenics, and he worked with Fromm-Reichmann
after her exile from Nazi Germany in 1934.
Fromm-Reichmann developed her own style
of treatment, which she called "psychoan-
alytically-oriented psychotherapy," which
indicated that she was departing from the
classical Freudian psychoanalytic procedure
in her treatment of schizophrenia. Many of
her essays on her treatment of schizophrenia
(written from 1939 onwards) are attempts to
describe the inner experiences of the patient
and the therapist working with such traditionally "difficult" patients. She described
the "loneliness" of the schizophrenic patient
and contradicted traditional psychoanalytic
notions that the person suffering from schizophrenia gladly seeks out his or her withdrawal from interpersonal relationships.
Fromm-Reichmann instead argued that the
schizophrenic is eager to reestablish relationships with others but is prevented by a
profound sense of mistrust that originates
from the earliest relationships with the mother.

Fromm-Reichmann was the first to use the
term "schizophrenogenic mother" to identify the mother's role in causing the disorder,
but it was only popularized through its later
use by psychoanalyst Trude Tietze, in 1949.
Fromm-Reichmann also contributed several
essays on her treatment of manic-depressive
psychosis in the late 1940s and early 1950s.
(See also COUNTERTRANSFERENCE.)

Fromm-Reichmann, F., *Psychoanalysis and Psychotherapy: Selected Papers*, D.M. Bullard
(ed.). Chicago: University of Chicago Press,
1959.

functional psychoses This is a term
popular since about 1915 to denote the group
of psychotic disorders that do not have a
known organic cause (etiology). Four primary groups of psychotic disorders have
been considered "functional." Dementia
praecox and manic-depressive psychosis have
long been described as the two main functional psychoses, although the acute recoverable psychoses and chronic paranoid psychoses have also been traditionally regarded
as functional psychoses. The term "functional" is also used to point out the importance of psychological or environmental factors in the development of these psychoses.
Functional psychoses are distinguished from
the "organic psychoses," which are psychotic disorders caused by known organic
disease processes in the brain (e.g., the dementias).

Perhaps the earliest use of the term "functional psychosis" is found in a psychiatric
textbook by German psychiatrist E. Mendel
in 1907:

> . . . there is a great difference of opinion
> amongst authors as to how to divide those
> mental diseases in which no anatomical find-
> ings have hiterto been met and which do not
> belong under any of the forms named. They
> are designated as functional psychoses, by
> which it is not said that anatomical changes do
> not exist, but only that we have so far been
> unable to verify them.

The term has not been used as frequently in the past decade or so, since the prevailing viewpoint is that both schizophrenia and bipolar disorder are essentially organic (e.g., genetic, biochemical) in origin. Thus, the dichotomy between "functional" and "organic" psychotic disorders is beginning to disappear.

Mendel, E., *Textbook of Psychiatry,* tr. W.C. Krauss. Philadelphia: F.A. Davis, 1907.

fundamental states of manic-depressive insanity   When elaborating his description of manic-depressive insanity (a term he originated), Emil KRAEPELIN noted that "manic-depressives" suffered only from a "periodical insanity" and thus were not psychotic all of the time. This was a major difference that separated manic-depressive insanity from dementia praecox, the other "functional psychosis" identified and named by him. However, Kraepelin noticed that manic-depressives seemed to fall into four main categories of personality types, or temperament, when they were in the "free intervals between the attacks" or if the full development of the disease had not yet occurred. These four manic-depressive "fundamental states" are as follows: (1) the "depressive temperament," which is characterized by a "permanent gloomy emotional stress in all the experiences of life"; (2) "manic temperament," the opposite of the depressive temperament, which Kraepelin also refers to as "constitutional excitement"; (3) the "irritable temperament," which is a mixture of the manic and depressed fundamental states in which these people exhibit a chronic hyper-sensitivity and irritability; and (4) the "cyclothymic temperament," which is characterized by the "frequent, more or less regular fluctuations of the psychic state to the manic or to the depressive side."

By identifying these fundamental temperaments, Kraepelin was supporting the contemporary idea that mental disorders may be grouped into categories that are actually spectrum disorders, i.e., that similarities can be found in the symptoms between certain psychotic disorders and less serious personality disorders, which may suggest that they are points on a spectrum of psychopathology. Bipolar disorder, for example, may share the same underlying disease process as BORDERLINE PERSONALITY DISORDER, and schizophrenia may likewise be a variant of SCHIZOTYPAL PERSONALITY DISORDER and SCHIZOPHRENIFORM DISORDER.

Kraepelin, E., *Manic-Depressive Insanity and Paranoia,* tr. R.M. Barclay, ed. G.M. Robertson. Edinburgh: E. & S. Livingstone, 1921.

fundamental symptoms of schizophrenia   When Eugen BLEULER coined the term "schizophrenia" and described this group of disorders in his famous 1911 textbook, he described them as being comprised of a group of "fundamental symptoms" that were "permanent," "specific" and "characteristic" of schizophrenia and not of any other mental disorder. Therefore, the fundamental symptoms are said to be pathognomonic of schizophrenia, according to Bleuler. These are in contrast to the ACCESSORY SYMPTOMS of schizophrenia (e.g., hallucinations and delusions), which may be found in other mental disorders as well. A shorthand label for these fundamental symptoms is THE FOUR AS, namely, AUTISM, AMBIVALENCE, AFFECTIVE DISTURBANCES and ASSOCIATION DISTURBANCES.

Bleuler, E., *Dementia Praecox, Or the Group of Schizophrenias,* tr. J. Zinkin. New York: International Universities Press, 1950; first published, 1911.

fury (or furor)   An excited state of uncontrollable violence and anger that has, since ancient times, been associated with the mental disorder of MANIA. Under Roman law, the Latin word *furor* referred to the mental disorder in which people (the *furiosi*) became manic and violent but were not legally responsible for their actions. The second major category of insanity in ancient Rome comprised those people who were mentally handicapped in a cognitive sense, such as the mentally retarded or, it is assumed, those others who experienced psychotic disorders that led to intellectual degeneration (the *mente capti*). They, too, were not responsible for their criminal acts. For almost 2,000 years "furor" or "fury" has been mentioned by authorities on mental illness as either a separate syndrome of its own or as a synonym for mania. In his 1801 textbook *A Treatise On Insanity,* Philippe PINEL confesses that patients of this type are extremely difficult to treat. He writes:

> I have found maniacal fury without delirium, which in France is called folie raisonnante, whether continued, periodical, or subject to irregular returns and independent of the influence of the seasons, the variety of the disorder most unyielding to the action of remedies. A madman of this description condemned himself to the most absolute confinement for eight years. During the whole of that time he was extremely agitated. He cried, threatened, and, whenever his arms were at liberty, broke to pieces whatever came in his way, without manifesting any error of the imagination, or any lesion of the faculties of perception, judgment and reasoning. Other madmen, subject to periodical accessions of extreme violence, are frequently sensible of the impending paroxysm, give warning of the necessity of their immediate confinement, announce the decline and termination of their effervescent fury, and retain during their lucid intervals the recollection of their extravagances.

As for the treatment of fury, Pinel recommends the following: "Opium, camphire (camphor) in large doses, sudden emersion in cold water, blisters, the moxa, and copious bleedings." However, almost four decades later (in 1838), Pinel's famous pupil, the French alienist J.E.D. ESQUIROL, devotes an entire chapter to "Fury" in his book *Mental Maladies,* primarily to put forth the the idea that fury is a symptom, not a separate disorder, and that it may be found in

many mental illnesses besides mania. "Fury . . . does not require special treatment," Esquirol writes, further arguing:

> It is because fury has been taken for insanity itself . . . that so many grave errors have been committed in the treatment of the furiously insane. They were bled to excess, with the intention of abating their vital force, and it was not perceived that the loss of blood augmented the evil, and that it composed the sick only by depriving them of the power of reaction, necessary for the solution of the disorder.
>
> This symptom has been the cause of the most general, as well as fatal errors in the treatment of the insane. Seeing among them only the furious, all the insane have been treated like dangerous and mischievous animals, ready to destroy and exterminate every thing; against whom it was necessary to protect society. Hence dungeons, cells, grates, chains and blows; means which, by exasperating the delirium, were a principal obstacle to its cure. Ever since these unfortunate people have been treated with kindness, the number of the furious has diminished to such a degree that, in hospitals well kept, and properly arranged, among many hundred insane people, not one can be found in a state of fury.

For the second half of the 19th century, "fury" as a separate form of insanity fell into disuse as a concept. However, it has long been noted (and is true today) that in certain manic states people can become irritable, hostile and, at times, violent. This can be true during certain manic phases of BIPOLAR DISORDER, a fact recognized by German psychiatrist Emil KRAEPELIN in the eighth edition of his famous *Textbook* on psychiatry (which appeared in four volumes between 1909 and 1915), in which he mentions the violent variety called the "raving mania" or "acute delirious mania."

Esquirol, J.E.D., *Mental Maladies, A Treatise On Insanity,* tr. E.K. Hunt. Philadelphia: Lea & Blanchard, 1845; first published, 1838.

Kraepelin, E., *Manic-Depressive Insanity and Paranoia,* tr. R.M. Barclay, ed. G.M. Robinson. Edinburgh: E. & S. Livingstone, 1921.

Pinel, P., *A Treatise On Insanity,* tr. D.D. Davis. Sheffield, England: W. Todd, 1806; first published, 1801.

G

Ganser's syndrome A rare psychotic syndrome (a cluster of symptoms) that likely occurs as a response to overwhelming stress. It has often been referred to as "prison psychosis," since, from the time it was first described by German psychiatrist Sigbert J. M. Ganser (1853–1931) in 1897, it has often (but not always) been found in people in confinement, primarily prisoners. Most of the case histories of the past several decades, however, have concerned people who are not confined and who are not prisoners.

The distinguishing hallmark of Ganser's Syndrome is the symptom of "approximate answers," i.e., blatantly incorrect, absurd and sometimes silly responses to direct questions that required a simple factual answer. In his 1897 lecture titled "A Peculiar Hysterical State," Ganser emphasized the "inability" of his patients (all prisoners) to "answer correctly the simplest questions which were asked of them, even though by many of their answers they have grasped, in a large part, the sense of the question, and in their answers they betray at once a baffling ignorance and a surprising lack of knowledge which they most assuredly once possessed or still possess." Ganser would ask his patients simple questions, and they would give the following responses to him: "Have you eyes? I have no eyes. How many fingers do you have? Eleven. How many legs does a horse have? Three." Ganser remarked on how these people would deliberately pass over the correct answer and select an obviously false one. He concluded, however, that they were not malingering, but that this was a genuine symptom of a mental disorder.

The symptom of approximate answers is sometimes referred to by the German word *Vorbeireden,* meaning "to talk past the point." However, Ganser never used this term himself. Further case studies of Ganser's syndrome have found that there is usually a clouding of consciousness, as well as reports of hallucinations, delusions and later periods of amnesia for the intervals when the symptoms of Ganser's syndrome were present. Although Ganser thought it was a form of hysteria, it is most often considered either a true psychotic disorder or simple malingering, an instance of FEIGNED INSANITY. However, due to reports of clouded consciousness, amnestic episodes and its possible origin as a reaction to extreme stress, it is classified among the nonspecific dissociative disorders under that category in DSM-III-R (1987). (See also FAXENSYNDROM.)

Auerbach, D.B., "The Ganser Syndrome," in C.H. Friedman & R.A. Faguet (eds.), *Extraordinary Disorders of Human Behavior.* New York: Plenum, 1982.
Ganser, S.J., "Über einen eigenartigen hysterischen dämmerzustand," *Arch. Psychiatr. Nervenkr.,* 30(1898), 633. (An English translation by C.F. Shorer appears in the *British Journal of Criminology,* 5(1965), 120.)

Genain quadruplets The Genain quadruplets are a rare set of monozygotic ("identical") sisters who all developed schizophrenia in the mid-1950s when they were in their twenties. They have been studied by David Rosenthal and his colleagues at the National Institute of Mental Health in Bethesda, Maryland, at periodic intervals ever since. At the time of their initial hospitalization at NIMH in the 1950s, they were extensively studied in the hope that they could provide clues to the genetic transmission of schizophrenia. Being monozygotic quadruplets, they were genetically identical. However, the four sisters all differed in the severity of their disorder, and this has remained true throughout their lives. They were last under extensive study at NIMH in

1981, but an update on their progress was published in *Schizophrenia Bulletin* in 1988 by NIMH scientists Allan Mirsky and Olive Quinn; it revealed that the then-57-year-old sisters "are faring about as well now as they ever have in their adult lives."

The name "Genain" is a pseudonym chosen by Rosenthal and is derived from the Greek for "dreadful gene." Likewise, the names for the sisters, given in birth order, were "Nora," "Iris," "Myra" and "Hester" and were chosen from the acronym NIMH. Rosenthal summarized the initial psychological and physiological studies conducted in the 1950s in his book, *The Genain Quadruplets* (1963). Rosenthal felt that the Genain quadruplets were evidence of the genetic determination of schizophrenic subtypes, since they all developed nonparanoid types of schizophrenia, thus fitting the pattern of monozygotic twins. The 1981 follow-up study at NIMH utilized all of the neurological and biochemical techniques of investigation that had been developed since the 1950s. He and his researchers found that there were similar biological and biochemical abnormalities in the quadruplets when compared to normals, but that their CT scans were all normal, showing no evidence of ventricular enlargement and little atrophy of brain tissue. (See also BRAIN ABNORMALITIES IN SCHIZOPHRENIA; BRAIN IMAGING TECHNIQUES; TWINS METHOD AND STUDIES.)

Mirsky, A.F. and Quinn, O.W., "The Genain Quadruplets," *Schizophrenia Bulletin*, 14(1988), 595–612.

Rosenthal, D., *The Genain Quadruplets*. New York: Basic Books: 1963.

gender differences in schizophrenia
It has long been observed that there are many differences between men and women who are afflicted with schizophrenia. This observation is almost a century old. In Emil KRAEPELIN's original description of DEMENTIA PRAECOX in the 1896 fifth edition of his famous textbook, *Psychiatrie*, he makes the observation that: "Men appear to be three times more likely than women to suffer from the forms of illness described here." In the 1980s, as researchers collected evidence on the heterogeneity of schizophrenia, gender differences became an increasingly important area of research. Some of the major findings can be summarized here: (1) men have an earlier age of onset for schizophrenia than women; (2) men with schizophrenia have a poorer premorbid history than women with schizophrenia; (3) males have more NEGATIVE SYMPTOMS than females; (4) neurocognitive functioning is different across many parameters between males and females with schizophrenia; (5) males have a poorer course of schizophrenia than females; (6) males have a poorer response to antipsychotic drugs than females; (7) males have more structural and functional brain abnormalities than women. Thus, by almost any measure, women with schizophrenia as a whole tend to do better than men with the disorder.

A special issue of *Schizophrenia Bulletin* published in 1990 was devoted to the theme of "Gender and Schizophrenia."

Goldstein, J.M. and Tsuang, M.T., "Gender and Schizophrenia: An Introduction and Synthesis of Findings," *Schizophrenia Bulletin*, 16:2 (1990), 179–184.

gender-identity confusion A commonly reported experience, usually during the onset of schizophrenia or during periods of exacerbations, in which a person becomes confused about which gender he or she is. They tend to feel themselves transforming into the opposite sex. If it occurs in a man, he may feel he is becoming a woman, and in extreme cases may report the feeling of being "pregnant." This symptom is not to be confused with the "switching" into an alternate personality of the opposite sex that sometimes occurs in multiple personality disorder, as this phenomenon is situation-specific and is not related to the pervasive sense of one's entire being undergoing the sexual transformation that is found in psychotic states.

gene   The word gene is derived from an ancient Greek word meaning "birth." It is often defined as the functional unit of heredity, or sometimes as an inherited "Mendelian factor" transmitted from parent to offspring. Each gene occupies a specific place on a CHROMOSOME, and this place is called the locus (plural: loci). Each gene is able to reproduce itself exactly at each cell division and is capable of directing the formation of an enzyme or other protein. Genes normally occur in pairs in all cells as a consequence of the fact that all chromosomes are paired (except the sex chromosomes X and Y of the male). If any one of a series of two or more different genes must occupy the same locus on a chromosome, it is referred to as an allele.

general paralysis of the insane   This was the name given to a mental and physical disorder suffered by large numbers of people admitted to asylums in the 19th century; early in this century the disorder was conclusively found to be the effects of the tertiary stage of syphilis. People suffering from general paralysis of the insane (often referred to as "paretics" due to the paresis, or muscular weakening, that characterized the disorder) would first experience difficulties in speaking, then movement problems, epileptic-like convulsions, then a more paralytic stage, which would develop to the point where these people would need constant help in feeding, dressing, hygiene and simply moving their bodies in any desired manner. Psychological symptoms would almost invariably begin with depression, then delusions (sometimes grandiose ones), then a degeneration of memory and other cognitive functions that rendered the sufferer psychologically—as well as physically—paralyzed.

It has been suggested by medical historian George Rosen that the condition may have been observed in the mentally ill as early as 1672 by English physician Thomas Willis (1621–1675), and a mental disorder with similar symptoms was also described by John HASLAM in 1798. The label "general paralysis of the insane" was given to the disorder in 1826 by French alienist Louis Calmeil (1798–1895). However, the progression of stages in the disorder were accurately described first by another French alienist, Antoine-Leurente Bayle (1799–1858), in 1822. As a result, this disorder was commonly known in France throughout the 19th century as *"la maladie de Bayle."* In reviewing the psychiatric literature of his day, German psychiatrist Wilhelm GRIESINGER (1817–1868) found that estimates from asylums in many European countries put the number of admissions of patients with this disorder at anywhere from 6% to 25% of total admissions by the 1860s, with France reporting the highest rates.

With the growing interest in the study of the brain and the nervous system in the latter half of the 1800s some researchers began to suspect that syphilis might be related to the cause of general paralysis of the insane. Although this hypothesis was controversial, a research study by German neurologist and psychiatrist Richard von Krafft-Ebing (1840–1902) strongly suggested such a link in 1897. In 1906 German bacteriologist August von Wassermann and his colleagues devised the diagnostic blood test for syphilis that still bears his name, and in 1913 the issue was finally laid to rest when the syphilitic organism was found in the brains of paretics by Noguchi and Moore.

The story of general paralysis of the insane, or "dementia paralytica" as it is sometimes called in the 20th-century psychiatric literature, may have important lessons for our present study of schizophrenia. Like the 19th-century disorder, schizophrenia also involves a complex disease process with both psychological and physiological symptoms. Like paresis, schizophrenia, too, has been the subject of controversy between those who believe it is environmentally caused (e.g., psychoanalytic and the early family systems theories) and those who have sought biological etiologies. Although the true cause or causes of schizophrenia is not yet known, advances in technology may bring the proof of the identifiable biological processes that are responsible for the disorder. (See also DEGENERATION.)

Bayle, A.L., *Traité des maladies du cerveau et de ses membranes*. Paris: 1826.

Noguchi, H. and Moore, J.W., "A Demonstration of Treponema Pallidum in the Brain in Cases of General Paralysis," *Journal of Experimental Medicine*, 17(1913), 232–238.

Rosen, G., *Madness In Society: Chapters in the Historical Sociology of Mental Illness*. Chicago: University of Chicago Press, 1968.

genetic counseling for schizophrenia

With the advances made in linking certain medical disorders to specific genes (e.g., Huntinton's chorea with chromosome 4, in 1983), more and more prospective parents have sought genetic counseling to discover the risks involved when there is a family history of a particular disease. This presents difficulties for those who seek genetic counseling for schizophrenia, since the patterns of transmission are still unknown. The only solid information that can presently be offered are risk factors calculated by certain computer programs (with names like RISKMF, LIPED and LINKAGE) that are based on a polygenetic or multifactorial model for the transmission of schizophrenia. These computer programs can calculate the risks for each combination of affected or unaffected family members, ranging from a risk of .9% (the base rate found in the general population) to over 50% (when both parents and other relatives have the illness). Given this lack of knowledge, should a genetic counselor ever advise schizophrenics or their mates *not* to have children? In this situation,

a well-known textbook on genetic counseling by Fuhrmann and Vogel argues that the risks are high enough even with present knowledge to always discourage having children. Others, however, may argue only that this advice should "usually" be given in this situation. For example, in a 1976 article a major figure in schizophrenia research, L. Erlenmeyer-Kimling, observes that, "Parenthood and schizophrenia tend to mix poorly." She adds the following explanation:

In addition to the genetic risks to the children of schizophrenic parents, there is considerable likelihood that any children of such parents will be exposed to a disrupted home environment, and frequently to a grossly unsuitable one. The birth of a child often exacerbates the patient's illness, and the responsibilities of bringing up the children tend to trigger further difficulties.

An experimental program for genetic counseling for schizophrenia was set up in London's Maudsley Hospital Genetic Clinic in 1983–84, with the results reported by Adrianne Reveley in 1985. Most of the cases inquired about the risk of potential offspring developing schizophrenia in situations where (a) one of the prospective parents was schizophrenic or (b) when a relative of one of the two prospective parents had schizophrenia. Contrary to the strong opinions of some scholars in the field, in practice, genetic counselors cannot scientifically make these decisions for people, and the staff at the Maudsley Clinic did not do so. Their philosophy should be remembered by those who either seek or give genetic counseling for schizophrenia: "It is not the role of a genetic counsellor to advise individuals, but rather to present the evidence of risk, and provide enough information for those seeking counsel to make their own decisions."

A similar situation presently exists for the genetic counseling of bipolar disorder. A review of this issue by Cadoret in 1976 (still valid today) concludes that such counseling might be so tentative at present as to be virtually useless. (See also GENETIC TRANS-MISSION.)

Cadoret, R.J., "The Genetics of Affective Disorder and Genetic Counseling," *Social Biology*, 23(1976), 116–122.

Erlenmeyer-Kimling, L., "Schizophrenia: A Bag of Dilemmas," *Social Biology*, 23(1976), 123–134.

Fuhrmann, W. and Vogel, F., *Genetic Counseling*, 3rd ed. New York: Springer-Verlag, 1982.

Reveley, A., "Genetic Counselling for Schizophrenia," *British Journal of Psychiatry*, 147 (1985), 107–112.

genetic heterogeneity This is one of the possible modes of the GENETIC TRANSMISSION of schizophrenia. It is also sometimes referred to as ETIOLOGIC HETEROGENEITY. The idea is that schizophrenia (or other psychotic disorders such as bipolar disorder) may be caused by any one of a number of single genes, located, perhaps, even on different chromosomes, each one of which is entirely capable of predisposing to the disease without the additional effect of other genes.

genetic markers of vulnerability In the search for BIOLOGICAL MARKERS OF SCHIZOPHRENIA and bipolar disorder, the assumption is that certain measurable physiological processes accompany specific diseases and, it is hoped, may be related to the cause of the disease. Furthermore, it is hoped that these characteristic biological markers are indeed true genetic markers for the disorder, that is, that the biological characteristic and the disease are genetically linked and follow related patterns of genetic transmission. Identifying such a biological characteristic (such as "smooth pursuit eye movement abnormalities" in schizophrenia) may then be considered a sign or a marker of the genetic vulnerability of the person with the marker for the disease to which it is linked.

According to a highly recommended report on *Behavioral Genetics* by the National Institute of Mental Health, a genetic marker must meet the following criteria:

1. The characteristic must be associated with an increased likelihood of the illness (although all people with the illness need not show the characteristic nor vice versa). It is then a marker for the illness, though not necessarily a genetic one.
2. It must be heritable and not be a secondary effect of the illness. That is, it must be genetic and not a result of having had the illness.
3. It must be observable (or evocable) in the well state in addition to the ill state. Since the marker is a predisposition to the illness, not a marker of the illness itself, we should expect it in at least some well relatives and the recovered ill.
4. Transmission of both the characteristic and the illness must be related within pedigrees. This demonstration shows the characteristic is a necessary or contributing genetic factor in an illness.

Therefore, the search for genetic markers is a quest for the underlying biological predisposition or vulnerability to a particular disease that is detectable in the afflicted person during periods of remission as well as when actively symptomatic. This shifts the attention of research away from studying just those periods when the disease is most visible.

There are several strategies for searching for genetic markers of vulnerability. In well-state studies, patients, either in remission or actively psychotic, along with their relatives who do not have psychotic disorders can be matched according to a marker they all share, and which distinguishes them from "normals" who do not have the marker nor the disorder. For example, EYE-MOVEMENT ABNORMALITIES may be such a marker for schizophrenia, since it has been found in many schizophrenics and their nonschizophrenic relatives and is thought to have a genetic basis. Or, such genetically vulnerable people and normals may be distinguished from one another if they have different re-actions to a specific drug that is experimentally administered for a short period, a technique known as a PHARMACOLOGIC CHALLENGE.

Once a suspected biological marker of vulnerability is identified, it can be analyzed according to how highly correlated the transmission of the marker and the disorder is in families. One of the most powerful statistical procedures for this is SEGREGATION ANALYSIS. In segregation analysis, the observed frequency of illness in a *sibship* (the group of all siblings of the afflicted person, and their parents) or in a *pedigree* (the multigenerational extended family group) is compared with a hypothetical pattern of inheritance that is based on a particular model of a mode of genetic transmission (for example, possible patterns based on the theory that only one gene is the cause of the disorder or the theory that more than one gene is, in combination, responsible for the disease). These complicated analyses are done by computer.

If a biological marker is identified that seems to be transmitted throughout a family in a highly similar manner to the way the disease is inherited, then the next strategy would be to link the marker to a single CHROMOSOME or to a location on a specific chromosome. The marker is then called a LINKED MARKER. This search for disease-related genes is done through a statistical procedure known as LINKAGE ANALYSIS. Linkage analysis is considered more sensitive than segregation analysis for detecting a single "locus" or place that is responsible for predisposition to the illness (monogenetic transmission), and it is less suited to a model of genetic transmission that hypothesizes that many genetic places or loci, plus perhaps the environment, may be responsible together for predisposition to the illness (polygenetic transmission). Therefore, the linkage of a particular disorder to a specific chromosome (such as the linkage of schizophrenia to abnormalities on chromosome 5) only lets us know where on the chromosome the genetic predisposition may originate, and does not necessarily tell us anything about the actual cause of the disorder, which may involve many factors, both genetic and environmental.

At present, it must be emphasized that there are no definite genetic markers for schizophrenia. (See also CANDIDATE GENES; CHROMOSOME ABNORMALITIES; GENETIC TRANSMISSION.)

National Institute of Mental Health, *Behavioral Genetics, Science Monographs No.2*, DHEW Publication No. (ADM) 80–876. Washington, D.C.: U.S. Gov't. Printing Office, 1980.

Pardes, H. et al., "Genetics and Psychiatry: Past Discoveries, Current Dilemmas, and Future Directions," *American Journal of Psychiatry*, 146(1989), 435–443.

genetics studies   The idea that "madness" or "insanity" is inherited in some way from generation to generation has been hypothesized for thousands of years. Although family patterns of disease were observed, the causes people attributed them to were not scientific. The "sins of the father" (or perhaps some other family member), which may have brought a Divine curse upon the family, were considered to be manifested in the mental illness of certain family members. Or people simply attributed the mental illness in an afflicted family to "bad blood."

Many of the earliest psychiatric manuals from the early 1800s all comment on the fact that some mental disorders are associated with certain families and not others. By mid-century, so many statistical studies had been compiled by researchers at various asylums that Wilhelm GRIESINGER could write in 1845:

Statistical investigations strengthen very remarkably the opinion generally held by physicians and the laity, that in the greater number of cases of insanity a hereditary predisposition lies at the bottom of the malady; and I believe that we might, without hesitation, affirm that there is really no circumstance more powerful than this.

With advances in the scientific theory that inherited characteristics were the result of a biological process of genetics, in the early 1900s more careful records were kept of family histories of people who exhibited mental illness. The language of genetics began to be used in theories about the cause of dementia praecox (schizophrenia) at about this time. For example, German psychiatrist Wilhelm Weygandt (1870–1939) writes in 1907 that, "I should like to put forward a tentative explanation of dementia praecox of my own . . . I would suggest that so far as the organic side is concerned the most plausible concept is one of autotoxic damage affecting genetically predisposed brains."

Perhaps the historical starting point for the modern study of the genetics of schizophrenia is the work of Ernst Rüdin, who published a study using the CONSANGUINITY METHOD in 1916. He found that there was a higher rate of schizophrenia in the relatives of the "proband" or "index case," as the afflicted person was called, than in the population as a whole. He also recognized that the suspected gene was passed along from generation to generation in a pattern that did not fit known patterns of genetic transmission (this is called NON-MENDELIAN PATTERNS OF TRANSMISSION). Further "family studies," as the consanguinity method is also called, were conducted in the following decades by others, most notably F.J. Kallmann, whose book *The Genetics of Schizophrenia* appeared in 1938. It is Kallmann's work that most scholars consider the true starting point for the scientific investigation of the genetics of schizophrenia.

Since Rüdin's work in 1916, most studies have shown that first-degree relatives (parents, siblings, children) of the afflicted person have at least a 10 times greater risk of developing schizophrenia than the general population, although some estimates in the mid-1980s have put this risk as high as 18 times greater. The risk for first-degree relatives of people with bipolar disorder has been found by some studies in the 1980s to be as high as 25 times greater than the general population.

During the 1960s, studies employing the ADOPTION METHOD were conducted to test the hypothesis that genetics was involved in the development of schizophrenia. Adoption studies that examined the siblings of an afflicted person, or the children of an afflicted person (who were adopted at birth and raised in families with no history of psychotic disorders), have all consistently found that the biological relatives of schizophrenics (who were adopted and raised in "normal" families) had a much higher rate of developing schizophrenia than the biologically-unrelated siblings in the adopting family.

A third type of genetics studies has employed the TWINS METHOD. The twins studies compare the CONCORDANCE RATE for a disorder in MONOZYGOTIC TWINS ("identical twins" who are assumed to share close to 100% of their genes) with that for the disorder in DIZYGOTIC TWINS (who are assumed to have about 50% of their genes in common). If schizophrenia or bipolar disorder is genetically transmitted, then the likelihood that both monozygotic twins would develop the disease, if one of them has it, should be much higher than the likelihood of the same thing happening in pairs of dizygotic twins. However, the rate for dizygotic twins in which at least one member is afflicted should still be higher than that for the general population because of the genetic vulnerability assumed in close relatives of people with a genetically transmitted disorder.

In fact, the difference in concordance rates between monozygotic and dizygotic twins strongly supports the hypothesis that there is a genetic component in the transmission of schizophrenia and bipolar disorder. The twins studies have consistently shown that there is a higher rate for monozygotic twins than dizygotic twins, and the rates for both are higher than that for the general population. Indeed, for schizophrenia, there is a 40 to 60-times greater risk for developing schizophrenia in monozygotic twins than in the general population—a strong confirmation that genetics are involved in the development of the disease. For bipolar disorder, monozygotic twins have a concordance rate of 79% and dizygotic twins a rate of 19%.

Besides the traditional family studies, adoption studies and twins studies, specific BIOLOGICAL MARKERS, which are often found in people with particular disorders, are analyzed to determine if they are true GENETIC MARKERS of the disease. With advances in technology in the field of MOLECULAR GENETICS, subtle MOLECULAR MARKERS (sometimes referred to as "polymorphic DNA markers") can be detected at the level of molecules, many of which have been identified and linked to most of the known major genes. For example, in the late 1980s there was considerable research on "restriction length polymorphisms" (RFLPs) as a molecular marker for schizophrenia. Identifying the molecular markers of schizophrenia and bipolar disorder might then lead to their localization on certain genes. Statistical methods of analysis, such as SEGREGATION ANALYSIS and LINKAGE ANALYSIS are employed in the search for the mode of GENETIC TRANSMISSION (still unknown in schizophrenia and bipolar disorder) and for the place (or "locus") on the suspected CHROMOSOME or chromosomes where the major genes that cause the predisposition to the disorder are located.

Certain molecular markers have led to the linkage of schizophrenia to chromosome 5 and to chromosome X, and bipolar disorder to chromosome 11 and chromosome X. Although there is presently a linkage to certain chromosomes, the actual genes that are responsible for the predisposition to the illness are not yet known. This is true for nonpsychiatric diseases that have also been linked to specific chromosomes. For example, although it has been known since 1983 that Huntington's Chorea was localized on chromosome 4, it is still not known what specific genes are responsible for the illness. Thus, despite reports in newspapers and magazines and on television, the gene that causes schizophrenia has not yet been discovered.

Other points to remember about the present state of knowledge from genetics studies are: (1) Since there is already thought to be more than one subtype of schizophrenia (and different variants of bipolar disorder), there is a significant possibility that there are many different genetic forms of schizophrenia (although, as a 1981 study by C. Scharfetter suggests, there is a tendency for people of a particular subtype of schizophrenia to have relatives that develop the same subtype); and (2) any pattern in the mode of genetic transmission of these disorders does not follow known patterns and is presently unknown, so it is impossible to definitely predict who will and will not develop schizophrenia, as only the probabilities are known for this.

Perhaps the best summary to date on genetics studies of schizophrenia can be found in a 1984 issue of *Schizophrenia Bulletin* (vol. 15, no. 3) titled "Advances in the Genetics of Schizophrenia." *Schizophrenia Bulletin* is published by the National Institute of Mental Health, and free back issues of this special issue (as available) and others may be obtained from the Schizophrenia Research Branch of NIMH at (301) 443-4707.

Griesinger, W., *Mental Pathology and Therapeutics,* tr. C.L. Robinson and J.Rutherford. New York: William Wood & Co., 1882; first published, 1845–65.

Reiss, D., Plomin, R., and Hetherington, E.M., "Genetics and Psychiatry: An Unheralded Window on the Environment," *American Journal of Psychiatry,* 148(1991), 283–291.

Scharfetter, C., "Subdividing the Functional Psychoses: A Family Heredity Approach," *Psychological Medicine,* 11(1981), 637–640.

Weygandt, W., "Critical Comments on the Psychology of Dementia Praecox," in J. Cutting and M. Shepherd (eds.), *The Clinical Roots of the Schizophrenia Concept: Translations of Seminal European Contributions on Schizophrenia.* Cambridge, U.K.: Cambridge University Press, 1987; first published as "Kritische Bemerkungen zur Psychologie der Dementia praecox," *Monatschrift für Psychiatrie und Neurologie,* 22(1907), 289–301.

genetic transmission   Despite more than 50 years of the study of the genetics of schizophrenia, the pattern of the transmission of the disease from family member to family member is unknown. Several possible models of the mode of genetic transmission of schizophrenia have been proposed.

There are, however, essentially two major varieties. One type of model proposes that a single major gene has defects that predispose an individual to a particular disease. This is known as a monogenetic transmission model. It is also sometimes called the "generalized single locus (GSL) model" or, by others, a "Mendelian pattern," since the defective gene in classical MENDELIAN TRANSMISSION patterns (the first genetic transmission patterns ever identified) is either a dominant gene, a recessive gene or a sex-linked gene (a single gene located on a sex chromosome). This is the oldest model for the genetic transmission of schizophrenia and was first proposed by Rosanoff and Orr in 1911. This monogenetic model of genetic transmission is the type more likely to be detected through LINKAGE ANALYSIS statistical procedures, which are considered more powerful than SEGREGATION ANALYSIS in the detecting of a single gene that may be responsible for the predisposition to schizophrenia.

As of 1989, more than 3,000 physical diseases (albeit somewhat rare ones) have been found to be monogenetic and are transmitted according to Mendelian patterns. Much research continues to be conducted in the hope that mental illnesses may also be transmitted in this "single gene" fashion.

The second type is polygenetic models of transmission, sometimes called "non-Mendelian models of transmission." The assumption here is that the genetic predisposition to a particular disease is the result of an additive effect. That is, the predisposition exists only through the combined effects of several genes. There are many physical characteristics that are polygenetically determined in all of us, such as height and intelligence. Furthermore, many physical illnesses such as diabetes are polygenetically determined. Mental disorders, especially schizophrenia and bipolar disorder, are likewise thought to be more likely to follow a polygenetic pattern of transmission. Computer models of transmission that also account for environmental factors in the development of the disease are called MULTIFACTORIAL THRESHOLD MODELS OF GENETIC TRANSMISSION, first proposed by Falconer in 1965 and adapted to schizophrenia by Gottesman and Shields in 1967. This is a form of a DIATHESIS-STRESS THEORY of schizophrenia.

Another idea that combines concepts from the monogenetic and polygenetic models is the GENETIC HETEROGENEITY of a particular disorder. The hypothesis here is that the same disease (schizophrenia) may be caused by any one of a number of genes located in different places (multiple loci). Any one of these genes alone would be sufficient to cause the disorder. Thus, while conflicting results of research may place the "schizophrenia-gene" at first on chromosome 5, then chromosome X, this may just be confirming evidence for the genetic heterogeneity of schizophrenia.

There continues to be much debate among researchers as to whether schizophrenia and the psychotic disorders follow a monogenetic or a polygenetic mode of transmission, or a "mixed model" of the two—a debate that is destined to be resolved by the research of the 1990s and beyond.

Falconer, D.S., "The Inheritance of Liability to Certain Diseases Estimated from the Incidence among Relatives,'' *Annals of Human Genetics,* 29(1965), 51–76.

Garver, D.L. et al., ''Schizophrenia and the Question of Genetic Heterogeneity,'' *Schizophrenia Bulletin,* 15(1989), 421–430.

Gottesman, I.I. and Shields, J., ''A Polygenetic Theory of Schizophrenia,'' *Proceedings of the National Academy of Sciences of the United States of America,* 58(1967), 199–205.

Rosanoff, A.J. and Orr, F.I., ''A Study in Insanity in the Light of Mendelian Theory,'' *American Journal of Insanity,* 68(1911), 221–261.

Rosenthal, D. and Kety, S., *The Transmission of Schizophrenia.* Oxford: Pergamon Press, 1968.

genome A combination of the words ''gene'' and ''chromosome,'' the word genome is the complete set of chromosomes derived from one parent; or it can refer to the total gene complement of a set of chromosomes found in higher life forms. On April 27, 1989, an announcement was made at Cold Spring Harbor Laboratory in New York state, a major genetics research center, that an international organization of geneticists was being formed to initiate an immense project to identify and define all human genes and genetic material. At present only a few thousand of the estimated 50,000 to 100,000 human genes are known, and therefore the task of the Human Genome Organization is to organize teams of scientists from around the world to systematically identify and map each human gene—thus providing a complete genetic picture of the human race. If the project to map the human genome is successful, it should have profound implications for understanding the causes of many diseases—especially mental disorders such as schizophrenia and bipolar disorder—and perhaps lead to the development of technology enabling early detection and prevention of these disorders.

genotype The genetic composition of an individual. It may also refer to a gene combination at any one locus or with respect to any specified combination of loci.

Germany Prevalence studies for schizophrenia conducted in the 1930s found prevalence rates ranging from 1.9 to 2.6 per thousand. Current evidence suggests that the prevalence rates have not changed in Germany since the 1930s.

Torrey, E.F., *Schizophrenia and Civilization.* New York: Jason Aronson, 1980.

Ghana The West African country of Ghana (formerly the Gold Coast) has been the subject of several schizophrenia prevalence studies since the 1940s. The most striking finding is that in one area of northern Ghana the prevalence of schizophrenia increased sharply between 1937 and 1963. Since this coincided with the pervasive introduction of Western cultural influences, the Ghana studies are often cited by E. Fuller Torrey as possible indications that schizophrenia is a ''disease of civilization.''

Torrey, E.F., *Schizophrenia and Civilization.* New York: Jason Aronson, 1980.

Gheel Colony Gheel, Belgium, has been the home of a shrine to Saint Dymphna, the patron saint of the mentally ill, since the 11th century. Many miraculous cures are said to have taken place there. However, by the 14th century the large number of mentally ill pilgrims was becoming unmanageable, and a hospital and humane system of family care were established. Mentally ill pilgrims would be placed in local households and be under the foster care of family members. Although as recently as the late 1930s it was reported that as many as 4,000 mentally ill persons were under foster care in the community, by the 1960s this number had been significantly reduced, with about 1,700 being served in 1970. However, the Belgian Ministry of Public Health still provides psychiatric services for these people in the Gheel Colony. The hospital that works with the families of the area is called the Rijkspsychiatrisch Ziekenhuis-Centrum voor Gezinsverpleging (the "State Psychiatric Hospital-Center for Family Care.").

The Gheel Colony is a remarkable example of how the severely mentally ill can be integrated into society as an alternative to institutionalization. Attempts to copy the "Gheel model" of care in Great Britain and the United States in the 19th century were known as the "cottage system" or as "boarding-out," but no successful long-term program based on the Gheel Colony has ever been devised.

American psychiatrist William Alanson White made a series of trips, beginning in 1906, to visit European hospitals for mental disease. In his memoirs, he gives a colorful description of the unique system of community care for the mentally ill at Gheel:

One of the most interesting of my visits was to Gheel, in Belgium, where the patients for the most part live with the families that make up this settlement. The hospital itself, the so-called *asile fermé*, occupies the central position. The little town of Gheel consists for the most part of a few stores on one side of a single street, and the country for twenty miles about is occupied by peasants who live upon and cultivate the land. This condition has been maintained over many centuries. The patients who are sent there are studied in the central asylum and if found to be sufficiently reliable are sent out to the little farm cottages, where they live with the peasant's families. The doctor makes his rounds once a month on his bicycle, sees the patient, chats with him and weighs him, the weight being considered one of the outstanding evidences that the patient is being properly cared for. I visited a number of these homes and found that the patient's room was a plain affair furnished only with a bed and a chair and perhaps a table and a rug, with a crucifix at the head of the bed. The patient himself, treated as a member of the family, could usually be found downstairs or nearby, engaged in the household work or the work of the farm.

Parry-Jones, W.L., "The Model of the Gheel Lunatic Colony and Its Influence on the Nineteenth-century Asylum System in Britain," in

A. Scull (ed.), *Madhouses, Mad-Doctors, and Madmen: The Social History of Psychiatry in the Victorian Era.* London: Athlone Press, 1981.

White, W.A., *William Alanson White: The Autobiography of a Purpose.* Garden City, N.Y.: Doubleday, Doran, 1938.

glossolalia   This is the technical term for the phenomenon of "speaking in tongues," the bizarre babbling and emission of sounds that is often part of an ecstatic religious ritual involving an altered state of consciousness. Although the phenomenon is ancient in origin, it is commonly observed in certain fundamentalist Christian or "charismatic" Roman Catholic gatherings, especially in the United States and Canada. The speech in glossolalia may seem like the NEOLOGISMS or WORD SALAD of a psychotic disorder, but it is in fact an innocuous situation-specific behavior that does not necessarily indicate a mental disorder.

Goodman, F., *Speaking in Tongues: A Cross-Cultural Study of Glossolalia.* Chicago: University of Chicago Press, 1972.

Goffman, Erving (1922–1988)   Goffman was a noted Canadian sociologist who is best remembered for his book *Asylums* (1961), which contained a series of essays on his research on the interactive effects of institutions and the persons who are confined and work in them. Goffman conducted his research between 1954 and 1957 as a visiting member of the Laboratory of Socio-environmental Studies of the National Institute of Mental Health in Bethesda, Maryland. For a period of one year (1955–56) he worked "undercover" in St. Elizabeth's Hospital in Washington, D.C., one of the country's largest mental hospitals with a census of over 7,000 patients. His depictions of the social world of the "hospital inmate," especially how this world is subjectively experienced by this person, offer a picture of how such institutions systematically dehumanize not only their "inmates," but the staff as well. He especially emphasized the ways in which inmates survive in the closed worlds of "total institutions" by "making-do" in a bad situation. The thesis of Goffman's book is that perhaps the most important influence on the behavior of a mental hospital patient is the institutional environment and *not* the illness, and that the reactions and adjustments of a patient in a mental hospital are similar to those of inmates in other types of institutions (e.g., prisons).

Goffman, E., *Asylums: Essays On the Social Situation of Mental Patients and Other Inmates*. New York: Doubleday, 1961.

Goldstein, Kurt (1878–1965)   A German psychiatrist perhaps most remembered for his studies of brain-damaged patients and schizophrenics. He proposed the idea that there were two essential types of thought, "concrete" and "abstract," and that brain-damaged people and schizophrenics had lost their capacity for abstract thought and instead exhibited concrete thought patterns. Goldstein felt that brain damaged people adopted the "concrete attitude" to avoid anxiety and "catastrophic reactions"—an agitated state of panic and rage that is a reaction to the frustrations brought on by the limitations imposed in thought and action by brain damage. His contribution to the study of schizophrenia was the further recognition of the fact that, at least in some forms of the disorder, it resembles an organic brain disease.

Goldstein, K. *The Organism*. New York: American Books, 1939.
———. "The Significance of Psychological Research in Schizophrenia," *Journal of Nervous and Mental Disease*, 97(1943), 261–279.

governess–psychosis   In the 19th century, when much less was known about the causes of the psychotic disorders, it was thought that certain occupations might predispose one to madness. Sometimes the exposure to certain chemicals or materials was the reputed cause, such as the chemical used

by hatters or shoemakers, or the vapors inhaled from the mining of lead (causing a form of insanity known in 19th-century Scotland as "mill-reeck"). However, most of the time no such material causes could be found. Artists, poets and other creative people are perhaps the best known example, but (at least in Europe) the profession of being a "governess" to the children of wealthy parents was also commonly regarded as possibly contributing to the development of a serious mental illness—especially dementia praecox (schizophrenia). In the conventional folk wisdom of the time, and even in psychiatric journals, it was commonly speculated that there was a mental disorder known as a "governess-psychosis." This topic was taken so seriously in the latter half of the 19th century that Eugen BLEULER felt the need to consider the issue in his chapter on "The Causes of the Disease" in his 1911 book, *Dementia Praecox, Or the Group of Schizophrenias:*

> For decades the idea has been preserved that governesses were especially prone to develop schizophrenia. Some authors even spoke of a "governess-psychosis"; and it has been maintained that governesses suffer a particularly severe (and unpleasant) form of the disease. There may be something in this, inasmuch as young women become governesses who have ambitions of raising their social standing beyond their capacities and among whom there must be many with schizophrenic predisposition. The treatment they often receive at the hands of their employers gives occasion for determining a schizophrenia. However, it must certainly be first established whether or not governesses really do suffer in greater numbers than members of other vocations.

(See also MAD HATTER, MAD AS A HATTER.)

Bleuler, E., *Dementia Praecox, Or the Group of Schizophrenias*, tr. J. Zinkin. New York: International Universities Press, 1950; first published, 1911.

grandiose type   One of the common types of delusional (paranoid) disorder identified by DSM-III-R (1978). Grandiose delusions are often those in which a person is convinced that they have some special ability or status that elevates them above all others. These may be delusions of unlimited riches, of the possession of special powers or abilities, or that the person has been given a divine calling of some sort. People may even believe that they are a famous person. However, in delusional disorder, these usually fixed delusions do not impair intellectual, social and occupational functioning as similar grandiose delusions do in the paranoid subtype of schizophrenia. The early 19th-century French descriptions of the mental disorder that Esquirol named MONOMANIA are perhaps most clearly found today in this grandiose type of delusional disorder. (See also PARANOID SCHIZOPHRENIA.)

grandiosity   An inflated belief about one's importance, worth, knowledge or identity. In the psychotic disorders, grandiose delusions are common, particularly in the paranoid subtype of schizophrenia (see PARANOID SCHIZOPHRENIA) and in the manic phase of bipolar disorder. A manic individual with grandiose delusions may believe that he or she has a "special message" or "talent" that no one in the world has, or may grossly overestimate their assets and create huge debts while on a shopping spree or in business transactions. People with the paranoid subtype of schizophrenia may believe that they are a famous rock music star (Mick Jagger and Madonna seem to be the favorites in American psychiatric hospitals) or are married to one.

Griesinger, Wilhelm (1817–1868)   A German psychiatrist who is regarded as the "father of biological psychiatry." Griesinger's famous 1845 textbook, *Mental Pathology and Therapeutics* (English translation, 1867), was a turning point in the history of psychiatry as it shifted the center of major scientific contributions in the field from France, whose *aliénistes* had dominated psychiatry in the first half of the 19th century, to Germany. German psychiatrists dominated the field well into the early 20th century.

Born in Stuttgart, Griesinger was educated in Germany, Switzerland and France. After finishing his medical studies he took a position at the Winnenthal asylum in Württemberg. His two years there seem to have been the only period in which he was involved in full-time clinical work with patients, as he held mainly administrative and teaching positions throughout the remainder of his life. His experience at Württemberg formed the basis of the ideas and observations of his famous 1845 book. After accepting a position as professor of medicine in Zurich in 1860, Griesinger was in charge of planning and supervising the construction of a large new hospital for the treatment of the mentally ill—the famous BURGHÖLZLI HOSPITAL, which Eugen BLEULER later managed in the early 20th century. He also founded a major psychiatric journal, which continues to be published today—the *Archiv für Psychiatrie und Nervenkrankheit*.

Griesinger made a major contribution to psychiatry with his strong emphasis on the brain and nervous system as the source of all mental disorders. His classifications of mental disorders and their clinical descriptions were widely adopted in Germany and elsewhere. His scientific philosophy still reigns today in our current research efforts to unlock the secrets of the psychotic disorders:

Insanity being a disease, and that disease being an affection of the brain, it can therefore only be studied in a proper manner from the medical point of view. The anatomy, physiology, and pathology of the nervous system, and the whole range of special pathology and therapeutics, constitute preliminary knowledge most essential to the medical psychologist.

Griesinger extensively revised his textbook, and this second edition was published in 1865.

Griesinger, W., *Mental Pathology and Therapeutics,* 2nd ed., tr. C.L. Robertson and J. Rutherford. New York: William Wood, 1882; 2nd ed. first published, 1865.

Griesinger, W., "The Care and Treatment of the Insane in Germany," *Journal of Mental Science,* 14(1868–69), 1–34.

Marx, O.M., "Wilhelm Griesinger and the History of Psychiatry: A Reassessment," *Bulletin of the History of Medicine,* 46(1972), 522–544.

group psychotherapy Group therapy came into vogue in the latter half of the 20th century, and from an administrative and therapeutic point of view it seemed the perfect treatment for institutionalized patients. Group meetings of a wide variety have been almost universally adopted by those who perform psychiatric services in institutional or quasi–institutional settings (e.g., aftercare programs), particularly since the resources do no exist to provide every patient with consistent individualized treatment.

Insight-oriented group therapy, which is designed to explore deeply personal emotional issues, has until recently been the primary mode of group-oriented treatment for institutionalized schizophrenics. Although patients with less serious psychiatric diagnoses (that is, non-psychotic disorders) may benefit from such emotionally intense group experiences, research shows that insight-oriented group psychotherapy may actually worsen psychotic symptoms. At best, as J.M. Kane concludes in 1989 in a major review of the research on the effectiveness of different treatments in schizophrenia,

> Many clinicians have suggested the value of group therapy during the inpatient phase of the treatment of schizophrenia. Several review articles have appeared on this topic . . . By and large, the results from studies designed to assess the impact of group therapy when used with or without medication have not been positive, though there are some exceptions.

Instead, much of the research indicates that the focus should be shifted from the idea that the disease process in schizophrenia is somehow being alleviated through insight-oriented group (or individual) therapy, as it most probably is not, to the idea that the focus of groups should be a structured program that teaches adaptive social and vocational skills. Likewise, the research indicates that insight-oriented family therapy (see FAMILY INTERACTION THEORIES), which views the cause of the illness in family interaction patterns, should instead be replaced by structured psychoeducational programs for family members that can teach them how their behavior affects the course of the schizophrenic relative's illness and how to accentuate the positive aspects of that influence. Such "family management strategies" can reduce the rate of relapse for schizophrenia (see EXPRESSED EMOTION).

Given the evidence that traditional insight-oriented "group therapy" is essentially useless in arresting the schizophrenic disease process, this knowledge should have profound effects on the treatment of schizophrenics in public institutions. For example, psychiatrists and psychologists would no longer be necessary for conducting "group therapy," since individuals with only a high school or college degree could be given specialized training in the methods of structured psychoeducational or supportive programming for schizophrenics. Such policies could have profound economic benefits since these people could be hired at far lower wages than clinical personnel and yet with the same therapeutic effect for the patients.

Conceptions of "group therapy" for the treatment of schizophrenics therefore have changed radically in the 1980s. When the patient is hospitalized during the acute stages of the psychosis, structured interaction with the patient, either individually or in a group situation, should be supportive and psychoeducational. However, research shows that inpatient "social skills" or "reality-adaptive-supportive therapy" or post-discharge "family management strategies" in combination with antipsychotic drugs are more effective than just the drugs alone; the research also indicates that the positive effects of these psychosocial strategies are only good for a year or so after discharge. Schizophrenia is, after all, in most of its manifestations a chronic brain disease of an unknown origin, and it appears that the organic disease process eventually counteracts the therapeutic gains of psychosocial treatment, no matter how intense or consistent the program may be. The true therapy of the future for schizophrenia will almost certainly be biologically-based. And although "group therapy" is almost universally mandated by the administrators of state hospitals as part of the "usual treatment" of institutionalized patients, it may one day be regarded as quaint and as ultimately useless as the "usual treatments" of the 19th century—bleeding, bathing and purging—seem to us today.

Kane, J.M., "Treatment of Schizophrenia," *Schizophrenia Bulletin,* 13(1987) 133–156.
Goldman, M.J., "Psychosocial Issues," *Schizophrenia Bulletin,* 13(1987), 157–172.

gustatory hallucination This is a hallucination of *taste.* People who report gustatory hallucinations often report an unpleasant taste in their mouth. This type of HAL-LUCINATION is less common than other types, particularly AUDITORY HALLUCINATIONS.

gyrator (or "gyrater") A mechanical device invented by Benjamin RUSH and used at the Pennsylvania Hospital in Philadelphia in the early 1800s. Based on the CIRCULAT-ING SWING used by English physician Joseph Mason Cox (1762–1822) at the Fishponds Private Lunatic Asylum in Stapleton, England, the gyrator was a machine on which a patient would apparently sit and be rapidly spun around by its gyrations to bring the blood to the brain. In his 1812 textbook, *Medical Inquiries and Observations Upon the Diseases of the Mind,* Rush describes his "gyrater" under the heading of "Exercise" as a recommended treatment:

EXERCISE. This should consist of swinging, seesaw, and an exercise discovered by Dr. Cox, which promises more than either of them, and that is, subjecting the patient to a rotary motion, so as to give a centrifugal direction of the blood towards the brain. He tells us he has cured eight persons of torpid madness by this mode of exercise. I have contrived a machine for this purpose in the hospital, which produces the same effects upon the body which are mentioned by Dr. Cox. These are vertigo and nausea, and a general perspiration. I have called it a Gyrater. It would be more perfect, did it permit the head to be placed at a greater distance from its center of motion. It produces great changes in the pulse.

Not satisfied with the "gyrater" he invented for use at the Pennsylvania Hospital, Rush provides the following suggestions for a more effective machine:

A cheap contrivance, to answer all its purposes, might easily be made, by placing a patient upon a board moved at its centre upon a pivot, with his head toward one of its extremities, and then giving it a rotary motion. The centrifugal force of the blood would exceed, in this way, that which it receives from the chair employed by Dr. Cox or from the gyrater in the Pennsylvania Hospital.

Many descriptions of Rush's "gyrater" incorrectly describe it as this latter machine suggested by Rush as an improvement on the gyrater.

Rush, B., *Medical Inquiries and Observations Upon the Diseases of the Mind.* Philadelphia: Kimber & Richardson, 1812.

H

hair pulling See TRICHTILLOMANIA.

Haiti See BOUFFÉE DÉLIRANTE AIGÜE.

Haldol Haldol is the trade name of halo-peridol, an ANTIPSYCHOTIC DRUG that is in the family of drugs known as butyrophenomes. It was first synthesized by Janssen in 1958.

Hallaran, William Saunders (1765?–1825)

Hallaran was the first Irish physician to write a clinical textbook on insanity. Although during his tenure at the asylum at Cork he recommended the non-restraint philosophy of moral medicine, he nonetheless advocated the use of the CIRCULATING SWING as a treatment for mental illness.

Hallaran, W.S., *Practical Observations On the Causes of Insanity*. Dublin: 1810.

hallucination

A hallucination is an event that is experienced as a sensory perception (e.g., the sound of a voice, the sight of someone or something) but, in fact, is not real. The relevant sensory organs, such as the ears or eyes, are not physically stimulated, yet the person reports a sensory experience. A hallucination is experienced as real, and it may be perceived as originating from outside a person's body (as with the usual sensory experiences of sight and sound), or it may be felt to come from within a person's own body. For example, a person may report "hearing voices," but the voices may be experienced as coming from within the head rather than from outside it. A delusional interpretation (if present) of a hallucination, may be consistent with a person's belief system or, if the person is psychotic, with his delusional system. Hallucinations are distinguished from delusions in that a hallucination is a disturbance of perception whereas a delusion represents a pathological distortion of normal ideation.

Hallucinations occur in the form of one or more of the five senses: sight (visual hallucinations), sound (auditory hallucinations, taste (gustatory hallucinations), touch (tactile hallucinations) and smell (olfactory hallucinations). Hallucinations can be mood congruent or mood incongruent in content, with either a manic or depressed mood. For example, a depressed individual who is also experiencing auditory hallucinations may hear voices telling him that he is worthless, useless or perhaps may urge self-mutilation or suicide.

Hallucinations are only to be considered a symptom of a psychotic disorder if there is also a clearly demonstrated break with reality in the mental state of the individual. Hallucinations are often thought of as immediately signifying that a person is psychotic, but this is not the case. People who have many other types of mental disorders, such as effective disorder and even personality disorder, can experience transient hallucinations. Even normal individuals can experience transient hallucinations from time to time. The most commonly reported hallucinatory experience reported in people without mental disorders is hearing a voice calling one's own name. Hallucinations that occur within the context of intense religious experiences are not necessarily to be considered a sign of mental illness.

The word "hallucination" first appeared in the English language in 1572 in a work by Johann Kaspar Lavater, referring to "ghostes and spirites walking by nyght" (in other words, "apparitions"). However, its original derivation is from a Greek word meaning "to wander in mind." J.E.D. ESQUIROL was the first to recognize the importance of hallucinations as a symptom of mental disorder in his 1838 textbook, *Des Maladies Mentales*. In the chapter, "Hallucinations," Esquirol constructs a definition of hallucinations that is still the basis of the one employed in the most current diagnostic manual of mental disorders—DSM-III-R (1987). Esquirol defines a hallucination as "a thorough conviction of the perception of a sensation, when no external object, suited to excite the sensation, has impressed the senses." Esquirol was also the first to emphasize the distinction between a hallucination and an ILLUSION, in which an actual external stimulus is misperceived or misinterpreted. A pupil of Esquirol's and a member of the "Esquirol Circle," A.J.F. BRIERRE DE BOISMONT, wrote the first comprehensive textbook on the clinical and cultural manifestations of hallucinations, and this book was translated into English and published in 1853.

Hallucinations (as well as delusions) were regarded as an important symptom of schizophrenia by many of the early authorities on schizophrenia, but they differed in regard to how necessary the presence of hallucinations in a person was to making the diagnosis of schizophrenia. For example, although many authorities have considered hallucinations, particularly auditory hallucinations, as a defining sign of schizophrenia (a German psychiatrist did with his FIRST-RANK SYMPTOMS in 1959), others have proposed that different symptoms might be better criteria for defining schizophrenia. Eugen BLEULER, for example, argued in 1911 that hallucinations and delusions are not among the four PRIMARY SYMPTOMS OF SCHIZOPHRENIA but instead are merely the ACCESSORY SYMPTOMS of the disorder. However, Bleuler realized how serious these accessory symptoms could be for the afflicted person. For as he remarks in his 1911 classic, *Dementia Praecox, Or the Group of Schizophrenias:*

> It is not often that the fundamental symptoms are so markedly exhibited as to cause the patient to be hospitalized in a mental institution. It is primarily the accessory phenomena which make his retention at home impossible, or it is they which make the psychosis manifest and give occasion to require psychiatric help.

Hallucinations, along with delusions, are considered to be the POSITIVE SYMPTOMS of schizophrenia and are characteristic of Type I schizophrenia, or BLEULER'S SYNDROME, as it is also called by British psychiatrist T.J. Crow (see CROW'S HYPOTHESIS). The most recent comprehensive review article on the theories and research findings on hallucinations was published in 1986 and was authored by G. Asaad and B. Shapiro. (See also TYPE I/TYPE II SCHIZOPHRENIA.)

Asaad, I. and Shapiro, B., "Hallucinations: Theoretical and Clinical Overview," *American Journal of Psychiatry,* 143(1986), 1088–1097.

Brierre de Boismont, A., *Hallucinations, or, The Rational History of Apparitions, Visions, Dreams, Ecstasy, Magnetism and Somnambulism.* Philadelphia: Lindsay & Blakiston, 1853.

Esquirol, J.E.D., *Mental Maladies, A Treatise On Insanity,* tr. E.K. Hunt. Philadelphia: Lea & Blanchard, 1845; first published, 1838.

Sarbin, T.R. and Juhasz, J.B. "The Historical Background of the Concept of Hallucination, *Journal of the History of the Behavioral Sciences,* 3(1967), 339–358.

hallucinatory verbigeration   This is the term given by Emil KRAEPELIN in the eighth edition (1909–1915) of his famous textbook, *Psychiatrie,* for the type of AUDITORY HALLUCINATION in which a patient hears essentially the same meaningless sentences over and over again. One of Kraepelin's patients wrote down the following nonsense sentences that he heard over and over again as an auditory hallucination: "For we ourselves can always hope that we should let ourselves pray other thoughts. For we ourselves wish to know who would let the swine's head be tormented to death with us foolishly."

Kraepelin, E., *Dementia Praecox and Paraphrenia,* tr. R.M. Barclay, ed. G.M. Robertson. Edinburgh: E. & S. Livingstone, 1919.

haloperidol   See HALDOL; ANTIPSYCHOTIC DRUGS.

handcuffs   Until the mid-1800s, many extreme methods of MECHANICAL RESTRAINT were still in use in European asylums. Handcuffs were included among these instruments, which were more often used for punitive measures than therapeutic ones. One variant on the form of handcuffs that we think of today was a type that would hook onto iron rings on a heavy iron belt that circled the waist. Handcuffs were routinely employed at the asylum in Middlesex, England, until English physician John CONOLLY, a leading figure of the NONRESTRAINT

MOVEMENT, became superintendent there in 1839.

harness, cruciform See CRUCIFORM STANCE; BED SADDLE.

Hartford Retreat An American private institution for the humane treatment of mental illness that was founded in Hartford, Connecticut, in 1824. It was based on the famous YORK RETREAT in England. For most of its first several decades, the Hartford Retreat admitted all patients who could pay and only a small portion of those who could not. However, these patients had to meet certain criteria and could not have a history of chronic mental illness. What's more, they would be discharged within six months regardless of their progress. Since "discharge rates" were often touted as "curability rates," the Hartford Retreat was praised by many, including Dorothea DIX and British author Charles Dickens, who visited it on his trip to America in 1842 and found it to be one of the few institutions in America that was worthy of merit.

However, when the retreat requested and received state funds in 1843, for the next two decades it shifted its role from one of a curative institution to a custodial one. More poor and chronic cases were admitted, and superintendents of the institution complained of the growing numbers of "filthy, noisy, or dangerous pauper lunatics" that filled its wards. In 1866 the state of Connecticut appropriated funds for a state asylum, allowing the Hartford Retreat to revert to a private institution for the wealthy. It later changed its name to the Institute for Living.

Rothman, D.J., *The Discovery of the Asylum: Social Order and Disorder in the New Republic*. Boston: Little, Brown, 1971.

Haslam, John (1764–1844) An apothecary and researcher at the BETHLEM ROYAL HOSPITAL ("Bedlam"), Haslam produced some of the finest of the early psychiatric manuals; the 1798 *Observations On Insanity* and its expanded second edition of 1809, retitled *Observations On Madness and Melancholy*. He performed autopsies on the patients at Bedlam and described his observations in his written works. He also provided clinical descriptions of what were later known as general paralysis of the insane and the chronic, more degenerative form of schizophrenia now described by British psychiatrist T.J. Crow as Type II schizophrenia (see TYPE I/TYPE II SCHIZOPHRENIA). Because Haslam and Philippe PINEL both seemed to provide the first descriptions of cases of this type of schizophrenia in 1809, Crow has given the name PINEL-HASLAM SYNDROME to Type II schizophrenia (see CROW'S HYPOTHESIS).

Haslam's descriptions of case histories seem to give a complete description of the disease process in CHRONIC SCHIZOPHRENIA, as we have come to know it, with an insidious onset in adolescence or early adulthood, classical signs and symptoms and a chronic deteriorating course. Prior to this time, many mental disorders had been described throughout the centuries, and although hallucinations and delusions had been commonly reported they had never been accompanied by descriptions of the developmental course of the disease. Therefore, Haslam and Pinel's simultaneous (but independent) publications of these case histories give us the first definite HISTORICAL EVIDENCE FOR SCHIZOPHRENIA as a distinct disease.

Haslam's descriptions in his 1798 book of what we now know as BIPOLAR DISORDER predate the French psychiatrist BAILLARGER's first thorough description in 1854 of a single disorder that combines both depressed and manic mood swings. When discussing "mania" and "melancholia" he insightfully asserts: "I would strongly oppose their being considered as opposite diseases." In a later passage in the same book Haslam gives a description of patients with bipolar disorder that is still accurate today:

. . . for we see every day the most furious maniacs suddenly sink into a profound melancholy; and the most depressed and miserable objects, become violent and raving. We have patients in the Bethlehem Hospital, whose lives are divided between furious and melancholic paroxisms, and who, under both states, retain the same set of ideas.

In his writings, Haslam recommended the "gentleness of manner and kindness of treatment" of the insane popularized by Pinel with his *traitement moral* ("moral treatment"). However, some of his activities at "Bedlam" were deemed abusive by a House of Commons investigation in 1815, and he was fired from the staff of that institution without a pension after more than 20 years' service. At the time of his dismissal he was 56 years old and is credited by historians with knowing more about mental illness than any of his contemporaries in Britain. His works on the clinical and legal aspects of mental illness remain classics in the field and were influential in the early days of psychiatry. (See also BEDLAM.)

Haslam, J., *Observations On Insanity, with Practical Remarks on the Disease, and an Account of the Morbid Appearances On Dissection.* London: F. & C. Rivington, 1798.
———, *Observations On Madness and Melancholy.* London: J. Callon, 1809.
———, *Medical Jurisprudence, As It Relates To Insanity, According to the Law of England.* London: 1809.
———, *Considerations on the Moral Management of Insane Persons.* London: Hunter, 1817.
Leigh, D., "John Haslam, M.D.—1764–1844, Apothecary to Bethlem," *Journal of the History of Medicine,* 10(1955), 17–44.

Hayner's wheel   A device that was originally designed as a form of treatment for mental illness but was more often used as a form of MECHANICAL RESTRAINT for agitated patients. The "hollow wheel," as it was also called, was a huge, padded circular treadmill on which a patient was forced to walk for hours or days at a time. The device was not unlike those we know today, which are commonly placed in the cages of pet mice or hamsters. With prodding from the "keepers" (as the psychiatric aides or attendants were called in those days), the patient would be "encouraged" to run the treadmill until exhausted. It was used in several German asylums in the 19th century, after its construction by a German psychiatrist named Hayner, who later renounced its use. Apparently, the idea for this machine was first proposed by one of the first German psychiatrists, Johann Christian Reil (1759–1813) of the University of Halle, who recommended many varieties of what he referred to as "non-injurious torture" as effective treatments for mental illness. In the 1890s, while at the Heidelberg Clinic, Emil KRAEPELIN acquired one of Hayner's wheels for the small museum of mechanical restraint that he set up for the medical students under his tutelage.

hebephrenia   One of the three distinct mental disorders, recognized in the last half of the 19th century, that Emil KRAEPELIN grouped together to form his unifying concept of DEMENTIA PRAECOX in 1896. Hebephrenia was the name given to a psychotic disorder identified by German psychiatrist Ewald Hecker (1843–1909) in 1871, which would begin in adolescence or adulthood and result in a rapid disorganization or DEGENERATION. Hecker believed that in this disorder a person's psychological state was arrested at the developmental stage of puberty, thus resulting in severe problems in late adolescence and early adulthood, when more mature psychological integration was required. Hecker derived the name of this disorder from "Hebe," the name of the ancient Greek goddess of youth.

Hecker is given credit by Kraepelin for being the first to point out the characteristic AGE AT ONSET in dementia praecox (schizophrenia). However, in his initial description of dementia praecox in 1896, Kraepelin does not completely accept Hecker's description of hebephrenia as a disorder in which a depressed state is followed by a manic state, after which mental degeneration quickly follows. Instead, Kraepelin accepts the expanded definition of hebephrenia proposed in a doctoral dissertation by Daraszkiewicz in 1892, which allows for the most severe cases—including the "depressed forms"—that end in profound mental deterioration.

Kraepelin later referred to hebephrenia as "silly dementia," since often a nonsensical, illogical "silliness" marks the dementia praecox patients with this subtype of the disorder. In the eighth edition (1909–1915) of his textbook, *Psychiatrie,* Kraepelin describes this variant of dementia praecox in the following manner:

> That form of dementia praecox which we have called above "silly dementia" is in many respects nearly related to simple insidious dementia. In its clinical picture there appears beside the progressive devastation of the psychic life *incoherence* in thinking, feeling, and action . . .
>
> The development of the disease is accomplished in almost four-fifths of the cases quite gradually; often an insidious change of the psychic personality precedes the appearance of more distinct morbid phenomena by many years. In the remaining patients the disorder begins in a subacute form; in a few cases it breaks out suddenly. In the preliminary stage there are sometimes nervous troubles, complaints of lassitude, headaches, feeling of giddiness, fainting-fits, irritability, disorders of sleep. The patients become absent-minded, forgetful, negligent; they tire easily, they cannot collect their thoughts any more; they appear lacking in ideas and understanding, they are silly and lazy; they fail in daily tasks, change their occupation, because it is too difficult for them, set aside their work, or give it up entirely.

Kraepelin's description of hebephrenia matches the current diagnostic subtype of schizophrenia known as the DISORGANIZED TYPE that can be found in DSM-III R (1987). The descriptions of hebephrenia as comprising an insidious onset with the full outbreak of psychotic symptoms in adolescence or early adulthood (usually between ages 15 and 25), and the resulting cognitive disintegration, are all incorporated in modern descriptions of CHRONIC SCHIZOPHRENIA or Type II schizophrenia (see CROW'S HYPOTHESIS), which is the nonparanoid variant of schizophrenia most related to BRAIN ABNORMALITIES and associated with a poor prognosis. (See also TYPE I/TYPE II SCHIZOPHRENIA.)

Daraskiewicz, (?). *Über Hebephrenie, insbesondere deren schwere Form.* Doctoral dissertation, University of Dorpat, 1892.

Hecker, E., "Die Hebephrenie," *Virchows Archiv für pathologische Anatomie,* 52(1871), 392–449.

Kraepelin, E., *Dementia Praecox and Paraphrenia,* tr. R.M. Barclay, ed. G.M. Robertons. Edinburgh: E. & S. Livingstone, 1919.

hebephrenic type   In the World Health Organization's ninth revision of the *International Classification of Diseases,* or ICD-9 (1978), this is one of the mental disorders classified under the category of schizophrenic psychoses. It is equivalent to the classical descriptions of HEBEPHRENIA and to current descriptions of the subtype of schizophrenia known as the DISORGANIZED TYPE, which is described in DSM-III-R (1987).

Heller's disease (or syndrome)   See CHILDHOOD SCHIZOPHRENIA; DEMENTIA INFANTALIS.

hemodialysis treatment of schizophrenia   Between the 1930s, when techniques for the CONVULSIVE THERAPIES, COMA THERAPY and PSYCHOSURGERY were being introduced, and the early 1970s, no new somatic treatment for schizophrenia was introduced. In the 1970s physician R. Cade noticed that the psychotic symptoms of a patient diagnosed with the paranoid subtype of schizophrenia had improved greatly after treatment with hemodialysis for a kidney disease. Cade and colleague J. Wagemaker Jr. theorized that the dialysis might have removed some sort of toxic substance from the blood of the patient that had been responsible for causing the psychotic symptoms. They followed up this observation by submitting to hemodialysis a group of patients who were diagnosed with schizophrenia but who did not have any kidney disease. They were encouraged by seemingly positive results and published them in 1977. However, several attempts at replication by other researchers have failed (most recently in 1983), suggesting that hemodialysis as a treatment for schizophrenia is not very effective and therefore is not recommended.

Carpenter, W.T. et al., "The Therapeutic Efficacy of Hemodialysis in Schizophrenia," *New England Journal of Medicine,* 308(1983), 669–675.
Wagemaker, J. and Cade, R., "The Use of Hemodialysis in Chronic Schizophrenia," *American Journal of Psychiatry,* 134(1977), 684–685.

hemorrhoids, production of as treatment   In his 1838 book on *Mental Maladies,* J.E.D. ESQUIROL recommends BLEEDING as a treatment for severe mental illness only if it is performed locally through cupping with leeches. For both the severe forms of depression ("lypemania or melancholy") and of mania, Esquirol recommends the application of leeches to the anus to produce hemorrhoids (varicose veins of the anus). He writes:

> Pursuing the atrabile into the circulation, the humorists deduce from blood-letting a general precept against melancholy . . . Nevertheless, we may have recourse to local sanguine evacuations; now at the epigastrium, when the stomach is the seat of an active irritation; now, to the vulva, when we wish to reestablish the menstrual flux; or to the anus, when we desire to renew a hemorrhoidal discharge; and finally to the head, when there are signs of cerebral congestion. I have sometimes applied leeches with success to the side of the head, when lypemaniacs complained of a fixed pain in the part.

This form of treatment is a vestige of the type of thinking that resulted from the influence of the HUMORAL THEORY of disease and mental illness, in which an excess of humors in the blood (a condition called *plethora*) needed to be drained off to restore a healthful balance in the patient.

Esquirol, J.E.D., *Mental Maladies. A Treatise On Insanity,*tr. E.K. Hunt. Philadelphia: Lea & Blanchard, 1845; first published, 1838.

heredity   See GENETICS STUDIES.

high-functioning schizophrenic   See AMBULATORY SCHIZOPHRENIC.

high-risk studies   Also called the "risk-for-schizophrenia" research, high-risk studies evaluate children who are considered to be at a higher than average statistical risk for developing schizophrenia later in life. These studies hope to clarify several questions that researchers have about the disease process in schizophrenia. For example, one hope is that by studying children before the onset of the disorder it will be possible to identify the initial, core "warning signs" of the full onset of the disorder and separate them from the later symptoms of the disorder. Furthermore, if specific environmental influences that precede the onset of schizophrenia can be identified, perhaps further research can then tell us whether schizophrenia can be prevented in vulnerable individuals by changing or altering these environmental influences in some way.

Most of the high-risk research has tended to use children with at least one biological parent who has schizophrenia. As the family studies research using the CONSANGUINITY METHOD to find evidence of the genetic transmission of schizophrenia have indicated, children with one schizophrenic parent have a lifetime risk of approximately 12%, whereas individuals who have two biological parents diagnosed with schizophrenia have a much higher risk, of 35% to 46%. Individuals with a schizophrenic biological parent also have a greater risk for developing one of the schizophrenia "spectrum'' disorders (e.g., schizotypal personality disorder, schizophreniform disorder, schizoaffective disorder).

However, it is estimated that 85% to 90% of all persons diagnosed with schizophrenia do not have a schizophrenic parent. Therefore, high-risk studies that use just the children of schizophrenic parents may not apply to the much larger number of individuals who will develop schizophrenia but who do not have schizophrenic parents. To take this possibility into account, a complementary research strategy using ''behavioral markers of risk'' has been developed, which defines an individual's risk status based on his or her own specific behavioral disturbances. The ongoing New York High-Risk Project, which is being conducted by researchers L. Erlenmeyer-Kimling and Barbara Cornblatt of the New York State Psychiatric Institute, has been studying two selected samples since the 1970s consisting of children of schizophrenics. This group periodically undergoes a battery of neuropsychological and psychophysiological tests that measure three primary ''biobehavioral domains'' of possible predictors of liability to psychopathology: attentional and information-processing capacities, neuromotor functioning, and psychophysiological processes. They theorize that these primary areas of disturbance create problems in social functioning as the child grows older. Their results have indicated greater problems in fine motor coordinations, attentions and information processing (AIP) in the children of schizophrenics.

Besides the presumed genetic risk factor in schizophrenia, risk factors related to the physical environment have long been explored in the high-risk studies as contributors to the development of schizophrenia. Some of the most suggestive childhood history factors that may increase the risk for developing schizophrenia are: (1) obstetrical complications; (2) the season of birth (a higher percentage of schizophrenics are born in the winter and spring months); (3) prenatal stress

of the mother; and (4) early exposure to certain viral infections.

In a major review of the evidence from 24 high-risk studies conducted since 1952, which was published in *Schizophrenia Bulletin* in 1988, researcher Joan Asarnow of the UCLA Neuropsychiatric Institute reaches the following conclusions about the state of our knowledge concerning children at-risk for schizophrenia:

- Some high-risk children can be distinguished from their peers by signs of neurointegrative problems, social impairments, and early symptomatology. Although some abnormalities can be identified as early as infancy, impairments are more pronounced in middle childhood and adolescence.
- Particular deficits in attention-information processing, neuromotor functions, and social behavior may be associated with specific risk for schizophrenia. The form of these deficits may vary with the age of the individual, and future work is needed to clarify developmental patterns within the same individuals. Other deficiencies are shown by children whose parents have other psychiatric disorders, as well as in samples of clinically disturbed children.
- Strong evidence currently exists from the risk-for-schizophrenia and general psychopathology literature that some attributes of the family environment are associated with increased risk for the onset of the disorder. These attributes include: family communication deviance, negative affective style, high expressed emotion, and general disturbance in the family environment. It is still unclear whether these family attributes hold specific risk for schizophrenia or are associated with increased risk for a variety of disorders and dysfunctions. However, the current evidence . . . points to the highest rates of schizophrenia spectrum disorders in individuals exposed to both disturbed rearing environments and genetic risk (inferred from the presence of

schizophrenia in at least one biological parent). Future studies need to explicate the mechanisms by which environmental attributes, individual attributes and genetic predisposition may interact to influence risk for schizophrenia.

A special issue of *Schizophrenia Bulletin* (vol. 13, no. 3) devoted to a review of the high-risk studies appeared in 1987. It provides the best overview of the continuing research in this field. Another, although much more technical, review of risk factor research was published by the National Institute of Mental Health in 1983. Copies of these publications may be requested (contingent upon supplies) by contacting the Schizophrenia Research Branch, NIMH, Rm 10C-06, 5600 Fishers Lane, Rockville, Maryland 20857.

Asarnow, J.R., "Children at Risk for Schizophrenia: Converging Lines of Evidence," *Schizophrenia Bulletin*, 14(1988), 613–631.

Cornblatt, B.A. and Erlenmeyer-Kimling, L., "Global Attentional Deviance as a Marker of Risk for Schizophrenia: Specificity and Predictive Validity," *Journal of Abnormal Psychology*, 94(1985), 470–486.

National Institute of Mental Health, *Risk Factor Research in the Major Mental Disorders*, DHHS Pub. No. (ADM)83-1068. Rockville, Md.: NIMH, 1983.

Watt, N.F. et al., *Children at Risk for Schizophrenia: A Longitudinal Perspective*. New York: Cambridge University Press, 1984.

Hill, Robert Gardiner (1811–1878) An English physician who served as the resident surgeon at the Lincoln Asylum in England. Known as a persuasive advocate of nonrestraint policies in the treatment of institutionalized patients, he put such policies into effect at Lincoln in 1838 and is given credit by Wilhelm GRIESINGER for being the first to do so. In an 1838 book he argues that, "in a properly constructed building, with sufficient number of suitable attendants, restraint is never necessary, never justifiable, and always injurious." (See also NON-

RESTRAINT MOVEMENT; MECHANICAL RESTRAINT; CHEMICAL RESTRAINT; ABUSE OF PSYCHIATRIC PATIENTS.)

Hill, R.G., *Total Abolition of Personal Restraint in the Treatment of the Insane*. London: Simpkin, Marshall, 1838.

———, *Lunacy: Its Past and Present*. London: Longman, Green, Reader & Dyer, 1870.

histamines One of the biogenic amines that are involved in the neurochemistry of the brain, particularly in its NEUROTRANSMITTERS. BENADRYL, one of the drugs used to treat some of the side effects of ANTIPSYCHOTIC DRUGS, works due to its effect as an antihistamine. (See also BIOGENIC AMINE HYPOTHESIS.)

historical evidence of schizophrenia If schizophrenia is truly a brain disease that has a strong basis in genetics, then there should be evidence that this severe mental disorder has afflicted people for hundreds, if not thousands, of years. "Madness" has been reported in every society on record to a greater or lesser degree, and descriptions of hallucinations, delusions and bizarre behavior are often reported in association with ancient mental disorders. In an attempt to trace schizophrenia back to ancient Babylonian accounts (3000 B.C.) or to early Sanskrit texts from India, translations of descriptions of mental illness were collected in articles published in 1985 by D.V. Jeste and his colleagues and in 1984 by C.V. Haldipur. But it is still unclear from this historical evidence that schizophrenia—as we know it, a disease with a particular course that begins in adolescence or early adulthood, with characteristic signs and symptoms and a chronic deteriorating course (at least in the type of schizophrenia that seems to be the most "genetic")—existed in ancient times. This point (and the larger ramifications of this entire issue) has been eloquently argued and documented by psychiatrist E. Fuller Torrey in his book *Schizophrenia and Civilization* (1980).

There are many reasons for this uncertainty. First, ancient descriptions of "madness," which involved delusional, hallucinating or confused individuals, could be accounts of any number of physical or mental disorders. For example, these symptoms could be produced by head trauma, brain infections, injury due to birth complications, strokes or any number of other known, organic mental disorders. Or, they could be descriptions of the other psychotic disorders, such as bipolar disorder or any of the acute reactive psychoses. What is missing in these ancient accounts are descriptions of the full course of the disease process over time.

Several changes in traditional thought developed in the 1600s (especially in England), which converged to change this state of affairs. First, societies began to incarcerate mentally ill people in central institutions (jails, hospitals) where many of them could be observed together for long periods of time. Secondly, physicians began to be put in charge of the care of the mentally ill in these institutions, as, for example, happened at the BETHLEM ROYAL HOSPITAL in England during the 17th century. And third, the concept of *disease* began to take on a new meaning, largely due to the influence of English physician Thomas Sydenham (1624–1689), often referred to as the "English Hippocrates," who emphasized the direct observation of illnesses and suggested their classification according to syndromes or groups of symptoms. This differed from centuries of the identification of diseases usually by a single symptom, as was the case with the mental disorder known as FURY. Throughout the 1700s physicians who doctored to the mentally ill ("mad-doctors," or "lunatic doctors," as their specialty of medical practice came to be known) contributed treatises and textbooks based on their idiosyncratic observations and classifications of the mentally ill.

Eventually, in 1809, the very first clinical descriptions of schizophrenia as we know it appeared in print. Working independently in their respective countries, John HASLAM of the Bethlem Royal Hospital in London and Philippe PINEL of the Salpêtrière asylum in Paris produced expanded second editions of books on mental illness, which had been published previously, that contain the first complete reports of what we now know as schizophrenia in its "chronic" (or Type II) form. The expanded second edition of Pinel's work, *Traité médico-philosophique sur l'aliénation mentale, ou la manie* (first edition, 1801), has never been translated into English. Pinel's description of DÉMENCE in the first edition, which strongly resembles the thought disorder of schizophrenia, was apparently illustrated with case material in the second edition that seemed to confirm this connection. However, the following case history, which is reproduced from Haslam's 1809 *Observations On Madness and Melancholy,* may be the first valid historical evidence in the English language that we have for schizophrenia:

there is a form of insanity which occurs in young persons; and, as far as these cases have been the subject of my observation, they have been more frequently noticed in females. Those whom I have seen, have been distinguished by prompt capacity and lively disposition; and in general have become the favorites of parents and tutors, by their faculty in acquiring knowledge, and by a prematurity of attainment. This disorder commences, about or shortly after, the period of menstruation, and in many instances has been unconnected with hereditary taint; as far as could be ascertained by minute enquiry. The attack is almost imperceptible; some months usually elapse before it becomes the subject of particular notice; and fond relatives are frequently deceived by the hope that it is only an abatement of excessive vivacity, conducing to a prudent reserve, and steadiness of character. A degree of apparent thoughtfulness and inactivity precede, together with a diminuation of the ordinary curiosity, concerning that which is passing before them; and they therefore neglect those objects and pursuits which formerly proved sources of delight and instruction. The sensibility appears to be considerably blunted; they do not bear the same affection towards their parents and relations; they become unfeeling to kindness, and careless of reproof. To their companions they show a cold civility, but take no interest whatever in their concerns. If they read a book they are unable to give any account of its contents; sometimes, with steadfast eyes, they will dwell for an hour on one page, and then turn over a number in a few minutes. It is very difficult to persuade them to write, which most readily develops their state of mind; much time is consumed and little produced. The subject is reportedly begun, but they seldom advance beyond a sentence or two: the orthography becomes puzzling, and by endeavoring to adjust the spelling the subject vanishes. As their apathy increases they are negligent of their dress and inattentive to personal cleanliness. Frequently they seem to experience transient impulses of passion, but these have no source in sentiment; the tears, which trickle down at one time, are as unmeaning as the loud laugh which succeeds them; and it often happens that a momentary gust of anger, with its attendant invectives, ceases before the threat can be concluded. As the disorder increases, the urine and feces are passed without restraint, and from the indolence which accompanies it, they generally become corpulent. Thus in the interval between puberty and manhood, I have painfully witnessed this hopeless and degrading change, which in a short time has transformed the most promising and vigorous intellect into a slavering and bloated idiot.

Haslam is describing what British psychiatrist T.J. Crow has named "Type II schizophrenia" or the PINEL-HASLAM SYNDROME: insidious onset, NEGATIVE SYMPTOMS (attention deficits, problems in information processing, apathy, poverty of speech, loss of curiosity in people and activities) and gradual cognitive deterioration. This *démence,* as Pinel called it, was later elaborated upon by French alienist B.A. Morel in his descriptions of mental DEGENERATION, and was used by Morel to coin the term *démence précoce* in 1852. Emil KRAEPELIN borrowed this term to describe our modern clinical picture of DEMENTIA PRAECOX in 1896.

Haldipur, C.V., "Madness in Ancient India: Concepts of Madness in Charaka Samhita (1st century A.D.)," *Comprehensive Psychiatry,* 25(1984), 335–344.

Haslam, J., *Observations On Madness and Melancholy.* London: J. Callon, 1809.

Jeste, D.V., "Did Schizophrenia Exist Before the Eighteenth Century?" *Comprehensive Psychiatry,* 26(1985), 493–503.

Pinel, P., *Traité médico-philosophique sur l'aliénation mentale,* 2nd ed. Paris: J.A. Brosson, 1809.

Torrey, E.F., *Schizophrenia and Civilization.* New York: Jason Aronson, 1980.

HIV CNS disease   A disease of the central nervous system (the brain and spinal cord) that is due to infection with the human immunodeficiency virus (HIV), implicated in acquired immunodeficiency syndrome (AIDS). The symptoms of such a disease process may resemble many mental disorders, including such psychotic disorders as schizophrenia and bipolar disorder. However, the most common symptom is DEMENTIA. The clinical signs and symptoms of the AIDS DEMENTIA COMPLEX were first clearly identified by B.A. Navia and his colleagues in 1986.

Bridge, T.P., Mirsky, A.F. and Goodwin, F.K., *Psychological Neuropsychiatric, and Substance Abuse Aspects of AIDS.* New York: Raven Press, 1988; *Advance in Biochemical Psychopharmacology,* vol. 44.

holergasia   A complete disorganization of mental activity. This was one of the many terms of psychological processes proposed by Swiss psychiatrist Adolph MEYER in the early 20th century that never became really popular and have since disappeared. Holergasia is probably equivalent to the FORMAL THOUGHT DISORDER of the DISORGANIZED TYPE of schizophrenia. Meyer, who came to the United States in 1892, was perhaps the most important figure in American psychiatry from about 1910 to 1940. His new name for schizophrenia, *parergasia*, was never adopted by anyone outside of his close circle of followers.

Meyer, A., Jelliffe, S.E. and Hoch, A., *Dementia Praecox, A Monograph*. Boston: Badger, 1911.

Hollingshead & Redlich   See SOCIAL DRIFT THEORY.

hollow wheel   See HAYNER'S WHEEL.

Horn's sack   An early German psychiatrist who worked in the Berlin asylum, Ernst Horn (1774–1848) is largely remembered as the inventor of a sack that was put over unmanageable patients in order to calm them down and place them under control. A patient died from suffocation in one of Horn's sacks, and the resulting court case earned Horn considerable notoriety. Horn's sack was a long, wide bag that was reinforced with oilcloth. Emil KRAEPELIN describes its use in his short historical book, *One Hundred Years of Psychiatry* (1917):

> The bag was pulled over the patient's head and tied beneath his feet. "It restrains the patient," explained Horn. "It shocks him by making him aware of his confinement and causes him to suspect or realize the fruitlessness of any attempt to stir up troubles." He also claimed that many restless, troublesome lunatics—even after other measures had failed to make them obedient, orderly and calm—responded to it by developing a more serene state of mind, by becoming more tractable, and by becoming more responsive to other, indirect, psychic treatments. Many patients who refused to eat were so impressed by the threat of the bag "that they took a new lease on life and began once more to enjoy the food which they had stubbornly refused."

Apparently, Horn was also an advocate of the CRUCIFORM STANCE, a standing form of the BED SADDLE.

Kraepelin, E., *One Hundred Years of Psychiatry*, tr. W. Baskin. New York: Philosophical Library, 1962; first published, 1917.

hospitalism   A term for the apathy and loss of ambition or creativity that was first noticed by Emelyn Lincoln Coolidge in 1909 in children who were hospitalized for a long time. Today we would refer to this as the effects of INSTITUTIONALIZATION. It is a type of "learned helplessness" that develops from being too dependent upon a caregiving staff in an institutional setting for too long a time.

In the 1940s the psychoanalyst René Spitz used this term to denote whatever physical or psychological disturbances occur in infants up to 18 months old who undergo a prolonged stay in a hospital or other similar institution where they are completely separated from their mother. Spitz did research in orphanages, nurseries and other institutions in which infants and young children were separated from their mothers. Spitz thought that when a baby is cared for in an institutional setting in which the caregivers are anonymous and for which no emotional link is established, the child will develop a series of disorders, which are collectively called "hospitalism." These disorders are: (1) retardation of bodily development; (2) retardation of body mastery; (3) retardation of adaptation to the world; (4) retardation of language ability; (5) a reduced resistance to disease; and (6) in the most extreme cases, emaciation and eventual death. Spitz thought the damage caused by this rupture in the earliest mother-child relationship was long-lasting and led to chronic problems, potentially including schizophrenia.

In studies of schizophrenia, the effects of institutionalization must be taken into account and separated from the observable behaviors of the schizophrenic subjects that are caused first and foremost by the disease process. This is the basis of the ACUTE CHRONIC DISTINCTION in schizophrenia research.

Coolidge, E.L., *Care of Infants Who Must Be Separated From Their Mothers Because of Some Especial Need On the Part of the Child*, Papers of the American Academy of Medicine, Conference on Prevention of Infant Mortality. Washington, D.C.: 1909.

Spitz, R.A., "Hospitalism—An Enquiry into the Genesis of Psychiatric Conditions in Early Childhood," *Psychoanalytic Study of the Child*, 1(1945), 53–74.

Hôtel-Dieu, L'   Founded in 1656, l'Hôtel Dieu is the oldest hospital in Paris. In 1660 the French Parliament declared that it should provide special accommodations for "mad men and women." In the early 1790s, during the French Revolution, many of the mentally ill patients were removed from the hospital and transferred to the care of Philippe PINEL at the Bicêtre Asylum. Prior to this time the patients there were subjected to BLEEDING so often that the technique was commonly referred to by the public as the *"traitement de l'Hôtel-Dieu."*

Hoxton madhouses   These were private "madhouses" in the Hoxton section of London, England. In the early 1700s practically all mentally ill in London were in one of the Hoxton madhouses. Like "Bellevue" in the United States, the word "Hoxton" took on the ominous meaning of a place of banishment for the mentally ill, and sometimes was used as a synonym for "madness" or "lunacy" itself. (See also PRIVATE MADHOUSES.)

Morris, A.D., *The Hoxton Madhouses*. London: 1958.

humoral theory of mental illness   This theory of health and disease is thought to have been formulated by Hippocrates (460–377 B.C.) and expanded upon by Galen (A.D. 129–199). The ancient Greek notion that the universe was comprised entirely of four elements (earth, air, fire, water), which were each associated with a particular quality (dry, cold, hot, moist), formed the basis of Hippocrates' empirical medicine. Hippocrates associated four essential characteristics—the humors (from the Latin word for moisture)—of the human body with combinations of the elemental qualities. These four humors were blood, yellow bile, black bile, and phlegm; their relative quantities in relation to one another led to good health or to disease. Each of these humors was then associated with its ascendancy during a particular season: spring (blood); summer (yellow bile); autumn (black bile); winter (phlegm). Galen later paired combinations of qualities to each of the humors and their seasons of ascendancy: blood was warm and moist, yellow bile warm and dry, black bile cold and dry and phlegm cold and moist.

Both physical and mental illnesses were considered by Galen to be caused by an excess of humors. What we would call acute diseases tended to be the result of an excess of blood or yellow bile, whereas an excess of black bile or phlegm was associated with more chronic ailments. Black bile in particular caused mental distress, and an excess of its produced MELANCHOLIA or "depression," as we know it. Black bile could build up in the blood, the stomach or elsewhere. Therefore Galen recommended what would later become the standard regimen for the institutionalized mentally ill, what Pinel referred to as the "usual treatment" of bleeding, bathing and purging. These treatments were recommended to either draw off the unwanted excess humor in certain disorders (by bleeding or purging) or to counteract the effects of the abnormal balance of humors (through temperature-specific baths or douches). Reestablishing the flow of blood in menstruation or from hemorrhoids with the use of leeches was thought by Galen to especially assist in the elimination of the disease-causing humor. Vestiges of the old Galenic humor theory of mental illness can especially be seen in the psychiatric texts of the first half of the 1800s, particularly in J.E.D. ESQUIROL's writings. (See also HEMORRHOIDS, PRODUCTION OF AS A TREATMENT.)

Jackson, S.W., "Galen—on mental disorders," *Journal of the History of the Behavioral Sciences,* 5(1969), 365–384.

hurry of the spirits   A term used popularly in 18th century England for "madness" or "lunacy." William BATTIE uses it in his famous 1758 book, *A Treatise On Madness.*

hydropathic institutions   In Europe (especially Germany) in the mid-1800s special clinics were set up to provide HYDRO-THERAPY to mentally ill people as an alternative to commitment to the traditional asylums. These "hydropathic" clinics or institutions could provide outpatient treatment. Thus, people who did not suffer from severe mental disorders did not have to be institutionalized to receive treatment—a very modern concept. However, the established psychiatric authorities of the time—notably Wilhelm GRIESINGER in Germany—strongly criticized these practices as potentially dangerous since they could be performed outside of the supervision of the medical profession. In the 1865 second edition of his *Mental Pathology and Therapeutics* (originally published in 1845), Griesinger expresses the following opinions about hydropathic institutions:

> In the first edition of this work, I have already expressed my opinion of the treatment in hydropathic institutions. Since then facts from all quarters have been elicited proving the injury which it generally inflicts on the mentally diseased. Most asylum physicians are in a position to contribute examples of this: Flemming, Erlenmeyer, Damerow, Sponholz, etc., have expressed themselves decidedly upon this point. This violent procedure seems much to favor the transition to general paralysis. The absurdity of sending patients to cold-water establishments, instead of into lunatic asylums, would be incredible were it not of daily occurrences, still, it is evident that, in certain cases, the occasional use of wet compresses, cold sitz-baths, and, above all, cold washing followed by dry friction, can, under special indications, be beneficially employed.

Despite these criticisms, hydropathic institutions did not disappear, but instead flourished in the 1880s and 1890s as places of treatment for those from the upper classes suffering from the Victorian Age malady of "nervousness" or NEURASTHENIA, the term for this condition coined by physician George Miller Beard (1839–1883) of New York in the 1870s. They specialized in a variety of hydrotherapeutic techniques involving both hot and cold bathing, including being wrapped alternately in hot and cold wet sheets, spraying from showering devices, and other such activities. The ancient spas at such places as Baden-Baden, Carlsbad and Marienbad, which offered natural thermal spring waters, were also popular as forms of hydrotherapy.

Drinka, G.F., *The Birth of Neurosis: Myth, Malady, and the Victorians.* New York: Simon & Schuster, 1984.
Griesinger, W., *Mental Pathology and Therapeutics,* tr. C.L. Robertson and J. Rutherford. New York: William Wood & Co., 1882; first published, 1845–65.

hydrotherapy   Literally "water therapy," since the late 19th century the term for the various types of BATHS or DOUCHES that were one of the primary modes of treatment of the institutionalized mentally ill. It was particularly used for those patients who had become agitated or unmanageable in some way. In the latter half of the 1800s "hydrotherapy" took on the meaning of a particular procedure for a tub bath, which became popular in German psychiatric institutions and then was copied in other places, including the United States. Special treatment rooms were set up that contained large tubs, which would be filled with water and usually heated to between 98 and 102 degrees Fahrenheit. However, cold water baths were sometimes prescribed as well. A thick canvas cover was stretched over the top of the tub and tethered along the rim of the tub, with a hole cut at one end to allow the patient's head to be exposed. A "bathmaster" or "bathmistress" would oversee the treatment sessions, during which a patient would be left immersed in the tub for hours or, in some cases of extreme agitation, days at a time. Not surprisingly, a state of relaxation resulted and behavioral compliance was restored.

While working at the psychiatric clinic at Heidelberg University between 1891 and 1903, Emil KRAEPELIN relied primarily on hydrotherapy for agitated patients, with great success. As he reports in his *Memoirs:*

> By procuring English fireclay tubs and by employing more staff and using the baths during the night, our equipment became more and more complete. The baths were especially successful when they were applied for weeks and months. Slowly, but surely, they became the most important method for dealing with states of agitation, and isolation became completely superfluous.

In the 1890s the primary authority on hydrotherapy in the United States was Dr. Simon Baruch of Bellevue Hospital in New York City. Hydrotherapy equipment was later instituted at St. Elizabeth's Hospital in Washington, D.C., after a visiting physician from there reviewed the hydrotherapy procedures at Bellevue in 1897. When William Alanson White became superintendent of St. Elizabeth's in 1904, he implemented a policy of eliminating the more inhumane forms of physical restraint (straight-jackets, bedsaddles, etc.) and promoted instead the use of hydrotherapy. By the 1920s hydrotherapy was the primary mode of treatment for institutionalized patients at St. Elizabeth's, and statistics show that between the summers of 1923 and 1924 a total of 106,816 warm-tub hydrotherapy sessions were prescribed for over 4,000 patients. Hydrotherapy declined in use in the 1930s when the COMA, CONVULSIVE and ELECTROSHOCK THERAPIES all came into vogue in institutions.

Kraepelin, E., *Memoirs,* tr. C. Wooding-Deane. Berlin: Springer-Verlag, 1987.

hyperkinesia Excessive movement and restlessness. When accompanied by impulsivity and poor attention span, it is a behavioral sign of a childhood disorder, which DSM-III-R (1987) labels attention-deficit hyperactivity disorder (ADHD). It is estimated that one-third of children who manifest ADHD (usually before age 4) continue to show signs of the disorder in adulthood. Hyperkinesis is also one of the traditional symptoms of CATATONIC EXCITEMENT.

hypnosis and psychosis In the 19th century a small number of physicians attempted to use hypnotism ("mesmerism") to treat "insanity" in institutionalized patients. For example, in the 1840s in India, British surgeon James Esdaile attempted to cure the mental illnesses of patients of the Calcutta Asylum during a six-month period, but was generally disappointed with the results. However, in a few cases, people with less debilitating disorders responded to Esdaile's hypnotic inductions. In one case, a man who had cut his throat during a MANIC EPISODE had emergency surgery performed on him by Esdaile while the patient was under "mesmeric anesthesia." British physician John Elliotson, who largely initiated the explosion of interest in mesmerism in England in 1837 and founded the *Zoist,* a mesmeric medical journal in 1843, recommended the use of hypnotism for HYSTERIA. In Paris, the famous hypnotic experiments (beginning in 1878) of neurologist Jean-Martin Charcot (1825–1893) with the institutionalized female patients of the Salpêtrière asylum led to the acceptance of hypnotism by the medical establishment.

In the 20th century there have been many research studies to determine: (1) if people with psychotic disorders can be hypnotized (questionable, due to problems in focusing attention noted particularly in schizophrenia) and (2) whether this may be a beneficial form of treatment. The leading authority on this issue is psychologist Elgin Baker of the Indiana University School of Medicine, who published a review of this issue in 1983. In reviewing the research Baker found that "psychotics" and "borderlines" were comparable to normal subjects and neurotic subjects in their ability to be hypnotized (hypnotic susceptibility). However, Baker recommends that hypnotism be used as one of many other possible treatment techniques in psychotherapy—and in accordance with an overall treatment plan that may even include ANTIPSYCHOTIC DRUGS, which apparently do not reduce the hypnotic susceptibility of psychotic patients.

Baker, E.L., "The Use of Hypnotic Techniques with Psychotics," *American Journal of Clinical Hypnosis,* 25(1983), 283–288.
Bramwell, J.M., *Hypnotism: Its History, Practice and Theory.* London: Alexander Moring, 1906.
Owen, A.R.G., *Hysteria, Hypnosis and Healing in the Work of J.-M. Charcot.* New York: Garrett, 1971.

hypochondriasis Sometimes called "hypochondria." The contemporary meaning of this disorder is of a preoccupation with the belief and accompanying fear that one has a serious disease; based on a misinterpretation of bodily sensations, when in fact physical examination and medical reassurances to the contrary present proof that one does not have the imagined disease. This belief is not of delusional intensity, so there is no break with reality. It is not known how many people develop this disorder, but the numbers of men and women afflicted seem to be equal, and it seems to follow a chronic course throughout a person's lifetime. Apparent predisposing factors seem to be a past history of an actual serious disease (e.g., a heart attack) in the person's life or in the life of a family member. In DSM-III-R this is listed as one of the somatoform disorders, a group of mental disorders that have physical symptoms, which at first seem to have a physical cause.

In the psychotic disorders, particularly schizophrenia, people may report odd physical symptoms in various parts of their bodies (e.g., the head, the genitals), which seems to be more common in the initial stages of the first definite onset of the disorder, or in periodic exacerbations in the first years of the disorder. This is especially true for those diagnosed with one of the three nonparanoid subtypes of schizophrenia, particularly the DISORGANIZED TYPE or HEBEPHRENIC TYPE that Emil Kraepelin called the "silly dementia." Although others often interpret these reports by schizophrenics as efforts at malingering or as hypochondriasis, this is generally not the case. Such reports seem to be the experience of genuine effects of the disease process on the nervous system.

"Hypochondria" has been used to describe mental disorders at least since the time of Galen, who may have been the first to use it. *Hypochondrium* is the Greek word for an area just below the lower ribs, and Galen believed this was the place of origin of one of the three forms of *melancholia.* Over the centuries the words "hypochondriasis" and "hypochondria" were used as synonyms for hypochondriacal melancholy, a type of depression accompanied by flatulence and gastrointestinal problems. In the late 1600s these terms were separated from melancholia (depression) by medical scholars, although hypochondriasis and melancholy were closely related well into the 1800s. However, the connection between an "imaginary illness" and hypochondria was apparent by the early 1600s to some medical scholars. By the 1800s, hypochondriasis differed from other, true forms of mental disorder, such as "hypochondriacal insanity," which were considered a more severe pathological development of "noninsane" hypochondriasis.

Perhaps the best history of hypochondriasis as a mental disorder was written by Stanley W. Jackson in his *Melancholia and Depression* (1986), in a chapter entitled "Hypochondriasis and Melancholia." Another useful source of information on hypochondriasis is an article by George Savage that was published in 1892 in Daniel Hack Tuke's two-volume *Dictionary of Psychological Medicine.*

Jackson, S.W., *Melancholia and Depression: From Hippocratic Times to Modern Times*. New Haven: Yale University Press, 1986.

Kenyon, F.E., "Hypochondriasis: A Survey of Some Historical, Clinical and Social Aspects," *International Journal of Psychiatry*, 2(1966), 308–326.

Savage, G.H., "Hypochondriasis and Insanity," in D.H. Tuke (ed.), *A Dictionary of Psychological Medicine*. Philadelphia: P. Blakiston & Son, 1892.

hypofrontality Also referred to as "cerebral metabolic hypofrontality," or "metabolic hypofrontality," it refers to the results of some studies of the patterns of blood flow in the brain, showing that some schizophrenics have a much lower than normal blood flow in the frontal lobe (specifically, the prefrontal regions) of the brain. The original study that discovered this abnormality was conducted by researchers Ingvar and Franzen and published in 1974. They determined this "hypofrontality" by using a then-new BRAIN IMAGING TECHNIQUE known as regional cerebral blood flow (rCBF). In people diagnosed with schizophrenia, the more "hypofrontal" they appeared, the more they were observed to manifest the NEGATIVE SYMPTOMS of schizophrenia (e.g., they were more withdrawn, there was greater "alogia" or poverty of speech, more disturbances in attention). The implication of this research is that this metabolic hypofrontality may be convincing evidence of a primary brain process (a lowered metabolism in the front part of the brain) that produces the observable symptoms of schizophrenia. However, the "hypofrontality" research has been somewhat inconsistent in that all of the studies using the rCBF brain imaging technique seem to replicate Ingvar and Franzen's original finding, but studies that use PET scans (positron emission tomography) to measure cerebral metabolism have been much less consistent. An excellent review of the hypofrontality research in schizophrenia appears in an article by Daniel Weinberger and Karen Berman.

Weinberger, D.R., and Berman, K.F., "Speculation on the Meaning of Cerebral Metabolic Hypofrontality in Schizophrenia," *Schizophrenia Bulletin*, 14(1988), 157–168.

hypomanic episode This is a less serious version of a fully developed MANIC EPISODE that is indicative of a MOOD DISORDER, particularly BIPOLAR DISORDER. The predominant mood in a hypomanic episode is usually described as expansive, elevated or irritable. A hypomanic episode is not serious enough to cause impairment in social and occupational functioning, and it does not develop into the sometimes psychotic features (delusions, hallucinations) that may accompany a manic episode.

hysteria "Hysteria" is the Greek word for uterus. From ancient times, a significant number of mental and physical disorders in women were believed to be caused by the wandering of a restless womb in the female body. Thus, there has always been a connection between hysterical symptoms and sexuality in women. Hysteria was initially identified by the Hippocratic school in the fifth century B.C. A large number of symptoms have been attributed to hysteria, many of which have survived into today's diagnostic manuals. Among the most ancient and most often reported symptoms have been spasms or convulsions, and feelings of choking due to the rise of an "hysterical ball" from the womb to the throat. In the 1700s and 1800s other symptoms indicative of an hysteric were added, such as the "vapors" (fainting, dizziness), paralysis of the limbs, loss of sensation in the skin (anesthesias), a deep suggestibility or gullibility and dissociative "trance-like" states of *absences* (as it was termed in France). The symptoms were often very changeable, alternating or appearing and disappearing without warning. Sometimes hysterics would also develop psychotic symptoms such as hallucinations, delusions and poor REALITY TESTING, leading 20th-century psychiatric manuals to refer to this as "hysterical psychosis."

"Hysteria" was generally an uncommon diagnosis in psychiatric institutions until the last quarter of the 19th century. The explosion of interest in this disorder was perhaps first evident in France, but soon spread to Germany, England and the United States. In a book on the French psychiatric profession in the 19th century, historian Jan Goldstein reports that at the Salpêtrière asylum for women in Paris, only 1% of the admissions for the two-year period 1841–1842 were given "hysteria" as a diagnosis, but in the period 1882–1883 a full 20.5% received that diagnosis. Also in this later period, two males were admitted to the Bicêtre asylum for men with this diagnosis, revealing a change in thinking about this "female malady."

The work of J.M. Charcot at the Salpêtrière in the 1870s legitimized hysteria as a distinct diagnostic category, and he identified four successive stages or "periods," which marked the fundamental nature of a "grand" hysterical attack (grande hystèrie): developing from physical rigidity, to spasmodic movements (grands mouvements), to a vividly dramatic, almost theatrical acting-out of intense emotional states (attitudes passionnelles), and then to a final delirious period in which the afflicted person laughed, cried and was otherwise highly labile until he or she returned to a more reasonable state. Charcot eventually recognized that hysteria was not a form of severe insanity (aliéne) but was instead a mental disorder that fell into a borderline area of partial normality (demi-fou). This also reflects the distinction, largely coming into vogue at about this time, between a PSYCHOSIS and a NEUROSIS. Sigmund Freud studied with Charcot in Paris in the winter of 1885–86, and as a result of his exposure to Charcot's hypnotic treatment of hysterics he and his mentor Joseph Breuer began to treat "hysterical neurosis" in their private practice patients in Vienna. In 1895 they published their famous book of such case histories, Studien Über Hysterie (Studies on Hysteria). Freud's theories about the

causes of hysteria in sexuality formed the basis of his "psychoanalysis" in the decades to come.

Due to the sometime psychosis-like symptoms in hysteria (disturbances in attention, "dreamy" or "indifferent" quality in interactions with others, delusions and hallucinations), there was much discussion at the turn of the century as to how it was related to Kraepelin's 1896 description of dementia praecox. One of the most important contributions made by Swiss psychiatrist and psychoanalyst C.G. JUNG was his detailed analysis of the similarities and differences between these two disorders in his 1907 monograph, Über die Psychologie der Dementia praecox: Ein Versuch (The Psychology of Dementia Praecox), particularly in his chapter on "Dementia Praecox and Hysteria." He pictured dementia praecox as the far more serious disorder and the one that was probably organic in origin.

In the 20th century, "hysteria" survived as a diagnosis as one of the "Neurotic Disorders" of the World Health Organization's ICD-9 (1978); and in DSM-III-R (1987) it was split up into no less than four different types of disorder. The variant that was formerly called "hysterical psychosis" is now called BRIEF REACTIVE PSYCHOSIS.

Goldstein, J., Console and Classify: The French Psychiatric Profession in the Nineteenth Century. Cambridge: Cambridge University Press, 1987.

Veith, I., Hysteria: The History of a Disease. Chicago: University of Chicago Press, 1965.

I

ICD-9   This is the acronym for the periodically revised manual produced by the World Health Organization entitled: The International Statistical Classification of Disease, Injuries, and Causes of Death. It is usually revised at 10-year intervals; the very first edition appeared in 1900 and the most recent—*ICD-9*—in 1977. A more detailed revision of *ICD-9* by major medical organizations in the United States, to make it more useful to clinicians, researchers, epidemiologists and others, is the *Clinical Modification* (or *ICD-9-CM*). With the growing importance of mental disorders, WHO produced in 1978 a special publication that included the chapter on mental disorders from *ICD-9* and a glossary and classification guide; it is perhaps the most useful summary of the *ICD-9* position on mental disorders.

Although DSM-III-R may be more widely used in clinical practice and research around the world, together with *ICD-9* these two manuals have become the standard classification systems for mental disorders in the 20th century. The special *ICD-9* mental disorders summary may be ordered from the World Health Organization, Division of Mental Health, 20 Avenue Appia, CH-1211 Geneva 27, SWITZERLAND (telephone: 91-36-17).

Commission on Professional and Hospital Activities, *The International Classification of Disease, 9th Revision, Clinical Modification*. Ann Arbor, Mich.: Commission on Professional and Hospital Activities, 1978.
World Health Organization, *Mental Disorders: Glossary and Guide to their Classification in Accordance with the Ninth Revision of the International Classification of Diseases*. Geneva: World Health Organization, 1978.

id   The Freudian "unconscious." Sigmund FREUD borrowed this term from a colleague, Georg Groddeck. Psychosis was viewed by Freud as the result of the ego's inadequate defenses against the id, thereby resulting in a flood of irrational, instinctually based "primary process" material—as appears, for example, in dreams.

ideas of reference   One of the most common symptoms of the psychotic disorders. It is an idea that certain events or people in a person's immediate environment have a magical "special meaning" for that person. For example, a song heard on the radio may be interpreted by a psychotic person as having been specifically played at that time to convey a special message to him or her. Ideas of reference are not as strong as DELUSIONS, nor are they as long-lasting. They tend to be transient and specific to the immediate situation the psychotic person finds him- or herself in at the moment.

idiot savant   See AUTISTIC SAVANTS.

idiot's cage   The name for an iron cage used to confine severely mentally ill and mentally retarded people for public display, usually as entertainment. Such cages were used well into the 1700s and had variations such as the BELGIAN CAGE that were used in the 1800s.

illogical thinking   This is the expression of thoughts that contain obvious inconsistencies and internal logical contradictions. Or, the reaching of blatantly incorrect conclusions, when given an initial premise. Everyone engages in illogical thinking, especially when fatigued or distracted. However, when illogical thinking is an outstanding characteristic of a person's thought patterns, it may be a sign of a mental disorder. It can be indicative of a NEUROSIS, where people may make consistently distorted judgments about themselves or others (which are based on reality), or it may be indicative of the FORMAL THOUGHT DISORDER that characterizes the psychotic disorders, particularly schizophrenia and the "schizophrenia-spectrum" mental disorders (e.g., schizotypal personality disorder, schizophreniform disorder).

illusion   This is a mistaken perception of an *actual* object or event in the environment. Illusions are different from HALLUCINATIONS, which do not have actual external stimuli for the sensory experience.

illusion des sosies   See CAPGRAS SYNDROME.

illusion of intermetamorphosis   See INTERMETAMORPHOSIS SYNDROME.

illusion of negative doubles   See CAPGRAS SYNDROME.

illusion of positive doubles   See FREGOLI'S SYNDROME.

immediacy hypothesis   This is the hypothesis that the behavior of people with schizophrenia is controlled primarily by stimuli immediate in their environment. "Normal" people are "controlled" by much wider and less immediate (i.e., not in the immediate environment) stimuli, according to this hypothesis, which is largely based on a radical behavioral interpretation of COGNITIVE STUDIES OF SCHIZOPHRENIA. This hypothesis was first put forth by Kurt Salzinger in 1966. (See also ATTENTION, DISORDERS IN.)

Salzinger, K., *Schizophrenia: Behavioral Aspects*. New York: John Wiley, 1973.

immersion therapy   See BATHS; HYDROTHERAPY.

impulsive character   See BORDERLINE SCHIZOPHRENIA.

incidence of schizophrenia   See EPIDEMIOLOGY.

incipient schizophrenia   An older term for that phase of the schizophrenic disease process when signs of the impending disorder first clearly make their appearance. This usually involves a clear deterioration in functioning before the active phase of the disorder. In DSM-III-R (1987) this is now called the PRODROMAL PHASE.

incoherence   Uncomprehensible speech. This term is applied when a person's speech is marked by ILLOGICAL THINKING, excessive use of incomplete sentences, tangential or irrelevant statements, or abrupt changes in the topic of conversation. Grammar may be distorted and word usage may be bizarre or idiosyncratic. Incoherence may be a sign of FORMAL THOUGHT DISORDER. It is commonly found in schizophrenia (particularly the DISORGANIZED TYPE) and in the ACUTE RECOVERABLE PSYCHOSES. Incoherence does not apply to an identifiable speech or language disorder such as an aphasia.

incomplete penetrance   In GENETICS STUDIES, the likelihood that a particular genetically transmitted abnormality (such as a disease) will be expressed depends on the degree of penetrance of that disorder. For example, with schizophrenia it may be that close biological relatives (such as MONOZYGOTIC TWINS) will carry the genetic predisposition to developing the disease, but genetic abnormalities that may produce the disease may not be expressed equally in the psychological and physiological development of these persons. For example, although the CONCORDANCE RATE for schizophrenia between monozygotic or "identical" twins is suggestively high, nonetheless one twin will often develop schizophrenia and the other will not, rendering them discordant for schizophrenia. This is an example of incomplete penetrance—the genetic defect does not fully "penetrate" or influence later "expressed" psychological and physiological development (in this case, in the genetically "identical" twin that does not develop schizophrenia). Because the modes of GENETIC TRANSMISSION for mental disorders are presently unknown, incomplete penetrance continues to be a major problem in genetics studies of these disorders.

incurable gallery, the   One of the four "galleries" (akin to cellblocks) that held the mentally ill patients at the BETHLEM ROYAL HOSPITAL ("BEDLAM").

inderal See PROPRANOLOL.

inderide See PROPRANOLOL.

index case In GENETICS STUDIES of schizophrenia, particularly the "family studies" using the CONSANGUINITY METHOD, the index case is the person who is diagnosed with the disorder. Such information as the possible risk for schizophrenia in relatives of a schizophrenic person are made by analyzing the relationships between the index case and other family members. Another term for the index case is the PROBAND.

India The prevalence rates for schizophrenia in India have been found to range from 2.2 to 5.6 per thousand. India is unusual in that the greater rates for schizophrenia have been found in the *higher* socioeconomic groups, which is unlike the pattern for most of the rest of the world, in which the higher rates are found in the lowest socioeconomic strata of society.

Torrey, E.F., "Prevalence Studies of Schizophrenia," *British Journal of Psychiatry,* 150(1987), 598–608.

indolamines A group of biogenic amines including the neurotransmitter SEROTONIN. The biogenic amines are implicated in the development of certain mental disorders, including schizophrenia, bipolar disorder and depression. (See also BIOGENIC AMINE HYPOTHESIS.)

induced psychotic disorder See FOLIE À DEUX.

infantile autism See AUTISM, INFANTILE.

infectious agent hypothesis See FOCAL INFECTION AS CAUSE OF PSYCHOTIC DISORDERS; VIRAL THEORIES OF SCHIZOPHRENIA.

infectious insanity See FOLIE À DEUX.

influenced psychosis See FOLIE À DEUX.

information processing in schizophrenia By employing metaphors and concepts derived from the computer sciences, COGNITIVE STUDIES OF SCHIZOPHRENIA have attempted to demonstrate the differences in the processes of thinking between people who are diagnosed with schizophrenia and those who are not. These studies examine the stages of information processing—essentially defined as the encoding, transformation, storage and retrieval of information for the purpose of regulating behavior—to determine at what stage or stages defects occur in schizophrenics that are unlike those found in most normals.

A comprehensive review of the literature of schizophrenia studies, conducted from an information-processing approach and compiled and analyzed by Canadian psychologists Leonard George and Richard Neufeld, appeared in *Schizophrenia Bulletin* in 1985. They conclude that the following traditional schizophrenic symptoms have the accompanying interpretations according to information processing theory:

Sensory and perceptual anomalies. Hallucinations may occur in conjunction with an interaction of several defects in information processing: a disruption in sensory processing, leading to the spontaneous retrieval of information in long-term memory; a predisposition toward representing this information as mental imagery; and the misattribution of these products of internal processing to external sources.

Body-image distortions. These may be misperceptions based on the result of a general sensory analysis dysfunction.

Loosening of associations. This anomaly may be related to studies that show a schizophrenic deficit in the implementation of the network of semantic relations in long-term memory.

Delusions. A large body of evidence indicates cognitive and perceptual differences between paranoid and nonparanoid schizophrenics, with the paranoid characterized by a "premature judgment" or "jump to conclusions" response set.

Movement abnormalities. These may be due to inadequate or inaccurate feedback information, or may reflect strategies for coping with attentional dysfunction. (See also AT-TENTION, DISORDERS IN.)

George, L. and Neufeld, R.W.J., "Cognition and Symptomatology in Schizophrenia," *Schizophrenia Bulletin,* 11(1985), 264–285.

informed consent Before any medical procedure is performed, physicians must legally obtain the informed consent of the patient to perform the procedure. This involves an explanation of the purpose of the procedure, how it is done, and the potential risks involved for the patient that may result from the procedure. If the patient agrees, the consent is then given in writing. Although obtaining informed consent usually presents no problem in most people who are about to undergo a medical procedure or treatment (e.g., surgery), for individuals who are suffering from a psychotic disorder there are dilemmas. Can a person who is having problems remaining in contact with "reality" and is unable to think clearly and comprehend difficult information truly give *informed* consent?

This is an ethical and legal issue that is continually debated not only in the psychiatric profession, but also in the legal system. For example, all of the present medical treatments for the psychotic disorders (antipsychotic drugs, electroconvulsive therapy, etc.) have side effects that affect either the immediate functioning of the individual (e.g., loss of memory after ECT) or his or her long-term health (e.g., tardive dyskinesia caused by years of treatment with antipsychotic drugs). Most studies confirm the obvious: Psychotic patients may say that they understand what is being explained to them, but in fact when they are given an objective examination afterward they reveal that they did not. The "lack of informed consent" before administering treatment to patients is one of the most common causes of legal action against psychiatrists.

Cohen, R.J. and Mariano, W.E., *Legal Guidebook in Mental Health.* New York: Free Press, 1982.
Irwin, M. et al., "Psychotic Patients' Understanding of Informed Consent," *American Journal of Psychiatry,* 142(1985), 1351–1354.

inheritance, modes of See GENETIC TRANSMISSION.

input dysfunction hypothesis This is one of the early "cognitive" interpretations of the behavior of schizophrenics that was put forth to explain deficits in attention (see ATTENTION, DISORDERS IN). In 1964, British psychologist Peter Venables proposed that schizophrenics suffer from an "input dysfunction" in their ability to focus attention. Essentially, he postulated that the ability to focus attention was related to levels of internal "arousal" in the nervous system. It is a well-known fact that for most of us, when we are nervous about performing some activity (such as public speaking, a job interview or taking a test), our ability to focus our attention may be affected. Venables proposes that in chronic nonparanoid schizophrenics there is a heightened arousal of the brain and nervous system (termed "cortical arousal"), which leads to an oversensitivity. Thus, when stimuli from the outside confronts the schizophrenic (even simple social interactions, for example), the person finds this to be "too intense," and he or she "shuts down." They may withdraw, become apathetic and feel a restriction in their range of feelings (these are now called NEGATIVE SYMPTOMS). The field of attention is then narrowed in these people. In contrast, acute schizophrenics suffer from a lowered level of cortical arousal when compared to normals, resulting in an expansion of attention that is so broad that they feel that they cannot shut anything out of awareness. Everything hits them at once, and they report feeling "flooded."

Venable's "input dysfunction theory" is only one of the many theories put forth in the 1960s about deficits in the ability of schizophrenics to focus attention. An excellent summary of these detailed theories, and of the research on all areas of "schizophrenic cognition," can be found in a classic volume by Loren J. and Jean P. Chapman, *Disordered Thought in Schizophrenia*.

Chapman, L.J. and Chapman, J.P., *Disordered Thought in Schizophrenia*. Englewood Cliffs, N.J.: Prentice-Hall, 1973.
Venables, P.H., "Input Dysfunction in Schizophrenia," in B.A. Maher (ed.), *Progress in Experimental Personality Research, vol. 1*. New York: Academic Press, 1964.

insane   A word derived from the Latin *insanus,* for "unsound (in mind)."

insanity   Originally termed "insanity of mind," this refers to the state of being insane. Presently, it has only a legal meaning (not a psychiatric one) relating to the soundness of mind of a person when involved in actions that have legal consequences. More generally, it has come to mean that a psychosis was present when a person committed such a legally consequent act. Throughout most of the 18th and 19th centuries, "insanity" was a generic term for all mental illnesses and was used in the same way that we rely on the term "mental disorders" today. Until the latter part of the last century, "lunacy" was a synonym also used by the psychiatric and legal professions to refer to mental illness. In 19th-century France, the distinction made was between *aliéne* and *demi-fou,* roughly our present distinction between a "psychosis" and "neurosis." Although a vast literature has existed since the early 1800s on the legal issues raised by acts committed by mentally ill offenders ("in-

sane" offenders), the word "insanity" was still being used in a quasi-psychiatric sense (at least in the United States) in the 1920s. In 1923, William Alanson White, the superintendent of St. Elizabeth's Hospital in Washington, D.C., and the foremost forensic psychiatrist in the country, argued forcefully in a book that the word "insanity" was entirely to be considered a legal term and had no medical meaning. White, as the president of the American Psychiatric Association at that time, was also instrumental in changing the name of the *American Journal of Insanity* to the *American Journal of Psychiatry* in 1922.

Although much has been written about the influence of American physician Isaac Ray in the 19th century in defining the nature of "insanity" for legal purposes, no single history of the development of forensic psychiatry as yet exists. (See also FEIGNED INSANITY; M'NAUGHTEN RULES.)

Hughes, J.S., *In the Law's Darkness: Isaac Ray and the Medical Jurisprudence of Insanity in Nineteenth-Century America*. New York: Oceana Publications, 1986.
Quen, J.M., "Isaac Ray and the Development of American Psychiatry and the Law," *Psychiatric Clinics of North America,* 6(1983), 527–537.
White, W.A., *Insanity and the Criminal Law*. New York: Macmillan, 1923.

insanity by contagion   See FOLIE À DEUX.

insanity defense   This is the legal defense in which a person may plead that he or she is not guilty for committing an alleged crime by reason of insanity. It apparently dates back to 13th-century English constitutional law, when it was popularly known as the "wild beast test," i.e., if people act like wild beasts they cannot be held accountable for their actions. Over the centuries the concept that a person could not be responsible for criminal acts because he or she was *non compos mentis* (mentally incompetent), usually due to being an "idiot" since birth or a "lunatic" thereafter, has undergone many changes. Our modern concepts of the insanity defense date back to the famous trial of Daniel M'Naughten in England in 1843 in which he was acquitted of a criminal act on the grounds of insanity. The judges in that trial relied primarily on the opinions in a book by American physician Isaac RAY, *A Treatise on the Medical Jurisprudence of Insanity* (1838), in which he advocated many reforms in the then-standard criminal laws and in the incompetency and commitment laws. The famous M'NAUGHTEN RULES, which later resulted from the trial, became the established criterion of "knowing right from wrong" for judging insanity.

The insanity defense has been disputed in the 1980s due to the "not guilty by reason of insanity" verdict against John Hinckley Jr., who attempted to assassinate President Ronald Reagan. Three states (Utah, Montana and Idaho) have abolished it completely, and many others have instituted major modifications that restrict its use. Twelve states have passed legislation allowing a variation on the verdict in the form of "guilty but insane."

A bimonthly periodical that follows the changes in the mental health laws is the *Mental Disability Law Reporter,* available from: the American Bar Association, 1800 M Street, N.W., Washington, DC 20036.

Lewinstein, S.R., "The Historical Development of Insanity as a Defense in Criminal Actions," *Journal of Forensic Science,* 14(1969), 275–293, 469–500.

Oppenheimer, H., *The Criminal Responsibility of Lunatics: A Study in Comparative Law.* London: Sweet & Maxwell, 1909.

institutionalization It has long been observed that many people who are diagnosed with schizophrenia and spend most of their time in institutions tend to get worse as the years go on. Patients become apathetic, submissive, resigned, emotionally flat and lose their sense of appropriateness in social behavior. But is this due to the disease process or is it due to the experience of being involuntarily (usually) hospitalized in an institution?

There have been many theories about the effects of hospitalization on the course of schizophrenia, and the ACUTE-CHRONIC DISTINCTION in schizophrenia research is partly designed to "control" for such institutionalization effects. For example, Erving GOFFMAN pictures the "inmates" of "total institutions" (mental hospitals, prisons, etc.) as undergoing a degrading devaluation of any sense of self-worth or identity, as being, essentially, brainwashed into the "role" of career mental patient. Others have viewed a hospitalized schizophrenic patient as holding a unique privilege—not responsible for his actions. Therefore, there may be every incentive to be sexually or aggressively inappropriate with others and to totally abdicate responsibility for self-care (feeding oneself, hygiene, etc.). Therefore, according to this view, patients are "rewarded" for acting "crazy" and manipulatible and remaining in the hospital—which may be more like a vacation resort than anything else. This latter position reflects the "impression management" theory of the effects of the institution on schizophrenics proposed by Braginsky and Braginsky in the late 1960s.

Controlled studies of the effects of institutionalization (chronicity) on schizophrenic patients have generally found that there is little evidence of intellectual deterioration that cannot be attributed to the disease process. Furthermore, the "zombie-like" appearance of some severe schizophrenics in institutions cannot entirely be attributed to the influence of ANTIPSYCHOTIC DRUGS since these behaviors match clinical descriptions of schizophrenics in institutions before the advent of this form of treatment. Some early studies of these effects, as well as a summary of the above theories, can be found in a 1973 book by Chapman and Chapman. However, given the often emotionally intense, noisy and frequently violent "holding-tank" environments of most large psychiatric institutions, it is difficult to see how living in such a setting could not have some effect on the mental health of the patient. (See also HOSPITALISM.)

Braginsky, B.M. and Braginsky, D.D., *Methods of Madness: The Mental Hospital As A Last Resort.* New York: Holt, Rinehart & Winston, 1969.
Chapman, L.J. and Chapman, J.P., *Disordered Thought in Schizophrenia.* Englewood Cliffs, N.J.: Prentice-Hall, 1973.

insulin coma (or shock) therapy   This was the most popular—and most consistently effective—form of treatment for acute schizophrenia from the mid-1930s to the late 1950s, when treatment with ANTIPSYCHOTIC DRUGS became dominant. This technique was invented by an Austrian psychiatrist, Manfred Joshua Sakel (1906–1957), who was working at the Lichterfield Hospital in Berlin with patients recovering from morphine addiction, between 1927 and 1933. To diminish the agitation and psychotic symptoms due to withdrawal, Sakel began giving them experimental doses of insulin, a relatively new drug—isolated and used for the treatment of diabetes only in 1922—whose full range of effects were not yet well known. He discovered that the higher doses did indeed relieve the agitative withdrawal symptoms, and when he found that doses that were high enough would induce a coma in patients—particularly in those patients who were also diagnosed with schizophrenia—he began to experiment in 1933 with induced insulin comas as a treatment for schizophrenia.

This therapy essentially regarded the induction of a hypoglycemic (abnormally low blood sugar) coma as a form of "shock" to the system of a schizophrenic patient. The modified procedure, which eventually came into use after Sakel published his results in 1934, required several months of treatments on an inpatient unit with a highly trained staff, since inattentiveness could lead to the death of the patient. In his book, *Interpretation of Schizophrenia* (1974), Silvano Ar-

ieti described the usual procedure for insulin treatment:

It consists of administration of insulin in progressively larger doses. One starts initially with 10 to 15 units and increases the dosage until the patient undergoes severe hypoglycemic shocks, which are characterized by comas and, less frequently, by epileptic seizures. The average coma producing dose is 100 to 150 units. The state of coma used to be terminated in the fourth or fifth hour by administration of an adequate amount of carbohydrates. Sugar was given orally if the patient was able to drink, or through tube feeding, or through an intravenous injection of a glucose solution. Now termination is obtained through the use of glucagon, in doses of 0.33 to 1 mg intravenously or intramuscularly. Small amounts generally awaken the patient, who is then able to drink a sugar solution. From a minimum of twenty to a maximum of eighty comas are generally produced, usually at a frequency of at least three times a week.

Sakel's theoretical explanation for why insulin coma therapy worked with acute schizophrenics was never considered adequate and was rejected by most. Nonetheless, the treatment seemed to be the first one that was consistently successful with people who were undergoing their very first episodes of psychosis. Chronic schizophrenics did not benefit at all from the treatment. Critics of this method have pointed out that most people undergoing their very first schizophrenic episodes respond to just about any form of treatment (or go into spontaneous remission anyway). Sakel immigrated to the United States in 1937, where insulin coma therapy became the primary treatment for schizophrenia for the next two decades.

Sakel, M., *The Pharmacological Shock Treatment of Schizophrenia.* New York: Nervous and Mental Diseases Monographs, 1936.
———, "New Treatment of Schizophrenia," *American Journal of Psychiatry,* 93(1937), 829–841.

intermetamorphosis syndrome   One of the rarest of the psychotic MISIDENTIFICA-

TION SYNDROMES, the intermetamorphosis syndrome involves the delusional belief that certain persons or objects have been interchanged. Rather than insisting that related persons are alien "impostors" (as in CAPGRAS SYNDROME), or that these strangers are, in reality, known persecutors who are inhabiting their bodies (FREGOLI'S SYNDROME), this delusion involves the belief that known persons have been interchanged or replaced by other known persons. For example, such a delusional person may insist that one's mother has been replaced by one's first-grade teacher, and so on. In the very first published case of the intermetamorphosis syndrome—by French psychiatrists P. Courboun and J. Tusques in 1932—a depressed woman with paranoid delusions of persecution insisted that her new coat had been replaced by a shabby, older one, that her two young hens had been replaced by older ones, and that various women had been metamorphosed into men, and the young into old. As with the other misidentification syndromes, intermetamorphosis syndrome may be the result of an ORGANIC MENTAL DISORDER or be found within the delusional systems of those diagnosed with the paranoid subtype of schizophrenia.

Courbon, P. and Tusques, J., "L'illusion d' intermétamorphose et de charmes," *Annales Medico-Psychologique*, 90(1932), 401.

interpersonal functioning   In any of the psychotic disorders, but particularly in schizophrenia, there is a marked deterioration in the ability to sustain relationships with other people. In fact, social withdrawal, emotional detachment and occupational problems often mark the beginning of the first full onset of schizophrenia. Since psychotic disorders, by their very definition, involve a disturbed relationship with the external demands of reality, this invariably leads to problems with others. Sometimes people may find themselves becoming preoccupied with bizarre ideas and fantasies

and will therefore shut out relationships. Other afflicted people may instead do the opposite: They may begin to cling to others, becoming almost child-like in their dependence on them. Or, they may begin to intrude upon strangers in public, demanding their attention and becoming physically too close to them, obviously making the strangers uncomfortable. These "inappropriate behaviors"—as the phrase is so often used in the psychiatric institutions of today—are often quite troublesome for the family members of schizophrenics and people with other psychotic disorders, and often leads the family to finally seek help for the individual.

introversion   A term coined by Swiss psychiatrist and psychoanalyst C.G. JUNG for a pervasive "attitude" toward the world in which one's "psychic energy" or "libido" is primarily directed inward toward the self and the internal world of one's own fantasies. Jung believed all people fit along a continuum from introversion to extroversion with, usually, one or the other as a dominant mode of approaching the world. Although introverted people were often very individualistic and were supposed to have a close relationship with the unconscious, they were often uncomfortable in groups or in social situations. In its extreme pathological form, introversion was thought to describe the withdrawal of many schizophrenic patients from the external world.

involuntary commitment   See COMMITMENT.

involutional psychosis   Also referred to as "involutional melancholia," this is a severe depression that has developed into a psychosis. Agitation, delusions, mood-congruent hallucinations and somatic preoccupations characterize this disorder. Although the terms "involutional psychosis" or "melancholia" are not used in DSM-III-R, involutional melancholia is listed in this manual as a major depressive episode, melancholic type. It is characterized by a loss of interest in activities, early morning awakenings, worse depression in the morning, significant weight loss or anorexia, and psychomotor retardation or agitation.

Ireland Along with parts of Croatia, and northern Sweden, western Ireland has one of the highest prevalence rates of schizophrenia in the world. Proportionately, Ireland has three times more people diagnosed with schizophrenia in psychiatric hospitals and three times more first admissions for schizophrenia than England. The schizophrenia first-admission rate is even three times that of the United States. Western and southwestern Ireland, which contain the poorer counties, have the highest schizophrenia rates. In these areas there is a one in 25 chance that a person will be hospitalized for schizophrenia at some point in their lives, making these rates the highest in the world. The counties most affected are Mayo, Kerry, Sligo, Roscommon, Galway, Clare, Cork and Waterford. Northern Ireland, which is part of the United Kingdom, has always maintained a lower rate of schizophrenia than in the south. Studies in the United States and Canada have consistently found that immigrants from Ireland have very high first-admission rates to psychiatric hospitals when compared to other ethnic groups.

Torrey, E.F., "Prevalence Studies of Schizophrenia," *British Journal of Psychiatry,* 150(1987), 598–608.

isolation Isolating agitated or violent people who are psychotic has long been a method of preventing them from harming themselves or others. It has been considered by many, over the centuries, as a more humane form of restraint than either physical or chemical methods. The famous "padded rooms" invented by the German physician Ferdinand AUTENREITH (1772–1835), which were lined with cork and rubber, were widely copied throughout European asylums in the 19th century as places to isolate patients.

Many institutions today still have isolation or "time-out rooms" for their more active patients.

In his 1838 classic, *Des Maladies Mentale,* ESQUIROL devotes many pages to a discussion of "isolation," but he uses the word in much the same way we use "hospitalization" today. His use of the term was to denote the isolating of the mentally ill person from his family by commitment in an institution for the "insane." Esquirol felt that the novelty of the new situation would have therapeutic value: "The first effect of isolation is, to produce new sensations, to change and break up the chain of ideas, from which the patient could not free himself. New and unexpected impressions strike, arrest, and excite his attention, and render him more accessible to those councils, that ought to bring him back to reason." Yet, after listing more virtues of commitment to an asylum for the insane, Esquirol also expresses some words of caution about "isolation":

> But, it may be said, that there are insane persons who are cured at home. This is true. These cures, however, are rare, and cannot impair the general rule. They prove only, that isolation, like all other curative means, ought always to be prescribed by a physician. I will say more, - that isolation has been fatal to some persons. And what shall we conclude from this? That we should recommend it with caution; especially when it is to be prolonged; and also, that it is the nature of the best and most useful things, not to be always exempt from inconveniences. To the wise, judicious and experienced physician does it belong, to foresee and prevent them.

A more commonly used term in the 20th century for isolating patients in separate rooms is seclusion.

Esquirol, J.E.D., *Mental Maladies, A Treatise on insanity,* tr. E.K. Hunt. Philadelphia: Lea & Blanchard, 1845; first published, 1838.

Israel Israel is a nation of immigrants. Since studies of schizophrenia prevalence rates in immigrant groups are subject to errors in statistical measurement because of the large number of variables to take into consideration, it has been difficult to determine reliable prevalence rates for schizophrenia in Israel.

Torrey, E.F., *Schizophrenia and Civilization*. New York: Jason Aronson, 1980.

Italy It has been noted at least since 1862, when W. Charles Hood published his book, *Statistics of Insanity*, that the rates of "insanity" in southern European countries were much lower than those in northern European countries. In fact, Hood found Italy to have the lowest rates in all of Europe. Although no conclusive prevalence rates have been calculated for Italy, it has been noted that, well into the 20th century, Italy had low hospitalization rates for schizophrenia as compared to other countries. Also, it has been found that the first-admission hospitalization rates for Italian immigrants in England and the United States are far lower than for other ethnic groups.

Torrey, E.F., *Schizophrenia and Civilization*. New York: Jason Aronson, 1980.

J

Janet, Pierre (1859–1947) A French philosopher and psychiatrist whose research on the nature of the unconscious mind and on psychotherapy makes him one of the most important figures in the history of psychology and psychiatry. He was appointed to teach philosophy at the Liceum of Le Havre in 1881 (at the age of 22) and did volunteer work at the local asylum, where he conducted research for his doctoral dissertation. His studies of the highly hypnotizable hysterical female patients there led to observations about the workings of the unconscious mind, which he incorporated into his disser-

tation and his classic book *L'Automatisme Psychologique (Psychological Automatisms)* (1889). He is best remembered for his descriptions of the psychological process known as DISSOCIATION, and how it worked in people under hypnosis, in those with hysteria and in those with multiple personalities. About 1980, when multiple personality disorder once again began to attract serious interest, the work of Janet likewise found new students. Janet wrote voluminously (in French) on a wide range of psychiatric, psychological and philosophical topics, but only a few of these works have ever been translated into English. There are many papers on paranoid schizophrenia that Janet produced in the 1930s and 1940s that still await translation.

Janet, P. *L'Automatisme psychologique*. Paris: Félix Alcan, 1889.

Perry, C. and Laurence, J.R., "Mental Processing Outside of Awareness: The Contributions of Freud and Janet," in K.S. Bowers and D. Meichenbaum (eds.), *The Unconscious Reconsidered*. New York: John Wiley, 1984.

Van der Hart, O. and Friedman, B., "A Reader's Guide to Pierre Janet on Dissociation: A Neglected Intellectual Heritage," *Dissociation*, 2(1989), 3–16.

Japan Japan and Sweden are the two countries in which the best data on the prevalence rates for schizophrenia have been collected. In Japan, the prevalence rates for schizophrenia have ranged form 2.1 to 2.3 per thousand. The lowest socioeconomic level in Japan has been found to have prevalence rates for psychotic disorders that are three to five times higher than the highest socioeconomic levels.

Torrey, E.F., *Schizophrenia and Civilization*. New York: Jason Aronson, 1980.

jealous type One of the variants of delusional (paranoid) disorder as listed in DSM-III-R (1987). It is a persistent, usually "nonbizarre" delusion in which a person is convinced that his or her spouse is being unfaithful—without any rational grounds for the suspicion. As this delusion can take on psychotic dimensions, such a person may take extraordinary measures to intervene and dissolve the fantasized relationship. He or she may keep the spouse locked in the house or may restrict that person's activities in other ways. The person with the delusional jealousy may secretly follow the spouse or have that person followed. In some cases the person with the psychotic delusion may physically harm the spouse. Although the delusion itself is so out of line with reality that it renders the person psychotic at times, no other FORMAL THOUGHT DISORDER or other sign of a psychosis is present. In its pure form, this delusion of jealousy has been called the OTHELLO SYNDROME.

jealousy, delusional See DELUSIONAL JEALOUSY.

Jung, Carl Gustav (1875–1961) A Swiss psychiatrist and psychoanalyst who formulated his own unique "analytical psychology" (first called "complex psychology"), after breaking with his mentor, Sigmund FREUD, in 1913. The son of a Protestant pastor in Basel, Switzerland, the young Jung originally wanted to become an archaeologist. After a vividly symbolic dream, he decided instead to pursue medicine, which was an offshoot of his fascination with the natural sciences. During his medical school years (specifically, in 1896), Jung became interested in the unusual trances and hypnotic phenomena of his 15-year-old cousin, who was a medium. In an attempt to analyze her behavior, he read widely in philosophy and spiritualism. In 1902, he based his doctoral dissertation on this work with her. In 1900, during his final examinations, he came across a psychiatry textbook written by German psychiatrist and neurologist Richard von Krafft-Ebing that convinced him he should study psychiatry—commonly regarded at the time as an "inferior" medical discipline. Jung passed his medical examinations and won a position at the BURGHÖLZLI HOSPITAL

under the direction of Eugen BLEULER in 1900.

From the beginning, Jung was interested in pursuing the psychological and symbolic meaning behind the psychotic disorders and not just their classification, which was the traditional occupation of psychiatry in those days. As Jung tells it in a lecture given in 1925:

> I told nobody that I intended to work out the unconscious phenomena of the psychoses, but that was my determination. I wanted to catch the intruders in the mind—the intruders that make people laugh when they should not laugh, and cry when they should not cry.

Jung remained at the Burghölzli for nine years. During this time he developed a worldwide scientific reputation for his famous "word-association test" experiments and for his 1907 monograph on the psychological processes involved in dementia praecox (*Über die Psychologie der Dementia Praecox*). It was likewise during these years that Bleuler was developing his ideas on "schizophrenia" (a term Bleuler first used in print in 1908), and Bleuler acknowledges the contributions of his assistant Jung in the preface to his famous book, *Dementia Praecox, Or the Group of Schizophrenias* (1911). Jung's later psychology was based largely on the dissociative experiences of his mediumistic cousin and his nine years of daily clinical work with institutionalized psychotic patients. He was particularly interested in the story-motifs and structures of schizophrenic hallucinations and delusions and how they seemed to correspond to the myths and fairy tales of centuries past. These organizing structural dominants of all psychological life, conscious and unconscious, he called "archetypes." In contrast, Freud (whom Jung was associated with from 1907 to 1913) based his theories of the structure and dynamics of the psyche on the neurotic patients he saw in the Viennese consulting room of his home and had only minimal contact with institutionalized patients.

Jung is famous for proposing that a "toxin" may be the actual cause of many of the seriously debilitating psychological symptoms of schizophrenia, although this toxin was first produced by the intense emotions of a psychological disturbance (i.e., a complex). He is also remembered for being perhaps the first to conduct individual psychotherapy with institutionalized schizophrenics; in his descriptions of his pre-psychoanalytic-period cases, he revealed a psychoeducational and rehabilitative approach rather than an insight-oriented one—an approach that is recommended for use with schizophrenics today. Although in his writings Jung sometimes refers to the successful treatment of "dementia praecox" in some patients, he later admitted that these were BORDERLINE CASES that did not develop into the full picture of this disorder. In a September 24, 1926, letter to an American psychiatrist who had asked about Jung's successful treatment of dementia praecox, Jung admits the limitations of his success:

> I suppose the news you heard of my successes in the treatment of Dementia praecox is greatly exaggerated. As a matter of fact I only treated a limited number of cases, and these were all what one might call in a liquid condition, that is, not yet congealed. I avoid the treatment of such cases as much as possible. It is true they can be treated, and even with the most obvious success, but such a success costs almost your own life. You have to make the most stupendous effort to reintegrate the dissociated psychic entities, and it is by no means a neat and simple technique which you can apply, but a creative effort with a vast knowledge of the unconscious mind.

Even in the face of the growing evidence for the organic basis of schizophrenia, until the end of his life Jung maintained that it may have an equally important psychological cause. His final statement on the issue was a letter sent to the chairman of a Symposium on Chemical Concepts of Psychosis (held in September 1957), clarifying his views on the issue; it was published in 1958. Jung asserts that the cause of schizophrenia is a "dual one: namely, up to a certain point psychology is indispensable in explaining the nature and the causes of the initial emotions which give rise to metabolic alterations. These emotions seem to be accompanied by chemical processes that cause specific temporary or chronic disturbances or lesions." (See also ABAISSEMENT DU NIVEAU MENTAL; BIOCHEMICAL THEORIES OF SCHIZOPHRENIA; BIBLIOTHERAPY; COMPLEX; DISSOCIATION.)

Jung, C.G., *Letters. 1:1906–1950*. Princeton: Princeton University Press, 1973.
———, *Analytical Psychology: Notes of the Seminar Given in 1925*. Princeton: Princeton University Press, 1989.
———, *The Collected Works of C.G. Jung*, 20 vols. Princeton: Princeton University Press, 1953–1979.

K

Kahlbaum, Karl Ludwig (1828–1899)

A German psychiatrist who was famous for grouping clusters of symptoms into observable "symptoms complexes," each of which would characterize a particular mental disorder. One of these disorders—CATATONIA—was first named by him in 1869, but only described in detail in his famous 1874 book on the subject. Catatonia was later added to paranoia and HEBEPHRENIA as the three disorders that were combined by Emil KRAEPELIN in 1896 to form DEMENTIA PRAECOX. A student of Kahlbaum's who worked closely with him, Ewald Hecker, later described one of the other syndromes that was included in the schizophrenia concept—hebephrenia.

Kahlbaum, K.L., *Die Katatonie oder das Spannungsirresein*. Berlin: Hirschwald, 1874. English-language edition: *Catatonia;* Baltimore: Johns Hopkins Press, 1973.

Kallman, Franz J. (1897–1965) Kallman was a German psychiatrist and researcher who, from 1928, directed neuropathology laboratories for psychiatric hospitals in Berlin. In 1936 he immigrated to the United States and brought his research on the genetics of mental disorders with him. A translated version of his manuscript was published in 1938, and it is considered by many contemporary scholars to be the first true starting point for the GENETICS STUDIES of schizophrenia. He also later became interested in the genetics of manic-depressive psychosis.

Kallmann, F.J., *The Genetics of Schizophrenia.* New York: J.S. Augustin, 1938.

Kandinsky-Clérambault syndrome. This is the type of delusional experience in which a person feels his or her mind is being controlled or influenced in some way by outside forces. It is a commonly reported experience in people diagnosed with schizophrenia. It was first described in 1890 by Viktor Chrisanfovich Kandinsky (1825–1889) and Gaétan de Clérambault (1872–1934).

Kanner, Leo (1894–1981) An Austrian-born psychiatrist who immigrated to the United States and became the "father of child psychiatry." He did research on IN-FANTILE AUTISM and CHILDHOOD SCHIZO-PHRENIA, which he thought, based on psychoanalytic theory, were caused by disturbances in early mother and child relationships. Kanner separated infantile autism from childhood schizophrenia in 1943, believing them to be two separate types of childhood disorder. Because of his pioneering work in this area, infantile autism is also called "Kanner's Syndrome."

Kanner, L., *Child Psychiatry.* Springfield, Ill.: Charles Thomas, 1942.

Kanner's syndrome See AUTISM, IN-FANTILE.

karyotype This is a chromosome that has been stained with a special substance and prepared so that it can be identified. Only since the early 1960s, when it was developed, has the process of karyotyping chromosomes made it possible to identify and study specific chromosomes.

katatonia See CATATONIA.

Kirkbride, Thomas Story (1809–1883) An American physician from Philadelphia and one of the original 13 founders of the AMERICAN PSYCHIATRIC ASSOCIATION. Kirkbride was the superintendent of the psychiatric section of the Pennsylvania Hospital for more than four decades (from 1840 until his death)—so long, in fact, that the institution became known by Philadelphia locals as simply "Kirkbride's." He became interested in the effects on the patients of the institutional environment's construction and of staff management styles; he firmly believed that, by designing and building pragmatic institutions, mental illness could be cured. His 1847 textbook on this issue (second edition, 1880), considered one of the most important American psychiatric textbooks of the 19th century, is divided into two primary parts: the first concerning the physical details of the ideal institution and the second detailing administrative procedures.

Kirkbride, T., *On the Construction, Organization, and General Arrangements of Hospitals for the Insane, with some Remarks On Insanity and its Treatment.* Philadelphia: Blakiston, 1880.
Tomes, N., *A Generous Confidence: Thomas Story Kirkbride and the Art of Asylum Keeping, 1840–1883.* Cambridge: Cambridge University Press, 1984.

Kitsune-Tsuki psychosis This is an unusual psychotic disorder native to Japan in which a person maintains the delusion that he or she has been possessed by a fox. Kitsune-Tsuki psychosis is an example of a "culture-bound syndrome." A European variation of this is LYCANTHROPY, in which a person believes he or she has been transformed into a wolf. Some psychiatric authorities on this syndrome have likened it to a BRIEF REACTIVE PSYCHOSIS marked by the "fox" delusion, and others have noted that it is similar to a POSSESSION SYNDROME.

Furukawa, F., and Bourgeois, M., Communications (16 Avril 1984): "Délires de possession par le renard au Japon (ou délire de Kitsune-Tsuke)," *Annales Médico-Psychologiques,* 142(1984), 677–687.

Korsakov's psychosis   More commonly known as "Korsakov's syndrome," this syndrome of amnesia is due to the deficiency of thiamine in the body caused by chronic alcoholism. In DSM-III-R (1987) it is called alcohol amnestic disorder. Once it appears, this syndrome follows a chronic course, and impairment may be so severe as to require lifelong custodial care. When thiamine is administered during a detoxification process before the syndrome is evident, it does not develop. Prior to the discovery that thiamine could reverse some of the other neurological signs that precede the amnesia of this syndrome, it routinely developed into its most severe forms. The syndrome is named after Sergei Sergeievich Korsakov (1853–1900), who was largely responsible for founding the discipline of psychiatry in Russia. He first described this syndrome in 1887 but called it *cerebropathia psychica toxemica.*

Kraepelin, Emil (1856–1926)   Perhaps the most important figure in psychiatry at the turn of the century, Kraepelin was a German psychiatrist, professor and researcher who maintained a strict biological point of view toward mental disorders. He was a professor in Germany for successive terms at the universities in Dorpat (starting in 1886), Heidelberg (1891) and Munich (1903–1922). Kraepelin is perhaps best remembered for his contributions to the classification of psychiatric syndromes. His famous textbook, *Psychiatrie,* underwent multiple revisions from the first edition (1883) to the eighth and final edition (1909–1915), and with each new revision Kraepelin clarified his thinking and introduced many ideas that are still used today. For example, Kraepelin first described and coined the terms for the two major FUNCTIONAL PSYCHOSES in successive revisions of his textbook: DEMENTIA PRAECOX was first discussed in the fifth edition (1896), and MANIC-DEPRESSIVE PSYCHOSIS in the sixth edition (1899). He separated the two based on their outcomes: Manic-depressive psychosis had a relatively good outcome, with many patients experiencing remissions; dementia praecox had a poor prognosis, following a chronic, degenerating course. In his first description of dementia praecox in 1896 he puts forth the very modern idea that it is a brain disease that is perhaps metabolic in origin, one in which the brain "autointoxicates" itself.

Kraepelin's influence on the practice of psychiatry was felt everywhere, as his classification system helped to unify the profession. In his memoirs, William Alanson White, one of the major figures in American psychiatry in the first third of the 20th century, tells of the confusing state of affairs in psychiatry in the 1890s prior to Kraepelin's work:

Of course we systematically labeled each patient according to the diagnosis that we thought best fitted him, but I am quite sure that nobody felt that he had accomplished much in so doing. The fact that whenever a physician from another institution visited the hospital one of the first questions was "What classification do you use?" indicates to my mind the very serious discontent with this state of affairs . . . When, therefore, Kraepelin's classification, based upon a new descriptive symptomatology and the course and outcome of the disease process, came to be known, it was hailed everywhere with joy. Here was a new lease on life for all of us, a new interest in psychiatry, new points of view. The whole subject was revivified and made more alive, and the patients correspondingly became more interesting.

When Kraepelin was at Munich, he oversaw the creation of an interrelated complex of research laboratories in 1918, the *Deutsche Forshungsanstalt für Psychiatrie*, all designed to stimulate research in the nervous and mental disorders. Many famous physicians were his assistants, including Alzheimer, Nissl and Aschaffenberg. The laboratories were concerned with combined research on problems in psychology, serology, chemistry, neuropathology, genetics and experimental therapy. Although these laboratories were distributed around Munich, they were eventually combined under one roof in March 1929, two years after Kraepelin's death.

No complete English language editions of Kraepelin's *Psychiatrie* have ever been published. However, several volumes of selected sections of these textbooks have been translated into English, as have his 1917 book on the history of psychiatry and his memoirs.

Havens, L.L., "Emil Kraepelin," *Journal of Nervous and Mental Disease,* 141(1965), 16–28.

Kraepelin, E., *Memoirs*. Berlin: Springer-Verlag, 1987.

———, *One Hundred Years of Psychiatry*. New York: Philosophical Library, 1962; first published, 1917.

White, W.A., *William Alanson White: The Autobiography of a Purpose*. Garden City, N.Y.: Doubleday, 1938.

L

lactation psychoses It was commonly believed by the ancients and by physicians well into the 1800s that the severe mental disorders suffered by women shortly preceding and especially directly following childbirth were related to the production (or lack of production) of milk. It had been thought for centuries that milk was diverted from the breasts to other areas of the body, especially the brain, causing these mental disorders. This process was sometimes called lacteal metastasis. J.E.D. ESQUIROL found these disorders to be so common that he devoted an entire chapter to them in his *Des Maladies Mentales* (1838), entitled "Mental Alienation of Those Recently Confined, and of Nursing Women." "Confinement" or "to be confined" is an 18th-century term for the period during which a woman was "confined" to her "child-bed" before and after giving birth. "The number of women who become insane after confinement, and during or after lactation, is much more considerable than commonly supposed," according to Esquirol. He noted that he was not talking about the much more common "milk fever," the transient delirium that takes place after confinement, but instead the more serious postpartum depressions and psychotic episodes that can occur.

Esquirol, after observations made during autopsies, asserted that no milk was ever found in the brain tissue of deceased women who suffered from postpartum psychoses. Although it was commonly observed that the suppression or diminution of milk production after birth was sometimes associated with the onset of the psychosis, Esquirol denied that the cause was related to milk being diverted to the brain. "Finally, it would be strange to find milk in the brain after confinement or lactation, when there was suppression of this secretion, as to find menstrual blood in the cavity of the cranium, in females who have become insane after the suppression of the menses." Esquirol admitted, however, that many of these women responded well to treatment, particularly when it was designed to reestablish lactation or menstruation following childbirth. He recommended enemas, emetics, warm hip-baths and, in the more extreme cases, to restore menstruation, the application of leeches to the vulva and cupping glasses to the thighs.

By the 20th century, however, the idea that psychoses occurring in women at about the time of birth were related to the lack of production of milk had been disregarded. Instead, the stress of pregnancy, and childbirth in particular, was thought to exacerbate an already existing underlying mental disorder such as schizophrenia or manic-depressive psychosis. This is the argument made by Eugen BLEULER in the fourth edition (1923) of his famous textbook *Lehrbuch der Psychiatrie* (first edition, 1916), in the section "Causes of Mental Diseases" in the English translation of 1924. Bleuler thus concludes: "The *lactation psychoses* have little practical significance." (See also BLEEDING; POSTPARTUM PSYCHOSIS; PUERPERAL INSANITY.)

Bleuler, E., *Textbook of Psychiatry*, 4th ed., tr. A.A. Brill. New York: Macmillan, 1924; first published, 1916.

Esquirol, J.E.D., *Mental Maladies: A Treatise on Insanity*, tr. E.K. Hunt. Philadelphia: Lea & Blakiston, 1845; first published, 1838.

Laing, Ronald David (1927–1989)

One of the most controversial psychiatrists of the 20th century, R.D. Laing is best remembered as a critic of the profession of psychiatry and a strong advocate of the often-neglected human rights of psychotic people. He was born and educated in Glasgow, Scotland, where he trained as a physician and a psychiatrist and served at the Glasgow Royal Mental Hospital. In 1957 he joined the famous Tavistock Clinic in London. However, by this time he had developed serious doubts about the profession of psychiatry. He felt there was a large gap between physicians and patients, and the meaning of people's lives was lost in dehumanizing clinical terms that placed them in an inferior position. Laing believed that society gave psychiatrists special powers over others that often led to abuse. His many books, starting with *The Divided Self* (1960), are thoughtful and provocative critiques of the present state of psychiatry. Beginning in June 1965 at Kingsley Hall, a community center in London, Laing and his colleagues began an experiment in which they lived with severely disturbed psychotics who would otherwise be locked up in mental institutions. There was no staff per se, no locked doors, no psychiatric treatment—just a group of people living together and trying to come to terms with one another. The atmosphere was described as being more like a "hippie commune" than a mental hospital ward. The Philadelphia Association, as this charitable organization was called, ended its experimental program at Kingsley Hall in May 1970.

Laing was often more criticized than applauded during his lifetime. His views were often regarded as mystical or downright dangerous for schizophrenics and others who, it was felt, might be led astray by Laing's antimedical, overly optimistic view of psychosis and its successful outcome. However, many of those sympathetic to his work introduced his radical ideas into practice and were collectively known as the "anti-psychiatry movement," a term that Laing says in his 1985 memoirs he never approved of. It was, however, invented by a colleague of Laing's, psychiatrist David Cooper, who set up an "anti-psychiatry ward" in a large mental hospital near London in 1962. Laing, however, was obviously sympathetic to the thesis of anti-psychiatry, namely, that the role of psychiatry is to exclude and repress those persons that society wants excluded and repressed.

Boyers, R. and Orrill, R. (eds.), *R.D. Laing and Anti-Psychiatry*. New York: Harper & Row, 1971.

Cooper, D., *Psychiatry and Anti-Psychiatry*. London: Tavistock Publications, 1967.

Laing, R.D., *Wisdom, Madness, and Folly: The Making of a Psychiatrist*. New York: McGraw-Hill, 1985.

language abnormalities in schizophrenia

One of the most distinctive signs of schizophrenia is a disturbance in language. Odd phrasing, loosening of associations, bizarre content of speech and the use of nonexistent words ("word salad") can all mark the person suffering from schizophrenia. To the extent that our spoken language reflects our thought processes, most studies of schizophrenic language are incorporated in research on FORMAL THOUGHT DISORDER, usually in the form of COGNITIVE STUDIES OF SCHIZOPHRENIA. One of the first books to appear on the subject of language abnormalities in schizophrenia was edited by J.S. Kasanin and published in 1944. Although abnormalities in language occur as a result of many mental disorders, studies by researcher Nancy Andreasen and colleagues at the University of Iowa suggest that alogia, the diminished capacity to think or express thoughts (also known as the NEGATIVE SYMPTOM of schizophrenia called "poverty of speech"), may be an especially important identifying indicator of schizophrenia and may also point to a poor prognosis. Because language ability is largely governed by the left hemisphere of the brain, there has been much speculation that schizophrenia may be the result of abnormalities in this area of the brain. (See also BRAIN ABNORMALITIES IN SCHIZOPHRENIA; LATERALITY AND SCHIZOPHRENIA.)

Andreasen, N.C., Hoffman, R.E. and Grove, W.M., "Language Abnormalities in Schizophrenia," in M.N. Menuck and M.V. Seeman (eds.), *New Perspectives in Schizophrenia*. New York: Macmillan, 1985.
Kasanin, J.S. (ed.), *Language and Thought in Schizophrenia*. Berkeley: University of California Press, 1944.

Lasègue's disease A rarely used 19th-century term for "persecution mania," the paranoid delusion that one is being deliberately persecuted by others when in fact there is no evidence to support this. It was initially described by Ernest Charles Lasègue (1816–1883) in 1852. Lasègue is more commonly remembered, however, for an article he published with J.P.J. Falret in 1877 that identified another psychotic delusional syndrome—FOLIE À DEUX.

lashing See FLOGGING.

latent psychosis This terms refers to the idea that a person has an underlying psychotic process that can break out into a full overt psychosis under the right circumstances. References to latent psychoses are found in the older psychiatric literature, but the idea is now generally subsumed under such terms as the "incipient" or "prodromal phases" of a psychotic disorder, particularly schizophrenia.

latent schizophrenia This term refers to people who exhibit odd or eccentric behavior, perhaps even with transient hallucinations and delusions, but who never develop the full symptomatology of schizophrenia. In DSM-III-R (1987), latent schizophrenia is called SCHIZOTYPAL PERSONALITY DISORDER—one of the "schizophrenia spectrum" disorders (including, for example), SCHIZOID PERSONALITY DISORDER and SCHIZOPHRENIFORM DISORDER) that seem to be related in some way to schizophrenia (see BORDERLINE CASES). "Latent schizophrenia" is still a valid diagnostic category in ICD-9 (1978), but it is not recommended for general use. *ICD-9* suggests that this label replace such previously used terms as "latent schizophrenic reaction," "borderline schizophrenia," "prepsychotic schizophrenia," "prodromal schizophrenia," "pseudoneurotic schizophrenia" and "pseudopsychopathic schizophrenia." The pre-1980 psychiatric literature speaks of "prepsychotic symptoms," which are summarized in a review by Docherty et al. (1978).

Eugen BLEULER, who coined and first used the term "schizophrenia" in a publication in 1908, also refers to "latent schizophrenia" for the first time in this same seminal classic. In his 1911 classic, *Dementia Praecox, Or the Group of Schizophrenias*, Bleuler notes in the introduction to his discussion of the "symptomatology" of schizophrenia that the symptoms can only be described when defining the clear-cut cases of the disorder and that "the milder cases, latent schizophrenics with far less manifest symptoms, are many times more common than the overt, manifest cases." He later emphasizes just how important the "subgroup" of schizophrenia known as "latent schizophrenia" is when compared with the other "schizophrenias:"

> There is also a latent schizophrenia, and I am convinced that this is the most frequent form, although admittedly these people hardly ever come for treatment. It is not necessary to give a detailed description of the various manifestations of latent schizophrenia. In this form, we can see in *nuce* all the symptoms and all the combinations of symptoms which are present in the manifest types of the disease. Irritable, odd, moody, withdrawn or exaggeratedly punctual people arouse, among other things, the suspicion of being schizophrenic.

People with latent schizophrenia may very well be those who are genetically predisposed for developing schizophrenia but never manifest the full symptoms of the disorder (See also BORDERLINE SCHIZOPHRENIA; INCOMPLETE PENETRANCE.)

Bleuler, E., *Dementia Praecox, Or the Group of Schizophrenias*, tr. J. Zinkin. New York: International Universities Press, 1950; first published, 1911.
———, *"Die Prognose der Dementia Praecox—Schizophreniegruppe,"* *Allgemeine Zeitschrift für Psychiatrie*, 65(1908), 436–464.
Docherty, J.P. et al., "Stages of Onset of Schizophrenic Psychosis," *American Journal of Psychiatry*, 135(1978), 420–426.

late-onset schizophrenia   Since the time of Emil KRAEPELIN, who relied on Ewald Hecker's description of the youthful age of onset of HEBEPHRENIA to help define his concept of DEMENTIA PRAECOX, schizophrenia has often been regarded as a disease that shows its first serious signs in late adolescence or early adulthood. Cases of persons developing schizophrenia after the age of 40, for example, were considered relatively uncommon. However, a recent comprehensive review of the research on this issue by M.J. Harris and D.V. Jeste suggests that late-onset schizophrenia may be more common than originally thought. Although they are careful to point out the possible faults in the more than 30 studies (mainly from Europe) they review, they nonetheless found that persons who develop late-onset schizophrenia (that is, after age 40) have the following characteristics:

(1) they tend to have predominant paranoid symptoms;
(2) they tend to be female rather than male;
(3) more instances of hearing loss or eye disease seem to occur among this group;
(4) prior to the full outbreak of the active phase of schizophrenia, these persons tend to have personalities that have strong "paranoid" or "schizoid" traits;
(5) the disease tends to follow a chronic course; and
(6) there is some alleviation of symptoms with ANTIPSYCHOTIC DRUGS.

Harris, M.J. and Jeste, D.V., "Late-onset Schizophrenia: An Overview," *Schizophrenia Bulletin*, 14(1988), 39–55.

laterality and schizophrenia   Most people are familiar with the media versions of the popular-psychology interpretations of "right brain" versus "left brain" functioning. It is roughly true that the left hemisphere of the brain is responsible for performing the more analytic, sequential, verbal and temporal sequencing functions, whereas the right hemisphere tends to serve more visual and spatial functions. The term "laterality" refers to the scientific evidence for this phenomenon. Since the 1960s, researchers have found that the two hemispheres of the human brain are not identical in many areas: Their respective structures (morphology) and biochemistry (proportions of various neurotransmitters) are not alike, and the two sides of the brain seem to serve different psychological functions. Laterality is found not only in humans, but also in other primates and mammals (such as rats).

Since Paul Broca (1824–1880) published his famous report in 1861 of the autopsy of a male patient from the Bicêtre asylum in Paris that localized the speech center of humans in the left hemisphere (now called "Broca's area"), language ability has commonly been assumed to be in this area of the brain. Furthermore, because approximately 93% of humans are right-handed, and speech has long been observed to be controlled by areas located in the hemisphere of the brain that is contralateral ("opposite-sided") to the dominant hand—the left hemisphere—it was thought that the language center could always be determined by handedness. However, although in the vast majority of cases language is largely centered in Broca's area in the left hemisphere, this is not always the case, particularly for left-handed people who prove to be right-hemisphere dominant. Many people seem to have functions such as language and even handedness distributed in unique patterns between the two hemispheres, and language and handedness may not even be related at all in some people. There are many differences in laterality between the sexes as well, with females appearing to be more like left-handed people in general, with more functions such as speech distributed in areas in both hemispheres. This is why it is thought that women and left-handed people in general can recover more completely from strokes (cerebral vascular accidents) than right-handed men.

Given the hypothesis that schizophrenia and, perhaps, the other psychotic disorders are brain diseases, is there evidence that they can be localized according to laterality in the brain?

The first evidence that laterality may be a factor in the psychotic disorders was found by neurologist P. Flor-Henry in 1969. Flor-Henry noticed in a study of temporal-lobe epilepsy (which can have many psychotic symptoms) that when the focal point of the seizure was in the left hemisphere, schizophrenia-like psychotic features would appear, whereas when the seizure focus was in the right hemisphere, the psychotic symptoms resembled those found in affective psychoses. When the epileptic patient had "bilateral foci," the psychotic symptoms seemed to be "schizo-affective" in nature. Based on Flor-Henry's initial study, there have been many other such neurophysiological studies of the psychotic disorders trying to link schizophrenia with the left hemisphere and bipolar disorder with the right hemisphere.

There have been many published reviews of the evidence suggesting that laterality may be related to schizophrenia, although not all of the evidence points conclusively to the left hemisphere as the source of dysfunction. This may be due to the fact that much of the research does not take schizophrenic subtype differences or gender differences into account. For example, paranoid schizophrenics are often distinguished from schizophrenics diagnosed with one of the nonparanoid subtypes on the basis of many perceptual and cognitive tasks in tests, but few studies take these subtype differences into account in laterality studies, generally only comparing generic "schizophrenics" with "normals" or other groups. This is true in the many neuropsychological studies, as well as those neurophysiological studies using measurements with the EEG and evoked potentials, regional cerebral blood flow (rCBF), position emission tomography (PET scans) and measurements of neurochemical differences to detect asymmetry between the hemispheres in the activity of certain neurotransmitters such as dopamine. However, an informed review of the major research into the issue of laterality and schizophrenia by psychiatric researcher Henry A. Nasrallah in 1986 provides the following cautious conclusion: "Overall the evidence for left hemisphere dysfunction and over-activation appears to be relatively better documented than other types of dysfunction, although it is by no means definitive."

Because schizophrenia seems to be characterized by language abnormalities, the left hemisphere is thought to be a prime candidate for the localization of the disease process. However, a number of studies point to the possibility that schizophrenia may be related to an "interhemispheric dysfunction," that is, it may be the result of disturbances in the way messages are passed and interpreted between the two hemispheres of the brain. A minority of studies even point to the right hemisphere as the source of dysfunctions in schizophrenia. Until more is understood about the importance of laterality in the functioning of the human brain, it may be difficult to conclusively resolve the question of laterality in the psychotic disorders.

Broca, R., "Remarques sur la siege de la faculte du langue articule," *Bull. Soc. Anat.*, 6(1861), 330–357.

Flor-Henry, P., "Psychosis and Temporal Lobe Epilepsy: A Controlled Investigation," *Epilepsia*, 10(1969), 363–395.

Nasrallah, H.A., "Is Schizophrenia a Left Hemisphere Disease?" in N.C. Andreasen (ed.), *Can Schizophrenia Be Localized in the Brain?* Washington, D.C.: American Psychiatric Press, 1986.

"Psychosis and Lateralization of the Brain," *The Lancet*, 2(1977), 1276–1277.

Wexler, B.E., "Cerebral Laterality and Psychiatry: A Review of the Literature," *American Journal of Psychiatry*, 137(1980), 279–291.

lazar house (lazaretto) See LEPER HOUSES.

leeches and leeching See BLEEDING.

legal issues in schizophrenia See COMMITMENT; CONFIDENTIALITY; INFORMED CONSENT; RIGHT TO TREATMENT; RIGHT TO REFUSE TREATMENT; INSANITY DEFENSE.

leg-locks A form of MECHANICAL RESTRAINT used in Europe until the mid-19th century. These were heavy iron clasps around each ankle or shin, linked by a chain or a thick metal ring.

leper houses Also known as "lazar houses" or "lazarettos" (particularly in Italy), these were asylums for lepers. After a drop in the incidence of leprosy in the 1500s, these places were used to contain the poor, the sick and the mentally ill—in other words, they were places of exile for all of society's undesirable elements. Many European asylums arose out of these former places of banishment for the lepers. According to French historian Michael Foucault, until about 1650 the mentally ill were not considered a "threat" to the existing "sane" society in Europe. After that time, the "Age of Reason" was on the rise, and for the first time the mentally ill were rounded up into institutions called "hospitals" to contain the socially displaced: the mentally ill, the poor, the disabled, the elderly, criminals, those with venereal diseases and political dissidents. These "hospitals" largely had no medical function but were essentially places of confinement. Foucault argues that the creation of these institutions was inspired by the older tradition of banishing lepers to leper houses and colonies.

Foucault, M. *Madness and Civilization: A History of Insanity in the Age of Reason.* New York: Random House, 1965.

leucotomy The name given by Portuguese neurologist Antonio Egas MONIZ for his intrusive PSYCHOSURGERY procedure in which the skull of a person is opened and the white fibers connecting the frontal lobe to the rest of the brain are severed. It is derived from two Greek words meaning "white" and "to cut." Moniz performed the first leucotomy on a human subject (a chronically depressed female patient from a local mental hospital in Portugal) on November 15, 1935. The first leucotomy performed in the United States was completed on September 14, 1936, in Washington, D.C., by American neurologists Walter FREEMAN and James Watts. In 1936, Freeman began to refer to the procedure as a "lobotomy" to separate himself from the shadow of Moniz and create an international reputation of his own. A leucotomy was a form of major surgery that involved opening the skull, whereas a technique devised by Freeman in 1946, the "trans-orbital lobotomy," only involved the penetration of an "ice pick" or similar instrument into the eye socket (the "orbit of the eye"), behind the eye and into the brain.

licensed houses   A 19th-century British term for those "private madhouses" that had obtained a license to house and provide limited care to the mentally ill. Licenses were obtained by petitioning the College of Physicians. These private madhouses generated a hefty profit for their operators, for their overhead could be kept quite low by providing the absolute minimum in food and custodial care for their mentally ill residents. This brisk and lucrative "trade in lunacy" finally degenerated to such inhumane conditions that a regulative body, the COMMISSIONERS IN LUNACY, was established in 1845 to monitor the private madhouses and ensure that they met minimum standards. (See also HOXTON MADHOUSES.)

Jones, K., *Lunacy, Law, and Conscience, 1744–1845: The Social History of the Care of the Insane.* London: Routledge & Kegan Paul, 1955.

Parry-Jones, W., *The Trade in Lunacy: A Study of Private Madhouses in England in the Eighteenth and Nineteenth Centuries.* London: Routledge & Kegan Paul, 1972.

life expectancy of schizophrenics   See MORTALITY.

limbic system   In most research on the areas of the brain that seem to be implicated in the disease process in schizophrenia, the one characteristic that does seem to unite them (even more than laterality) is the fact that most of these areas are interconnected in the brain according to what has been identified as the "limbic system." The limbic system (also sometimes called the "visceral brain"), which involves a number of structures that lie deep below the surface of the brain (the cortex), was long considered to be one of the oldest parts of the brain and the one that governs many of the primitive, instinctual functions. Recent neurological research now considers the limbic system to be a major integrative system, where raw sensations are selected and integrated and sent to sites throughout the brain. The limbic system is composed of such subcortical structures as the hippocampus, amygdala, hypothalamus, mammillary bodies, the olfactory area and bordering areas of the frontal and temporal lobes. Much of the work that identified the role of the limbic system as this large integrated network was conducted by neurologist Paul MacLean in the 1940s.

The evidence that schizophrenia involves abnormalities in the limbic system and its connections come from a wide variety of areas. EEG studies have shown abnormalities in the limbic areas of the brain, and brain structure abnormalities and neurochemical disturbances have been found in these areas. Because there is still much more to be learned about the functions of the brain as a whole, more research needs to be conducted to understand exactly how the limbic system is involved in the organic disease process of schizophrenia and to determine the meaning of these disparate research findings from many different areas when taken as a whole.

In his 1988 book psychiatrist E. Fuller Torrey writes that one of the "four established facts" about the causes of schizophrenia is that "the limbic system and its connections are primarily affected."

MacLean, P.D., "Psychosomatic Disease and the 'Visceral Brain,' " *Psychosomatic Medicine*, 11(1949), 338–353.

Torrey, E.F., and Peterson, M.R. "Schizophrenia and the Limbic system," *The Lancet*, 2(1974), 942–946.

Torrey, E.F., *Surviving Schizophrenia: A Family Manual*, 2nd ed. New York: Harper & Row, 1988.

linkage In genetics, "linkage" refers to the tendency of two ALLELES at different places (loci) on the same CHROMOSOME to be inherited together. The closer they are together, the lesser the chances of a genetic recombination occurring between them. Therefore, there is a greater probability that they will be inherited together. For example, in the search for the gene or genes that predispose to schizophrenia, it may well be that the abnormal gene responsible for a BIOLOGICAL MARKER OF SCHIZOPHRENIA (for example, eye movement abnormalities) may be "linked"—because of its physical closeness—to the actual disease gene that produces schizophrenia.

linkage analysis In genetics research, linkage analysis is a complex statistical procedure that is used to search for (1) the mode of genetic inheritance and (2) the approximate chromosomal location of major genes predisposing to mental disorders, particularly schizophrenia and bipolar disorder. SEGREGATION ANALYSIS is another statistical technique used in genetics research to do this. A succinct description of linkage analysis is provided in a 1989 article in *Schizophrenia Bulletin* by researcher David Garver and his colleagues:

> Linkage analysis assigns to *each pedigree* a score that is relevant to the odds of linkage or association of the studied feature with the affected disease state. The commonly used measure of such linkage or association of feature and the affected state is the "lod score," which is the logarithm of the odds of linkage. Assuming for the moment that a syndrome such as "schizophrenia" is the result of a single disease rather than several diseases (i.e., is

homogeneous), the lod scores from each pedigree with schizophrenia are summed to achieve a total lod (likelihood) score for the linkage of the studies feature to schizophrenia. Traditionally, a lod score of +3 or greater has been evidence for linkage of a studied feature to the disease. A lod score of –2 or less is cause for rejection of linkage. A lod score of +3 is similar to rejecting the null hypothesis of no relationship between the studied feature and the affected state with a p value of 0.001; while a –2 lod score is comparable to rejecting linkage at the $p = 0.01$ level. Very high probabilities are necessary because of the multiple comparisons that are at the heart of linkage analysis. Lod values between –2 and +3 are indeterminant, and require more or larger pedigrees and/or enhanced information carried in studied features.

Since all of the methods of statistical analysis must assume certain characteristics about the nature of the phenomenon they are analyzing, the method of linkage analysis that is generally used assumes that the disease under study (e.g., schizophrenia) operates according to genetic homogeneity— that is, it assumed that there is one primary locus (place) that contains the defect that predisposes to the development of the illness. The conflicting research reports that either support or reject the locus of the schizophrenia disease gene on chromosome 5 all tend to use this traditional form of linkage analysis, and this leads some researchers to conclude that this is evidence of the GENETIC HETEROGENEITY of schizophrenia—that is, that it may arise independently from multiple genetic loci. (See also GENETIC TRANSMISSION.)

Garver, D.L. et al., "Schizophrenia and the Question of Genetic Heterogeneity," *Schizophrenia Bulletin*, 15(1989), 421–430.

linkage studies With advances in the field of MOLECULAR GENETICS in the 1970s, genetic researchers began to search for the places (loci) where the genes for common medical disorders (including schizophrenia) were located on chromosomes. They used an approach based on the concept of LINK-

AGE. The basic idea behind linkage studies is that two genes lying close together on a chromosome tend to be inherited together—that is, they are "linked." If a major disease gene is the cause of a disease that runs in families or predisposes family members to it, and if a specific "marker" gene can be traced in a family through several generations, then a linkage study can be done. If the disease under study and the marker are inherited together in a family, it can be inferred that the disease gene lies very near (i.e., is linked to) the "marker" gene. LINKAGE ANALYSIS can then be done to determine whether the linkage between the marker and the disease is significant. In order to trace the marker, the marker must be *polymorphic*—that is, it must have various forms (ALLELES) that are inherited in a simple pattern of MENDELIAN TRANSMISSION so that it can be determined from which parent and grandparent the family member has inherited the gene.

In the 1980s the most fruitful of these molecular or genetic markers have been DNA markers, specifically *restriction fragment length polymorphisms* (RFLPs). RFLPs are now being identified in order to map the entire human GENOME. With the use of RFLPs, some researchers have identified a possible link of the gene or genes that cause schizophrenia with CHROMOSOME ABNORMALITIES on chromosome 5. (See also MOLECULAR MARKERS.)

linked markers   See MOLECULAR MARKERS; GENETIC MARKERS OF VULNERABILITY.

lithium   Lithium is the most commonly used drug for the treatment of recurrent affective (or mood) disorders such as BIPOLAR DISORDER or recurrent unipolar depression, MANIC EPISODES or acute HYPOMANIC EPISODES. A naturally occurring salt, lithium was discovered in 1817 by Swedish chemist John A. Arfvedson (1792–1841). Medical uses began to be applied in 1858 for the treatment of such conditions as gout and urinary calculi. It was later combined with bromides and used as a sedative. In 1940 lithium chloride was administered to cardiac patients as a salt substitute, but the severe toxic reactions they developed strongly discouraged researchers from conducting further studies on this drug. However, psychopharmacologist J.F.J. Cade continued research with lithium and in 1949 published the first scientific report of the antimanic effects of lithium. In a study of agitated psychotic patients, Cade found that 10 manic patients responded favorably to lithium, 6 schizophrenic and chronically depressed psychotic patients did not, and 1 patient's symptoms reappeared after the lithium was stopped. Due to the continued fears of the toxic effects of lithium, its use for the treatment of affective disorders was not approved in the United States until 1970.

It is not clearly understood how lithium works to produce its results in behavioral changes. However, it is estimated that between 70% and 80% of people with "typical" bipolar disorder respond favorably to lithium therapy. This means, however, that 20% to 30% of people experiencing mania do not respond to lithium. Lithium may take one to two weeks to be fully effective, but after the acute symptoms of a disorder lessen, lithium maintenance therapy can reduce the number, severity and frequency of episodes. The side effects of long-term lithium therapy may cause various endocrine abnormalities (thyroid problems, diabetes mellitus), kidney damage, cardiac reactions, skin problems, gastrointestinal problems and some central nervous system problems such as fine hand tremors and other neuromuscular problems. Because lithium can be lethal at toxic levels, blood levels of the substance must be assessed regularly to avoid dangerous concentrations.

Baldessarini, R.J., *Chemotherapy in Psychiatry: Principles and Practice*. Cambridge: Harvard University Press, 1985.

Cade, J.F.J. "Lithium—Past, Present, and Future," in F.N. Johnson and S. Johnson (eds.), *Lithium in Medical Practice*. 1978.

————, "Lithium Salts in the Treatment of Psychotic Excitement," *Medical Journal of Australia*, 11(1949), 349–352.

lobectomy A form of extreme surgery in which an entire lobe of the brain is removed. Although this procedure was sometimes performed to remove tumors and halt their spread in the brain, in the 1930s it was suggested that it might be an effective form of PSYCHOSURGERY for some mentally ill persons, specifically if the frontal lobe of the brain was removed. A full lobectomy was first performed on the chimpanzees Becky and Lucy in June 1934 at the Yale primate research laboratory by John Fulton and Carlyle Jacobsen. The entire frontal mass of the brain was extracted and a cottonoid (a sterile, oil-soaked cotton wad) was put in its place to fill in the space left in the skull and to support the remaining sections of the brain. At an international conference in London in August 1935, Fulton and Jacobsen reported on the behavioral changes that were observed in these animals as a result of the lobectomy. They inspired Portuguese neurologist Antonio Egas MONIZ to suggest at their presentation that lobectomies be performed on humans. The horrified response of most of the participants caused him to modify his views, but on his return to Portugal after the conference he devised a less radical procedure, the LEUCOTOMY, which merely severed the connections of the frontal lobe to the rest of the brain, and performed the first psychosurgery on a human subject in November 1935. (See FREEMAN, WALTER; TRANSORBITAL LOBOTOMY.)

lobotomy The term that American neurologist Walter FREEMAN invented to replace LEUCOTOMY, the name given by Portuguese neurologist Antonio Egas MONIZ for his famous psychosurgical procedure that severed the white fibers connecting the frontal lobe to the rest of the brain. Freeman suggested the name change at a meeting of the Southern Medical Association in Baltimore in November 1936, and it was first used in a published article in 1937. Because leucotomy referred to the severing of specific fibers, "lobotomy" was suggested as a more general term for any psychosurgical procedure that involved the cutting of the nerve fibers of a lobe of the brain.

Freeman, W.J. and Watts, J., "Prefrontal Lobotomy in the Treatment of Mental Disorders," *Southern Medical Journal*, 30(1937), 23–31.

lock hospitals A term popular in England for LEPER HOUSES and later asylums for the mentally ill in which persons would be involuntarily "locked in."

locus In genetics research, the word *locus* (plural, *loci*) is often used to refer to the place where a particular gene (or genes) is located.

lod score See LINKAGE ANALYSIS.

longitudinal studies These are also known as "long-term follow-up" studies. Particular groups of patients, or cohorts, are identified and followed throughout the course of their lives. The best studies follow patients from childhood (such as the HIGH-RISK STUDIES), although most have simply followed patients diagnosed with a particular illness. The purpose of these studies is to provide a picture of the natural course of a disease, identifying its characteristics throughout the life cycle of an individual. A special issue of *Schizophrenia Bulletin* devoted to a comprehensive review of such studies appeared in 1988 (Vol. 14, No. 4). (See also COURSE OF SCHIZOPHRENIA.)

loosening of associations This is one of the primary symptoms of the major psychotic disorders, particularly schizophrenia. It is considered a sign of FORMAL THOUGHT DISORDER. Loosening of associations refers to the verbal expression of thoughts that are disjointed and jump from one subject to another without any relationship whatsoever; in addition, the speaker demonstrates no awareness of the disconnection of these thoughts. When loosening of associations is severe, the person may be perceived as speaking nonsense or gibberish and may be incoherent.

Eugen BLEULER thought that such ASSOCIATION DISTURBANCES were one of the "primary symptoms" of schizophrenia that uniquely characterized it when compared with other mental disorders. He recognized the importance of loosening of associations in his first publication (1908) that introduced the concept of schizophrenia and its divergence from Kraepelin's notion of DEMENTIA PRAECOX. Bleuler writes:

On the psychological side the most fundamental disorder appears to be a change in associations. In schizophrenia it is as if the physiological inhibitions and pathways have lost their significance. The usual paths are no longer preferred, the thread of ideas very easily becomes lost in unfamiliar and incorrect pathways. Associations are then guided by random influences, particularly by emotions, and this amounts to a partial or total loss of logical function. In the acute stages associations are broken up into little fragments, so that in spite of constant psychomotor excitement, no kind of action is possible because no thought is followed through, and because a variety of contradictory drives exist side by side and cannot be synthesized under one unitary or affective point of view.

Disturbances in associations are also related to disturbances in attention and are more commonly found in the nonparanoid subtypes of schizophrenia that are characterized by such NEGATIVE SYMPTOMS. However, loosening of associations can also sometimes appear in MANIC EPISODES or in the ACUTE RECOVERABLE PSYCHOSES. (See also PRIMARY SYMPTOMS OF SCHIZOPHRENIA; the FOUR AS.)

Bleuler, E., "The Prognosis of Dementia Praecox: The Group of Schizophrenias" (1908), in J. Cutting and M. Shepherd (eds.), *The Clinical Roots of the Schizophrenia Concept: Translations of Seminal European Contributions On Schizophrenia*. Cambridge: Cambridge University Press, 1987.

loxapine   See DIBENZOXAZEPINE.

lunacy, lunatic   Derived from the Latin word for moon—*luna*—these terms were used for centuries to reflect the belief that mental disorders were caused by the influence of the moon. Both terms were in common usage until the mid- to late 19th century, when the term INSANITY replaced them as a generic reference to "mental illness" or "mental disorders," as we would term them today. The mentally ill were called "lunatics," and the physicians who administered aid to them were sometimes called "lunatic-doctors." Whereas "lunacy" was a term used in medical and legal texts and organizations (e.g., COMMISSIONERS IN LUNACY), the popular term "madness" was not used in these official capacities.

lunacy trials   Beginning with Illinois in 1867, many states passed "jury trial commitment" laws that entitled a person to be judged insane by a body of his or her peers before being involuntarily committed to an institution. These began as the result of the influence of Elizabeth Packard, whose husband had her committed to the Illinois State Asylum at Jacksonville for three years simply for disagreeing with him on philosophical issues. Although Illinois repealed its "lunacy trial" bill in 1892, many states still had such laws on the books well into the 20th century. There were many critics of the lunacy trials, who felt that they caused unnecessary public embarrassment to the patient and that they cast the mentally ill person into the role of a criminal. The First International Congress of Mental Hygiene, a congregation of the organizations of the Mental Hygiene Movement founded by Clifford BEERS, condemned the practice of lunacy trials in 1930. A long transcript of such a lunacy trail and a description of the events that transpired, including the incarceration of a Philadelphia businessman who was eventually set free by the jury, can be found in the 1869 autobiographical account by Ebenezer Haskell. (See also COMMITMENT.)

Haskell, E., *The Trial of Ebenezer Haskell, in Lunacy, and His Acquittal before Judge Brewster, in November, 1868, together with a Brief Sketch of the Mode of Treatment of Lunatics in Different Asylums in This Country and in England, with Illustrations, including a Copy of Hogarth's Celebrated Painting of a Scene of Old Bedlam, in London, 1635*. Philadelphia: E. Haskell, 1869.

lycanthropy Described since ancient times as a form of "melancholia," lycanthropy is a mental disorder in which an individual believes that he or she has been transformed into an animal, especially a wolf. This disorder has also been referred to as "werewolfism," in reference to the Anglo-Saxon term (literally, a "man-wolf"). Lycanthropy was long thought to be an extinct disorder, but at least 18 individual cases have been reported since 1975. Most of these cases concern people who have been diagnosed with one of the psychotic disorders, usually paranoid schizophrenia, depression with psychotic features or bipolar disorder. In the past century, such terms as *insania zoanthropica, zoanthropy* and *cyanthropy* have been used occasionally in psychiatric texts to refer to this exotic disease of the mind. Modern case histories of lycanthropy and its psychological significance can be found in a recent book by Richard Noll.

Jackson, S.W., *Melancholia and Depression: From Hippocratic Times to Modern Times*. New Haven: Yale University Press, 1986.
Keck, P.E. et al., "Lycanthropy: Alive and Well in the Twentieth Century, *Psychological Medicine*, 18(1988), 113–120.
Noll, R., *Vampires, Werewolves and Demons: Twentieth Century Reports in the Psychiatric Literature*. New York: Brunner/Mazel, 1991.

Verdoux, H. et al., "La Lycanthropie: Une pathologie contemporaine?" *Annales de Psychiatrie*, 4:2(1989), 178–179.

lypemania This is J.E.D. ESQUIROL's term for MELANCHOLIA, a group of disorders that we now refer to as depression. Depressed or "melancholic" persons were referred to as "lypemaniacs."

M

---

mad-business This was the 17th- and 18th-century term used for any profession that dealt with "mad-people" or "madmen." This included physicians, apothecaries and others who were responsible for the custodial care of the mentally ill, as well as the entire system of private "mad-houses" (after 1845 called LICENSED HOUSES) in England.

mad–doctor Also known as "lunaticdoctors," mad-doctors were physicians who provided medical care to the mentally ill. This term was popular in the late 1600s and, colloquially, into the 1800s. Our current usage of the term is different, referring instead to representations of psychotic scientists or physicians in literature and in motion pictures. For example, the profane experiments of the grandiose Dr. Victor Frankenstein, as described in the book *Frankenstein, Or, the Modern Prometheus* by Mary Shelley in 1816, may be the first such depiction of this image, and it has been carried into this century in many films, notably in the many roles played with such zeal by actor Lionel Atwill in the 1930s and 1940s.

Mad Hatter, mad as a hatter The "Mad Hatter" was a popular character in Lewis Carroll's *Alice in Wonderland* (1865), and it is because of this book that we are familiar with this term today. However, the expression "mad as a hatter" predates this book, although there are conflicting views as to how it originated. Some have argued (namely William Hazlitt) that the expression comes from a 17th-century eccentric named John Hatter. Another view is that a 17th-century hatter by the name of Robert Crab is the original "mad hatter," since he developed grandiose religious delusions and proclaimed himself a prophet after receiving head wounds in 1642 during the English civil war. However, modern interpretations suggest that the profession of hatmakers may have had more than its share of psychotic individuals due to the toxic effect of a substance they all commonly employed in making felt hats—mercuric nitrate—which may have induced an ORGANIC MENTAL DISORDER that included such psychotic symptoms as delusions and hallucinations.

Spalding, K., "Poisoning from Mercurous Nitrate Used in the Making of Felt Hats," *Modern Language Review*, 46(1951), 442.

madness   An Old English word first appearing in the 1300s, "mad" or "madness" has always referred to mental disorder, extreme foolishness or folly or an insane rage or fury. It has always been used as part of everyday conversation, but with the rise of the profession of psychiatry in the 1800s the terms "lunacy" and then "insanity" were almost exclusively used in the official sense. Hence, there were more often commissions on "lunacy" or journals of "insanity," but no such uses seem to have been made of the coarser term "madness." The word is still used today (as is its 16th-century synonym, "crazy," which is derived from a French word meaning "cracked") in this coarse sense.

mad-shirt   A sacklike garment that was used as a form of mechanical restraint for unmanageable patients. It is described as a close-fitting cylindrical garment, usually made of canvas or other strong material, which was pulled down over the head of the indi-

vidual and fastened tightly below the knees. It is reported to have been in use at the Pennsylvania Hospital in Philadelphia in the early 19th century. (See also HORN'S SACK; STRAITJACKET.)

magical thinking   This refers to the unusual belief that some people may have in which they feel that their thoughts, words or actions can influence other people or events in the physical world in such a way that defies our known physical laws of cause and effect. Sometimes this can reach delusional proportions and become a fixture of the person's belief system about him- or herself and the world. For example, a person with grandiose paranoid delusions may insist that he or she personally caused the 1989 San Francisco earthquake and will do so again if he or she is not immediately released from involuntary commitment to a hospital. Loren J. Chapman and Jean P. Chapman, two noted schizophrenia researchers from the University of Wisconsin in Madison, theorize that magical ideation in undiagnosed people in the general population is a strong indicator of "psychosis-proneness," particularly to schizophrenia. They have developed a 30-item Magical Ideation Scale with such items as "I think I could learn to read other people's minds if I wanted to" (keyed true), and "The hand motions that strangers make seem to influence me at times" (keyed true). They are conducting long-term studies to test their hypothesis that magical thinking in undiagnosed persons may be a sign of later schizophrenia. These persons may in fact be the type referred to with the labels LATENT SCHIZOPHRENIA, SCHIZOTYPAL PERSONALITY DISORDER or BORDERLINE SCHIZOPHRENIA.

According to DSM-III-R (1987), magical thinking is found only in "children, in people in primitive cultures, and in Schizotypal Personality Disorder, Schizophrenia, and Obsessive Compulsive Disorder." However, perfectly normal people with spiritual or religious beliefs that involve magical thinking should not be considered mentally ill. Furthermore, a legitimate branch of science known as *experimental parapsychology* investigates anomalies in the physical world that may be evidence for extrasensory perception or psychokinesis, and therefore reports of such experiences by persons who are not suffering from one of the psychotic disorders should be critically examined with an open mind to these possibilities.

Chapman, L.J. and Chapman, J.P., "Psychosis-Proneness," in M. Alpert (ed.), *Controversies in Schizophrenia*. New York: Guilford Press, 1985.

magnetic resonance imaging One of the BRAIN IMAGING TECHNIQUES currently used in research on the psychotic disorders, particularly schizophrenia. In MRI (its common acronym), a high-strength magnetic field works on the hydrogen atoms located in the brain. Once "oriented," radio frequency pulses are bounced off the hydrogen atoms. The resonant echoes are detected and, with the aid of computer analysis, can be constructed into an image of the inner structure of the brain. MRI has advantages over the use of the CT SCAN in that it can better identify the differences between gray matter and white matter in the brain. The first published study of schizophrenia using MRI was reported by R.C. Smith and colleagues in 1984.

Smith, R.C., "Nuclear Magnetic Resonance in Schizophrenia: A Preliminary Study," *Psychiatry Research*, 12(1984), 137–147.

Mahler's syndrome See SYMBIOTIC PSYCHOSIS.

malaria therapy See FEVER THERAPY.

malingering The intentional faking of psychological or physical symptoms for some ulterior motive (e.g., to receive worker compensation instead of returning to work, or to avoid military duty). It is quite common for many relatives and friends of mentally ill persons—particularly those with schizophrenia or severe depression—to unjustly accuse them of malingering to avoid the responsibilities of life. Strongly expressed sentiments of this sort by family members of schizophrenics can actually worsen the person's very real condition and increase the probability of relapse. However, with more education about mental illness, such misconceptions will hopefully diminish. (See also FEIGNED INSANITY.)

malvaria A new subtype of schizophrenia proposed by psychedelic researcher Abraham Hoffer in 1963 that was supposedly characterized by a "mauve factor." The idea never took hold and was never seriously considered by mainstream psychiatry. (See also TRANSMETHYLATION HYPOTHESIS.)

Hoffer, A., "Malvaria: A New Psychiatric Disease," *Acta Psychiatrica Scandinavica*, 39 (1963), 335–366.

mania One of the oldest terms for a type of mental illness, "mania" is included in the existing medical texts from ancient Greece and Rome as one of the three major types of mental disorders along with "melancholia" and "phrenitis." Phrenitis seems to resemble our present-day descriptions of ORGANIC MENTAL DISORDERS since it includes delirium and fever (such as, perhaps, in acute phases of encephalitis or meningitis), whereas the other two types do not. Since classical times, "mania" has been used as a general term for "madness," but particularly those instances of madness in which the person was highly excitable, unable to sleep for days at a time, perhaps grandiose in beliefs and otherwise uncontrollable or wild. "Mania" is an ancient Greek word related to a similar word for "to be mad" and not to the Greek word for the moon as is sometimes reported. Like "melancholy," mania included many different syndromes that we consider distinct today, but there was a core cluster of symptoms for each of these ancient forms of mental disorder that we still refer to by these same names today. Throughout the centuries there have been many different interpretations of mania, leading up to modern conceptions of bipolar disorder, which was given its first detailed descriptions in France in 1854. Perhaps the single best source of information in English on the history of mania is the chapter entitled "The Various Relationships of Mania and Melancholia" in the book *Melancholia and Depression* by Stanley W. Jackson of Yale University.

LITHIUM is the drug of choice in the treatment of mania, and it is estimated that 70% to 80% of manic persons respond to lithium therapy. Current research has linked abnormalities in the processing of the neurotransmitter acetylcholine to mania. (See also BIPOLAR DISORDER; MANIC-DEPRESSIVE PSYCHOSIS.)

Diethelm, O., "Mania: A Clinical Study of Dissertations before 1750," *Confina Psychiatrica*, 13(1970), 26–49.

Jackson, S.W., *Melancholia and Depression: From Hippocratic to Modern Times*. New Haven: Yale University Press, 1986.

Swann, A.C. (ed.), *Mania: New Research and Treatment*. Washington, D.C.: American Psychiatric Press, 1986.

mania sine delirio Literally, "mania without delirium." This refers to a MANIC EPISODE in which the consciousness of the afflicted person is not clouded (see DELIRIUM), nor is thinking permanently impaired. This is perhaps the most ancient definition of MANIA that exists. Sometimes in the older psychiatric literature, the word *delirium* means a disturbance in the rational thinking processes (e.g., delusions) and may not refer specifically to our modern concept of delirium as an organic disease of the brain. Philippe PINEL devoted an entire section to this "species of mental derangement" in his 1801 classic textbook, *Traite médico-philosophique sur l'aliénation mentale, ou la manie,*

in which he referred to it in French as *manie sans délire*. According to Pinel, this type of mania "may be either continued or intermittent. No sensible change in the functions of the understanding; but perversion of the active faculties, marked by abstract and sanguinary fury, with a blind propensity to acts of violence." Due to the problems in institutional management created by such agitated "maniacs," it is not surprising that they frequently received the more extreme "treatments," such as extensive BLEEDING, the CAUTERY TREATMENT, the BATH OF SURPRISE and DOUCHING with cold water. J.E.D. ESQUIROL describes the treatment of a typical maniac in the following passage from his 1838 textbook:

> A maniac becomes furious during the night, and utters frightful howls. At two o'clock in the morning, I order the douche, and whilst the cold water is falling upon his head, inundating his body, he appears to be greatly pleased and thanks us for the kindness we have shown him; becomes composed; and sleeps remarkably well the rest of the night.

Esquirol, J.E.D., *Mental Maladies: A Treatise on Insanity*, tr. E.K. Hunt. Philadelphia: Lea and Blanchard, 1845; first published, 1838.

Pinel, P., *A Treatise on Insanity*, tr. D.D. Davis. Sheffield, England: W. Todd, 1806; first published, 1801.

manic-depressive psychosis One of the two major psychotic disorders (along with schizophrenia) characterized by a major disturbance in mood. Manic-depressive psychosis consists of one or more manic episodes combined with alternating periods of depression. Although this psychotic disorder is now officially called BIPOLAR DISORDER, it is still more commonly referred to as "manic-depressive illness" or "psychosis." The term "manic-depressive psychosis" *(das manisch-depressive Irresein)* was first used by Emil KRAEPELIN in 1899 in the sixth edition of his often-revised textbook *Psychiatrie*. He used it to refer to a group of disorders that contained manic states, depressed states and mixed states; he was convinced that the disorders in this group were all due to a single underlying disease process, and hence they were not really separate mental disorders. This term replaced the one he introduced in his famous fifth edition of 1896—periodic psychosis (das periodische Irresein)—in which he grouped "circular insanity," mania and melancholia together into the same class of FUNCTIONAL PSYCHOSES. The periodic psychoses were characterized by their good prognosis, in contrast to DEMENTIA PRAECOX (also proposed for the first time in the fifth edition of 1896), which was the class of functional psychoses characterized by a certain course of intellectual and functional degeneration. The distinction between manic, mixed and depressed forms proposed by Kraepelin are still largely used in current diagnostic manuals such as DSM-III-R (1987).

Kraepelin, E., *Manic-Depressive Insanity and Paranoia*, tr. R.M. Barclay; ed. G.M. Robertson. Edinburgh: E. & S. Livingstone, 1921.
———, *Psychiatrie: Ein Lehrbuch für Studirende und Ärzte*, 5th ed. Leipzig: Johann Ambrosias Barth, 1896.
———, *Psychiatrie: Ein Lehrbuch für Studirende und Ärzte*, 6th ed., 2 vols. Leipzig: Johann Ambrosias Barth, 1899.

manic episode   This is the *DSM-III-R* (1987) term for the ancient disorder of MANIA. It is a distinct period of time in which a person's mood is "elevated, expansive, or irritable." However, unlike the less-serious HYPOMANIC EPISODE, a manic episode is severe enough to cause significant problems in one's occupation, or in social relationships of all types, and may require hospitalization and treatment with LITHIUM to prevent harm to self or others. People so afflicted usually resist all efforts to be treated because they do not recognize that they are ill. There are many other symptoms of a manic episode, including a highly inflated (and often delusional) sense of self-worth or grandiosity; a decreased need for sleep; pressured speech, in which the person becomes incessantly talkative; the feeling of "racing thoughts" or a flight of ideas; distractibility; the inability to stop moving or to stop doing things; or excessive impulsive behavior that is pleasurable but may have painful consequences (such as shopping sprees, taking irrational business risks, sexual promiscuity, substance abuse). Manic episodes are an essential feature of BIPOLAR DISORDER.

MAO activity   See ENZYME DISORDER HYPOTHESIS.

marital schism   See FAMILY INTERACTION THEORIES.

marital skew   See FAMILY INTERACTION THEORIES.

marital status of schizophrenics   It has long been observed that most people with severe mental disorders that are admitted to psychiatric hospitals are unmarried. For example, even in 1812, American physician Benjamin Rush could conclude, based on the patient statistics of the Pennsylvania Hospital in Philadelphia, "Single persons are more predisposed to madness than married people." Almost all studies of the first admission rates of psychiatric hospitals in recent decades have likewise shown that more unmarried than married people have serious psychiatric illnesses, and that this unmarried rate is consistently higher among males than females. In schizophrenia, these high rates are related to the age of onset of illness (it is generally earlier than in bipolar illness) and the subtype of schizophrenia (the unmarried rate is higher for the nonparanoid subtypes). According to a comprehensive review by Letten Saugstad of Norway published in 1989, the single to married ratio in schizophrenia is 7.7:1 for males, and 4.5:1 for females, and for manic-depressive psychosis (bipolar disorder) the ratios were a far lower 1.5:1 for males and 1.3:1 for females. The likelihood of a schizophrenic person remaining married is directly related to the severity and course of illness, with those people with the worst prognosis obviously having the greater marital disruptions and divorces. Thus, in schizophrenia, being single or divorced is associated with a poor prognosis for the illness.

Eaton, W.W., "Marital Status and Schizophrenia," *Acta Psychiatrica Scandinavica,* 52 (1975), 320–329.
Saugstad, L.F., "Social Class, Marriage, and Fertility in Schizophrenia," *Schizophrenia Bulletin,* 15(1989), 9–43.

masturbation   Practically until the 20th century masturbation, also referred to as "onanism," was thought to help cause mental disorders or worsen their symptoms. For example, in J.E.D. ESQUIROL's 1838 textbook, *Mental Maladies,* a chart comparing the "physical causes" of MANIA among the patients of the Salpêtrière with those of the Bicêtre hospitals in Paris lists masturbation as the cause of insanity in a total of 16 cases. Elsewhere in his book he writes: "Masturbation, that scourge of human kind, is more frequently than is supposed, the cause of insanity, especially among the rich." Patients who were excessive masturbators would be subjected to various techniques of mechanical restraint, including the wearing of MUFFS or STRAITJACKETS. (See also CHIRO-MANIA.)

Englehart, H.T., "The Disease of Masturbation: Values and the Concept of Disease," *Bulletin of the History of Medicine,* 48(1974), 239–248.
Gilbert, A.N., "Doctor, Patient, and Onanist Diseases in the Nineteenth Century," *Journal of the History of Medicine,* July 1975, 217–234.
Hare, E.H., "Masturbation and Insanity," *Journal of Mental Science,* 108(1962), 16.
Macdonald, R., "The Frightful Consequences of Onanism: Notes on the History of a Delusion," *Journal of the History of Ideas,* 28(1967), 423–431.

Maudsley, Henry (1835–1918)   A British psychiatrist, editor of the *Journal of Mental Science* and the benefactor and foun-

der of the famous Maudsley Hospital in London, Henry Maudsley was perhaps the most important figure in British psychiatry from the 1870s until his death. He was married to the daughter of the man who had previously dominated psychiatry in Britain, John CONOLLY, the leader of the NONRESTRAINT MOVEMENT. Like his contemporary, Wilhelm GRIESINGER in Germany, Maudsley believed in the physiological basis of all mental disorders and particularly emphasized the role of heredity in transmitting these disorders. His first book, *The Physiology and Pathology of Mind* (1867), was considered a turning point in British psychiatry due to this biological perspective. In this book he proposed that there were "two great divisions" in the "varieties of insanity," namely *"Affective* and *Ideational,"* and these were distinguished on the basis of whether or not a person had delusions (delusions being a sign of an ideational insanity). He was much criticized for his chapter in that book entitled "Insanity in Early Life," because it was not generally accepted in those times that children could develop psychotic disorders. Although he recommended the earliest possible treatment of people with mental disorders in settings that removed them from their families, he also believed that the most chronic mental patients should be discharged from asylums and cared for at home. As treatment, Maudsley recommended baths, emetics and purgatives, a good diet and the use of opium.

Unlike his cheerful and empathic father-in-law, John Conolly, Maudsley was often described as arrogant, aloof, somewhat mean-spirited and bitter. In 1896, at the age of 60, Maudsley's rather pessimistic view of life was reflected in this confessional passage about his career:

A physician who had spent his life in administering to diseased minds might be excused if, asking at the end of it whether he had spent his life well, he accused the fortune of an evil hour which threw him on that track of work. He could not well help feeling something of bitterness in the certitude that one-half the diseased he had dealt with never could get well, and something of the misgiving in the reflection whether he had done real service to his kind by restoring the other half to do reproductive work. Nor would the scientific interest of his studies compensate entirely for the practical uncertainties, since their revelation of the structure of human nature might inspire a doubt whether, notwithstanding impassioned aims, paeans of progress, endless pageants of self-illusions, its capacity of degeneration did not equal, and might someday exceed, its capacity of development.

Maudsley, H., "Insanity in Relation to Criminal Responsibility," *Alienist and Neurologist,* April 17, 1896.

————, *The Physiology and Pathology of Mind.* New York: D. Appleton, 1867.

mechanical restraint   Throughout history, the mentally ill have been abused and generally mistreated, both before and after the rise of institutional care in the late 1700s and especially during the early 1800s. More often than not, the human needs of the mentally ill (who were viewed as wild, like beasts) were met with FLOGGINGS and lashings, placement in cages or restraint by chains. Masks and gags that would keep talkative patients silent were perfected by Ferdinand AUTENREITH in Germany in the late 1700s. Various machines based on the CIRCULATING SWING or the GYRATOR were used to spin patients into obedience, as would the "hollow wheel" (HAYNER'S WHEEL) treadmill. Another 17th-century invention, by Mac-Bride in England, was the "straight-waist-coat," later known as the STRAITJACKET, and this in turn inspired other variations by other asylum keepers, including the sacklike mechanical restraints known as HORN'S SACK or the MAD-SHIRT that would be placed over the unmanageable patient's head in order to subdue him or her. Despite the widespread influence of the NONRESTRAINT MOVEMENT in Europe beginning in the 1840s, many such inhumane devices of mechanical restraint as the straitjacket, MUFFS or the BED SADDLE survived into the 20th century.

Part of the reason that the use of mechanical restraints was so common in the treatment of the mentally ill was due to the prevailing belief in those days that mental illness was incurable. According to Emil KRAEPELIN in his book *One Hundred Years of Psychiatry* (which is actually an excellent history of the use of mechanical restraints), it was only about 1820 that the idea took hold in Europe (and presumably the United States) that some cases of mental illness might be treatable and that some patients could be rehabilitated. Mechanical restraints, although often portrayed as "treatments" that led to "cures," were in fact merely coercive methods to subdue difficult patients during periods of crisis. Philippe PINEL made the first steps to correct the torturous treatment of the mentally ill by freeing dozens of patients from their chains on May 24, 1789 (with his male nurse, Pussin), and by advocating the practice of "moral medicine." Yet rehabilitative treatment for these patients was not begun until two decades later.

When Emil Kraepelin served at the Heidelberg Clinic from 1891–1903, he used no coercion with his patients—a standard philosophy of the time that was not everywhere practiced to the letter. To demonstrate to his medical students how much had changed in the institutional treatment of the mentally ill, he set up a small museum of mechanical restraints. Kraepelin relates in his memoirs:

> The revolution caused by the systematical introduction of bed rest, the frequent use of baths, and finally the newer narcoleptics and tranquilizers was striking. To give the students an idea of these advances, I began collecting means of mechanical restraint, for example, straightjackets, chairs, footcuffs, muffs, gloves, and so on with corresponding illustrations from the old asylums and made a little museum, which I showed the students during the semester. I managed to get some chains, which had once been used to chain a patient.

Perhaps the only form of mechanical restraint still in use today is the FOUR-POINT

RESTRAINT or FIVE-POINT RESTRAINT used for brief, supervised periods. Seclusion or isolation rooms are still used in some institutions as well. However, many patients and patient advocates charge that the modern equivalent of these mechanical restraints is in reality the use of ANTIPSYCHOTIC DRUGS as a form of CHEMICAL RESTRAINT to keep patients manageable in an institutional setting.

Illustrations of almost all of the forms of mechanical restraint ever used are reproduced in a useful book by A.A. Roback and Thomas Kiernan.

Kraepelin, E., *One Hundred Years of Psychiatry.* New York: Philosophical Library, 1962; first published, 1917.

Roback, A.A. and Kiernan, T., *Pictorial History of Psychology and Psychiatry.* New York: Philosophical Press, 1969.

médicine mentale Literally "mental medicine." This was one of the earliest terms used in France for the professional discipline of psychiatry. By the 1820s, the status of *médicine mentale* was debated in many circles. During this time J.E.D. ESQUIROL argued that former methods of studying human nature, particularly "metaphysical philosophy," completely ignored the "physical man." *Médicine mentale* was thus based on a physiological foundation, as evidenced by the methodology used by Esquirol and Philippe PINEL in their investigations of the causes of mental illness: namely, autopsies.

medical disorders that mimic psychotic disorders It has long been known that some physical illnesses can have serious effects on the mental health of an individual. Some of the more serious diseases can actually produce symptoms that, upon first presentation, may look like one of the psychotic disorders. A person may be disoriented and confused, act bizarrely and experience hallucinations and delusions but then be found to be suffering only from a treatable physical ailment. The following medical disorders are those most likely to resemble a psychotic disorder, particularly schizophrenia:

Viral encephalitis. This is literally a "viral infection of the brain." Such brain infections can resemble schizophrenia in their earliest stages of infection. The most commonly reported viruses implicated are cytomegalovirus, measles, coxsackie, herpes simplex, Epstein-Barr and equine encephalitis. As we know from the history of the disorder that used to be called the GENERAL PARALYSIS OF THE INSANE, cerebral syphilis can resemble schizophrenia in its most advanced stages, though it is rarely encountered today. The suspected viral cause of the psychosis can be confirmed with a spinal tap (lumbar puncture). The human immunodeficiency virus (HIV) can cause mental deterioration (dementia), and individuals who are seropositive for HIV and manifest the AIDS DEMENTIA COMPLEX may be diagnosed with AIDS solely on the basis of this dementia.

Brain tumors. The most likely place for the growth of a tumor that would cause schizophrenia-like symptoms is on the pituitary gland, but some temporal lobe tumors may also do this. The correct diagnosis can be made with a CT scan and can be cured by surgery if the tumor is detected early enough.

Temporal lobe epilepsy. This type of epilepsy has long been reported to include psychotic symptoms (delusions and hallucinations) in some people.

Thyroid disease. Any disease process involving the hormones and their role in the nervous system of human beings (neuroendocrinopathy) can cause psychosis-mimicking symptoms. Primary hypothyroidism is perhaps the most commonly misdiagnosed medical disorder that mimics a psychiatric disorder, because it involves so many symptoms that resemble a severe depression (depressed mood, weight loss, sleep disturbances and, in its most extreme forms, delusions and hallucinations). Thyroid disease can be mistaken for the mood disorders and, in some cases, schizophrenia.

Huntington's disease. A genetically transmitted disease that strikes in mid-life, Huntington's disease in its earliest stages is perhaps more persistently misdiagnosed as schizophrenia than is any other medical disorder. When the characteristic abnormal movements begin later in the disease ("choreiform movements"), the actual diagnosis is usually made without difficulty.

Multiple sclerosis. Multiple sclerosis has much in common with schizophrenia. Like schizophrenia, it often begins in people between the ages of 18 and 40. In its earliest stages, patients may report feeling "tired" or "weak" a lot of the time, may become depressed and may undergo a certain amount of intellectual deterioration. Multiple sclerosis is commonly misdiagnosed in its early stages, but as the disease progresses the characteristic symptoms become obvious.

There are a number of other medical disorders that may produce symptoms resembling schizophrenia, though less commonly. These may include the following medical disorders: stroke (cerebral vascular accident, or CVA); metal poisoning (e.g., mercury, lead); insecticide poisoning (e.g., organophosphorous compounds); Wilson's disease; tropical infections; acute intermittent porphyria, metachromatic leukodystrophy; lupus erythematosus; normal pressure hydrocephalus; hepatic encephalopathy; pellagra; pernicious anemia; leptospirosis and sarcoidosis.

Extein, I. and Gold, M.S., *Medical Mimics of Psychiatric Disorders.* Washington, D.C.: American Psychiatric Press, 1986.
Jefferson, J.W. and Marshall, J.R., *Neuropsychiatric Features of Medical Disorders.* New York: Plenum Press, 1981.
Whybrow, P.C. et al., "Mental Changes Accompanying Thyroid Gland Dysfunction," *Archives of General Psychiatry,* 20(1969), 48–63.

medical model of mental disorders
This is the prevailing philosophical position in our culture on the nature of mental disorders. Mental disorders are viewed as equivalent to physical "illnesses," which can be "diagnosed" and "treated." Critics of the medical model, such as American psychiatrist Thomas Szaz, believe the "myth of mental illness" has outlived its usefulness as a way to conceptualize the social and psychological phenomena we label "sick." Other models of mental disorder can be based on other premises. For example, in other cultures (or subcultures within our own society), supernatural models may be more accepted, with mental disorders viewed as the result of spirits or demons that must be exorcised.

The psychotic disorders had been assumed to be brain diseases since the 19th century. However, due to the great influence in American psychiatry of psychoanalysis and FAMILY INTERACTION THEORIES throughout most of the 20th century, which emphasized the social and cultural causes of schizophrenia, the medical model did not really gain prominence again in schizophrenia research until the 1970s with the advent of new BRAIN IMAGING TECHNIQUES and other technological advances in the field of biochemistry and genetics.

Siegler, M. and Osmond, H., *Models of Madness, Models of Medicine.* New York: Macmillan, 1974.

medical restraint   See CHEMICAL RESTRAINT.

Meduna, Ladislas Joseph von (1896–1964)   The inventor of METRAZOL SHOCK THERAPY, one of the several forms of CONVULSIVE THERAPIES developed for the treatment of schizophrenia in the 1930s. Meduna was a Hungarian psychiatrist from Budapest who noticed that his schizophrenic patients who were also epileptic had a remission of symptoms following seizures. He then developed the otherwise unsupported theory that schizophrenia and epilepsy were physiologically incompatible, and therefore, if convulsive seizures could be artificially induced, the symptoms of schizophrenia could be reduced. To induce seizures, Meduna used a camphor derivative known as cardiazol (trade name: Metrazol). His first published report of his experiments appeared in a German psychiatric journal in 1935. Meduna immigrated to the United States in 1939 where he assumed a faculty position at Loyola University Medical School. Metrazol shock therapy was used in many American hospitals in the late 1930s before the introduction of ELECTROSHOCK THERAPY largely replaced it as a mode of treatment.

megavitamin therapy Megavitamin therapy for schizophrenia was first reported in a publication by psychiatrist Abraham Hoffer and his colleagues in 1957. On the basis of the TRANSMETHYLATION HYPOTHESIS, a BIOCHEMICAL THEORY OF SCHIZOPHRENIA, they reasoned that a toxic substance was created when the neurotransmitter epinephrine was metabolized in the brain. This toxic metabolite—adrenochrome—was thought to be responsible for producing the symptoms of schizophrenia. To block the production of adrenochrome, schizophrenic patients were administered high doses of niacin (vitamin B-3). In later studies, the doses of niacin were raised even higher and combined with ECT and other somatic treatments. The literature on megavitamin therapy is voluminous, and highly controversial, with most knowledgeable assessments of this area of research tending to discount the claims of lasting therapeutic success with megavitamin therapy.

In 1968 Linus Pauling, a Nobel laureate in chemistry, coined the term *orthomolecular psychiatry* to refer to the treatment of mental disorders through nutritional changes. Pauling argues in his first paper on the subject that mental illness is the result of chemical imbalances in the brain that could be corrected through a proper diet and nutri-

tional supplements. Pauling speaks of creating an "orthomolecular environment of the mind" that eliminates the altered subjective experiences of psychosis (which, in orthomolecular psychiatry is called "metabolic dysperception"). Orthomolecular therapy grew in the 1970s among its adherents, and a wide variety of vitamins and minerals have been used in the treatment of schizophrenia and other disorders. These research reports have been reported in such publications as the *Journal of Orthomolecular Psychiatry*.

Although it is entirely possible—and even probable—that nutrition may affect the development and the course of schizophrenia and other psychotic disorders, due to its lack of conclusive evidence, orthomolecular treatment is considered at present to be outside the mainstream of psychiatry. (See also FOOD ALLERGIES AS A CAUSE OF PSYCHOSIS.)

Hawkins, D. and Pauling L., *Orthomolecular Psychiatry: Treatment of Schizophrenia*. San Francisco: Freeman, 1973.

Hoffer, A. et al., "Treatment of Schizophrenia with Nicotinic Acid and Nicotinamide," *Journal of Clinical and Experimental Psychopathology*, 18(1957), 131–158.

Pauling, L., "Orthomolecular Psychiatry," *Science*, 160(1968), 265–271.

melancholia Like MANIA, melancholia is one of the most ancient forms of mental disorder known throughout history. Although down through the centuries it has often served as an umbrella label for a wide variety of different types of mental disorders, at its core has generally been a cluster of symptoms that we now call depression. The word is derived from an ancient Greek term for a mental disorder characterized by long periods of fear and depression. Some of the disorders that have been called "melancholia" throughout history include modern psychotic disorders that we know as bipolar disorder or depression with psychotic features. The most comprehensive description of the millennia-old history of melancholia can be found in an excellent book on the subject by Yale University historian of psychiatry Stanley W. Jackson.

Jackson, S.W., *Melancholia and Depression: From Hippocratic Times to Modern Times*. New Haven: Yale University Press, 1986.

Mellaril   This is the trade name for the ANTIPSYCHOTIC DRUG known as thioridazine, which is included in the chemical class of drugs known as the piperidines.

Mendelian transmission   The modern science of genetics is based upon the work of an Austrian biologist and Augustinian monk, Gregor Johann Mendel (1822–1884). In his experiments with peas grown in the garden of the monastery at Brünn he discovered lawful patterns of heredity in the ways certain characteristics, or traits, were transmitted from generation to generation in the plants. Classical Mendelian transmission is monogenetic transmission—that is, a single gene with dominant and recessive ALLELES distributes certain traits (called Mendelian traits) in a typical fashion: Three offspring have the dominant characteristic for every individual with a recessive trait. It has long been known that the genetic predisposition to the psychotic disorders is passed on from generation to generation in a NON-MENDELIAN PATTERN OF TRANSMISSION that is, as yet, not well understood. (See also GENETIC TRANSMISSION.)

Mental After-Care Association   An organization devoted to providing housing and care for patients who were discharged from mental hospitals. It was founded in 1879 by the chaplain for the Colney Hatch Asylum in England, the Reverend Henry Hawkins. Many prominent British psychiatrists of the time were members including Henry MAUDSLEY.

mental alienation   Mental illness. Although used in a different context for centuries, it was not until the 1800s that mental alienation *(aliénation mentale)* became a medical term. With legislative reforms in France in 1838, the term began to refer to the legal status of insanity *(folie)*. At about this time it became popular with physicians who treated the mentally ill as a term for severe mental illness. The term "mental alienation" first began appearing in English medical texts about 1860, and it was at about this time that the term "alienist" began to be popularly used to describe a physician who specialized in the treatment of the mentally ill. In English, "mental alienation" referred to mental disorders that were not diseases of the brain (as was delirium). Along with the concepts of "insanity" and "dementia," the old concept of mental alienation helped to form the concept of PSYCHOSIS in the latter half of the 19th century.

Berrios, G.E., "Historical Aspects of Psychoses: 19th-century Issues," *British Medical Bulletin*, 43(1987), 484–498.

mental disorder   This is now the officially accepted term for what has been called in the past "mental illness," "psychiatric disorder" or "mental diseases." The word *disorder* is used to make the concept more neutral and to specifically downplay the assumption of a medical model of madness that is communicated with the words "illness" or "disease."

DSM-III-R (1987) is very specific in its definition of a mental disorder, and it is worth repeating here:

In *DSM-III-R* each of the mental disorders is conceptualized as a clinically significant behavioral or psychological syndrome or pattern that occurs in a person and that is associated with the present distress (a painful symptom) or disability (impairment in one or more important areas of functioning), or a significantly increased risk of suffering death, pain, disability, or an important loss of freedom. In addition, this syndrome or pattern must not be merely an expectable response to a particular event, e.g., the death of a loved one. Whatever its original cause, it must currently be considered a manifestation of a behavioral, psychological, or biological dysfunction in the persons. Neither deviant behavior, e.g., political, religious, or sexual, nor conflicts that are primarily between the individual and society are mental disorders unless the deviance or conflict is a symptom of a dysfunction in the person, as described above.

mental hospitals See ASYLUMS.

Mental Hygiene Movement Since the

reform era of the mid-1800s, in the United States and Europe there was a growing concern surrounding the treatment and possibly even the prevention of mental disorders. The term that came to be used for this concept—mental hygiene—was coined and first used in a book in 1843 by William C. Sweetwater, an American physician. It was later also used by Isaac RAY as the title of a book on this subject published in 1863. However, in this century the term "mental hygiene" has come to be associated with an American reformer, Clifford BEERS.

At the turn of the century, American businessman Clifford Beers suffered a mental disorder that led to his hospitalization in private and then in public institutions. The horrors of his treatment led him to seek reforms in the treatment of the mentally ill once he had recovered. The first step was the publication of his vivid autobiography, *A Mind That Found Itself,* in March 1908. On May 6, 1908, Clifford Beers met with 13 other interested men and women in New Haven and founded the Connecticut Society for Mental Hygiene. The objectives they agreed upon that day have influenced all other mental health organizations since that time and have remained a vital plan of action for community responses to mental illness in society:

The chief purpose of the Society shall be to work for the conservation of mental health; to help prevent nervous and mental disorders and mental defects; to help raise the standards of care for those suffering from any of these dis-

orders or defects; to secure and disseminate reliable information on these subjects; to cooperate with federal, state, and local agencies or officials and with public and private agencies whose work in any way relates to that of a society for mental hygiene.

The public response to this new organization was impressive (helped, no doubt, by Beers' shocking book), and groups began to spring up in other areas of the country and, later, in other countries. By 1909, Beers formed the National Committee for Mental Hygiene and had the support of such prominent figures as psychologist and philosopher William James and psychiatrist Adolph Meyer. In 1930, the First International Congress on Mental Hygiene met in Washington, D.C. Later, this organization once again changed its name to the National Council for Mental Hygiene. It is now known as the National Mental Health Association (address: 1021 Prince Street, Alexandria, Virginia 22314; phone: 703-684-7722).

Historical essays on the Mental Hygiene Movement and its influence can be found in the supplement included in later editions (starting in 1953) of Beers' book.

Beers, C., *A Mind That Found Itself: An Autobiography.* New York: Longman, Green, 1908.

messiah complex See AMENOMANIA; MONOMANIA.

metabolic disorder hypothesis In biological terms, the word *metabolism* refers to tissue change, that is, to the sum of the chemical changes occurring in the tissue of the body. It has been proposed since Emil KRAEPELIN's first description of DEMENTIA PRAECOX in 1896 that this disorder may be metabolic in nature. Kraepelin theorized that an inherited abnormal metabolic process led to the brain's "autointoxication" (i.e., the brain poisons itself), which then produced the observable symptoms of a psychotic disorder. The term "metabolic disorders" is a generic term often used to refer to a wide variety of physiological diseases. The BIO-

CHEMICAL THEORIES OF SCHIZOPHRENIA are largely based on the metabolic disorder hypothesis, especially the DOPAMINE HYPOTHESIS. So is research that is conducted that measures the regional cerebral blood flow (rCBF) and has found evidence of brain abnormalities in its discovery of "cerebral metabolic hypofrontality" (see BRAIN ABNORMALITIES IN SCHIZOPHRENIA; HYPOFRONTALITY).

Most of the schizophrenia research conducted according to the metabolic disorder hypothesis searches for the following types of information (listed by researcher Herbert Meltzer in 1979):

1. Increased incidence of excessive levels of abnormal substances in patients compared with controls.
2. Increased synthesis or decreased metabolism of these compounds, preferably in tissue culture.
3. Demonstration that the enzymatic abnormality was distributed among the patient's relatives in accordance with the known genetics of the disorder.
4. Evidence that the defect can produce the specific impairments associated with schizophrenia.
5. Evidence that correction of the metabolic abnormalities was clinically useful.

Meltzer, H.Y., "Biochemical Studies in Schizophrenia," in L. Bellak (ed.), *Disorders of the Schizophrenic Syndrome*. New York: Basic Books, 1979.

Metrazol shock therapy One of the chemically induced forms of the CONVULSIVE THERAPIES of schizophrenia, invented by Hungarian psychiatrist Ladislas von Meduna (1896–1964) in the early 1930s. Believing that schizophrenia and epilepsy were physiologically incompatible, Meduna reasoned that the artificial induction of seizures in schizophrenic patients would alleviate their symptoms. He then set out to do this through chemical means by administering an initial intravenous dose of 3 c.c. of cardiazol (Me-

trazol) with an increase of 1 c.c. if a convulsion was not induced in the patient. Achieving what he interpreted as a convincing success, he published his results in 1935. The treatment spread quickly, and by 1938 literally thousands of schizophrenic patients in Europe and the United States had been treated with Metrazol shock therapy, both in institutions and in private practice. Metrazol shock therapy was much easier to administer than the INSULIN COMA (OR SHOCK) THERAPY of Manfred Sakel (1900–1957), which required hospitalization for months at a time and a highly trained staff to administer and monitor the potentially life-threatening treatments.

Metrazol is a derivative of camphor, a substance used since the 18th century on institutionalized mentally ill patients. In fact, the earliest use of a chemically induced convulsion therapy for mental illness was reported by British physician William Oliver in 1785. Oliver administered a high dose of camphor to a patient experiencing a manic episode in order to sedate him, but instead the patient experienced a convulsion. However, his manic symptoms seemed to miraculously disappear. But when the same patient was suffering from depression two years later, the same treatment had no effect. Oliver's report of convulsive treatment was cited occasionally in early psychiatric manuals, but it does not seem that it inspired others to apply the method as a formal treatment for mental disorders until Meduna's work in the 1930s.

In a 1938 article that reviews the research on Metrazol shock therapy to date and gives a report on the treatment of 35 patients in a private practice setting, Philadelphia psychiatrist N.W. Winkleman of the University of Pennsylvania Medical School gives the following vivid description of what Metrazol shock therapy was like:

The technic of the therapy as advised by von Meduna consists of two injections per week. Within a few seconds to minutes after the intravenous injection of 3 c.c to 10 c.c of metrazol, the patients usually give a short cough. This is followed in rapid succession by generalized body twitching, opening of the mouth, frequently with a cry, generalized convulsive seizures of the entire body, intense rigidity, gradual closing of the mouth with such vigor that frequently the patients have bitten through a wooden tongue depressor. Then cyanosis, dyspnea, apnea occur until finally after a few seconds of cessation of breathing the patient suddenly inspires and relaxes. The mouth gag is usually kept in the mouth rather tightly until the patient returns to full consciousness and frequently the patient makes sucking movements on the mouth gag. The patients are frequently in a confused state which lasts for a variable period after the convulsion is at an end. They may struggle to get out of bed or they may talk in an incoherent manner. Frequently they are confused for a period up to two hours and are then able to be up and around and are then given their food after three or four hours.

The convulsions (sometimes called "Metrazol storms") were often so severe that some patients experienced shoulder and jaw dislocations, with reports that sometimes teeth would actually break in the process. To prevent shoulder dislocations, Winkleman and A.M. Rechtman, a Philadelphia orthopedic surgeon, invented a leather "belt" or "restraining device" that fastened the wrists of a person to the hips so that the arms would be immobile during convulsions. A picture of this device, which resembles MECHANICAL RESTRAINTS used in the 18th and 19th centuries, can be found in Winkleman's article.

The primary drawback to Metrazol shock therapy was that the convulsion did not occur immediately after the injection of the drug, during which time the patient was conscious and experiencing feelings of intense fear and terror that were a side effect of the drug. Furthermore, sometimes convulsions could not be produced, and these patients would remain in an agitated state for days until another treatment could be applied. ELECTROSHOCK THERAPY quickly replaced Metra-

zol shock therapy after 1938 because it induced immediate unconsciousness and convulsions and was therefore considered more humane. (See also MEDUNA, LADISLAS JOSEPH VON.)

Oliver, W., "Account of the Effects of Camphor in a Case of Insanity," *London Medical Journal,* 6(1785), 120–130.

von Meduna, L., *Konvulsionstherapie der Schizophrenie.* Halle: Marhold, 1937.

———, "Versuche über die biologische Beeinflüssung des ablaufes der Schizophrenie. I. Campher- und Cardazolkampfe," *Zeitschrift für Neurologie und Psychiatrie,* 152(1935), 235–262.

Winkleman, N.W., "Metrazol Treatment in Schizophrenia: A Study of Thirty-five Cases in Private Practice, Complications and Their Prevention," *American Journal of Psychiatry,* 95 (1938), 303–316.

Meyer, Adolph (1866–1950)   A Swiss neurologist and psychiatrist who emigrated to the United States in 1892 after completing his medical studies, Adolph Meyer was perhaps the single most influential figure in American psychiatry from about 1895 to the 1940s. He established many links between American and European psychiatrists, and he was instrumental in modernizing the medical school teaching of psychiatry. He became a professor of psychiatry at the Johns Hopkins Hospital in Baltimore, Maryland, in 1910 and director of the famous Henry Phipps Psychiatric Clinic in 1913.

He coined the term "psychobiology" to describe his approach to psychiatry, which emphasized that a person's mental state was influenced by biological and environmental factors. Meyer liked to emphasize the lifelong history of a person and his or her subjective experience of a disease. His influence can be seen in the first standard American diagnostic manual for mental disorders, *DSM-I* (1952), in which many of the disorders were labeled as various types of "reactions"—a reflection of Meyer's philosophy that all mental disorders were psychological responses (reactions) to the environment, past experience or biological processes.

Meyer attempted to replace traditional terms for mental disorders and other psychiatric terms with his own idiosyncratic vocabulary (for example, *parergasia* for schizophrenia, *thymergasia reactions* for manic-depressive psychosis, *holergasic disorders* for the psychotic disorders, *ergasiology* for psychobiology and *ergasiatry* for psychiatry). None of these terms, however, ever gained wide acceptance.

Lidz, T., "Adolph Meyer and the Development of American Psychiatry," *American Journal of Psychiatry,* 123(1966), 320–332.
Meyer, A., *The Collected Papers of Adolph Meyer,* 4 vols., ed. E.E. Winters. Baltimore: The Johns Hopkins University Press, 1951.

milieu therapy   The idea behind milieu therapy is that by creating a specially designed "therapeutic environment" for patients with severe mental illness, the course of the disease can be affected in a positive way. This idea is as old as those of the earliest pioneers of reform in the MORAL TREATMENT of mental illness, namely Philippe PINEL in France, Vincenzo CHIARUGI in Italy and especially William Tuke in England, whose YORK RETREAT may have been the first true attempt at such a therapeutic environment. Since the early 19th century there have always been small private institutions that have attempted to provide such environments, but it was not until the 1930s and 1940s that the concept of constructing special wards or buildings for the purpose of milieu therapy came about.

American psychiatrist Harry Stack Sullivan may be given credit for stimulating the use of milieu therapy with his 1931 publication describing his special unit for young males with acute schizophrenia. However, it was the work of T.F. Main with neurotics at the Cassel Hospital in England that popularized the notion of the "therapeutic community," a term coined by Main in a 1946 paper. This approach demanded a more active participation by the patients in the management of the environment and emphasized three elements: (1) a flattening of the hierarchical structure of authority; (2) the blurring of role differentiations between staff and patients; and (3) the cultivation of open communication in order to minimize differences between the social life within the institution and that of the world outside. Many such experimental wards and units for the treatment of schizophrenia were initiated using this approach.

The environments of many psychiatric institutions have undergone extensive transformations since the 1950s in order to make them more "therapeutic." However, as a specific mode of treatment for schizophrenia and the psychotic disorders, the measurable positive effects of such an environment have been small in research studies. Hence milieu therapy has been criticized by researchers Van Putten and May in a 1976 review of the research literature: "Milieu therapy has increasingly become an ideology rather than a defined method of treatment sustained to a large extent not by scientific evaluation but by a steady flow of rhetoric and by humanitarian and emotional justifications." Nonetheless, in conjunction with other forms of treatment, it seems incontrovertible that a more humane environment can only help those who are suffering from severe mental disorders.

Main, T.F., "The Hospital as a Therapeutic Institution," *Bulletin of the Menninger Clinic,* 19(1946), 66–70.
Sullivan, H.S., "Socio-psychiatric Research: Its Implication for the Schizophrenia Problem and for Mental Hygiene," *American Journal of Psychiatry,* 10(1931), 977–991.
Van Putten, T. and May, P.R.A., "Milieu Therapy of the Schizophrenias," in L.J. West and D.E. Flinn (eds.), *Treatment of Schizophrenia: Progress and Prospects.* New York: Grune & Stratton, 1976.

misidentification syndromes   These are a group of syndromes characterized by delusions that persons or objects in the environment are something other than what their true nature is. Familiar persons can be regarded as imposters (as in CAPGRAS SYNDROME), strange persons can become known persons who are believed to be persecuting the delusional person (FREGOLI'S SYNDROME) or persons in the delusional individual's immediate environment can become other known individuals (such as in the INTERMETAMORPHOSIS SYNDROME, in which a doctor, for example, can be mistaken for a first grade teacher). All of the misidentification syndromes are generally part of one of the psychotic disorders and are not diagnostic categories themselves.

"The Delusional Misidentification Syndromes," *Biblioteca Psychiatrica*, 164(1986), 1–153.

M'Naughten Rules A legal interpretation named after Daniel M'Naughten (?– 1865), the man whose celebrated trial legitimized the legal verdict "not guilty by reason of insanity," also referred to as the "M'Naughten Rules." M'Naughten (also spelled McNaughton) was a British joiner who apparently led a solitary existence for most of his life. As an adult he developed paranoid delusions that he had enemies who were trying to kill him. He also complained of violent headaches, which leaves open the possibility that he may have been suffering from one of the MEDICAL DISORDERS THAT MIMIC PSYCHOTIC DISORDERS. In any event, his paranoid delusions also began to take on a political nature. He became convinced that the members of the Tory party were the persecutors who were out to get him, and to fight back he attempted to assassinate British Prime Minister Sir Robert Peel (1788–1850) but instead mistakenly shot Edward Drummond, the prime minister's secretary. In his subsequent trial in 1843 he was found not guilty by reason of insanity—a historic judicial decision that caused considerable public outrage. The House of Lords then required the judges in the M'Naughten trial to provide a written explanation of how they reached their controversial decision. Their

criteria for judging a criminal not guilty by reason of insanity have been referred to as the M'Naughten Rules and have greatly influenced legislation in Great Britain and in the United States.

M'Naughten himself was involuntarily committed to the BETHLEM ROYAL HOSPITAL, where he was incarcerated for the remainder of his life. The attempted assassination of President Ronald Reagan in 1981 by John Hinckley, Jr., caused a similar public outcry when he too was found not guilty by reason of insanity—based, in part, on the more than a century of legislation influenced by the M'Naughten Rules. (See also INSANITY DEFENSE.)

Quen, J.M., "An Historical View of the M'Naughten Trial," *Bulletin of the History of Medicine*, 42(1968), 43–51.
West, D.J. and Walk, A. (eds.), *Daniel McNaughton: His Trial and the Aftermath*. Ashford, Kent: Headley Brothers for the British Journal of Psychiatry, 1977.

mode of inheritance In GENETICS STUDIES, the pattern of inheritance (e.g., dominant or recessive) of a particular ALLELE.

molecular genetics Developed in the 1970s, this is the branch of genetics research that employs new technologies to study the processes of genetics at the molecular level.

molecular markers These are certain biochemical substances, identified by their molecules, that can be traced throughout a family to see if they are "markers" that are genetically transmitted along with the disease genes of a particular medical or mental disorder. If the disease and the marker are found to be inherited together in a family, it can be inferred that the disease gene lies very near (is linked to) the marker gene. In the 1970s, non-DNA markers (mainly protein polymorphisms) were often used in LINKAGE STUDIES. However, with advances in molecular genetics technology in the 1980s, DNA molecules themselves were used as markers through *recombinant DNA* techniques. DNA, or deoxyribonucleic acid, is found in the nucleus of each animal and vegetable cell and is considered to be the repository of hereditary characteristics. DNA is structured in a chainlike fashion, and so recombinant DNA techniques involve the insertion into the chain, through chemical or biological means, of a sequence (a whole or partial chain of DNA) not originally biologically present in that chain. The resulting form of DNA is then called recombinant DNA.

By cutting up the DNA into fragments and mounting them in the same relative sequence that they were in originally, another previously identified DNA fragment can be used as a "probe" to see if it is related to any of the cut-up fragments. Thus, by systematically comparing DNA slices whose positions in the human GENOME are already known with those tens (if not hundreds) of thousands that are as yet unknown, a map can be made point by point using these molecular markers. There are non-DNA and DNA molecular markers.

DNA markers are composed of individual variations of DNA that are present on many areas of each chromosome. These variations are detectable through special restriction enzymes that cut the DNA only when they recognize a specific base pair sequence. These fragments of DNA are called *restriction fragment length polymorphisms* (RFLP), the first of which was identified by geneticists Y.W. Kan and A.M. Dozy in 1978. The DNA marker (RFLP) is actually the combination of various-sized fragments resulting from a restriction enzyme's cutting of the DNA. These fragments are first separated by size and then identified by binding them to radioactive DNA probes so that a characteristic "banding pattern" is seen. These are also called "polymorphic patterns" because they reflect the various forms (alleles) that are inherited in a simple Mendelian pattern so that it can be determined from which parent and grandparent an individual has inherited the marker.

As of 1989, it was estimated that about 3,000 RFLP loci, or positions, have been mapped, with new discoveries occurring weekly. These DNA markers, RFLPs, are thought to provide a virtually limitless supply of molecular linkage markers that can be used to construct a detailed map of the entire human genome. Once RFLPs are identified and located with respect to one another on a "linkage map," any disease that seems to be genetically transmitted in a family can be tested for linkage to markers on this map. The new technologies for creating such a map through the use of RFLPs was first outlined in a paper by geneticists D. Botstein and colleagues in 1980.

With the discoveries of possible relationships between CHROMOSOME ABNORMALITIES on chromosome 5 with schizophrenia, many researchers have begun to map the RFLPs in the suspected abnormal region of that chromosome.

Botstein, D. et al., "Construction of a Genetic Linkage Map in Man Using Restriction Fragment Length Polymorphisms," *American Journal of Human Genetics,* 32(1980), 314–331.

Kennedy, J.L. et al., "Molecular Genetics Studies in Schizophrenia," *Schizophrenia Bulletin,* 15(1989), 383–391.

molindone   See DIHYDROINDOLONE.

monasteries   For many centuries in Europe, monasteries served as hospitals for the sick and the poor. Although the Roman Catholic church banned the practice of medicine by the clergy (particularly such treatments as BLEEDING) in the early 13th century, monks were still allowed to provide food and shelter to the needy. The mentally ill were among those cared for by the various religious institutions, and some of them later became asylums for the mentally ill (as was the case for the BETHLEM ROYAL HOSPITAL). (See also ALMS HOUSES; BASKET MEN.)

Moniz, Egas (Antonio Caetano de Abrere Freire) (1874–1955)   A Portuguese neurologist who performed the first PSYCHOSURGERY (a term he coined) on a human being (a LEUCOTOMY) on November 15, 1935. For the invention of this procedure he won a Nobel Prize in physiology and medicine in 1949. Moniz spells out his rationale for the leucotomy in the first book on psychosurgery, *Tentatives Opératoires dans le Traitement de Certaines Psychoses (Experimental Surgery in the Treatment of Certain Psychoses)*, which was published in France in the spring of 1936: "To cure these patients it is necessary to destroy the arrangements of cellular connections, more or less fixed, that must exist in the brain and particularly those that are linked with the frontal lobes." Moniz's work inspired Walter FREEMAN to perform the first leucotomy in the United States and to popularize the practice of psychosurgery.

Considering the later repudiation of psychosurgery as a therapeutic technique for severe mental disorders, a procedure that left thousands of patients permanently brain damaged, Moniz met a rather ironic death. In December 1955, at the age of 81, he was beaten to death in his private practice office by one of his patients. In fact, this particular patient was supposed to be Moniz's last before retiring from medical practice.

Moniz, E., *Tentatives Opératoires dans le Traitement de Certaines Psychoses*. Paris: Masson, 1936.

monoamine oxidase (MAO) An enzyme that breaks down neurotransmitters such as norepinephrine and serotonin. The inhibition of this enzyme in the functioning of the brain produces an antidepressant effect, and the MAO inhibitors were therefore the first drugs to be used in the treatment of depression. In schizophrenia, low levels of this enzyme have been associated with the disorder (see ENZYME DISORDER HYPOTHESIS), although it has been questioned whether platelet MAO can be used as a BIOLOGICAL MARKER OF SCHIZOPHRENIA.

monomania A term for a very popular psychiatric diagnosis in France in the 1830s and 1840s, monomania referred to a type of mental disorder in which a person would have fixed, and often grandiose, ideas that did not correspond to reality. Although the person maintained these delusions, no other sign of mental deterioration was present. Save for these pockets of delusions in their thought pattern, the persons affected were otherwise considered rational. After J.E.D. ESQUIROL introduced the term around 1810, "monomania" quickly caught on with intellectuals as a cultural metaphor for political, religious and other social extremism. In his 1838 book, *Des Maladies Mentales*, Esquirol identified several subtypes of monomania, generally depending upon the content of the primary delusions, the cause of the disorder or its behavioral consequences: for example, *theomania* (religious delusions), *erotic monomania* or *erotomania* (erotic delusions), *monomania resulting from drunkenness, incendiary monomania* (pyromania) and *homicidal monomania*.

Although monomania was the most popular diagnosis given in French asylums in the 1830s and 1840s (rivaled only by the GENERAL PARALYSIS OF THE INSANE), the condition was criticized by many alienists for being too general and thus virtually disappeared by the end of the century. Perhaps the most specific modern equivalent to monomania is the delusional (paranoid) disorders listed in DSM-III-R, particularly the "grandiose type." However, the category was so broad that it might have also included cases of what we may now term paranoid schizophrenia or bipolar disorder.

The best and only English-language history of this 19th-century psychotic disorder is the chapter entitled "Monomania" in a 1987 book by Jan Goldstein on the French psychiatric profession in the 19th century.

Goldstein, J., *Console and Classify: The French Psychiatric Profession in the Nineteenth Cen-*

tury. Cambridge: Cambridge University Press, 1987.

monosymptomatic hypochondriacal psychosis

A proposed psychotic disorder, especially in Europe, in which a person maintains a psychotic hypochondriacal delusional system that is distinct from the rest of the personality. The single delusion usually contains one of the three following themes: FORMICATION (a tactile hallucination in which the person feels that bugs are crawling under his or her skin); dysmorphophobia (the delusional belief that one is misshapen and unattractive); or the ''olfactory reference syndrome'' (the delusion that one emits a foul body odor).

Munro, A. and Chamara, J., ''Monosymptomatic Hypochondriacal Psychosis: A Diagnostic Check List Based on 50 Cases of the Disorder,'' *Canadian Journal of Psychiatry*, 27(1982), 374–376.

monozygotic twins

''Identical twins.'' Monozygotic twins share all of their genes in common, whereas ''fraternal twins'' share only half of their genetic heritage. Therefore, the CONCORDANCE RATE for genetically transmitted disorders is much higher in monozygotic twins than in fraternal, or dizygotic, twins.

mood

This term refers to a pervasive and long-lasting emotion that seems to color a person's perception of the world and of the self. The most commonly experienced moods are anxiety, elation (elevated mood), depression (dysphoric mood), anger (irritable mood) and euphoria (euphoric mood). In an expansive mood, a person may just blurt out whatever emotions he or she may be feeling at the time, and this often includes grandiose overevaluations of self-importance. When a person is not experiencing an elevated or a depressed mood, the term for this is euthymic mood, that is, mood in the ''normal'' range of experience.

mood disorders

An umbrella term introduced in DSM-III-R in 1987 to apply to the group of disorders previously termed the AFFECTIVE DISORDERS. These include the BIPOLAR DISORDERS (cyclothymia, and the three types of bipolar disorders: mixed, manic and depressed) and the depressive disorders (formerly called unipolar depression). The mood disorders have been found to have seasonal patterns in which the mood disorder returns during a particular 60-day period every year.

moon, influence of on madness

Since classical times it was thought that the moon caused madness or made it worse, and the idea of ''lunacy'' in the ancient sense of the word did not really die out until the 1800s. Although many of the 18th-century authors of the earliest psychiatric texts (such as John HASLAM) expressed their skepticism of this theory of the cause of mental illness, American physician Benjamin RUSH did not dismiss it outright. Instead, he concocted a pseudoscientific theory that mental illness gives some people a ''sixth sense'' that renders them more sensitive to moonlight and to the changes in the temperature and density of the air when the moon was full. In his 1812 book on the diseases of the mind Rush writes:

> The moon, when full, increases the rarity of the air and the quantity of light, each of which I believe acts upon sick people in various diseases, and, among others, in madness . . . The inference from these facts is, that the cases are few in which mad people feel the influence of the moon, and that when they do, it is derived chiefly from an increase of its light . . . It is possible, further, that in the few cases in which the light of the moon, or the rarity of the air, is felt by deranged persons in a hospital, that their noise, by keeping a number of patients in neighboring cells awake, and in a state of inquietude from the want of sleep, may have contributed to establish that general belief in the influence of the moon upon madness, which has so long obtained among physicians.

Oliver, J.F., "Moonlight and Nervous Disorders: A Historical Study," *American Journal of Psychiatry*, 99(1943), 579–584.

Rush, B., *Medical Inquiries and Observations upon the Diseases of the Mind*. Philadelphia: Kimber & Richardson, 1812.

moral insanity A term introduced in English by psychiatrist and anthropologist James Cowles Prichard in 1835 to refer to a type of mental illness in which a person would exhibit severe disturbances in emotions or engage in highly pathological or self-destructive behaviors but would not have any intellectual impairment (i.e., no FORMAL THOUGHT DISORDER). Thus, a person had the ability to reason yet would engage in irrational behaviors. Unlike another popular diagnosis in Europe at that time, MONOMANIA, there were no delusions in a particular subject area or any hallucinations relating to those specific delusions.

In his book *A Treatise on Insanity and Other Disorders Affecting the Mind*, Prichard defines "moral insanity" in the following way:

> . . . a morbid perversion of the natural feelings, affections, inclinations, temper, habits, moral dispositions, and natural impulses, without any remarkable disorder or defect of the intellect or knowing and reasoning faculties, and particularly without any insane illusion or hallucination . . . The individual is found to be incapable, not of talking or reasoning upon any subject proposed to him, for this he will often do with great shrewdness and volubility, but of conducting himself with decency and propriety in the business of life.

Although Prichard based his idea of a moral insanity on many similar ideas proposed perhaps as early as the 17th century, his concept that there was no intellectual impairment came under attack by other medical authorities. However, by 1850 the debate had shifted from the intellectual versus emotional issue to the irrational behavior of such persons, specifically on how "moral insanity" was related to immoral and criminal actions. Thus, by the 20th century, the original meaning of Prichard's "moral insanity" as essentially a synonym for an "emotional illness" was eliminated from the psychiatric vocabulary and was reduced to our modern notions of "sociopathic personalities," "psychopathic personalities" and, as they are now called, "antisocial personalities"—that is, persons who repeatedly engage in acts destructive to themselves or others (e.g., criminal activities) without any realization of the consequences of their actions or any seeming ability to feel empathy for those persons who become the "victims" of their antisocial behaviors.

The term "moral insanity" was first used in German *(moralische Insanie)* in 1819 by J.C.A. Grohmann (1769–1847) to describe a particular symptom.

Carlson, E.T. and Dain, N., "The Meaning of Moral Insanity," *Bulletin of the History of Medicine*, 1962, 130–140.

Prichard, J.C., *A Treatise on Insanity and Other Disorders Affecting the Mind*. London: Sherwood, Gilbert & Piper, 1835.

moral treatment The treatment of mental illness through means other than physical ones (e.g., bleeding, bathing and purging). Perhaps the best modern translation of the meaning of "moral treatment" is a broad interpretation of our word *psychotherapy* but also may refer to modern ideas of MILIEU THERAPY. *Traitement moral* is the name for the revolutionary philosophy for the treatment of the mentally ill proposed by the great French reformer and physician Philippe PINEL in his 1801 book, *Traite médico-philosophique sur l'aliénation mentale, ou la manie* (English translation of 1806 entitled *A Treatise on Insanity*).

Moral treatment, as prescribed by Pinel, did not solely mean an ethical approach to treating the mentally ill, nor did it mean a method of treatment that instructed patients in ethics. Since the early 1800s the French word *moral* had several meanings, especially referring to that which was psychological in nature and not physical. Thus, Pinel could talk of the "passions" (emotions) as a "moral cause" of mental illness.

In his book, Pinel advocates an understanding of the character of the patient and his or her humane treatment. Coercion and mechanical restraints were to be banned except in extreme circumstances. Pinel also thought that by improving the physical environment of asylums that patients would improve, and so he advocated the supervised daily cleaning of the patients' cells. Certain physical activities were recommended as beneficial to patients, such as exercise, work, experiencing beautiful scenery and listening to soft, melodious music. Although these ideas seem quaint and rather obvious today, in Pinel's time the mentally ill were thought to have brain lesions that rendered them to a bestial level, and were therefore incurable. Hence, treatment to improve or rehabilitate the mentally ill in any permanent sense was not considered a rational idea.

Thus, the trend toward "moral medicine," as it was sometimes called, began with Pinel and finally culminated in a general interest throughout Europe in rehabilitating treatments about the year 1820. The NON-RESTRAINT MOVEMENT that began in the 1830s in England was directly inspired by Pinel in France (and at about the same time by Chiarugi in Italy and Tuke in England). Our continuing efforts today to improve the daily life of the mentally ill person and to discover new methods of treatment and rehabilitation are a continuation of the *traitement moral* of Pinel.

Bockoven, J.S., *Moral Treatment in American Psychiatry*. New York: Springer, 1963.

Carlson, E.T. and Dain, N., "The Psychotherapy That Was Moral Treatment," *American Journal of Psychiatry*, 117(1960), 519–524.

Riese, W., "An Outline of a History of Ideas in Psychotherapy," *Bulletin of the History of Medicine*, 25(1951), 442–456.

morbid jealousy See OTHELLO SYNDROME.

Moreau de Tours, Jacques Joseph (1804–1884) A French alienist who was part of the "Esquirol Circle." He wrote his 1830 doctoral thesis on MONOMANIA under the supervision of J.E.D. ESQUIROL. He is best remembered for his self-experimentation with hashish and cannabis to produce ALTERED STATES OF CONSCIOUSNESS that helped him gain insight into mental illness. In his 1845 book on these experiments, he introduced the concept of DISSOCIATION for the first time. Moreau de Tours is considered the first medical researcher to use drugs to produce an "artificial psychosis," although reports of the creation of an "artificial insanity" through the use of chemical substances date from at least the experiments of the Paracelsian iatrochemist Jan Baptista van Helmont (1577–1644). (See also PSYCHOTOMIMETIC.)

Moreau de Tours, J.J., *Du hachisch et de l'aliénation mentale: Etudes psychologiques*. Paris: Fortin, Masson, & Cie, 1845.

Morel, Benedict Augustin (1809–1873) A French psychiatrist who worked under Jules FALRET at the Salpêtrière hospital in Paris. He wrote several important psychiatric texts during his career, but he is best remembered for his theory that many mental diseases were the result of physical, intellectual and moral (emotional) DEGENERATION. Morel coined the term *demence precoce* in 1852 to refer to rapid degeneration, and this concept was later borrowed by Emil KRAEPELIN when describing DEMENTIA PRAECOX in 1896.

Morel, B.A., *Etudes cliniques: Traité théorique et pratique des maladies mentales*. Nancy: Grimblot; Paris: J.-B. Baillière, 1852.

mortality in schizophrenia Since the first mortality studies of people with schizophrenia were published in 1934, it has been known that schizophrenia is a life-shortening disease. In fact, in a major review of the mortality research on schizophrenia that was published in 1989, researcher Peter Allebeck of Huddinge, Sweden, concludes that the overall death rate is about twice that of the general population. In the studies of institutionalized schizophrenic patients prior to the invention of ANTIPSYCHOTIC DRUGS, tuberculosis was the major cause of death. However, starting in the 1950s, most patients were treated with antipsychotic medication and were returned to the community through DEINSTITUTIONALIZATION. As these patients are no longer monitored on a daily basis by medical staff, and often cast into the community with little or no social support, it is not surprising that suicide has become the leading cause of death for persons with schizophrenia. In fact, some estimates are so high that it is estimated that perhaps 10% to 13% of schizophrenics commit suicide. A second major cause of death is accidents. Young white schizophrenic men with high levels of premorbid functioning and high expectations are particularly at risk.

Other studies have been conducted to see if the high mortality rates in schizophrenics are due solely to suicides and accidental deaths. It has been found that the death rate due to "natural" cardiovascular disorders is also higher in schizophrenics than in the general population. Other studies have shown that institutionalized psychiatric patients (regardless of diagnosis) have a higher mortality as a whole than the general population.

Allebeck, P., "Schizophrenia: A Life-Shortening Disease," *Schizophrenia Bulletin*, 15(1989), 81–89.

Caldwell, C.B. and Gottesman, I.I., "Schizophrenics Kill Themselves Too: A Review of Risk Factors for Suicide," *Schizophrenia Bulletin*, 4(1990), 571–589.

Malzberg, B., *Mortality among Patients with Mental Disease*. New York: State Hospital Press, 1934.

mosaicism A term used in GENETICS STUDIES that refers to the condition of having a mixture of normal and abnormal chromosomes. A person who has mosaicism has various amounts of normal cells and trisomies (cells with three chromosomes), resulting in varying degrees of illness.

motion pictures, depictions of psychosis in Persons with psychotic disorders have been portrayed in Greek classical tragedy, Elizabethan and Jacobean plays, stage melodramas and Gothic novels of the 18th and 19th centuries and 20th-century feature films. Perhaps the first extensive portrayal of the interior world of psychosis in motion pictures is the famous German expressionist film of 1919 *The Cabinet of Dr. Caligari*. In the surprise ending to this dreamlike film the audience learns that the entire story was merely the delusion of an institutionalized psychotic patient.

In a book on the portrayal of insanity in the feature film, authors Michael Fleming and Roger Manvell identify several major "themes of madness" that have often reflected prevailing societal attitudes toward mental illness and the psychiatric profession. These are: (1) the family and madness (*A Woman Under the Influence*, 1974); (2) institutionalization of the mad (*The Snake Pit*, 1948; *One Flew over the Cuckoo's Nest*, 1975); (3) possession as madness (*The Exorcist*, 1973; *Three Faces of Eve*, 1957); (4) the struggle between love and aggression (*Bad Timing: A Sensual Obsession*, 1980); (5) the love of aggression (*M*, 1931; *Straw Dogs*, 1971); (6) violence against women (*Psycho*, 1960); (7) murder and madness (*White Heat*, 1949; *Badlands*, 1974); (8) war and madness (*The Deer Hunter*, 1978); (9) drugs and madness (*The Lost Weekend*, 1945); (10) paranoia and madness (*The Caine Mutiny*, 1954; *Repulsion*, 1965); (11) sanity as madness, madness as sanity (*Harvey*, 1950; *The King of Hearts*, 1966) and (12) madness and the psychiatrist (*Dressed to Kill*, 1980). Fleming and Manvell's book also provides a synopsis of 150 films dealing in one way or another with the problems of mental illness.

Prior to *The Cabinet of Dr. Caligari,* many shorter. films appeared that depicted psychiatric patients, asylums and psychiatrists. Perhaps the earliest American film to depict a psychotic individual is the 1904 one-reeler *The Escaped Lunatic.* The Biograph publicity bulletin for this film reveals that it is about

> the escapades of an insane man who imagines himself to be Napoleon I. He escapes from the asylum by a miraculous jump from a third story window, and is pursued across the country by the keepers through a series of ludicrous adventures, until finally disgusted at the chase, he jumps back into the window of the asylum, and is very comfortably reading a newspaper when the tired and mud-spattered keepers enter.

A subsequent one-reel film made in 1906, *Dr. Dippy's Sanitarium,* is the first American film to depict a mental health professional other than an attendant (a "keeper"). The first motion picture image of a psychiatrist is the one we still often see depicted in comedies and cartoons today: bearded (often with a goatee), wearing pince-nez glasses and somewhat portly with a distinctive formal continental European bearing. As in *The Escaped Lunatic,* there is a psychotic individual who grandiosely believes he is Napoleon, but there is also a depiction of a woman with HYSTERIA who resembles a somnambulist, gliding about in a flowing white gown with her extended arm holding a candle in its holder. Whereas *Dr. Dippy's Sanitarium* appears to be the first film portrayal of a psychiatrist, the first literary appearances of the figure of the alienist can be found at least as early as 1861 in the novels of Oliver Wendell Holmes.

As with the mentally ill, psychiatrists have been depicted in films in a number of different ways. In their book *Psychiatry and the Cinema,* Krin and Glen O. Gabbard propose that psychiatrists have been portrayed in three primary ways: as the "alienist," the "quack" or the "oracle."

Recent trends in motion pictures and television have unjustly overemphasized the "homicidal maniac" stereotype of people suffering from psychotic disorders—particularly in films in the horror genre. Many advocacy groups for the mentally ill have formally objected to these unrealistic portrayals and have attempted to counter these negative stereotypes with factual information about mental illness for the general public.

Fleming, M. and Manvell, R., *Images of Madness: The Portrayal of Insanity in the Feature Film.* Cranbury, N.J.: Associated University Presses, 1985.

Gabbard, K. and Gabbard, G.O., *Psychiatry and the Cinema.* Chicago: University of Chicago Press, 1987.

moxa   See CAUTERY TREATMENT.

MRI   See MAGNETIC RESONANCE IMAGING.

muffs   A form of MECHANICAL RESTRAINT in which a patient's hands were bound together at the wrists in a thick, tubular canvas casing. In his autobiography, Clifford BEERS describes his experience of being forced to wear muffs every night during his first few weeks in a "sanitarium" while the attendant who watched over him slept:

> . . . I was subjected to a detestable form of restraint that amounted to torture. To guard me at night while the remaining attendant slept, my hands were imprisoned in what is known as a "muff." A muff, innocent enough to the eyes of those who have never worn one, is in reality a relic of the Inquisition. It is an instrument of restraint which has been in use for centuries and even in many of our public and private institutions is still in use. The muff I wore was made of canvas, and differed in construction from a muff designed for the hands of fashion only in the inner partition, also of canvas, which separated my hands, but allowed them to overlap. At either end was a

strap which buckled tightly around the wrist and was locked.

Beers, C., *A Mind That Found Itself: An Autobiography*. New York: Longman, Greens, 1908.

multifactorial threshold model of genetic transmission

This is the hypothetical model of the genetic transmission of schizophrenia first proposed in detail by I.I. Gottesman and J. Shields in 1967. Essentially, the multifactorial threshold model suggests that schizophrenia is caused primarily by the additive effect of a large number of genes of small effect, in addition to certain environmental (but somewhat less powerful) influences. This is a type of *polygenetic* model of transmission and is sometimes called *complex development* (as opposed to another type of polygenetic model, GENETIC HETEROGENEITY). Genetic influences are assumed to account for 80% of the development of schizophrenia, and environmental factors 20%. This is a more complex revision of older DIATHESIS-STRESS THEORIES of the cause (etiology) of schizophrenia. In the multifactorial model, it is assumed that schizophrenia only becomes fully developed in those persons in whom a critical threshold of liability is exceeded (i.e., in those persons in whom enough of the disease-causing genes have added together, plus enough of the right environmental causes have been introduced—thus pushing the person's nervous system "over the edge," as it were, to provoke the onset of the illness).

In this model, the chance of developing this disorder is normally distributed throughout the population. On the average, relatives of schizophrenics are at greater risk than the general population, and therefore a greater proportion of these people have a liability that exceeds the threshold. This model predicts that those schizophrenic persons who have the most severe manifestations of the disorder (i.e., those with the highest liability) will have the greatest proportions of relatives who will be affected. This is a feature of the model that corresponds to the findings of twin studies and consanguinity studies of schizophrenia. This model also makes the prediction that a person is at greater risk for developing schizophrenia if two or more persons in the family are affected.

There have been several criticisms of this model. One is that the specific environmental causes of schizophrenia are hard to pin down. Second, all of the genes that combine their effects may not be of equal importance, for there may be a single major gene that has a far greater effect upon the risk for schizophrenia than the other "polygenes." This second idea is the basis for a "mixed model" of genetic transmission, first proposed as a possible mode of GENETIC TRANSMISSION for schizophrenia by Paul Meehl in 1972.

Gottesman, I.I. and Shields, J.A., "A Polygenic Theory of Schizophrenia," *Proceedings of the National Academy of Sciences of the United States of America*, 58(1967), 199–205.

McGue, M. et al., "The Transmission of Schizophrenia under a Multifactorial Threshold Model," *American Journal of Human Genetics*, 35(1983), 1161–1178.

Meehl, P.E., "A Critical Afterward," in I.I. Gottesman and J.A. Shields, *Schizophrenia and Genetics: A Twin Study Vantage Point*. New York: Academic Press, 1972.

multiple insanity   See FOLIE À DEUX.

multiple personality and schizophrenia

Many people often confuse schizophrenia with having "split personalities." Although schizophrenia literally means "split-mind," schizophrenia is a very distinct disorder from multiple personality disorder. An expanded diagnosis definition of multiple personality disorder (MPD) made its first appearance in *DSM-III* in 1980 as one of the new category of mental disorders known as the DISSOCIATIVE DISORDERS. Prior to 1980, multiple personality was considered to be rare, with only about 200 cases reported in the psychiatric literature. However, since that time it is estimated that more than 6,000 cases have been diagnosed.

Multiple personality was far more commonly recognized prior to 1910, and reports of this disorder virtually disappeared between 1910 and 1975. It has been suggested that this was due to the fact that most people with MPD were misdiagnosed with schizophrenia, the then-new diagnosis that Bleuler was popularizing at that time as a much more inclusive disorder than Emil Kraepelin's DEMENTIA PRAECOX. In 1988, a major study by Canadian psychiatrist Colin Ross found that in a sample of 236 persons diagnosed with MPD, almost 41% had once previously been diagnosed with schizophrenia. It was found that many FIRST-RANK SYMPTOMS that are thought to characterize schizophrenia also characterize MPD. People with multiple personality disorder experience delusions, experiences of being influenced, feeling that their thoughts were being broadcast from their heads, feeling that their thoughts were being withdrawn from their heads, and they also report auditory hallucinations (which are thought to be the "alternate personalities" talking to one another inside the person's body). All of these are also commonly reported in schizophrenia.

Rosenbaum, M., "The Role of the Term Schizophrenia in the Decline of the Diagnosis of Multiple Personality," *Archives of General Psychiatry*, 37(1980), 1383–1385.

Ross, C. and Norton, G.R., "Multiple Personality Disorder Patients with a Prior Diagnosis of Schizophrenia," *Dissociation*, 1(1988), 39–42.

multiple sclerosis and schizophrenia
Multiple sclerosis (MS) is a neurological disease primarily of body musculature and movement but with certain psychological effects as well. Although it is quite distinct from schizophrenia in its total picture, there are nonetheless many similarities between the two disorders that may point to a common type of cause for them. For example, the age of onset in both MS and schizophre-

nia is at its peak in the early to mid-20s, with a range between ages 15 and 45. The course of the two diseases is very similar, with periods in which the symptoms are very active (exacerbations) often interspersed, at least in the earlier stages, with partial or total disappearance of the symptoms for short periods (remissions). The highest pockets of the disease seem to be distributed in the Northern Hemisphere, particularly in Europe and North America. All of these points of correspondence were discussed in a 1988 paper on this topic by psychiatrist J.R. Stevens that was published in *Schizophrenia Bulletin*. Her interpretation of the similarities between MS and schizophrenia is that they both may be neurological disorders that are caused by viruses. (See also VIRAL THEORIES OF SCHIZOPHRENIA.)

Stevens, J.R., "Schizophrenia and Multiple Sclerosis," *Schizophrenia Bulletin*, 14(1988), 231–241.

Munchausen's syndrome   This is a type of mental disorder in which the person fakes a serious physical illness, constructs an elaborate system of lies to account for it and then must wander from city to city after all of the emergency room staff of one city finally "catches on" to the pathological lying of the patient, who then repeatedly enacts the same scenario for other physicians. In DSM-III-R (1987) this is known as a factitious ("not genuine") disorder with physical symptoms. Other proposed names for this syndrome have been "hospital addicts" and "hospital hoboes." In 1951 R. Asher published the first description of this disorder and named it after an 18th-century German baron, Hieronymus Carl Friedrich von Münchausen (1720–1797), who became famous for telling tall tales of exotic adventures to his friends. There have been cases on record of such persons even faking psychotic disorders such as schizophrenia just to be admitted to a psychiatric hospital. Although these persons are not found to be out of touch with reality, no one theory has been put forth that adequately explains their behavior.

Asher, R., "Munchausen's Syndrome," *Lancet*, 1(1951), 339.

museums, psychiatric In the United States there are several small museums that contain items relating to the treatment of institutionalized people with psychotic disorders. The better collections can be found in the Midwest. The museum at the Menninger Institute in Topeka, Kansas, maintains a collection of restraining devices, including straitjackets and photographs from old asylums from around the world. The Medical History Museum in Indianapolis, Indiana, is notable for the exquisite architectural detailing from psychiatric wards. The St. Joseph's State Hospital Museum in Kirksville, Missouri, has a collection of restraining devices and other items, which chronicle the history of psychiatric treatment from the 15th century to the present. This museum also contains a unique exhibit featuring 1,446 objects that were surgically removed from a psychiatric patient's gastrointestinal tract, including nuts, bolts, spoon handles, nails, stones, pins, pieces of glass and a thimble.

Lipp, M., *Medical Landmarks USA*. New York: McGraw-Hill, 1990.

music therapy The act of listening to or playing music as a treatment for mental illness. In 1727 the first book devoted to music therapy appeared in print, *Medicina Musica* (the shortened title of the expanded 1729 edition), written by an English apothecary named Richard Browne. He recommended its use in calming "maniacal" patients. Philippe Pinel in France recommended it as a form of his MORAL TREATMENT of mental illness, and this suggestion was repeated by many other authors of psychiatric books. Music therapy remains a part of most

psychiatric institutions today and helps to make them more humane places to live.

mustard pack A form of treatment developed in the late 1800s that involved adding "crude mustard" to wet sheets in which agitated patients were packed. It is said that the technique of packing agitated mentally ill people in wet sheets was invented in 1840 by a Silesian peasant named Priessnitz who gained a reputation for favorably treating disease by packing people in cold, wet sheets. It was apparently first used to treat mental illness in 1860 by an English physician, Lockhart Robinson, at the Sussex County Asylum in England.

In the traditional wet pack, a cold, wet sheet is wrapped around the naked body of a patient, who is then rolled up in two or three blankets. In the mustard pack (apparently first used on the mentally ill by another English physician, S. Newington), two handfuls of crude mustard are tied in a cloth, put in hot water and then squeezed, then wrapped around the abdomen or legs, with a blanket then wrapped around this. Because the mustard acted as an irritant to the skin, this was quite an unpleasant procedure to experience. Packing in wet sheets was a technique that continued to be used until well into the 20th century and probably did not disappear until the advent of ANTIPSYCHOTIC DRUGS in the 1950s.

Williams, D., "Baths," in D.H. Tuke (ed.), *A Dictionary of Psychological Medicine*. London: J. & A. Churchill, 1892.

mystic paranoia See FOLIE À DEUX.

myth of mental illness In 1960 American psychiatrist Thomas Szaz published a paper in which he argues that the concept of "mental illness" is, in reality, a myth. Szaz insists that the term is used to stigmatize anyone who deviates from certain psychological, ethical or legal norms. "We call people physically ill when their body-functioning violates certain anatomical and physiological norms; similarly, we call people mentally ill when their personal conduct violates certain ethical, political and social norms.'' Furthermore, since (at that time) there was very little evidence for the physiological basis of the various mental disorders, they are not medical disorders that should be treated with medical procedures. Hence, there is no such thing in reality as a purely ''mental illness.''

Szaz gained notoriety for his notion of the ''myth of mental illness,'' and his many publications that question the standard operating procedure of psychiatrists and the mental health system created much animosity towards him. Nonetheless, the value in his writing is that he dared to ''question authority,'' and his works stimulated a good deal of discussion about psychiatric procedures, patients' right to refuse treatment, and other significant issues with medical and legal implications.

Szaz, T., ''The Myth of Mental Illness,'' *American Psychologist*, 15(1960), 113–118.

N

National Alliance for the Mentally Ill
Currently the largest and most active self-help advocacy organization for families and friends of people suffering from serious mental illness in the United States. As of 1989, NAMI had 75,000 members in 850 local chapters throughout the country. NAMI can be reached at 1901 North Fort Myer Drive, Suite 500, Arlington, Virginia 22209-1604 (telephone: 703-524-7600).

National Institute of Mental Health
The primary research and information organization in the United States devoted to the study of mental disorders. It was established by the National Mental Health Act

passed by the U.S. Congress in 1946 but did not formally begin operation until 1949. NIMH distributes federally mandated grant money to states and institutions for research on mental disorders. Since 1954, NIMH has devoted a major effort to schizophrenia research with the establishment of the NIMH Laboratory of Psychology and Psychopathology at the NIMH campus in Bethesda, Maryland. From 1955 to 1966 the laboratory carried out a program of research on the nature of the behavioral deficits in schizophrenia, initiated by David Shakow, who was then Chief of the Laboratory. David Rosenthal (who succeeded Shakow as chief in 1977) and Seymour Kety conducted other studies on the genetics of schizophrenia, the most famous of which is the case of the GENAIN QUADRUPLETS. Rosenthal's work on the genetic factors in the development of schizophrenia helped to define the nature of the transmission of schizophrenia. Under A.F. Mirsky, the current Chief of the Laboratory of Psychology and Psychopathology, schizophrenia research is concentrating on the autonomic, psychophysiological and event-related brain potential investigations of schizophrenia patients, as well as a long-term follow-up study of a high-risk population in Israel. (See also EEG STUDIES OF SCHIZOPHRENIA; HIGH RISK STUDIES.)

Mirsky, A.F., ''Research on Schizophrenia in the NIMH Laboratory of Psychology and Psychopathology, 1954–1987,'' *Schizophrenia Bulletin*, 14(1988), 151–156.

Navane   The trade name of thiothixene, an ANTIPSYCHOTIC DRUG that belongs to the class of such drugs known as the thioxanthenes. Navane is available in oral or injectable form.

negative symptoms   The symptoms of schizophrenia that are best conceptualized as ''defects''—that is, as something ''taken away'' from the personality of the afflicted person. The negative symptoms seem to most resemble those types of symptoms found in people with brain damage due to other causes, and as such, negative symptoms have been correlated to structural BRAIN ABNORMALITIES IN SCHIZOPHRENIA by British researcher Timothy Crow in 1980 and are the hallmark of "Type II" schizophrenia. Prominent negative symptoms are: (1) poverty of speech (alogia); (2) restricted affect and diminished emotional range; (3) diminished interest in the environment and a reduction in curiosity; (4) diminished sense of purpose; and (5) a diminished interest in social interaction with others. POSITIVE SYMPTOMS, on the other hand, are those symptoms that seem to be "added to" the personality, such as hallucinations and delusions.

The distinction between negative and positive symptoms has its origins in 19th-century neurology. Perhaps the first use of these terms was by the British neurologist J.R. Reynolds in 1858. They became popularized, although not in a sense directly appropriate to schizophrenia, by the famous British neurologist John Hughlins Jackson, who discussed them in 1894 as part of the FACTORS OF INSANITIES. The explicit application of these concepts to schizophrenia can be credited to a paper published in 1974 by J.S. Strauss, W.T. Carpenter and J.J. Bartko.

Negative symptoms characterize the most chronic forms of schizophrenia, and their early signs indicate a poor prognosis. ANTIPSYCHOTIC DRUGS have a minimal effect in diminishing or reversing negative symptoms. At present, there is no fully effective treatment for these symptoms. (See also CROW'S HYPOTHESIS; DEFICIT SYMPTOMS/SYNDROME.)

Berrios, G.E., "Positive and Negative Symptoms and Jackson: A Conceptual History," *Archives of General Psychiatry*, 42(1985), 95–97.

Reynolds, J.R., "On the Pathology of Convulsions, with Special Reference to Those of Children," *Liverpool Medico-Chirurgical Journal*, 2(1858), 1–14.

Strauss, J.S., Carpenter, W.T. and Bartko, J.J., "The Diagnosis and Understanding of Schizophrenia: III. Speculations on the Processes That Underlie Schizophrenic Symptoms and Signs," *Schizophrenia Bulletin*, 1, Experimental Issue 11(1974), 61–69.

negativism, schizophrenic   A concept put forth in 1910 by Eugen BLEULER to account for the baffling and often frustrating "contrary" or "oppositional" behavior of people with schizophrenia. Such reactions often infuriate those responsible for the care of people with schizophrenia, who may frequently forget that such actions are expressions of the disease itself. The best example of this is the primary schizophrenic symptom of AMBIVALENCE, in which an impulse is balanced by contrary ones, thus paralyzing the willful activity of the schizophrenic. In his 1911 book, Bleuler notes that in "negativism," "the patients cannot or will not do what is expected of them (passive negativism); or they do just the very opposite or, at least, something else than what is expected (active or contrary negativism)." Bleuler largely attributed this negativism to the nature of the disease rather than to the intentions of the patient. Bleuler's concept of negativism was criticized in 1911 by his former assistant, C.G. JUNG, who was then a disciple of Sigmund FREUD's and who thus interpreted such "negativism" according to the psychoanalytic concept of an unconscious (but meaningful) *resistance*. "Negativism" is no longer discussed in the modern literature of schizophrenia.

Bleuler, E., *Dementia Praecox, Or the Group of Schizophrenias*, tr. J. Zinkin. New York: International Universities Press, 1950; first published, 1911.

———, "Zur Theorie des schizophrenen Negativismus," *Psychiatrisch-neurologische Wochenschrift* (Halle), 12(1910–1911), 171–195.

Jung, C.G., "A Criticism of Bleuler's Theory of Schizophrenic Negativism" (1911), in *The Collected Works of C.G. Jung*, vol. 3. Princeton: Princeton University Press, 1960.

negligent release   In the United States, there have been many legal suits brought against institutions and responsible psychiatrists for releasing patients who then go on to do harm to themselves or others. In such "negligent release" suits, the charge is that psychiatric authorities released individuals to the community who were still dangerous and in need of commitment.

neologisms The expression of neologisms (literally meaning "new words,") by people with psychotic disorders (particularly schizophrenia) is a clear sign of FORMAL THOUGHT DISORDER. A person may create entirely new words, distort actual words or give new and unusual meanings to words that already have an accepted meaning.

neurasthenia A word coined by New York neurologist George Miller Beard in 1869 for a type of "nervousness" disorder that could be treated by HYDROTHERAPY, weak electrical currents and rest. It was considered a uniquely American neurotic disorder, for "nervous exhaustion" was brought about the "wear and tear" on the nervous system induced by overwork. In the upper classes MASTURBATION was also thought by Beard to be a significant cause of neurasthenia, although among members of the lower classes, as Beard points out in his 1884 book *Sexual Neurasthenia*, this was not the case because, for example, "Strong, phlegmatic Irish servant-girls may begin early the habit of abusing themselves and keep it up for years, but with little apparent harm." Whereas Beard thought many of the vague and mild symptoms were part of an actual nervous disease, many of his contemporaries rejected them as mild and easily reversible symptoms of tiredness or out-and-out signs of malingering and attention seeking. Special private sanitariums, retreats, spas and hydropathic institutions were set up in the late 1800s to treat individuals, largely female and from the upper classes of society, who suffered from "nervousness" or neurasthenia.

Neurasthenia is still included as a diagnostic category in the World Health Organization's ICD-9 (1978). It is defined as "a neurotic disorder characterized by fatigue, irritability, headaches, depression, insomnia, difficulty in concentration, and a lack of capacity for enjoyment (anhedonia). It may follow or accompany an infection or exhaustion, or arise from continued emotional stress."

Beard, G.M., *American Nervousness*. New York: Putnam's, 1881.
———, *Sexual Neurasthenia: Its Hygiene, Causes, Symptoms, and Treatment*, ed. A.D. Rockwell, New York: Treat: 1884.
Drinka, G.F., *The Birth of Neurosis: Myth, Malady, and the Victorians*. New York: Simon & Schuster, 1984.

neurohistopathic hypothesis This is the assumption in schizophrenia research that microscopic structures in the brain cells of schizophrenics should be significantly different from those found in the brains of people without schizophrenia. This idea has been proposed since at least the beginning of the century and was investigated by the researchers working under Emil KRAEPELIN in Munich at that time (which led to Alzheimer's discoveries of the cellular changes in the brains of people with presenile dementia). However, most studies of microscopic changes in the brains of schizophrenic persons have not proved to be consistent in findings until very recently. In the 1980s, at least 10 studies have been published that found significant pathological changes at the cellular level in the brains of schizophrenics. With new advances in the technology for neuropathological techniques, the search for microscopic changes in the brain cells of schizophrenics promised to be a fruitful area of research in the 1990s and beyond.

Kirch, D.G., "Anatomical Neuropathology in Schizophrenia: Post-mortem Findings," in H.A. Nasrallah and D.R. Weinberger (eds.), *The Neurology of Schizophrenia*. Amsterdam: Elsevier, 1986.

Stevens, J.R., "Neuropathology of Schizophrenia," *Archives of General Psychiatry,* 39(1982), 1131–1139.

neuroimaging techniques See BRAIN IMAGING TECHNIQUES.

neuroleptic This is another word for any drug that changes the mental state of anyone who ingests it. It is often used synonymously with the term "psychotropic." The term "neuroleptics" is sometimes used as an alternative name for ANTIPSYCHOTIC DRUGS as well, although technically it can refer to antianxiety or antidepressant drugs.

neuroleptic malignant syndrome This is a rare but serious disorder that may be a side effect from the use of ANTIPSYCHOTIC DRUGS. The symptoms of this disorder are fever, muscular rigidity, stupor, autonomic dysfunction (increased pulse, sweating and respiration) and, occasionally, respiratory distress. NLMS, as it is sometimes abbreviated, develops suddenly over a 24- to 72-hour period anywhere from hours to months after the initiation of therapy with antipsychotic drugs. At present, it is difficult to predict who will or will not develop NLMS, because a person who had previously undergone a period of treatment without developing the syndrome may suddenly develop it during other treatment periods. Neuroleptic malignant syndrome is often associated with the use of high-potency antipsychotic drugs. It is more common in young adult males with psychotic disorders and in persons with organic mental disorders. The use of antipsychotic drugs must be discontinued immediately if NLMS occurs, for about 15% to 20% of the patients who develop this disorder die. The exact cause of the disorder is unknown; however, it can now be treated with such drugs as bromocriptine and dantrolene.

Caroff, S.N., "The Neuroleptic Malignant Syndrome," *Journal of Clinical Psychiatry,* 41 (1980), 79–83.

Levinson, J.L., "Neuroleptic Malignant Syndrome," *American Journal of Psychiatry,* 142 (1985), 1137–1145.

neuropsychological studies of schizophrenia In the 1970s special batteries of psychological tests were devised to assess brain functioning in persons suspected of having an organic brain dysfunction. These "neuropsychological tests" targeted such processes as memory, perception, concept formation, visual-spatial ability, attention span and intelligence to see if they were disrupted in ways that were characteristic of brain-damaged individuals who took such tests. Perhaps the two most famous of these batteries are the Halstead-Reitan battery and the Luria-Nebraska battery. Major reviews of the more than 100 studies of the performance of persons with schizophrenia on neuropsychological tests have confirmed that "chronic" and "nonparanoid" schizophrenics are indistinguishable from persons who have known brain damage that is diffuse rather than focal (i.e., spread throughout the brain rather than localized damage in one place). Perhaps the most succinct conclusion to be drawn from these neuropsychological studies has been reached by schizophrenia researchers T.E. Goldberg and D.R. Weinberger: "Schizophrenic patients perform like organic patients because they too have brain disease."

Goldberg, T.E. and Weinberger, D.R., "Methodological Issues in the Neuropsychological Approach to Schizophrenia," in H.A. Nasrallah and D.R. Weinberger (eds.), *The Neurology of Schizophrenia.* Amsterdam: Elsevier, 1986.
Seidman, J., "Schizophrenia and Brain Dysfunction: An Integration of Recent Neurodiagnostic Findings," *Psychological Bulletin,* 94(1983), 195–238.

neurosis In contemporary usage, the term "neurosis" refers to a wide variety of mental disorders that do not involve a break with reality (as in PSYCHOSIS) and do not have an apparent organic basis. However, this term has changed its meaning over the past two centuries, and even now there is some controversy about the actual meaning of the word.

The word *neurosis* was first used by English physician William Cullen in 1776 in his book *Synopsis Nosologiae Methodical.* It was derived from the Greek for "disorder of the neuron (brain cell)." Following Cullen, throughout most of the 19th century "neuroses" referred to a large class of diseases that included present-day neurotic and psychotic disorders, neurological disorders and many other medical disorders. The defining characteristics of the neuroses were a disorder of the "general" functions of the central nervous system and the lack of fever in an individual. Thus, throughout the 19th century, a "neurosis" was a disease of the brain and nervous system, whereas a "psychosis" (particularly in Germany) originally referred to the psychological aspects of a mental state.

However, by the year 1900, the term "neurosis" began to take on more of the meaning of a "psychological disorder" without reference to its organic nature, and thus the types and number of neuroses were greatly reduced. "Psychosis" began to be used instead to refer to the growing number of mental disorders that were organic in nature (e.g., dementia praecox). At about this time Sigmund FREUD began to redefine the neuroses (which he also termed *psychoneuroses*) according to psychoanalytic theory—specifically, that the neuroses were mental disorders that were caused by an unconscious conflict. This latter meaning of neuroses became the standard during much of the 20th century, and the "neurotic disorders" were a common part of most diagnostic manuals. However, in 1980, the American Psychiatric Association's DSM-III eliminated the term "neurosis" because of its theoretical assumptions based on psychoanalysis and instead introduced a largely atheoretical and neutral descriptive termi-

nology, using various classifications of "mental disorders" to account for the more traditional neuroses.

The World Health Organization's ICD-9 (1978), however, still uses the category termed "neurotic disorders" and defines them in the following way:

> The distinctions between neurosis and psychosis is difficult and remains subject to debate. However, it has been retained in view of its wide use.
>
> Neurotic disorders are mental disorders without any demonstrable organic basis in which the patient may have considerable insight and has unimpaired reality testing, in that he usually does not confuse his morbid subjective experiences and fantasies with external reality. Behavior may be greatly affected although usually remaining within socially acceptable limits, but personality is not disorganized. The principal manifestations include excessive anxiety, hysterical symptoms, phobias, obsessional and compulsive symptoms, and depression.

López Piñero, J.M., *Historical Origins of the Concept of Neuroses,* tr. D. Berrios. Cambridge: Cambridge University Press, 1983.

neurotransmitter   Any specific chemical agent released by one brain cell or neuron (the pre-synaptic cell) when it is stimulated that crosses the gap between neurons (the synapse) to stimulate or inhibit a neighboring brain cell (the post-synaptic cell). About 60 such neurotransmitters are currently known. Since evidence has been accumulating that many mental disorders may be the result of chemical imbalances that cause disturbances in the ways in which messages are transmitted in the nervous system, much research has centered on the role of neurotransmitters in causing these disorders. For example, the DOPAMINE HYPOTHESIS is one such theory of the cause of schizophrenia that is based on the actions of a specific neurotransmitter.

neurotransmitter disorder as a cause of schizophrenia   The first theory of the cause of schizophrenia that is based on the hypothesis of a neurotransmitter disorder was put forth by biochemists D.W. Wooley and E. Shaw in 1954. They proposed that a decrease in the (then) newly discovered transmitter serotonin (5HT) may be related to the development of schizophrenia. Part of the reason for this was that LSD was thought to be a powerful serotonin agonist, and at that time the "psychedelic model" of psychosis was in vogue, which suggested that schizophrenic experience was related to the experiences of those who ingested hallucinogenic substances. This hypothesis was not seriously considered for very long and was largely replaced by the DOPAMINE HYPOTHESIS in 1963. Other neurotransmitters that have been implicated as possible causes of schizophrenia are norepinephrine, GABA and the endorphins.

Wooley, D.W. and Shaw, E., "A Biochemical and Pharmacological Suggestion about Certain Mental Disorders," *Proceedings of the National Academy of Sciences of the United States of America,* 40(1954), 228–231.
———, "A Biochemical and Pharmacological Suggestion about Certain Mental Disorders," *Science,* 119(1957), 587–588.

night attendant service Until 1829, it was customary for patients in almost all asylums throughout Europe and the United States to be locked in their cells or strapped or chained to their beds for the night without supervision. The death of such a restrained patient in that year at the Lincoln Asylum in England led to the eventual adoption of "night attendants" who would keep watch over such mechanically restrained patients. However, this policy was not adopted in every British asylum nor throughout Europe on a large scale for many years. Even in the 20th century, reports of unsupervised patients in restraints continue to surface from time to time. However, the general policy in psychiatric institutions today is that physically restrained patients must be continually supervised by at least one staff member.

NIMH See NATIONAL INSTITUTE OF MENTAL HEALTH.

nitrogen inhalation therapy This is one of the forms of COMA THERAPY that were developed in the 1930s as a type of treatment for schizophrenia. Introduced by Franz A. Alexander and colleagues in 1939, this form of treatment involved having schizophrenic patients breathe in pure nitrogen to reduce the amount of oxygen in the brain (cerebral hypoxia) in order to induce a comatose state. It never became popular, for ELECTROSHOCK THERAPY and INSULIN COMA (OR SHOCK) THERAPY, introduced just prior to the invention of nitrogen inhalation therapy, had already taken root and were considered much more successful in the treatment of schizophrenia.

Alexander, F.A.D. and Himwich, H.E., "Nitrogen Inhalation Therapy for Schizophrenia," *American Journal of Psychiatry,* 94(1939), 643–655.

nitrogen metabolism disorder hypothesis This is the hypothesis put forth by the Norwegian psychiatric researcher R. Gjessing in 1938 that the catatonic subtype of schizophrenia is caused by a primary disturbance of nitrogen metabolism that causes a shift back and forth from positive to negative balances of nitrogen in the body of a catatonic. Gjessing discovered that by administering the drug thyroxin, these metabolic shifts could be prevented with therapeutic results. Unfortunately, the nitrogen metabolism disorder hypothesis as a cause of schizophrenia was found to apply only to the very small group of persons suffering from periodic catatonia, and thus Gjessing's findings were not generalizable to the other subtypes of schizophrenia. However, Gjessing is given credit for being the first to provide a reliable theory for a specific physiological disease process that leads to the development of a form of schizophrenia, as well as for the first rational pharmacological treatment for this disorder.

Gjessing, R., "Disturbances of Somatic Functions in Catatonia with a Periodic Course and Their Compensation," *Journal of Mental Science*, 84(1938), 608–621.

nonallelic genetic heterogeneity Because many mental disorders—in particular, schizophrenia and bipolar disorder—seem to constitute a spectrum of disorders rather than a single disease entity, it has been thought that there are different genetic causes of these disorders that nevertheless manifest similar symptoms when they are evident in a person. This has been called ETIOLOGIC HETEROGENEITY. One reason for etiologic heterogeneity may be nonallelic genetic heterogeneity, which refers to the fact that although two or more persons may manifest the same symptoms of a particular disease, and therefore may have the same diagnosis, nonetheless different genes may be affected in different individuals to cause the disorder. In other words, the differences are not caused by alternate forms of the same gene (alleles). Nonallelic genetic transmission has been hypothesized for the psychotic disorders.

noninjurious torture This is the self-explanatory term used by German physician Johann Christian Reil (1759–1813) to refer to his philosophy of the treatment of institutionalized patients with mental disorders. Although Reil was more of a philosopher than a clinician and had no extensive experience in treating the mentally ill, he nonetheless wrote a 500-page volume in 1803 outlining his suggestions for the psychological treatment of such patients. He advocated the use of fear and intimidation to shock patients back into rationality, as well as the BATH OF SURPRISE, sudden loud noises, FLOGGING with a whip, the use of the straitjacket and a whole host of other "treatments."

Reil, J.C., *Rhapsodien über die Anwendung der psychischen Curmethode auf Geisteszerruttungen*. Leipzig: 1803.

non-Mendelian patterns of transmission This term is used as an umbrella for a wide variety of theories of genetic transmission that do not fit strict "single gene" patterns that are known to characterize classical MENDELIAN TRANSMISSION. The psychotic disorders follow non-Mendelian patterns of genetic transmission. All theories that resort to the hypothesis that more than one gene is implicated in the transmission and development of a particular disorder (i.e., *polygenetic theories*) can be referred to as non-Mendelian.

nonparanoid schizophrenia Since the beginning of the century, schizophrenia has generally been divided into a paranoid subtype and three nonparanoid subtypes, which are currently known as the disorganized type, the catatonic type and the undifferentiated type. It has long been observed that those schizophrenics with nonparanoid diagnoses tended to be more disorganized and have more FORMAL THOUGHT DISORDER than the paranoid subtype; they tended to have an earlier onset (on average, by as much as 10 years) and a poorer prognosis than the paranoid subtype; and they tended to exhibit a more diffuse set of symptoms than the paranoid subtype. Starting in the 1970s and 1980s, research psychologists conducted numerous studies that found significant differences between paranoid and nonparanoid schizophrenics in many areas. On cognitive, perceptual and problem-solving tests, paranoids and nonparanoids have shown consistent differences. Nonparanoids tend to exhibit a more conservative response style than paranoids, who often "jump to conclusions" without having enough of the relevant information to make a logical decision on tasks presented on various tests.

Many of these differences between nonparanoid and paranoid schizophrenics that have been found in COGNITIVE STUDIES OF SCHIZOPHRENIA support the notion that schizophrenia is not a unitary disorder but may instead be several different disorders.

The psychological evidence also correlates with other evidence that points to neurophysiological differences between the two as well. In GENETICS STUDIES, there is also evidence to indicate that nonparanoid schizophrenics tend to "breed true"—that is, nonparanoid schizophrenia seems to be transmitted from relative to relative more consistently in affected families than in those families in which a paranoid schizophrenic member exists, which does not necessarily mean that there will be a preponderance of afflicted family members with the paranoid subtype of schizophrenia

A major issue of *Schizophrenia Bulletin* devoted to reviewing the research on the differences between nonparanoid and paranoid was published in 1981 (vol. 7, no. 4).

Kendler, K.S. and Davis, K.L. "The Genetics and Biochemistry of Paranoid Schizophrenia and Other Paranoid Psychoses," *Schizophrenia Bulletin,* 7(1981), 689–709.

Magaro, P.A., "The Paranoid and the Schizophrenic: The Case for Distinct Cognitive Style," *Schizophrenia Bulletin,* 7(1981), 632–661.

nonrestraint movement   This term was used by English physician John CONOLLY to describe the great shift in the philosophy and treatment of the institutionalized mentally ill in the 19th century that advocated the absolute minimum use of MECHANICAL RESTRAINTS. Although the philosophy of MORAL TREATMENT and moral medicine had been given lip service since the time of Philippe PINEL around 1801, a truly humane approach to the institutionalized mentally ill was not adopted by the vast majority of European asylums that still restrained most patients whether they were violent or not. First-person descriptions of conditions in asylums in the early 1800s attest to these terrible abuses. Considered incurable by most, and no better than animals, the mentally ill were feared by many. Although some institutions began experimenting with nonrestraint policies, it was not until John Conolly successfully adopted such policies at the Hanwell Asylum

in England between 1839 and 1843 that the issue was discussed in earnest around the world. His ideas caught the imagination of the public, due largely to strong support from publications such as *The Lancet* and the *Times* of London.

When Conolly first arrived at the Hanwell Asylum, he found the following items and immediately abolished them: 51 leather straps, 10 leather muffs, 2 screw-gags, 2 extra-strong chain leg-locks, 353 handcuffs and leg-locks, 49 restraint-chairs (similar to the American physician Benjamin Rush's TRANQUILLIZER) and 78 leather-and-ticking restraint-sleeves. Despite loud cries of criticism, Conolly implemented his experimental program with great success. His methods were copied by most English asylums and then by European and American institutions in the years that followed. Our modern policies of nonrestraint except in the most extreme circumstances is directly due to the influence of John Conolly and his nonrestraint movement.

Marx, O.M., "Descriptions of Psychiatric Care in Some Hospitals during the First Half of the 19th Century," *Bulletin of the History of Medicine,* 1967, 208–214.

Zilboorg, G., *A History of Medical Psychology.* New York: W.W. Norton, 1941.

nonsense syndrome   See GANSER'S SYNDROME.

norepinephrine and schizophrenia
The neurotransmitter norepinephrine (or "noradrenaline"), a catecholamine (like dopamine), has been studied for a possible link to schizophrenia. Some studies have found increased levels of norepinephrine (NE) in the brain, blood and cerebro-spinal fluid of schizophrenics. Some studies have even connected these increased blood plasma levels of NE with POSITIVE SYMPTOMS and the paranoid subtype of schizophrenia. However, further studies that replicate these findings need to be done before any firm conclusions can be reached.

Hornykiewicz, O. "Brain Catecholamines in Schizophrenia—A Good Case for Noradrenaline," *Nature*, 299(1982), 484–486.

Norway See SCANDINAVIA.

nosology This is the study of the classification of medical and mental disorders. The logic that underlies classification schemes has changed over the centuries to reflect cultural influences and scientific advances in any given age. The nosology of schizophrenia has undergone little change since Eugen BLEULER's division of schizophrenia into the four familiar subtypes that form the basis of our modern nosological system for mental disorders. (See also FIRST-RANK SYMPTOMS.)

O

obsession A persistent, intrusive, generally undesirable idea, mental image or impulse that cannot be willfully eliminated through logical or rational thought. Although obsessions are the hallmark of obsessive-compulsive disorder, which is not one of the psychotic disorders, obsessions may nonetheless be found in psychotic disorders such as schizophrenia. The term was first used in its modern psychiatric sense by the French alienist Benedict Augustin MOREL in 1860.

occupational therapy Perhaps the earliest form of therapy for the mentally ill. Since the days of ancient Egypt, afflicted persons have traditionally been given physical activities or manual labor to perform. This "occupational therapy" has probably derived from the observation that persons with debilitating mental illnesses just seem to get worse if they are left alone to vegetate without becoming involved in meaningful activities. With the rise of the philosophy of "moral treatment" in the early 1800s, many institutions for the insane developed work programs involving their residents. In his 1801 *A Treatise on Insanity*, Philippe PINEL noted that his patients at the Bicêtre in Paris "were supplied by the tradesmen of Paris with employments which fixed their attention." By the 20th century, the term "occupational therapy" came into vogue and developed a professional status, with "occupational therapists" now part of practically every inpatient psychiatric unit or hospital. The current focus has shifted to more of a rehabilitation model, so that activities are designed to (ideally) teach skills that enable the patient to find employment when he or she is discharged and returned to the community. For the most chronic forms of mental illness (such as schizophrenia), this goal is not so realistic; nonetheless, anyone who has ever been employed in a psychiatric inpatient facility would no doubt agree with the observation made by C.G. JUNG in 1939 that "the results of occupational therapy in mental hospitals have clearly shown that the status of the hopeless cases can be enormously improved." (See also FARMING AS TREATMENT.)

Jung, C.G., "On the Psychogenesis of Schizophrenia," *Journal of Mental Science*, 85(1939), 999–1011.

odor of the insane For centuries it was believed that mentally ill people may have a particular odor that distinguishes them from others. This idea was given a certain short-lived credibility in a book by English physician George Man Burrows (1771–1846), who ran his own private asylum known as the Clapham Retreat. In his 1828 *Commentaries on Causes, Forms, Symptoms and Treatment of Insanity* he asserted that "mania" could be diagnosed by a particular odor, that of fermenting henbane. Needless to say, there is no scientific validation of this idea. However, in modern times, persons under treatment for a psychotic disorder are often characterized by the strong odor of "thorazine breath" that is part of the olfactory environment of many psychiatric inpatient units.

olfactory hallucinations These are hallucinations of smell. Olfactory hallucinations are not commonly reported among people with psychotic disorders, but they can occur. More commonly they occur along with such neurological disorders as convulsive disorders, especially those due to temporal lobe lesions (temporal lobe epilepsy) or uncinate gyrus fits. They have also been reported in person's suffering from migraines or Parkinson's disease.

Asaad, G. and Shapiro, B., ''Hallucinations: Theoretical and Clinical Overview,'' *American Journal of Psychiatry*, 143(1986), 1088–1097.

olfactory reference syndrome This is the delusion in which a person is convinced (falsely) that he or she is emitting a strong, foul body odor, such as a fecal or rotting-flesh stench. It is a delusion and not an OLFACTORY HALLUCINATION. It can be a part of a psychotic disorder, or it can be a part of a less serious disorder known as the monosymptomatic hypochondriacal syndrome.

oligophrenia See PROPFSCHIZOPHRENIA.

oligosymptomatic types A term coined by psychiatrist Silvano ARIETI in 1959 to describe ''very mild'' cases of schizophrenia. Arieti distinguishes the oligosymptomatic forms of the four subtypes of schizophrenia from BORDERLINE CASES by noting that the latter are not psychotic, whereas the mild cases of schizophrenia are psychotic. Arieti's term never gained prominence in psychiatric terminology.

Arieti, S., *Interpretation of Schizophrenia*, 2nd ed. New York: Basic Books, 1974.

onset of psychosis See AGE AT ONSET.

opium Opiates were commonly used in the 18th and 19th centuries as a form of CHEMICAL RESTRAINT to quell the agitation of certain persons confined to asylums. In the 20th century, the search for other somatic treatments eventually led to the discovery of ANTIPSYCHOTIC DRUGS, thus finally eliminating the use of opiates persons with psychotic disorders.

Orap See PIMOZIDE.

organicity in schizophrenia See BRAIN ABNORMALITIES IN SCHIZOPHRENIA.

organic mental disorders This is the generic name for a group of mental disorders that have a known or presumed organic cause. For example, such disorders as alcohol withdrawal delirium or multi-infarct dementia would be classified as organic mental disorders. In DSM-III-R (1987), a distinction is made between organic mental disorders and ORGANIC MENTAL SYNDROMES.

organic mental syndromes This term refers to a cluster of psychological or behavioral signs and symptoms whose cause is unknown. These signs and symptoms are those that have long been identified by physicians as due to the dysfunctioning of the brain. For example, an individual who enters a hospital may exhibit the signs and symptoms of delirium or dementia, but the exact cause may be unknown. Such behavior may be due to the influence of a stroke, substance abuse or other toxicity or perhaps even a brain tumor or other neurological disease. In this case, a tentative diagnosis of an organic mental syndrome is given until the source of brain dysfunction is known, at which time it is rediagnosed as an organic mental disorder.

organic psychosis See FUNCTIONAL PSYCHOSIS.

orthomolecular theory See MEGAVITAMIN THERAPY.

Othello syndrome   This is an delusional syndrome in which the dominant delusion is that one's spouse or sexual partner is secretly unfaithful. When this delusion of infidelity occurs in its purest form, it is often called the Othello syndrome after the Shakespearean character whose jealousy was the central delusion that led to his madness. Other names that have been given to this delusional syndrome are "sexual jealousy," "the erotic jealousy syndrome," "morbid jealousy" and "psychotic jealousy." In all of these cases the jealous person maintains a psychotic delusion that accompanies a significant break from reality. However, there are persons who are generally not suffering from a psychotic disorder who may be jealously obsessed with the past sexual activity of their mates, but there is no delusion about any current infidelity. In this case the syndrome is called "retrospective ruminative jealousy." In DSM-III-R (1987), the Othello syndrome is included under the label "delusional (paranoid) disorder, jealous type." The best summary of the psychiatric literature on this disorder is found in the chapter titled "The Othello Syndrome" in a textbook by M.D. Enoch and W.H. Trethowan.

Enoch, M.D. and Trethowan, W.H., *Uncommon Psychiatric Syndromes,* 2nd ed. Bristol, England: John Wright & Sons, 1979.

oubliettes   A term popular in the 19th and early 20th centuries for the primitive seclusion cells that were used to contain agitated or violent patients in mental hospitals. They were usually cylindrical pits large enough for only one person that were dug into the basement floor and covered with a heavy metal grate. Such oubliettes once existed in the basement of the Center Building of St. Elizabeth's Hospital in Washington, D.C. The word is derived from the French verb *oublier,* meaning "to forget." Such inhumane forms of seclusion were also more commonly called "strong rooms."

outpatient care   The concept that mentally ill persons could still live in the community and yet come to a clinic or hospital for outpatient treatment was first put into practice by the Pennsylvania Hospital in Philadelphia (at its Pine Street location) in November 1885. Although "nerve clinics" offering primarily HYDROTHERAPY and various tonics were established almost two decades earlier in Philadelphia (1867) and Boston (1873) for what would later be called NEURASTHENIA, Pennsylvania Hospital was the first mental hospital to offer an outpatient department. The clinic was operated by the medical staff of the Department for the Insane of the Philadelphia Hospital. The concept that such a clinic could be used for *preventing* the development of more serious mental illness was quite revolutionary for its time. Historian of the Pennsylvania Hospital Thomas. G. Morton writes in 1897 that

> . . . the service was regarded at that time as experimental. . . . It was undertaken under a conviction that in a city of one million inhabitants, a large number were suffering from premonitory symptoms of insanity as nervous prostration and depression, who might receive timely advice and treatment, and that a further development of mental disorder might thus be arrested.

In England the first outpatient departments were opened at Saint Thomas' Hospital in London, and at the Wakefield Asylum, in 1890.

Morton, T.G. *History of the Pennsylvania Hospital.* Philadelphia: 1897.

outpatient commitment   This is a legal procedure allowed in about two-thirds of the ·United States in which a person is committed to treatment in an outpatient program rather than a psychiatric hospital. This differs from "conditional release," in which a person who is already committed and residing in a psychiatric hospital is released to the community on the condition that he or she follows through with an outpatient treatment program. Outpatient commitment has been used infrequently due to the extra responsibility it places on psychiatrists, who must first initiate a legal proceeding and go to court to testify. Psychiatrist E. Fuller Torrey is an advocate of outpatient commitment.

Torrey, E.F., *Surviving Schizophrenia*, 2nd ed. New York: Harper & Row, 1988.

ovariotomy The surgical removal of the ovaries in a woman was thought to be a cure for severe mental disorders. French surgeon Jules Émile Péan (1830–1898) performed the first ovariotomy in France in 1864 and performed what may have been the first such operation for the treatment of hysteria in 1882. In the late 19th century it was performed on women suffering from HYSTERIA following the theory of Jean Martin Charcot that the disorder had a sexual basis. Hysterectomies and ovariotomies were also considered a cure for schizophrenia according to the focal theory of infection of American psychiatrist Henry Cotton, who performed such operations on patients with schizophrenia at the Trenton State Hospital in New Jersey around 1920. (See also FOCAL INFECTION AS CAUSE OF PSYCHOTIC DISORDERS.)

P

pacifick medicines The 18th-century term for drugs given to the mentally ill to "calm" or perhaps "subdue" them. They were commonly derivatives of OPIUM. The modern term for such drugs might be "tranquilizers." (See also PHARMACOTHERAPY OF THE PSYCHOTIC DISORDERS; PHENOTHIAZINE.)

Packard, Elizabeth Parsons Ware See COMMITMENT.

packing (as treatment) Until well into the 20th century, a common method for treating agitated persons with mental disorders. It involved packing the patients in wet sheets, usually cold, and then wrapping them further in several blankets. Sometimes these sheets were saturated with mustard, which acted as an irritant and thus caused such agony in patients that they eventually succumbed to exhaustion. This practice is said to have been invented in 1840 by a Silesian peasant named Priessnitz, who gained a reputation for treating physical illness by applying cold-water wet packs. This technique was first used on the mentally ill in 1860 in the Sussex County Asylum in England by Dr. Lockhart Robinson. It was finally judged an inhumane form of treatment and abandoned in the 20th century.

Williams, D., "Baths," in D.H. Tuke (ed.), *A Dictionary of Psychological Medicine*, Vol. 1. London: J. & A. Churchill, 1892.

padded room A single-person room lined with rubber and cork in which agitated mental patients were incarcerated. The first padded room was invented by Ferdinand Autenreith (1772–1835) for use in German asylums. Throughout the 19th century and into the 20th, practically every large institution for the care of the mentally ill possessed such a room for the seclusion of violent or agitated patients.

paleologic thought A term coined by Silvano ARIETI for the type of primitive logic that underlies the thought processes of all schizophrenics. It is the particular laws of this type of logic that Arieti proposes lead to delusions. Arieti also argues that the thought processes of very young children and people in primitive societies also manifest this type of logic. Paleologic thought was believed to be a developmentally earlier type of thinking than Aristotelian logic, which Arieti says is the "usual logic of the normal human being."

Arieti, S., *Interpretation of Schizophrenia*, 2nd
ed. New York: Basic Books, 1974.

Papua New Guinea   In 1929, physician
and anthropologist C.G. Seligman reported
that he found no cases of psychotic disorders
in Papua New Guinea native villages living
a traditional life-style but found several cases
among those "natives" who were in close
contact with Europeans. A major study conducted by E. Fuller Torrey, B.G. Burton-
Bradley and colleagues in the early 1970s
found that the prevalence rates for schizophrenia differed greatly across the country.
However, Torrey concludes: "Papua New
Guinea provides another case study in which
schizophrenia appears to be more common
in areas with longer contact with Western
civilization and rare in areas with little such
contact."

Torrey, E.F., *Schizophrenia and Civilization*. New
York: Jason Aronson, 1980.

paralytic insanity   See GENERAL PARAL-
YSIS OF THE INSANE.

paranoia   A psychotic disorder described
since antiquity in which a person maintains
a delusion that is usually persecutory or
grandiose in nature and clearly does not
correspond with reality. It is derived from
an ancient Greek term for "folly" or "madness," but the term did not carry the meaning of a persecutory delusion for the ancient
Greeks as it does today. Hippocrates referred
to paranoia as a mental illness marked by
cognitive deterioration. The first modern description of paranoia as a psychotic disorder
was given by the German physician Karl
KAHLBAUM in his classic textbook *Grup-
pierung der psychischen Krankheiten (The
Grouping of Psychic Diseases)*, which was
published in Danzig (today, Gdansk, Poland) in 1863. Although Emil KRAEPELIN
included "dementia paranoides" as one of
the three subtypes of the progressively degenerative disorder known as DEMENTIA

PRAECOX in 1896, in the 6th edition (1899)
of his *Psychiatrie* he describes "paranoia"
as a distinct illness from dementia praecox,
especially since paranoia did not include
"marked mental deterioration, clouding of
consciousness or involvement of the coher-
ence of thought." Furthermore, the delusions in paranoia were found by Kraepelin
to be different from those found in dementia
praecox:

> The delusions in dementia praecox are ex-
> tremely fantastic, changing beyond all reason,
> with an absence of system and a failure to har-
> monize them with events of their past life; while
> in paranoia the delusions are largely confined
> to morbid interpretations of real events, are
> woven together into a coherent whole, gradu-
> ally becoming extended to include even events
> of recent date, and contradictions and objec-
> tions are apprehended and explained.

Although the concept and the word are
thousands of years old, "paranoia" is still
included in modern diagnostic manuals. DSM-
III-R (1987) currently lists a separate category for delusional (paranoid) disorders, as
well as schizophrenia, paranoid type. In 1981,
Schizophrenia Bulletin (vol. 7, no. 4) devoted an entire special issue to "paranoia"
and its relationship to schizophrenia.

Kendler, K.S. and Tsuang, M.T., "Nosology of
Paranoid Schizophrenia and Other Paranoid
Psychoses," *Schizophrenia Bulletin*, 7(1981),
594–610.
Simon, B., *Mind and Madness in Ancient Greece:
The Classical Roots of Modern Psychiatry*.
Ithaca: Cornell University Press, 1978.

paranoia erotica   A now-defunct term
for EROTOMANIA, it was coined and first
described by psychiatrist L. Bianchi in 1906.
He felt that this type of delusional syndrome
could sometimes occur alone without any
other evidence of a psychotic disorder and
that it "occurred often in individuals of
defective sexual life, not much inclined to
copulation, sometimes in old maids who
have never had an opportunity of marrying."

Bianchi, L., *A Textbook of Psychiatry*, tr. J.H. MacDonald. London: Baillière, Tindall, & Cox, 1906.

paranoid cognitive style

A concept derived from COGNITIVE STUDIES OF SCHIZOPHRENIA, it refers to the fact that people diagnosed with paranoid schizophrenia have a unique way of responding to perceptual, cognitive and behavioral tasks in experiments. Paranoid cognitive style is characterized by a "jump to conclusions" strategy—that is, such persons give a response to an ambiguous stimulus (for example) without really having enough information in the first place to make a reasonable correct response. Paranoid cognitive style is also marked by a certain rigidity of thought processes and a reliance on verbal information processing.

Magaro, P.A., "The Paranoid and the Schizophrenic: The Case for Distinct Cognitive Style," *Schizophrenia Bulletin*, 7(1981), 632–661.

paranoid-nonparanoid distinction, the

It has become clear after decades of research that there are some fundamental differences between the paranoid subtype of schizophrenia and the three nonparanoid subtypes. Persons with the nonparanoid forms of this disorder tend to be more disorganized and to have more formal thought disorder, more overall cognitive deterioration, an earlier age of onset and a poorer prognosis than those persons diagnosed with the paranoid subtype. In cognitive, perceptual and behavioral studies of schizophrenia, many differences have been demonstrated to exist between these two major divisions of schizophrenia. Much of this research has been summarized in the special 1981 issue of *Schizophrenia Bulletin* (vol. 7, no. 4) devoted to "Paranoia."

paranoid personality disorder

This is a nonpsychotic disorder in which a person maintains a pervasive and unwarranted tendency, beginning before early adulthood, to interpret the words and actions of people as deliberately demeaning or threatening. These sorts of persons often expect to be hurt or exploited in some ways by others, read "hidden meanings" into the harmless remarks or actions of others and are generally hypersensitive and easy to anger. They usually bear grudges forever, are generally somewhat humorless and are often interested in mechanical devices or electronics. Such persons are often sensitive to rank and often are jealous of those in positions of power and disdain those persons of lower rank. It is not exactly known how this personality disorder is related to schizophrenia, paranoid type, or to the delusional (paranoid) disorders.

paranoid schizophrenia, or paranoid type

This has traditionally been one of the subtypes of dementia praecox and schizophrenia. When Emil Kraepelin first described DEMENTIA PRAECOX in 1896 as a mental disorder that was marked by its rapid mental disintegration or an "early" or presenile "degeneration," he identified three subtypes of this disease, one of which he called DEMENTIA PARANOIDES. Dementia paranoides was marked by its bizarre, disorganized delusions; the presence of hallucinations; the presence of FORMAL THOUGHT DISORDER; the deterioration of the personality; and a chronic course leading to eventual dementia. When Eugen Bleuler widened the definition of dementia praecox and changed its name to SCHIZOPHRENIA, he kept the "paranoid type" as one of the variations of this disorder.

Currently, in DSM-III-R (1987) the paranoid type of schizophrenia is defined as a type of schizophrenia in which there is a "preoccupation with one or more systematized delusions or with frequent auditory hallucinations related to a single theme." Because the paranoid subtype is characterized by delusions and hallucinations, it is said that POSITIVE SYMPTOMS are the hallmark of this variant. Furthermore, reflecting the vast psychological research of COGNITIVE

STUDIES OF SCHIZOPHRENIA, the 1987 revision of this diagnostic manual notes that the Paranoid Type has none of the following characteristics that are found in the three nonparanoid subtypes, many of which are NEGATIVE SYMPTOMS: "incoherence, marked loosening of associations, flat or grossly inappropriate affect, catatonic behavior, grossly disorganized behavior." The AGE AT ONSET tends to be later for persons developing the paranoid subtype of schizophrenia. In addition, the prognosis for persons with this diagnosis seems to be better than that for persons diagnosed with the other forms of schizophrenia, especially in the areas of occupational functioning and the capacity for independent living. GENETICS STUDIES of schizophrenia have suggested that paranoid schizophrenia is not as likely to "breed true" as is NONPARANOID SCHIZOPHRENIA. Therefore, in those families in which a paranoid schizophrenic member exists, it does not necessarily mean that there will be a preponderance of afflicted family members with the paranoid subtype of schizophrenia.

Kendler, K.S. and Tsuang, M.T., "Nosology of Paranoid Schizophrenia and Other Paranoid Psychoses," *Schizophrenia Bulletin*, 7(1981), 594–610.

paraphrenia   The term, no longer in use, for a type of paranoid mental disorder that was introduced by Emil Kraepelin in the 8th edition of his *Psychiatrie*, which was published in four volumes between 1909 and 1913. Paraphrenia is a paranoid psychotic disorder in which people may present fantastic or bizarre delusions that are somewhat organized and accompanied by hallucinations; but, unlike the paranoid form of dementia praecox, FORMAL THOUGHT DISORDER is usually absent, and there is little or no deterioration of the rest of the personality. Like dementia praecox, Kraepelin thought that paraphrenia was a chronic disorder, but that unlike dementia praecox it did not lead to dementia. Kraepelin identified four subtypes of paraphrenia: *systematica* (the most common type); *expansive; confabulans;* and *phantastica*. In terms of the severity of the paranoid psychotic disorders described by Kraepelin, paraphrenia occupies a midpoint between paranoid dementia praecox (the most severe disorder) and paranoia (the least severe of the three).

Kendler, K.S., and Tsuang, M.T., "Nosology of Paranoid Schizophrenia and Other Paranoid Psychoses," *Schizophrenia Bulletin*, 7(1981), 594–610.

parataxic distortion   A term used by American psychiatrist and psychoanalyst Harry Stack Sullivan (1892–1949) to identify one of the three developmental modes of experience through which all humans pass: the prototaxic, the parataxic, and the syntaxic. Experiences in the parataxic mode are often fragmented, momentary states of being that have no logical connections or relationship between them. Sullivan thought that this mode of experience, usually found only in very young children, characterized many schizophrenic adults, leading to distorted interpretations of interpersonal situations. This happens by incorrectly inferring causal relationships between events that are actually independent. If parataxic distortions are not corrected, Sullivan felt that the schizophrenic would then receive less and less "consensual validation" and that this lack of respect and validation for the thoughts and feeling of the afflicted person would only serve to increase problems in his or her day-to-day interpersonal relationships.

Sullivan, H.S., *The Interpersonal Theory of Psychiatry*, ed. H.S. Perry and M. L. Gawel. New York: W.W. Norton, 1953.

parergasia   A term coined by Adolph MEYER for schizophrenia. Meyer, who was perhaps the single most influential figure in American psychiatry from about 1895 until the 1940s, attempted to rename all of the major mental disorders based on concepts from his own theory of "psychobiology."

None of his proposed terms—including this one—were ever adopted by mainstream psychiatry.

paresis   See GENERAL PARALYSIS OF THE INSANE.

Parkinson's syndrome   The cluster of Parkinsonian symptoms that is induced as a side effect of treatment with ANTIPSYCHOTIC DRUGS. The signs and symptoms are very much like those found in Parkinson's disease, which was first described by British physician and surgeon James Parkinson (1755–1824) in 1817 in his treatise *Essay on the Shaking Palsy*. However, Parkinson's disease is caused by an unknown pathological process of the nervous system, whereas Parkinson's syndrome is a drug-induced disorder.

Parkinson's syndrome is characterized by a triad of signs: tremor, rigidity and akinesia (also called bradykinesia). The tremor is worse when the person's afflicted body part is at rest, and it is usually found in the hands, often with the thumb rubbing against the pad of the index finger to produce a "pill-rolling" movement. However, the wrists, elbows, head or almost any other body part can experience tremor. Rigidity is the increase in the normal resting tone of a body part and is usually only detectable upon physical examination. Akinesia (an absence of motion) or bradykinesia (a slowness of motion) are more commonly found earlier in Parkinson's syndrome than in Parkinson's disease. The bradykinetic person may have a masklike face, with diminished expressiveness and less frequent eye blinking. The body is turned "en bloc," as if the person were a solid mass without joints. The slowed movements may make the person seem apathetic or "zombie-like," and drooling can often occur.

Parkinson's syndrome can develop in persons who are taking antipsychotic drugs within weeks to months after the beginning of therapy. Women and elderly persons are the most commonly affected. Treatment for this syndrome may include lowering the dosage of antipsychotic drugs, switching to a less potent drug and/or introducing an antiparkinsonian agent such as amantadine (trade name Symmetrel), benztropine (Cogentin), biperiden (Akineton), diphenhydramine (Benadryl) or trihexyphenidyl (Artane).

Gelenberg, A.J., "Psychoses," in E.L. Bassuk, S.C. Schoonover and A.J. Gelenberg (eds.), *The Practitioner's Guide to Psychoactive Drugs*, 2nd ed. New York: Plenum, 1983.

pathogen   Something that causes a disease process.

pathognomonic   Certain signs and symptoms are said to be pathognomonic of a particular disease if they alone can identify the presence of that particular disease. Although this may be true for many medical disorders whose physiological basis is quite well known and can be diagnosed through physical measurements, such is not the case for mental disorders. For example, because delusions and hallucinations can occur in many disorders (and sometimes in normal persons), they would not be considered pathognomonic of schizophrenia. No single symptom alone is pathognomonic of schizophrenia. (See also FIRST-RANK SYMPTOMS.)

pathognomy   A 19th-century pseudoscience that, like phrenology and PHYSIOGNOMY, influenced the development of psychiatry as a science. Pathognomy (also called "movable physiognomy") was the study of the various expressions of the human face as they reflect different emotions and underlying musculature, and particularly as they reflect the inner emotional states of the mentally ill. The internationally acclaimed Scottish anatomist, physiologist and neurologist Sir Charles Bell (1774–1842) of Edinburgh was one of the earliest to take a scientific interest in the expressions of mentally ill persons, and in his 1806 book, *Essays on* *the Anatomy of Expressions in Painting,* he compares the expressions of "madness" with those found in "lower animals" and attributed them to fear and terror. Bell was a gifted illustrator and included a sketch of a typical "outrageous maniac" that he observed on a visit to the Bethlem Hospital ("Bedlam") in July 1805. In his book he gives advice to painters on "what ought to be represented as the prevailing character and physiognomy of a madman," and in doing so, Bell sets the following scene:

> You see him lying in his cell regardless of every thing, with a death-like fixed gloom upon his countenance. When I say it is a death-like gloom, I mean a heaviness of the features without knitting of the brows or actions of the muscles.
> If you watch him in his paroxysm you may see the blood working to his head; his face acquires a darker red; he becomes restless; then rising from his couch he paces his cell and tugs his chains. Now his inflamed eye is fixed upon you, and his features lighten up into an inexpressible wildness and ferocity.

The famous Scottish physician Alexander Morison (1779–1866), who in 1822 delivered the first formal lectures in psychiatry in Great Britain, published a textbook in several editions that discussed the pathognomy of mental illness and included a series of relevant illustrations of patients who represented various diagnostic categories. In his *Outlines of Lectures on Mental Diseases* (1826), Morison writes: "The appearance of the face, it is well known, is intimately connected with, and dependent upon, the state of mind." He continued his research on the pathognomy of mental disorders and in 1840 published a textbook with 108 original drawings of the facial expressions of the mentally ill, *The Physiognomy of Mental Diseases.* Many of the expressions depicted would be similar to those seen on the faces of persons with psychotic disorders in the psychiatric hospitals and wards of today.

Gilman, S.L., *Seeing the Insane.* New York: John Wiley & Sons, 1982.

pauper lunatics   A term especially popular in the 19th century for the destitute mentally ill. An analogous term today might be the "homeless mentally ill."

Pavlov's theory of schizophrenia   The famous Russian physiologist Ivan Pavlov (1849–1936), who influenced the field of learning by establishing the importance of the autonomic nervous system in the phenomenon known as "conditioned reflexes" (the discovery of which led to a Nobel Prize in 1904), became interested in schizophrenia after several visits to a Russian psychiatric hospital in 1918. Pavlov was particularly interested in catatonic patients and in his writings compared them to animals that had been experimentally conditioned. In early articles (1919), he interpreted the behavior of catatonic schizophrenics as resulting from an inhibition of the cerebral cortex of the brain, specifically a motor inhibition (inhibition of voluntary movement). Later (1930) Pavlov theorized that schizophrenia was a chronic state of hypnosis caused by hereditary and learned weakness of the cells of the cerebral cortex. Pavlov felt that the disease might begin as a learned response, but later becomes organic in nature.

Pavlov, I.P., "Last Communications on the Physiology and Pathology of the Superior Nervous Activity," *Journal of Mental Science,* 80 (1934), 187–197.

peas therapy   Yet another of the bizarre somatic treatments for psychotic disorders and other mental disorders in the 18th and 19th centuries, peas therapy involved the creation of a head wound into which strings of dried peas would be inserted. It was thought that this would work as a counterirritant to the irritation of the brain within the skull that was causing the insanity. It was reportedly used by the famous Scottish physician James Cowles Prichard (1786–1848), who in his day was one of the most eminent alienists in Britain.

pedigree   A diagramed ancestral line of descent (a "family tree") that is used in GENETICS STUDIES to analyze the inheritance of psychiatric disorders or other associated characteristics. It is often more difficult to determine correct pedigree information for genetics studies of psychiatric disorders than for studies of other types of illnesses. Often family members may be inaccessible or uncooperative, or, as in the case of people with schizophrenia, who tend to produce fewer children than normals, the families may simply be too small to do a thorough study. Researchers often try to minimize the limitations to pedigree studies by locating and studying "geographical isolates," that is, communities that have been in one place for many generations and have not interbred very much with groups from other areas. The geographical isolation itself, as well as consanguineous marriages (marriages within the same bloodlines), helps to minimize the probability that the illness that is being studied for its possible genetic transmission is due to more than one genetic variant. Such an approach was taken, for example, in famous studies of bipolar disorder among the Amish and of schizophrenia in northern Sweden.

Pardes, H. et al., "Genetics and Psychiatry: Past Discoveries, Current Dilemmas, and Future Directions," *American Journal of Psychiatry,* 146(1989), 435–443.

pediluvia   One of the inhumane somatic treatments for mental illness used in the 19th century in which the legs of patients were plunged into vats of water containing an irritating substance.

pellagrous insanity   Pellagra is a disease caused by a deficiency of niacin. The term is derived from two Italian words meaning "skin" and "rough." Pellagra was first described in the 1730s in Spain, and its symptoms include diarrhea, dermatitis and in its latter stages, mental disorders such as depression and dementia. Thus, many per-

sons who survived into the final stages of this disorder needed institutional care, usually in psychiatric hospitals. Although cases of pellagra are relatively uncommon today, it was estimated that in 1917 there were 125,000 cases of pellagra in the United States, primarily in the southeastern states. However, it was estimated that only 4% to 10% of persons with pellagra ("pellagrins") went on to develop the psychotic disorder known as "pellagrous insanity."

Cooper, T.C., "Pellagrous Insanity," *American Journal of Insanity,* 1928, 945–952.

penetrance   In GENETICS STUDIES, the proportion of persons with a given GENOTYPE that actually manifest a particular PHENOTYPE.

peptides and schizophrenia   A peptide is an intermediate level of biochemical synthesis between amino acids and proteins. A protein is composed of one or more peptides. Some of these protein particles have been demonstrated to have significant effects on behavior. Neuropeptides have been demonstrated to act as NEUROTRANSMITTERS, and therefore it has been suggested that a neuropeptide abnormality in the brain might be a possible or contributing cause of schizophrenia. However, in an informed review of the existing studies thus far by Herbert Meltzer in 1987 concludes, "It should be clear from this brief review that there is as yet no clear evidence for a neuropeptidergic mechanism in schizophrenia." Nonetheless, the exploration of the relationship between neuropeptides and schizophrenia is strongly recommended as a possibly fruitful area of research for the future.

Meltzer, H.Y., "Biological Studies in Schizophrenia," *Schizophrenia Bulletin,* 13(1987) 77–111.

perceptual anomalies in schizophrenia
It has long been known that persons who are undergoing a brief psychotic episode or who

have a chronic psychotic disorder have quite a different sensory experience of the world than those who are not psychotic. Although many attempts have been made by clinical observers (as well as by writers in fictional treatments of madness) to understand and describe this "other worldliness" of psychosis, it was not until the 1960s that the first scientific studies attempted to find a measure that could quantify the phenomenology of the ALTERED STATES OF CONSCIOUSNESS found in psychosis, and specifically in schizophrenia. The perceptual anomalies caused by the ingestion of hallucinogenic substances such as peyote or LSD led to their early label as "psychotomimetic" or "psychosis-mimicking" drugs. Disorders of attention in schizophrenia have often suggested that a "filtering" mechanism that separates out meaningful from peripheral information is dysfunctional in persons with schizophrenia, and so along these lines some theorists have suggested that "perceptual dyscontrol" may be a useful way of attempting to describe and understand the mysterious symptoms of this psychotic disorder (see ATTENTION, DISORDERS IN).

In a 1976 paper published in *Schizophrenia Bulletin,* psychiatrist Lionel Corbett lists the following perceptual anomalies found in people with schizophrenia:

1. Changes in stimulus intensity control:
   • Enhancement; increased vividness of sounds, colors, appetite, even to the point of pain.
   • Diminution; sensations become muted; awareness is deadened.
2. Shifts in quality: Objects change size, faces swell, printed words rearrange themselves and zigzag; sudden changes in gestalts occur.
3. Abnormal concomitant perceptions: Each true stimulus is accompanied by a second sensation; for example, every word heard is associated with a pain in the head.

4. Abnormal perceptual alienation: Things and people look strangely different; voices sound unreal; the world looks fresh, exciting and overpoweringly beautiful or uncanny and menacing. Sometimes perceptions lose their meaning, so that sounds, faces and speech do not make any sense.
5. Splitting of perceptions: For example, a bird is heard chirping, but the bird and its song seem separated as though they do not belong together.
6. Loss of perceptual constancy: Depth perception and perspective are lost, so that everything looks two-dimensional and flat. Buildings seem to be crumbling, the steepness of stairs cannot be judged, the edges of rooms curve.
7. Failure of gating: The perceptual world is flooded with uncontrolled images, originating both internally and externally.
8. Abnormal time perception: Time speeds, slows, stands still, or the moment expands into eternity. Events become discontinuous, or time sensation becomes erratic.
9. Abnormal space perception: For example, micropsia, macropsia, dysmegalopsia; space expands.
10. Distortion of bodily perception: The limbs feel light or heavy, or as though they are coming apart. The nose, hands, face, feet or hips seem to have changed size. The skin texture or body odor seems different, the head feels odd or numb.
11. Hallucinations, including hallucinatory memory.
12. Changes in the perception of emotion: The experience of having lost all feelings; changes in the feeling tone of perceptions—for example, the touch of normal objects becomes charged with unpleasant affect. Sometimes percepts become unduly imbued with ecstatic, wonderful feelings.

Corbett, L., "Perceptual Dyscontrol: A Possible Organizing Principle for Schizophrenia Research," *Schizophrenia Bulletin*, 2(1976), 249–265.

perceptual delusions See DELUSIONAL PERCEPTION.

perinatal factors hypothesis Because genetics cannot account for 100% of the causes of schizophrenia, many theorists have postulated that there may be environmental causes of this brain disease. One possibility that has attracted attention is that certain factors surrounding the birth of the person who later develops schizophrenia may contribute to or actually cause the disease itself. Among the first to investigate these perinatal factors was researcher W. Pollin and colleagues in the mid-1960s. Many other investigators have followed suit and have examined a variety of possible factors in the development of schizophrenia. For example, in examining birth weight as a perinatal factor, it has been found that in those pairs of monozygotic twins ("identical twins") discordant for schizophrenia (that is, one has it and the other doesn't), the "normal" twin is usually the one who weighed more at birth and is usually born first. Other studies (conducted in the 1970s by Sweden's Thomas F. McNeil and colleagues) indicate that birth complications are more likely to have occurred in the ill twin of monozygotic twins discordant for schizophrenia, thus suggesting that given identical genes, environmentally induced injuries may influence the later expression of the illness.

Other perinatal factors that have been investigated in schizophrenia research are the mother's nutritional status at the time of the birth of the child, complications arising during the delivery of the child, possible hypoxia due to postnatal apnea in the newborn, intracranial hemorrhages, the immediate postnatal living environment of the newborn and possible exposure to infectious diseases. Currently, new research on perinatal factors is being conducted in the area of fetal neural development. (See also FETAL NEURAL DEVELOPMENT AND SCHIZOPHRENIA.)

Lyon, M. et al., "Fetal Neural Development and Schizophrenia," *Schizophrenia Bulletin*, 15 (1989) 149–160.
McNeil, T.F., "Perinatal Factors in the Development of Schizophrenia," in H. Helmschen and F. Henn (eds.), *Biological Perspectives of Schizophrenia*. Chichester, England: John Wiley & Sons, 1987.
Pollin, W. et al., "Life History Differences in Identical Twins Discordant for Schizophrenia," *American Journal of Orthopsychiatry*, 36(1966), 492–509.

persecutory delirium See DELUSIONS, PERSECUTORY.

persecutory type According to DSM-III-R (1987), the variant of delusional (paranoid) disorder in which the predominant theme of the person's delusion is that the afflicted person (or someone that he or she is close to) is being deliberately mistreated or threatened in some way. Persons with this disorder may continually complain to landlords, the police or the FBI, for example, about being mistreated. Persons with this disorder are often resentful and angry and may become violent toward those they believe are persecuting them. This is the most commonly reported subtype of delusional (paranoid) disorder. (See also PARANOIA.)

perseveration The tendency to continue to repeat a particular behavior long after it is necessary to perform it. Persons with brain damage often perseverate, since it seems that the ability to inhibit an impulse to perform an action once it has started is impaired, thus causing the organically impaired person to ritually repeat the same activity over and over again. Due to the evidence for the underlying organic basis of schizophrenia, it is not surprising to at times find such behaviors in people with this disorder.

pervasive developmental disorders
See CHILDHOOD SCHIZOPHRENIA.

PET scan   A type of BRAIN IMAGING TECHNIQUE or neuroimaging technique that measures regional brain metabolism. The acronym stands for positron emission tomography, and the first published report of its use was in a paper by L. Sokoloff in 1977. PET scans examine functional changes in the brain, specifically: (a) biochemical changes such as oxygen metabolism, glucose metabolism and changes in neurotransmitter receptor numbers; and (b) changes in physiological parameters, such as regional blood flow and blood volume.

PET uses computer-generated images, displayed as if they were slices of the brain. These images serve to map and quantify metabolic changes throughout the brain. Through either intravenous or inhaled means, the subject is administered "tracer agents" that have been tagged with a short-lived (usually two to four hours) positron-emitting isotope. A variety of brain functions can be studied with PET since hundreds of different tracer agents can be tagged with positron-emitting isotopes. The PET scanner follows the course of the positron emissions and translates these signals into pictures.

The first published report of the use of PET in schizophrenia research was a preliminary report on a single chronic schizophrenic subject by T. Farkas and colleagues in 1980. The first published controlled study of PET using schizophrenics and normal control subjects was produced by M.S. Buchsbaum and colleagues in 1982. PET scan studies have confirmed the finding of HYPOFRONTALITY in schizophrenia, as suggested by METABOLIC DISORDER HYPOTHESIS studies of schizophrenia. Schizophrenia research using PET is currently being conducted in many research centers, and it is a central focus of research being conducted at the Section on Clinical Brain Imaging, Laboratory of Cerebral Metabolism, the National Institute of Mental Health, Bldg. 10,

4N317, 9000 Rockville Pike, Bethesda, MD 20892.

Buchsbaum, M.S. et al., "Cerebral Glucography with Positron Tomography: Use in Normal Subjects and in Patients with Schizophrenia," *Archives of General Psychiatry*, 39(1982), 251–259.

Cohen, R.M. et al., "From Syndrome to Illness: Delineating the Pathophysiology of Schizophrenia with PET," *Schizophrenia Bulletin*, 14 (1988), 169–177.

Farkas, T. et al., The Application of [18F] 2-deoxy-2-fluoro-D-glucose and Positron Emission Tomography in a Study of Psychiatric Conditions," in J.V. Passonneau et al. (eds.), *Cerebral Metabolism and Neural Function*. Baltimore: Williams & Wilkins, 1980.

pharmacologic challenge   A method employed in GENETICS STUDIES to search for markers of vulnerability by administering drugs in subclinical doses for a limited period of time. A selected drug is given both to persons who are thought to be genetically vulnerable to the later development of a disease and to normals. If the two groups respond differently, then the difference in response is attributed to genetic differences. At that point, response differences to a particular drug can be used as a useful marker of vulnerability. No such marker has yet been discovered for schizophrenia using a pharmacologic challenge. A suggestive finding of a possible marker of vulnerability for bipolar disorder was indicated in a pharmacologic challenge study by E. Gershon and associates in 1979 using the drug arecoline, a cholinergic agonist.

Gershon, E.S. et al., "Pharmacogenetics and Pharmacologic Challenge Strategy in Clinical Research: Studies of D-Amphetamine and Arecoline," in B. Saletu et al. (eds.), *Neuro-Psychopharmacology*. New York: Pergamon, 1979.

pharmacotherapy of the psychotic disorders   Pharmacotherapy is the treatment of disease using drugs. In the treatment of mental illness, OPIUM and camphor were used as early as the 18th century on institutionalized patients. By the 1840s, physicians were using bromides as sedative agents in asylums. Like the ANTIPSYCHOTIC DRUGS of today, the bromides did alleviate anxiety in patients as a short-term effect, but their long-term use caused central nervous system disturbances. By the end of the 19th century a new crop of sedatives began to be used in psychiatric facilities, especially paraldehyde, urethane, sulfonal and chloral hydrate. At the turn of the century Emil KRAEPELIN began to experiment with new forms of pharmacotherapy for mental illness, and he is credited with establishing the first laboratory for testing such drugs in humans. The next wave of pharmacotherapeutic agents was composed of various barbiturates, which served to replace all previously administered drugs in psychiatric hospitals. Their mood-altering properties and addictive potential led to their widespread use until the development of the PHENOTHIAZINES in 1949.

phenocopy   An individual who exhibits a trait that is due to nongenetic factors.

phenomenology of schizophrenic experience   See ALTERED STATE OF CONSCIOUSNESS; PERCEPTUAL ANOMALIES IN SCHIZOPHRENIA; SUBJECTIVE EXPERIENCES OF SCHIZOPHRENIA.

phenothiazine   Technically, the parent chemical compound for the synthesis of a large number of antipsychotic drugs, including promethazine and chlorpromazine. By the late 1940s, researchers had discovered all the major chemical groups that are currently used in psychopharmacology. At about this time it was discovered that promethazine, a phenothiazine derivative, effectively potentiated the sedative properties of barbiturates (the type of drugs primarily used for mental illness for the first half of the 20th century) when used together but was useless when used alone. Therefore, researchers sought to develop other phenothiazines that might have a stronger effect. This was achieved in 1949 when Charpentier synthesized chlorpromazine (trade name: Thorazine). By 1952 the antipsychotic effect of this drug had been documented in published reports, and it was approved for use with persons with psychotic disorders in the United States in 1954.

phenotype   An observable trait in a person, physical or behavioral, surmised to be due to genetics.

Philadelphia Association, the   See LAING, RONALD DAVID.

photophilia in schizophrenia   It has been reported by many observers of people with psychotic disorders that they sometimes exhibit photophilic (sun-loving) or photophobic (sun-avoiding) tendencies. Schizophrenics in particular have been observed in sun-gazing activities, sometimes resulting in damage to the retina. Psychiatrist Hector Gerbaldo suspects that people with schizophrenia have a decreased sensitivity to light, and that this may be important later in understanding the relationship between schizophrenia and photosensitive neuroendocrine processes (neural and hormonal processes that are stimulated by sunlight). It has been hypothesized that psychotic symptoms may be tied in with natural biological rhythms, and therefore the study of photophilia in schizophrenia may shed light on chronobiological studies of the psychotic disorders.

Gerbaldo, H., Thaker, B. and Cassady, S., "Sun Gazing and Photophilia in Schizophrenia," *American Journal of Psychiatry,* 148(1991), 693.

physical abnormalities in schizophrenia   Many investigators looking for "biological markers" of schizophrenia have found minor physical abnormalities in schizophrenia, confirming, somewhat, the approach of the study of PHYSIOGNOMY. Minor physical anomalies (PAs) are often defined in research studies as slight defects of the head, hands, mouth, hair, eyes, ears and feet. Generally, most researchers believe that these anomalies are due to perinatal factors and are associated with injury or unusual development during the first trimester of pregnancy, since this is the most critical period for the development of the epidermis, hair, ears, nose and eyes (see PERINATAL FACTORS HYPOTHESIS). Between 1967 and 1989 the only five studies of PAs in schizophrenics that have ever been conducted have all found positive results. In a 1989 study by M.F. Green and colleagues at the UCLA Research Center in Camarillo, California, schizophrenic patients had significantly more physical anomalies than the normal control group subjects. They also found that the most common anomalies in schizophrenics were anomalies of the mouth and unusual head circumference, especially in woman. In addition, the more prevalent physical anomalies were found in those persons, especially males, who had an earlier age of onset for schizophrenia. None of these anomalies, particularly the head circumference anomalies, were found to be related to cognitive performance, confirming a conclusion that Philippe PINEL made in 1801: "I have also taken, by means of a caliber compass, the dimensions of the heads of different persons of both sexes, who had been, or who were at the time in a state of insanity. I generally observed that the two most striking varieties, the elongated and the spheroidal skulls are found indifferently and bearing, at least, no evident relation to the extent of the intellectual faculties."

Green, M.F., "Minor Physical Anomalies in Schizophrenia," *Schizophrenia Bulletin,* 15 (1989) 91–99.
Pinel, P. *A Treatise on Insanity,* tr. D.D. Davis Sheffield, England: W. Todd, 1806; first published, 1801.

physical disease and schizophrenia
The belief in the existence of a relationship between physical and mental illness has a long history. Indeed, throughout the centuries it has been reported that severe physical illnesses can sometimes alleviate the symptoms of mental illness, as was the basis for the rationale for FEVER THERAPY. Many studies have examined the risk factors for specific physical illnesses to which persons with schizophrenia may or may not be susceptible. A 1988 review of this vast area of research by psychologist Anne Harris of Arizona State University has concluded that: (a) persons with schizophrenia may be at increased risk for breast cancer and possibly for cardiovascular disease; (b) persons with schizophrenia seem to have a decreased risk for developing rheumatoid arthritis or lung cancer (even in light of the fact that so many of them are heavy smokers); and (c) the overall risk for cancer is, however, greater in persons with paranoid schizophrenia than in those diagnosed with the other subtypes. The problem with these studies, however, is that the risk factors for particular disease may one day be found to have nothing to do with the schizophrenic disease process per se in individuals but instead may be determined by the effects of antipsychotic medication or other as yet unknown confounding factors.

Harris, A.H., "Physical Disease and Schizophrenia," *Schizophrenia Bulletin,* 14(1988), 85–96.

physiognomy The attempt to gain insight into a person's character or personality based on his or her physical characteristics (particularly facial expressions) dates from at least Aristotle, who, in the *Physiognomica* (a book attributed to him), suggested that people have the temperament of animals they may resemble. In 1775, J.K. Lavater published his *Physiognomische Fragmente,* which attempted to construct a classification system of character based on facial expressions. In a later work published in Paris, *L'Art de connaitre les hommes par la physionomie* (1806), Lavater explains that "physiognomy is the science or knowledge of the correspondence between the internal and external man, the visible superficies and the invisible contents. Franz Joseph Gall's (1758–1828) influential pseudoscience of *phrenology* (which dominated psychiatric thought between the 1820s and 1840s) likewise drew attention to the relationship between physiology and mental faculties, with the structure of the skull allegedly related to structural characteristics of the brain that were correlated with specific mental functions. Phrenology had a profound effect on the history of psychiatry, since it conclusively introduced the (then) controversial notion that the mind had a primarily physiological basis in the brain.

It has long been proposed that specific psychotic disorders could be diagnosed in part through the physical characteristics of a particular individual. This early protoscientific attempt to understand the "biological markers" of mental illness involved the study and classification of the physiognomy of the "insane." Philippe PINEL devoted considerable effort to measuring the size and shapes of the heads of many of his institutionalized patients as well as of "a great number of skulls in different museums," finding only a relationship between skull size and shape and mental retardation. He devotes a whole section to the topic—"Of Malconformation of the Skulls of Maniacs and Idiots"—in his 1801 *A Treatise on Insanity*. Pinel's pupil, J.E.D. ESQUIROL (1772–1840) maintained a large collection of plaster casts of the faces of institutionalized patients at the Salpêtrière in Paris. During the early 1820s, another member of the "Esquirol Circle," Etienne-Jean Georget (1795–1828), commissioned the painter Géricault to paint 10 studies of "lunatics," all of which were "monomaniacs." Later in the 19th century, Cesare Lombroso (1836–1909) studied criminal behavior and believed that certain physical characteristics in a person were "stigmata of degeneracy" that could identify the "criminal type."

In the 20th century, German psychiatrist Ernst Kretschmer (1888–1964) correlated body type and constitution with specific mental disorders in his famous book *Körperbau und charakter* (1921). The ASTHENIC TYPE was thought to characterize schizophrenics. In the United States, American psychologist William H. Sheldon (1899–1977) correlated various psychotic disorders with body types and proposed that certain very thin individuals called ectomorphs would be more likely to develop schizophrenia than endomorphs, who were heavier and more likely to develop manic-depressive psychosis. Similarly, American psychiatrist Alexander Lowen, a disciple of Wilhelm Reich's "bioenergetics analysis," combined physiognomy and psychoanalytic thought by identifying the "schizophrenic character" and the "schizoid character" in his writings of the 1950s.

Cooter, R., "Phrenology and the British Alienists, ca. 1825–1845," in A. Scull (ed.), *Madhouses, Mad-Doctors, and Madmen: The Social History of Psychiatry in the Victorian Era*. London: Athlone Press, 1981.

Goldstein, J., *Console and Classify: The French Psychiatric Profession in the Nineteenth Century*. Cambridge: Cambridge University Press, 1987.

Lowen, A., *Physical Dynamics of Character Structure: Bodily Form and Movement in Analytic Therapy*. New York: Grune & Stratton, 1958.

Sheldon, W.H., *The Varieties of Human Physique*. New York: Harper Brothers, 1940.

pica   The eating of nonfood substances (e.g., dirt, paint chips, hair, cloth). Pica can sometimes be the result of a person's psychotic disorder, particularly in severe cases of chronic schizophrenia.

pimozide   The generic name of a type of ANTIPSYCHOTIC DRUG from the class of BU-

TYROPHENOMES. The trade name of pimo-zide is Orap.

Pinel, Philippe (1745–1826)   A French alienist and one of the most important figures in the development of modern psychiatry. In 1793, following the French Revolution, Pinel was appointed chief physician at the Bicètre asylum in Paris, where he became famous for freeing more than 50 male patients from their chains. In 1795 he became the head of the other major asylum in Paris at that time, the Salpètrière, where he was also known for his humane philosophy of treatment, which he later called the MORAL TREATMENT. His 1801 textbook, *Traité médico-philosophique sur l'alienation mental ou la manie,* is one of the long-standing classics of psychiatry and had a profound effect on the classification and treatment of the mentally ill worldwide. He is credited (along with John HASLAM of England) with providing the first complete description of a case of schizophrenia in 1809.

Goldstein, J., *Console and Classify: The French Psychiatric Profession in the Nineteenth Century.* Cambridge: Cambridge University Press, 1987.
Riese, W., *The Legacy of Philippe Pinel: An Inquiry into Thought on Mental Alienation.* New York: Springer, 1969.

Pinel-Haslam syndrome, the   The proposed name for the type of schizophrenia that according to CROW'S HYPOTHESIS is called "Type II" schizophrenia—the type that is characterized by NEGATIVE SYMPTOMS, is more organically based and has an earlier onset and a more chronic course. This term was first proposed by M. Altschule in 1967 as a replacement for the term "schizophrenia." (See also HISTORICAL EVIDENCE OF SCHIZOPHRENIA.)

Altschule, M.D., "Whichophrenia, or the Confused Past, Ambiguous Present, and Dubious Future of the Schizophrenia Concept," *Journal of Schizophrenia,* 1(1967), 8–17.

placebo   A harmless, impotent substance that can be given to a patient and affects that person through suggestion. Placebos are important in testing the efficacy of new drugs, since control groups given the placebo should not show any difference in affect, behavior or other areas, where as those persons in the experimental group who are given an actual drug should indeed show such differences. The word is derived from a liturgical hymn from the Roman Catholic church, specifically, the first antiphon of the vespers for the dead:"Placebo Domino in regione vivorum" ("I shall be pleasing to the Lord in the land of the living").

Platelet MAO activity hypothesis   See ENZYME DISORDER HYPOTHESIS.

Poland   Although no conclusive studies have been conducted in Poland, the prevalence rate for schizophrenia is estimated to be higher than in most countries. This is based on data from Australia, England and the United States which concludes that Polish immigrants (as well as Russian and, in some studies, Swedish immigrants) have very high rates of first admission to psychiatric hospitals when compared with other ethnic groups.

Torrey, E.F., *Schizophrenia and Civilization.* New York: Jason Aronson, 1980.

Polygenetic theory   See DIATHESIS-STRESS THEORIES.

polydipsia   This is a medical term for frequent drinking because of excessive thirst. Polydipsia is a commonly observed behavior in people with psychotic disorders. Although studies have indicated that 6% of 17% of all chronically ill psychiatric patients manifest this behavior, 69% to 83% of people diagnosed with schizophrenia do so. Both relatives and institutional caretakers of people with schizophrenia can acknowledge that this is a very common activity, but the reason for it still remains a matter of conjecture. Irrational or psychotic thoughts that encourage drinking, the mouth dryness caused by antipsychotic drugs, and the hyperactivity of the thirst centers in the hypothalamus in the brain have all been posited as contributing to this behavior. However, polydipsia can be dangerous, as it can lead to abnormally low concentrations of sodium ions in the circulating blood, which is a condition known as hyponatremia. The constant drinking of water can lead to water intoxication, with such symptoms as confusion, lethargy, the worsening of psychotic symptoms, and even death. Perhaps the earliest case report of a person with schizophrenia engaging in dangerous polydipsia was reported in 1938 by Barahal, who described an example "in which a female dementia praecox patient drank excessive quantities of tap water resulting in edema, coma, convulsions, with subsequent recovery." Other terms for this syndrome have been "compulsive water drinking," "self-induced water intoxication and psychosis," "psychogenic polydipsia," "primary polydipsia" and "psychosis-intermittent hyponatremia-polydipsia (PIP) syndrome." The primary treatment remains fluid restriction and the removal of exacerbating factors.

Barahal, H.S., "Water Intoxication in a Mental Case," *Psychiatric Quarterly,* 12(1938), 767–771.
Illowsky, B.P. and Kirch, D.G., "Polydipsia and Hyponatremia in Psychiatric Patients," *American Journal of Psychiatry,* 145(1988), 675–683.

polypharmacy The mixing of several drugs in one prescription. Psychiatrists are often cautious about the possible dangers of such a practice, since care must be taken when prescribing, for example, an antipsychotic, an antidepressant and an antiparkinsonian drug all at the same time.

poor houses See ALMS HOUSES.

portmanteau word This is a word that has two separate meanings "packed" into it in a forced fit. Persons with psychotic disorders, particularly schizophrenia, can sometimes create such NEOLOGISMS that are usually quite meaningless. For example, the "pillfill" might be a word for the little plastic cup in which a nurse hands a patient his or her medication. Author Lewis Carroll coined the term in his novel *Through the Looking Glass* (1872).

positive symptoms Specifically, delusions and hallucinations. Positive symptoms have been postulated to be the characteristic symptoms of "Type I" schizophrenia by British researcher Timothy Crow and are thought to be related to increased dopamine receptors in the brain. However, CROW'S HYPOTHESIS has been challenged by prominent schizophrenia researcher Herbert Meltzer of Case Western Reserve University, who argues that the connection between increased dopamine activity and positive symptoms is not clear-cut, and indeed dopamine activity may be related to negative symptoms as well. (See also NEGATIVE SYMPTOMS; FACTORS OF INSANITIES, THE.)

Berrios, G.E., "Positive and Negative Symptoms and Jackson: A Conceptual History," *Archives of General Psychiatry,* 42(1985), 95–97.
Meltzer, H.Y., "Dopamine and Negative Symptoms in Schizophrenia: A Critique of the Type I–II Hypothesis," in M. Alpert (ed.), *Controversies in Schizophrenia.* New York: Guilford Press, 1985.

possession syndrome Since antiquity there have been numerous reports of persons who claim to be "possessed" by evil spirits. French alienist J.E.D. ESQUIROL referred to this syndrome in the 19th century as CACODEMONOMANIA. Case histories of such persons continue to appear from time to time in modern psychiatric literature. More than likely, such persons are experiencing a DISSOCIATIVE DISORDER in which a person's consciousness, memory and identity are split into two or more separate personality states or personalities. Many persons who were thought to be "possessed" over the centuries may have instead been afflicted with multiple personality disorder, with the switching of alternate personalities leading to a supernatural explanation. However, in persons with schizophrenia, it is not uncommon to encounter reports that the person feels "possessed" or has delusions about being possessed by evil spirits, malevolent family members, and so on.

The belief in possession is so widespread that an exhaustive study of 488 randomly selected societies in 1968 by cultural anthropologist Erika Bourguignon of Ohio State University found that 74% of them had some sort of belief in possession, and many had ritualized forms of "possession trance" that were accepted among religious practitioners. Due to the influx of many immigrants into the United States and Canada from South America and the Caribbean, where there are many cultures that promote such beliefs and religious practices, clinicians are encountering more and more examples of such cases.

Bourguignon, E., *Possession*. San Francisco: Chandler & Sharp, 1976.

Goodman, F.D., *How about Demons? Possession and Exorcism in the Modern World*. Bloomington: Indiana University Press, 1988.

McAll, R.K., "Demonosis or the Possession Syndrome," *International Journal of Social Psychiatry*, 17(1971), 150–158.

Noll, R., *Vampires, Werewolves and Demons: Twentieth Century Case Reports in the Psychiatric Literature*. New York: Brunner/Mazel, 1991.

postpartum psychosis   The phenomenon that still occurs from time to time in which a psychotic episode (usually a psychotic depression) or more serious psychotic disorder (such as schizophrenia or bipolar disorder) seems to be induced by the stress of childbirth. It was first described by the French physician Charles Lepois (1563–1633), who thought it was due to an excess

(plethora) of dark humors (see HUMORAL THEORY OF MENTAL ILLNESS). Well into the 1800s some physicians believed that the severe mental disorders suffered by women shortly preceding and especially directly following childbirth were related to the production (or lack of production) of milk (see LACTATION PSYCHOSES). In 1838 French alienist J.E.D. ESQUIROL observed that fully one-twelfth of the women admitted to the Salpêtrière in Paris became psychotic after giving birth.

Research into the types of psychotic disorders that are brought on by childbirth has resulted in conflicting conclusions over the years. In a major study published in 1969 by Protheroe in England, almost twice as many cases of manic-depressive psychosis were reported as cases of schizophrenia. In some previous studies, more cases of schizophrenia were reported as postpartum or PUERPERAL INSANITY. One of the best sources of information on postpartum psychotic disorders is the chapter titled "Postpartum Schizophrenic Psychoses" in Silvano ARIETI's book *Interpretation of Schizophrenia* (1974). Today, with the use of synthetic hormones, ANTIPSYCHOTIC DRUGS and psychotherapy, such psychotic episodes in women rarely become chronic illnesses.

Arieti, S., *Interpretation of Schizophrenia*, 2nd ed. New York: Basic Books, 1974.

Protheroe, C., "Puerperal Psychoses: A Long-Term Study, 1927–1961," *British Journal of Psychiatry*, 115(1969), 9–30.

poverty of content of speech   Another of the NEGATIVE SYMPTOMS of schizophrenia. According to DSM-III-R (1987), this is "speech that is adequate in amount but conveys little information because of vagueness, empty repetitions, or use of stereotyped or obscure phrases."

poverty of speech   One of the NEGATIVE SYMPTOMS of schizophrenia, it is a reduction in the amount and frequency of speech.

predisposing factors   Any fact of a person's life, whether genetic or environmental, that may increase the likelihood that that person will develop a specific disease. For example, in both schizophrenia and bipolar disorder, a family history that includes several afflicted persons with the same psychotic disorder is a strong predisposing factor to the possible development of the disease. (See also HIGH-RISK STUDIES.)

prefrontal lobotomy   See LOBOTOMY.

pregnancy delusions   A commonly encountered type of delusion found in both women and men with severe psychotic disorders, usually schizophrenia. A man may claim, for example, that he has been pregnant for nine years.

In persons who may not have psychotic disorders, there have been many cases on record of women who have developed a psychosomatic syndrome in which they may fully believe they are pregnant and at times mysteriously manifest many of the symptoms of pregnancy but may not actually be so. With this mysterious syndrome—called pseudocyesis (a term coined by John Mason Good in his *Physiological System of Nosology* in 1823)—women may report morning sickness or feeling fetal movements, and, incredibly, the abdomen may enlarge and the breasts may enlarge and actually begin to produce milk. This psychosomatic disorder has been reported since 300 B.C. when Hippocrates, the father of medicine, wrote about women "who imagined they were pregnant, seeing the menses suppressed and the matrices swollen," treating 12 such cases himself. Although modern technology has allowed the early detection of pregnancy and has eliminated most cases of pseudocyesis, the continued rare occurrence of such cases has led to a new scientific name for the syndrome: the *galactorrhea-amenorrhea hyperprolactinemia syndrome,* or GAHS. A related syndrome in men is *couvade,* from the French for to "brood" or "hatch," and

it essentially refers to what is conventionally known as "sympathetic labor pains."

Enoch, M.D. and Trethowan, W.H., *Uncommon Psychiatric Syndromes,* 2nd ed. Bristol, England: John Wright, 1979. (The chapter on the "Couvade" syndrome is an exemplary resource.)
Small, G.W., "Pseudocyesis: An Overview," *Canadian Journal of Psychiatry,* 31(1986), 452–457.

premorbid functioning   The physical, psychological and interpersonal level of functioning of a person before the first clear signs of a mental disease process are apparent. Another, older term for this is "premorbid personality." In schizophrenia it has generally been found that persons with the paranoid subtype have a higher level of premorbid functioning than those with the nonparanoid subtypes. Premorbid functioning is a factor in the PROCESS-REACTIVE DISTINCTION IN SCHIZOPHRENIA, with "process" schizophrenics being characterized by poor premorbid history and "reactive" schizophrenics having a much better premorbid level of functioning. (See also AGE AT ONSET; COURSE OF SCHIZOPHRENIA.)

prenatal factors   See FETAL NEURAL DEVELOPMENT AND SCHIZOPHRENIA; PERINATAL FACTORS HYPOTHESIS.

prepsychotic panic   A commonly reported phenomenon by people who later develop a full psychotic episode or disorder. It is the crucial point in the person's life when he or she realizes that his or her experiences of the world are aberrant, and this engenders a sense of isolation and loneliness. Fear, terror and sheer panic are experienced by the individual who experiences the world as splitting or crumbling. It may very well be the point at which the person realizes he or she is losing control and will soon no longer be able to function in a healthy way. Many people enter treatment at this point and can be helped with pharmacotheraphy and psychotherapy, although many still go on to develop a psychosis. American psychiatrist Harry Stack Sullivan described just such a "schizophrenic panic," which he thought was the result of an extreme injury to self-esteem or sense of self. Silvano ARIETI describes this initial stage of "prepsychotic panic" in the development of a full case of schizophrenia as follows: "when the patient starts to perceive things in a different way, is frightened on account of it, appears confused, and does not know how to explain 'the strange things that are happening.'"

Arieti, S., *Interpretation of Schizophrenia*, 2nd ed. New York: Basic Books, 1974.
Sullivan, H.S., *Conceptions of Modern Psychiatry*. New York: Norton, 1953.

prepsychotic personality   See LATENT SCHIZOPHRENIA.

pressured speech   This is one of the hallmarks of a MANIC EPISODE. It occurs when a person is rapidly talking in great bursts and is difficult, if not impossible, to interrupt. Often the person is speaking very loudly and emphatically and without any prompting from anyone else. Indeed, such persons may continue to speak even though no one is listening. Beside manic episodes, pressured speech may occur in persons who are diagnosed with schizophrenia, an organic mental disorder, major depression with psychomotor agitation, other psychotic disorder or in short-term reactions to stress.

prevalence of schizophrenia   See EPIDEMIOLOGY.

primary process   According to Sigmund FREUD, this is the type of psychological process that is characteristic of the unconscious. From the point of view of psychoanalysis, primary process is the most primitive and infantile form of psychological activity, and it is most evident in dreams, fantasies and hallucinations. A psychotic episode or psychotic disorder would then be considered the eruption or intrusion of this primitive and infantile mode of experience into consciousness. Primary process is to be distinguished from secondary process, which is the more logical, sequential and rational form of thought that typifies normal waking consciousness. The principal drive behind primary process, according to Freud, is the pleasure principle, whereas the primary motivation behind secondary process is the reality principle. Freud developed the distinction between primary and secondary process as early as 1895 in his "Project for a Scientific Psychology" but developed these ideas in more detail in his book, *The Interpretation of Dreams*.

Laplanche, J. and Pontalis, J.B., *The Language of Psycho-Analysis*, tr. D. Nicholson-Smith. New York: W.W. Norton, 1973.

primary symptoms of schizophrenia   See FUNDAMENTAL SYMPTOMS OF SCHIZOPHRENIA.

primitive thinking   See MAGICAL THINKING.

prison psychosis   See GANSER'S SYNDROME.

private madhouses   Common in France, Germany and especially Britain in the 18th and 19th centuries, these were privately owned "madhouses" for mentally ill people with money. Those without money—the "pauper lunatics"—sometimes had their costs paid by local church parishes. The earliest of the private madhouses was developed in England in 1615 (the Kingsdown house at Box, closed finally in 1940), but they did not become a popular practice until the next century. Most were owned by businessmen, not medical professionals, and many were run by women—usually the wives, widows and daughters of the owners. Some of these private madhouses were passed on for many generations within the same family.

Private madhouses were a profit-making enterprise, and scandals and abuses were frequent. In 1706 British author Daniel Defoe wrote an essay calling for the abolition of private madhouses because of the inhumane treatment prevalent in so many of them. It was finally a novel, *Hard Cash,* by British author Charles Reade (1814–1884), that ignited the movement for reform in the 1860s. *Hard Cash* (first published in England in 1863, and then in the United States in 1864 under the title *Very Hard Cash*) is the story of a sane young man who is diabolically committed to a private asylum by his business associates who covet the young hero's wealth. Reade based the novel on an actual incident in his own life in which he was instrumental in gaining the release of a young man who was wrongfully committed to a private madhouse. Prior to being released as a novel, Reade's *Hard Cash* was first serialized in a periodical edited by Charles Dickens, *All the Year Round,* and both of these men were attacked by the *British Medical Journal* for being irresponsible in making "diabolical charges upon the character of all medical men connected with the management of lunatics."

Ackerknecht, E.H., "Private Institutions in the Genesis of Psychiatry," *Bulletin of the History of Medicine,* 60(1986), 387–399.
Parry-Jones, W.L., *The Trade in Lunacy: A Study of Private Madhouses in England in the Eighteenth and Nineteenth Centuries.* London: Routledge & Kegan Paul, 1972.

proband In GENETICS STUDIES, the proband is the person in a given PEDIGREE diagnosed with the disease. Relationships between that person and others in the family are then studied to determine possible patterns of genetic transmission. Another name for proband is INDEX CASE or "propositus" (plural: probands or propositi).

process-reactive distinction in schizophrenia, the This distinction is one attempt to further differentiate the possible subtypes of schizophrenia. The process-re-

active distinction divides persons with schizophrenia into two groups based on differences in premorbid personality, the course of the disease and its PROGNOSIS. The idea is that the premorbid history of a person who develops schizophrenia and the rapidity with which the first symptoms appear are related to how well or ill the person eventually becomes in the course of his or her lifetime. Therefore, it is also sometimes referred to as the "poor premorbid/good premorbid" distinction, or, by some, the "poor prognosis/good prognosis" distinction (see PREMORBID FUNCTIONING).

Eugen BLEULER first discussed the differences between psychotic disorders that were based on a "morbid reaction to an affective experience" (such as an emotional shock or stressor), which he called *reactive psychoses* or *situation psychoses,* and those psychoses based on a "morbid process in the brain," which he termed *process psychoses* or *progressive psychoses.* However, as Bleuler notes in the fourth edition (1923) of his *Textbook of Psychiatry,* "no (diagnostic) division can be based on these classes because the two symptomatologies intermingle."

However, based on Bleuler's observation about psychotic disorders in general, the idea was further developed by others that some persons with schizophrenia could have a variety of the disease caused by an organic disease of the brain and another variety that seemed to be induced as a reaction to stress or other environmental factors. Revising some proposals for studying the problem of prognosis in schizophrenia first put forth in a 1937 article, G. Langfeldt in a 1956 paper proposed that schizophrenics who had a poor premorbid history (that is, a long-term history of poor social, occupational and psychological functioning perhaps dating from childhood) be called *process schizophrenics.* Furthermore, Langfeldt also argued that these persons generally had a poor prognosis and a lifelong history of long-term institutionalization. Langfeldt noticed that there was another type of schizophrenia characterized by persons who may have had a generally good premorbid history and who develop an acute onset of symptoms rather than the slow, insidious development of symptoms found in process schizophrenics. Furthermore, these persons had a better chance of recovery than those with process schizophrenia. Langfeldt called this reactive disorder *schizophreniform psychosis*.

Throughout the years the process-reactive distinction has been given many other names as well. These clinical dichotomies have been termed: true schizophrenia/schizophreniform; demential praecox/schizophrenia; typical schizophrenia/atypical schizophrenia; chronic schizophrenia/episodic schizophrenia; degenerative schizophrenia/psychogenic schizophrenia.

Decades of research that has divided schizophrenia into these two forms has proven useful, for significant differences have been found between the two types of persons with schizophrenia. Process schizophrenics tend to perform more poorly on cognitive, perceptual and behavioral tasks in experiments. Reactives perform closer to normals on these tasks. Process schizophrenics are also more likely to have NEGATIVE SYMPTOMS, which is to be expected if this is a form of the disorder that seems to be the most organic and genetically based (much like the "Type II" schizophrenia of CROW'S HYPOTHESIS). Reactive schizophrenics tend to demonstrate a fuller range of affect and have shorter hospitalizations and fewer admissions than process schizophrenics. The paranoid subtype of schizophrenia tends to be more common among those in the reactive category, whereas the nonparanoid subtypes tend to be found among those considered process schizophrenics.

The process-reactive distinction has been extremely important for understanding schizophrenia since one of the most consistent research findings is that the premorbid level of social functioning is *the* most important factor in determining the prognosis of cases of schizophrenia, although it is not 100% predictive and must be considered with other factors. Indeed, this finding is one of the most firmly substantiated lines of evidence in all of psychiatry regarding the prognosis of psychotic disorders. This vast literature is reviewed by J. Higgins in a 1969 article, and in 1977 an entire issue of *Schizophrenia Bulletin* (Vol. 3, No. 2) was devoted to the issue of the premorbid adjustment aspect of the process-reactive distinction.

Bleuler, E., *Lehrbuch der Psychiatrie*, 4th ed. Berlin: Springer, 1923. (English translation, 1924).

Higgins, J., "Process-Reactive Schizophrenia," *Journal of Nervous and Mental Disease*, 149 (1969), 450–465.

Langfeldt, G., "The Prognosis in Schizophrenia and the Factors Influencing the Course of the Disease," *Acta Psychiatrica et Neurologica Scandinavica Supplementum*, no. 13 (1937).

———, "The Prognosis in Schizophrenia," *Acta Psychiatrica et Neurologica Scandinavica Supplementum*, no. 110 (1956).

prodromal phase   According to DSM-III-R, schizophrenia is characterized by a course with a *prodromal phase*, an *active phase*, and a *residual phase*. The prodromal phase is the period prior to the full expression of psychotic symptoms (delusions, hallucinations, etc.) in which there is a clear deterioration in a person's previous level of functioning. Often during this period the person will tend to withdraw from social situations, perhaps begin to exhibit poor grooming and hygiene or express odd or bizarre ideas. Often the person's affect will become rather blunted, or he or she may express it inappropriately (e.g., laughing to him- or herself in the middle of a serious discussion). Sometimes he or she will have perceptual abnormalities and may seem to have lost a zest for life by developing a lack of initiative or energy. Insensitive family members or friends may accuse the person of being "lazy" when in fact this is not really the case. Often those who know the person who is undergoing the prodromal phase of schizophrenia will comment on that fact that he or she "is no longer the same person." The length of the prodromal phase is extremely variable, perhaps weeks in some cases to many years in others. The poor premorbid adjustment of "process schizophrenics" (see the PROCESS-REACTIVE DISTINCTION IN SCHIZOPHRENIA) may be due to the presence of the prodromal phase of the illness. (See also AGE AT ONSET.)

prognosis The foretelling of the probable course or outcome of a disease.

In BIPOLAR DISORDER, the prognosis is poorer and the course of the disease is more chronic for those who have a mixed or "rapid cycling" episode (that is, two or more complete cycles of a manic and a major depressive episode that succeed each other without a period of remission within a year). Persons who respond to LITHIUM may have a more chronic course, but due to the positive effects of pharmacotherapy, they may be able to maintain a higher level of functioning and thus have a better outcome than those persons with bipolar disorder who do not respond to lithium.

Much attention has been paid to the prognosis of schizophrenia. Indeed, Emil KRAEPELIN's classification of the psychotic disorders was based on prognosis, with dementia praecox representing the types of psychosis that follow a chronic degenerating course and MANIC-DEPRESSIVE PSYCHOSIS being the type of psychotic disorder that has a better outcome. Within the field of schizophrenia research specifically, the concept of "poor prognosis/good prognosis" types of schizophrenia has been examined and confirmed (see PROCESS-REACTIVE DISTINCTION IN SCHIZOPHRENIA, THE).

In *Surviving Schizophrenia: A Family Manual*, psychiatrist E. Fuller Torrey lists the following factors, which, when considered together in an individual's unique history, help to determine whether that person fits in the good prognosis or the poor prognosis group:

1. *History of adjustment prior to onset of illness*. This has often been regarded as perhaps the most important factor. If the person seemed relatively normal prior to the obvious onset of schizophrenia, then the chances for a better outcome are greater than for those who may have seemed "odd," withdrawn or delinquent since childhood.

2. *Gender*. Women have a much better prognosis for schizophrenia than men. Women have a later AGE AT ONSET than men, shorter hospital stays and fewer relapses (see GENDER DIFFERENCES IN SCHIZOPHRENIA).

3. *Family history*. A family history of schizophrenia often indicates a poor prognosis, especially if the blood relationship is close between the INDEX CASE and the affected relatives. A good outcome is suggested by no family history of schizophrenia or psychiatric disorders, or, as it turns out, if there is a history of depression or bipolar illness in the family.

4. *Age of onset*. The earlier schizophrenia develops and is diagnosed in a person, the worse the potential outcome will be. Alternatively, those persons who develop schizophrenia relatively late (especially after age 30) have a much better prognosis.

5. *Suddenness of onset*. If the first symptoms come on rapidly, then the prognosis is much better than if the symptoms developed over a period of months or years.

6. *Precipitating events*. If there is a definite stressful situation or event that is pointed to as the starting point for the onset of the schizophrenic symptoms, the prognosis is good. This corresponds to the "reactive schizophrenia" notion of a subtype that may be more environmentally induced and less genetically and organically based.

7. *CT scan findings*. If a person who is diagnosed with schizophrenia is given a CT scan and the ventricles of the brain are found to be enlarged, this is an in-

dication of poor prognosis. If the CT scan results are normal, then the prognosis is much better.

8. *Response to medication.* One of the strongest indicators of prognosis is response to ANTIPSYCHOTIC DRUGS. If the initial response to antipsychotic medication is weak, then the prognosis is far worse, especially since these drugs are the first line of defense against the debilitating effects of schizophrenia.

9. *Clinical symptoms.* Torrey lists a number of symptoms that may appear during the first schizophrenic episode that he states "can be used as predictive factors." Initial symptoms that indicate a good outcome are the presence of: (a) paranoid symptoms; (b) catatonic symptoms; (c) depression or other emotions; (d) a previous diagnosis of schizoaffective disorder; (e) symptoms that are not typical of schizophrenia; (f) confusion ("I don't understand what is happening to me!" is an example Torrey gives). Initial symptoms that indicate a poor outcome are the presence of: (a) NEGATIVE SYMPTOMS such as flat or blunted affect, apathy, extreme social withdrawal, poverty of speech, blocking, etc.; (b) obsessive and compulsive symptoms. (See also COURSE OF SCHIZOPHRENIA; HIGH-RISK STUDIES; LONGITUDINAL STUDIES.)

Stephens, J. H., "Long Term Prognosis and Follow-up in Schizophrenia," *Schizophrenia Bulletin*, 4(1978), 25–47.

Torrey, E. F., *Surviving Schizophrenia: A Family Manual*, 2nd ed. New York: Harper and Row, 1988.

projection In Sigmund FREUD's psychoanalysis, projection is a defense mechanism in which feelings, qualities or wishes that the person refuses to recognize or are rejected in him- or herself are expelled ("projected") from the self and located in another person, group or thing. Projection is one of the most primitive of the defense mecha-

nisms and is prevalent in the psychotic disorders, particularly those involving PARANOIA or paranoid delusions. In fact, Freud first became aware of the phenomenon of projection in 1895–96 when studying the mental processes involved in paranoia.

projective tests Psychological tests that attempt to infer qualities of an individual's personality by analyzing the free responses he or she gives to selected stimuli. The idea is based on Freud's concept of PROJECTION. The answers given on a projective test are thought to contain information about the unconscious wishes, fears and desires within a person, as well as give an idea of how, at a more conscious level, the person constructs reality and how approaches are taken to problem solving. Projective tests give a good idea of how strong a person's defense mechanisms are, thereby indicating how strong the ego is and how well the person can deal with the demands of life and of reality. Projective tests can use structured stimuli (such as words for the Word Association Test, or charcoal drawings for the Thematic Apperception Test) or unstructured stimuli (such as the various inkblot tests, especially the Rorschach). What is interesting about the history of projective tests is that they were first developed by clinicians using institutionalized people with dementia praecox (schizophrenia) and other serious mental disorders.

C. G. JUNG (1875–1961), the Swiss psychiatrist and psychoanalyst, was the first to use a projective test for diagnostic purposes with people with mental disorders. Even though the Word Association Test had been used by others in previous studies to study the way the "normal," rational, conscious mind words, Jung used the association test to discover the unconscious feelings, wishes, fears and desires that revealed something about the deeper aspects of the human personality. He experimentally demonstrated the phenomenon of COMPLEXES using these tests, and his published research (which appeared in journals between 1904 and 1910) made him world famous.

Swiss psychiatrist Hermann Rorschach (1884–1922) initially invented an inkblot test to examine the fantasy capacity of successful art students versus less talented ones. Although Rorschach conducted his initial experiments with the inkblots in 1911, over the years he experimented with more than 300 psychiatric patients in asylums and clinics in Switzerland as well as normal persons. Many of the institutionalized patients had psychotic disorders, such as schizophrenia and manic-depressive psychosis, and so it is with these types of patients that Rorschach fine-tuned his famous test. He finally published the results of his studies in 1921 in his famous book *Psychodiagnostik (Psychodiagnostics)*.

The interpretation of projective tests for the purposes of diagnosing schizophrenia (or other psychotic disorders) is too detailed to summarize here, and those interested in pursuing this issue further should consult the book by I. B. Weiner listed below.

Jung, C. G., *Experimental Researches: The Collected Works of C. G. Jung, Vol. 2*. Princeton: Princeton University Press, 1973.

Rabin, A. I., "Projective Methods: A Historical Introduction," in A. I. Rabin (ed.), *Assessment with Projective Techniques: A Concise Introduction*. New York: Springer, 1981.

Rorschach, H., *Psychodiagnostik*. Bern und Leipzig: Ernst Bircher Verlag, 1921.

Weiner, I. B., *Psychodiagnosis in Schizophrenia*. New York: Wiley, 1966.

prolonged sleep therapy See SLEEP TREATMENT.

propfschizophrenia A now-defunct term for a type of schizophrenia that was only thought to be found in a small number of persons who were mentally retarded. It was considered to have an onset after puberty and was characterized by paranoid episodes with delusions and hallucinations. "Propfhebephrenia" is another term formerly used for the same concept. "Oligophrenia" was a term used for "mental defective" or "idiots" (as the mentally retarded were termed earlier in this century), and propfschizophrenia was often referred to as a variety of this class of disorders.

propositus See PROBAND.

propranolol An antianxiety drug that is better known by its trade names, Inderal or Inderide. Originally approved for use in lowering blood pressure, preventing attacks of angina pectoris and controlling certain cardiac arrhythmias, propranolol has not officially been labeled by the FDA as a treatment for anxiety or psychiatric disorders. However, its use for such conditions is widespread.

protein factors hypothesis Since the time of Emil KRAEPELIN, the search for a toxin or other substance that was to be found in the blood of schizophrenics has been reported from time to time. In many studies the blood or urine of schizophrenics has been analyzed, and substances that were assumed to be protein factors have been singled out as being possibly related to the cause of the disorder, or at least to the expression of its symptoms. Often these substances were isolated and then injected into other organisms (e.g., cells, plants, animals), which then changed their usual behavior, thus indicating that quite possibly these substances were affecting the behavior of humans.

Frohman, C. E. et al., "Evidence of a Plasma Factor in Schizophrenia," *Archives of General Psychiatry*, 2(1960), 255–262.

pseudoabstraction A characteristic of the thought and language of some schizophrenics who begin to use polysyllabic, highly abstract words, perhaps taken from philosophy or the sciences, but without using them meaningfully or in the proper context. Silvano ARIETI remarks that in a patient who is exhibiting pseudoabstraction, "If we ask him to explain what he means with these big words, he will be unable to do so. He will use other big words to accentuate the feeling of confusion . . . Various German authors have very appropriately called this characteristic 'talking on stilts.' ''

Arieti, S., *Interpretation of Schizophrenia*, 2nd ed. New York: Basic Books, 1974.

pseudocyesis See PREGNANCY DELUSIONS.

pseudodementia Sometimes a person may exhibit signs and symptoms of an ORGANIC MENTAL SYNDROME such as dementia without having any underlying brain disease process. Sometimes persons who are experiencing a major depressive episode may appear to have dementia due to the seriousness of the vegetative signs. In rarer cases, the PRODROMAL PHASE of schizophrenia may resemble dementia in extreme instances.

pseudodementia syndrome See GANSER'S SYNDROME.

pseudologia fantastica The clinical term for "pathological lying." The term is coined from two Greek words meaning "elaborate false speech."

pseudoneurotic schizophrenia See BORDERLINE SCHIZOPHRENIA.

pseudoschizophrenia syndrome A type of epilepsy that resembles schizophrenia and is supposedly characterized by its "hypnoid states." This concept has never gained wide usage. Although the relationship between convulsive disorders such as epilepsy and schizophrenia have been investigated, no support has ever been found for a pseudoschizophrenia syndrome.

Zec, N.R., "Pseudoschizophrenic Syndrome," *Psychiat. et. Neurol.*, 149(1965), 197–209.

psychedelic experiences in schizophrenia With the advent of the "psychedelic revolution" in the mid-1960s, the metaphors supplied by the types of experiences reported by persons who had ingested hallucinogenic substances (e.g., LSD, peyote) came to be applied to numerous areas of human experience. In particular, the psychedelic metaphors were applied to the subjective experience of psychosis. Because many persons in the PRODROMAL PHASE of schizophrenia and other psychotic disorders report perceptual anomalies and other phenomena related to ALTERED STATES OF CONSCIOUSNESS, many investigators during this period began to turn their attention to the similarities between drug-induced hallucinatory states of consciousness and psychotic experience (see PERCEPTUAL ANOMALIES IN SCHIZOPHRENIA). The most notable attempt at such a comparison was published by Malcom Bowers and Daniel X. Freedman in 1966.

Due to a long-standing tradition of romanticizing "madness," psychotic experiences were compared with psychedelic experiences as possible "transcendent" experiences, notably by R.D. LAING. However, in a sharp critique of Laing's "psychedelic model" of schizophrenia, Miriam Siegler, Humphrey Osmond and Harriet Mann constructed a detailed comparison of the subjective experiences of psychedelic experiences with those of schizophrenia and found many disturbing differences. They make the analogy of the difference between good dreams, bad dreams and nightmares, with psychosis represented by the latter and psychedelic experiences by the first two. With the metaphoric fad of the 1960s no longer in fashion, the "psychedelic model" of schizophrenia is no longer discussed in the literature on this disorder.

Bowers, M. and Freedman, D.X., "Psychedelic Experiences in Acute Psychosis," *Archives of General Psychiatry*, 15(1966), 240–248.

Laing, R.D., "Transcendental Experience in Relation to Religion and Psychosis," *Psychedelic Review*, 6(1965), 7–15.

Siegler, M. and Osmond, H., *Models of Madness, Models of Medicine*. New York: Macmillan, 1974.

Siegler, M., Osmond, H. and Mann, H., "Laing's Models of Madness," in R. Boyers and R. Orrill (eds.), *R. D. Laing and Anti-Psychiatry*. New York: Harper & Row, 1971.

psychesthenia A disorder caused by the "exhaustion" of the nervous system. It is related to the concept of NEURASTHENIA in that the "wear and tear" of the "nerves" was thought to lead to a "nervous breakdown," which may result in some cases in more serious disorders such as schizophrenia or one of the other psychotic disorders. Pierre JANET introduced the term in 1903 in his book *Les obsessions et la psychasthénie.*

psychiatric social work In many instances it is the nonmedical professionals such as social workers who are in the "front lines" of the battle against the inhumane treatment of the mentally ill. It was only in the 1920s that the specialization of psychiatric social work came into existence, largely through the proliferation of "child guidance clinics" in the United States and England. In the decades since, psychiatric social workers have provided critical services for people with mental disorders in virtually every aspect of community care. In the United States, the professional organization of social workers is the National Association of Social Workers, 7981 Eastern Avenue, Silver Spring, MD 20910, telephone: (301) 565-0333.

psychiatry The medical profession devoted to the study and treatment of mental disorders. The word "psychiatry" was first used in English in 1846 to refer to this profession. Other terms have been "medical psychologist" or "alienist," and in an earlier age these physicians were also known as "mad-doctors" or "lunatic doctors." The word is derived from the German term *psychiaterie*, which was first used in 1803 by the physician and student of mental illness Johannes Christian Reil (1759–1813) in a book entitled *Rhapsodies in the Application of Psychic Methods in the Treatment of Mental Disturbances*. The word *psychiatrie* was first used by Johann Christian Heinroth (1773–1843), and Ernst von Feuchtersleben (1806–1849) used the term *psychiatrics* for the profession in 1845.

Hunter, R.A. and Macalpine, I. (eds.), *Three Hundred Years of Psychiatry, 1535–1860: A History Presented in Selected English Texts*. Oxford: Oxford University Press, 1963.

psychoanalysis See DIRECT ANALYSIS.

psychoanalytic theories of schizophrenia Sigmund FREUD coined the term *psychoanalysis* in 1896 to refer to his philosophy and system of therapy that was based on a careful analysis of internal unconscious processes. Although Freud did treat some manic-depressives, he never treated schizophrenic patients (unlike his colleague, C.G. JUNG, who held a position in a psychiatric hospital for nine years). Freud was very pessimistic about the treatment of schizophrenia with psychoanalysis and tended to discourage it. He left few writings on the subject, but this gap was filled by those psychoanalysts who came after him, notably Karl Abraham, Paul Federn, Melanie Klein, Frieda Fromm-Reichmann, Leland Hinsie, John Rosen (see DIRECT ANALYSIS), Otto Fenichel and Harold Searles.

According to Freud, schizophrenia involves a withdrawal of libido from the objects of the external world and into the self. This withdrawal of energy into the self was termed by Freud a regression into a state of *primary narcissism* similar to that found in infants in a period before there is any differentiation between ego, superego or id and before there is any discriminative ability between the inner and outer worlds. Because of this, Freud believed no *transference* could take place between the schizophrenic patient and the analyst, and therefore no treatment could be possible. Because the regression to a state of primary narcissism characterized psychoses, he called them *narcissistic neuroses* (as opposed to *transference neuroses,* which were the usual phenomenon in psychoanalysis). Freud wrote in 1924 that in the narcissistic neuroses "the resistance is unconquerable" and that psychoanalytic techniques therefore "must be replaced by others; and we do not know yet whether we shall succeed in finding a substitute."

The central aspect of the schizophrenic experience, according to most psychoanalytic theorists, is the initial break with reality, after which the ego returns to its original infantile, undifferentiated state in which it is submerged or dissolved wholly or partially into the id. Although such regressions may be found in normals, the schizophrenic regresses to a fixation point in development that is further back than any encountered in the neuroses.

A useful summary of many of the psychoanalytic theories of schizophrenia and of psychosis is provided by Silvano Arieti in his book *Interpretation of Schizophrenia.*

Arieti, S., *Interpretation of Schizophrenia,* 2nd ed. New York: Basic Books, 1974.

psychological research Although the search for the biological basis for schizophrenia and the psychotic disorders has been a primary focus of investigation since the 18th century (see ABLATION STUDIES), psychological experiments have given us much useful information on cognition, perception, learning, language, memory and behavior in these disorders. The current trend is to correlate the overall findings of these studies and match this knowledge with the new discoveries gained by biochemical techniques, brain imaging and other areas of scientific inquiry.

Francis Galton founded the first psychological laboratory in England in 1884, and his Anthropometric Laboratory collected data on more than 9,000 subjects. Galton charged his subjects a fee for providing them with their test results. However, the first laboratory designated solely for the application of the experimental method to psychology was founded in Leipzig, Germany, by Wilhelm Wundt in 1879. In the 1880s, many Americans flocked to Germany to learn the experimental method (generally from Wundt), and subsequently between 1888 and 1895 many universities and hospitals set up "psychological laboratories" to conduct research. Harvard University was probably the first to do so in the United States, but the eminent American philosopher and psychologist William James (1842–1910), who taught at Harvard, was not impressed with the experimental method. Ridiculing the stereotypical obsessive-compulsive style of the Germans, James snidely remarks in the first volume of his landmark *Principles of Psychology* (1890), "This method taxes patience to the utmost, and could hardly have arisen in a country whose natives could be *bored.* Such Germans as Weber, Fechner, Vierordt and Wundt obviously cannot . . . ."

A useful summary of the psychological research on schizophrenia can be found in a review article by A.I. Rabin, Stuart Doneson and Ricky Jentons in L. Bellak's *Disorders of the Schizophrenic Syndrome.*

Boring, E.G., *A History of Experimental Psychology.* New York: Century Company, 1929.
James, W., *The Principles of Psychology,* 2 vols. New York: Henry Holt, 1890.
Rabin, A.I. et al., "Studies of Psychological Functions in Schizophrenia," in L. Bellak (ed.), *Disorders of the Schizophrenic Syndrome.* New York: Basic Books, 1979.

psychomotor agitation Excessive movement that is associated with inner tension. Often the activity is repetitious and nonproductive. When the agitation is at a high level, some persons may scream, shout or complain loudly. People with psychomotor agitation can be seen pacing, pulling at their clothes or hair, wringing their hands, being unable to sit in one place for more than a few seconds, etc. When this type of behavior is a side effect of antipsychotic drugs, the behavior is called AKATHESIA.

psychoneurosis   A nonpsychotic mental disorder of a purely psychological (and not organic) origin. The word was introduced by Swiss neuropathologist Paul Charles Dubois (1848–1918) and was often used by Sigmund FREUD.

psychopathology   The study of mental disorders. Despite the fact that mental disorders have been reported since antiquity, the clinical and descriptive categories now in use were only developed in the 19th century.

Berrios, G. E., "Descriptive Psychopathology: Conceptual and Historical Aspects," *Psychological Medicine*, 11(1984), 677–688.

psychose passionelle   See EROTOMANIA.

psychosis   Today, psychosis refers to a mental disorder in which there is gross impairment in reality testing (a "break with reality") and the creation of a new reality. Although the word "psychoses" first appeared in the early part of the 19th century, it has only been used in this sense since the end of that century, encompassing phenomena that were formerly described by the terms "insanity," "alienation" and "dementia." Throughout most of the 19th century the word "neuroses" referred to an enormous class of diseases that included all the insanities, most neurological conditions, all the present-day neuroses and some medical disorders—thus, they were considered "organic" in origin. The word "psychoses" instead referred to psychological or experiential states, and the terms "neuroses" and "psychoses" were not dichotomous and did not depend upon one another for definition. By the end of the 1800s the new classifica-

tory systems of Karl KAHLBAUM and especially Emil KRAEPELIN introduced the modern concept of psychosis and drastically reduced the number of the "insanities."

Two classification dichotomies that were popular in the 19th century and survived into the early part of the 20th are (a) functional vs. organic psychoses (see FUNCTIONAL PSYCHOSES); and (b) exogenous (in neurology, diseases due to toxins and infections) vs. endogenous psychoses (due to inner or constitutional factors), a distinction that Kraepelin introduced into psychiatry in the 1896 edition of his famous textbook.

The DSM-III-R rationale for the current diagnostic categories for the various psychotic disorders can be found in a 1989 article by Kenneth S. Kendler and colleagues.

Berrios, G.E., "Historical Aspects of Psychoses: 19th-century Issues," *British Medical Bulletin*, 43(1987), 484–498.
Kendler, K.S., et al., "Psychotic Disorders in *DSM-III-R*," *American Journal of Psychiatry*, 146(1989), 953–962.

psychosis gene   See EINHEITSPSYCHOSE; GENETIC TRANSMISSION.

psychosis of association   See FOLIE À DEUX.

psychosocial stressors   Psychological or social sources of stress that can exacerbate mental disorders, including psychotic disorders. Severe tragedies (the death of loved ones) can even lead to the development of such disorders, as can the developmental phases of life (e.g., the stresses of adolescence, childbirth). The types of psychosocial stressors that clinicians are advised by DSM-III-R (1987) to document by severity are: (a) conjugal (marital and nonmarital): for example, engagement, marriage, discord, separation, divorce, death of a spouse; (b) parenting; (c) other interpersonal problems; (d) occupational; (e) financial; (f) living circumstances, for example, change in residence; (g) developmental phases of life; (h) physical illness or injury; (i) family factors.

psychosurgery   A word coined by Egas MONIZ in 1936 to describe the treatment of mental disorders through surgery on the brain. (See also FREEMAN, WALTER.)

psychotherapy of schizophrenia   Because people with schizophrenia have so many personal problems associated with daily living, most find themselves in some form of psychotherapy at some point in their lives, and this can be supportive for them. The earliest recorded cases of individual psychotherapy with schizophrenic persons can be attributed to Swiss psychiatrist and psychoanalyst C. G. JUNG at the BURGHÖLZLI HOSPITAL in Switzerland. There is a vast literature on the psychotherapy of schizophrenia, and the various therapeutic modalities that have been tried include individual, group, family and a whole host of "brandname" psychotherapeutic orientations.

Throughout most of the century the emphasis has been on the alleviation of the disease process itself with psychotherapy, but with the new emphasis on the organic basis of schizophrenia (and the discouraging results of psychotherapy on the disease itself), this goal is no longer deemed justified. Instead, the focus has shifted to improving the psychosocial adaptation of individuals with schizophrenia, their vocational functioning and the subjective well-being of these persons. Also, family therapy approaches have shifted away from viewing family dynamics as the cause of schizophrenia and now focuses instead on the potential influence of the family on the course of the illness and how family members may be taught strategies to make that influence more positive and reduce relapses (see EXPRESSED EMOTION).

In general, the well-controlled scientific research on the influence of psychotherapy on schizophrenics has tended to conclude that insight-oriented individual or group psychotherapy may be too intense for such individuals and perhaps worsen symptoms. Indeed, E. Fuller Torrey goes so far as to label psychoanalysis, insight-oriented therapy and group psychotherapy as "ineffective treatments" in his book *Surviving Schizophrenia: A Family Manual* (1988). It is now generally recommended that psychotherapeutic treatments be psychoeducational and supportive in nature and used as an adjunct to treatment with ANTIPSYCHOTIC DRUGS. (See also FAMILY INTERACTION THEORIES; GROUP PSYCHOTHERAPY.)

Kane, J.M., "Treatment of Schizophrenia," *Schizophrenia Bulletin,* 13(1987), 133–156.

psychotic disorders   According to the most recent revision of the most widely used diagnostic manual for mental disorders, DSM-III-R (1987), the following diagnoses constitute the current psychotic disorders recognized by psychiatry:

Brief reactive psychosis;

Delusional (paranoid) disorder;

Induced psychotic disorder;

Major depressive episode with psychotic features;

Manic episode with psychotic features;

Organic delusional disorder;

Organic hallucinosis;

Schizoaffective disorder;

Schizophrenia;

Schizophreniform disorder;

and Psychotic disorder not otherwise specified.

psychotic jealousy   See OTHELLO SYNDROME.

psychotogenic drugs Literally, "psychosis-causing drugs." With the severe and widespread substance-abuse epidemic following the "psychedelic revolution" of the 1960s, psychiatric facilities around the world have been flooded with individuals, many of them young (see YOUNG ADULT CHRONIC PATIENTS), whose substance abuse has led to permanent psychotic disorders. Such persons with a psychotic disorder and a history of chronic substance abuse are called *dually diagnosed* patients. Current research studies are beginning to find that premorbid psychotogenic drug use (e.g., cocaine, PCP, LSD, marijuana) contributes to the development of psychotic disorders and may hinder the effectiveness of ANTIPSYCHOTIC DRUGS (a phenomenon called "neuroleptic refractoriness"), especially at the beginning of the illness.

Bowers, Jr., M.B. et al., "Psychotogenic Drug Use and Neuroleptic Response," *Schizophrenia Bulletin*, 16(1990), 81–87.

psychotomimetic Literally "psychosis-mimicking." Hallucinogenic (psychedelic) drugs were for a time referred to as "psychotomimetic drugs" because it was thought they could mimic the subjective experience of psychosis in anyone who ingested them. Prior to the banning of research using psychedelic drugs in the 1960s, some investigators administered such drugs to research subjects so as to better understand various dimensions of the psychotic disorders (see PSYCHOTOGENIC DRUGS). This sort of research has a long history dating from the 17th century. In Immanuel Kant's published lectures on "anthropology" (what we would now call empirical psychology), he cites the efforts of researchers to induce an "artificial insanity" through psychotomimetic drugs:

On the other hand, attempts to observe oneself in a condition which approaches derangement, produced in oneself voluntarily and by physical means, in order to better understand the involuntary through such observations, indicate that one has understanding enough to investigate the sources of the phenomenon. But it is dangerous to perform experiments with the mind, and to make it disordered to a certain extent, for the sake of observing it and investigating its nature by means of the features which may be discovered in such experiments. Thus Helmont reports, after consuming a certain dose of *napell* (a poisonous root), having the unmistakable feeling as if he thought in his stomach. Another doctor increased his consumption of camphor, little by little, until it appeared to him as if everything along the street were in a great tumult. Still others have experimented on themselves with opium so long that they felt a weakening of the mind whenever they stopped using more of this brain-stimulant. An artificial insanity can easily become a real one.

Kant, I., *The Classification of Mental Disorders*, tr. C.T. Sullivan. Doylestown, Penn.: The Doylestown Foundation, 1964 [1798].

psychotropic See NEUROLEPTIC.

puerperal insanity Another name for POSTPARTUM PSYCHOSIS.

pulse Since the days of ancient Greece and Rome and well into the 19th century, it was commonly believed that a physician could diagnose mental disorders simply by taking the afflicted person's pulse and determining the heartbeat rate. In his famous textbook of 1812, American physician Benjamin Rush of Philadelphia reports that: ". . . seven-eighths of all the deranged patients in the Pennsylvania Hospital in the year 1811 had frequent pulses, and that a pardon was granted to a criminal by the President of the United States, in the year 1794, who was suspected of counterfeiting madness, in consequence of its having been declared by three physicians that that symptom constituted an unequivocal mark of intellectual derangement."

The diagnostic importance of the pulse was still so highly regarded at the end of the last century that 20 columns were given to it in Daniel Hack Tuke's famous *Dictionary of Psychological Medicine.*

Rush, B., *Medical Inquiries and Observations upon the Diseases of the Mind.* Philadelphia: Kimber & Richardson, 1812.

Tuke, D.H., "Pulse," in D.H. Tuke (ed.), *A Dictionary of Psychological Medicine.* London: Churchill, 1892.

purging One of Pinel's three USUAL TREATMENTS for mental disorders around 1800, purgatives were given to patients to help them expell bad humors or other bodily toxins that were thought to be the cause of mental illness. Purgatives have been used for thousands of years for the treatment of mental illness, and the herb *hellbore* was used for this purpose until the end of the 19th century.

pyknic type One of the four physiological types identified by Ernst Kretschmer in the 1920s. It was a thick-torsoed type with rounded shoulders that tended to resemble an orangutan. Most pyknic types were thought by Kretschmer to be "circulars" (manic-depressives). (See also ASTHENIC TYPE; ATHLETIC TYPE.)

R

race and schizophrenia In the United States, blacks have a higher rate of schizophrenia than do whites. This conclusion has been confirmed across many studies. However, psychiatrist E. Fuller Torrey argues in his book *Surviving Schizophrenia: A Family Manual* that this may have more to do with geography and socioeconomic status than with racial differences or racism. Most of the studies that have found a higher rate in blacks have been conducted in dense urban areas, but those studies done in rural areas find that the schizophrenia rates in whites and blacks are the same. Therefore, Torrey concludes, "This argues strongly against race as being the cause of the difference. Rather it suggests that it is because blacks live in the inner city, and not because they are black, that they have a higher schizophrenia rate."

Torrey, E.F., *Surviving Schizophrenia: A Family Manual.* New York: Harper & Row, 1988.

rauwolfia alkaloids In 1931, Indian physicians Ganneth Sen and Katrick BOSE reported administering an alkaloid isolated from the plant *Rauwolfia serpentina* to psychotic patients, but with unremarkable results. The drug's relative weakness as an antipsychotic and its propensity for causing depression has led to its rare usage today as a treatment for schizophrenia. The drug was originally developed for its hypotensive and sedative properties. By 1950 the useful properties of the drug in treating high blood pressure and psychosis were recognized in the West and the compound taken from it was named reserpine (trade name: Raudixin); it is the oldest antipsychotic drug known.

Sen, G. and Bose, K., "Rauwolfia Serpentina: A New Indian Drug for Insanity and High Blood Pressure," *Indian Medical World,* 2(1931), 194–201.

Ray, Isaac (1807–1881) An American physician and legal scholar, Ray was one of the original 13 founders of the American Psychiatric Association. His classic textbook, *Treatise on the Medical Jurisprudence of the Insane* (1838), is considered to be perhaps the most influential American psychiatric text of the 19th century.

Hughes, J.S., *In the Law's Darkness: Isaac Ray and the Medical Jurisprudence of Insanity in Nineteenth Century America.* New York: Oceana Publications, 1986.

rCBF The acronym for *regional cerebral blood flow*, a measurement used to study the relationship between cerebral metabolism and psychiatric disorders. (See also METABOLIC DISORDER HYPOTHESIS.)

reactive schizophrenia See PROCESS-REACTIVE DISTINCTION IN SCHIZOPHRENIA, THE.

reality testing The ability to "test" or evaluate the external world ("reality") objectively and to distinguish it from the internal psychological state. It is also the ability to discriminate ego boundaries between what is the self and what is non-self (the "I" vs. the "not-I"). The term was coined by Sigmund FREUD in 1911 as *Realitätsprüfung*. The hallmark of PSYCHOSIS is that reality testing is impaired.

recessive In GENETICS STUDIES, the opposite of DOMINANT.

recombination The process by which a pair of homologous chromosomes exchange sections yielding a new combination of genes.

recoverable psychosis According to the classification system of Emil KRAEPELIN, the group of recoverable psychoses was characterized by its primary entity, MANIC-DEPRESSIVE PSYCHOSIS. These were psychotic disorders that had exacerbations and remissions but did not lead to the gross cognitive deterioration of chronic, progressively worsening disorders such as dementia praecox.

recovery with defect The term describes those persons whose basic personality is permanently altered after recovery from their primary mental disorder. Today, such a condition in schizophrenia might be termed the RESIDUAL PHASE. This term was coined by the German physician K.G. Neumann (1744–1850).

reference, ideas of See IDEAS OF REFERENCE.

refrigerator mother The name for the cold, rejecting mother who would thereby induce *autism* in her child. (See also AUTISM, INFANTILE.)

regression A concept introduced by Sigmund FREUD in 1900 in his classic book *The Interpretation of Dreams,* although he did not use the word until much later. Essentially, regression means a reversion to earlier forms of thought, object-relationships or behavior that the individual had previously experienced. Thus, according to psychoanalysis, persons with psychotic disorders are "regressed" because they show signs of returning to infantile modes of thought, behavior and experience. (See also PSYCHOANALYTIC THEORIES OF SCHIZOPHRENIA.)

relapse, signs of Those people with schizophrenia who seem to fare the best are those who are aware of the signs of an impending relapse of an active phase of the illness and who therefore seek help. In a useful study of relapse by Marvin Herz and Charles Melville published in 1980, they found the following signs and symptoms of relapse to be the most frequently reported by patients and their families:

Patients Reported:	Percent
being tense and nervous	80
eating less	72
trouble concentrating	70
trouble sleeping	67
enjoying things less	65
restlessness	63
not able to remember things	63
depression	61
being preoccupied with one or two things	60
seeing friends less	60
being laughed at, talked about	60

Families Reported:	Percent
being tense and nervous	83
restlessness	79
trouble concentrating	76
depression	76
talking in a nonsensical way	76
loss of interest in things	76
trouble sleeping	69
enjoying things less	68
being preoccupied with one or two things	65
not able to remember things	60
hearing voices, seeing things	60

It is extremely important for family members and persons with schizophrenia to recognize these signs of relapse and to seek medical help immediately.

Herz, M.I. and Melville, C., "Relapse in Schizophrenia," *American Journal of Psychiatry*, 137(1980), 801–805.

Herz, M., "Prodromal Symptoms and the Prevention of Relapse in Schizophrenia," *Journal of Clinical Psychiatry*, 46(1985), 22–25.

religious delusions   Religious delusions are quite common in the psychotic disorders, but especially in the paranoid subtype of schizophrenia. Persons may believe, for example, that they are God, Jesus Christ or a prophet who relates messages from God to the world. Many of these delusions are also grandiose in nature.

remission   The abatement of an illness. In schizophrenia, the period after a remission may still evidence residual deficits from the illness. Full remissions from schizophrenia apparently do occur, but they are extremely rare and the few that are on record are an issue of controversy. A return to full premorbid functioning is also rare in schizophrenia. (See also RESIDUAL PHASE.)

Renfield's syndrome   A term first used by Richard Noll (1991) to refer to clinical VAMPIRISM, since contemporary reports of

people with this disorder seem to develop the same sequence of symptoms as the human vampire Renfield in Bram Stoker's novel, *Dracula* (1897).

Noll, R., *Vampires, Werewolves and Demons: Twentieth Century Case Reports in the Psychiatric Literature*. New York: Brunner/Mazel, 1991.

repression   A term used by Sigmund FREUD (*Verdrängung* in the original German) for a psychological operation in which a person attempts to push away, expel or keep in the unconscious representations (thoughts, images, memories) that are connected to an instinct. Repression occurs when it is determined that the expression of an instinctual urge, which is probably in itself pleasurable (e.g., sex), may have painful consequences. Repression is considered one of the most basic defense mechanisms for keeping threatening materials out of conscious awareness. Freud once wrote that "the theory of repression is the cornerstone on which the whole structure of psychoanalysis rests." According to psychoanalytic theory, the failure of repression in the psychotic disorders leads to hallucinations and bizarre and inappropriate behavior. (See also PSYCHOANALYTIC THEORIES OF SCHIZOPHRENIA.)

Laplanche, J. and Pontalis, J.B., *The Language of Psycho-Analysis*, tr. D. Nicholson-Smith. New York: Norton, 1973.

research diagnostic criteria (RDC)   In an effort to ensure that diagnostic groups of persons with mental disorders have the same characteristics across different studies performed in different settings, several attempts have been made to set standard guidelines for selecting subjects for research. An early system was the FEIGHNER RESEARCH CRITERIA, but currently the most widely accepted criteria is the Research Diagnostic Criteria developed at the New York Psychiatric Institute. When research studies refer to "RDC schizophrenics," they are referring to schizophrenic subjects that fit the RDC definitional guidelines.

Endicott, J. et al., "Diagnostic Criteria for Schizophrenia: Reliabilities and Agreement between Systems," *Archives of General Psychiatry,* 39(1982), 864–889.

Spitzer, R.L., Endicott, J. and Robins, E., "Research Diagnostic Criteria: Rationale and Reliability," *Archives of General Psychiatry,* 35(1978), 773–782.

residual phase According to DSM-III-R (1987), the course of schizophrenia is characterized by a PRODROMAL PHASE, an active phase and a residual phase. The residual phase follows the active phase of the illness. In many ways the clinical picture of the residual phase resembles many of the signs and symptoms of the initial prodromal phase, except that the blunting or flattening of affect and a marked impairment in social and occupational functioning are found. Some delusions and hallucinations may persist in the residual phase, but they may not be accompanied any longer by strong affect (e.g., a strong screaming reaction to the hearing of voices may not be found in the residual phase). The most common course of schizophrenia is a disease process characterized by acute exacerbations of symptoms followed by periods of residual impairment between active phases of the illness. During the first years of the disorder (some say 5 to 10 years), the residual impairment between episodes increases and then seems to plateau at some point for the remainder of the person's life.

restraints See CHEMICAL RESTRAINTS; MECHANICAL RESTRAINTS.

retrospective ruminative jealousy A (usually) nonpsychotic delusional disorder related to the OTHELLO SYNDROME in which a person is obsessed with the past sexual activities of the current sexual partner or spouse. However, there is no delusion about present infidelity.

RFLP See MOLECULAR MARKERS.

right to refuse treatment In the United States, the legal principle has developed over a series of cases since 1975 that holds that no one admitted to a psychiatric facility for treatment, whether the commitment was voluntary or involuntary, can be forced to submit to any form of treatment against his or her will unless it is determined that a life-and-death emergency exists.

Applebaum, P.S., "The Right to Refuse Treatment with Antipsychotic Medications: Retrospect and Prospect," *American Journal of Psychiatry,* 145(1988), 413–419.

right to treatment In the United States, the legal principle has developed that when a psychiatric facility has assumed the responsibility of providing treatment for a person, that facility is then legally obligated to provide adequate treatment for that individual.

risk factors These are elements present in the history of individuals with a given psychiatric disorder (such as schizophrenia) that may then be early signs of the development of a future disorder if they are present in the history of other individuals. The probabilities of developing a given disease are estimated for some risk factors. Risk factors for schizophrenia include: perinatal factors; family history of schizophrenia; SEASONALITY OF BIRTH; and possibly infectious processes. Of these risk factors for schizophrenia, genetics constitute the strongest influence (see also GENETICS STUDIES).

Kety, S.S. and Kinney, D.K., "Biological Risk Factors in Schizophrenia," in National Institute of Mental Health, *Risk Factor Research in the Major Mental Disorders.* DHHS Pub. No. (ADM) 83-1068. Rockville, Md.: National Institute of Mental Health, 1983.

ritualistic behavior Sometimes people with schizophrenia are described as engaging in ritualistic behavior—that is, they repeat stereotyped actions based, perhaps, on MAGICAL THINKING. For example, such a person may repeatedly take off all of his or her clothes, crouch down on the floor in a praying position, and then get up and put the clothes back on, only to continually repeat these actions over and over again for long periods of time.

Rorschach test See PROJECTIVE TESTS.

Rosen, John See DIRECT ANALYSIS.

rotatory machines See CIRCULATING SWING; GYRATOR.

Rush, Benjamin (1746–1813) The first American physician to specialize in mental disorders. In fact, his profile appears in the logo of the AMERICAN PSYCHIATRIC ASSOCIATION. He graduated from the Presbyterian College of New Jersey (later renamed Princeton) when he was 15 years old and later went to Edinburgh and received a medical degree from the university there in 1768. During his stay in Scotland and England, Rush visited the major psychiatric hospitals of his day, including the BETHLEM ROYAL HOSPITAL, and was influenced by English physician William Cullen's ideas on the classification and treatment of mental disorders. Rush was a signer of the Declaration of Independence, and as physician at the Pennsylvania Hospital in Philadelphia (starting in 1783), he was the leading American physician of his day. Rush's own son John became insane at the age of 30 and was admitted to the Pennsylvania Hospital as a "lunatic," and he remained there until his death 27 years later.

Besides conducting an abundance of research on all aspects of medicine, Rush took a particular interest in diseases of the human mind. Rush's treatments covered a wide range from the "moral treatment" (influenced in Philadelphia, no doubt, by the Quakers) of institutionalized patients to some fairly terrifying methods of BLEEDING and MECHANICAL RESTRAINT, including his famous invention the stationary "coercion-chair" or TRANQUILLIZER and the GYRATOR. His 1812 textbook was the only American textbook on psychiatry for more than 70 years.

Goodman, N.G., *Benjamin Rush: Physician and Citizen, 1746–1813.* Philadelphia: University of Pennsylvania Press, 1934.
Rush, B., *Medical Inquiries and Observations on the Diseases of the Mind.* Philadelphia: Kimber & Richardson, 1812.

Sakel, Manfred Joshua (1906–1957) The inventor of INSULIN COMA THERAPY for schizophrenia.

Salpêtrière, la The famous Paris asylum for insane females. Although it was a place of incarceration for socially undesirable females since 1656, following the French Revolution of the early 1790s it became primarily a hospital for mentally ill women. The Salpêtrière played an important role in the history of psychiatry, for Philippe PINEL made many of his clinical observations as head of the institution in the 1790s and Jean Martin Charcot established a neurological clinic there in 1878. It was there that Charcot developed an interest in hypnotism and HYSTERIA.

Scandinavia The Scandinavian countries contain areas with some of the highest prevalence rates of schizophrenia in the world. This fact was observed as early as 1862 in a book by W. Charles Hood, *Statistics of Insanity,* in which he reported that the northern European countries had the highest rates of insanity and the southern European countries had the lowest. The Scandinavian countries, particularly Sweden, have been found to have prevalence rates for schizophrenia that are two to three times that of the United States. The highest prevalence rates for any area of the world have been found in northern Sweden in two studies that were conducted 25 years apart by J.A. Böök and colleagues. The rural area of Sweden that was north of the Arctic Circle was found by Böök to have a prevalence rate of 9.5 per thousand. Other Swedish studies have found lower rates, but these are still quite high when compared with other areas of the world. High rates have also been found in areas of Norway and Finland, but somewhat less so for Denmark.

Böök, J.A., "Schizophrenia in a Northern Swedish Population, 1900–1975," *Clinical Genetics,* 14(1978), 373–394.
Torrey, E.F., "Prevalence Studies of Schizophrenia," *British Journal of Psychiatry,* 150(1987), 598–608.

schizoaffective disorder The term "schizoaffective" was coined by Kasanin in 1933 to describe cases of BORDERLINE SCHIZOPHRENIA. Kasanin's concept was accepted for a time as a possible fifth subtype of schizophrenia. According to DSM-III-R (1987), it is now a psychotic disorder that has symptoms of both a schizophrenic and a mood disturbance, and at other times with psychotic symptoms but without mood symptoms. The diagnosis is made only if the criteria for schizophrenia or for a mood disorder cannot be met and if it cannot be determined if an organic factor is responsible for this confusing mixture of symptoms. Family studies indicate that schizoaffective disorder is distinct from BIPOLAR DISORDER but that it may bear a closer relationship to schizophrenia. There are two subtypes of schizoaffective disorder: schizoaffective disorder, bipolar type, which, with its current or previous manic episode, makes it more closely related to a mood disorder than to schizophrenia; and schizoaffective disorder, depressive type, which does seem to be more closely related to schizophrenia.

The typical age of onset for schizoaffective disorder is early adulthood. The course of the disorder tends to be chronic, but the prognosis is better than that for schizophrenia, and worse than that for a mood disorder. It is not known how prevalent this disorder is, but it is less common than schizophrenia. Some family studies have indicated that there is an increased risk of schizophrenia in the first-degree biological relatives of people with this disorder.

Kasanin, J., "The Acute Schizo-affective Psychoses," *American Journal of Psychiatry,* 97(1933), 97–106.
Williams, P.V. and McGlashan, T.H., "Schizoaffective Psychosis. I. Comparative Long-Term Outcome," *Archives of General Psychiatry,* 44(1987), 130–137.
McGlashan, T.H. and Williams, P.V., "Schizoaffective Psychosis. II. Manic, Bipolar and Depressive Subtypes," *Archives of General Psychiatry,* 44(1987), 138–139.

schizoid personality disorder According to DSM-III-R (1987), the defining characteristic of this nonpsychotic mental disorder is "a pervasive pattern of indifference to social relationships and a restricted range of emotional experience and expression, beginning in early adulthood and present in a variety of contexts." These people appear to be cold and aloof, and they do not seem to desire or enjoy close relationships with other people. They almost always choose solitary activities and occupations, and they express little desire for sexual relationships with others. A person who meets the criteria for schizoid personality disorder must have demonstrated a lifelong course, and even though many of the signs and symptoms may resemble the PRODROMAL PHASE of schizophrenia, it is not thought that persons with this personality disorder go on to develop schizophrenia.

schizomimetic Behavior in a person that mimics or resembles the signs and symptoms of schizophrenia but in fact is not due to the presence of that disorder.

schizophrene An obsolete term for persons with schizophrenia. We now call them "schizophrenics." An analogous outmoded term for persons with bipolar disorder is "circulars."

schizophrenia A term coined by Swiss psychiatrist Eugen BLEULER to replace the term DEMENTIA PRAECOX for the most prevalent group of the psychotic disorders. In the 1890s Emil KRAEPELIN had unified what were previously separate disorders—hebephrenia, catatonia and paranoia (of a specific type)—under the general heading of dementia praecox, which he regarded as all chronic and progressively degenerative diseases. Thus, the basis of Kraepelin's classification was the *prognosis* of these disorders.

Bleuler disagreed with the overtly negative prognosis as the defining characteristic of this disorder and instead renamed it *schizophrenia* (from two Greek words meaning "to split" and "mind") to stress what for him was the fundamental nature of these psychotic disorders: the splitting or dissociation of psychic functions (for which Bleuler used the German word *Spaltung*).

Although Bleuler had been using the word "schizophrenia" in clinical presentations and lectures at the BURGHÖLZLI HOSPITAL in Zurich, Switzerland, where he was the chief physician, he introduced the concept in print in a 1908 article titled "The Prognosis of Dementia Praecox: The Group of Schizophrenias *(Die Prognose der Dementia Praecox—Schizophreniegruppe)*." In the first paragraph of that historic article, in which he questions the importance of Kraepelin's idea of prognosis, Bleuler writes:

In using the term dementia praecox I would like it to mean what the creator of the concept meant it to mean. To treat the subject from any other point of view would serve no purpose, but I would like to emphasize that Kraepelin's dementia praecox is not necessarily either a form of dementia or a disorder of early onset. For this reason, and because there is no adjective or noun that can be derived from the term dementia praecox, I am taking the liberty of using the word *schizophrenia* to denote Kraepelin's concept. I believe that the tearing apart or splitting of psychic functions is a prominent symptom of the whole group and I will give my reasons for this elsewhere.

So what is "split" *(Spaltung)* in schizophrenia? Bleuler argues that it is primarily encountered in the disturbance of associations that characterize normal trains of thought, although there are also splits in the normal functions of affect and of behavior (especially relating to the external world). Thus, the FOUR AS (associations disturbances, autism, ambivalence, affective disturbances) that constitute the FUNDAMENTAL SYMPTOMS OF SCHIZOPHRENIA according to Bleuler are all manifestations of the splitting of psychic functions.

In 1911 Bleuler published his classic book that still influences our current thinking about schizophrenia: *Dementia Praecox oder die Gruppe der Schizophrenien (Dementia Praecox, or the Group of Schizophrenias)*. In it, Bleuler defines his conception of the disease in the following way:

By the term "dementia praecox" or "schizophrenia" we designate a group of psychoses whose course is at times chronic, at times marked by intermittent attacks, and which can stop or retrograde at any stage, but does not permit a full *restitutio ad integrum*. The disease is characterized by a specific type of alteration of thinking, feeling, and relation to the external world which appears nowhere else in this particular fashion.

Bleuler divided the clinical picture of schizophrenia into its "fundamental symptoms" *(Grund-symptome)*, which were caused directly by the disease process itself, and its accessory symptoms *(Akzessorische Symptoms)*. The fundamental symptoms (the "four As") are present to some degree during the entire course of the illness, whereas the secondary symptoms (delusions, hallucinations, transient catatonic episodes, behavioral disturbances) come and go throughout the course of the illness and are found in other mental disorders as well. In addition, Bleuler added a fourth subtype of the disease—"simple schizophrenia"—that had been proposed by Otto Diem in 1904.

A new way of conceptualizing schizophrenia was proposed by German psychiatrist Kurt Schneider in 1939 based on the idea that certain core symptoms were pathognomonic of schizophrenia and that the presence of any one of these FIRST-RANK SYMPTOMS was enough for making the diagnosis of the disease.

The current clinical picture of schizophrenia provided in DSM-III-R (1987) still owes much to Bleuler's concept of four subtypes. The paranoid type and the catatonic type still bear the same names as in Bleuler's time, although the HEBEPHRENIC TYPE is now called the disorganized type, and "simple schizophrenia" is replaced by an "undifferentiated type." According to *DSM-III-R:*

The essential features of this disorder are the presence of characteristic psychotic symptoms during the active phase of the illness and functioning below the highest level previously achieved (in children or adolescents, failure to achieve the expected level of social development), and a duration of at least six months that may include characteristic prodromal or residual symptoms. At some phase of the illness Schizophrenia always involves delusions, hallucinations, or certain characteristic disturbances in affect and the form of thought. The diagnosis is made only when it cannot be established that an organic factor initiated and maintained the disturbance. The diagnosis is not made if the symptoms are due to a Mood Disorder or Schizoaffective Disorder.

Schizophrenia is also characterized in the current diagnostic manual as having a three-stage course composed of a PRODROMAL PHASE, an active phase and a RESIDUAL PHASE.

Schizophrenia remains the most prevalent of the psychotic disorders (see EPIDEMIOLOGY), and although it is almost certain that it is a brain disease with a strong genetic component, the actual cause of schizophrenia is unknown.

Bleuler, E., *Dementia Praecox oder die Gruppe der Schizophrenien,* a volume in G. Aschaffenburg (ed.), *Handbuch der Geisteskrankheiten.* Leipzig: F. Deuticke, 1911.
———, "Die Prognose der Dementia Praecox—Schizophreniengruppe," *Allgemeine Zeitschrift für Psychiatrie,* 65(1908), 436–464.

Cutting, J. and Shepherd, M. (eds.), *The Clinical Roots of the Schizophrenia Concept: Translations of Seminal European Contributions on Schizophrenia.* Cambridge: Cambridge University Press, 1987. (Contains an almost complete translation of Bleuler's 1908 article.)

schizophreniform disorder According to DSM-III-R (1987), persons with this disorder have identical signs and symptoms of schizophrenia, except that they last less than six months and there is a full recovery from the disorder. The true relationship of these mysterious short-term psychotic disorders with schizophrenia is unknown. (See also ACUTE RECOVERABLE PSYCHOSIS.)

schizophrenogenic mother Due to the influence of psychoanalysis and, later, FAMILY INTERACTION THEORIES, it was thought that the behavior of certain family members—particularly the mother—was responsible for causing a schizophrenic breakdown in children. The term "schizophrenogenic mother" (although previously used in a paper by Frieda FROMM-REICHMANN) was introduced into the mainstream by psychoanalytic psychiatrist Trude Tietze in a 1949 published study of 25 mothers of schizophrenic patients. They were all seen as "domineering" and with "warped psychosexual development" that psychologically injured their children. Today, it is clear that there is no scientific evidence to support the notion of the schizophrenogenic mother.

Tietze, T., "A Study of Mothers of Schizophrenic Patients," *Psychiatry,* 12(1949), 55–65.

schizotaxia A term coined by psychologist Paul Meehl in 1962 to refer to the genetically transmitted "neural integrative defect" that predisposes a whole class of individuals to develop schizotypy or schizophrenia. Schizotaxia, according to Meehl, is the only thing that is inherited in schizophrenics, and it does not necessarily lead to the development of this disorder unless there are certain environmental factors that also push the individual in the direction of psychopathology. Schizotypy refers to the unusual personality organization that these environmental influences may cause, but persons who are schizotypes still may not necessarily develop schizophrenia. Instead, Meehl suggests: "It seems likely that the most important causal influence pushing the schizotype toward schizophrenic decompensation is the schizophrenogenic mother."

Meehl first proposed these ideas in a Presidential Address to the American Psychological Association in September 1962, and the idea of "schizotaxia, schizotypy, schizophrenia" was important in developing later diathesis stress models of schizophrenia and of the role of genetics in SPECTRUM DISORDERS.

Meehl, P., "Schizotaxia, Schizotypy, Schizophrenia," *American Psychologist,* 17(1962), 827–838.

schizotypal personality disorder This type of personality disorder best exemplifies what Paul Meehl meant by "schizotypy" (see SCHIZOTAXIA). According to DSM-III-R (1987), the person with schizotypal personality disorder displays a "pervasive pattern of peculiarities of ideation, appearance, and behavior and deficits in interpersonal relatedness, beginning by early adulthood and present in a variety of contexts, that are not severe enough to meet the criteria for schizophrenia." These persons may exhibit IDEAS OF REFERENCE, be extremely uncomfortable in social situations, exhibit extremely odd beliefs or engage in magical thinking, may look odd or unkempt, talk to themselves, speak oddly, have no close friends, have silly or inappropriate affect or perhaps even be a little suspicious or paranoid. It is estimated that approximately 3% of the population of the United States has this disorder and that it is more common among the FIRST-DEGREE RELATIVES of persons with schizophrenia. (See also LATENT SCHIZOPHRENIA;

SLUGGISH SCHIZOPHRENIA; SIMPLE SCHIZOPHRENIA.)

schizotypy See SCHIZOTAXIA.

schizovirus According to the VIRAL THEORIES OF SCHIZOPHRENIA, there is a possibility that some individuals with schizophrenia develop the disorder due to a chronic infectious agent of the nervous system. Although such a possibility had been noted by Emil KRAEPELIN at the turn of the century, the hypothesis was not investigated seriously until E. Fuller Torrey resurrected this notion with a series of studies at the National Institute of Mental Health in the 1970s. In a 1988 article he reports, "My psychiatric research colleagues regarded the efforts whimsically as the search for the 'schizovirus' or 'schizococcus.'" However, as Torrey admits, there is yet very little direct evidence to link viruses with schizophrenia. Yet, he writes, "The search for the putative 'schizovirus' continues. Whether the quest will eventually lead to Jason's fabled Golden Fleece, or merely be another blind alley down which schizophrenia research has wandered, remains to be seen."

Torrey, E.F., "Stalking the Schizovirus," *Schizophrenia Bulletin,* 14(1988), 223–229.
Torrey, E.F. and Peterson, M.R., "Slow and Latent Viruses in Schizophrenia," *Lancet,* 2(1973), 22–24.

Schnauzkrampf Interest in the PHYSIOGNOMY of mental illness was a major concern in the 19th century. In schizophrenic people with CATATONIA, it was reported by German psychiatrist Karl KAHLBAUM that they tended to exhibit a protrusion of the lips that resembled an animal snout *(Schnauzkrampf).*

Schneider, Kurt (1887–1967) A German psychiatrist who made a lasting influence on the clinical diagnosis of schizophrenia with his proposal that there were certain pathognomonic FIRST-RANK SYMPTOMS that could be used to identify the disorder. Schneider was noted for his phenomenological approach to mental disorders, as was his mentor, Karl Jaspers.

Scotland Scotland has a higher prevalence rate for schizophrenia than England, its neighbor to the south. The observation that there has always been more ''insanity'' among the Scottish dates at least from the mid-19th century. A schizophrenia prevalence study by Mayer-Gross in Scotland, in which 56,231 persons were surveyed, found a prevalence rate of 4.2 per thousand.

Torrey, E.F., *Schizophrenia and Civilization.* New York: Jason Aronson, 1980.

seasonal affective disorder The observation that depression and mania are sensitive to seasonal and environmental influences has been reported for at least 2,000 years. Hippocrates noted in the 4th century B.C. that ''it is chiefly in the changes of season which produce diseases, and in the seasons the great changes are from cold or heat.'' As early as 1801, French alienist Philippe PINEL noted winter and summer onsets for mood disorders. DSM-III-R (1987) now includes criteria for ''seasonal pattern'' in mood disorders such as BIPOLAR DISORDER or recurrent major depression in which it must be established that, through the years, there has been a regular appearance of an episode of the disorder in a given 60-day period of the year. In a 1989 review of all of the research studies that link seasonal patterns to mood disorders, it was found that there are two primary, opposite seasonal patterns of annual mood disorders, namely depression: those with winter depression (onset during September, October and November) and summer depression (onset during March, April and May). It is estimated that seasonal affective disorder has been found to occur in about 16% to 38% of all persons who experience recurrent depression. The

vast majority of persons (83%) who develop SAD (the apt acronym for seasonal affective disorder) are females in their 30s. It is generally important to identify those persons who suffer from recurrent winter depression because they have been found to respond to a novel form of treatment—phototherapy (bright light administered to such persons for varying lengths of time and intensity of brightness).

Rosenthal, N.E. and Blehar, M.C. (eds.), *Seasonal Affective Disorder and Phototherapy.* New York: Guilford, 1989.

Rosenthal, N.E. and Wehr, T.A., ''Seasonal Affective Disorders,'' *Psychiatric Annals,* 17(1987), 670–674.

Wehr, T.A. and Rosenthal, N.E., ''Seasonality and Affective Illness,'' *American Journal of Psychiatry,* 146(1989), 829–839.

seasonality of births One of the most consistent findings in schizophrenia research is that there is a seasonal excess of births in the winter and early spring months (roughly January to March) of people who go on to develop schizophrenia later in life. This observation was first made by German researcher M. Tramer in 1929.

The largest sample of schizophrenic births studied to date (a total of 53,584 schizophrenics) was published by E. F. Torrey and colleagues in 1977. In examining the patterns according to individual months and by regions of the United States, the following was found: In the New England states, December, April and May were the peak months for schizophrenic births; in the Midwest, December, January, March and April had the most births; and in states in the South there was a less pronounced seasonal birth effect. Overall, January seems to be the peak month for the birth of persons who develop schizophrenia, with the numbers for December and March also being elevated. This winter/early spring effect is also found in the Southern Hemisphere of the earth, with most studies showing that a greater excess of schizophrenic births occur from September to November (the Southern Hemisphere spring) than at any other time.

Bipolar disorder may also be related to season of birth, but the studies that confirm this do not show as strong an effect as there is for schizophrenia. Again, the critical season is January to March, and quite possibly April also shows an excess of births of persons who go on to develop bipolar disorder in later life.

The persons with schizophrenia who are born during times of seasonal excess may be different from other types of schizophrenics. Some evidence suggests that the seasonal effect is associated with a subgroup of schizophrenics who have an early onset of psychosis, less genetic loading for schizophrenia (based on family history of the disease) and, paradoxically, may have a better prognosis (see PROCESS-REACTIVE DISTINCTION IN SCHIZOPHRENIA for why this is a paradox). It is hypothesized that a seasonal factor—possibly a virus—causes damage during fetal neural development and may later manifest as schizophrenia.

Boyd, J.H. et al., "Season of Birth: Schizophrenia and Bipolar Disorder," *Schizophrenia Bulletin,* 12(1986), 173–186.
Dalen, P., *Season of Birth: A Study of Schizophrenia and Other Mental Disorders.* Amsterdam: Elsevier/North Holland, 1975.
Torrey, E.F. and Bowler, A.E., "The Seasonality of Schizophrenic Births: A Reply to Marc S. Lewis," *Schizophrenia Bulletin,* 16(1990), 1–3.
Tramer, M., "Uber die biologische Bedeutung des Geburtsmonates, insbesondere für die Psychoseerkrankung," *Schweitzer Archiv für Neurologie und Psychiatrie,* 24(1929), 17–24.

secondary process See PRIMARY PROCESS.

secondary symptoms of schizophrenia
See ACCESSORY SYMPTOMS.

segregation analysis This is a major statistical method used in population genetics research that compares the observed frequency of an illness in a pedigree with a pattern that would occur if a hypothesized mode of genetic inheritance (e.g., one of the patterns of monogenetic transmission or polygenetic transmission) were accurate. Although there are limitations to segregation analyses, such analyses on diverse phenotypes in relevant pedigrees have been able to reject the "single-locus model" (that is, the idea that *all* cases of schizophrenia have a common single cause and that *no* familial resemblance is environmentally determined). It has also ruled out the strict polygenetic inheritance model (that is, that schizophrenia is caused by the additive effect of many genes in *all* cases).

Garver, D.L. et al., "Schizophrenia and the Question of Genetic Heterogeneity," *Schizophrenia Bulletin,* 15(1989), 421–430.

seleniasmus Yet another synonym for lunacy. The word is derived from the name for the Greek goddess of the moon, Selene.

self-image in schizophrenia According to Silvano ARIETI, a person's self-image consists of three components: body image, self-identity and self-esteem. In schizophrenia, all three of these components are disrupted. There are body image distortions and perceptual anomalies, GENDER-IDENTITY CONFUSION, and a loss of self-esteem that can be so severe that it may precipitate the PREPSYCHOTIC PANIC that may then lead to a psychosis. American psychiatrist Harry Stack Sullivan devoted considerable work to exploring the development of self and self-image, which he felt originated in the child's passive incorporation of reflected appraisals from significant adults. Several papers on the transformation of self-image in the person stricken with schizophrenia were published in a special issue of *Schizophrenia Bulletin* (vol. 15, no. 2) in 1989 devoted to the theme "Subjective Experiences of Schizophrenia and Related Disorders."

Estroff, S.E., "Self, Identity, and Subjective Experiences of Schizophrenia," *Schizophrenia Bulletin,* 15(1989), 189–198.

self-injurious behavior, or self-mutilation   The deliberate cutting, scratching, burning, tearing or other action performed against one's own body. Self-mutilation is a serious sign of extreme internal distress in many of the persons who do it. It is a side effect of many psychiatric disorders, especially in the psychotic disorders, the dissociative disorders, borderline personality disorder, sexual masochism and the eating disorders bulimia and anorexia nervosa. Self-injurious behavior (SIB) is also quite commonly seen in the mentally retarded, and studies have reported that as many as 40% of the institutionalized mentally retarded, especially those with a rare enzyme deficiency known as Lesch-Nyhan syndrome, bang their heads, chew their fingers, lips or the skin of other parts of their body and abuse themselves in a multitude of other ways. A special issue of the professional journal *Analysis and Intervention in Developmental Disabilities* (vol. 2, no. 1) published in 1982 was devoted to the topic of self-injurious behavior.

Favazza, A., *Bodies under Siege: Self-Mutilation in Culture and Psychiatry.* 1990.

serotonin and schizophrenia   Serotonin is a neurotransmitter that functions in both the central and the peripheral nervous systems. In the peripheral nervous system (PNS) it functions as a vasoconstrictor. In the central nervous system (CNS) it has many functions, primarily the inhibition of certain brain areas during sleep.

The chemical name for serotonin is 5-hydroxytryptamine, or 5HT. Serotonin was the basis for the first theory of a NEURO-TRANSMITTER DISORDER AS A CAUSE OF SCHIZOPHRENIA, which was proposed in a paper by biochemists D. W. Wooley and E. Shaw in 1954. In a 1988 review of the vast literature of research studies on the relationship between serotonin and schizophrenia that appeared in *Schizophrenia Bulletin,* it was proposed that all of the conflicting results of these studies took on new meaning when examined according to CROW'S HYPOTHESIS of a Type I and Type II schizophrenia. The authors of the review conclude that serotonin may be related to such features of Type II schizophrenia as NEGATIVE SYMPTOMS, degenerative brain changes and chronicity. In addition, because some studies conducted in the mid-1980s have suggested that certain drugs that are 5HT agonists have an antipsychotic effect on some negative symptoms, the authors recommend that future pharmacotherapy of schizophrenia should include a 5HT-blocking component as well as the traditional dopamine-blocking agents that constitute most ANTIPSYCHOTIC DRUGS in use. Serotonin has also been implicated in the MANIC EPISODES of bipolar disorder, and it has been found that some antiserotonin drugs have an antimanic effect.

Bleich, A. et al., "The Role of Serotonin in Schizophrenia," *Schizophrenia Bulletin,* 14(1988), 297–314.
Davis, J.M. et al., "Differential Diagnosis and Treatment of Mania," in A.C. Swann (ed.), *Mania: New Research and Treatment.* Washington, D.C.: American Psychiatric Press, 1986.
Wolley, D.W. and Shaw, E., "A Biochemical and Pharmacological Suggestion about Certain Mental Disorders," *Proceedings of the National Academy of Sciences of the United States of America,* 40(1954), 228–231.

sex differences in schizophrenia   See GENDER DIFFERENCES IN SCHIZOPHRENIA.

sexual jealousy   See OTHELLO SYNDROME.

shamanism and schizophrenia   Shamanism is a magico-religious tradition that has been reported for centuries in simple societies that are based on hunting, gathering and fishing. The shaman is an individual who deliberately enters an altered state of consciousness (through drugs, drumming, dancing, fasting) in order to induce visionary states in which he performs certain culturally prescribed actions, usually either healing or divination. Unfortunately, especially prior to the "psychedelic era" of the 1960s, the only frame of reference most anthropologists possessed for understanding the unusual experiences these people had during their visions was psychiatric diagnostic manuals. Thus, such experiences were long interpreted as signs of psychosis, and the myth grew that shamans were nothing more than severely disturbed individuals who may even be psychotic, but whose society has a role for them and therefore they are accepted and "healed" to some extent.

A widely cited 1967 paper by Julian Silverman did much to promote this pathologizing of shamans by comparing the experiences of the altered states of consciousness in the early training of the shaman with the symptoms of acute schizophrenia. Unfortunately, Silverman's paper was taken as the final word on the issue for almost two decades. However, a 1983 paper by clinical psychologist Richard Noll strongly criticized this assumption on phenomenological grounds, and now anthropological studies of religion no longer view the experiences of shamans as "schizophrenic" or "psychotic."

Noll, R., "Shamanism and Schizophrenia: A State-Specific Approach to the 'Schizophrenia Metaphor' of Shamanic States," *American Ethnologist*, 10(1983), 443–459.

———, "What Have We Really Learned about Shamanism?" *Journal of Psychoactive Drugs*, 21(1989), 47–50.

Silverman, J., "Shamanism and Acute Schizophrenia," *American Anthropologist*, 69(1967), 21–31.

shared delusional (or paranoid) disorder See FOLIE À DEUX.

shock therapy See ELECTROSHOCK THERAPY.

sibship The group of all siblings of the afflicted person and their parents.

sign The sign of an illness is an objective indicator of a pathological condition. This differs from a SYMPTOM in that the sign of a disorder is observed by an examiner and is not a subjective report by the individual. For example, a runny nose is the sign of the common cold, whereas the feeling of discomfort or fever are symptoms of this illness.

silly dementia See HEBEPHRENIA.

simple schizophrenia The fourth subtype of schizophrenia added by Eugen BLEULER to the original three of paranoia, hebephrenia and catatonia grouped together by Emil KRAEPELIN as DEMENTIA PRAECOX. This subtype was outlined by Swiss psychiatrist Otto Diem in 1903. Diem worked under Bleuler at the BURGHÖLZLI HOSPITAL, and the idea for his article may have been suggested by Bleuler as an elaboration of an earlier idea by Czech psychiatrist Arnold Pick (1851–1924). In the English translation (in Cutting and Shepard's book) of his original article, Diem acknowledges the "characteristic mental debility" of Kraepelin's dementia praecox in the three original subtypes and then proposes that "there is one further condition which leads to the same end state, to the same disorder of intelligence and affect." Diem calls this *dementia simplex*, or "simple schizophrenia." Diem notes that, after puberty, "the onset of this particular form of the illness is habitually simple, insidious and without warning signs, and the illness progresses without acute progressive attacks and remissions. There are no definite affective disturbances of a manic or a melancholic nature, no hallucinations or delusional ideas, and none of the other characteristic symptoms of the other forms of dementia praecox . . . such as catalepsy, affectations, mannerisms, stereotypies, negativism and mutism." The term "simple schizophrenia" entered the official psychiatric diagnostic manuals and remained there for many years. However, it is no longer considered one of the four main subtypes of schizophrenia and is instead currently referred to as schizotypal personality disorder.

Black, D.W. and Boffeli, T.J., "Simple Schizophrenia: Past, Present, Future," *American Journal of Psychiatry,* 146(1989), 1267–1273.

Diem, O., "The Simple Dementing Form of Dementia Praecox," ("Die einfach demente Form der dementia Praecox"), *Archiv Für Psychiatrie und Neruenkrankheiten,* 37(1903), 111–187. Translated and reprinted in J. Cutting and M. Shepherd (eds.) *The Clinical Roots of the Schizophrenia Concept.* Cambridge: Cambridge University Press, 1987.

simulated insanity   See FEIGNED INSANITY.

sleep studies   It has often been remarked how "dreamlike" the hallucinatory and confusional states of some persons with schizophrenia seem to be. This has led researchers to explore the psychophysiology of sleep and to see if people with schizophrenia manifest any significant differences in the normal stages of sleep or in REM (rapid eye movement) sleep that is associated with dreaming. A 1977 review of this vast experimental literature by Mendelson et al. concluded that investigators "have failed to establish any unique or even consistent abnormalities in the sleep of schizophrenic patients." However, a later reassessment of this conclusion by Buchsbaum in 1979 suggests that the highly contradictory results of the study of sleep in persons with schizophrenia may simply indicate the great diversity in the sleep neurophysiology of persons with psychotic disorders and perhaps warrants more carefully controlled studies with larger sample sizes of schizophrenic subjects. Although the issue of REM sleep differences in schizophrenics when compared with normals is still controversial, Buchsbaum does suggest that one fairly consistent finding is that people with schizophrenia have much lower amounts of delta, or stage IV, sleep than do people without this disorder.

Buchsbaum, M.S., "Neurophysiological Aspects of the Schizophrenic Syndrome," in L. Bellak (ed.), *Disorders of the Schizophrenic Syndrome.* New York: Basic Books, 1979.

Mendelson, W.B., Gillin, J.C. and Wyatt, R.J., *Human Sleep and Its Disorders.* New York: Plenum, 1977.

Reich, L. et al., "Sleep Disturbance in Schizophrenia," *Archives of General Psychiatry,* 32(1975) 51–55.

sleep treatment   In the 1920s, Swiss psychiatrist Jakob Kläsi introduced the first somatic treatment specifically for schizophrenia. It was referred to as "prolonged sleep therapy." He used barbiturates to induce continuous periods of sleep of one week or longer in persons with schizophrenia. They were only allowed to be awakened for eating and performing other bodily functions. Kläsi reported good results with his sleep treatment, but it never became an accepted treatment. The strong sedatives he used were rather toxic and would result in respiratory complications, especially pneumonia.

Kläsi, J., "Ober die therapeutische Anwendung per 'Dauernarkose' mittels sominifens bei Schizophrenen," *Z. Neurol. Psychiatr.,* 74(1922), 557–592.

sluggish schizophrenia   In the Soviet Union, perhaps 40% of all persons labeled with "schizophrenia" are within the form of the disorder identified as "sluggish schizophrenia." In many ways this concept is compatible with Eugen BLEULER's concept of LATENT SCHIZOPHRENIA, which he presented in 1911. In Soviet psychiatry, there is a long-established tradition of studying "soft" forms of schizophrenia. In 1969, A.V. Snezhnevsky and colleagues published an influential book that introduced a new classification system for the various schizophrenias, including the new concept of "sluggish schizophrenia." Sluggish schizophrenia is not viewed as an initial or PRODROMAL PHASE of schizophrenia, but instead it is an independent diagnostic category characterized by a slowly progressive course, subclinical manifestations in the latent period, overt psychopathological symptoms in the active period. Then follows a period in which the POSITIVE SYMPTOMS decrease and the NEGATIVE SYMPTOMS predominate the clinical presentation during the stabilization of the patient. In the United States, "sluggish schizophrenia" may have been called SIMPLE SCHIZOPHRENIA or by its currently accepted name, SCHIZOTYPAL PERSONALITY DISORDER.

The diagnosis of "sluggish schizophrenia" has long been claimed by Soviet dissidents to be the excuse for putting countless political prisoners into Soviet mental hospitals for punishment. During the week of June 30, 1989, the Reuters news agency reported from Moscow that the current issue of an influential Moscow journal, the *Literary Gazette,* published an article by writer Leonid Zagalsky that for the first time publicly named and condemned the two top Soviet psychiatric authorities and their mentor, A.V. Snezhnevsky, for condoning the imprisonment in mental hospitals of otherwise healthy persons under the label "sluggish schizophrenia." (See also ABUSE OF PSYCHIATRIC PATIENTS; BORDERLINE SCHIZOPHRENIA.)

Smulevich, A.B., "Sluggish Schizophrenia in the Modern Classification of Mental Illness," *Schizophrenia Bulletin,* 15(1989) 533–539.

Snezhnevsky, A.V. (ed.), *Shizofrenia: Klinika i Patogenez.* Moscow: Meditsina, 1969.

smoking and schizophrenia As anyone who has ever visited or worked in a psychiatric hospital will know, persons with schizophrenia tend to smoke a great deal. Some have even been seen to smoke two or more cigarettes at a time, and many persons chain-smoke so much that their lips and fingers are stained with nicotine. Cigarettes are the currency of the psychiatric hospital, and all sorts of economic transactions (including prostitution) are based on them. One study of outpatients with schizophrenia found that 88% of them were regular smokers, a number three times higher than the nonpsychiatric control group subjects in the study and still far higher than persons who are diagnosed with other psychiatric disorders. It is not known why nicotine addiction is so prevalent in persons with schizophrenia, nor is it known why, paradoxically, lung cancer does not seem to be a major cause of death among schizophrenics despite their years of heavy daily smoking. (See also PHYSICAL DISEASE AND SCHIZOPHRENIA.)

Hughes, J.R. et al., "Prevalence of Smoking among Psychiatric Outpatients," *American Journal of Psychiatry,* 143(1986), 993–997.

social drift theory See SOCIOECONOMIC STATUS AND SCHIZOPHRENIA.

social skills training The poor social interactions of people who develop schizophrenia adds considerably to the often terrible quality of their lives and alienates them from other members of the community. Social adjustment has repeatedly been found to be a relatively strong predictor of relapse, rehospitalization and long-term outcome. Therefore, since the 1970s and 1980s in particular, there has been a strong emphasis on teaching persons with schizophrenia certain "social skills" that may help prevent relapse of rehospitalization as they continue to adjust to life with such a chronic and debilitating disease. Social skills that are often trained are learned abilities such as making eye contact, the content of speech, voice inflection and facial expression. The training techniques often include modeling new behaviors, role playing, homework and even training in social perception in order to help keep such persons from misinterpreting the expressions and actions of others.

Many studies have indicated that social skills training procedures are effective in teaching some persons with schizophrenia new skills, and that such newly learned behaviors can be maintained for varying periods of time. Some studies have even associated some forms of social skills training with reduced rates of relapse. However, due to the organic nature of the disease, it is difficult to maintain such learned skills once the person with schizophrenia is no longer monitored and trained consistently within a structured program, and therefore those persons who would most benefit from such training are strongly encouraged to be involved in such programs as often as possible.

Bellak, A.S. (ed.), *Schizophrenia: Treatment, Management, Rehabilitation.* New York: Grune & Stratton, 1984.

Morrison, R.I. and Bellak, A.S., "The Social Functioning of Schizophrenic Patients: Clinical and Research Issues," *Schizophrenia Bulletin,* 13(1987), 715–726.

socioeconomic status and schizophrenia

One of the most overwhelming pieces of evidence that we have about schizophrenia is that it occurs at an unusually high rate in the lowest socioeconomic strata of urban communities. However, there are several different interpretations of this finding. One of them is the famous "social drift" explanation—that is, that persons who develop schizophrenia tend not to be able to function very well in the social or occupational spheres and therefore tend to "drift" downward to the lower socioeconomic layers of society. An alternative hypothesis asserts that it is the unhealthful and stressful living conditions of persons of low socioeconomic levels (e.g., living in a ghetto) that produces the disorder.

Perhaps another explanation may involve a mixture of these two theories, in that if schizophrenia is a genetic disease, then previous generations have gotten sick and have already drifted downward in socioeconomic status over the generations, and therefore a higher concentration of persons with this disorder should be found at these lower levels of society.

Faris and Dunham published the first major study of the relationship between schizophrenia and socioeconomic status in 1939 and gave the first evidence for the inverse relationship between class and schizophrenia. Their research was corroborated by Hollingshead and Redlich in 1958, in their famous book *Social Class and Mental Illness,* in which they present the "social drift" hypothesis. In 1980 epidemiologist W.W. Eaton published a review of 17 studies conducted throughout the world and found that 15 of them confirmed the same conclusion that Faris and Dunham reached in 1939: that schizophrenia forms a concentric pattern, with the highest admission rates for schizophrenia in the central slum areas of the city with the lowest socioeconomic status and then diminishing rates as one looks farther and farther from the inner-city slums to the higher-status suburbs.

Eaton, W.W., "A Formal Theory of Selection for Schizophrenia," *American Journal of Sociology,* 86(1980), 149–158.

Faris, R.E.L. and Dunham, H.W., *Mental Disorders in Urban Areas.* Chicago: Chicago University Press, 1939.

Hollingshead, A.B. and Redlich, F.C., *Social Class and Mental Illness: A Community Study.* New York: John Wiley & Sons, 1958.

Kohn, M.L., "Social Class and Schizophrenia: A Critical Review," in D. Rosenthal and S.S. Kety (eds.), *The Transmission of Schizophrenia.* Oxford: Pergamon Press, 1968.

Saugstad, L.F., "Social Class, Marriage, and Fertility in Schizophrenia," *Schizophrenia Bulletin,* 15(1989), 9–43.

somatic delusions

Delusions involving the body. An example is the delusion that one has a hole in the middle of one's body through which the wind is blowing. Another type may be a PREGNANCY DELUSION.

somatic type

One of the subtypes of the psychotic disorder known as delusional (paranoid) disorder in which a person may have the delusion that he or she has some physical defect, disorder or disease.

Soviet Union The prevalence rate for schizophrenia in the Soviet Union is considered high when compared with other countries. Studies of Russian immigrants to Australia, England and the United States have found high first-admission rates to psychiatric hospitals when compared with other ethnic groups. A recent review article on SLUGGISH SCHIZOPHRENIA by a prominent Soviet psychiatrist reports that researchers have found prevalence rates that range from 1.44 per thousand to 5 per thousand in the Soviet Union.

Smulevich, A.B., "Sluggish Schizophrenia in the Modern Classification of Mental Illness," *Schizophrenia Bulletin*, 15(1989), 533–539.
Torrey, E.F., "Prevalence Studies of Schizophrenia," *British Journal of Psychiatry*, 150 (1987), 598–608.

spectrum disorders Influenced by Paul Meehl's DIATHESIS-STRESS THEORY of "schizotaxia, schizotypy, schizophrenia" and by the later GENETICS STUDIES of David Rosenthal and Seymour Kety, it has been suggested that many persons may inherit a genetic defect (schizotaxia, in Meehl's words) that may then give rise to a spectrum of disorders, all the way from a schizoid personality disorder to schizotypal personality disorder to schizophrenia. In other words, a spectrum of related disorders from the least serious to the most serious may be due to similar or related genetic factors. The evidence supporting a spectrum concept of schizophrenia is that first-degree biological relatives of persons with schizophrenia have a greater risk of developing schizotypal personality disorder or paranoid personality disorder or other schizophrenia-spectrum disorders.

spinning chair See CIRCULATING SWING.

spontaneous remission Although many clinicians have reported rare cases of spontaneous remission in cases of schizophrenia, DSM-III-R (1987) cautions that "a return to full premorbid functioning in this disorder is not common. Full remissions do occur, but their frequency is currently a subject of controversy."

spread eagle cure In 19th-century America this was a technique used in all asylums and prisons for agitated patients or inmates. The procedure involved stripping the violent patient of all clothes and throwing him flat on his back. Four men would take hold of each of the limbs and spread them out at right angles from the body. A physician or an attendant would then stand up on a chair or a table and pour buckets of ice-cold water on the restrained person's face until he is completely subdued. In some instances, the shock was so great that death resulted. A picture of this torturous procedure appears in Emil Kraepelin's book *One Hundred Years of Psychiatry*.

Kraepelin, E., *One Hundred Years of Psychiatry*, tr. W. Baskin. New York: Philosophical Library, 1962; first published, 1917.

stadium melancholicum This is the 19th-century term for the depression that sometimes precedes the onset of a psychotic disorder. German psychiatrist Wilhelm GRIESINGER writes in his book, *Mental Pathology and Therapeutics:* "The *stadium melancholicum* which precedes insanity is by some physicians designated as the period of incubation, or "prodromal stadium . . . (that) the stage of incubation has almost always a depressive character is interesting and of great importance." (See also PRODROMAL PHASE.)

Griesinger, W., *Mental Pathology and Therapeutics,* 2nd ed., tr. C.L. Robertson. New York: William Wood, 1882.

State Care Act of 1890 This was the legislative act passed by Congress that divided each of the United States into districts and mandated a state hospital for each of the districts. With this act, the term "asylum" was replaced by the term "hospital" in reference to these institutions.

Stelazine The trade name for trifluoperazine, an ANTIPSYCHOTIC DRUG within the class of such drugs known as the piperazine phenothiazines.

stereotypy Long observed to be a behavioral sign of psychotic disorders, particularly schizophrenia, stereotypy refers to seemingly meaningless repetitive acts that are rigidly performed over and over again, as if engaged in an idiosyncratic ritual. One of the first psychiatrists to find a symbolic meaning in the stereotypies of psychotic individuals was C.G. JUNG, who, in his autobiography, *Memories, Dreams, Reflections* (1962), relates the story of a quiet old woman who made strange repetitive sewing motions with her hands. In trying to understand what possible meaning the action could have had for her, he investigated her past and found out that many years previously, the woman had suffered the onset of her psychosis after losing a lover who happened to make shoes—hence the source of her sewing motions. Psychoanalyst Frieda FROMM-REICHMANN writes in a 1942 paper that "the seemingly meaningless and inappropriate stereotyped actions of schizophrenics are meaningful, as are the rest of their communications. They serve to screen the appropriate emotional reactions that are at their bottom . . . They are a means of defense against non-acceptance and rebuff."

Fromm-Reichmann, F., "A Preliminary Note on the Emotional Significance of Stereotypes in Schizophrenics" (1942), in D.M. Bullard (ed.), *Psychoanalysis and Psychotherapy: Selected Papers of Frieda Fromm-Reichmann*. Chicago: Chicago University Press, 1959.

Storch's theory of schizophrenic cognition Alfred Storch was a German psychologist who published one of the first comprehensive studies of the peculiarities of thought and language in schizophrenia. Storch was a pupil of the comparative psychologist Heinz Werner. In his 1922 book (published in an English translation in 1924), Storch compared the similarities between the thought processes of schizophrenics and those of persons in primitive societies. He compared the magical worlds of persons living in such societies and the delusional worlds of schizophrenics, especially their preoccupations with religious and mystical issues. Such comparisons are today considered invalid due to the ethnocentrism that colors them. Persons who live in preliterate societies are as "normal" in their thought processes as "normal" persons are in our own, and mental illness is known in these societies and is recognized as such.

Storch, A., *The Primitive Archaic Forms of Inner Experiences and Thought in Schizophrenics*. New York and Washington, D.C.: Nervous and Mental Disease Publishing Company, 1924.

straitjacket, or straight-waistcoat A form of MECHANICAL RESTRAINT invented by a man named MacBride in England in the 1700s for restraining agitated patients in asylums. The heavy canvas coat had sleeves that wrapped around the body and could be tied in the back. Such forms of restraint were used well into the 20th century and may still be in use in some places even today. (See also CAMISOLE.)

street drug psychosis A psychotic disorder whose onset is related to the use of PSYCHOTOGENIC DRUGS. (See also SUBSTANCE ABUSE.)

street people A term for vagrants of all sorts, but especially the homeless mentally ill persons who live on the streets. It is an American term that came into vogue in the 1980s. A 19th-century term for the same class of individuals was PAUPER LUNATICS.

stress It is clear that stress is related to the onset and relapse of many mental and physical disorders. However, a direct connection between stressful life events and the development of schizophrenia has not been demonstrated. Given that about 80% of the cause of schizophrenia is now estimated to be from genetic factors (see GENETICS STUDIES), it is probably true that part of the remaining 20% may be related to physically or emotionally stressful environmental influences that contribute to the exacerbation of the disease process. However, a major review of the stress issue in schizophrenia published in 1985 has concluded that "there is no good evidence that life stress is causally related to episodes of schizophrenia." (See also BRIEF REACTIVE PSYCHOSIS.)

Gruen, R. and Biron, M., "Stressful Life Events and Schizophrenia," *Neuropsychobiology,* 12 (1984), 206–208.
Tennant, C.C., "Stress and Schizophrenia: A Review," *Integrative Psychiatry,* 1985, 248–261.

strong rooms   See OUBLIETTES.

subjective experiences of schizophrenia   With its emphasis on biological and biochemical factors in the development of mental disorders (and the psychotic disorders in particular), psychiatry has been criticized for ignoring the actual experience of an illness by the afflicted person. Indeed, psychiatry has been accused of viewing the notion of the "self" as perhaps a bit mystical, and most professional psychiatric journals today have less and less space for detailed "case histories" of individual experiences. Most studies of the subjective experience of schizophrenia agree on the alterations in the sense of "self" that the disease process produces. Hearing voices, perceptual anomalies, odd beliefs, intrusive thoughts, strange feelings (or lack thereof)— all of these highly self-threatening phenomena have been documented in the various reports of persons with psychotic disorders (see PERCEPTUAL ANOMALIES IN SCHIZOPHRENIA). By understanding what actually goes on inside the thoughts and emotions of a person with schizophrenia, we can all develop a deeper empathy for the afflicted person and interact with him or her in a much more genuinely supportive manner.

Based on their work in the United Kingdom, McGhie and Chapman's 1961 paper on attention disturbances is an exemplary study of the inner experiences of schizophrenics and what these reports may mean from a theoretical point of view. The "psychedelic era" generated new interest in purported PSYCHEDELIC EXPERIENCES IN SCHIZOPHRENIA, which then led to a series of studies comparing drug-induced states with psychotic states of consciousness. In the United States, psychiatrist Malcom Bowers' book, *Retreat from Sanity: The Structure of Emerging Psychosis,* published in 1974, provided clinicians and the general public with a series of vivid case histories of what it must be like to undergo a psychotic episode. An excellent collection of historical accounts of the subjective experience of mental illness, particularly of institutionalization, was published by Dale Peterson in 1982, containing a comprehensive bibliography of first-person accounts of experiences with "madness." Indeed, most of the major attempts to study the subjective experiences of people with schizophrenia were published in the 1960s and 1970s—prior to the revolution in BRAIN IMAGING TECHNIQUES and GENETICS STUDIES that have shifted the focus to the purely organic view of this disease. In an effort to resurrect interest in the more human and experiential side, in 1989 *Schizophrenia Bulletin* (Vol. 15, No. 2) devoted an entire special issue to the theme "Subjective Experiences of Schizophrenia and Related Disorders." However, one of the best and most readily accessible accounts of the subjective experience of schizophrenia can be found in the chapter titled "The Inner World of Madness: View from the Inside" in the second edition (1988) of E. Fuller Torrey's *Surviving Schizophrenia: A Family Manual.*

Bowers, M., *Retreat from Sanity: The Structure of Emerging Psychosis*. New York: Human Sciences Press, 1974.

Freedman, B.J., "The Subjective Experience of Perceptual and Cognitive Disturbances in Schizophrenia," *Archives of General Psychiatry*, 30(1974), 333–340.

Freedman, B.J. and Chapman, L.J., "Early Subjective Experience in Schizophrenia Episodes," *Journal of Abnormal Psychology*, 82(1973), 46–54.

Kleinman, J.E. et al., "A Comparison of the Phenomenology of Hallucinogens and Schizophrenia from Some Autobiographical Accounts," *Schizophrenia Bulletin*, 3(1977), 560–586.

McGhie, A. and Chapman, J., "Disorders of Attention and Perception in Early Schizophrenia," *British Journal of Medical Psychology*, 34(1961), 103–115.

Peterson, D. (ed.), *A Mad People's History of Madness*. Pittsburgh: University of Pittsburgh Press, 1982.

substance abuse   Psychiatric facilities the world over have been deluged since the 1960s with a new type of patient—the "dual diagnosis" patient who is often young, a substance abuser, and perhaps even schizophrenic. Considering the prevalence of illicit drug use in our society by adolescents, and given the fact that it is usually in late adolescence or early adulthood that the first serious onset of schizophrenia has been documented for almost a century, the combination ("comorbidity") of schizophrenia and substance abuse is perhaps the rule and not the exception in today's treatment centers. The issues that are often raised are whether certain drugs actually do initiate the onset of schizophrenia, how they affect its course and how a history of substance abuse with PSYCHOTOGENIC DRUGS may affect treatment, especially with antipsychotic drugs.

In a major review of the impact of substance abuse on schizophrenia, researchers Winston Turner and Ming T. Tsuang of the Brockton/West Roxbury V.A. Medical Center in Brockton, Massachusetts, arrived at the following conclusions regarding the present state of scientific knowledge about this relationship:

1. It is evident that substance abuse may profoundly affect the course and outcome of schizophrenia, but the true impact remains largely undefined.

2. There is some evidence that drugs tend to hasten the age of onset of psychosis, but it is unclear whether the effect is to precipitate latent or subliminal psychotic behavior or to initiate psychosis in persons who would not have had a psychotic episode if they did not abuse drugs.

3. Drug abuse just before hospitalization is fairly common, and the drugs of choice do not appear to be random, but it has yet to be determined whether the specific benefits the schizophrenic patients are receiving from the drugs differ from those experienced by persons who do not have schizophrenia.

4. The relationship between characteristics of drug abuse (drug type, quantity and frequency of drug abuse) and the degree of psychopathology, manifestations of the disease and long-term outcome has yet to be addressed.

5. Drugs may be precipitating relapse and subsequent rehospitalization among those persons with schizophrenia who are in remission and who would otherwise remain outside of the hospital.

A special issue of *Schizophrenia Bulletin* was published in 1990 that was devoted to the theme "Substance Abuse Comorbidity in Schizophrenia."

Turner, W.M. and Tsuang, M.T., "Impact of Substance Abuse on the Course and Outcome of Schizophrenia," *Schizophrenia Bulletin*, 16 (1990), 87–95.

subtype   An identifiable variant of a particular disease. In schizophrenia there are four main subtypes (paranoid, disorganized, catatonic and undifferentiated). Bipolar disorder has been estimated to have as many as four to six different subtypes.

suicide and schizophrenia   See DEPRES-
SION; MORTALITY IN SCHIZOPHRENIA.

Sullivan's theory of schizophrenia
American psychiatrist Harry Stack Sullivan
(1892–1949) was an empathetic therapist
and close observer of the lives of schizophrenics. Sullivan helped to "humanize"
the image of the schizophrenic, especially
in psychoanalytic circles, where such persons were often regarded as untreatable or
extremely difficult at best. It has been suggested in recent biographies of Sullivan that
he himself suffered a breakdown of some
sort as a young adult and that this is the
source of his lifelong interest and insights
into schizophrenia. Sullivan's primary emphasis was on the interpersonal dynamics of
human life and how this related to the intra-
personal dynamics that had long been the
pursuit of psychoanalysis. A person's concept of "self" was largely derived from the
"reflective appraisals" of the immediate
caretakers of the infant and young child. If
there is something wrong in the upbringing
of the child (e.g., an overanxious, cold or
simply pathological mother), the child will
grow up with poor self-esteem and engage
in distorted interpretations of social interactions, a phenomenon that Sullivan calls
PARATAXIC DISTORTION.

Sullivan is famous for his conception of
the development of "self" as a dissociative
(splitting) process into the "good me," "bad
me" and "not me." Any experiences from
early childhood (especially from the mother)
that are associated with disapproval or hu-
miliation are personalized in the self as the
"bad me," and the child then tries to dis-
sociate these experiences from consciousness so that they become "not me" or unconscious. In the initial phase of schizophrenia
this natural dissociative process breaks down,
and a state of PREPSYCHOTIC PANIC occurs.
The personality becomes disorganized, and
all of those terrible associations of the "bad
me" that were forced into becoming "not
me" suddenly erupt into consciousness. The

terror that ensues is equivalent to that of the
infant for the bad mother. Sullivan proposed
that the reason so many cases of schizophrenia seem to begin in adolescence is that this
is a period in which so many blows are
leveled at a person's self-esteem, and the
resurgence of that which had been dissociated induces the psychosis.

Sullivan, H.S., *Conceptions of Modern Psychia-
try*, New York: Norton, 1953.
———, *Schizophrenia as a Human Process*. New
York: Norton, 1962.

sulpiride   This is a drug that has been
used to treat schizophrenia in Europe for
many years but has not yet been approved
for use in the United States. It comes from
a class of drugs—the benzamides—completely different from those in current usage.

surgery   See COLUMBIA-GREYSTONE PROJ-
ECT; FOCAL INFECTION AS A CAUSE OF
SCHIZOPHRENIA; LEUCOTOMY; LOBECTOMY;
LOBOTOMY; PSYCHOSURGERY; TOPECTOMY;
TRANSORBITAL LOBOTOMY.

Sweden   See SCANDINAVIA.

swinging chair   See CIRCULATING SWING.

symbiotic bond   According to one of the
FAMILY INTERACTION THEORIES, that of
Theodore Lidz, when an elementary relationship is established between a therapist
and a schizophrenic patient, the patient
sometimes develops an attitude of total dependency on the therapist that is similar to
that between the newborn infant and mother.
Unfortunately for the patients (at least according to Lidz), they had mothers who
treated them parasitically, so that there was
no psychological separation between child
and mother, almost as if the child were an
appendage of the mother. Lidz called this
the "symbiotic bond." Thus, in therapy, the
person was likely to resume this symbiotic
attitude toward the therapist. (See also
TRANSFERENCE.)

Lidz, R.W. and Lidz, T., "Therapeutic Considerations Arising from the Intense Symbiotic Needs of Schizophrenic Patients," in M. Brody and T. Redlick, *Psychotherapy with Schizophrenics*. New York: International Universities Press, 1952.

symbiotic psychosis This was a syndrome proposed by child psychoanalyst Margaret Mahler to describe a psychotic disorder of childhood that may resemble schizophrenia. It has also been called the "Mahler syndrome." According to Mahler, it occurs in children who have reached a level of development in which they are able to differentiate and individualize from the mother (usually ages two to four) but cannot proceed to a full separation. Whenever separation is attempted, panic ("separation anxiety") sets in. Mahler writes: "The symbiotic psychotic syndrome is aimed at restoring the symbiotic-parasitic delusion of oneness with the mother and thus serves a function diametrically opposite to that of the autistic mechanism." Mahler says that the psychosis may be insidious and may not be detected until school age. The primary symptoms of REGRESSION are catatonia-like temper tantrums and states of panic.

Mahler, M.S., *On Human Symbiosis and the Vicissitudes of Individuation*, Vol. 1, *Infantile Psychosis*. New York: International Universities Press, 1968.

symptom Generally, a symptom is any manifestation of a pathological condition. Although a strict interpretation of this word is that it refers only to subjective complaints of distress, it may, in some instances, also refer to objective pathological conditions (see also SIGN).

syndrome A cluster of symptoms that commonly appear together and constitute a recognizable condition. The term "syndrome" is often less specific than the words "disease" or "disorder." "Disease" is used when a specific etiology (cause) of an illness

is known, or if its specific organic disease process is known. Most mental disorders therefore are in fact "syndromes" rather than "diseases."

synesthesia A condition in which a sensory experience normally associated with one modality occurs when another modality is stimulated. For example, a loud, sudden sound might produce visual images of lights flashing or swirling colors. Such experiences have been reported with the use of hallucinogens and in acute psychotic episodes. (See also PSYCHEDELIC EXPERIENCES IN SCHIZOPHRENIA.)

syphilitic psychosis See GENERAL PARALYSIS OF THE INSANE.

T

tactile hallucinations A hallucination of "touch." Often a tactile hallucination involves something that is felt on or under the skin, and a delusional interpretation of the sensory experience usually accompanies a tactile hallucination. FORMICATION is a specific type of tactile hallucination in which something (usually "bugs") is felt to be crawling just below the surface of the skin. Formication is commonly reported in alcohol withdrawal delirium and in withdrawal from cocaine intoxication.

Taiwan The prevalence rate for schizophrenia in Taiwan has been found to be 2.2 per thousand. Studies of prevalence rates for schizophrenia among the aboriginal population has been found to be among the lowest rates in the world—0.9 per thousand.

Torrey, E.F., *Schizophrenia and Civilization*. New York: Jason Aronson, 1980.

tangentiality A feature of the peculiar thought processes found in schizophrenia and in schizotypal personality disorder in which a person does not stick to one topic when speaking but gets pulled off into tangential currents of thought. Usually these are topics that are unrelated to the main point of the conversation, but the person seems unable to focus attention enough to stay consistent with the main topic.

taraxein hypothesis   In 1957 a research study by Heath and coworkers announced that they had isolated an abnormal blood protein in the serum of people with schizophrenia that they called taraxein. When they injected this protein into monkeys, it apparently produced abnormal behavior. Furthermore, when injected into normal human subjects, Heath claimed that this substance induced a temporary psychotic disorder that mimicked schizophrenia. It was claimed that taraxein was in the gamma immunoglobulin (IgG) of persons with schizophrenia and that it acted as an antibody against antigens that were present in the person's own limbic system in the brain. Therefore, since it interfered with brain functioning, it was argued that taraxein was a probable cause of schizophrenia, making it an autoimmune disease. Heath's findings have not been replicated by other laboratories despite several tries, but neither have they been completely refuted. (See also AUTOIMMUNE HYPOTHESIS; PROTEIN FACTORS HYPOTHESIS.)

Heath, R.G. et al., "Effect on Behavior in Humans with the Administration of Taraxein," *American Journal of Psychiatry*, 114(1957), 14–24.
Heath, R.G. and Krupp, I.M., "Schizophrenia as an Immunologic Disorder: Demonstration of Antibrain Globulins by Fluorescent Antibody Techniques," *Archives of General Psychiatry*, 16(1967), 1–9.

tardive dyskinesia   In the 1970s it was recognized that the long-term use of ANTIPSYCHOTIC DRUGS caused certain irreversible side effects. One of the most serious is tardive dyskinesia, which is characterized by abnormal and involuntary movements involving the tongue, jaw, lips, face, extremities and sometimes the trunk. The person may grimace, frown, blink excessively, make snakelike movements with the tongue and pucker or smack the lips repeatedly. Patients who are elderly are more susceptible to developing tardive dyskinesia than younger ones. Tardive dyskinesia is in many ways the opposite of PARKINSON'S SYNDROME in that the former is a disorder of extra and unnecessary movement, whereas the latter involves a reduction in movement. Furthermore, pharmacotherapy that makes one better usually makes the other worse. The best prevention of tardive dyskinesia is to make sure that antipsychotic drugs are absolutely necessary before administration. Cutting back the dosage level of antipsychotic drugs may temporarily worsen the symptoms of tardive dyskinesia, but this will eventually subside. (See also ANTIPARKINSONIAN DRUGS.)

temperament   See FUMDAMENTAL STATES OF MANIC-DEPRESSIVE INSANITY.

temporary psychosis   See BORDERLINE PERSONALITY DISORDER; BRIEF REACTIVE PSYCHOSIS.

theomania   A type of MONOMANIA identified by J.E.D. ESQUIROL in 1938 for the category of persons with a psychotic disorder that includes those "who believe that they are God, who imagine that they have conversations and intimate communications with the Holy Spirit, angels and saints, and who pretend to be inspired, and to have received a commission from heaven to convert men." This disorder is in distinction to CACODEMONOMANIA, which involves the delusional belief of contact with "evil" forces.

Esquirol, J.E.D., *Mental Maladies: A Treatise on Insanity*, tr. E.K. Hunt. Philadelphia: Lea and Blanchard, 1945; first published, 1838.

therapeutic community   See MILIEU THERAPY.

thioridazine See MELLARIL.

thioxanthenes The class of ANTIPSY-CHOTIC DRUGS that includes thiothixene (trade name: Navane) and chlorprothixene (Tarac-tan).

thorazine The trade name for CHLOR-PROMAZINE, which, in 1954, was the first ANTIPSYCHOTIC DRUG approved for use in the United States. It is named after the Norse god of Thunder, Thor.

thought broadcasting A delusion common in schizophrenia in which the person believes or experiences his or her own internal thoughts as being broadcast from one's head as they are occurring so that others can hear them.

thought disorder See FORMAL THOUGHT DISORDER.

thought insertion Another common delusion found in persons in schizophrenia, it is the delusion that thoughts belonging to other persons or entities are being inserted into one's mind.

thought withdrawal One of the most common delusions found in schizophrenia, "thought withdrawal" is the belief that thoughts have been removed from one's head.

thrashing See FLOGGING.

Three Christs of Ypsilanti Social psychologist Milton Rokeach published his famous study of the impact that three paranoid schizophrenic men, who all believed they were Jesus Christ, had on one another when they were placed together in the same bedroom, same workplace and same cafeteria table at Ypsilanti State Hospital in Michigan from July 1959 to August 1961. The purpose was to record the changes in each of the men, who all claimed the same delusional identity. Although no one improved in any

overall sense, two of the Christs modified their self-identities a bit to avoid conflict, whereas the third ended up becoming more firmly entrenched in his identity, even to the point of denying that the other two were alive (see COTARD'S SYNDROME). Rokeach concludes in the final sentence of his books: "And, finally, we have learned that even when a summit of three is composed of paranoid men, deadlocked over the ultimate in human contradiction, they prefer to seek ways to live with one another in peace rather than destroy one another."

Rokeach, M., *The Three Christs of Ypsilanti: A Psychological Study.* New York: Alfred A. Knopf, 1964.

thyroid disease masking as psychosis See MEDICAL DISORDERS THAT MIMIC PSYCHOTIC DISORDERS.

token economy See BEHAVIOR THERAPY.

topectomy A PSYCHOSURGERY procedure invented by J. Lawrence Pool, a research assistant in the Department of Neurology at Columbia University in 1947. The term is derived from two Greek words meaning "place" and "excision." An attempt to create a more conservative form of psychosurgery, topectomy involved destroying parts of the frontal cortex itself rather than severing the white fibers below (as in a LEUCOTOMY). It considerably reduced the chances of hemorrhaging and therefore the likelihood that a patient would become a zombie-like vegetable, as was the case in many psychosurgical patients of Walter FREEMAN. The topectomy was one of the forms of psychosurgery studied by the COLUMBIA-GREYSTONE PROJECT in 1947 and was performed on patients of the New Jersey State Hospital in Greystone Park, New Jersey.

Tory rot An 18th- and early-19th-century American psychotic disorder identified by

Benjamin Rush to refer to those "insane" persons who did not believe in the value of the American Revolution. Rush was convinced that these people were mentally ill and that they died from their insanity. It is not known if Rush involuntarily committed any of these people to the Pennsylvania Hospital in Philadelphia, which would have made them political prisoners.

Lloyd, J.H., "Benjamin Rush and His Critics," *Annals of Medical History,* 2(1930), 470–475.

toxin theory   The century-old idea that a particularly poisonous chemical, probably produced by the body itself, acts on the brain and nervous system in such a way that it produces the symptoms of dementia praecox or schizophrenia. In his first description of dementia praecox in 1896, Emil KRAEPELIN proposes that it is due to a metabolic disorder involving such a possible "autointoxication" by a toxin produced in the body. Likewise, C.G. JUNG proposed that a "toxin" was the cause of this disease in his 1906 book, *The Psychology of Dementia Praecox.* Many modern theories of the cause of schizophrenia are still based on this basic idea. (See also AUTOIMMUNE HYPOTHESIS; BIOCHEMICAL THEORIES OF SCHIZOPHRENIA; PROTEIN FACTORS HYPOTHESIS; TARAXEIN HYPOTHESIS; MEGAVITAMIN THERAPY.)

tranquillizer   A form of MECHANICAL RESTRAINT invented by American physician Benjamin RUSH in 1808. Also called a "coercion chair," it was designed to restrain agitated or violent patients. The device was an instrument of torture in which a person would sit upright in a chair, arms shackled to the arms of the chair and feet clasped by the ankles in a device at the bottom of the chair; it had a wooden block that could be raised or lowered and would fit over the head of the person, making him or her completely immobile. In his 1812 treatise, Rush extols the virtues of the use of the "tranquillizer" for violent patients:

Confinement by means of a strait waistcoat or of a chair which I have called a tranquillizer. He submits to them both with less difficulty than to human force, and struggles less to disengage himself from them. The tranquillizer has several advantages over the straight waistcoat or mad shirt. It opposes the impetus of blood towards the brain, it lessens muscular action every where, it reduces the force and the frequency of the pulse, it favours the application of cold water and ice to the head, and warm water to the feet, both of which I shall say presently are excellent remedies in this disease; it enables the physician to feel the pulse and to bleed without any trouble, or altering the erect position of the patient's body; and, lastly, it relieves him, by means of a close stool, half filled with water, over which he constantly sits, from the feetor and filth of his alvine evacuations.

Since Rush's time, the word "tranquillizer" has been part of the slang of asylums and mental hospitals, referring to just about any method that quiets an agitated patient. It is thought that this is the source of our use of the word "tranquilizer" for sedative medications. A graphic reproduction of the famous illustration of Rush's device appears on the cover of the book cited below by Sander Gilman.

Gilman, S.L., *Seeing the Insane.* New York: John Wiley & Sons, 1982.
Rush, B., *Medical Inquiries and Observations upon the Diseases of the Mind.* Philadelphia: Kimber & Richardson, 1812.

transcultural studies of schizophrenia
See CROSS-CULTURAL STUDIES.

transference   A term invented by Sigmund FREUD for his method of psychoanalysis that refers to the re-experiencing and PROJECTION of unconscious, infantile wishes onto another person (usually the analyst). In fact, the establishment, the modalities, the interpretation and the resolution of the transference are what defines the "cure" in psychoanalysis. Freud used the German word *Übertragung* to refer to this process, which he refers to in the 1895 book he co-authored with Joseph Breuer, *Studies on Hysteria.* According to PSYCHOANALYTIC THEORIES OF SCHIZOPHRENIA, psychotic individuals were unable to establish a positive *transference neurosis* toward their analyst in psychoanalysis, and therefore, treatment of such persons was next to impossible. Others have noted that, instead, a SYMBIOTIC BOND sometimes forms as a transference. (See also FROMM-REICHMANN, FRIEDA; COUNTERTRANSFERENCE.)

transmethylation hypothesis   One of the biochemical theories about the cause of schizophrenia (see BIOCHEMICAL THEORIES OF SCHIZOPHRENIA). This theory was first proposed by Humphrey Osmond and J. Smythies in 1952 in which they suggested that schizophrenia was caused by a toxic hallucinogenic substance, naturally produced in the brain, through the faulty methylation of adrenaline. Later, along with Abraham Hoffer, this theory was elaborated in 1959 by Osmond, who then claimed that the toxic substance was adrenochrome, but later studies could never find adrenochrome in the bodily fluids of persons with schizophrenia. An informed literature review of the research studies of the transmethylation hypothesis of schizophrenia published in 1978 concluded that there was no support for this theory.

Hoffer, A. and Osmond, H., "The Adrenochrome Model and Schizophrenia," *Journal of Nervous and Mental Disease,* 123(1959), 18–35.

Luchins, D. et al., "A Review of Nicotinic Acid, N-methylated Indoleamines and Schizophrenia," *International Pharmacopsychiatry,* 13 (1978), 16–33.

Osmond, H. and Smythies, J., "Schizophrenia: A New Approach," *Journal of Mental Science,* 98(1952), 309–315.

transorbital lobotomy   The famous "ice pick technique" of PSYCHOSURGERY invented by psychiatrist Walter FREEMAN in 1946 as an alternative to the formal surgical procedures that involved the opening of the skull. Transorbital lobotomies avoided this by lodging an ice pick–type instrument behind the orbit of the eye and into the frontal lobes, where a few quick strokes could damage enough of the brain tissue to achieve the desired tranquilizing effect. Freeman first used this technique on outpatients in his Washington, D.C., office in 1946 against the advice of his associate, James Watts, who refused to cooperate with him. For these first patients Freeman did use an actual ice-pick from his kitchen drawer at home, and this historic kitchen utensil is in the collection of the James W. Watts and Himmelfarb Health Sciences Library of George Washington University in Washington, D.C. The development of the transorbital lobotomy technique led to the mass brain damaging of thousands of institutionalized psychiatric patients in the 1940s and 1950s.

treatment refractoriness   Despite the many positive reports about the beneficial effects of treating people with schizophrenia with ANTIPSYCHOTIC DRUGS, there are still patients who are refractory to this form of therapy. Those who are not helped by antipsychotic drugs range in estimates from 5% to 25% of schizophrenics. These estimates do not include the 15% or so of schizophrenic patients who improve with just placebo treatment in double-blind studies of antipsychotic drugs. The definition of "treatment refractoriness" in the treatment of schizophrenia has become an important issue in the United States because the availability of the new antipsychotic drug CLOZAPINE is dependent upon this primary screening criterion for its use with patients. The noted schizophrenia researcher Herbert Y. Meltzer suggests that treatment refractoriness be defined in the following way:

> Schizophrenic patients who do not return to their best premorbid level of functioning—adjusted for the disrupted effect of "time out" from their previous activities, for the effects

on self-esteem and confidence, and for the reactions of their environment that might occur with any mental illness—should be considered treatment resistant to the extent that their previous level of functioning is further impaired.

Meltzer, H.Y., "Commentary: Defining Treatment Refractoriness in Schizophrenia," *Schizophrenia Bulletin,* 16(1990), 563–565.

Brenner, H.D. et al., "Defining Treatment Refractoriness in Schizophrenia," *Schizophrenia Bulletin,* 16(1990), 551–561.

trepanation (or trephination)   Perhaps the earliest form of PSYCHOSURGERY for epilepsy and mental disorders, this technique involved the removal of a (usually) circular piece of the skull for the purposes of surgical treatment of the brain. Trephined skulls dating from Neolithic times have been found in Europe and among the ruins of the great civilizations of the world, including the ancient Incas. During the Middle Ages trepanning continued as a treatment and was done by using carpenters' drills. Sir William Osler (1848–1919) writes in a 1921 book, *The Evolution of Modern Medicine,* that "the operation was done for epilepsy, infantile convulsions, headache and various cerebral disease believed caused by confined demons, to whom the hole gave a ready method of escape."

Horrax, G., *Neurosurgery—An Historical Sketch.* Springfield, Ill.: Charles C. Thomas, 1952.

trichtillomania   An infrequently observed but not uncommon behavior observed in people with psychotic disorders (and with other types of mental disorders) is the compulsive pulling out of one's hair, resulting in bald patches on the scalp or on other parts of the body. In DSM-III-R trichtillomania is included among the impulse control disorders. Trichtillomania was first described by the French physician Hallopeau in 1889. Most studies of trichtillomania have concluded that it is: (1) a chronic disorder, which (2) frequently involves multiple hair sites and (3) which is highly correlated with the presence of another mental disorder (for example, major depression, the mental disorder with which trichtillomania is most closely correlated).

Christenson, G.A. et al., "Characteristics of 60 Adult Chronic Hair Pullers," *American Journal of Psychiatry,* 148(1991), 365–370.

Hallopeau, M., "Alopécie par grattage (trichomanie ou trichtillomanie)," *Annales Dermatol. Venerol.,* 10(1889), 440–441.

trust vs. mistrust   The first of the eight stages of "psychosocial development" outlined by neo-Freudian psychoanalyst Erik Erikson. It is believed that persons with psychotic disorders, particularly schizophrenia, tend to "regress" to this basic stage of development, which is why it is so hard for them to form relationships with others or to adequately perform REALITY TESTING. Erikson writes: "In *adults* the impairment of basic trust is expressed in a basic *mistrust.* It characterizes individuals who withdraw into themselves in particular ways when at odds with themselves and with others. These ways, which are not often obvious, are more strikingly represented by individuals who regress into psychotic states in which they sometimes close up, refusing food and comfort and becoming oblivious to companionship."

Erikson, E.H., *Identity and the Life Cycle.* New York: International Universities Press, 1959.

tuberculosis and psychosis   The idea has often been put forth that certain diseases are incompatible and cannot be found in the same person. This was the untested hypothesis behind the CONVULSIVE THERAPY idea in the 20th century that epilepsy and schizophrenia could not be found together in the same person. In the 18th and 19th centuries, it was believed that those persons who developed pulmonary tuberculosis were not likely to develop a psychotic disorder. No scientific support for this theory has ever been put forth.

However, in the 1930s, the opposite hypothesis was put forth: namely, that tuberculosis might be the cause of certain mental diseases, including schizophrenia. In 1933, Austrian researcher E. Löwenstein published a paper describing a new and more sensitive technique for the detection of Koch's bacillus (the cause of tuberculosis) and suggested that he could establish a diagnosis of tuberculosis in cases that may not, on first appearance, look like tuberculosis. Included among these were some mental disorders, including schizophrenia. For a few years following this announcement, the hypothesis was discussed that schizophrenia and tuberculosis may be related after all, but no confirming evidence was ever put forth. (See also PHYSICAL DISEASE AND SCHIZOPHRENIA.)

Hunter, R.A. and Widdicombe, J.G., "Tuberculosis and Insanity: Historical and Experimental Observations on the Straight-waistcoat as Collapse Therapy," *St. Bart's Hospital Journal*, 61(1957) 113–119.

Löwenstein, E., "Über Tuberkelbasillämie bei Nervenkrankheiten," *Wein. Klin. Wchschr.* 46 (1933), 228–231.

twins method and studies Studying pairs of twins in which one or both members have schizophrenia or bipolar disorder has been an important area in GENETICS STUDIES of these psychotic disorders. Indeed, they have been so fruitful that NIMH genetics researcher David Rosenthal has concluded that "the twins studies probably have contributed our most reliable data regarding the inheritance of schizophrenia."

Twins studies compare the CONCORDANCE RATE for schizophrenia in pairs of monozygotic ("identical") twins with the rate found in dizygotic ("fraternal") twins. In fact, it was Rosenthal himself who pioneered the scientific study of schizophrenic twins for their possible information regarding genetic transmission, publishing the first study using

the strategy of comparing the concordance rate of monozygotic twins in 1962. In some later studies, the rate in first-degree biological relatives is also compared.

There are two major assumptions behind the twins studies: (a) that monozygotic twins share all the same genes, whereas dizygotic twins only have about half of their genes in common; and (b) that both varieties of twin pairs are exposed to the same prenatal and postnatal environmental influences. Therefore, given these two assumptions, it would be expected that monozygotic twins would show a greater concordance for genetically transmitted diseases of all types than dizygotic twins—which is, indeed, the case.

According to a review of genetics studies of schizophrenia by K.S. Kendler in 1986, the twins studies of schizophrenia have fairly consistently reported a three-times greater risk for developing schizophrenia in the monozygotic twins of persons with schizophrenia than in the dizygotic twins of afflicted persons. Furthermore, the risk for developing schizophrenia is 40% to 60% greater in these monozygotic twins than in the general population. Other studies have demonstrated that monozygotic twins reared apart from each other are concordant for schizophrenia (that is, both twins have it) at about the same rate as those who are raised together, thus strongly confirming the role of genetics over the environment. Still, there are monozygotic twins who are discordant for schizophrenia, and future research must determine why this is so if schizophrenia is a genetically transmitted disease.

For bipolar disorder, twins studies also point to a strong genetic component for the transmission of the illness. A famous Danish twins study of manic-depressive disorders published in 1977 found that there was a 79% concordance rate for bipolar illness in the monozygotic twins of persons diagnosed with this disorder, in contrast to a concordance rate of only 19% in the dizygotic twins of persons diagnosed with bipolar disorder.

Bertelsen, A. et al., "A Danish Twin Study of Manic-Depressive Disorders," *British Journal of Psychiatry*, 130(1977), 330–351.

Kendler, K.S., "Genetics of Schizophrenia," in A.J. Frances and R.J. Hales (eds.), *Psychiatry Update: American Psychiatric Association Annual Review*, vol. 5. Washington, D.C.: American Psychiatric Press, 1986.

Rosenthal, D., "Problems of Sampling and Diagnosis in the Major Twin Studies of Schizophrenia," *Journal of Psychiatric Research*, 1 (1962), 116–134.

two-syndrome concept of schizophrenia   See CROW'S HYPOTHESIS.

Type I/Type II schizophrenia   See CROW'S HYPOTHESIS.

U

unconscious   According to PSYCHOANALYTIC THEORIES OF SCHIZOPHRENIA (and of psychosis in general), such a psychotic disorder is produced when previously repressed contents (images, feelings, thoughts, memories) that have been unconscious and therefore out of awareness erupt into consciousness. In essence, the unconscious rips through the weakened defense mechanism of the ego. According to such theories, the contents of the psychotic symptoms (delusions, hallucinations, bizarre behaviors) are all meaningful because they are symbolic expressions of unconscious conflicts that seek resolution in this extreme manner.

undifferentiated type   This is one of the four subtypes of schizophrenia currently recognized by DSM-III-R (1987), and it is probably the most common diagnosis given to people with schizophrenia (with the paranoid subtype close behind). The essential features of this subtype are prominent psychotic features such as delusions, hallucinations, for-mal thought disorder, incoherence or grossly disorganized behavior, but it may combine features of two or more of the other subtypes, or features that simply cannot fit into the diagnostic descriptions of the other subtypes. Hence, "undifferentiated type" is a garbage pail diagnosis, usually reserved, however, for those who more closely match the nonparanoid forms of schizophrenia.

undoing   One of the psychological defense mechanisms identified by Sigmund FREUD in his theory of psychoanalysis. It is perhaps better referred to as "undoing what has been done," since this is a vivid description of what occurs. In undoing, a conflicted, ambivalent person makes an attempt to erase past thoughts, words or behaviors, as if they never occurred, by making use of thoughts, words or behaviors having the opposite meaning. In this sense, undoing involves a bit of MAGICAL THINKING, and although Freud described undoing as a defense mechanism often seen in persons who are obsessive-compulsive (as in the famous case of the "Rat Man") it is also observed in persons with psychotic disorders, particularly schizophrenia. (See also AMBIVALENCE.)

unitary psychosis   See EINHEITSPSYCHOSE.

United States   Worldwide prevalence rates for schizophrenia have been found to range from less than 1 to 17 per thousand persons. However, most studies conducted worldwide—including those in the United States—fall within the 2 to 5 per thousand range. In the United States, specific prevalence rates from research studies have ranged from 1.1 (among the rural Hutterites, a closed religious community) to 4.7 (if age corrected, from 2.1 to 6.4) per thousand. The highest rates of schizophrenia are found in the urban areas and among the lowest socioeconomic strata of American society. E. Fuller Torrey has suggested that preliminary evidence shows that the prevalence rate for schizophrenia in the United States may have risen since 1950 and recommends that more comprehensive research be carried out to investigate this possibility.

Torrey, E.F., "Prevalence Studies of Schizophrenia," *British Journal of Psychiatry,* 150 (1987), 598–608.

"usual treatment, the" Philippe Pinel's phrase that he used several times in his 1801 book, *A Treatise on Insanity,* to describe the treatment of institutionalized persons with mental disorders in the 18th and early 19th centuries—namely, "bleeding, bathing and purging."

Utica crib A form of MECHANICAL RESTRAINT originally developed in France by a physician named Aubanel in 1845 but first used in the United States at the Utica State Hospital in New York State upon the recommendation of its superintendent, Amariah Brigham, one of the original 13 founders of the American Psychiatric Association. It was a crib bed, but with a hinged lid that could be locked, keeping the patient confined in a horizontal position.

V

V.A. hospitals Hospitals in the United States for veterans of military service. They are managed under the auspices of the Veterans' Administration, and their psychiatric wards serve as an adjunct to the state hospital system for the mentally ill.

vampirism, clinical Although it is quite rare, there have been actual case reports of people with psychotic disorders engaging in clinical vampirism—that is, the ingestion of blood, whether one's own or the blood of others. Clinical vampirism is actually a "blood fetish" that often develops in childhood,

when the child finds the taste of his own blood enjoyable. Then, after puberty, these pleasurable feelings become associated with sexual activities, usually masturbation. The typical course starts with autovampirism, causing bleeding from one's own body through simple cuts or scrapes, to then opening major blood vessels to drink one's own blood. In some people, the fetish graduates to true clinical vampirism—the desire to drink the blood of others. Psychologist Richard Noll has suggested this syndrome be named RENFIELD'S SYNDROME, after the character in Bram Stoker's *Dracula*. People with schizophrenia have been reported to have engaged in clinical vampirism, but this is an extremely rare occurrence.

Benezech, M. et al., "Cannibalism and Vampirism in Paranoid Schizophrenia," *Journal of Clinical Psychiatry,* 42(1981), 7.

Noll, R., *Vampires, Werewolves and Demons: Twentieth Century Case Reports in the Psychiatric Literature*. New York: Brunner/Mazel, 1991.

Prins, H., "Vampirism—A Clinical Condition," *British Journal of Psychiatry,* 146(1985), 666–668.

variable expressivity In GENETICS STUDIES, if the same genetically transmitted abnormality produces different manifestations for either genetic or nongenetic reasons, it is said that this abnormality is characterized by variable expressivity. For example, the finding in schizophrenia research that smooth-pursuit eye movement abnormalities have been found in 60% of persons with schizophrenia and in 55% of their first-degree biological relatives might be an example of variable expressivity, because in many instances there are persons with schizophrenia who do not have abnormal smooth-pursuit eye movement but their nonschizophrenic relatives do (see EYE MOVEMENT ABNORMALITIES IN SCHIZOPHRENIA). All this may really mean is that an underlying process (or "latent trait," perhaps) may induce a disorder in the brain that produces either schizophrenia, smooth-pursuit eye movement abnormalities or both. These three possibilities illustrate the variable expressivity of this underlying process or trait.

Holzman, P.S., "Eye Movement Dysfunction and Psychosis," *International Review of Neurobiology*, 27(1985), 179–205.

vasomotor theory of psychosis   In the late 1800s, German neurologist and psychiatrist Theodore Meynert (1833–1892) proposed that the psychotic disorders were caused by pathological changes in the circulatory system. His theory of psychosis was thus based entirely on a physiological basis, but no scientific evidence was ever produced. Meynert's extreme emphasis on the physical causes of all disorders—mental and physical—had a profound influence on one of his medical school pupils in Vienna, the young Sigmund Freud, who took his first psychiatry classes with Meynert.

Meynert, T.H., *Klinische Vorlesunger über Psychiatrie*, Vienna: 1890.

ventriculomegaly   Literally, "enlarged ventricles," a common characteristic of persons with Type II schizophrenia. (See also BRAIN ABNORMALITIES IN SCHIZOPHRENIA.)

verbigeration   A term for the repetitious, meaningless speech of persons with psychotic disorders. It was first introduced by German psychiatrist Karl KAHLBAUM in 1874. In the English translation of the fourth edition of Eugen BLEULER's famous textbook on psychiatry, he defines this psychotic behavior in the following way: "The stereotype of speech, or *verbigeration*, always repeats the same words or sentences, often entirely senseless ones."

violence and schizophrenia   Contrary to the popular negative stereotype of the mentally ill as "psycho killers," it is probably not true that persons with schizophrenia are more violent toward others than those persons who do not have this disease. It is true that those persons with schizophrenia that do tend to be violent toward others are of the paranoid subtype or have transient paranoid delusions, are undermedicated or have ingested street drugs of some sort. It is also true that persons with schizophrenia have a higher rate of crimes against property than persons in the general population. In addition, persons with schizophrenia have higher rates of violence against themselves in the form of suicide when compared with the general population, and perhaps even for acts of self-mutilation, although there are no statistics for this latter observation. Although a prior history of violence is the best predictor of future violence in individual cases, it is still next to impossible for clinicians to accurately predict future acts of "dangerousness" or of violence.

McNiel, D.E. and Binder, R.L., "Predictive Validity of Judgments of Dangerous in Emergency Civil Commitment," *American Journal of Psychiatry*, 144(1987), 197–200.

Rada, R.T., "The Violent Patient: Rapid Assessment and Management," *Psychosomatics*, 22(1981), 101–109.

Weaver, K.E., "Increasing the Dose of Antipsychotic Medication to Control Violence," *American Journal of Psychiatry*, 140(1983), 1274.

Yesavage, J.A., "Inpatient Violence and the Schizophrenic Patient: An Inverse Correlation between Danger-Related Events and Neuroleptic Levels," *Biological Psychiatry*, 17(1982), 1331–1337.

viral theories of schizophrenia   Since the turn of the century, it has often been suggested that infectious agents might be the cause of schizophrenia. Both Emil KRAEPELIN and Eugen BLEULER commented on the fact that infectious processes might play a role in the development of schizophrenia. When it was discovered conclusively at around that time that the syndrome known as the GENERAL PARALYSIS OF THE INSANE was caused by tertiary syphilis, similar infectious agents were sought for dementia praecox (schizophrenia). Most of the research centered on bacteria (see FOCAL INFECTION AS A CAUSE OF PSYCHOTIC DISORDERS and TUBERCULOSIS AND PSYCHOSIS), since viruses were not well understood at the time.

After the First World War, worldwide outbreaks of influenza and Von Economo's encephalitis drew attention once again to this hypothesis, since postencephalitic patients seem to have the same signs and symptoms of schizophrenia. However, after the 1920s, the rise of psychoanalytic, psychosocial and family interaction theories of the causes of schizophrenia drew attention away from possible organic causes, such as viruses. It wasn't until the 1950s that interest once again briefly revived, only to subside until the 1970s, when research on the role of infectious agents in the development of many physical diseases began to uncover some promising results.

E. Fuller Torrey is responsible for drawing attention once again to the viral hypothesis of schizophrenia, after he became aware of some research that demonstrated that "slow" or latent viruses could cause central nervous system diseases after remaining latent in the body for perhaps 20 years or more. Such research continues into the possible viral causes of multiple sclerosis and many other diseases of the central nervous system. Torrey began research at the National Institute of Mental Health in the early 1970s by collecting the blood and cerebral spinal fluid (CSF) from persons with schizophrenia and then analyzing these fluids to detect evidence of a viral presence. His first publication on this viral hypothesis appeared in 1973.

Although other infectious agents such as bacteria, rickettsiae and fungi cannot be ruled out, viruses are prime suspects in schizophrenia for several reasons: (1) their frequent neurotropism, that is, their affinity for neural tissue; (2) their ability to remain latent in brain tissue for many years, perhaps even decades; (3) they can attack very specific areas of the brain (often the limbic system, which is implicated in schizophrenia) and leave others untouched; (4) their propensity to produce relapses and remissions; and (5) their ability to alter the enzymatic functions of brain cells without causing visible structural damage to the cells that could be picked up, for example, by BRAIN IMAGING TECHNIQUES or neuropathological methods. They have even been found to cause changes in the neurotransmitter of the brain, perhaps even producing the biochemical changes that produce the symptoms of schizophrenia.

There are several viral models as possible causes of schizophrenia. Some of them are based on the idea that an *in utero* infection of the fetus may affect fetal neural development and therefore result in schizophrenia later in life. This theory fits in with the research on perinatal factors as contributing causes to schizophrenia. Other theories propose that the mother or even the father may be an asymptomatic carrier that transmits the virus across the placenta during pregnancy. The SEASONALITY OF BIRTHS of persons who develop schizophrenia also fits well with a viral theory, since many viral infections are seasonal, and the excess of schizophrenic births in late winter to spring may be a reflection of prenatal infection. The fact that schizophrenia runs in families may be attributed to viral theories as well, since persons may be inheriting a genetic predisposition to being affected by a particular virus, or the virus may actually be transmitted on the gene itself (as is the case in retroviruses).

However, despite the logic of viral theories of schizophrenia, the research has not been very fruitful. In 1988, E. Fuller Torrey concluded in his review of the issue: "Despite the theoretical attractiveness of infectious agents as etiologic models, there is as yet little direct evidence with which to link them to schizophrenia. This may be because laboratory technology is not yet sensitive enough, we have not yet looked for the correct infectious agent, or the infectious hypothesis is simply wrong. In addition, adoption studies suggest that if infectious agents are involved in such cases, transmission of the agent must occur in utero or at birth.'' (See also MULTIPLE SCLEROSIS AND SCHIZOPHRENIA.)

Morozov, P.V. (ed.), *Research in the Viral Hypothesis of Mental Disorder.* Basel, Switzerland: Kerger, 1983.

Torrey, E.F., ''Stalking the Schizovirus,'' *Schizophrenia Bulletin,* 14(1988), 223–229.

Torrey, E.F. and Peterson, M.R., ''Slow and Latent Viruses in Schizophrenia,'' *Lancet,* 2 (1973), 22–24.

visual hallucinations   Hallucinations of sight. These may include *formed* images (such as people or alligators) or *unformed* images (such as flashes of light). Visual hallucinations have often been attributed to an organic cause, such as the presence of drugs in the person's system, or perhaps a metabolic disorder or an infection. In schizophrenia, auditory hallucinations have been the most commonly reported type. However, a 1989 study found that visual hallucinations may occur in 32% to 56% of persons with schizophrenia at some point in their illness, and that they are usually associated with auditory hallucinations, delusions and thought disorder. They found that visual hallucinations were slightly more prevalent in the nonparanoid forms of schizophrenia than in the paranoid forms but that this difference was not statistically significant in the study. They suggest that most clinicians do not ask about visual hallucinations (the most common interview question is often, ''Do you hear voices?''), and that probably accounts for why they are so infrequently discussed in the literature of schizophrenia.

Bracha, H.S. et al., ''High Prevalence of Visual Hallucinations in Research Subjects with Chronic Schizophrenia,'' *American Journal of Psychiatry,* 146(1989), 526–528.

von Meduna   See MEDUNA, LADISLAS JOSEPH VON.

vorbeireden   See GANSER'S SYNDROME.

vulnerability model of schizophrenia
What do all of the various theories of schizophrenia (genetic, environmental, developmental, learning, neurophysiological) have in common? Can they be unified in some way? These were the questions asked by researchers Joseph Zubin and Bonnie Spring, who propose in a 1977 paper that the concept of *vulnerability* is the common link between all of these theories. They write: ''The vulnerability model proposes that each of us is endowed with a degree of vulnerability that under suitable circumstances will express itself in an episode of schizophrenia illness.'' However, the researchers ''distinguish between *vulnerability* to schizophrenia, which we regard as a relatively permanent, enduring trait, and *episodes* of schizophrenic disorder, which are waxing and waning states.'' Thus, they suggest that both vulnerability and episodic ''markers'' (biological, genetic, environmental) must be found. Since the publication of this article, the concept of ''vulnerability'' in this wider, more general sense is often referred to in the literature of schizophrenia.

Zubin, J. and Spring, B., ''Vulnerability—A New View of Schizophrenia,'' *Journal of Abnormal Psychology,* 86(1977) 103–126.

W

water drinking, excessive, in persons with schizophrenia   See POLYDIPSIA.

water therapy   See HYDROTHERAPY.

wet sheets   See PACKING (AS TREATMENT).

whipping   See FLOGGING.

Williamsburg Eastern Lunatic Asylum   The first official asylum for the mentally ill to be founded in the United States. It was established in Williamsburg, Virginia, in 1773, and was open to all levels of society except slaves.

witchcraft   It has often been reported, especially in psychiatric textbooks, that the most prevalent theory of the causes of mental illness (and particularly the psychotic disorders) was a supernatural one based on "demons" or malevolent "spirits." Furthermore, it has often been reported that most of those people who died during the Great Witch Hunt in Europe, between about 1500 and 1650, were mentally ill. However, research by psychologist Thomas Schoeneman has demonstrated that these assertions, despite wide report in psychiatric textbooks, are untrue and that the evidence shows that most of the people who were executed for witchcraft were poor women with a sharp tongue and a bad temper, or old and unmarried—or that, in some areas, just about anyone was suspect.

Schoeneman, T.J., "The Mentally Ill Witch in Textbooks of Abnormal Psychology: Current Status and Implications of a Fallacy," *Professional Psychology: Research and Practice*, 15 (1984), 299–314.

withdrawal, social   This is one of the most commonly reported signs of schizophrenia and is present long before the definite outbreak of a psychosis in many persons. Social withdrawal is therefore part of the PRODROMAL PHASE of schizophrenia and can later develop into one of the chronic NEGATIVE SYMPTOMS of this disorder. Such persons may shun contact with others, for example, or be unable to interact or make eye contact when in the presence of others.

word salad   A very descriptive term for an abnormality of language that can be found in some persons with schizophrenia or with certain types of aphasias. A person speaking word salad just seem to toss out words without regard to their meaning, making unusual and meaningless combinations and perhaps even creating NEOLOGISMS.

work (as therapy)   See FARMING (AS TREATMENT); OCCUPATIONAL THERAPY.

World Health Organization   One of the semi-autonomous organizations created by the United Nations, the World Health Organization (WHO) has been instrumental in sponsoring epidemiological and CROSS-CULTURAL STUDIES of schizophrenia and other mental disorders. WHO, 20 Avenue Appia, CH-1211 Geneva 27, Switzerland (telephone: 791-36-17).

World Health Organization, *Schizophrenia: An International Follow-up Study*. Chichester, England: John Wiley & Sons, 1979.

World Psychiatric Association   An international association made up of national associations of psychiatrists from various countries. It was founded in 1961 and is currently based in Copenhagen, Denmark. *WPA:* Kommunehospitalet, DK-1399 Copenhagen K, Denmark (telephone: 45-33-938500, ext. 3390).

Y

York Retreat   The famous humane institution for the insane founded in 1792 by the Religious Society of Friends in York, England. Founded by William Tuke (1732–1822), it helped to put into practice the MORAL TREATMENT of the institutionalized mentally ill in England, as was shortly thereafter the case in Philippe PINEL's France and Vincenzo CHIARUGI's Italy. The emphasis was on occupational therapy and good food and sanitary conditions, with MECHANICAL RESTRAINTS used rarely, if at all. William

Tuke's grandson, Samuel Tuke (1784–1857), wrote a glowing description of the treatment of the mentally ill at the Retreat, and after its publication in 1813 it helped influence Parliament to investigate conditions in British asylums.

Daniel Hack Tuke (1827–1895), one of the leading psychiatrists in England in the 19th century, was the son of Samuel and the grandson of William Tuke.

Tuke, S., *Description of the Retreat*. London: 1813.

young adult chronic patient   With the ever-increasing problem of patients presenting with the dual diagnosis of a traditional psychotic disorder (schizophrenia, bipolar disorder, schizoaffective disorder) and a history of substance abuse since the 1960s, more and more young persons who are nonetheless following a *chronic* course of illness have made up a large percentage of the admissions to psychiatric facilities. This person has been labeled by psychiatrist Bert Pepper as the "young adult chronic patient." A young adult chronic patient is defined as one who is between 18 and 35 years old, abuses alcohol and drugs, is sexually active, has unpredictable and sometimes violent behavior, has frequent suicidal thoughts, often has children with whom there is little or no relationship, often has been arrested, cannot seem to hold down a job and is attention-seeking but also tends to reject treatment. (See also SUBSTANCE ABUSE.)

Pepper, B., "The Young Adult Chronic Patient: Population Overview," *Journal of Clinical Psychopharmacology*, 5(1985), 3S to 7S.

APPENDIXES

APPENDIXES

APPENDIX I

THE CARE OF PERSONS WITH SCHIZOPHRENIA IN THE UNITED STATES

Table 1. Clients/patients under care on a single day with a diagnosis of schizophrenia by type of program and type of mental health organization, United States, 1986.

Table 2. Clients/patients admitted with a diagnosis of schizophrenia by type of program and type of mental health organization, United States, 1986.

Table 3a. Inpatient programs: Percent distribution of clients/patients under care on a single day with a diagnosis of schizophrenia by selected client/patient characteristics, United States, 1986.

Table 3b. Outpatient programs: Percent distribution of clients/patients under care on a single day with a diagnosis of schizophrenia by selected client/patient characteristics, United States, 1986.

Table 3c. Partial care programs: Percent distribution of clients/patients under care on a single day with a diagnosis of schizophrenia by selected client/patient characteristics, United States, 1986.

Table 4a. Inpatient programs: Percent distribution of clients/patients admitted with a diagnosis of schizophrenia by selected client/patient characteristics, United States, 1986.

Table 4b. Outpatient programs: Percent distribution of clients/patients admitted with a diagnosis of schizophrenia by selected client/patient characteristics, United States, 1986.

Table 4c. Partial care programs: Percent distribution of clients/patients admitted with a diagnosis of schizophrenia by selected client/patient characteristics, United States, 1986.

(SOURCE: *Schizophrenia Bulletin,* 1989, vol. 15, no. 1)

Table 1. Clients/Patients Under Care on a Single Day with A Diagnosis of Schizophrenia[1] by Type of Program and Type of Mental Health Organization, United States, 1986

Type of Program & Mental Health Organization	Number & Percent Diagnosed with Schizophrenia		Total Number Under Care	Schizophrenia as a Percent of Total Under Care
	No.	%	No.	%
Total	387,874	100.0	1,808,245	21.5
Inpatient programs	73,064	18.8	193,291	37.8
State & county mental hospitals	58,066	15.0	111,110	52.3
Private psychiatric hospitals	1,872	0.5	24,084	7.8
Multiservice mental health organizations	2,070	0.5	5,852	35.4
VA medical centers	5,707	1.5	17,372	32.9
Non-Federal general hospitals with separate psychiatric services	5,349	1.4	34,873	15.3
Outpatient programs	265,768	68.5	1,489,651	17.8
State & county mental hospitals	17,401	4.5	51,938	33.5
Private psychiatric hospitals	5,081	1.3	48,717	10.4
Multiservice mental health organizations	163,130	42.1	851,228	19.2
VA medical centers	17,433	4.5	74,427	23.4
Non-Federal general hospitals with separate psychiatric services	29,035	7.5	203,930	14.2
Residential treatment centers for emotionally disturbed children	720	0.2	10,158	7.1
Freestanding outpatient mental health clinics	32,968	8.5	249,253	13.2
Partial care programs	49,043	12.6	125,303	39.1
State & county mental hospitals	1,564	0.4	3,909	40.0
Private psychiatric hospitals	1,178	0.3	2,966	39.7
Multiservice mental health organizations	36,589	9.4	90,307	40.5
VA medical centers	1,882	0.5	8,384	22.4
Non-Federal general hospitals with separate psychiatric services	5,157	1.3	11,074	46.6
Residential treatment centers for emotionally disturbed children	*	*	2,827	*
Freestanding partial care programs	2,426	0.6	5,836	41.6

[1] Clients/patients under care with a diagnosis of schizophreniform disorder are included in the figures reported for schizophrenia.
* Five or fewer sample cases; estimate not shown because it does not meet standards of reliability.

Table 2. Clients/Patients Admitted with a Diagnosis of Schizophrenia[1] by Type of Program and Type of Mental Health Organization, United States, 1986

Type of Program & Mental Health Organization	Number & Percent Diagnosed with Schizophrenia		Total Number of Admissions	Schizophrenia as a Percent of Total Admissions
	No.	%	No.	%
Total	495,416	100.0	4,168,081	12.0
Inpatient programs	323,925	65.4	1,691,172	19.2
State & county mental hospitals	105,303	21.3	345,032	30.5
Private psychiatric hospitals	17,089	3.4	211,180	8.1
Multiservice mental health organizations	25,916	5.2	94,928	27.3
VA medical centers	43,989	8.9	181,814	24.2
Non-Federal general hospitals with separate psychiatric services	131,628	26.6	858,218	15.3
Outpatient programs	128,321	25.9	2,294,806	5.6
State & county mental hospitals	9,317	1.9	48,946	19.0
Private psychiatric hospitals	3,332	0.7	84,208	4.0
Multiservice mental health organizations	66,541	13.4	1,355,518	4.9
VA medical centers	9,597	1.9	59,815	16.0
Non-Federal general hospitals with separate psychiatric services	23,746	4.8	298,607	8.0
Residential treatment centers for emotionally disturbed children	1,491	0.3	24,343	6.1
Freestanding outpatient mental health clinics	14,297	2.9	423,369	3.4
Partial care programs	43,170	8.7	161,481	26.7
State & county mental hospitals	3,370	0.7	9,429	35.7
Private psychiatric hospitals	572	0.1	6,147	9.3
Multiservice mental health organizations	30,444	6.1	107,718	28.3
VA medical centers	1,303	0.3	4,169	31.3
Non-Federal general hospitals with separate psychiatric services	5,415	1.1	25,913	20.9
Residential treatment centers for emotionally disturbed children	366	0.1	3,248	11.3
Freestanding partial care programs	1,700	0.3	4,857	35.0

[1] Clients/patients admitted with a diagnosis of schizophreniform disorder are included in the figures reported for schizophrenia.

Table 3a. Inpatient Programs: Percent Distribution of Clients/Patients under Care on a Single Day with a Diagnosis of Schizophrenia[1] by Selected Client/Patient Characteristics, United States, 1986

Selected Client/Patient Characteristics	Total	State & County Mental Hospitals	Private Psychiatric Hospitals	Multi-service	VA Medical Centers	Non-Federal General Hospitals
Total	73,064	58,066	1,872	2,070	5,707	5,349
Percent						
Male	64.2	61.4	59.7	68.2	99.6	56.8
White	64.4	62.7	85.6	70.6	68.3	69.3
Under 18	1.1	*	14.6	*	—	1.5
18–24	8.6	8.3	16.3	12.6	*	15.3
25–44	60.9	61.4	47.9	67.1	57.9	59.9
45–64	21.1	20.5	15.2	17.2	31.8	20.3
65+	8.3	9.0	*	*	8.8	3.0
Voluntary	31.9	22.8	65.4	35.0	76.8	70.4
Prior psychiatric inpatient care	91.6	93.1	74.8	83.6	92.7	82.9
No fee	38.5	46.0	*	35.6	7.2	4.8
Blue Cross/other private insurance	3.8	1.0	55.8	9.6	—	18.3
Medicare	22.9	25.7	30.8	11.4	—	18.6
Medicaid	8.2	6.0	*	14.6	—	39.0
VA	8.0	*	—	*	92.8	*
Individual therapy	66.6	64.0	93.5	71.5	66.0	85.1
Group therapy	53.7	51.2	68.1	58.8	58.4	69.0
Drug therapy	90.3	91.1	87.3	88.3	79.0	96.4

[1]Clients/patients under care with a diagnosis of schizophreniform disorder are included in the figures reported for schizophrenia.
*Five or fewer sample cases; estimate not shown because it does not meet standards of reliability.

Table 3b. Outpatient Programs: Percent Distribution of Clients/Patients under Care on a Single Day with a Diagnosis of Schizophrenia[1] by Selected Client/Patient Characteristics, United States, 1986

Selected Client/Patient Characteristics	Total[2]	State & County Mental Hospitals	Private Psychiatric Hospitals	Multi-service	VA Medical Centers	Non-Federal General Hospitals	Free-standing Outpatient Clinics
				Type of Mental Health Organization			
Total	265,768	17,401	5,081	163,130	17,433	29,035	32,968
Percent							
Male	54.8	51.1	79.2	50.7	96.4	40.7	63.6
White	69.7	63.7	74.7	68.2	75.6	68.7	76.3
Under 18	0.0	*	—	—	—	—	*
18–24	9.1	13.2	*	11.3	*	*	8.0
25–44	50.4	51.4	71.1	50.9	54.0	44.3	48.1
45–64	35.2	29.0	15.1	33.2	31.9	46.9	42.5
65+	5.2	6.3	*	4.6	11.6	7.7	*
Voluntary	93.7	75.4	100.0	95.5	95.8	93.8	92.3
Prior psychiatric inpatient care	72.5	73.1	30.5	72.8	73.2	90.0	61.0
No fee	15.9	56.9	—	11.3	3.8	*	38.8
Blue Cross/other private insurance	2.9	3.0	*	2.8	—	*	4.8
Medicare	14.9	7.1	25.0	18.8	—	19.3	*
Medicaid	33.7	17.8	*	37.3	—	44.9	31.0
VA	6.6	—	*	*	96.2	—	*
Individual therapy	54.0	70.0	59.0	51.9	68.7	43.0	56.9
Group therapy	18.3	36.2	3.0	13.7	13.0	32.9	24.2
Drug therapy	74.2	75.9	85.8	74.4	77.4	73.5	69.7

[1] Clients/patients under care with a diagnosis of schizophreniform disorder are included in the figures reported for schizophrenia.
[2] Figure includes 720 clients/patients in residential treatment centers for emotionally disturbed children.
*Five or fewer sample cases; estimate not shown because it does not meet standards of reliability.

Table 3c. Partial Care Programs: Percent Distribution of Clients/Patients Under Care on a Single Day With a Diagnosis of Schizophrenia[1] by Selected Client/Patient Characteristics, United States, 1986

Selected Client/Patient Characteristics	Total[2]	Type of Mental Health Organization					
		State & County Mental Hospitals	Private Psychiatric Hospitals	Multi-service	VA Medical Centers	Non-Federal General Hospitals	Free-standing Partial Care
Total	49,043	1,564	1,178	36,589	1,882	5,157	2,426
Percent							
Male	55.5	41.7	44.1	52.5	86.2	62.0	65.7
White	71.5	92.7	80.4	69.6	74.9	76.8	64.8
Under 18	1.0	*	*	*	—	*	*
18–24	7.7	8.2	2.2	7.9	*	8.2	9.3
25–44	53.4	21.5	60.0	53.6	48.1	65.4	45.6
45–64	29.4	51.9	36.2	28.9	42.0	17.7	36.4
65+	8.5	16.0	*	8.9	9.6	7.4	3.5
Voluntary	95.3	88.8	94.7	94.7	100.0	98.1	98.0
Prior psychiatric inpatient care	81.5	90.3	84.6	79.7	93.2	84.4	85.4
No fee	15.9	42.8	*	14.4	34.7	*	34.1
Blue Cross/other private insurance	1.9	*	10.0	1.6	—	1.7	*
Medicare	7.7	8.2	9.2	6.8	—	18.0	*
Medicaid	50.2	25.4	7.0	54.7	—	61.5	35.9
VA	3.4	—	—	1.0	65.3	1.0	*
Individual therapy	57.3	59.8	53.6	56.2	56.3	69.1	50.0
Group therapy	66.3	87.9	76.7	63.0	54.4	88.6	60.4
Drug therapy	68.0	69.1	69.7	71.2	64.0	70.1	18.9

[1]Clients/patients under care with a diagnosis of schizophreniform disorder are included in the figures reported for schizophrenia.
[2]Figure includes 247 clients/patients in residential treatment centers for emotionally disturbed children.
*Five or fewer sample cases; estimate not shown because it does not meet standards of reliability.

Table 4a. Inpatient Programs: Percent Distribution of Clients/Patients Admitted with a Diagnosis of Schizophrenia[1] by Selected Client/Patient Characteristics, United States, 1986

| Selected Client/Patient Characteristics | Total | Type of Mental Health Organization | | | | |
		State & County Mental Hospitals	Private Psychiatric Hospitals	Multi-service	VA Medical Centers	Non-Federal General Hospitals
Total	323,925	105,303	17,089	25,916	43,989	131,628
Percent						
Male	67.3	69.2	67.4	64.4	96.0	56.8
White	62.8	49.6	61.5	75.3	66.4	69.2
Under 18	1.1	*	*	*	—	1.5
18–24	12.0	10.3	16.7	12.9	*	15.3
25–44	65.1	71.7	62.7	70.8	62.1	59.9
45–64	17.9	11.9	11.8	14.9	29.2	20.3
65+	4.0	5.8	*	*	4.8	3.0
Voluntary	55.2	26.0	50.0	39.9	90.4	70.4
Prior psychiatric inpatient care	86.4	91.3	80.9	83.3	88.8	83.0
No fee	23.9	57.9	*	19.8	10.3	4.8
Blue Cross/other private insurance	10.7	2.1	36.5	8.0	—	18.4
Medicare	15.5	16.6	20.8	18.1	—	18.6
Medicaid	19.2	6.9	*	13.6	—	39.0
VA	12.2	*	—	*	87.4	*
Individual therapy	74.3	66.9	84.3	67.7	60.1	85.1
Group therapy	51.6	31.9	54.3	48.8	47.1	69.0
Drug therapy	90.1	84.7	89.5	89.7	84.5	96.5

[1] Clients/patients admitted with a diagnosis of schizophreniform disorder are included in the figures reported for schizophrenia.
*Five or fewer sample cases; estimate not shown because it does not meet standards of reliability.

Table 4b. Outpatient Programs: Percent Distribution of Clients/Patients Admitted with a Diagnosis of Schizophrenia[1] by Selected Client/Patient Characteristics, United States, 1986

Selected Client/ Patient Characteristics	Total[2]	Type of Mental Health Organization					
		State & County Mental Hospitals	Private Psychiatric Hospitals	Multi-service	VA Medical Centers	Non-Federal General Hospitals	Free-standing Outpatient Clinics
Total	128,321	9,317	3,332	66,541	9,597	23,746	14,297
Percent							
Male	67.8	69.2	81.4	67.9	97.4	55.8	61.8
White	68.3	66.1	95.1	67.1	68.1	69.5	64.0
Under 18	*	—	*	*	—	—	—
18–24	25.2	22.8	*	35.6	*	14.4	14.3
25–44	48.1	65.3	29.6	40.2	74.4	50.8	56.6
45–64	21.1	11.9	*	17.8	17.5	32.9	23.3
65+	4.3	—	*	4.2	5.4	*	*
Voluntary	91.4	87.5	70.5	93.7	95.9	97.5	78.7
Prior psychiatric inpatient care	73.5	82.8	100.0	74.5	81.1	68.7	62.2
No fee	16.7	55.5	—	14.7	9.1	*	25.1
Blue Cross/other private insurance	9.1	*	*	8.2	—	*	*
Medicare	6.8	*	*	4.1	—	*	*
Medicaid	29.1	32.1	*	30.5	—	31.0	42.1
VA	7.3	*	—	*	90.9	*	—
Individual therapy	44.8	25.9	56.5	51.8	40.3	35.0	40.7
Group therapy	6.8	*	*	6.0	3.9	11.1	*
Drug therapy	43.1	35.3	27.9	38.5	66.0	63.5	23.0

[1] Clients/patients admitted with a diagnosis of schizophreniform disorder are included in the figures reported for schizophrenia.
[2] Figure includes 1,491 clients/patients in residential treatment centers for emotionally disturbed children.
* Five or fewer sample cases; estimate not shown because it does not meet standards of reliability.

Table 4c. Partial Care Programs: Percent Distribution of Clients/Patients Admitted with a Diagnosis of Schizophrenia[1] by Selected Client/Patient Characteristics, United States, 1986

Selected Client/Patient Charactersitics	Total[2]	Type of Mental Health Organization					
		State & County Mental Hospitals	Private Psychiatric Hospitals	Multi-service	VA Medical Centers	Non-Federal General Hospitals	Free-standing Partial Care
Total	43,170	3,370	572	30,444	1,303	5,415	1,700
Percent							
Male	63.3	53.7	59.4	65.1	94.8	54.0	59.9
White	72.4	71.4	97.6	71.6	71.8	73.6	71.6
Under 18	0.4	*	*	*	—	—	*
18–24	15.7	*	*	18.8	*	*	14.0
25–44	59.6	61.4	58.0	58.0	72.6	68.3	54.4
45–64	22.4	24.9	20.3	21.0	19.5	29.1	22.2
65+	1.8	—	—	2.0	*	—	*
Voluntary	91.1	90.9	97.7	89.7	96.9	96.5	94.1
Prior psychiatric inpatient care	83.6	91.5	91.1	83.3	89.6	82.6	69.6
No fee	17.0	33.3	—	16.7	22.2	*	29.2
Blue Cross/other private insurance	3.2	*	42.0	1.6	—	10.2	*
Medicare	11.5	*	27.8	10.9	—	16.8	*
Medicaid	40.7	29.4	*	45.8	—	39.3	28.8
VA	3.0	*	—	*	77.8	—	*
Individual therapy	60.3	59.5	76.9	59.8	54.3	68.3	39.5
Group therapy	65.6	60.4	78.1	62.8	61.5	83.1	66.1
Drug therapy	58.4	56.5	74.5	57.7	68.1	67.6	34.1

[1]Clients/patients admitted with a diagnosis of schizophreniform disorder are included in the figures reported for schizophrenia.
[2]Figure includes 366 clients/patients in residential treatment centers for emotionally disturbed children.
*Five or fewer sample cases; estimate not shown because it does not meet standards of reliability.

APPENDIX II

The National Institute of Mental Health (NIMH) administers the federal government's major program of support for research in mental health. NIMH conducts and supports research in the etiology, treatment, and prevention of mental illnesses and research on many public health problems related to mental health. The many biological, genetic, psychological, social, and environmental factors that affect and shape mental health and mental illnesses are studied through NIMH-supported research in hospitals, universities, mental health centers, and community settings.

The schizophrenia-related research grants that appear below have been categorized under the administrative program of the NIMH Schizophrenia Research Branch (SRB) that was involved with its monitoring. The listing includes the title, grant number, total cost during fiscal years 1987 and 1989, name of principal investigator (PI), institution, city, and state. (The grants are presented in alphabetical order by PI.)

NIMH SCHIZOPHRENIA-RELATED RESEARCH GRANTS, FISCAL YEAR 1987

BIOLOGICAL AND CLINICAL FACTORS PROGRAM

INVESTIGATOR INITIATED RESEARCH GRANTS

Neuropsychiatric Mechanisms Underlying Flat Affect
MH 37952; $194,120

Alpert, Murray
New York University
New York, NY

Phenomenology and Classification of Schizophrenia
MH 31593; $372,303

Andreasen, Nancy A.
University of Iowa
Iowa City, IA

NMR Imaging in the Major Psychoses
MH 40856; $176,694

Andreasen, Nancy A.
University of Iowa
Iowa City, IA

The OR, DR, and SR in Schizophrenia and Depression
MH 28594; $124,438

Bernstein, Alvin S.
SUNY at Downstate Medical Center
Albany, NY

(SOURCES: *Schizophrenia Bulletin*, 1989, Vol. 15, No. 1; *Schizophrenia Bulletin*, 1990, Vol. 16, No. 4)

Circling: As a Probe of Lateral DA
Activity in Schizophrenia
MH 43537; $76,826

Bracha, Haim S.
University of California
La Jolla, CA

Sensory Gating and Habituation in
Schizophrenia
MH 42228; $156,154

Braff, David L.
University of California
La Jolla, CA

PET Studies in Schizophrenia
MH 42647; $220,336

Brodie, Jonathan D.
New York University Medical Center
New York, NY

Studies of Attention in Schizophrenia
MH 40071; $240,132

Buchsbaum, Monte S.
University of California
Irvine, CA

Feasibility Study of a Bar Detector
System for SPECT I
MH 43598; $31,786

Chang, Wei
University of Iowa
Iowa City, IA

Hemispheric Dysfunction in Psychosis
MH 39469; $105,638

Chapman, Loren J.
University of Wisconsin
Madison, WI

A Rational Use of Plasma HVA in
Mental Illness
MH 37922; $82,747

Davis, Kenneth L.
Mount Sinai School of Medicine
New York, NY

Nuclear Magnetic Resonance in
Schizophrenia
MH 37820; $157,374

DeMyer, Marian K.
Indiana University
Indianapolis, IN

Hemispheric Activation and Emotion in
Families of Schizophrenics
MH 43587; $34,689

Doane, Jeri A.
Yale University
New Haven, CT

Prospective Study of Children of
Schizophrenic Parents
MH 19560; $580,707

Erlenmeyer-Kimling, L.
Research Foundation for Mental Hygiene,
  Inc.
New York, NY

Electrophysiology of Sensory Gating in
Schizophrenia
MH 38321; $142,558

Freedman, Robert
University of Colorado
Denver, CO

Autoimmune Phenomena and Psychotic
Relapse in Schizophrenia
MH 41883; $149,080

Ganguli, Rohan
University of Pittsburgh
Pittsburgh, PA

A Neurobehavioral Study of
Schizophrenia
MH 42191; $213,829

Gur, Raquel E.
University of Pennsylvania
Philadelphia, PA

Sex Differences in Schizophrenia
MH 43613; $98,456

Haas, Gretchen L.
Cornell University Medical College
New York, NY

Schizophrenic Cognition: A Longitudinal Study
MH 26341; $99,689

Harrow, Martin
Michael Reese Hospital and Medical
   Center
Chicago, IL

Tyrosine Hydroxylase Phosphorylation and Schizophrenia
MH 43620; $33,919

Haycock, John W.
Louisiana State University
New Orleans, LA

Collaborative Biological Research in Schizophrenia
MH 31154; $1,094,732

Holzman, Philip S.
McLean Hospital
Belmont, MA

Psychomotility and Cognitive Style in the Schizophrenias
MH 31340; $199,322

Holzman, Philip S.
Harvard University
Cambridge, MA

Adoption Study Analyses of the Etiology of Schizophrenia
MH 41582; $151,223

Holzman, Philip S.
McLean Hospital
Belmont, MA

Longitudinal ERP Studies of Schizophrenics and Siblings
MH 42769; $122,093

Josiassen, Richard C.
Temple University
Philadelphia, PA

Biology of Schizophrenia and Mood Disorders in Families
MH 43687; $34,750

Keshavan, Matcheri S.
University of Pittsburgh
Pittsburgh, PA

Autonomic OR in Schizophrenia
MH 40803; $43,325

Levinson, Douglas F.
Medical College of Pennsylvania
Philadelphia, PA

Validation of Negative Symptoms: Data Analysis
MH 42485; $18,848

Lewine, Richard R.J.
Emory University
Atlanta, GA

Prospective Study of Psychobiology in Schizophrenia
MH 41646; $224,182

Lieberman, Jeffrey A.
Long Island Jewish Medical Center
New Hyde Park, NY

Debrisoquin as an Agent for the Study of Psychotic State
MH 40935; $177,185

Maas, James W.
University of Texas
San Antonio, TX

Functional Asymmetry, Cognitive Deficiencies and the Genetics of Schizophrenia
MH 42266; $82,912

Markow, Therese A.
Arizona State University
Tempe, AZ

**Neurophysiological Studies of
Schizophrenia
MH 40799; $200,131**

McCarley, Robert W.
Harvard Medical School
Boston, MA

**Temporal Integration in the
Schizophrenic Spectrum
MH 43593; $36,500**

Merritt, Rebecca D.
Purdue Research Foundation
West Lafayette, IN

**Developmental Processes in
Schizophrenic Disorders
MH 37705; $172,412**

Nuechterlein, Keith H.
University of California
Los Angeles, CA

**A 24-Year Followup of Children of
Schizophrenic Mothers
MH 41469; $284,860**

Parnas, Josef S.
Psykologisk Institut
Copenhagen, Denmark

**The Application of Genetic Strategies to
Neuroimaging
MH 43740; $109,382**

Resnick, Susan M.
University of Pennsylvania
Philadelphia, PA

**PET Analysis of Dopamine$_2$ Receptors in
Schizophrenia
MH 41205; $176,250**

Sedvall, Göran C.
Karolinska Institute
Stockholm, Sweden

**Electrophysiological Studies of
Psychiatric Disorder
MH 12507; $352,601**

Shagass, Charles
Temple University
Philadelphia, PA

**Vulnerability to Schizophrenia
Neurobehavioral Aspects
MH 43615; $106,170**

Steinhauer, Stuart R.
University of Pittsburgh
Pittsburgh, PA

**Biological Markers in Discordant
Monozygotic Twins
MH 41176; $198,727**

Torrey, E. Fuller
Friends Medical Science Research Center
Baltimore, MD

**Drug Response and Genetic Factors in
Schizophrenia
MH 41874; $241,255**

Tsuang, Ming T.
Harvard Medical School
Boston, MA

**Gender and Schizophrenia:
Epidemiologic Implications
MH 42604; $97,428**

Tsuang, Ming T.
Harvard Medical School
Boston, MA

**^{11}C-N-Methylspiperone PET Scans in
Schizophrenia
MH 40362; $49,907**

Tune, Larry E.
The Johns Hopkins University
Baltimore, MD

**Alprazolam-Neuroleptic Treatment in
Schizophrenia
MH 43612; $81,471**

Wolkowitz, Owen M.
University of California
San Francisco, CA

Quantitative Receptor Imaging in Schizophrenia
MH 42821, $283,588

Wong, Dean F.
The Johns Hopkins University
Baltimore, MD

Behavioral and rCBF Studies of Memory in Psychopathology
MH 39599; $193,796

Wood, Frank B.
Wake Forest University
Winston-Salem, NC

Sleep and REM Phasic Events in the Schizophrenias
MH 37252; $183,504

Zarcone, Vincent P., Jr.
Stanford University
Stanford, CA

Dopamine Functional Subtypes of Schizophrenia
MH 40293; $164,743

Zemlan, Frank P.
University of Cincinnati
Cincinnati, OH

CAREER DEVELOPMENT AND RESEARCH TRAINING

Major Psychosis: Phenomenology, Behavior, and Genetics
MH 00625; $60,750

Andreasen, Nancy C.
University of Iowa
Iowa City, IA

Context Disturbance in Schizophrenia: Models and Measures
MH 00673; $57,526

Cohen, Jonathan D.
Stanford University
Stanford, CT

Autoimmune Mechanisms in Schizophrenia
MH 00626; $63,482

Ganguli, Rohan
University of Pittsburgh
Pittsburgh, PA

Neuronal Phosphoproteins in Neuropsychiatric Disorders
MH 00671; $71,741

Grebb, Jack A.
New York University Medical Center
New York, NY

Regional Brain Activity and Psychopathology
MH 00586; $60,750

Gur, Raquel E.
University of Pennsylvania
Philadelphia, PA

Molecular Neurobiology of Schizophrenia
MH 00682; $51,948

Kaufmann, Charles A.
Columbia University
New York, NY

Cognitive and Psychomotor Disorders in Psychopathology
MH 00460; $67,230

Levin, Smadar
McLean Hospital
Belmont, MA

Schizophrenia in High-Risk Populations
MH 00619; $60,556

Mednick, Sarnoff A.
University of Southern California
Los Angeles, CA

Biological Studies of the Major Psychoses
MH 47808; $60,264

Meltzer, Herbert Y.
Case Western Reserve University
Cleveland, OH

RSDA Training Program in PET and
Schizophrenia Research
MH 00723; $70,618

Tune, Larry E.
The Johns Hopkins University
Baltimore, MD

PHARMACOLOGIC AND SOMATIC TREATMENTS PROGRAM

INVESTIGATOR INITIATED RESEARCH GRANTS

Dopamine and Chronic Antipsychotic
Drug Treatment
MH 28216; $89,609

Bowers, Malcolm B., Jr.
Yale University
New Haven, CT

Chlorpromazine, Immunogenetics and
Tardive Dyskinesia
MH 39528; $65,040

Canoso, Rosa T.
Beth Israel Hospital
Boston, MA

Outpatient Treatment: Targeted vs.
Maintenance Medication
MH 35996; $200,520

Carpenter, William T., Jr.
University of Maryland
Baltimore, MD

The Efficacy of Carbamazepine in
Psychiatric Outpatients
MH 42582; $80,072

Carpenter, William T., Jr.
University of Maryland
Baltimore, MD

Antipsychotic Drug-Induced Dyskinesias
MH 36657; $119,113

Casey, Daniel E.
Medical Research Foundation of Oregon
Portland, OR

The Course of Dyskinesia
MH 32675; $218,940

Cole, Jonathan O.
Boston Mental Health Foundation
Boston, MA

Drug Holidays in Chronic Neuroleptics:
An Animal Model
MH 39961; $61,772

Ellison, Gaylord D.
University of California
Los Angeles, CA

Biological Studies of Psychotic Disorders
MH 08618; $568,928

Friedhoff, Arnold J.
New York University
New York, NY

Striatal Transmission Imbalance in
Tardive Dyskinesia
MH 42429; $150,159

Friedman, Eitan
Medical College of Pennsylvania
Philadelphia, PA

Epidemiologic Studies of Tardive
Dyskinesia
MH 39665; $170,475

Glazer, William M.
Yale University
New Haven, CT

Intermittent vs. Maintenance Medication
in Schizophrenia
MH 37343; $185,440

Herz, Marvin I.
SUNY at Buffalo
Albany, NY

Drug-Induced Movement Disorders in Schizophrenia
MH 43586; $91,398

Hoffman, William F.
Oregon Health Sciences University
Portland, OR

Pharmacotherapy of Distress in Recovering Schizophrenia
MH 39166; $453,646

Hogarty, Gerard E.
University of Pittsburgh
Pittsburgh, PA

Treatment of Neuroleptic Nonresponsive Schizophrenia
MH 42929; $186,601

Johns, Celeste A.
Long Island Jewish Medical Center
New Hyde Park, NY

Prospective Study of Tardive Dyskinesia Development
MH 32369; $239,281

Kane, John M.
Long Island Jewish-Hillside
   Medical Center
New Hyde Park, NY

Prospective Study of Tardive Dyskinesia in the Elderly
MH 40015; $189,241

Kane, John M.
Long Island Jewish-Hillside Medical
   Center
New Hyde Park, NY

Psychoactive Drug Levels in Depressed Schizophrenics
MH 42679; $16,952

Kramer, Mark S.
VA Medical Center
Coatesville, PA

Prediction of Relapse in Schizophrenia
MH 38880; $172,236

Lieberman, Jeffrey A.
Long Island Jewish-Hillside Medical
   Center
New Hyde Park, NY

Management of Risk for Relapse in Schizophrenia
MH 41573; $165,135

Marder, Stephen R.
University of California
Los Angeles, CA

The Neuroleptic Threshold Dose in Acute Schizophrenia
MH 41254; $210,737

McEvoy, Joseph P.
University of Pittsburgh
Pittsburgh, PA

Neuroleptic Effects on Regional Cerebral Blood Flow
MH 41961; $184,674

Mukherjee, Sukdeb
Research Foundation for Mental
   Hygiene, Inc.
New York, NY

Clinical Psychopharmacology Computer Laboratory
MH 32457; $110,075

Overall, John E.
University of Texas
Houston, TX

Tardive Dyskinesia Outcome— Persistence or Resolution?
MH 41802; $157,168

Richardson, Mary Ann
Research Foundation for Mental Hygiene,
   Inc.
Albany, NY

**Fluphenazine Blood Levels, Efficacy,
and Pharmacokinetics
MH 41585; $154,616**

Simpson, George M.
Medical College of Pennsylvania
Philadelphia, PA

**Prolactin/Fluphenazine Levels in
Maintenance Schizophrenia
MH 42445; $145,370**

Simpson, George M.
Medical College of Pennsylvania
Philadelphia, PA

**Adjunctive Imipramine in Depressed
Schizophrenics
MH 34309; $222,538**

Siris, Samuel G.
Mount Sinai University
New York, NY

**Psychotropic Drugs: Competency and
Commitment in Mentally Ill
MH 41735; $119,561**

Stanley, Barbara H.
John Jay College—CUNY
New York, NY

**GABA Agonist Therapy in Tardive
Dyskinesia
MH 37073; $155,010**

Tamminga, Carol A.
University of Maryland
Baltimore, MD

**Haloperidol Kinetics in Persistent
Psychosis
MH 37264; $114,175**

Tamminga, Carol A.
University of Maryland
Baltimore, MD

**Regional Brain Glucose Utilization
Before and After Neuroleptic**

**Withdrawal in Schizophrenic Patients
With and Without Tardive Dyskinesia
MH 42234; $192,387**

Tamminga, Carol A.
University of Maryland
Baltimore, MD

**Haloperidol Blood Levels and Effects in
Schizophrenia
MH 41772; $236,059**

Volavka, Jan
Research Foundation for Mental Hygiene,
   Inc.
Albany, NY

CAREER DEVELOPMENT AND RESEARCH TRAINING

**Chemical Factors in Abnormal Behavior
MH 14024; $59,584**

Friedhoff, Arnold J.
New York University
New York, NY

**Prospective Study of Psychobiology in
Schizophrenia
MH 00537; $63,277**

Lieberman, Jeffrey A.
Long Island Jewish-Hillside Medical
   Center
New Hyde Park, NY

**Pharmacologic Characterization of
Borderline Disorders
MH 00658; $61,479**

Soloff, Paul H.
University of Pittsburgh
Pittsburgh, PA

COOPERATIVE AGREEMENTS

**Treatment Strategies in Schizophrenia
MH 39998; $393,450**

Bellack, Alan S.
Medical College of Pennsylvania
Philadelphia, PA

Treatment Strategies in Schizophrenia
MH 40007; $380,045

Glick, Ira D.
Cornell University
New York, NY

Treatment Strategies in Schizophrenia
MH 40042; $365,396

Hargreaves, William A.
University of California
San Francisco, CA

Computed Tomography Study of
Schizophrenia
MH 42321; $20,884

Jacobs, Marc
University of California
San Francisco, CA

Treatment Strategies in Schizophrenia
MH 39992; $302,580

Kane, John M.
Long Island Jewish-Hillside Medical
  Center
New Hyde Park, NY

Computed Tomography Study in
Schizophrenia
MH 42271; $16,203

Lieberman, Jeffrey A.
Long Island Jewish Medical Center
New Hyde Park, NY

Treatment Strategies in Schizophrenia
MH 40597; $341,763

Ninan, Philip T.
Emory University
Atlanta, GA

Computed Tomography Study of
Schizophrenia
MH 42298; $51,496

Ninan, Philip T.
Emory University
Atlanta, GA

Computed Tomography Study of
Schizophrenia
MH 42305; $16,790

Sweeney, John
Cornell University Medical College
New York, NY

Computed Tomography Study of
Schizophrenia
MH 42304; $26,001

Yadalam, Kashinath G.
Medical College of Pennsylvania
Philadelphia, PA

PSYCHOSOCIAL TREATMENT AND REHABILITATION PROGRAMS

INVESTIGATOR INITIATED RESEARCH GRANTS

Social Skill and Schizophrenia
MH 38636; $221,709

Bellack, Alan S.
Medical College of Pennsylvania
Philadelphia, PA

A Functional Analysis of Family
Therapy in Schizophrenia
MH 41577; $151,962

Bellack, Alan S.
Medical College of Pennsylvania
Philadelphia, PA

Risk Factors Associated With Mortality
in Schizophrenia
MH 43652; $34,750

Black, Donald W.
University of Iowa
Iowa City, IA

Schizophrenic Offspring From Birth to
Adulthood
MH 31653; $76,332

Fish, Barbara
University of California
Los Angeles, CA

Boarding Homes and Relapse in Chronic Schizophrenics
MH 43689; $37,250

Fox, Jeanne C.
University of Virginia
Charlottesville, VA

Coping Behavior in Schizophrenia
MH 08744; $202,974

Goldstein, Michael J.
University of California
Los Angeles, CA

Environmental-Personal Treatment of Schizophrenia
MH 30750; $255,152

Hogarty, Gerard E.
University of Pittsburgh
Pittsburgh, PA

Expressed Emotion and Relapse in Schizophrenic Patients
MH 42782; $217,178

Hooley, Jill M.
Harvard University
Cambridge, MA

The Course of Schizophrenia
MH 34365; $87,146

Strauss, John S.
Yale University
New Haven, CT

Long-Term Community Treatment of Young Schizophrenics
MH 40886; $218,407

Test, Mary Ann
University of Wisconsin
Madison, WI

Finnish Adoptive Family Study of Schizophrenia
MH 39663; $183,840

Wynne, Lyman C.
University of Rochester
Rochester, NY

CAREER DEVELOPMENT AND RESEARCH TRAINING

Understanding the Course of Psychiatric Disorder
MH 00340; $62,897

Strauss, John S.
Yale University
New Haven, CT

NIMH SCHIZOPHRENIA-RELATED RESEARCH GRANTS, FISCAL YEAR 1989

DIVISION OF BASIC BRAIN AND BEHAVIORAL SCIENCES

Pharmacology or Dopamine Receptors in Mammalian Brain
MH 34006; $261,783

Baldessarini, Ross J.
Harvard University
McLean Hospital
Belmont, MA

Biological Substrates and Correlates of Schizophrenia
MH 00423; $61,097

Benes, Francine M.
Harvard University
Mailman Research Center
McLean Hospital
Belmont, MA

Quantitative Cytoarchitectural Studies of Schizophrenic Cortex
MH 42261; $93,824

Benes, Francine M.
Harvard University
Mailman Research Center
McLean Hospital
Belmont, MA

Brain Tissue Resource for Neuropsychiatric Research
MH 31862; $547,168

Bird, Edward D.
Harvard University
McLean Hospital
Belmont, MA

Neurological Brain Abnormalities in Schizophrenia
MH 44188; $654,661

Bunney, William E., Jr.
University of California
College of Medicine
Irvine, CA

Neuroscience Center for Research in Schizophrenia
MH 44211; $641,728

Carpenter, William T., Jr.
University of Maryland
Maryland Psychiatric Research Center
Baltimore, MD

Antipsychotic Drug Effects: Tests of NE Versus DA Mechanism
MH 42543; $128,010

Cohen, Bruce M.
Harvard University
Mailman Research Center
McLean Hospital
Belmont, MA

Dopamine Receptors, Antipsychotic Drugs and Schizophrenia
MH 00316; $60,410

Creese, Ian N.
Rutgers University
Newark, NJ

Emotional Reactivity and Frontal Brain Asymmetry
MH 43454; $220,991

Davidson, Richard
University of Wisconsin
Madison, WI

Dopamine System Interaction and Schizophrenia
MH 45124; $88,348

Deutch, Ariel Y.
Yale University
School of Medicine
New Haven, CT

Effect of Neurotensin on Dopamine Release in the CNS
MH 42934; $78,970

Dwoskin, Linda P.
University of Kentucky
Lexington, KY

Postdoctoral Training in Emotion Research
MH 18931; $146,347

Ekman, Paul
University of California
San Francisco Medical Center
San Francisco, CA

Genetic and Neurobiological Investigation of Schizophrenia
MH 44212; $679,896

Freedman, Robert
University of Colorado Health Sciences
    Center
Denver, CO

Hypothalamic Neuropeptides and
Schizophrenia
MH 45480; $149,313

Gabriel, Steven
Bronx Veterans Administration Medical
  Center
Bronx, NY

Cortical Mechanisms in Schizophrenia
MH 44866; $1,880,345

Goldman-Rakic, Patricia
Yale University
School of Medicine
New Haven, CT

Dopamine-Neuropeptide Coexistence and
Mental Function
MH 43230; $354,870

Goldstein, Menek
New York University Medical Center
New York, NY

In Vitro Electrophysiology of Midbrain
Dopamine Neurons
MH 42217; $70,766

Grace, Anthony A.
University of Pittsburgh
Pittsburgh, PA

Automatic Mechanisms for Detection
and Identification
MH 42465; $124,688

Graham, Frances
University of Delaware
Newark, DE

Actions of Clozapine—A More Effective
Antipsychotic
MH 42868; $125,524

Gudelsky, Gary A.
Case Western Reserve University
Cleveland, OH

Drug Mechanism in Neuronal Dopamine
Organization
MH 28942; $295,890

Heller, Alfred
The University of Chicago
Chicago, IL

Brain Dopamine Regulation of Male Sex
Behavior in Rats
MH 40826; $126,485

Hull, Elaine M.
State University of New York
Buffalo, NY

Cognitive Neuropsychology
MH 18215; $55,969

Hulse, Stuart
The John Hopkins University
Baltimore, MD

CA2+ Antagonists and Brain Dopamine
Receptor Regulation
MH 42894; $101,022

Janowsky, Aaron J.
Veterans Medical Center Research Service
Portland, OR

Phencyclidine Psychopharmacology:
Model for Schizophrenia
MH 00631; $99,834

Javitt, Daniel C.
Albert Einstein College of Medicine
New York, NY

Neurotransmitter Disorders in
Schizophrenia
MH 43852; $105,132

Joyce, Jeffrey N.
University of Pennsylvania
School of Medicine
Philadelphia, PA

Regulation of Mesolimbic Dopamine by
Endogenous Compounds
MH 40817; $108,798

Kalivas, Peter W.
Washington State University
Pullman, WA

Mesoamygdaloid Dopamine Neurons and Antipsychotic Drugs
MH 39967; $153,515

Kilts, Clinton D.
Duke University
Durham, NC

The Function and Process of Individual Differences in Emotion Response Intensity
MH 42057; $49,473

Larsen, Randy
Purdue University
West Lafayette, IN

In Vivo Pharmacology of Dopamine Receptor Subtypes
MH 00708; $77,962

Leslie, Catherine
University of Virginia
Charlottesville, VA

Dopaminergic Innervation of Primate Neocortex
MH 43784; $139,296

Lewis, David A.
University of Pittsburgh
Western Psychiatric Institute and Clinic
Pittsburgh, PA

Late Behavior and EEG Effects of Antipsychotic Medication
MH 39057; $106,666

Lifshitz, Kenneth
Nathan S. Kline Institute
Research Foundation for Mental Hygiene, Inc.
Orangeburg, NY

Encoding Processes on Complex Visual Stimuli
MH 41637; $83,175

Loftus, Geoffrey
University of Washington
Seattle, WA

Psychoendocrine Studies of Diagnosis and Bereavement
MH 00346; $62,181

Mason, John W.
Yale University
School of Medicine
Veterans Administration Medical Center
West Haven, CT

Autoreceptor Regulation of Dopamine Release
MH 41551; $112,631

Masserano, Joseph M.
University of Colorado Health Science Center
Denver, CO

Mechanisms in Dopamine Receptor Sensitivity Regulation
MH 00656; $70,129

Miller, Jeannette
New York University
New York, NY

Neurotensin—An Endogenous Neuroleptic-Like Peptide
MH 39415; $127,450

Nemeroff, Charles B.
Duke University
Durham, NC

Desensitization of Dopamine D_2 Receptors
MH 45372; $100,888

Neve, Kim A.
Oregon Health Sciences University
Portland, OR

Development of Potentially Selective Dopamine Agonists
MH 42705; $93,015

Nichols, David E.
Purdue University
West Lafayette, IN

Neuroleptic Interaction With Dopamine Receptor Subtypes
MH 44799; $106,814

Randall, Patrick K.
University of Texas
Austin, TX

Mesocorticolimbic Dopamine Neurons In Vitro
MH 44736; $87,731

Rayport, Stephen G.
Columbia University Medical Center
New York, NY

The Genetic Control of Dopamine-Containing Neurons
MH 00655; $60,264

Roffler-Tarlo, Suzanne K.
Tufts University
Boston, MA

Antipsychotic Drugs and Control of Dopaminergic Neurons
MH 14092; $208,680

Roth, Robert H.
Yale University
New Haven, CT

Early Development of Temperamental Self-Regulation
MH 43361; $111,385

Rothbart, Mary
University of Oregon
Eugene, OR

Electrochemical Studies of Antipsychotic Drug Action
MH 42759; $75,769

Schenk, James O.
Yale University
School of Medicine
New Haven, CT

Development of the Nigrostriatal Dopaminergic Axons
MH 44887; $36,500

Shults, Clifford
University of California
Veterans Administration Medical Center
San Diego, CA

Role of Dopamine in Early Striatal Development
MH 45342; $24,863

Snyder-Keller, Abigail
Wadsword Center for Labs and Research
Albany, NY

Memory as Affected by Injury, Disease, and ECT
MH 24600; $187,629

Squire, Larry
University of California, San Diego
La Jolla, CA

Schizophrenia and Afferent Control of Dopamine Neurons
MH 45286; $114,539

Tepper, James M.
Rutgers University
Center for Molecular and Behavioral
  Neuroscience
Newark, NJ

Molecular Cloning of Dopamine Receptor
MH 45019; $176,950

Todd, Richard D.
Washington University
St. Louis, MO

Neuroleptic and Dopamine-Colocalized Peptide Gene Expression
MH 43854; $134,345

Uhl, George R.
The Johns Hopkins University
Baltimore, MD

The Mode of Action of Antipsychotic Drugs
MH 00378; $60,993

Wang, Rex
SUNY at Stony Brook
Stony Brook, NY

**Behavioral and Biochemical Correlates
of Dopamine
MH 42148; $149,401**

Weiss, Benjamin
The Medical College of Philadelphia—
  EPPI
Philadelphia, PA

**Nucleus Accumbens Neurons and
Schizophrenia
MH 40832; $78,867**

White, Francis J.
University of Illinois
Champaign, IL

DIVISION OF BIOMETRY AND APPLIED SCIENCES

**Mental Health Services Study:
Capitation Payments System
MH 40053; $377,000**

Babigian, Haroutun M.
University of Rochester Medical Center
Rochester, NY

**Capitated Payment System for
Involuntary Clients
MH 44686; $152,975**

Bigelow, Douglas A.
Oregon Health Sciences University
Portland, OR

**Management and Treatment of Insanity
Acquitees in Oregon
MH 42221; $168,118**

Bloom, Joseph D.
Oregon Health Sciences University
Portland, OR

**Research Scientist Development Award,
Level II
MH 00842; $64,400**

Bond, Gary R.
Purdue University
Indianapolis, IN

**Cost Effectiveness of PACT Programs
MH 46624; $263,796**

Burns, Barbara J.
Duke University Medical Center
Durham, NC

**Comparing Programs for Monitoring
NGRIs
MH 44258; $90,304**

Callahan, Lisa
Policy Research Associates, Inc.
Delmar, NY

**Evaluation of Treatments for the
Homeless Mentally Ill
MH 43248; $218,539**

Calsyn, Robert J.
University of Missouri
St. Louis, MO

**Service Uses and Homelessness in
Chronic Mental Illness
MH 44705; $249,981**

Caton, Carol L.
Columbia University
New York, NY

**Efficacy of Two Models of Vocational
Service to the Chronically Mentally Ill
MH 44913; $130,851**

Cook, Judith A.
Thresholds Research Institute
Chicago, IL

**Substance Abuse in the Severely
Mentally Ill
MH 46363; $79,425**

Corse, Sara J.
Mercy Catholic Medical Center
Misericordia Hospital
Philadelphia, PA

Videotape Recording of Psychiatric Inpatient Assaults
MH 44662; $99,544

Crowner, Martha L.
Manhattan Psychiatric Center
Ward's Island, NY

Enhancing Research Capacity in State Mental Health Agencies—California
MH 46296; $135,311

DeRisi, William
California Department of Mental Health
Sacramento, CA

Tailoring Treatment for the Chronically Mentally Ill
MH 44691; $90,602

Dozier, Mary
Trinity University
San Antonio, TX

ADAMHA Research Scientist Development Award, Level II
MH 00839; $66,877

Drake, Robert
Dartmouth University Medical Center
Hanover, NH

Long-Term Course of Severely Mentally Ill in Four Service Systems
MH 44653; $133,883

Eaton, William W.
The Johns Hopkins University
School of Hygiene and Public Health
Baltimore, MD

Comparisons of Treatment: Research to Enhance SMHA Capacity
MH 46306; $144,270

Essock, Susan M.
Connecticut Department of Mental Health
Hartford, CT

Income Maintenance, Dependence, and Service System Use
MH 40314; $277,904

Estroff, Sue
University of North Carolina
School of Medicine
Chapel Hill, NC

Consequences of Cost Containment Policies for Mental Health
MH 44407; $123,723

Frank, Richard G.
The Johns Hopkins University School of
   Hygiene and Public Health
Baltimore, MD

Mental Health Services Research Center
MH 43555; $412,888

Greenley, James R.
University of Wisconsin
Mental Health Research Center
Madison, WI

Assessment-Based Augmentation of the Case Management Process
MH 46364; $102,314

Gudeman, Howard
Hawaii State Hospital
Honolulu, HI

Cost-Effectiveness of Services for Severely Mentally Ill
MH 45072; $267,859

Jerrell, Jeanette
Western Consortium for Public Health
Berkeley, CA

Cost-Effectiveness of Substance Abuse Treatment for Severely Mentally Ill
MH 46331; $302,817

Jerrell, Jeanette
Western Consortium for Public Health
Berkeley, CA

Self-Help and Severe Mental Illness
MH 45218; $206,408

Kaufmann, Caroline L.
University of Pittsburgh
Western Psychiatric Institute and Clinic
Pittsburgh, PA

**Validation of a Mental Health Service
System Model
MH 44878; $181,206**

Leff, H. Stephen
Human Services Research Institute
Cambridge, MA

**Conditional Prediction and the
Management of Dangerousness
MH 40030; $597,747**

Lidz, Charles
University of Pittsburgh
Western Psychiatric Institute and Clinic
Pittsburgh, Pa

**Attitudes Toward the Homeless/
Homeless Mentally Ill
MH 46101; $321,336**

Link, Bruce G.
Columbia University
Psychiatric Epidemiology Training Program
New York, NY

**Capitating Noninstitutionalized
Schizophrenic Medicaid Recipients
MH 43410; $223,166**

Lurie, Nicole
University of Minnesota
School of Public Health
Minneapolis, MN

**Center for Research on Care of Severely
Mentally Ill
MH 43458; $284,313**

McFarland, Bentson H.
Oregon Health Sciences University
Portland, OR

**Center for Research on the Organization
and Financing Care for the Severely
Mentally Ill
MH 43450; $346,717**

Mechanic, David
Rutgers University
Institute for Health, Health Care Policy and
   Aging Research
New Brunswick, NJ

**Relationships Between General Medicine
and Mental Health Specialty
MH 44654; $168,696**

Mechanic, David
Rutgers University
Institute for Health, Health Care Policy and
   Aging Research
New Brunswick, NJ

**Enhancing Research Capacity in State
Mental Health Agencies
MH 46307; $185,072**

Mowbray, Carol T.
Michigan Department of Mental Health
Lansing, MI

**Formal and Informal Mental Health
Services Networks in Robert Wood
Johnson Demonstration Sites
MH 44839; $288,078**

Paulson, Robert
University of Cincinnati
School of Social Work
Cincinnati, OH

**Treating Substance Abuse Among
Chronic Mental Patients
MH 46335; $231,789**

Penk, Walter E.
University of Massachusetts Medical
   Center
Worcester, MA

**A Multilevel Network Model for Mental
Health Services
MH 00849; $55,575**

Pescosolido, Bernice A.
Indiana University
Bloomington, IN

A Network-Episode Model for Mental
Health Services
MH 44780; $52,175

Pescosolido, Bernice A.
Indiana University
Bloomington, IN

Evaluating Two Methods of Providing
24-Hour Emergency Psychiatric Care
MH 46324; $112,395

Pokorny, Lois J.
Oklahoma Department of Mental Health
Oklahoma City, OK

The National Self-Help Research Center
MH 46399; $359,856

Powell, Thomas J.
University of Michigan
School of Social Work
Ann Arbor, MI

Mental Illness, Service Use, and
Homeless Careers
MH 46104; $384,432

Robertson, Marjorie J.
Medical Research Institute of San
   Francisco
Berkeley, CA

Service Effects on Patient Outcomes: An
Exploratory Study
MH 44708; $141,306

Rosenfield, Sarah
Rutgers University
Institute for Health, Health Care Policy and
   Aging Research
New Brunswick, NJ

Integrated Services for Mentally Ill
Chemical Abusers
MH 46327; $272,015

Rosenthal, Richard N.
Beth Israel Medical Center
New York, NY

Services in Systems: Impact on Client
Outcomes
MH 46348; $128,095

Roth, Dee
Ohio Department of Mental Health
Columbus, OH

Center on the Organization and
Financing of Care for Severely
Mentally Ill
MH 43694; $358,015

Scheffler, Richard M.
University of California
School of Public Health
Berkeley, CA

Informed Service Strategy in Psychiatry
Emergency Evaluation
MH 37310; $152,300

Segal, Steven P.
Institute for Scientific Analysis
San Francisco, CA

Impacts of Differing Reimbursement
Mechanisms for Intensive Case
Management Services on the Process and
Outcomes of Treatment
MH 46365; $868,682

Shern, David
New York State Office of Mental Health
Research Foundation for Mental
   Hygiene, Inc.
Albany, NY

Statistical Theory and Methods for
Prospective Payment
MH 43214; $191,060

Siegel, Carole
Nathan S. Kline Institute for Psychiatric
   Research
Orangeburg, NY

Mental Health Scientist Development
Award, Level II
MH 00843; $57,348

Smith, G. Richard
University of Arkansas for the Medical
   Sciences
Little Rock, AR

Case Management for Funded Homeless CMI: Two Models
MH 46162; $447,079

Solomon, Phyllis L.
Hahnemann University
Philadelphia, PA

Medicaid, Payment Limits, and Care of the Mentally Ill
MH 44881; $280,702

Soumerai, Stephen B.
Harvard Medical School
Boston, MA

Assessing the Impact of Insanity Defense Reform
MH 38329; $263,415

Steadman, Henry J.
New York State Office of Mental Health
Albany, NY

Center on Organization and Financing of Care for the Severely Mentally Ill
MH 43703; $657,226

Steinwachs, Donald M.
The Johns Hopkins University
School of Hygiene and Public Health
Baltimore, MD

Medicaid Financing for the Severely Mentally Ill
MH 44865; $176,369

Steinwachs, Donald M.
The Johns Hopkins University
School of Hygiene and Public Health
Baltimore, MD

Predictors of Service Use by Homeless Shelter Residents
MH 45109; $100,349

Struening, Elmer L.
New York State Psychiatric Institute
Research Foundation for Mental
   Hygiene, Inc.
New York, NY

Scaled Measures of Burden and Benefits
MH 44690; $111,287

Struening, Elmer L.
New York State Psychiatric Institute
Research Foundation for Mental
   Hygiene, Inc.
New York, NY

Continuity of Care, Residence, and Family Burden
MH 44683; $238,333

Tessler, Richard C.
University of Massachusetts
Amherst, MA

Family, Mental Illness and Homelessness
MH 00834; $60,891

Tessler, Richard C.
University of Massachusetts
Amherst, MA

Rural Homelessness in Ohio: Five-Year Replication Study
MH 46111; $230,097

Toomey, Beverly G.
Ohio State University
Columbus, OH

Center for Cross-Cultural Research
MH 44214; $105,125

Trevino, Fernando M.
University of Texas
Galveston, TX

Psychiatric Disorder and Help-Seeking Among Blacks
MH 45258; $38,304

Williams, David R.
Yale University
New Haven, CT

A Treatment Outcome Study
MH 43029; $340,380

Wilson, Nancy
Division of Mental Health Department of
    Institutions
Denver, CO

Intensive Case Management for Chronic
Mentally Ill
MH 44648; $115,442

Worley, Nancy K.
University of Pennsylvania
School of Nursing
Philadelphia, PA

DIVISION OF CLINICAL
RESEARCH

MH Schizophrenia Research Manpower
MH 00728; $66,096

Adler, Lawrence E.
University of Colorado Health Sciences
    Center
Denver, CO

Neuropsychiatric Mechanisms
Underlying Flat Affect
MH 37952; $129,514

Alpert, Murray
New York University Medical Center
New York, NY

Clinical Research Center for the Study
of Neurobiology and Phenomenology of
Major Psychoses
MH 43271; $1,272,153

Andreasen, Nancy C.
University of Iowa
Iowa City, IA

Major Psychosis: Phenomenology,
Behavior, and Genetics
MH 00625; $56,431

Andreasen, Nancy C.
University of Iowa
Iowa City, IA

NMR Imaging in the Major Psychoses
MH 40856; $622,381

Andreasen, Nancy C.
University of Iowa
Iowa City, IA

Phenomenology and Classification of
Schizophrenia
MH 31593; $418,220

Andreasen, Nancy C.
University of iowa
Iowa City, IA

Cortical Folding in Temporal Lobes of
Schizophrenics
MH 45594; $26,246

Armstrong, Este
Armed Forces Institute of Pathology
Washington, DC

Familial Psychiatric Disorders and
Attention in Schizophrenia
MH 45112; $246,216

Asarnow, Robert F.
University of California, Los Angeles
Neuropsychiatric Institute
Los Angeles, CA

Gene Markers in Schizophrenia and
Other Psychoses
MH 44115; $293,690

Baron, Miron
New York State Psychiatric Institute
Research Foundation for Mental
    Hygiene, Inc.
New York, NY

A Functional Analysis of Family
Therapy in Schizophrenia
MH 41577; $170,061

Bellack, Alan S.
Medical College of Pennsylvania—EPPI
Philadelphia, PA

Social Skill and Schizophrenia
MH 38636; $210,766

Bellack, Alan S.
Medical College of Pennsylvania—EPPI
Philadelphia, PA

Treatment Strategies in Schizophrenia
MH 39998; $413,400

Bellack, Alan S.
Medical College of Pennsylvania—EPPI
Philadelphia, PA

The OR, DR, and SR in Schizophrenia
and Depression
MH 28594; $171,417

Bernstein, Alvin S.
SUNY at Downstate Medical Center
Brooklyn, NY

Dopamine and Chronic Antipsychotic
Drug Treatment
MH 28216; $110,090

Bowers, Malcolm B., Jr.
Yale University
School of Medicine
New Haven, CT

Circling: As a Probe of Lateral DA
Activity in Schizophrenia
MH 43537; $80,699

Bracha, H. Stefan
University of Arkansas
Veterans Administration Medical Center
Neuropsychiatric Research Laboratory
North Little Rock, AR

Sensory Gating and Habituation in
Schizophrenia
MH 42228; $203,521

Braff, David L.
University of California
San Diego Medical Center
La Jolla, CA

Long-Term Community Rehabilitation of
Schizophrenics
MH 43640; $119,955

Brekke, John S.
University of California, Los Angeles
School of Social Work
Los Angeles, CA

PET Studies in Schizophrenia
MH 42647; $237,826

Brodie, Jonathan D.
New York University Medical Center
New York, NY

Epidemiology of Newly Diagnosed
Psychotic Disorders
MH 44801; $667,638

Bromet, Evelyn J.
SUNY at Stony Brook
Stony Brook, NY

PET Imaging of Performance Tasks in
Schizophrenia
MH 43229; $301,702

Buchsbaum, Monte S.
University of California
College of Medicine
Irvine, CA

Studies of Attention in Schizophrenia
MH 40071; $360,371

Buchsbaum, Monte S.
University of California
College of Medicine
Irvine, CA

Molecular Genetic Study of Manic-
Depression and Schizophrenia
MH 42643; $259,692

Byerley, William F.
University of Utah Medical Center
Salt Lake City, UT

Antecedents of Positive and Negative Schizophrenia
MH 09929; $11,500

Cannon, Tyrone D.
University of California, Los Angeles
Los Angeles, CA

Chlorpromazine, Immunogenetics, and Tardive Dyskinesia
MH 39528; $62,560

Canoso, Rosa T.
Beth Israel Hospital
Veterans Administration Medical Center
Boston, MA

Clinical Research Center for the Study of Classification and Course of the Schizophrenias
MH 40279; $208,233

Carpenter, William T., Jr.
University of Maryland
Maryland Psychiatric Research Center
Baltimore, MD

Outpatient Treatment: Targeted vs. Maintenance Medication
MH 35996; $237,590

Carpenter, William T., Jr.
University of Maryland
Maryland Psychiatric Research Center
Baltimore, MD

The Efficacy of Carbamazepine in Psychiatric Outpatients
MH 42582; $55,145

Carpenter, William T., Jr.
University of Maryland
Maryland Psychiatric Research Center
Baltimore, MD

Antipsychotic Drug-Induced Dyskinesias
MH 36657; $214,089

Casey, Daniel E.
Medical Research Foundation of Oregon

Oregon Regional Primate Research Center
Portland, OR

Cognitive Markers of the Predisposition to Schizophrenia
MH 44062; $115,304

Chapman, Loren J.
University of Wisconsin
Madison, WI

Markers of Psychosis and Psychosis Proneness
MH 00743; $60,361

Chapman, Loren J.
University of Wisconsin
Madison, WI

Studies of Psychosis-Prone Young Adults and Psychotics
MH 31067; $165,311

Chapman, Loren J.
University of Wisconsin
Madison, WI

Positron Emission Tomography of the Brain in Schizophrenia
MH 440783; $91,574

Cleghorn, John M.
McMaster University
Hamilton, Ontario, Canada

Diagnostic Center for Linkage Studies of Schizophrenia
MH 46276; $211,500

Cloninger, C. Robert
Washington University
School of Medicine
St. Louis, MO

Context Disturbance in Schizophrenia: Models and Measures
MH 00673; $97,071

Cohen, Jonathan D.
Stanford University
Stanford, CA

The Course of Dyskinesia
MH 32675; $260,075

Cole, Jonathan O.
Boston Mental Health Foundation, Inc.
McLean Hospital
Belmont, MA

Lexical Decision and Evoked Potentials
in Schizophrenia
MH 45331; $31,279

Condray, Ruth
University of Pittsburgh
Veterans Administration Medical Center
Pittsburgh, PA

A Subtype of Schizophrenia Defined by
Attention Deficits
MH 43321; $97,119

Cornblatt, Barbara A.
Columbia University
New York State Psychiatric Institute
Research Foundation for Mental
   Hygiene, Inc.
New York, NY

A Genetic Study of Schizophrenia Using
DNA Probes
MH 43212; $87,804

Crowe, Raymond R.
University of Iowa
Iowa City, IA

Toward a Rational Use of Plasma HVA
in Schizophrenia
MH 37922; $142,497

Davidson, Michael
Mt. Sinai School of Medicine
New York, NY

Nuclear Magnetic Resonance in
Schizophrenia
MH 37820; $171,129

DeMyer, Marian K.
Indiana University Foundation
Indianapolis, IN

Risk and Protective Factors in Recovery
From Schizophrenia
MH 44991; $93,033

Doane, Jeri A.
Yale University
New Haven, CT

Drug Holidays in Chronic Neuroleptics:
An Animal Model
MH 39961; $103,215

Ellison, Gaylord D.
University of California, Los Angeles
Los Angeles, CA

Prospective Study of Children of
Schizophrenic Parents
MH 19560; $563,542

Erlenmeyer-Kimling, L.
Columbia University
New York State Psychiatric Institute
Research Foundation for Mental
   Hygiene, Inc.
New York, NY

Electrophysiology and Neuroimaging in
Schizophrenia
MH 45113; $104,568

Erwin, Roland J.
University of Pennsylvania
Philadelphia, PA

PET Analysis of Dopamine-D_2 Receptors
in Schizophrenia
MH 41205; $150,889

Farde, Lars
Karolinska Institute
Stockholm, Sweden

Biophysical Analysis of Neuroleptics'
Behavioral Effects
MH 43429; $93,850

Fowler, Stephen C.
University of Mississippi
University, MS

Treatment Strategies in Schizophrenia
MH 40007; $392,027

Frances, Allen
Cornell University Medical College
New York Hospital
Payne Whitney Clinic
New York, NY

Electrophysiology of Sensory Gating in
Schizophrenia
MH 38321; $166,126

Freedman, Robert
University of Colorado Health Sciences
  Center
Denver, CO

Biological Studies of Psychotic Disorders
MH 08618; $562,703

Friedhoff, Arnold J.
New York University
School of Medicine
New York, NY

Chemical Factors in Abnormal Behavior
MH 14024; $60,823

Friedhoff, Arnold J.
New York University
School of Medicine
New York, NY

Clinical Research Center for the Study
of Organic Affective and Schizophrenic
Disorders
MH 35976, $997,595

Friedhoff, Arnold J.
New York University Medical Center
New York, NY

Cognitive Brain Potentials: Normal and
Abnormal
MH 00510; $61,722

Friedman, David
Columbia University
New York, NY

Autoimmune Mechanisms in
Schizophrenia
MH 00626; $64,732

Ganguli, Rohan
University of Pittsburgh
Western Psychiatric Institute and Clinic
Pittsburgh, PA

Autoimmune Phenomena and Psychotic
Relapse—Schizophrenia
MH 41883; $340,048

Ganguli, Rohan
University of Pittsburgh
Western Psychiatric Institute and Clinic
Pittsburgh, PA

Antidepressants: Behavior and
Hippocampal Transmitters
MH 00188; $61,398

Geyer, Mark A.
University of California, San Diego
School of Medicine
La Jolla, CA

Epidemiologic Studies of Tardive
Dyskinesia
MH 39665; $230,415

Glazer, William M.
Yale University
Connecticut Mental Health Center
New Haven, CT

Mechanism of Abnormal Water
Excretion in Schizophrenia
MH 43618; $96,515

Goldman, Morris B.
The University of Chicago Medical Center
Chicago, IL

Coping Behavior in Schizophrenia
MH 08744; $148,816

Goldstein, Michael J.
University of California, Los Angeles
Los Angeles, CA

Psychological Research on Schizophrenic Conditions
MH 14584; $190,720

Goldstein, Michael J.
University of California, Los Angeles
Los Angeles, CA

Neuronal Phosphoproteins in Neuropsychiatric Disorders
MH 00671; $71,524

Grebb, Jack A.
Rockefeller University
New York University Medical Center
New York, NY

Early Visual Processing in Schizophrenia
MH 43292; $79,259

Green, Michael F.
University of California Research Center
Camarillo State Hospital
Camarillo, CA

Sensory Processing, Sensory Gating, and Schizophrenia
MH 45177; $32,111

Grillon, Christian
Yale University
New Haven, CT

A Neurobehavioral Study of Schizophrenia
MH 42191; $310,675

Gur, Raquel E.
University of Pennsylvania
Philadelphia, PA

Clinical Research Center for the Study of Regional Brain Function in Schizophrenia
MH 43880; $1,473,648

Gur, Raquel E.
University of Pennsylvania
Philadelphia, PA

Regional Brain Activity and Psychopathology
MH 00586; $62,791

Gur, Raquel E.
University of Pennsylvania
Philadelphia, PA

Sex Differences in Schizophrenia
MH 43613; $125,450

Haas, Gretchen L.
Cornell University Medical College
New York Hospital
Payne Whitney Clinic
New York, NY

Treatment Strategies in Schizophrenia
MH 40042; $457,799

Hargreaves, William A.
University of California
San Francisco General Hospital
San Francisco, CA

Schizophrenic Cognition: A Longitudinal Study
MH 26341; $21,018

Harrow, Martin
Michael Reese Hospital and Medical Center
Chicago, IL

Intermittent vs. Maintenance Medication in Schizophrenia
MH 37343; $90,119

Herz, Marvin I.
SUNY at Buffalo
Erie County Medical Center
Buffalo, NY

Drug-Induced Movement Disorders in Schizophrenia
MH 43586; $99,389

Hoffman, William F.
Oregon Health Sciences Center
Portland, OR

Environmental-Personal Treatment of Schizophrenia
MH 30750; $506,186

Hogarty, Gerard E.
University of Pittsburgh
Western Psychiatric Institute and Clinic
Pittsburgh, PA

Pharmacotherapy of Distress in Recovering Schizophrenia
MH 39166; $115,319

Hogarty, Gerard E.
University of Pittsburgh
Western Psychiatric Institute and Clinic
Pittsburgh, PA

Collaborative Biological Research in Schizophrenia
MH 31154; $868,921

Holzman, Philip S.
Harvard University
McLean Hospital
Belmont, MA

Linkage Analysis in Pedigrees at Risk for Schizophrenia
MH 44876; $372,746

Holzman, Philip S.
Harvard University
McLean Hospital
Belmont, MA

Psychomotility and Cognitive Style in the Schizophrenias
MH 31340; $227,873

Holzman, Philip S.
Harvard University
McLean Hospital
Belmont, MA

Expressed Emotion and Relapse in Schizophrenic Patients
MH 42782; $167,016

Hooley, Jill M.
Harvard University
Cambridge, MA

Asymmetric Cerebral Reaction to d-Amphetamine
MH 09686; $11,500

Hoptman, Matthew J.
The University of Chicago
Chicago, IL

Epidemiology and Course of First Episode Schizophrenia
MH 44643; $137,085

Iacono, William G.
University of Minnesota
Minneapolis, MN

Computed Tomography Study of Schizophrenia
MH 42321; $4,178

Jacobs, Marc
University of California
San Francisco General Hospital
San Francisco, CA

PCP and Extracellular Dopamine in Brain
MH 00727; $78,649

Jauch, Diana
University of Maryland
Maryland Psychiatric Research Center
Baltimore, MD

Late Onset Schizophrenia: A Neuropsychiatric Study
MH 43693; $184,472

Jeste, Dilip
University of California, San Diego
La Jolla, CA

Risk Factors for Tardive Dyskinesia in Older Patients
MH 45131; $264,764

Jeste, Dilip
University of California, San Diego
La Jolla, CA

Role of Corticosterone in a Model of Psychosis
MH 44454; $36,750

Johnson, Michel
University of Utah
Salt Lake City, UT

Longitudinal ERP Studies of Schizophrenia and Siblings
MH 42769; $132,046

Josiassen, Richard C.
Medical College of Pennsylvania
Philadelphia, PA

Clinical Research Center for the Study of Schizophrenia
MH 41960; $558,887

Kane, John M.
Long Island Jewish-Hillside Medical
  Center
Glen Oaks, NY

Prospective Study of Tardive Dyskinesia Development
MH 32369; $180,330

Kane, John M.
Long Island Jewish-Hillside Medical
  Center
Glen Oaks, NY

Prospective Study of Tardive Dyskinesia in the Elderly
MH 40015; $209,271

Kane, John M.
Long Island Jewish-Hillside Medical
  Center
Glen Oaks, NY

Treatment of Neuroleptic Nonresponsive Schizophrenia
MH 42929; $200,818

Kane, John M.
Long Island Jewish-Hillside Medical
  Center
Glen Oaks, NY

Treatment Strategies in Schizophrenia
MH 39992; $309,995

Kane, John M.
Long Island Jewish-Hillside Medical
  Center
Glen Oaks, NY

Diagnostic Center for Schizophrenia Linkage Studies
MH 46289; $242,999

Kaufmann, Charles A.
Columbia University
New York State Psychiatric Institute
New York, NY

Molecular Neurobiology of Schizophrenia
MH 00682; $78,694

Kaufmann, Charles A.
Columbia University
New York State Psychiatric Institute
New York, NY

Genetic Epidemiology of Schizophrenia in Ireland
MH 41953; $571,190

Kendler, Kenneth S.
Virginia Commonwealth University
Richmond, VA

Genetic Studies of Psychiatric Disorders
MH 39239; $431,857

Kidd, Kenneth K.
Yale University
School of Medicine
New Haven, CT

Cholecystokinin-Containing Systems in Primate Thalamus
MH 09671; $7,914

Kritzer, Mary F.
Yale University
New Haven, CT

Clinical Trial Methodology in Schizophrenia
MH 42959; $94,597

Laska, Eugene M.
Nathan S. Kline Institute for Psychiatric Research
Research Foundation for Mental Hygiene, Inc.
Orangeburg, NY

Schizophrenia Clinical Research Training
MH 18914; $63,183

Levine, Jerome
University of Maryland
Maryland Psychiatric Research Center
Baltimore, MD

Schizophrenia, Heterogeneity, and Brain Sex Differences
MH 44151; $252,215

Lewine, Richard R. J.
Grady Memorial Hospital
Atlanta, GA

Clinical Research Center for the Study of Schizophrenia
MH 30911; $885,104

Liberman, Robert P.
Rehabilitation Medical Service
Brentwood Veterans Administration Medical Center
Los Angeles, CA

Clozapine Treatment of Severe Tardive Dyskinesia
MH 45122; $187,218

Liebermann, Jeffrey A.
Long Island Jewish-Hillside Medical Center
Glen Oaks, NY

Computed Tomography Study in Schizophrenia
MH 42271; $2,627

Lieberman, Jeffrey A.
Long Island Jewish-Hillside Medical Center
Glen Oaks, NY

Prediction of Relapse in Schizophrenia
MH 38880; $198,877

Lieberman, Jeffrey A.
Long Island Jewish-Hillside Medical Center
Glen Oaks, NY

Prospective Study of Psychobiology in Schizophrenia
MH 00537; $61,290

Lieberman, Jeffrey A.
Long Island Jewish-Hillside Medical Center
Glen Oaks, NY

Prospective Study of Psychobiology in Schizophrenia
MH 41646; $254,982

Lieberman, Jeffrey A.
Long Island Jewish-Hillside Medical Center
Glen Oaks, NY

Tardive Dyskinesia: Free Radical Mechanisms and Vitamin E
MH 45142; $73,152

Lohr, James B.
University of California, San Diego
Veterans Administration Medical Center
La Jolla, CA

Quantitative Assessment of Visual Function in Schizophrenia
MH 43662; $26,910

Maclin, Edward L.
Columbia University
New York State Psychiatric Institute
Foundation for Mental Hygiene, Inc.
New York, NY

Motor and Limbic System Integration in Schizophrenia
MH 00806; $45,544

Majumdar, Lisa A.
University of Rochester
Rochester, NY

Schizophrenia Academic Award
MH 00824; $77,210

Malaspina, Delores
Columbia University
New York State Psychiatric Institute
New York, NY

Management of Risk for Relapse in Schizophrenia
MH 41573; $350,314

Marder, Stephen R.
University of California Rehabilitation
    Service
Los Angeles, CA

Functional Asymmetry, Cognitive Deficiencies, and the Genetics of Schizophrenia
MH 42266; $81,169

Markow, Therese A.
Arizona State University
Tempe, AZ

Neurophysiological Studies of Schizophrenia
MH 40799; $185,428

McCarley, Robert W.
Harvard Medical School
Brockton, MA

The Neuroleptic Threshold Dose in Acute Schizophrenia
MH 41254; $165,879

McEvoy, Joseph P.
University of Pittsburgh
Western Psychiatric Institute and Clinic
Pittsburgh, PA

Fetal Viral Infection and Adult Schizophrenia
MH 37692; $185,599

Mednick, Sarnoff A.
University of California, Los Angeles
Los Angeles, CA

Schizophrenia in High-Risk Populations
MH 00619; $62,645

Mednick, Sarnoff A.
University of California, Los Angeles
Los Angeles, CA

Biological Studies of the Major Psychoses
MH 47808; $60,264

Meltzer, Herbert Y.
Case Western Reserve University
Cleveland, OH

Neuroleptic Effects on Regional Cerebral Blood Flow
MH 41961; $195,261

Mukherjee, Sukdeb
Columbia University
New York State Psychiatric Institute
Research Foundation for Mental
    Hygiene, Inc.
New York, NY

RCT—An Enriched Psychosocial Therapy for Schizophrenia
MH 43323; $83,945

Munroe-Blum, Heather
McMaster University
Hamilton, Ontario,
Canada

Genetic Influences on Normal Attentional Development
MH 45195; $105,180

Myles-Worsley, Marina
University of Utah Medical Center
Salt Lake City, UT

Flat Affect in Schizophrenia
MH 44116; $127,655

Neale, John M.
SUNY at Stony Brook
Research Foundation of SUNY
Stony Brook, NY

Computed Tomographic Study of
Schizophrenia
MH 42298; $14,908

Ninan, Philip T.
Emory University Clinic
Atlanta, GA

Treatment Strategies in Schizophrenia
MH 40597; $106,400

Ninan, Philip T.
Emory University Clinic
Atlanta, GA

Developmental Processes in
Schizophrenic Disorders
MH 37705; $23,495

Nuechterlein, Keith H.
University of California, Los Angeles
Neuropsychiatric Institute
Los Angeles, CA

Brain Development in Schizophrenics
and Their Siblings
MH 43650; $145,030

Olson, Stephen C.
Ohio State University Research Foundation
Columbus, OH

Linkage Analysis Methods in
Schizophrenia
MH 44292; $218,454

Ott, Jurg
Columbia University
New York State Psychiatric Institute
Research Foundation for Mental
  Hygiene, Inc.
New York, NY

Clinical Psychopharmacology Computer
Laboratory
MH 32457; $133,995

Overall, John E.
University of Texas Medical School
Houston, TX

Biobehavioral Heterogeneity in
Schizophrenia
MH 44877; $113,883

Pandurangi, Anand K.
Virginia Commonwealth University
Richmond, VA

A 24-Year Followup of Children of
Schizophrenic Mothers
MH 41469; $154,072

Parnas, Josef S.
Psykologisk Institut
Kommunehospitalet
Copenhagen, Denmark

Neuroimaging and Neuropsychologic
Impairment in Psychosis
MH 43775; $241,376

Pearlson, Godfrey D.
The Johns Hopkins University Hospital
Baltimore, MD

PET D$_2$ Receptor, MRI, and CT in Late
Life Schizophrenia
MH 43326; $282,324

Pearlson, Godfrey D.
The Johns Hopkins University Hospital
Baltimore, MD

Family Studies of Schizophrenia and
Neuropsychology
MH 43666; $93,981

Pogue-Geile, Michael F.
University of Pittsburgh
Pittsburgh, PA

**Genetic-Epidemiologic Studies of
Schizophrenia
MH 45588; $999,999**

Pulver, Ann E.
The Johns Hopkins University
School of Medicine
Baltimore, MD

**Heterogeneity of Schizophrenia
MH 35712; $198,899**

Pulver, Ann E.
The Johns Hopkins University
School of Medicine
Baltimore, MD

**Physiology and Plasticity of CNS
Synapses in the Rat
MH 00705; $64,962**

Rayport, Stephen G.
Columbia University
New York State Psychiatric Institute
New York, NY

**The Application of Genetic Strategies to
Neuroimaging
MH 43740; $130,457**

Resnick, Susan M.
University of Pennsylvania
Philadelphia, PA

**A Twin Study of Nosology and Etiology
in Schizophrenia
MH 44359; $127,598**

Reveley, Adrianne M.
Institute of Psychiatry
London, England

**Quantitative Genetics of Clinical
Psychopathology
MH 37685; $162,207**

Rice, John
Washington University
St. Louis, MO

**Neurochemical Indicators of Tardive
Dyskinesia Vulnerability
MH 44153; $230,884**

Richardson, Mary Ann
Nathan S. Kline Institute for Psychiatric
    Research
Research Foundation for Mental
    Hygiene, Inc.
Orangeburg, NY

**Tardive Dyskinesia Outcome—
Persistence or Resolution
MH 41802; $80,631**

Richardson, Mary Ann
Nathan S. Kline Institute for Psychiatric
    Research
Research Foundation for Mental
    Hygiene, Inc.
Orangeburg, NY

**Schizophrenia Research Training
MH 18870; $109,175**

Rieder, Ronald O.
Columbia University
New York State Psychiatric Institute
New York, NY

**Putative Genetic Markers in
Schizophrenia
MH 09668; $11,500**

Rothfeld, Jill
New York University
Chappaqua, NY

**Membrane Dysfunction in Schizophrenia
MH 43385; $280,722**

Rotrosen, John
New York University
Veterans Administration Medical Center
New York, NY

**Childhood Risk Factors for Adult
Mental Disorders
MH 43274; $291,281**

Schwartzman, Alex
Concordia University
Montreal, Quebec,
Canada

**PET Analysis of D_1-Dopamine Receptors
in Schizophrenia
MH 44814; $275,000**

Sedvall, Göran C.
Karolinska Institute and Hospital
Stockholm, Sweden

**Electrophysiological Studies of
Psychiatric Disorder
MH 12507; $236,959**

Shagass, Charles
Temple University Health Science Center
Philadelphia Psychiatric Center
Philadelphia, PA

**Schizophrenia: Clinical Symptoms and
Brain Mechanisms
MH 00746; $68,989**

Shenton, Martha E.
Massachusetts Mental Health Center
Boston, MA

**The Relationship Between Schizotypal
Personality Disorder and Schizophrenia
MH 42827; $216,919**

Siever, Larry J.
Mt. Sinai Hospital
New York, NY

**Collaborative Training Program in
Schizophrenia Research
MH 18932; $73,300**

Simpson, George M.
Medical College of Pennsylvania
Philadelphia, PA

**Fluphenazine Blood Levels, Efficacy and
Pharmacokinetics
MH 41585; $216,869**

Simpson, George M.
Medical College of Pennsylvania
Philadelphia, PA

**Prolactin/Fluphenazine Levels in
Maintenance Schizophrenia
MH 42445; $41,765**

Simpson, George M.
Medical College of Pennsylvania
Philadelphia, PA

**Adverse Effects of Neuroleptics in
Schizophrenia
MH 09711; $34,500**

Singh, Hardeep
Medical College of Pennsylvania
Philadelphia, PA

**Adjunctive Imipramine in Depressed
Schizophrenics
MH 34309; $181,455**

Siris, Samuel G.
Long Island Jewish-Hillside Medical
  Center
Glen Oaks, NY

**Pharmacologic Characterization of
Borderline Disorders
MH 00658; $62,208**

Soloff, Paul H.
University of Pittsburgh
Western Psychiatric Institute and Clinic
Pittsburgh, PA

**Genes of the Catecholamine System and
Schizophrenia
MH 44276; $161,491**

Sommer, Steve S.
Mayo Foundation
Rochester, MN

Vulnerability to Schizophrenia Neurobehavioral Aspects
MH 43615; $114,300

Steinhauer, Stuart R.
University of Pittsburgh
Western Psychiatric Institute and Clinic
Pittsburgh, PA

The Course of Schizophrenia
MH 34365; $109,079

Strauss, John S.
Yale University
School of Medicine
New Haven, CT

Understanding the Course of Psychiatric Disorder
MH 00340; $89,951

Strauss, John S.
Yale University
School of Medicine
New Haven, CT

Computed Tomographic Study of Schizophrenia
MH 42305; $19,307

Sweeney, John A.
Cornell University Medical College
New York Hospital
New York, NY

Eye Tracking Abnormalities in Schizophrenia
MH 42969; $105,899

Sweeney, John A.
Cornell University Medical College
New York Hospital
New York, NY

GABA Agonist Therapy in Tardive Dyskinesia
MH 37073; $151,926

Tamminga, Carol A.
University of Maryland
Maryland Psychiatric Research Center
Baltimore, MD

Haloperidol Kinetics in Persistent Psychosis
MH 37264; $120,656

Tamminga, Carol A.
University of Maryland
Maryland Psychiatric Research Center
Baltimore, MD

Regional Brain Glucose Utilization
MH 42234; $86,371

Tamminga, Carol A.
University of Maryland
Maryland Psychiatric Research Center
Baltimore, MD

Long-Term Community Treatment of Young Schizophrenics
MH 40886; $222,000

Test, Mary Ann
University of Wisconsin
School of Social Work
Madison, WI

Eye Movement Measurements in Schizophrenia
MH 43031; $81,793

Thaker, Gunvant K.
University of Maryland
Maryland Psychiatric Research Center
Baltimore, MD

Biological Markers in Discordant Monozygotic Twins
MH 41176; $108,159

Torrey, E. Fuller
Friends Medical Science Research Center
Bethesda, MD

Drug Response and Genetic Factors in Schizophrenia
MH 41874; $235,597

Tsuang, Ming T.
Harvard Medical School
Brockton/West Roxbury Veterans
    Administration Medical Center
Brockton, MA

**Gender and Schizophrenia:
Epidemiologic Implications
MH 42604; $100,699**

Tsuant, Ming T.
Harvard Medical School
Brockton/West Roxbury Veterans
   Administration Medical Center
Brockton, MA

**Linkage Studies of Schizophrenia
MH 46318; $177,891**

Tsuang, Ming T.
Harvard Medical School
Brockton/West Roxbury Veterans
   Administration Medical Center
Brockton, MA

**Schizophrenia: Psychopathology and
Heterogeneity
MH 43518; $295,349**

Tsuang, Ming T.
Harvard Medical School
Brockton/West Roxbury Veterans
   Administration Medical Center
Brockton, MA

**Subtyping Schizophrenia: An
Epidemiological Approach
MH 44277; $393,501**

Tsuang, Ming T.
Harvard Medical School
Brockton/West Roxbury Veterans
   Administration Medical Center
Brockton, MA

**[11]C-N-Methylspiperone PET Scans in
Schizophrenia
MH 40362; $50,633**

Tune, Larry E.
The Johns Hopkins University
School of Medicine
Baltimore, MD

**RSDA Training Program in PET and
Schizophrenia Research
MH 00723; $70,564**

Tune, Larry E.
The Johns Hopkins University
School of Medicine
Baltimore, MD

**Haloperidol Blood Levels and Effects in
Schizophrenia
MH 41772; $232,455**

Volavka, Jan
Nathan S. Kline Institute
Research Foundation for Mental
   Hygiene, Inc.
Orangeburg, NY

**Developmental Precursors of
Schizophrenia
MH 44342; $36,627**

Walker, Elaine F.
Emory University
Atlanta, GA

**Neuroleptic Noncompliance in
Schizophrenia
MH 43635; $90,678**

Weiden, Peter J.
Long Island Jewish-Hillside Medical
   Center
Glen Oaks, NY

**Pharmacological Approach to
Nonresponsive Schizophrenia
MH 46700; $122,129**

Wilson, William H.
Oregon Health Sciences University
Dammasch State Hospital
Wilsonville, OR

**Alprazolam—Neuroleptic Treatment in
Schizophrenia
MH 43612; $97,760**

Wolkowitz, Owen M.
University of California, Langley Porter
San Francisco, CA

**Quantitative Receptor Imaging in
Schizophrenia
MH 42821; $112,802**

Wong, Dean F.
The Johns Hopkins University Hospital
Baltimore, MD

**Behavioral and rCBF Studies of Memory
in Psychopathology
MH 39599; $166,903**

Wood, Frank B.
Wake Forest University
Bowman Gray School of Medicine
Winston-Salem, NC

**Finnish Adoptive Family Study of
Schizophrenia
MH 39663; $179,915**

Wynne, Lyman C.
University of Rochester
School of Medicine and Dentistry
Rochester, NY

**Computed Tomographic Study of
Schizophrenia
MH 42304; $4,147**

Yadalam, Kashinath G.
Medical College of Pennsylvania—EPPI
Philadelphia, PA

**Membrane Phospholipids Role in
Schizophrenia
MH 43742; $87,614**

Yao, Jeffrey K.
University of Pittsburgh Veterans
 Administration Medical Center
Pittsburgh, PA

DIVISION OF EDUCATION AND SERVICE SYSTEMS LIAISON

**Mental Health Service Demonstration
MH 43583; $164,845**

Biddle, David
South Carolina Department of Mental
 Health
Columbia, SC

**Vision for a Model Mental Health
System—Community Support Program,
South Carolina
MH 44487; $525,000**

Biddle, David
South Carolina Department of Mental
 Health
Columbia, SC

**Friends of the Homeless Project—Share
the Bounty
MH 44569; $129,976**

Blanch, Andrea K.
Office of Mental Health
Albany, NY

**Peer Specialists as Members of ICM
Teams
MH 46140; $349,938**

Blanch, Andrea K.
Office of Mental Health
Albany, NY

**Wisconsin's Community Support
Program Consumer-Operated Services
MH 44531; $110,250**

Carpenter, Elaine
Wisconsin Department of Health and
 Social Services
Madison, WI

**Maryland Mental Health Services
MH 43628; $136,630**

Carter, Alison
Maryland Department of Health and
 Mental Hygiene
Baltimore, MD

**Mental Health Services Demonstration
Grants—Community Support Program
for Adults
MH 44548; $167,160**

Copland, Rodney
Vermont Department of Mental Health
Waterbury, VT

Mental Health Services Demonstration Grant
MH 43668; $155,257

Corcoran, Maureen
Ohio Department of Mental Health
Columbus, OH

Community Support Program Comprehensive Community Systems Change Project
MH 44537; $335,000

Crockett, Judith
Division of Mental Health
Honolulu, HI

Mental Health Services Demonstration Project
MH 46082; $349,782

Dean-Johnson, Barbara
Office of Mental Health
Harrisburg, PA

Supported Housing Project
MH 44526; $150,000

Dietrich, Ann
Rhode Island Department of Mental Health
   and Mental Retardation
Cranston, RI

Local Consumer-Operated Demonstration Project
MH 44549; $167,618

DiFranco, Bonnie
Great Rivers Mental Health Center
St. Louis, MO

Assertive Case Management for Dually Diagnosed Clients
MH 46072; $384,329

Drake, Robert E.
West Central Services
Lebanon, NH

Community Support Program Local Consumer-Operated Services Demonstration Grant
MH 44505; $169,152

Engelby, Chris
Department of Institutions
Denver, CO

Experimental Analysis of Assertive Community Treatment
MH 46062; $349,439

Essock, Susan
Connecticut Department of Mental Health
Hartford, CT

Young Adult Mentally Ill With Substance Abuse Problem
MH 43534; $125,718

Fraser, Mary
Division of Mental Health
Salt Lake City, UT

Community Support Program Housing Demonstration Project in Milwaukee, WI
MH 44567; $163,255

Fray, Ray
Department of Health and Social Services
Madison, WI

Community Support Program Young Adult Demonstration
MH 43460; $145,000

Hill, Walter
California Department of Mental Health
Sacramento, CA

Mental Health Services Demonstration Grant Young Adults
MH 43498; $178,707

Jimmerson, Beverly
New Mexico Health and Environment
   Department
Santa Fe, NM

Community Support Program Local Supportive Housing Demonstration Project
MH 44564; $145,912

Johnson, Gary
Department of Social and Health Services
Olympia, WA

Community Support Program Local Consumer-Operated Service Demonstration Project
MH 44499; $52,057

Johnson, Ted J.
Mental Health and Center Rehabilitation
    Services
Charleston, WV

Community Support Program Local Supportive Housing Demonstration Grant
MH 44547; $155,487

Kramer, Elmer
State of Oregon Mental Health Division
Salem, OR

Marion County CSS Local Demonstration Serving Severely Mentally Ill With Substance Abuse Problems
MH 43571; $146,912

Kramer, Elmer
State of Oregon Mental Health Division
Salem, OR

Community Support Program Local Consumer-Operated Services Demonstration Project
MH 44562; $135,000

Krygier, LuRee
State of Oregon Mental Health Division
Salem, OR

Mental Health Services Demonstration Grants/Community Support Program
MH 44545; $159,442

Lewis, Grace
Ohio Department of Mental Health
Columbus, OH

Community Support Program Community Services Demonstration Project
MH 46145; $289,548

Lilly, George W.
West Virginia Department of Health
Charleston, WV

New Hampshire Community Support Program Local Consumer-Operated Demonstration Project
MH 44503; $77,828

Longgood, Bret
Division of Mental Health and
    Developmental Services
Concord, NH

Community Support Program Local Consumer Service Demonstrations
MH 44583; $52,500

Miller, Larry D.
Department of Mental Health
Indianapolis, IN

Community Support Program Young Adult Demonstration
MH 43667; $121,505

Miller, Larry D.
Department of Mental Health
Indianapolis, IN

Northeast Eastern Indiana District Community Support Program Enhancement Project
MH 44558; $563,000

Miller, Larry D.
Department of Mental Health
Indianapolis, IN

Rural Assertive Community Treatment Project
MH 46060; $340,402

Miller, Larry D.
Department of Mental Health
Indianapolis, IN

Cost-Effectiveness of Case Management for the Homeless
MH 46160; $350,000

Morse, Gary A.
Malcolm Bliss Mental Health Center
St. Louis, MO

Community Treatment/Support for the Mentally Ill and Chemically Dependent Demonstration Grant
MH 43468; $104,973

Mowbray, Carol T.
Michigan Department of Mental Health
Lansing, MI

Enhancing Vocational Opportunities
MH 46081; $240,697

Mowbray, Carol T.
Michigan Department of Mental Health
Lansing, MI

Community Support Program Consumer-Operated Demonstration Project
MH 44566; $79,395

Neff-Daniels, Marianne
Department of Social and Health Services
Olympia, WA

Consumer Providers in Crisis Response Systems
MH 46065; $257,888

Pennington, Margaret A.
Division of Mental Health
Frankfort, KY

Community Support Program Young Adult Demonstration
MH 43461; $140,686

Peterson, Paul D.
Department of Social and Health Services
Olympia, WA

Controlled Study of Two Case Management Models
MH 46059; $346,441

Ralph, Ruth O.
Department of Mental Health and Mental Retardation
Augusta, ME

Community Support Program Young Adult Local Demonstration Grant
MH 43596; $175,000

Schorske, Bonnie
Division of Mental Health and Hospital
Princeton, NJ

Mental Health Services Demonstrations
MH 43430; $117,128

Speier, Tony
Office of Mental Health
Louisiana Health and Human Services Division
Baton Rouge, LA

Expanding Futures Consumer Support Group—Greenhouse Center
MH 44559; $134,765

Townsend, Wilma
Department of Mental Health
Columbus, OH

Community Support Program Demonstration Grant for Young Adults With Substance Abuse Problems
MH 43463; $155,000

Wenner, Dennis
Tennessee Department of Mental Health and Mental Retardation
Division of Mental Health Service
Nashville, TN

**Mental Health Services Demonstration:
Community Support Program Tennessee
MH 44488; $72,100**

Wenner, Dennis
Tennessee Department of Mental Health
    and Mental Retardation
Division of Mental Health Service
Nashville, TN

**Helping Psychiatrically Labeled to Help
Themselves
MH 44528; $169,182**

Wygal, Susan
Department of Mental Health and Mental
    Retardation
Augusta, ME

**Community Support Program Consumer
Case Management Project
MH 46146; $328,012**

Zarit, Mozell
Department of Mental Health
Sacramento, CA

**Community Support Program Local
Consumer-Operated Demonstration
MH 44512; $126,590**

Zarit, Mozell
Department of Mental Health
Sacramento, CA

OFFICE OF THE DIRECTOR

**Demonstration Program for Homeless
Mentally Ill Women in New York City
MH 44388; $890,641 (2 yr)**

Bethea, Vernon T.
New York State Office of Mental Health
Albany, NY

**The Course of Homelessness Among the
Seriously Mentally Ill
MH 46121; $383,580**

Burnam, Audrey
The RAND Corporation
Santa Monica, CA

**Older Homeless Women
MH 45780; $140,586**

Cohen, Carl I.
State University of New York Health
    Science Center
Brooklyn, NY

**Community Mental Health and Support
Service for the Homeless
MH 44393; $893,682 (2 yr)**

Corbin, Ruth R.
Department of Health and Rehabilitative
    Alcohol, Drug Abuse and Mental Health
Tallahassee, FL

**Assertive Case Management for Dually
Diagnosed Clients
MH 46077; $384,923**

Drake, Robert E.
New Hampshire Department of Health and
    Human Services
Concord, NH

**Integration Service System Approach to
Advert Homelessness
MH 44383; $1,086,366 (2 yr)**

Fielder, Rita
Illinois Department of Mental Health
Mental Illness Division
Chicago, IL

**Women and Children in the Continuum
of Residential Stability
MH 46106; $462,479**

Fischer, Pamela J.
The Johns Hopkins University
Baltimore, MD

**Cuyahoga County Homeless Study
MH 44361; $1,243,423 (2 yr)**

Hernandez, Carol
Ohio Department of Mental Health
Columbus, OH

Multnomah County Social Service Division Demonstration Service Incarcerate
MH 44379; $473,164 (2 yr)

Krieger, Dale
State of Oregon Mental Health
Salem, OR

Attitudes Toward the Homeless Mentally Ill
MH 46101; $322,077

Link, Bruce G.
Columbia University
New York, NY

Cost Effectiveness of Case Management for the Homeless
MH 46166; $365,776

Morse, Gary A.
Malcolm Bliss Mental Health Center
St. Louis, MO

The Homeless Mentally Ill: A Multi-County Approach
MH 44373; $915,790 (2 yr)

Mowbray, Carol T.
Michigan Department of Mental Health
Lansing, MI

A Proposal to Fund a Model Program for Homeless Adults
MH 44387; $925,046 (2 yr)

Pierson, Henry C., III
South Carolina Department of Mental
  Health
Community Services
Columbia, SC

Mental Illness Service Use and Homeless Careers
MH 46104; $384,432

Robertson, Marjorie J.
Medical Research Institute of San
  Francisco
Berkeley, CA

Case Management for Jailed Homeless Chronically Mentally Ill: Two Models
MH 46162; $447,079

Solomon, Phyllis L.
Hahnemann University
Philadelphia, PA

Mental Health Services Demonstration Grant for Homeless Mentally Ill
MH 44389; $811,753 (2 yr)

Stuckey, Grace H.
Department of Mental Health
Mental Retardation and Substance Abuse
  Services
Office of Mental Health
CSP Unit
Richmond, VA

Rural Homelessness in Ohio: A Five-Year Study
MH 46111; $227,056

Toomey, Beverly G.
The Ohio State University
Columbus, OH

Community Support Program Demonstration Grant for Mentally Ill Homeless
MH 44380; $713,470 (2 yr)

Wenner, Dennis
Department of Mental Health and Mental
  Retardation
Division of Mental Health Service
Nashville, TN

APPENDIX III

RESOURCES

United States
National Associations, Institutes, Organizations and Government Agencies
Community Support Groups

Canada
National Associations, Institutes, Organizations and Government Agencies
Community Support Groups

Australia and New Zealand
United Kingdom
National Associations, Institutes, Organizations and Government Agencies
Community Support Groups

Ireland
Community Support Groups

International Organizations

UNITED STATES

NATIONAL ASSOCIATIONS, INSTITUTES, ORGANIZATIONS AND GOVERNMENT AGENCIES

Academy of Psychosomatic Medicine

Evelyne Hallberg, Executive Director
5824 N. Magnolia
Chicago, IL 60660
Telephone: (312) 784-2025
Facsimile: Not available

Alcohol and Drug Problems Association of North America, Inc.

Karst J. Besteman, Executive Director
444 N. Capitol Street, N.W., Suite 181
Washington, DC 20001
Telephone: (202) 737-4340
Facsimile: Not available

Alcohol, Drug Abuse, and Mental Health Administration (ADAMHA)

Frederick K. Goodwin, M.D.,
    Administrator
5600 Fishers Lane
Rockville, MD 20857
Telephone: (301) 443-3783
Facsimile: (301) 443-1719

American Academy for Cerebral Palsy and Developmental Medicine

John A. Hinckley, Executive Director
P.O. Box 11086
Richmond, VA 23230
Telephone: (804) 282-0036
Facsimile: (804) 282-0090

American Academy of Child and Adolescent Psychiatry

Virginia Q. Anthony, Executive Director
3615 Wisconsin Avenue, N.W.
Washington, DC 20016
Telephone: (202) 966-7300
Facsimile: (202) 966-2891

American Academy of Clinical Psychiatrists

Alicia A. Munoz, Executive Secretary
P.O. Box 3212
San Diego, CA 92103
Telephone: (619) 298-4782
Facsimile: (619) 298-3601

American Academy of Family Physicians

Robert Graham, M.D., Executive Vice-
President
8880 Ward Parkway
Kansas City, MO 64114
Telephone: (816) 333-9700
Facsimile: (816) 822-0580

American Academy of Medical Administrators

Thomas R. O'Donovan, Ph.D., President
30555 Southfield Road, Suite 150
Southfield, MI 48076
Telephone: (313) 540-4310
Facsimile: Not available

American Academy of Neurology

Jan W. Kolehmainen, Executive Director
2221 University Avenue, S.E., Suite 335
Minneapolis, MN 55414
Telephone: (612) 623-8115
Facsimile: (612) 623-3504

American Academy of Pediatrics

James E. Strain, M.D., Executive Director
P.O. Box 927
Elk Grove Village, IL 60009-0927
Telephone: (312) 288-5005
Facsimile: (312) 228-5097

American Academy of Psychiatrists in Alcoholism and Addictions

Edward Kaufman, M.D., President
P.O. Box 376
Greenbelt, MD 20770
Telephone: (301) 220-0951
Facsimile: Not available

American Academy of Psychiatry and the Law

Jonas R. Rappeport, M.D., Medical
Director
1211 Cathedral Street
Baltimore, MD 21201
Telephone: (301) 539-0379
Facsimile: (301) 547-0915

American Academy of Psychoanalysis

Vivian Mendelsohn, Executive Director
30 East 40th Street, Room 206
New York, NY 10016
Telephone: (212) 679-4105
Facsimile: Not available

American Anorexia/Bulimia Association, Inc.

Coaron Willinger, Executive Director
133 Cedar Lane
Teaneck, NJ 07666
Telephone: (201) 836-1800
Facsimile: Not available

American Anthropological Association

Eugene L. Sterud, Executive Director
1703 New Hampshire Avenue, N.W.
Washington, DC 20009
Telephone: (202) 232-8800
Facsimile: Not available

American Association for Counseling and Development

Patrick J. McDonough, Ed.D., Executive
Director
5999 Stevenson Avenue
Alexandria, VA 22304
Telephone: (703) 823-9800
Facsimile: (703) 823-0252

American Association for Geriatric Psychiatry

George T. Grossberg, M.D., President
P.O. Box 376A
Greenbelt, MD 20770
Telephone: (301) 220-0952
Facsimile: Not available

American Association for Marriage and Family Therapy

Mark R. Ginsberg, Ph.D., Executive
  Director
1717 K Street, N.W., Suite 407
Washington, DC 20006
Telephone: (202) 429-1825
Facsimile: (202) 331-0699

American Association for Partial Hospitalization

Joan Hyman, Executive Director
1411 K Street, N.W., Suite 1000
Washington, DC 20005
Telephone: (202) 347-1649
Facsimile: Not available

American Association for Social Psychiatry

Harold M. Visotsky, M.D., President
303 E. Superior Street
Chicago, IL 60611
Telephone: (312) 908-8049
Facsimile: (312) 908-3134

American Association for the Advancement of Science

Meetings Office
1333 H Street, N.W.
Washington, DC 20005
Telephone: (202) 326-6448
Facsimile: (202) 289-4021

American Association for the History of Medicine, Inc.

Arthur J. Viseltear, Ph.D., M.P.H.,
  Secretary-Treasurer
Yale School of Medicine, 333 Cedar Street
New Haven, CT 06510-8015
Telephone: (203) 785-4338
Facsimile: Not available

American Association of Chairmen of Departments of Psychiatry

Jeffrey L. Houpt, M.D., Secretary-
  Treasurer
Box AF, Emory University School of
  Medicine
Atlanta, GA 30322
Telephone: (404) 727-5630
Facsimile: (404) 727-0473

American Association of Community Psychiatrists

Gordon H. Clark, Jr., M.D., President
88 Gale Avenue
Laconia, NH 03246
Telephone: (603) 524-3211 (X240)
Facsimile: Not available

American Association of Directors of Psychiatric Residency Training, Inc.

Peter M. Zeman, M.D., Executive
  Secretary
400 Washington Street
Hartford, CT 06106
Telephone: (203) 241-6856
Facsimile: Not available

American Association of General Hospital Psychiatrists

Mary O'Loughlin, Executive Secretary
Wyman 3, Mount Auburn Hospital
Cambridge, MA 02238
Telephone: (617) 499-5008
Facsimile: Not available

American Association of Neuropathologists

Reid R. Heffner, Jr., M.D., Secretary-
  Treasurer
462 Grider Street
Buffalo, NY 14215
Telephone: (716) 898-3117
Facsimile: Not available

American Association of Orthomolecular Medicine
(A Division of the Huxley Institute for Biosocial Research)

Mary E. Haggerty, Executive Director
900 North Federal Highway, Suite 330
Boca Raton, FL 33432
Telephone: (407) 393-6167
Facsimile: Not available

American Association of Pastoral Counselors

C. Roy Woodruff, Ph.D., Executive
  Director
9508 A Lee Highway
Fairfax, VA 22031
Telephone: (703) 385-6967
Facsimile: (703) 352-7725

American Association of Psychiatric Administrators

Steve Rachlin, M.D., President
Department of Psychiatry, Nassau County
  Medical Center
Hampstead Turnpike, East Meadow, NY
  11554
Telephone: (516) 542-3885
Facsimile: Not available

American Association of Psychiatric Services for Children

Sydney Koret, Ph.D., Executive Director
1200-C Scottsville Road, Suite 225
Rochester, NY 14624
Telephone: (716) 235-6910
Facsimile: Not available

American Association of Psychiatrists From India

Anjali Pandya, M.D., Executive Secretary
855 Bruce Drive
East Meadow, NY 11554
Telephone: (516) 292-9741
Facsimile: Not available

American Association of Sex Educators, Counselors and Therapists

David G. Lister, Executive Director
435 N. Michigan Ave., Suite 1717
Chicago, IL 60611
Telephone: (312) 644-0828
Facsimile: (312) 644-8557

American Association of Suicidology

Julie Perlman, M.S.W., Executive Officer
2459 South Ash
Denver, CO 80222
Telephone: (303) 692-0985

American Association on Mental Retardation

M. Doreen Croser, Executive Director
1719 Kalorama Road, N.W.
Washington, DC 20009
Telephone: (202) 387-1968

American Bar Association

Jill Wine-Banks, Executive Vice-President
750 North Lake Shore Drive
Chicago, IL 60611
Telephone: (312) 988-5130
Facsimile: (312) 988-4664

American Board of Forensic Psychiatry, Inc.

Jonas R. Rappeport, M.D., Executive
  Director
1211 Cathedral Street
Baltimore, MD 21201
Telephone: (301) 539-0872
Facsimile: (301) 547-0915

American Board of Medical Specialties

Donald G. Langsley, M.D., Executive
  Vice-President
One Rotary Center, Suite 805
Evanston, IL 60201
Telephone: (312) 491-9091
Facsimile: (312) 475-6240

American Board of Psychiatry and Neurology, Inc.

Stephen C. Scheiber, M.D., Executive
Secretary
500 Lake Cook Road, Suite 335
Deerfield, IL 60015
Telephone: (708) 945-7900
Facsimile: (708) 945-1146

American College Health Association

Stephen D. Blom, Executive Director
15879 Crabbs Branch Way
Rockville, MD 20855
Telephone: (301) 963-1100
Facsimile: Not available

American College of Emergency Physicians

Colin C. Rorrie, Jr., Ph.D., Executive
Director
P.O. Box 619911
Dallas, TX 72561-9911
Telephone: (214) 550-0911
Facsimile: (214) 580-2816

American College of Mental Health Administration

Deena Morey-Tetrault, Administrative
Assistant
P.O. Box 66
White River Junction, VT 05001
Telephone: (603) 646-5858
Facsimile: Not available

American College of Neuropsychopharmacology

Oakley Ray, Ph.D., Secretary
Box 1823-Station B
Nashville, TN 37221
Telephone: (615) 327-7200
Facsimile: (615) 327-7078

American College of Occupational Medicine

Donald L. Hoops, Ph.D., Executive
Director
55 West Seegers Road
Arlington Heights, IL 60005
Telephone: (312) 228-6850
Facsimile: (312) 228-1856

American College of Physicians

John Ball, M.D., J.D., Executive Vice-
President
Independence Mall West
Philadelphia, PA 19106-1572
Telephone: (215) 351-2400
Facsimile: Not available

American College of Psychiatrists

Alice Conde Martinez, Executive Director
P.O. Box 365
Greenbelt, MD 20770
Telephone: (301) 345-3534
Facsimile: Not available

American College of Psychoanalysts

Harold Mann, M.D., Secretary General
2006 Dwight Way #304
Berkeley, CA 94704
Telephone: (415) 845-7957
Facsimile: Not available

American College of Surgeons

Fred C. Spillman, Convention Manager
55 East Erie Street
Chicago, IL 60610
Telephone: (312) 664-4050
Facsimile: (312) 440-7014

American Council on Education

Robert H. Atwell, President
One Dupont Circle, N.W., Suite 801
Washington, DC 20036
Telephone: (202) 939-9300
Facsimile: (202) 833-4760

American Dental Association

Thomas J. Ginley, Ph.D., Executive
  Director
211 East Chicago Avenue
Chicago, IL 60611
Telephone: (312) 440-2701
Facsimile: (312) 440-7488

American Federation for Clinical Research, Eastern Section

Patricia A. McFadden, Account Executive
6900 Grove Road
Thorofare, NJ 08086
Telephone: (609) 848-1000
Facsimile: (609) 853-5991

American Geriatrics Society

Linda Hiddemen Barondess, Executive
  Vice-President
770 Lexington Avenue, Suite 400
New York, NY 10021
Telephone: (212) 308-1414
Facsimile: (212) 832-8646

American Group Psychotherapy Association, Inc.

Marsha S. Block, Chief Executive Officer
25 East 21st Street, 6th Floor
New York, NY 10010
Telephone: (212) 477-2677
Facsimile: Not available

American Health Care Association

Paul R. Willging, Ph.D., Executive Vice
  President
1201 L Street, N.W.
Washington, DC 20005
Telephone: (202) 842-4444
Facsimile: (202) 842-3860

American Hospital Association

Rhonda Goldstein, Director of Section for
  Psychiatric and Substance Abuse
  Services
840 N. Lake Shore Drive
Chicago, IL 60611
Telephone: (312) 280-6495
Facsimile: (312) 280-5979

American Institute of Biological Sciences

Dr. Charles M. Chambers, Executive
  Director
730 11th Street, N.W.
Washington, DC 20001-4584
Telephone: (202) 628-1500
Facsimile: (202) 628-1509

American Medical Association

James H. Sammons, M.D., Executive
  Vice-President
535 N. Dearborn Street
Chicago, IL 60610
Telephone: (312) 645-5000
Facsimile: (312) 645-4184

American Medical Care and Review Association

Ronald A. Hurst, Executive Vice-President
5410 Grosvenor Lane, Suite 210
Bethesda, MD 20814
Telephone: (301) 493-9552
Facsimile: (301) 530-2211

American Medical Student Association

Paul R. Wright, Executive Director
1890 Preston White Drive
Reston, VA 22091
Telephone: (703) 620-6600
Facsimile: (703) 620-5873

American Medical Women's Association

Eileen McGrath, Executive Director
801 N. Fairfax Street, Suite 400
Alexandria, VA 22314
Telephone: (703) 838-0500
Facsimile: (703) 549-3864

American Mental Health Fund

Jack Hinckley, Chairman
David George, President
3299 Woodburn Road, Suite 335
Annandale, VA 22003-1275
Telephone: (703) 573-2200
Facsimile: Not available

American Neurological Association

Linda J. Wilkerson, Association Manager
2221 University Ave., S.E., Suite 350
Minneapolis, MN 55414
Telephone: (612) 378-3290
Facsimile: (612) 623-3504

American Nurses' Association

Barbara Redman, R.N., Executive Director
2420 Pershing Road
Kansas City, MO 64108
Telephone: (816) 474-5720
Facsimile: (816) 471-4903

American Occupational Therapy Association

Jeanette Bair
1383 Piccard Drive
Rockville, MD 20850
Telephone: (301) 948-9626
Facsimile: (301) 948-5512

American Orthopsychiatric Association

Herbert A. Sohn, Ph.D., Executive
  Director
19 West 44th Street, Suite 1616
New York, NY 10036
Telephone: (212) 354-5770
Facsimile: (212) 302-9463

American Pediatric Society

Catherine DeAngelis, M.D., Secretary-
  Treasurer
Johns Hopkins Hospital, Dept. of
  Pediatrics, CMSC 2-124
Baltimore, MD 21205
Telephone: (301) 955-5942
Facsimile: Not available

American Psychiatric Association

Melvin Sabshin, M.D., Medical Director
1400 K Street, N.W.
Washington, DC 20005
Telephone: (202) 682-6000
Facsimile: (202) 682-6114

American Psychoanalytic Association

Helen Fischer, Administrative Director
309 East 49th Street
New York, NY 10017
Telephone: (212) 752-0450
Facsimile: Not available

American Psychological Association

Raymond D. Fowler, Ph.D., Chief
  Executive Officer
1200 17th Street, N.W.
Washington, DC 20036
Telephone: (202) 955-7660
Facsimile: (202) 331-0437

American Psychopathological Association

Nancy C. Andreasen, M.D., Ph.D.
Department of Psychiatry, The University
  of Iowa College of Medicine
500 Newton Road, Iowa City, IA 52242
Telephone: (319) 356-1553
Facsimile: Not available

American Psychosomatic Society, Inc.

George K. Degnon, Executive Director
6728 Old McLean Village Drive
McLean, VA 22101
Telephone: (703) 556-9222
Facsimile: (703) 556-8729

American Public Health Association

William H. McBeath, M.D., Executive
  Director
1015 15th Street, N.W.
Washington, DC 20005
Telephone: (202) 789-5600
Facsimile: (202) 789-5661

**American Schizophrenia Association
(A Division of the Huxley Institute for
Biosocial Research)**

Mary E. Haggerty, Executive Director
900 North Federal Highway, Suite 330
Boca Raton, FL 33432
Telephone: (407) 393-6167
Facsimile: Not available

American School Health Association

Dana A. Davis, Executive Director
7263 State Rt 43
Kent, OH 44240
Telephone: (216) 678-1601
Facsimile: Not available

**American Society for Adolescent
Psychiatry**

David Lewis, Executive Director
5530 Wisconsin Avenue, N.W., Suite
1149
Washington, DC 20815
Telephone: (301) 652-0646
Facsimile: (301) 656-0989

**American Society for Psychosomatic
Obstetrics and Gynecology**

Donna Stewart, M.D.
St. Michael's Hospital, 30 Bond Street
Toronto, Ontario, Canada M5B 1W8
Telephone: (416) 864-5137
Facsimile: Not available

American Society of Addiction Medicine

James F. Callahan, Ph.D., Executive
Director
5225 Wisconsin Avenue, N.W.,
Suite 409
Washington, DC 20016
Telephone: (202) 244-8948
Facsimile: Not available

American Society of Clinical Hypnosis

William F. Hoffmann, Jr., Executive Vice-
President
2250 East Devon Avenue, Suite 336
Des Plaines, IL 60018
Telephone: (312) 297-3317
Facsimile: Not available

**American Society of Group
Psychotherapy and Psychodrama**

George K. Degnon, Executive Director
6728 Old McLean Village Drive
McLean, VA 22101
Telephone: (703) 556-9222
Facsimile: (703) 556-8729

American Society of Law and Medicine

Sharin Paaso, Associate Director
765 Commonwealth Avenue, 16th Floor
Boston, MA 02215
Telephone: (617) 262-4990
Facsimile: (617) 437-7596

**American Society of Psychoanalytic
Physicians**

Janice Wright, Executive Director
4804 Jasmine Drive
Rockville, MD 20853
Telephone: (301) 929-1623
Facsimile: Not available

American Sociological Association

William V. D'Antonio, Executive Officer
1722 N Street, N.W.
Washington, DC 20036
Telephone: (202) 833-3410
Facsimile: Not available

Association for Academic Psychiatry

Mary O'Loughlin, Administrative Assistant
Wyman 3, Mount Auburn Hospital
Cambridge, MA 02238
Telephone: (617) 499-5008
Facsimile: Not available

Association for Child Psychoanalysis

Robert D. Gillman, M.D., President
P.O. Box 5935
Washington, DC 20016
Telephone: (202) 363-7849
Facsimile: (202) 363-7849

Association for Clinical Psychosocial Research

Gerald Klerman, M.D., President
Payne Whitney Clinc, 525 East 68th Street
New York, NY 10021
Telephone: (617) 746-3675
Facsimile: (617) 746-0931

Association for Convulsive Therapy

Donald P. Hay, M.D., Executive Director
7040 North Green Bay Avenue
Milwaukee, Wisconsin 53209
Telephone: (414) 351-2688
Facsimile: Not available

Association for Medical Education and Research in Substance Abuse

David C. Lewis, M.D., Director
AMERSA National Office, Brown
  University, Box G
Providence, RI 02912
Telephone: (401) 863-3173
Facsimile: Not available

Association for Retarded Citizens of the United States

Alan Abeson, Ed.D., Executive Director
2501 Avenue J
Arlington, TX 76006
Telephone: (817) 640-0204
Facsimile: (817) 633-6459

Association for the Advancement of Psychoanalysis

Jeanne Smith, M.D., President
329 East 62nd Street
New York, NY 10021
Telephone: (212) 838-8044
Facsimile: Not available

Association for the Advancement of Psychotherapy

Stanley Lesse, M.D., President
114 East 78th Street
New York, NY 10021
Telephone: (212) 288-4466

Association for the Care of Children's Health

Beverly H. Johnson, R.N., Executive
  Director
3615 Wisconsin Avenue, N.W.
Washington, DC 20016
Telephone: (202) 244-1801

Association of American Indian Physicians

Terry Hunter, Executive Director
10015 S. Pennsylvania, Building D
Oklahoma City, OK 73159
Telephone: (405) 692-1202

Association of American Medical Colleges

Robert G. Petersdorf, M.D., President
One Dupont Circle, N.W., Suite 200
Washington, DC 20036
Telephone: (202) 828-0400
Facsimile: (202) 785-5027

Association of Directors of Medical Student Education in Psychiatry

John Racy, M.D., President
1501 North Campbell Avenue
Tucson, AZ 85724
Telephone: (602) 626-6512
Facsimile: (602) 626-4884

Association of Gay and Lesbian Psychiatrists

Peggy Hanley-Hackenbruck, M.D.,
  President
1732 S.E. Ash
Portland, OR 97214
Telephone: (503) 235-7072

Association of Korean American Psychiatrists

Kyung Sun Noh, M.D., President
907 South Wolcott
Chicago, IL 60612
Telephone: (312) 413-1728
Facsimile: Not available

Association of Mental Health Administrators

Nancy Gordon, Director
640 North Lake Shore Drive, Suite 1103W
Chicago, IL 60611
Telephone: (312) 943-2751
Facsimile: (312) 943-3791

Association of Mental Health Clergy

George E. Doebler, M. Div., Executive
   Director
12320 River Oaks Point
Knoxville, TN 37922
Telephone: (615) 544-9704
Facsimile: (615) 544-8888

Association of Mental Health Librarians

Elizabeth P. Emily, President
Highland Hospital Medical Library, P.O.
   Box 1101
Asheville, NC 28802-1101
Telephone: (704) 254-3201
Facsimile: (704) 258-8095

Association of Military Surgeons of the United States

Lt. General Max B. Bralliar, Executive
   Director
9320 Old Georgetown Road
Bethesda, MD 20814
Telephone: (301) 897-8800
Facsimile: Not available

Association of Polish Psychiatrists and Neurologists in America

Stanley Golec, M.D.
6442 Calhoun Street
Dearborn, MI 48126
Telephone: (313) 582-0071
Facsimile: Not available

Association of Professional Sleep Societies

Lori J. Lingl, Meeting Coordinator
604 Second Street, S.W.
Rochester, MN 55902
Telephone: (507) 287-6006
Facsimile: (507) 287-6008

Autism Society of America

Thomas Nerney, Executive Director
1234 Massachusetts Avenue, N.W., Suite
   C1017
Washington, DC 20005
Telephone: (202) 783-0125
Facsimile: (202) 783-7435

Behavior Therapy and Research Society

Harriet Rosemoff, Administrative Secretary
3200 Henry Avenue
Philadelphia, PA 19129
Telephone: (215) 849-0607
Facsimile: Not available

Black Psychiatrists of America

Thelisa Harris, M.D., President
664 Prospect Avenue
Hartford, CT 06105
Telephone: (203) 236-2320
Facsimile: Not available

Bulimia Anorexia Self-Help, Inc.

Felix E.F. Larocca, M.D., President
6125 Clayton Avenue, Suite 215
St. Louis, MO 63139
Telephone: (314) 567-4080
Facsimile: (314) 768-3794

Central Neuropsychiatric Association

Larry E. Tripp, M.D., Secretary-Treasurer
3707 Gaston Avenue, Suite 418
Dallas, TX 75246
Telephone: (214) 824-2273

Child Welfare League of America, Inc.

David S. Liederman, Executive Director
440 1st Street, N.W., Suite 310
Washington, DC 20001
Telephone: (202) 638-2952
Facsimile: (202) 638-4004

Christian Medical and Dental Society Psychiatry Section

Don Gent, M.D., President
P.O. Box 830689
Richardson, TX 75083-0689
Telephone: (214) 783-8384
Facsimile: Not available

Committee on Problems of Drug Dependence, Inc.

Martin W. Adler, Ph.D., Executive
  Secretary
Temple University School of Medicine,
  Department of Pharmacology
3420 North Broad Street, Philadelphia, PA
  19140
Telephone: (215) 221-3242
Facsimile: (215) 221-4135

Council of Medical Specialty Societies

Richard S. Wilbur, M.D., Executive Vice-
  President
P.O. Box 70
Lake Forest, IL 60045
Telephone: (312) 295-3456
Facsimile: (312) 295-3759

Council of State Governments

Carl W. Stenberg, Executive Director
P.O. Box 11910
Lexington, KY 40578
Telephone: (606) 231-1939
Facsimile: (606) 231-1858

Eastern Psychiatric Research Association

Robert Cancro, M.D., President
550 First Avenue
New York, NY 10016
Telephone: (212) 340-6214
Facsimile: (212) 340-8135

Educational Commission for Foreign Medical Graduates

Marjorie P. Wilson, M.D.
3624 Market Street, 4th Floor
Philadelphia, PA 19104-2685
Telephone: (215) 386-5900
Facsimile: (215) 387-9963

Epilepsy Foundation of America

William M. McLin, Executive Vice-
  President
4351 Garden City Drive, Suite 406
Landover, MD 20785
Telephone: (301) 459-3700
Facsimile: (301) 577-2684

Group for the Advancement of Psychiatry

Carolyn Robinowitz, M.D., President
1400 K Street, N.W.
Washington, DC 20005
Telephone: (202) 682-6331

ICD-International Center for the Disabled

John B. Wingate, Executive Director
340 East 24th Street
New York, NY 10010
Telephone: (212) 679-0100

Institute of Medicine/National Academy of Sciences

Samuel O. Thier, M.D., President
2101 Constitution Avenue, N.W.
Washington, DC 20418
Telephone: (202) 334-3300
Facsimile: (202) 334-1694

Institutes of Religion and Health

Dr. Roger W. Plantikow, President
3 West 29th Street
New York, NY 10001
Telephone: (212) 725-7850
Facsimile: Not available

Joint Commission on Accreditation of Healthcare Organizations

Dennis S. O'Leary, M.D., President
875 North Michigan Avenue
Chicago, IL 60611
Telephone: (312) 642-6061
Facsimile: (312) 642-9136

Mental Health Materials Center

Alex Sareyan, President
9 Willow Circle
Bronxville, NY 10708
Telephone: (914) 337-6596
Facsimile: Not available

Milton H. Erickson Foundation, Inc.

Jeffrey K. Zeig, Ph.D., Director
3606 North 24th Street
Phoenix, AZ 85016
Telephone: (602) 956-6196
Facsimile: (602) 954-8974

National Alliance for Research on Schizophrenia and Depression

Gwill Newman
208 South LaSalle Street, Suite 1428
Chicago, IL 60604
Telephone: (312) 641-1666
Facsimile: (312) 236-7741

National Association for Music Therapy, Inc.

Edward L. Norwood, R.M.T., Executive
    Director
505 11th Street, S.E.
Washington, DC 20003
Telephone: (202) 543-6864
Facsimile: Not available

National Association of Private Psychiatric Hospitals

Robert L. Thomas, Executive Director
1319 F Street, N.W., Suite 1000
Washington, DC 20004
Telephone: (202) 393-6700
Facsimile: (202) 783-6041

National Association of Social Workers

Mark G. Battle, A.C.S.W., Executive
    Director
7981 Eastern Avenue
Silver Spring, MD 20910
Telephone: (301) 565-0333
Facsimile: (301) 587-1321

National Association of State Mental Health Program Directors

Harry C. Schnibbe, Executive Director
1101 King Street, Suite 160
Alexandria, VA 22314
Telephone: (703) 739-9333
Facsimile: (703) 548-9517

National Association of State Mental Health Research Institutes

William T. Carpenter, Jr., M.D.,
    Secretary-Treasurer
P.O. Box 21247
Baltimore, MD 21228
Telephone: (301) 455-7101
Facsimile: Not available

National Association of Veterans Administration Chiefs of Psychiatry

Thomas Horvath, M.D., Chief, Psychiatry
    Service (116A)
Bronx VA Medical Center, 130 W.
    Kingsbridge Road
Bronx, NY 10468
Telephone: (212) 584-9000; Federal
    Telephone System: 663-1663
Facsimile: (212) 933-2121

National Board of Medical Examiners

Robert L. Volle, Ph.D., President
3930 Chestnut Street
Philadelphia, PA 19104
Telephone: (215) 349-6400
Facsimile: (215) 349-6400 ext. 279

National Center for Clinical Infant Programs

Eleanor S. Szanton, Ph.D., Executive
  Director
733 15th Street, N.W., Suite 912
Washington, DC 20005
Telephone: (202) 347-0308
Facsimile: (202) 347-3724

National Coalition of Arts Therapy Associations

David Johnson, Ph.D., Chairman
505 11th Street, S.E.
Washington, DC 20003
Telephone: (202) 543-6864
Facsimile: Not available

National Congress of Parents and Teachers

Robert N. Woerner, Executive
  Administrator
700 North Rush Street
Chicago, IL 60611
Telephone: (312) 787-0977
Facsimile: (312) 787-8342

National Consortium of Chemical Dependency Nurses

Randy Bryson, R.N., Executive Director
975 Oak Street, Suite 675
Eugene, OR 97401
Telephone: 1-800-876-2236
Facsimile: (503) 345-7297

National Council of Community Mental Health Centers

Charles G. Ray, Executive Director
12300 Twinbrook Parkway, Suite 320
Rockville, MD 20852
Telephone: (301) 984-6200
Facsimile: Not available

National Council on Alcoholism, Inc.

Hamilton Beazley, President
12 West 21st Street, 8th Floor
New York, NY 10010
Telephone: (212) 206-6770
Facsimile: (212) 645-1690

National Council on Compulsive Gambling

Jean Chasen-Falzon, M.A., C.A.C.,
  Executive Director
445 West 59th Street, Room 1523N
New York, NY 10019
Telephone: (212) 765-3833
Facsimile: Not available

National Council on the Aging, Inc.

Daniel Thursz, President
600 Maryland Avenue, S.W., West Wing
  100
Washington, DC 20024
Telephone: (202) 479-1200
Facsimile: (202) 479-0735

National Depressive and Manic Depressive Association

Lorraine Richter, Corresponding Secretary
53 West Jackson
Chicago, IL 60604
Telephone: (312) 939-2442
Facsimile: (312) 726-0934

National Guild of Catholic Psychiatrists

Thomas K. Ciesla, M.D., President
1301 20th Street, Suite 212
Santa Monica, CA 90404
Telephone: (213) 315-0300
Facsimile: Not available

National Institute of Mental Health (NIMH)

5600 Fishers Lane
Rockville, MD 20857
Telephone: (301) 443-3673
Facsimile: (301) 443-2203

Lewis L. Judd, M.D., Director

James D. Lawrence, Executive Officer and
   Director
Office of Resource Management

Leroy Goldman, Acting Director
Office of Policy Analysis and Coordination

Marsha Corbett, Director
Office of Scientific Information

Lyle W. Bivens, Ph.D., Director
Division of Basic Sciences

Darrel A. Regier, M.D., M.P.H., Director
Division of Clinical Research

Jack D. Burke, M.D., M.P.H., Director
Division of Biometry and Applied Sciences

James W. Stockdill, Director
Division of Education and Service Systems
   Liaison

Eleanor C. Friedenberg, Director
Division of Extramural Activities

Steven Paul, Ph.D., Director
Division of Intramural Research Programs

National Institute on Aging

T. Franklin Williams, M.D., Director
9000 Rockville Pike
Bethesda, MD 20892
Telephone: (301) 496-9265
Facsimile: (301) 496-2525

National Institute on Alcohol Abuse and Alcoholism

Enoch Gordis, M.D., Director
5600 Fishers Lane, Room 16-105
Rockville, MD 20857
Telephone: (301) 443-3885
Facsimile: (301) 443-7043

National Institute on Drug Abuse

Charles R. Schuster, Ph.D., Director
5600 Fishers Lane, Room 10-05
Rockville, MD 20857
Telephone: (301) 443-6480
Facsimile: (301) 443-1726

National League for Nursing

Pamela J. Maraldo, Ph.D., R.N.,
   Executive Director
10 Columbus Circle
New York, NY 10019
Telephone: (212) 582-1022
Facsimile: (212) 541-9547

National Medical Association

William C. Garrett, Executive Vice-
   President
1012 10th Street, N.W.
Washington, DC 20001
Telephone: (202) 347-1895
Facsimile: Not available

National Mental Health Association

Preston J. Garrison, Executive Director
1021 Prince Street
Alexandria, VA 22314
Telephone: (703) 684-7722
Facsimile: (703) 684-5968

National Mental Health Consumers Association

Joseph A. Rogers, President
311 South Juniper Street
Philadelphia, PA 19107
Telephone: (215) 735-2465
Facsimile: Not available

National Rehabilitation Association

Robert E. Brabham, Ph.D., Executive
  Director
633 S. Washington Street
Alexandria, VA 22314
Telephone: (703) 836-0850
Facsimile: (703) 836-2209

Pan American Health Organization

Carlyle Guerra de Macedo, M.D., Director
525 23rd Street, N.W.
Washington, DC 20037
Telephone: (202) 861-3200
Facsimile: (202) 223-5971

Philippine Psychiatrists of America

James Campbell, M.D., President
4430 North 53rd Street
Phoenix, AZ 85018
Telephone: (662) 227-5551
Facsimile: Not available

Physicians for Social Responsibility

Maureen T. Thornton, Executive Director
1000 16th Street, N.W., Suite 810
Washington, DC 20036
Telephone: (202) 785-3777
Facsimile: (202) 785-3942

Recovery, Incorporated (The Association of Nervous and Former Mental Patients)

Mary Jane Maggio, Executive Director
802 North Dearborn Street
Chicago, IL 60610
Telephone: (312) 337-5661
Facsimile: Not available

Sex Information and Education Council of the U.S. (SIECUS)

Debra W. Haffner, M.P.H., Executive
  Director
32 Washington Place, Suite 52
New York, NY 10003
Telephone: (212) 673-3850
Facsimile: Not available

Society for Neuroscience

Nancy Beang, Executive Director
11 Dupont Circle, N.W., Suite 500
Washington, DC 20036
Telephone: (202) 462-6688
Facsimile: (202) 234-9770

Society of Behavioral Medicine

Judith C. Woodward, Executive Director
P.O. Box 8530
Knoxville, TN 37996
Telephone: (615) 974-5164
Facsimile: Not available

Society of Biological Psychiatry

David L. Dunner, M.D., Secretary-
  Treasurer
Harborview Medical Center ZA-15
Seattle, WA 98104
Telephone: (206) 223-3425
Facsimile: (206) 223-3997

Society of Professors of Child and Adolescent Psychiatry

Norbert B. Enzer, M.D., President
3615 Wisconsin Avenue, N.W.
Washington, DC 20016
Telephone: (202) 966-7300
Facsimile: Not available

Southern Medical Association

William J. Ranieri, Executive, Vice-
  President
P.O. Box 190088
Birmingham, AL 35219-0088
Telephone: (205) 945-1840
Facsimile: (205) 942-0642

Southern Psychiatric Association

Margo S. Adams, Executive Secretary
P.O. Box 10002
Tallahassee, FL 32302
Telephone: (904) 222-8404
Facsimile: (904) 561-6320

U.S. Department of Health and Human Services

James O. Mason, M.D., Assistant
   Secretary for Health
200 Independence Avenue, S.W., Room
   716-G
Washington, DC 20201
Telephone: (202) 245-7694
Facsimile: (202) 245-6274

U.S. Veterans Administration

Paul Errera, M.D., Director
Mental Health and Behavioral Sciences
   Service
810 Vermont Avenue, N.W., Room 915
Washington, DC 20420
Telephone: (202) 233-3416
Facsimile: (202) 233-2807

Western Interstate Commission for Higher Education, Mental Health Program

Meredith Davis, Program Director
P.O. Drawer P
Boulder, CO 80302
Telephone: (303) 497-0256
Facsimile: (303) 497-0291

COMMUNITY SUPPORT GROUPS

National Mental Health Consumer's
Association (NMHCA)
311 S. Juniper St., Rm. 902
Philadelphia, PA 19107

National Alliance for the Mentally Ill
   (NAMI)
1901 N. Fort Myer Dr., Suite 500
Arlington, VA 22209
(703) 524-9094

AMI, Alabama
2061 Fire Pink Ct.
Birmingham, AL 35244
(205) 987-8338

AMI, Arizona
PO Box 60756
Phoenix, AZ 85082
(602) 244-8166

AMI, Alaska
4050 Lake Otis Pkwy., #103
Anchorage, AK 99508
(907) 561-3127

AMI, Arkansas
4313 W. Markham
Little Rock, AR 72205
(501) 661-1548

AMI, California
1111 Howe Ave., Suite 475
Sacramento, CA 95825
(916) 567-0163

AMI, Colorado
1100 Fillmore St.
Denver, CO 80206
(303) 321-3104

AMI, Connecticut
62 Alexander St.
Manchester, CT 06040
(203) 643-6697

AMID
2500 West Fourth St.
Wilmington, DE 19803
(302) 427-0787

Friends of St. Elizabeth's AMI
514 First St., SE
Washington, DC 20003
(202) 546-1162

AMI, Threshold DC
422 8th Street, S.E.,
Washington, DC 20003
(202) 546-0646

AMI, Florida
400 S. Dixie Highway #14
Lake Worth, FL 33460
(305) 582-1835

AMI, Georgia
1256 Briarcliff Rd. NE, Rm. 412-S
Atlanta, GA 30306
(404) 894-8860

AMI, Hawaii
1612 Kuhilani St.
Honolulu, HI 96821
(808) 737-9069

AMI Boise Chapter
313 N. Allumbaugh
Boise, ID 83704
(208) 386-9432

Coalition, AMI Illinois State
1728 S. 6th
Springfield, IL 62703
(312) 297-9966

AMI, Indiana
Rt. #1, Box 406-B
Lake Village, IN 46349
(219) 992-3720

AMI of Iowa
Box 495
Johnston, IA 50131
(515) 225-8666

AMI, Kansas
4811 W. 77th Pl.
Prairie Village, KS 66208
(913) 642-4389

AMI, Kentucky
PO Box 5367
Louisville, KY 40205
(502) 896-1877

AMI, Louisiana
2431 So. Acadian Thruway, #420
Baton Rouge, LA 70808

AMI of Maine
PO Box 2130
Bangor, ME 04401

AMI of Maryland
2114 N. Charles St.
Baltimore, MD 21218
(301) 235-2511

AMI of Massachusetts
164 Canal St.
Boston, MA 02211
(617) 367-8890

Michigan, State AMI of
1602 Granger
Ann Arbor, MI 48104
(313) 663-1150

AMI of Minnesota
1595 Selby Ave., #103
Minneapolis, MN 55104
(612) 645-2948

Mississippi AMI
3500 Hwy. 90 E.
Ocean Springs, MS 39564
(601) 960-7477

Missouri Coalition of AMI
40 E. 107th St.
Kansas City, MO 64114
(816) 941-0285

MONAMI
PO Box 1021
Helena, MT 59624
(406) 443-7871

AMI of Nebraska
RR # 1
Ivandale, NE 68952
(402) 291-9483

Nevada AMI
PO Box 85373
Las Vegas, NV 89185
(702) 457-7238

AMI of New Hampshire
10 Ferry St.
Concord, NH 03301
(603) 225-5359

New Jersey AMI
400 Rt. 1, #10
Monmouth Junction, NJ 08852
(201) 329-2888

AMI of New Mexico
7701 Wyoming NE
Albuquerque, NM 87109
(505) 983-2584

AMI of New York
260 Washington Ave.
Albany, NY 12210
(800) 950-3228

AMI, North Carolina
4900 Water Edge Dr., #170
Raleigh, NC 27606
(919) 859-2201

North Dakota AMI
1720 5th Ave. NE #D-7
East Grand Forks, ND 56721
(218) 773-8712

AMI of Ohio
65 South Fourth St., #305
Columbus, OH 43215
(614) 464-2646

Oklahoma AMI
525 NW 13th
Oklahoma City, OK 73103
(405) 239-6264

Oregon Alliance of Advocates for the
    Mentally Ill
3400 Market St., #266
Salem, OR 97301
(503) 270-7774

AMI of Pennsylvania
2149 N. 2nd St.
Harrisburg, PA 17110
(717) 238-1514

AMI of Rhode Island
421 Bellevue Ave., #2B
Newport, RI 02840
(401) 621-4588

South Carolina AMI
PO Box 2538
Columbia, SC 29202
(803) 736-1542

South Dakota AMI
Box 221
Brookings, SD 57006
(605) 692-5673

Tennessee AMI
1900 N. Winston Rd., #511
Knoxville, TN 37919
(615) 531-8264

TEXAMI
400 W. 15th St., #619
Austin, TX 78701
(512) 474-2225

Utah AMI
PO Box 58047
Salt Lake City, UT 84158
(801) 583-2500

AMI of Vermont
Box 305
Vernon, VT 05354
(802) 862-6683

Virginia AMI
PO Box 1903
Richmond, VA 23215
(804) 225-8264

Family Support Network (AMI)
PO Box 11523
St. Thomas, VI 00801
(809) 776-2442

AMI of Washington State
1629 SE 244th St.
Kent, WA 98031
(206) 854-1797

West Virginia AMI
25 Clinton Hills
Triadelphia, WV 26059
(304) 242-8850

AMI of Wisconsin
1245 E. Washington Avenue, #76A
Madison, WI 53703
(608) 257-5888

Wyoming AMI (WYAMI)
519 Elk Mountain
New Castle, WY 82701
(307) 464-5521

CANADA

NATIONAL ASSOCIATIONS, INSTITUTES, ORGANIZATIONS AND GOVERNMENT AGENCIES

Canadian Association for Community
   Living
4700 Keele St.
Downsview, Ontario M3J 1P3
Canada
(416) 661-9611

Canadian Medical Association
1876 Alta Vista Drive
Ottawa, Ontario K1G 3Y6
Canada
(613) 731-9013

Canadian Mental Health Association
2160 Yonge St., 3rd Floor
Toronto, Ontario M4S 2Z3
Canada
(416) 484-7750

Canadian Psychiatric Association
294 Albert St., Suite 204
Ottawa, Ontario K1P 6E6
Canada
(613) 234-9857

Royal College of Physicians and Surgeons
   of Canada
74 Stanley Ave.
Ottawa, Ontario K1M 1P4
Canada
(613) 746-8177

COMMUNITY SUPPORT GROUPS

Canadian Friends of Schizophrenics
95 Barber Greene Rd., #39
Don Mills, Ontario M3C 3E9
Canada

(Local chapters serve all Canadian
   provinces)

AMI-QUEBEC Alliance for the Mentally
   Ill
C P 145
Succ. Cote-Des-Neiges
Montreal, Quebec
Canada
(514) 731-8059

AUSTRALIA AND NEW ZEALAND

Royal Australian and New Zealand College
   of Psychiatrists
101 Rathdowne St.
Carlton, Victoria
Australia 3053
(03) 6635466

UNITED KINGDOM

NATIONAL ASSOCIATIONS, ETC.

British Medical Association
Tavistock Square
London WC1H 9JP
United Kingdom
(01) 387-4499

Royal College of Psychiatrists
17 Belgrave Square
London SW1X 8PG
United Kingdom
(01) 235 2351

Royal Society of Medicine
One Wimpole Street
London W1M 8AE
United Kingdom
(01) 408-2119

SUPPORT GROUPS

England
National Schizophrenia Fellowship
78 Victoria Road
Surbiton, Surrey KT6 4NS

Scotland
National Schizophrenia Fellowship
40 Shandwick Place
Edinburgh EH2 4RT

Northern Ireland
National Schizophrenia Fellowship
Advice Center, Bryson House
Bedford Street
Belfast, Northern Ireland

IRELAND

SUPPORT GROUPS

Schizophrenia Association of Ireland
4 Fitzwilliam Place
Dublin 2

INTERNATIONAL ORGANIZATIONS

International Federation for Medical
    Psychotherapy
Psychiatrische Universitatspoliklinik
Murtenstrasse 21
CH-3010 Berne
Switzerland

International Academy of Law and Mental
    Health
3419 rue Simpson
Montreal, Quebec H3G 2J6
Canada
(514) 932-4988

International Association for the Scientific
    Study of Mental Deficiency
73 Merrion Road
Dublin 4
Ireland
Tel: 694706/264444

International College of Psychosomatic
    Medicine
Department of Psychiatry
Middlesex Hospital
London W1N 8AA
United Kingdom
(01) 380 9477

International Committee Against Mental
    Illness
PO Box 1921, Grand Central Station
New York, NY 10163
(212) 340-6214

International Council on Social Welfare
Koestergasse 1/29
A-1060 Vienna
Austria
Tel.: Vienna 0222/587 81 64

World Association for Psychosocial
  Rehabilitation
Bangour Village Hospital
Broxburn
West Lothian EH52 6LW
Scotland
UK
Tel: 050 681 301

World Federation for Mental Health
Eugene Brody, M.D.
Sheppard Pratt Hospital
PO Box 6815
Baltimore, MD 21285-6815
(301) 938-3180

World Health Organization
20 Avenue Appia
CH-1211 Geneva 27
Switzerland
Tel: 791 36 17

World Medical Association
28 Avenue des Alpes
01210 Ferney-Voltaire
France
Tel: 50-40-75-75

World Psychiatric Association
Kommunehospitalet
DK-1399 Copenhagen K
Denmark
Tel: 45 33 938500 (x3390)

INDEX